Sport and Society
A Student Introduction

Edited by

Barrie Houlihan

2nd edition

SAGE Publications
Los Angeles · London · New Delhi · Singapore

SAGE Publications Ltd
1 Oliver's Yard
55 City Road
London EC1Y 1SP

SAGE Publications Inc.
2455 Teller Road
Thousand Oaks, California 91320

SAGE Publications India Pvt Ltd
B 1/I 1 Mohan Cooperative Industrial Area
Mathura Road, New Delhi 110 044

SAGE Publications Asia-Pacific Pte Ltd
33 Pekin Street #02-01
Far East Square
Singapore 048763

Library of Congress Control Number: 2007925701

British Library Cataloguing in Publication data

A catalogue record for this book is available
from the British Library

ISBN 978-1-4129-2135-0
ISBN 978-1-4129-2136-7 (pbk)

Typeset by C&M Digitals (P) Ltd., Chennai, India
Printed in Great Britain by TJ International Ltd, Padstow, Cornwall
Printed on paper from sustainable resources

Contents

List of Figures

List of Tables

List of Boxes

Contributors

Mahfoud Amara is Lecturer in Sport and Leisure Policy and Management at the School of Sport and Exercise Sciences, Loughborough University. His principal research area is comparative sports policy with a specific focus on sport in Arabo-Muslim countries and communities.

John Amis is an Associate Professor in the Department of Management at the University of Memphis. He also holds courtesy appointments in the Department of Health & Sport Sciences and the Center for Community Health. Amis's research interests centre predominantly on issues of organisational and institutional change, particularly the role of individuals in interpreting and realizing change. His work has been published in *Academy of Management Journal, Organizational Research Methods, Journal of Applied Behavioral Science, European Marketing Journal, Journal of Sport Management, Leisure Studies* and *European Sport Management Quarterly*.

David L. Andrews is an Associate Professor of Physical Cultural Studies in the Department of Kinesiology at the University of Maryland at College Park, and an affiliate faculty member of the Departments of American Studies and Sociology. He is Assistant Editor of the *Journal of Sport & Social Issues*, and on the editorial board of a number of journals including the *Sociology of Sport Journal* and *Leisure Studies*. He has published on a variety of topics related to the critical analysis of sport as an aspect of contemporary commercial culture. His recent publications include *Sport-Commerce-Culture: Essays on Sport in Late Capitalist America* (Peter Lang, 2006), *East Plays West: Essays on Sport and the Cold War* (with S. Wagg, Routledge, 2007) and *Sport, Culture, and Advertising: Identities, Commodities, and the Politics of Representation* (with S.J. Jackson, Routledge, 2005).

Kathleen Armour is a Reader in Physical Education & Sport Pedagogy in the School of Sport & Exercise Sciences, Loughborough University. Her main research area is career-long professional learning for physical education teachers and coaches. She is also engaged in evaluation research into physical education and sport initiatives for young people funded by both public and corporate bodies.

Ben Carrington teaches sociology at the University of Texas at Austin, where he is also the Associate Director of the Center for European Studies, and is a Carnegie Visiting

Research Fellow at Leeds Metropolitan University. He is co-editor, with Ian McDonald, of '*Race*', *Sport and British Society* (Routledge, 2001).

Mike Collins is Visiting Professor at the University of Gloucestershire, and Visiting Research Fellow at Loughborough University, was Head of Research, Strategy and Planning at the Sports Council for many years, and Senior Lecturer in Loughborough's School of Sport & Exercise Sciences for 16 years. He is author of *Sport and social exclusion* (Routledge, 2002) and editor of and major contributor to *Examining Sports Development* (Routledge, forthcoming). Besides those topics, his research interests include sport and its social, environmental and economic impacts, and the structure and role of voluntary sport and its relationships with the other sectors.

Paulo David is Regional Representative for the Pacific of the Office of the United Nations High Commissioner for Human Rights (OHCHR) based in Suva, Fiji Islands. He has worked for over 15 years in the field of human rights and specialises in the rights of the child. He is the author of *Human Rights in Youth Sport: a Critical Review of Children's Rights in Competitive Sports* (Routledge, 2005).

Peter Donnelly is Director of the Centre for Sport Policy Studies, and a Professor in the Faculty of Physical Education and Health, at the University of Toronto. His research interests include sport politics and policy issues (including the area of children's rights in sport), sport subcultures and mountaineering (history). His recent books include *Taking Sport Seriously: Social Issues in Canadian Sport* (1997; 2nd edition, 2000) and *Inside Sports* (1999) and the Canadian edition of *Sports in Society* (2004, both with Jay Coakley).

Ian Henry is Professor of Leisure Policy and Management and Director of the Centre for Olympic Studies and Research at Loughborough University. His research interests lie in the field of sport and leisure policy and politics and his recent publications include *Transnational Research in Sport: Globalisation, Governance and Sport Policy* (Routledge, 2007)

Barrie Houlihan is Professor of Sport Policy in the Institute of Sport and Leisure Policy at Loughborough University. He has written widely in the area of sport policy and recent publications include *The Politics of Sports Development: Development of Sport or Development through Sport?* (with Anita White, Routledge, 2002), *Elite Sport Development: Policy Learning and Political Priorities* (with Mick Green, Routledge, 2005) and *Sport Policy: a Comparative Analysis of Stability and Change* (with N.A. Bergsgard, P. Mangset, S.I. Nødland and H. Rommetvedt, Butterworth–Heinemann, 2007).

Guy Jackson was formerly a Lecturer in the Institute of Sport and Leisure Policy, Loughborough University, where his main research interests were in the interrelationship between sport and tourism and in the area of sports development and management. As a researcher he undertook studies for a wide range of national and local agencies and a number of sports governing bodies. He left Loughborough University in 2006 to take up the post of Manager of the National Cricket Centre for the England and Wales Cricket Board.

Ruth Jeanes is a Research Associate working at the Institute of Youth Sport, Loughborough University. She works on a range of national evaluation projects examining youth sport and physical activity initiatives. Her research interests include gender identity, young people and football. She is also interested in ways of conducting research with young people and developing interactive methods and new approaches to collect data with children.

Tess Kay is Senior Research Fellow in the Institute of Youth Sport at Loughborough University. Her research focuses on the relationship between sport, leisure and social structure and the use of sport to promote inclusion, especially among children and young people. She has undertaken research into sport and family, sport and gender, sport and community development in the UK, and the use of sport in HIV/AIDS education in Africa. She is the author with Michael Collins of *Sport and Social Exclusion* (Routledge, 2003), Managing Editor of *Leisure Studies* journal, and is currently editing a volume on *Fathering through Sport and Leisure* (Routledge, 2009).

David Kirk is currently Dean of the Carnegie Faculty and Professor of Physical Education and Youth Sport at Leeds Metropolitan University. He has held academic appointments at Loughborough University, the University of Queensland and Deakin University. His research interests include curriculum change in physical education, young people's experiences of sport, and situated learning in physical education and sport.

Tara Magdalinski is a Senior Lecturer at University College Dublin. She has published widely in sports studies and focuses on the cultural construction of performance enhancement, the role of nature in the bodies and site of the Sydney 2000 Olympics, and the corporate motives of Olympic education. Her first book, co-edited with Timothy Chandler, *With God on their Side: Sport in the Service of Religion*, was published by Routledge in July 2002.

Ian McDonald teaches sociology and politics at the Chelsea School, University of Brighton. He is co-editor, with Ben Carrington, of '*Race', Sport and British Society* (Routledge, 2001).

Milena M. Parent is an Assistant Professor at the School of Human Kinetics, University of Ottawa. Her research interests include organisation theory, stakeholder management and event management. She is co-author of the textbook *Understanding Sport*

Organizations, 2nd edition (Human Kinetics, 2006) with Trevor Slack. She has also published in the *Journal of Sport Management, Journal of Business Ethics, Journal of Sport Finance* and *European Sport Management Quarterly.*

Murray Phillips teaches in the Sport Studies Department in the School of Human Movement Studies at the University of Queensland. His research interests are in the epistemological status of sport history, sport and gender, the football codes, swimming and coaching history. He is the author of *From Sidelines to Centre Field: a History of Sports Coaching in Australia* (University of South Wales Press, 2000).

Robert Pitter is an Associate Professor in Kinesiology at Acadia University. His research and publications focus on sport, recreation and physical activity in three areas: government policy, social inequality and social identities/meanings. He is co-editor of *Sporting Dystopias: the Making and Meaning of Urban Sport Cultures* (with R. Wilcox, D.L. Andrews and D. Irwin, SUNY Press, 2003).

Martin Polley is Senior Lecturer in Sport at the University of Southampton. He is the author of *Moving the Goalposts: a History of Sport and Society Since 1945* (Routledge, 1998), *A-Z of Modern Europe since 1789* (Routledge, 2000) and *Sports History: a Practical Guide* (Palgrave, 2007), and editor of the five-volume *The History of Sport in Britain 1880–1914* (Routledge, 2004). He has also published numerous articles on various aspects of sports history, including diplomacy, national identity and amateurism. He is a past Chairman of the British Society of Sports History.

Holger Preuss is Junior Professor at the Johannes Gutenberg-Universität Mainz, Germany. There he teaches Sports Sociology and Sports Economics and is a member of the 'Research Team Olympia'. Since 2006 he has been a Visiting Professor at the Beijing Sport University and since 2007 International Scholar in Sports Management at SUNY Cortland, State University of New York. His research focuses on economic impacts of mega sport events, especially the economic implications of hosting the Olympic Games from Munich 1972 to Beijing 2008.

Leigh Robinson is a Lecturer in Sport and Leisure Management in the Institute of Sport and Leisure Policy at Loughborough University. Her main research area is the management of sport and leisure organisations. She is the author of *Managing public sport and leisure services* (Routledge, 2003) and recent publications include 'Customer expectations of sport organisations' (*European Sport Management Quarterly* 2006). She is the Chief Editor (with J. Camy) of an IOC-funded project 'Managing Olympic Sport Organisations'.

Parissa Safai is an Assistant Professor in the School of Kinesiology and Health Science at York University. Her research interests focus on sport at the intersection of risk, health and healthcare including: sport's 'culture of risk'; the development and social organisation of sport and exercise medicine in Canada; and the social determinants of athletes' health.

Michael Silk is Senior Lecturer at the University of Bath. His research and scholarship centres on the production and consumption of space, the governance of bodies, and the performative politics of identity within the context of neo-liberalism. He has recently published a number of book chapters and journal articles in *Media, Culture, Society, Journal of Sport & Social Issues, Sociology of Sport Journal, International Review for the Sociology of Sport, Sport, Culture and Society, International Journal of Media & Cultural Politics, Media Culture: A Review, Journal of Sport Management* and *Cultural Studies - Critical Methodologies*.

Trevor Slack is a Professor at the University of Alberta and Adjunct Professor at the University of Ottawa. In 2002 he suffered a stroke. He has published three books since that time. He has published in such sports and leisure journals as *Journal of Sport Management; International Journal of Sports Marketing & Sponsorship; Sport Management Review; European Sport Management Quarterly; International Review for the Sociology of Sport; Journal of Leisure Research; Leisure Studies; Culture, Sport Society* and *International Journal of Sport Finance*. He has also published in *Organization Studies, Journal of Management Studies, Human Relations, European Journal of Marketing, Journal of Applied Behavioral Science* and the *Academy of Management Journal*. He has also published a number of books and chapters on the management of sport.

David Stead is a Lecturer in Sociology of Sport in the School of Sport and Exercise Sciences at Loughborough University. Formerly concerned with youth sport policy, he currently researches globalisation and sport, the personal and professional experiences of elite athletes and the interrelationship between sport and the media. His publications include '"Rite de passage" or passage to riches? The motivation and objectives of Nordic/Scandinavian players in English league soccer' (with Prof. Joseph Maguire, *Journal of Sport & Social Issues*, 2000).

Nigel Thomas is Head of Sport and Exercise at Staffordshire University. He began his career in higher education following 10 years in local authority and governing body sports development roles, specifically focusing on the development of opportunities for young disabled people. His research interests include the media coverage of disability sport and the integration of children with special educational needs into mainstream physical education. In 2004 he completed his PhD at Loughborough University on the policy process in disability sport.

Mike Weed is Professor of Sport in Society and Director of Research in the Department of Sport Science, Tourism and Leisure at Canterbury Christ Church University, UK. He is interested in all aspects of the relationship between sport and tourism, but particularly in the experiences of sports tourists. He is the Editor of the *Journal of Sport & Tourism*, and is author/editor of *Sports Tourism: Participants, Policy and Providers* (Elsevier, 2004), *Sport & Tourism: A Reader* (Routledge, 2007) and *Olympic Tourism* (Elsevier, 2007).

Kevin Young is Professor of Sociology at the University of Calgary. He has published on a variety of sports-related topics such as violence, gender and subcultural identity. His books include *Sport and Gender in Canada* (Oxford University Press, 2007), *Theory, Sport & Society* (Elsevier, 2002), *Sporting Bodies, Damaged Selves: Sociological Studies of Sports-Related Injury* (Elsevier, 2004) and *Global Olympics: Historical and Sociological Studies of the Modern Games* (Elsevier, 2005). He has served on the editorial boards of several journals, such as the *International Review for the Sociology of Sport, Sociology of Sport Journal, Soccer and Society* and *Avante*, as well as on the Executive Board of the North American Society for the Sociology of Sport. He is currently serving a second four-year, elected term as Vice-President of the International Sociology of Sport Association.

Introduction

BARRIE HOULIHAN

THE GROWTH OF INSTITUTIONAL AND POLICY COMPLEXITY

In the fairly recent past, the late 1950s and early 1960s, the number of roles that an individual might fulfil in relation to sport was limited to those such as participant, spectator, consumer of sports news and reports mainly through the newspapers and radio, or voluntary club administrator or official. There were few professional athletes and even fewer professional administrators; the symbiotic relationship between the television companies and sport was only just emerging; and the rampant commercialisation of sport, especially football, was still some years away. The organisational infrastructure of sport was similarly simple. National governing bodies of sport and their clubs were the organisational core of the sports system in the UK; the government considered sport as an area of social activity that did not warrant treatment as a matter of public policy; and the schools were left to provide a combination of physical training and some sports. The involvement of the state in sport was sporadic, substantially limited to the occasional committee of inquiry into a sports-related problem (such as the Moelwyn–Hughes Report in 1946 which followed the collapse of safety barriers at Bolton FC's ground), a police presence at major sports events and the Queen handing over the trophy to the winners of the FA Cup Final.

Today, however, the picture is radically different: the roles have multiplied, the infrastructure is much more complex and the state is now at the heart of sport. Individuals consume sport in a broad variety of ways through spectating, both at home and as travelling fans, and participation. Paulo David's contribution complements Collins' opening chapter by providing an analysis of the extent to which sport, an opportunity for enjoyment, socialising and personal development for so many young people, is, for some, an arena for the degradation, abuse and the denial of basic human rights.

Tess Kay and Ruth Jeanes trace the recent history of women's exclusion from sport and draw attention to the variety and subtlety of the debates that seek to explain female under-representation as participants, officials, coaches and administrators. The depth and persistence of patriarchy within contemporary sport are amply exposed. Of especial significance is that the authors point to the paradox, according to which many women perceive participation in sport as 'contradictory to femininity', while those who do participate experience little role conflict and report a sense of empowerment reflected in increased self-esteem, personal development, physical power and well-being.

Parissa Safai picks up and develops the idea of well-being in her chapter on the relationship between sport and health. As she makes clear, the assumptions about the beneficial effects of sport have largely gone unchallenged. More specifically, she investigates the interrelationship between pain, injury, gender and elite-level sport. Her chapter is complemented by that of Kevin Young who explores the complex relationship between sport and violence. Moving beyond the limited focus of the existing literature on violence on the field of play and spectator violence, Young uncovers a much more extensive and complex pattern of sports violence. In particular, he argues that a sociological understanding of sports violence requires an examination of the interconnection between class, race and ethnicity, gender, and regionality.

In his chapter on sport and disability Nigel Thomas reviews the persisting tension between medical and social models of disability and the power of those models, almost exclusively designed by the able-bodied, to determine the parameters of sports participation. But what comes across most strongly from Nigel Thomas's chapter is the complexity of the politics of disability sport. Not only is there a multiplicity of disability sports organisations, but there is also a marked lack of consensus regarding the strategy for widening opportunities for disability sport, in particular whether disability sport should be organised separately or work more closely with mainstream sports governing bodies. These debates take place against a backdrop of consistent and continuing success of UK elite athletes in the Paralympic Games.

The significance of acknowledging the ideological context within which issues in sport are discussed is emphasised in the contribution from Ben Carrington and Ian McDonald. In their critique of the evolution of public policy towards race and ethnicity in sport, the authors trace the slow shift away from an assumption that the route to more equitable participation lay in uncovering and addressing the constraints to be found within ethnic communities to an acknowledgement of the barriers to participation evident within sports institutions. The anti-racism efforts of major sports, such as cricket, and the impact of the New Labour government are evaluated and lead the authors to conclude that while there is evidence of progress in tackling racism and inequity in opportunities, 'discrimination continues to structure the reality of sport for black and ethnic minorities in Britain in complex and often contradictory ways'.

In their chapter on physical education and sport, Kathleen Armour and David Kirk provide ample illustration of the extent to which contemporary practice in physical education has been shaped by the sharply contested history of the subject. Not only was there disagreement over the form of physical 'education' best suited to different social classes (sports for the children at fee-paying schools and military drill for those in the state system), but there was, and to an extent still is, a fierce debate about the value of physical education within the curriculum and the relationship between physical education and sport. Of particular importance is their discussion of the contemporary emphasis on the capacity of physical education and school sport to deliver non-PE and sport objectives such as improved academic attainment and improved behaviour. The final contribution to Part Two by David Andrews, Michael Silk and Robert Pitter explores the relationship between sport, urban space, health and other socio-economic indicators. The continuing association between sports participation and socio-economic status is amply demonstrated through the examination of soccer as an element of suburban lifestyle and status segregation.

If the recurring themes that run through Chapters 4 to 12 are public policy, access and exclusion, then the next seven chapters in Part Three 'The impact of commercialisation' give greater weight to the significance of business for contemporary sport. Business has always been involved in sport, but the intensity and ubiquity of the business presence in sport is a phenomenon of the late twentieth century. Yet far from usurping the position of the state, business involvement with sport has prompted closer public sector involvement with the state often seeking to regulate corporate activity in sport. Leigh Robinson provides an overview of the increasingly close relationship between sport and commerce and explores not just the variety of involvement, from online betting to sponsorship, but also the impact on professional sport and the structure of the sports industry. The author explores the unique characteristics that make sport so attractive to the commercial sector and discusses whether the relationship is best described as dependence, symbiosis, manipulation, mutual benefit or exploitation. Whatever description is preferred, the reader is left in no doubt as to the significance of the sport and leisure industry to the national economy.

Some of the themes introduced by Leigh Robinson are developed in more detail in David Stead's examination of the relationship between sport and the media. This relationship is the axis around which commercial interest in sport revolves. In addition to raising issues of audience manipulation through the media presentation of sports events, David Stead also explores the key question of access to sports products that are increasingly delivered in a pay-to-view format. The issues the author raises have a clear resonance with the earlier discussions of social exclusion. Given the pace of commercialisation and the investment by governments in national governing bodies of sport, it is important to understand the significance of organisational change for the way in which sport is managed. John Amis and Trevor Slack not only supply a conceptual language for the analysis of sports organisations, but also provide a wealth of examples drawn from both the commercial and voluntary sectors. Of especial importance is the analysis of the change in the structure of sports organisations from voluntarily run, simply structured and poorly resourced 'kitchen table' bodies to professionally managed, structurally differentiated and well-resourced boardroom organisations in which volunteers play an increasingly marginal role.

The professionalisation of both the participation in, and the administration of, sport is nowhere more clearly exemplified than in relation to the issue of doping. The rewards of sporting success, the proliferation of specialists (dieticians, masseurs, coaches, doctors, physiologists, etc.) within an athlete's entourage and the global character of the sports competition circuit have all made the successful development of an effective anti-doping policy more challenging. Barrie Houlihan discusses the attempts to develop a global policy response to doping and illustrates the extent to which anti-doping efforts by sports organisations have been supported, and occasionally submerged, by the regulatory activity of states.

Mike Weed and Guy Jackson then examine the rapidly growing phenomenon of sports tourism. Following a review of the nature of tourism supply and demand, the authors explore the impact of sports tourism. As is made clear, the hosting of major sports events can have substantial impacts on the local economies and environments, a point which Holger Preuss emphasises in relation to the hosting of the Olympic Games. However, as the authors also make clear, the sport tourism market is still in its infancy and is certainly not limited to the hosting of major events. While the clear impetus for market expansion has come from the commercial sector and from governments keen to attract lucrative mega-events, there is also the potential to use sports tourism to achieve other objectives more closely associated with sport for all and fitness and health. In his analysis of the Olympic Games, Holger Preuss explores in detail the argument that the hosting of the Olympic Games is an unalloyed benefit for the local community. The author shows clearly that while one might reach a conclusion that, on balance, the net benefits of hosting the Games outweigh the costs, the beneficiaries and those who bear the costs are often different groups in a community. Not surprisingly, business interests and the local or regional state are often able to use the Games to achieve organisational objectives associated with profit or urban regeneration, but the costs are often borne by poorer local residents who are displaced to make way for stadiums and who can rarely afford the ticket price for the Games themselves. Holger Preuss's chapter provides a powerful illustration of the close association between commercial interests and state power.

The final contribution to this part of the book considers the relationship between sport and the environment. Michael Collins uses a series of case studies to highlight both the positive and negative impacts of sport on the environment. Linking with a number of conclusions from Holger Preuss's chapter, the author examines the potential for sport, and especially the hosting of major events, to facilitate the rapid regeneration of inner-city industrial areas. In addition, Michael Collins illustrates how competing uses of the countryside for sport can be reconciled, but also how relations between sporting and non-sporting users of the countryside can break down. Acknowledging that sport can generate significant negative environmental impacts, the author makes it clear that sport can also bring substantial environmental benefits if managed sensitively. The reclamation of brownfield sites for stadiums and mineral quarries for sailing, climbing and shooting, the development of community forests and the deliberate protection of biodiversity in the design of golf courses, all attest to the potential for commerce and sport to prosper without inflicting environmental damage.

The fourth part of the book encourages the reader to consider the pattern of sport in their own country and culture in comparison to that in other industrialised countries and in other cultures and also in relation to the emergence of supranational and global institutions affecting sport. Trevor Slack and Melina Parent's discussion of aspects of sport in the United States and Canada paints a vivid picture of the extent to which commercialisation in the United States dominates intercollegiate sport and also the degree to which the role of the public sector has been marginalised. Although the public sector is still more prominent in Canada, the trend is towards greater commercialisation and a greater reliance on voluntary community provision. Of especial interest are the problems created for professional sport in Canada as a result of the economic power of the United States. The chapter also provides an interesting insight into the privileged position ascribed to the (usually male) high school athlete and the corrosive effect on broader school values.

Murray Phillips and Tara Magdalinski provide another point of comparison in their discussion of the sports system and culture in Australia. After stripping away the rhetoric that pervades many discussions of sport in Australia, they reveal a sports system and culture which disadvantages women and discriminates against Aboriginal athletes. The authors also describe a society where the mythology of Australian sport has such a strong hold that few questioned the substantial sums of public money that were used to underwrite the Sydney Olympic Games. Not only does Australia exemplify the strengthening role of government in managing the sports system, but it also illustrates the impact of increasing commercialisation. Perhaps of especial interest is their discussion of the interweaving of immigrant identities with a sense of Australian identity.

Identity is also an important aspect of Ian Henry's discussion of the increasingly prominent role of the European Union in sport. Given that so many of the world's major sports events are located in member states of the European Union, the impact of EU involvement in sport extends well beyond its boundaries and comprises an increasingly important element of the context of sport for many countries. The EU has shown itself to be an effective regulator of both commercial sports interests and also of aspects of public provision.

Moreover, the EU has a strong interventionist tradition and, as the author makes clear, has ambitions to define a European model of sport which will stand in opposition to the highly commercialised North American model outlined by Trevor Slack and Melina Parent and also referred to by Leigh Robinson and David Stead.

The themes of identity and culture provide the foundation for Mahfoud Amara's discussion of sport and Islam. After outlining key aspects of Islamic theology, the author considers the debates among Islamic scholars about the place of sport, and especially recreational and elite sport, in Islamic life. Mahfoud Amara also discusses the influence of Islamic thought on public policy for sport in Islamic countries.

The last contribution to this part and the final chapter in the book is Barrie Houlihan's examination of globalisation and sport. In the opening section of this introduction emphasis was placed on the extent to which the context for modern sport had altered at the national level, with the steady rise in governmental interest in sport running in parallel with global commercialisation. The final chapter explores the process and outcome of globalisation and suggests that while the significance of globalising pressures is undeniable, the direction of change and the consequences for sport and for communities are far less clear. Nevertheless, while the trajectory of globalisation might be obscured, the role of the state as both an engine and a mediator of globalisation is clear.

CONCLUSION

At one time it was often argued that sport was an oasis in an increasingly complex and compromised society. Sporting values were clear (and laudable) and sporting practice made the concept of 'free time' a reality. As this volume shows, if this perception was ever valid, it certainly is no longer today. Sport, sports organisations and sports practice are at the heart of a number of major social issues either in their own right as sites of tension over social values such as gender equity, racial/ethnic equality and social inclusion, or as policy instruments of government, such as those designed to achieve economic regeneration or gain diplomatic prestige. While each of the chapters in the book can be read independently, they provide strong collective evidence of the need to see sport located at the core of our consideration of many contemporary social issues, as an integral part of the industrial economy, and an increasingly valuable political resource. In the preface to his landmark study of the relationship between cricket and West Indian society, C.L.R. James famously adapted lines written by Kipling to ask 'What do they know of cricket who only cricket know?' It is the foundation of this volume that not only can our understanding of sport be enriched by using perspectives developed across a range of disciplines, but also the study of sport can also cast substantial light on major contemporary social and economic issues.

Part One

Perspectives on Sport

1

Sport and Social Theory

PETER DONNELLY

[T]he discovery of sociology can change your life. It can help you to understand the social forces you confront, the forces that constrain and free you as you go about living your life. This under-standing offers a liberating potential: To gain insight into how these social forces influence your life allows you to stand somewhat apart from at least some of them, and thereby exert more creative control over your own life. (Henslin, 1999: 1–2)

OVERVIEW

- » *Sociological theory*
- » *Structure and agency in sociology*
- » *Synthesis*
- » *Theoretical history of sociology of sport*
- » *Methods of sociological analysis*
- » *The future of sociology of sport*

In the epigraph, Henslin is paraphrasing from Berger's (1963) *Invitation to Sociology*. Discovering the sociology of sport can also change your life – if you are an athlete, and/or a student in sport studies or the sport sciences. It can help you to understand the social forces that affect your involvement in sport and physical activity, and that knowledge may help you to exert more control over your participation. This chapter is concerned with the fundamental aspect of understanding in sociology – social theory. It begins with an extended example, a demonstration of the way in which an analysis of the relationship between sport and social class reveals the two main schools of thought in sociology. The example outlines the strengths and weaknesses of these two approaches, and shows how they are connected to political decisions that are made about health, sport and physical activity. This is followed by a synthesis of the two schools of thought showing how, in combination, they provide a much clearer understanding of the ways in which social forces influence participation. The latter part of the chapter presents a brief history of the development of sociological thought in the sociology of sport, and a short analysis of the methods used in research in the sociology of sport. The chapter concludes with some ideas about the future of this field of study.

One of the most important bodies of research in the sociology of sport concerns the relationships between sport and social inequality – how does social inequality affect access to and participation in sports and physical activity? Research consistently shows not only that, in multicultural societies, racial minorities enjoy more limited access to sports and physical activity than the racial majority population, but also that racial minority participation tends to be limited to specific sports that are stereotypically associated with particular racial minorities. Similarly, research consistently shows that girls and women have lower rates of participation in sports and physical activity than boys and men; and that the higher a person's income and/or level of education (social class), the more likely he, and increasingly she, is to participate in sport and physical activity. This leads to the **first** point to be made about such relationships: no one is characterised only by their race/ethnicity, their gender, or their social class: 'Each of us has a gender, a social class background, a racial/ethnic affiliation, and a variety of other social characteristics that serve as advantages or disadvantages in the various structural and cultural circumstances of our lives, and we relate to each other on the basis of ours and theirs' (Donnelly, 1996). Thus, any examples of research accounting for only one of these characteristics must be seen as partial.

Second, interpreting statistical relationships is tricky. They show that a is related to b; they do not show that a caused b. Thus, we need to be cautious before assuming that, and interpreting the reasons why there are relationships between sport and social inequality. If we find a relationship between, for example, wearing brown shoes and achieving high marks in examinations, we have no problem seeing it as a meaningless relationship – it is highly unlikely that wearing brown shoes caused the higher marks. Other relationships may lead us to suppose causality. If, for example, we found a relationship between bodybuilding and feelings of sexual inadequacy, we might think that there are reasons to expect such a relationship. It is certainly a theme that has recurred in some fitness industry advertising, where bodybuilding is supposed to relieve such feelings.

The explanation of such relationships is referred to in science (including the social sciences) as a theory. It is the best, currently accepted, explanation of the available evidence of a relationship or a natural phenomenon – why the apple fell from the tree; why the bath water rises when you get in; why everyone is soon aware that there is a flatulent person in the seminar room. New evidence may confirm the theory, or lead to newer explanations – the theory of creation becomes the theory of evolution; Newtonian physics is supplemented by the theory of relativity. In the natural sciences, the process of explanation is continual, and in many cases relatively straightforward. The process of explanation in the social sciences – social theory – is not nearly so straightforward. As Giddens notes:

1   We cannot approach society, or 'social facts', as we do objects or events in the natural world, because societies only exist in so far as they are created and re-created in our own actions as human beings …
2   … Atoms cannot get to know what scientists say about them, or change their behaviour in light of that knowledge. Human beings can do so. Thus, the relation between sociology and its 'subject-matter' is necessarily different from that involved in the natural sciences. (1982: 13–15)

Thus, our theory about bodybuilders is easily overturned by 'sexually inadequate' individuals who decide to stop participating in bodybuilding because of what it might reveal about their sexual adequacy, or by 'sexually adequate' individuals who do not give much credence to the theory and decide to become involved in bodybuilding for other reasons.

THE TWO SOCIOLOGIES

To return to the relationship between social class and participation, sociological explanations tend to fall into one of the two main historical approaches to social theory – what we refer to here as *agency theories* and *structure theories* (sometimes called social action theories and social system theories). Our explanation is easier if we place participation in sport and physical activity in the larger context of health, and if we start with the idea of *agency*. A major justification for participation – for the existence of public and private fitness centres and for government expenditure on sport and physical activity – is that we are supposed to be responsible for our own health. A number of neo-liberal governments now claim that they can no longer afford public funding for health care for a population that does not take some responsibility for its own health. Thus we find a whole catalogue of advice, demands and moral suasion designed to encourage people to become more active and take better care of themselves. The following is a recent example, from the British Chief Medical Officer, Liam Donaldson:

TEN TIPS FOR BETTER HEALTH

1   Don't smoke. If you can, stop. If you can't, cut down.
2   Follow a balanced diet with plenty of fruit and vegetables.
3   Keep physically active.
4   Manage stress: e.g. talk things through, make time to relax.
5   If you drink alcohol, do so in moderation.

6   Cover up in the sun, and protect children from sunburn.
7   Practise safer sex.
8   Take up cancer screening opportunities.
9   Be safe on the roads: follow the Highway Code.
10 Learn the First Aid ABC – airways, breathing, circulation. (Cited in Raphael, 2001a: A8)

None of these 'tips' is unfamiliar to us. We have heard similar messages often, in the media, in government statements, in health and physical education classes. The messages take many of the well-known causes of illness, injury and premature death and suggest how to avoid them. And what they all have in common is the assumption of individual responsibility and choice with regard to lifestyle decisions.

Agency, or action, refers to the freedom that individuals enjoy to act in a manner of their own choosing. It refers to behaviour that is not thought to be determined by outside forces; and it tends to be associated with individualism, voluntarism and free will. At its extreme, it leads to statements such as Margaret Thatcher's view of 'society': 'There is no such thing as society, only individuals'. Sportspeople, and students of sport, often concur with this view of society. They produce, observe and are impressed by individual efforts; some even tend to see team sports only as a collection of individuals temporarily working together. They are often impressed by psychological explanations of motivation, individual effort, and success or failure. Furthermore they are likely to be convinced that individuals ought to be active and live healthy lifestyles because people are, or ought to be, responsible for their own health; and they are likely to attribute ill health or overweight to personal shortcomings and failures on the part of the individual. In sociological terms, agency theories tend to focus more on the ways in which individuals create and give meaning to their world. Sociological theories emphasising this approach include: ethnomethodology, methodological individualism, phenomenology and some of the other interpretive sociologies (cf. Donnelly, 2000).

Agency theories represent one of what Dawe (1970) termed 'the two sociologies'. Standing in contrast are structure theories, which are based on the premise that our actions are determined by social forces and social structures. Sociological theories emphasising this approach include: some forms of Marxism, structuralism and some forms of structural functionalism. At its extreme this approach argues that, so powerful are the institutions, social processes and social forces that govern people's lives, individual actions (agency) are ineffectual. However, the emphasis given to structure in sociology tends to be on relationships between social structures, or on social relations, rather than individuals.[1]

If we return to our social class, health and physical activity example, a search of the literature indicates that a great deal of solid evidence is ignored when the causes of illness, injury and premature death are attributed only to lifestyle choices. Numerous articles in leading medical journals, and a great deal of evidence summarised in books such as Evans et al. (1994) *Why Are Some People Healthy and Others Not?* and reports such as Raphael's (2001b) *Inequality Is Bad for Our Hearts*, suggest that (in addition to genetics) poverty and lack of education are far better predictors of disease than inappropriate lifestyle choices. In other words, these data indicate that social structure (e.g. the class system, social inequality and social relations between the social classes) is a better predictor of disease than agency. The evidence is summarised by Giddens:

> Working class people have on average lower birth weight and higher rates of infant mortality, are smaller at maturity, less healthy, and die at a younger age than those in higher class categories. Major types of mental disorder and physical illness including heart disease, cancer, diabetes, pneumonia and bronchitis are all more common at lower levels of the class structure than towards the top. (1989: 215)

The magnitude of the effect is quite striking. Raphael (2001b) cites a study in Toronto, Canada, which showed that one's chance of dying from a heart attack increased 10 per cent for each drop of $10,000 in income.

Raphael (2001a: A8) notes that '23% of all premature years of life lost prior to age 75 in Canada can be attributed to income differences'. Of these lost years, 22 per cent result from heart attack and stroke, 17 per cent from injuries and 14 per cent from cancers. Thus, 'the material conditions under which we live – especially during childhood – are far greater determinants of whether we die from illness than our adult "lifestyle choices"' (Raphael, 2001b: A8). Evans et al. (1994) show that 'top people live longer', and they do so despite statistical controls for 'lifestyle choices' such as smoking and physical activity. Current views of this difference point, not to greater knowledge of health care due to higher levels of education, or the ability to purchase 'better' nutrition and health care, but to the sense of being in control of one's life:

> Higher incomes are related to better health not only because wealthier people can buy adequate food, clothing, shelter and other necessities, but also because wealthier people have more choices and control over decisions in their lives. The sense of being in control is intrinsic to good health. (National Forum on Health, 1997)

This sense of the effects of structure (the social and material conditions of our lives) rather than agency (our lifestyle choices) led David Gordon at Bristol University to devise the rather tongue-in-cheek:

ALTERNATIVE TEN TIPS FOR BETTER HEALTH

1   Don't be poor. If you can, stop. If you can't, try not to be poor for long.
2   Don't have poor parents.
3   Own a car.
4   Don't work in a stressful, low-paid manual job.
5   Don't live in damp, low-quality housing.
6   Be able to afford to go on a foreign holiday and sunbathe.
7   Practise not losing your job and don't become unemployed.
8   Take up all benefits you are entitled to, if you are unemployed, retired or sick or disabled.

9 Don't live next to a busy major road or near a polluting factory.
10 Learn how to fill in the complex housing benefit/asylum forms before you become homeless and destitute. (Cited in Raphael, 2001a: A8)

Population activity studies – which define some people as 'inactive' or 'sedentary' – raise serious concerns about research that is usually based on middle-class assumptions about white-collar jobs and exercise as a lifestyle choice – they often only measure recreational physical activity:

> Housework, child care, manual labour, work that involves being on your feet, and the activities that some define as leisure and others as a chore (e.g. gardening) ... [which] account for the majority of energy expenditure of Canadians – remain unrecorded in most surveys. (Donnelly and Harvey, 1996)

Since lower-income people are far more likely to be involved in manual work or work that involves standing, to use public transport, and to have less access to child care and house cleaning and maintenance services, assumptions about and measures of 'inactive' populations are likely to be misleading.[2]

THE TWO SOCIOLOGIES: A SYNTHESIS

This extended example provides an ideal account of 'the two sociologies' – what Gouldner (1975) referred to as 'man on his back' (structure) and 'man fighting back' (agency). Each provides a highly plausible explanation of the relationship between social class and sport and physical activity, and each is well supported by evidence. As individuals (agents) we ought to make healthy lifestyle choices; but can we be blamed for the circumstances of our lives – for having poor parents or for having to live and work in unhealthy environments? Those adopting an agency perspective attribute lower levels of participation among lower-class individuals to a lack of motivation, and a lack of concern for personal health and well-being. Structural interpretations are likely to point to involvement in manual labour, low incomes, low education levels, and other structural and environmental circumstances in the lives of low-income people to explain lower levels of participation. In addition to the dilemma this creates, each interpretation is quite political, another element of sociological theory that must be considered. Agency explanations of the relationship, when attempting to account for the failure of some people to participate in sport and physical activity, or engage in other healthy lifestyle practices, can have the following consequences:

- **they lead to victim-blaming – moral sanctions, or threats to withdraw health care from individuals who appear to have made unhealthy lifestyle choices;**
- **they lead to patronising attitudes about individuals who are considered not to know better, or to be too weak-willed to make healthy lifestyle choices; and**

- they lead to poor policy decisions with regard to creating education programmes, public service advertising campaigns, and the provision of sport and fitness programmes and facilities that do not take into account the circumstances of people's lives.

Structural explanations of the relationship, when attempting to account for the failure of some people to participate in sport and physical activity, or to engage in other healthy lifestyle practices, can have the following consequences:

- they lead to criticisms about cuts to public spending on programmes and facilities, when such programmes and facilities were not necessarily ones that were supported by all individuals;
- they lead to compassion, and occasionally patronising attitudes, about the structural circumstances of people's lives without any real sense of how to involve people in changing those structural circumstances; and
- they lead to poor policy decisions with regard to creating sport and fitness programmes and facilities which address some of the structural barriers to participation, but often fail to take into account individual needs, interests and choices.

In political terms, agency interpretations are preferred by the neo-conservative end of the political spectrum while structural interpretations are preferred by the social democratic end of the spectrum. Unfortunately, the political centre often combines the worst of both approaches (see Box 1.1).

Box 1.1 An example of the relationships between structure and agency

Consider the example of Women Organizing Activity for Women (WOAW), a programme of physical activity for low-income single mothers with pre-school children developed in British Columbia, Canada, by Wendy Frisby. An enlightened group of health, physical activity and recreation professionals and academics met, together with representatives of the target population, to plan the programme. The details of the programme were developed, and were about to be finalised, when the mothers announced that they would not be able to participate. When asked why, they in turn asked, 'who will look after our children?' It became clear that none of the academics or professionals had considered the issue of child care. Child care provisions were added to the programme, and it became a success because the participants also had an opportunity to determine the form of the programme. (The most popular activities reflected the interests and structural conditions of the lives of the target population – see if you can guess the two most popular activities before you check the

(Cont'd)

end note.⁴) Without the participation of the target population in the decision-making process day care provision would not have been made, very few people would have become involved in the programme, and the professionals and academics might have concluded that low-income mothers of pre-school children were not interested in physical activity programmes, and further concluded that, therefore, there was no need to make provision of such programmes. The participants were interested, but were also far more aware than the usual policy makers of the structural circumstances of their lives. Without their input, even a well-meaning policy decision would have failed.

In sociology, the struggle to develop a synthesis, or a compromise, between 'the two sociologies' has been under way for some time. In fact, 150 years ago Marx recognised that: 'Men make their own history [agency], but they do not make it just as they please; they do not make it under circumstances chosen by themselves, but under circumstances directly encountered, given and transmitted from the past [structure]' (1852/1991: 15). Thompson and Tunstall asked: 'Do the two approaches of social systems and social action theory simply correspond to our own ambivalent experience of society as something that constrains us and yet also something that we ourselves construct?' (1975: 476). Berger and Luckmann's (1967) ideas about 'the social construction of reality', Giddens' structuration theory, the theoretical work of Pierre Bourdieu, and the critical cultural studies developed at the Centre for Contemporary Cultural Studies at Birmingham University, have all consciously attempted to effect this compromise.³ For Berger and Luckmann, 'society forms the individuals who create society [social construction of reality] in a continuous dialectic' (Jary and Jary, 1995: 664). Giddens argues that 'societies only exist in so far as they are created and re-created in our own actions [agency] as human beings' (1982: 13), and he resolves the dilemma by proposing the 'duality of structure' – '"structure" is both the medium and the outcome of the actions which are recursively organized by structures' (Abercrombie et al., 2000: 8). Bourdieu's approach is evident in the work of one of his former students, Loïc Wacquant's (1992) study of boxing in an African American neighbourhood of Chicago. Wacquant locates the actions (agency) of the boxers within the class and racial structures of the United States, and the subculture of the boxing gym. Although each of these theoretical approaches has influenced the sociology of sport, it is *critical cultural studies* which have had the greatest impact on the field in the last 20 years.

The relationship between social class and participation in sport and physical activity is much more complex than it is possible to explain by either agency or structure interpretations alone. Individuals do choose whether to participate or not, if the circumstances of their lives permit such a choice. And even if the choice is available to an individual, a whole host of circumstances from that person's past (e.g. whether his/her family had been involved in sport, or had encouraged participation; the person's experiences in school physical education classes, etc.) and present (e.g. whether transportation and child care are available; whether they are safe; and whether people are made to feel welcome and comfortable participating) may affect his/her decision. Donnelly and Harvey (1996: 23–4) outline the structural barriers to participation in sport and physical activity, which they classify as:

- *infrastructural barriers* – associated with the material means of access (e.g. cost, available transportation, time, etc.);
- *superstructural barriers* – associated with ideas about access (e.g. policies, knowledge, prejudice, etc.); and
- *procedural barriers* – associated with the course of action available to individuals to attain access (e.g. social support, citizens' rights, organisational structure and management style).

In addition, two types of access are identified:

- *participational access* – when individuals have information; when they are able to cope with procedures associated with access (e.g. registration); and when they meet competent staff who are sensitive to diversity; and
- *representational access* – when participants (i.e. those with participational access) are also present in the structure and decision-making process.

Donnelly characterised the latter as 'a fully democratised sport and leisure environment [which] include(s) both the right to participate, regardless of one's particular set of social characteristics, and the right to be involved in determination of the forms, circumstances and meanings of participation' (1993: 417). In other words, the *agency* of participants is involved in creating and recreating the *structural* circumstances of their participation.

ANOTHER EXAMPLE

An additional example, involving athletes' use of performance-enhancing drugs, shows, first, how agency and structure interpretations have become a part of our everyday lives and, second, how social theory helps to resolve these overly simplified interpretations of human behaviour. An athlete has to decide to ingest or inject a banned substance; it is a conscious act, and the athlete is almost always aware that it is an illegal act in the world of sport.[5] Thus, given the assumption of agency, it is appropriate to blame the athlete, who is attempting to win by illegal means, and to impose what sanctions there are available.

This would be fine if athletes lived alone in a vacuum, but they are also a part of society and act within and are influenced by its structures. Those defending rather than blaming athletes for taking banned substances may point to the larger cultural and structural context in which athletes now live:

- the 'culture of excellence' which only values winning;
- the medicalisation of society, in which drugs are developed and sold for a whole range of conditions that were not previously defined as 'medical';
- the rationalisation of the body, in which athletes' bodies are treated and trained as 'objects' somehow removed from the personhood of the athletes;
- the professionalisation of sport, which has added income to the prestige of winning (in a culture of excellence) – a dangerous combination encouraging individuals to take risks in order to be the best; and
- public demand for records, and for more spectacular athletic performances.

In addition, they might consider the subculture of sport, and look at drug use from an athlete's perspective. In 1991, after the Ben Johnson scandal and the exposures of the Dubin Inquiry, Canadian sprinter Angella Issajenko made the following statement: 'Athletes will do whatever they have to to win. They know that random testing is in [introduced in Canada as a result of the Dubin Inquiry], and they are still prepared to take the risk.'

The elements that help to explain such risk taking from an athlete's perspective include:

- *positive deviance* – athletes overconforming to the norms of sport (Hughes and Coakley, 1991), which includes taking such risks in order to win;
- *the social relations of sport*, which often involve controlling relationships between coaches and athletes, and may extend to a coach's implicit or explicit condoning of drug use;
- *an athlete's commitment to sport*, which involves so much time, cost and sacrifice on the part of the athlete, and his/her family, and which may lead to an athlete seeking an 'edge' in order to justify their sacrifices;
- *the structure of sport*, in which government and sponsor funding, and a place on national teams, are only available to athletes who achieve and maintain a certain level of performance;
- *the abusive nature of sport*, which always includes punishing one's body, and which may include abusive dietary practices, a variety of therapies (some ethically questionable) for the rapid rehabilitation of injured athletes, and 'psychodoping' (Coakley, 1992), creates a context in which the use of 'natural' chemicals (e.g. testosterone, HGH) seems normal; and
- *the athlete information network*, in which information is informally and easily shared among athletes competing internationally – information concerning drugs and 'supplements', who is using drugs, what they are using and in what dosages, and how they are getting away with it.

So, is it the athlete's fault? Is it society's fault? Or is the fault in the system of sport that we have created? Of course, the 'fault' (a word which implies that we have already judged the situation, so 'cause' might be a better term) lies in all three. The society in which the athlete lives, and the social formations and networks in which the athlete trains and competes, exist in a dialectical relationship with the athlete. Decisions made by the athlete cannot be independent of those contexts; the athlete will make a decision about the use of banned substances, but that decision can only be understood in light of the circumstances in which it is made.

The simple assignment of blame/cause to the athlete or the system makes a good pub argument, and is carried out in the media.[6] But, as we have seen here, it is quite asociological. To paraphrase Douglas et al., 'human actions [cannot only] be explained in terms of concrete individual factors (such as individual will, choice, or the concrete situations individuals face) or in terms of something outside of the individual (such as culture or social structure) that determines or causes what they will do' (1980: 183). Our understanding of human behaviour can only be developed when we tease out the complex interactions between individuals and the social structures in which they live. And, as Henslin notes: 'This understanding offers a liberating potential: To gain insight into how these social forces influence your life allows you to stand somewhat apart from at least some of them, and thereby exert more creative control over your own life' (1999, p. 2).

THE DEVELOPMENT OF THE SOCIOLOGY OF SPORT

In many ways, the theoretical development of theory in the sociology of sport parallels the process outlined above. Separate and often unreflexive concerns with structure and agency in the early stages of development eventually lead to a more sophisticated synthesis of the two in more recent research.[7] A separate subdiscipline of sociology recognised as the sociology of sport began to emerge in the mid-1960s in the United States (Kenyon and Loy, 1965; Loy and Kenyon, 1969). Its origins were in both sociology and physical education, its practitioners were often advocates for, and fans of, sport and, as a consequence, little of the early work was critical in nature. This is problematic since sociology is often considered to be a 'critical' science – everyday assumptions about social relations, and aspects of social life that are considered to be 'common sense', are exposed to analysis to determine whether such assumptions and aspects of common sense are supported by evidence.[8] The development of the sociology of sport can be traced through three relatively distinct phases of theory, interpretation and explanation: namely, reflection, reproduction and resistance.

Reflection

The early, uncritical work in the sociology of sport was rooted in the assumption that 'sport reflects society' or, to put it another way, 'sport is a mirror [or microcosm] of society' (the reflection thesis). This view is not incorrect; in fact, it is quite obvious. How could a major cultural institution such as sport not reflect the societies in which it is practised? If the economy is capitalist, and women have less social power than men in a particular society, is it likely that the major cultural institutions such as sport will be characterised by socialist economic principles and gender equity? This approach was connected to structural functionalism, the predominant theory at the time in US sociology, and the most significant initial influence on sociology of sport almost everywhere that it began to emerge. And within structural functionalism:

> If there was a theme that seemed to best articulate the mission of the sociology of sport in the early period, it was socialization. It was inclusive: Within it one could look at 'sex' differences, race differences, child development, who entered into organized sport and how, categoric differences in enculturation, moral development, and so forth. (Ingham and Donnelly, 1997: 367)

Thus, sport was considered to be beneficial and functional. Through sport individuals learned how to become members of their social system – to set goals, maintain discipline, manage aggression and adapt to change.[9]

Since structural functionalism, especially as expressed in the work of Talcott Parsons, is often considered to flip-flop between agency and structure (as opposed to subsequent attempts to discover a synthesis between the two), this was evident in the sociology of sport. Agency was evident in the assumed voluntary nature of social action – individuals participated in sport, and behaved in the ways they did, because that was their choice. The emphasis on individuals was also evident in the close relationship between the sociology and psychology of sport during their early manifestations; and in the early studies of sport from a symbolic interactionist perspective, which examined the individual actors' definitions of the situation and creation of meaning in sport subcultures. In contrast, the individual disappeared when analyses turned to structure, deriving from Parsons's later emphasis on social systems. The sociology of sport focused on social processes (e.g. socialisation, social change), and social institutions such as sport and the related institutions (e.g. education, politics). This also represented a more valid adaptation of Parsons's system needs (see note 9).

While the reflection thesis is accurate, it is also obvious, and passive, but not necessarily uncritical (if one takes a dim view of gender inequity, that criticism is unlikely to stop short of criticising sport). The consensus view outlined above came to be challenged by a conflict view of sport which focused on social problems, and began to emphasise the sexist, racist and exploitative nature of sport (cf. Hoch, 1972; Scott, 1971) – issues that reflected those concerns in the larger society. Sport was seen as the new 'opiate of the masses' (in the nineteenth century Karl Marx had referred to religion as the 'opiate of the masses'), socialising individuals into an uncritical acceptance of status quo inequities.

Reproduction

It soon became evident that the reflection thesis did not explain the relationship between sport and society. However, although it only served to describe a status quo, it was an important initial stage for the sociology of sport. It helped to overcome a view that sport was a distinct sphere, somehow separate from, and perhaps even transcending, social life (e.g. Novak, 1976). The rather primitive Marxism of the conflict perspective was an important transitional stage, leading those concerned with a critical sociology of sport, and those critical of the status quo in sport, to search for more sophisticated theoretical tools. They found them in European sociological theory, and in a sociology of sport that was emerging in France and Germany. Work by Brohm (1978), Rigauer (1969) and Vinnai (1973), in English translations, began to have a powerful impact on North American and British sociology of sport, and became part of what Ingham and Donnelly (1997) referred to as the 'critical shift' in the subdiscipline.

The European neo-Marxist critique of sport argued that sport socialised individuals into work discipline, hyper-competitiveness and assertive individualism. In other words, sport not only reflected capitalist society, but also helped to reproduce it, to reproduce dominant social and cultural relations in society as a whole (Hargreaves, 1986). The idea of social reproduction was drawn, in part, from Bourdieu and Passeron's (1970) work on education, in which they demonstrated how the French educational system helped to reproduce the social class structure of French society. Thus, in the sociology of sport, rather than passively mirroring society, sport could now be seen as actively helping to maintain a particular set of power relations in an inequitable society.[10]

A further shift in the sociology of sport in the 1980s led to far greater attention being paid to gender and race than to social class, and here the reproduction thesis proved to be invaluable. Sport came to be seen as a 'school for masculinity' – at a time of rapidly changing gender relations and increasing social power for women, sport was considered to be one of the last bastions of masculine power. In addition to helping to reproduce gender relations, sport also came to be viewed as one of the barriers to changing race relations – helping to maintain the notion that certain racial characteristics (mental and physical) existed, and promoting stereotypical views of them. However, the reproduction thesis is rooted in structural thinking. There is no agency evident in analyses that focus on social processes and social relations of power. The reproduction thesis came to be considered as an accurate and dynamic, but partial attempt to characterise the relationship between sport and society.

Resistance

The reproduction thesis characterises a dynamic, but one-way relationship between sport and society. If the status quo is effectively reproduced from generation to generation, then no changes in the relative power of social groups, and their social and cultural relations, will occur. Individuals are rendered as passive agents: either as falsely conscious consumers of the new 'opiate of the masses' (namely, sport), unaware of the forces involved in producing and reproducing inequality and maintaining their subordinate status; or 'as passive learners "molded" and "shaped" by "society"' (Coakley, 1993: 170). If individuals are to play some part in understanding, giving meaning to and shaping their destiny, then it is necessary to reintroduce agency. Despite the overwhelming differences in social power that exist between a wealthy ruling elite and everyone else, we are not powerless. The resistance thesis attempts to capture the two-way process in which reproductive forces are resisted – in which agency confronts structure.

The first, and still one of the more valuable attempts to characterise this process, to synthesise agency and structure in the sociology of sport, is Gruneau's (1983) *Class, Sport, and Social Development*. His solution is developed from the ideas of Gramsci, Williams and Bourdieu. The resistance thesis, sometimes referred to as hegemony theory, is rooted in Antonio Gramsci's ideas about social power. Before Gramsci, hegemony referred to the straightforward domination of, for example, one nation or social class over another. Gramsci recognised that hegemony worked in more subtle ways, often aided by the compliance of those in the subordinate position.[11] As Williams noted:

> A lived hegemony is always a process … Moreover … it does not just passively exist as a form of dominance. It has continually to be renewed, recreated, defended, and modified. It is also continually resisted, limited, altered, challenged by pressures not all its own … That is to say, alternative political and cultural emphases, and the many forms of opposition and struggle, are important not only in themselves but as indicative features of what the hegemonic process has in practice had to control. (1977: 112–13)

These ideas permitted sport to be seen as not only dominated by elites such as the International Olympic Committee, FIFA, sporting goods manufacturers and media conglomerates, but also 'contested terrain', as the 'site of struggles' over 'the forms, circumstances and meanings of participation' (Donnelly, 1993: 417; see also Donnelly, 1988).

In the resistance thesis, individuals are seen as active, self-reflexive agents (a) who 'might quite consciously value sports as meaningful and beneficial aspects of their lives, while at the same time being aware that ruling groups attempt to use sport as an instrument of control' (Hargreaves, 1982: 43; see also Gruneau, 1983: 151–2); (b) who have the capacity to change the conditions under which they practise sport and recognise and change the conditions that maintain their subordinate status; and (c) whose attempts at resistance sometimes have an opposite effect, serving to reinforce the conditions of their subordination (cf. Donnelly, 1988). Thus, the resistance thesis focuses on sport as an aspect of culture, produced (socially constructed) by the participants but not always in the manner of their own choosing. Critical cultural studies of sport have examined, among other things, sport subcultures, sport media, gender and racial relations in sport, and more recently globalisation processes. As such, these studies become part of the 'struggles', because they expose the hegemonic process. For example, some studies of gender and the media (Cluer et al., 2001; Duncan and Messner, 2000) appear to show that a sustained, evidence-based critique of media sources regarding their marginalisation and trivialisation of women's sports is having an impact in terms of increasing and more equitable sports coverage for women.

A NOTE ON FIGURATIONAL SOCIOLOGY

This discussion of agency and structure in sociological theory – as evidenced in the sociology of sport – would not be complete without taking note of the important contribution of the work of Norbert Elias and Eric Dunning to this field of study (e.g. Dunning, 1999; Elias and Dunning, 1986). Their work, and that of others following Elias's figurational (or process) approach to sociology (e.g. Maguire, 1999), have been prominent in sport studies in the UK and The Netherlands, and increasingly in Japan. Rather than attempting a synthesis/dialectical relationship between agency and structure, or the individual and society, Eliasian sociologists argue that these are artificial distinctions. Their focus is on constantly changing social configurations produced by the interactions among interdependent individuals, and on the social processes that are simultaneously produced by, and produce, these social configurations. Work in this area of theory tends to take a much longer-term historical view of social processes than other sociologies, and important research on sport is evident in analyses of such processes as globalisation, democratisation, sportisation (the process by which sports developed and spread), parliamentarisation, and the civilising process. In addition to studying the development of sport (and specific sports such as rugby and boxing), Elias, Dunning and others are best known in the sociology of sport for their work on soccer hooliganism, the globalisation of sport, and health and injury issues in sport.

A NOTE ON METHODOLOGY

The growing sophistication of sociological theory (for the interpretation of data) occurred in parallel with the use of increasingly sophisticated sociological methods (for the collection of data).[12] Some of these methods were developed in sociology, but others have been borrowed from history, anthropology and literary studies. Perhaps the best known of these is survey research, employing written or oral questionnaires. Methods range through various forms of textual analysis (from content analysis to discourse analysis), to observation, participant observation and in-depth interviewing. The last group of methods is now often referred to as ethnography – an in-depth analysis of a social setting or social phenomenon in an attempt to understand it from the participants' perspectives. Growing sophistication is most evident in the use of multiple methods, not just for the purposes of 'triangulation' (Denzin, 1970) – where various methods are used in order to determine the validity of results from one of the methods – but also in recognition of the complexity of social phenomena, and the need to obtain as many sources of data as possible in order to generate a more complete understanding.

For example, a comprehensive study of Olympic television coverage might include analyses of the following:

- *The audience* – a broad-based audience survey to determine who they are and what they watched (this might include secondary analysis of the media's own audience surveys); in-depth interviews with selected audience members to discover the meanings they attached to the coverage; focus groups of audience members to discuss their observations of Olympic coverage; and participant observation with individuals or groups watching the Olympics in order to understand how they watch, what they see, and how they interpret what they see.
- *The content* – quantitative content analyses to determine exactly what was shown, when and for how long; and more qualitative textual or discourse analyses to discover how sports were shown, and what meanings were given to the coverage by the broadcasting crews, the sponsors, etc. This could include analyses of the commentary, the content, and the way in which that content was selected and presented, and in commercial media sources, the types of advertising shown.
- *The production* – in order to discover how Olympic broadcasts are made, a researcher (or research team) might interview key production staff; examine (content and textual analysis) broadcast policy documents produced by the International Olympic Committee, the local organising committee, the host broadcaster, sponsors and advertising agencies, and the actual broadcaster (CBC, BBC, etc.); and observe planning and production meetings, editing and production suites, and on-site commentary and electronic news-gathering crews.

Even if the research team decides to limit its research to one Olympic sport, it is evident that a complete study – taking into account the three primary elements of media analysis (production, content and audience) – is a complex and expensive undertaking.

Similarly with reference to the example given above, a research project on the use of banned substances in sport using, for example, a critical cultural studies perspective, might take into account:

- the perspectives of the athletes (using participant observation and in-depth interviews);
- the perspectives of those individuals who 'support' high-performance athletes (coaches, medical staff, psychologists and other sport scientists, agents, sponsors, sport organisation officials, the media, family and friends, etc.);

(These first two sources of data involve the researcher gaining, and honouring, a great deal of insider information and trust in what has traditionally been a secretive and closed system of sport.)

- the structure of the sport system; and
- the values of the society that support the sport system and the athletes.

And such a study might ask searching questions about power relations and vested interests in that sport system; or why athletes are the main focus for punishment for taking banned substances and rarely the suppliers of drugs, the suppliers of information about their use, and those who turn a blind eye to undetected use because their position and income depend on the performances of athletes.

FUTURE TRENDS IN THE SOCIOLOGY OF SPORT

Predicting future trends is always risky, especially at the time of writing when the events of 11 September 2001 appear to be having a long-term impact on, for example, processes of globalisation, and systems of surveillance and social control. The sociology of sport is also an extremely wide-ranging and active field of research, so any predictions must also be partial. However, the following issues seem to be attracting attention:

- the globalisation of sport, including its relationship to local and regional sport practices, and to issues of identity;
- continuing critical analysis of the commercialisation of sport, including the parts played by sponsors, media conglomerates and national and international sports organisations;
- growing interest in the contradiction between sport as a healthy practice and the high degree of risk and injury evident in many sporting practices, and the institutionalisation of sports medicine;
- the interests in commercialisation and health also combined in growing research interest in labour practices and legal issues in sport and sports-related industries;
- the production of sporting mega-events (Olympics, World Cups, etc.), including the involvement of various levels of government, citizen involvement (or lack of), the development and construction industries, the spaces that are dedicated to such events, the legacy of such events, and environmental concerns;
- a revival of interest in social class, and its intersections with gender and ethnocultural heritage, in relation to sport and physical activity practices and barriers (e.g. the earlier example of WOAW concerns the intersections of class, gender and age/ parenthood);
- an increasing body of research on sport policy and policy-related issues ranging from the use of sport to combat social ills such as obesity and social exclusion, to the

continuing struggle for resources between high-performance sport and sport for all, to the use of sport as a foreign policy tool in programmes of sport development, and development through sport;

• growing interest in postmodern analyses of sport, which have provided important cautions with regard to the politics of research methods, and with regard to the types of claims and generalisations that can be drawn from sociological research.

Social theory provides the interpretive tools for analysis of these and many other issues of interest to those involved in the sociology of sport.

CHAPTER SUMMARY

» There are two main schools of thought in the sociology of sport, one which emphasises agency, the freedom of individuals to act in a manner of their own choosing, and the other which emphasises structure, the extent to which individual actions are constrained by social forces and social structures.
» A synthesis of these two schools of thought is possible whereby variation in participation in sport, for example, may be explained in terms of the involvement of participants as agents in creating and recreating the structural circumstances of their participation.
» Sociology of sport has moved through a number of phases of analysis – reflection, reproduction and, most recently, resistance.
» Future concerns within the sociology of sport include globalisation, critical analysis of commercialisation, the tension between health and injury in sport, mega-events and social exclusion.

FURTHER READING

Henslin (1999) provides a sound introduction to the major concepts and schools of thought in sociology and Donnelly (2000) illustrates their application in the sociology of sport. Wacquant's (1992) analysis of boxing in the black community of Chicago illustrates the insights to be gained from a synthesis of structure and agency approaches in sociology. Ingham and Donnelly (1997) provide an overview of the development of the sociology of sport.

NOTES

1 While the focus of this chapter is on sociology and sociological theory, it should be pointed out that social thought regarding the structure and agency dilemma is evident in all of the social sciences – anthropology, political economy, history and even economics.

2 Of course, physical activity does not automatically lead to good health, as many coal miners, injured athletes and anorexic figure skaters could attest. We do have concerns about the health of those involved in heavy physical work, and physical activity, in unhealthy environments. Ingham put this in perspective with regard to recreational physical activity when he wrote: 'The fusion of new right ideology and right-thinking common sense … promotes a lifestyle which exhorts us to save our hearts by jogging in the arsenic filled air of Tacoma' (1985: 50). His comment has proven to be prophetic since a fairly recent California study shows a direct link between lung disease and air pollution among children involved in outdoor sports: 'the most active children in high-smog communities developed asthma at a rate three times that of children in the low-smog areas' (Mittelstaedt, 2002: A8).

3 However, as Jary and Jary have noted, despite many disagreements regarding the relationships between the two concepts, and problems of definition, 'most forms of sociological theory can be located … as recognizing the importance of both structural determinacy and individual agency' (1995: 663–4).

4 The two most popular activities were dance (reflecting a need for pleasure and sociability) and self-defence (reflecting another reality in the lives of some low-income women).

5 Athletes in East Germany in the 1970s were often not aware that they were being given banned substances; and, until athletes were warned about contamination of health food supplements, a number of those who tested positive for nandrolone were probably unaware that they had ingested a performance-enhancing drug. This example of the structural circumstances in which athletes use drugs is drawn from Donnelly (1991).

6 Readers might wish to try a similar case study, exposing explanations of athletic success, for example, to detailed analysis. Is it only a result of individual effort involving both mental determination and physical prowess? Or is it a result of a sophisticated talent recognition and sport development system using all of the most up-to-date knowledge, equipment and personnel from sport science and coaching science?

7 Parts of this section are drawn from Donnelly (1996), who develops reflection, reproduction and resistance theses from Alan Ingham and John Loy, and from Ingham and Donnelly (1997). The section provides a simplified description of the development of this field of study.

8 Students often view criticism as destructive. However, in science criticism is considered to be a constructive process involved in the development of knowledge. In the social sciences, criticism often exposes the assumptions and power relations that exist in everyday views of what is considered to be 'common sense'. Lazarsfeld (1949) exposed the dangers of 'common sense' when he revisited the findings of a well-known study of the American soldier in World War II. He presented a series of findings of the study (e.g. 'As long as the fighting continued, men were more eager to be returned to the States than they were after the German surrender') that appeared to be 'common sense' (of course, they didn't want to be killed); and then revealed that he had reversed all of the findings (the eagerness to return to the United States increased after the surrender – during the war, there was an important job to be done; after the war, they wanted to get on with their lives). Since both the false and the actual findings can be explained by 'common sense', the actual data, and the way in which they are interpreted, are shown to be of far more importance than 'common sense'.

9 The system needs identified by Parsons – adaptation, goal attainment, integration and pattern maintenance – were intended to apply to aspects of social systems (e.g. pattern maintenance was related to socialising institutions such as families and schools), but were often presented in the sociology of sport in terms of the socialisation of individuals.

10 It is interesting to note, however, that focus on the reproduction of social class had a far more significant impact on the sociology of education than the sociology of sport.

11 Subordinate compliance may be determined by feelings of powerlessness, or by the belief that the social order is appropriate (such beliefs often being encouraged by institutions such as education, politics, religion and the media). In British terms, it has been noted that the Conservative Party, often considered to represent the interests of wealth, would never be elected without a working-class 'deference vote'. And the widespread support for the Royal Family often surprises outside observers who see royalty as enshrining ideas of inherited privilege, rather than merit.

12 Following work by Ingham and Gruneau, Donnelly (1996) presented three levels of analysis – categorical, distributive and relational – that tend to parallel the reflection, reproduction and resistance theses.

REFERENCES

Abercrombie, N., Hill, S. and Turner, B. (2000) *The Penguin Dictionary of Sociology*. 4th edn. London: Penguin.

Berger, P. (1963) *Invitation to Sociology*. New York: Bantam.

Berger, P. and Luckmann, T. (1967) *The Social Construction of Reality*. London: Allen Lane.

Bourdieu, P. and Passeron, J.-C. (1970) *Reproduction in Education, Society and Culture*. London: Sage.

Brohm, J.-M. (1978) *Sport: a Prison of Measured Time*. London: Ink Links.

Cluer, S., Donnelly, P. and MacNeill, M. (2001) 'Lessons learned: a case study of CBC television coverage of men's and women's diving at the Sydney Olympics'. Paper presented at the North American Society for the Sociology of Sport Annual Conference, San Antonio, TX, 31 October–3 November.

Coakley, J. (1992) 'Burnout among adolescent athletes: a personal failure or a social problem?', *Sociology of Sport Journal*, 9: 271–85.

Coakley, J. (1993) 'Sport and socialization', *Exercise and Sport Sciences Reviews*, 21: 169–200.

Dawe, A. (1970) 'The two sociologies', *British Journal of Sociology*, 21: 207–18.

Denzin, N. (ed.) (1970) *Sociological Methods: a Source Book*. Chicago: Aldine.

Donnelly, P. (1988) 'Sport as a site for "popular" resistance', in R. Gruneau (ed.), *Popular Cultures and Political Practices*. Toronto: Garamond Press, pp. 69–82.

Donnelly, P. (1991) 'The culture of excellence: drug use by high performance athletes'. Paper presented at the Annual Conference of the International Committee for the Sociology of Sport, Tallin, Estonia, 26–29 June.

Donnelly, P. (1993) 'Democratization revisited: seven theses on the democratization of sport and active leisure', *Loisir et société/Society and Leisure*, 16: 413–34.

Donnelly, P. (1996) 'Approaches to social inequality in the sociology of sport', *Quest*, 48: 221–42.

Donnelly, P. (2000) 'Interpretive approaches to the sociology of sport', in J. Coakley and E. Dunning (eds), *Handbook of Sports Studies*. London: Sage, pp. 77–91.

Donnelly, P. and Harvey, J. (1996) *Overcoming Systemic Barriers to Access in Active Living*. Report prepared for Fitness Branch, Health Canada, and Active Living Canada.

Douglas, J., Adler, P., Fontana, A., Freeman, C. and Kotarba, J. (1980) *Introduction to the Sociologies of Everyday Life*. Boston: Allyn & Bacon.

Duncan, M. and Messner, M. (2000) *Gender in Televised Sports: 1989, 1993 and 1999*. Los Angeles: Amateur Athletic Foundation of Los Angeles.

Dunning, E. (1999) *Sport Matters: Sociological Studies of Sport, Violence and Civilization*. London: Routledge.

Elias, N. and Dunning, E. (1986) *Quest for Excitement: Sport and Leisure in the Civilizing Process*. Oxford: Basil Blackwell.

Evans, R., Barer, M. and Marmor, T. (1994) *Why Are Some People Healthy and Others Not? The Determinants of Population Health*. NewYork: Aldine de Gruyter.

Giddens, A. (1982) *Sociology: a Brief but Critical Introduction*. London: Macmillan.

Giddens, A. (1989) *Sociology*. Cambridge: Polity Press.

Gouldner, A. (1975) *For Sociology: Renewal and Critique in Sociology Today*. Harmondsworth: Penguin.

Gruneau, R. (1983) *Class, Sport, and Social Development*. Amherst, MA: University of Massachusetts Press.

Hargreaves, J. (1982) 'Sport, culture and ideology', in J. Hargreaves (ed.), *Sport, Culture and Ideology*. London: Routledge & Kegan Paul, pp. 30–61.

Hargreaves, J. (1986) *Sport, Power, and Culture*. New York: St Martin's Press.

Henslin, J. (ed.) (1999) *Down to Earth Sociology: Introductory Readings*. 10th edn. New York: Free Press.

Hoch, P. (1972) *Rip Off the Big Game: the Exploitation of Sports by the Power Elite*. Garden City, NY: Doubleday.

Hughes, R. and Coakley, J. (1991) 'Positive deviance among athletes: the implications of overconformity to the sport ethic', *Sociology of Sport Journal*, 8 (4): 307–25.

Ingham, A. (1985) 'From public issue to private trouble: well-being and the fiscal crisis of the state', *Sociology of Sport Journal*, 2: 43–55.

Ingham, A. and Donnelly, P. (1997) 'A sociology of North American sociology of sport: disunity in unity, 1965–1996', *Sociology of Sport Journal*, 14: 362–418.

Jary, D. and Jary, J. (1995) *Collins Dictionary of Sociology*. 2nd edn. Glasgow: Harper Collins.

Kenyon, G. and Loy, J. (1965) 'Toward a sociology of sport: a plea for the study of physical activity as a sociological and social psychological phenomenon', *Journal of Health, Physical Education, and Recreation*, 36: 24–5, 68–9.

Lazarsfeld, P. (1949) 'What is obvious?', *Public Opinion Quarterly*, 13: 378–80.

Loy, J. and Kenyon, G. (eds) (1969) *Sport, Culture, and Society.* Toronto: Collier-Macmillan.

Maguire, J. (1999) *Global Sport: Identities, Societies, Civilizations.* Oxford: Polity Press.

Marx, K. (1852/1991) *The Eighteenth Brumaire of Louis Bonaparte.* New York: International Publishers.

Mittelstaedt, M. (2002) 'Smog linked to asthma in children', *Globe & Mail*, 2 February: A8.

National Forum on Health (1997) *Canada Health Action: Building on the Legacy*, 2 vols. Ottawa: Public Works and Government Services.

Novak, M. (1976) *The Joy of Sports.* New York: Basic Books.

Raphael, D. (2001a) 'Staying healthy in Canada: what's missing?', *Guelph Mercury*, 7 September: A8.

Raphael, D. (2001b) *Inequality Is Bad for Our Hearts: Why Low Income and Social Exclusion are Major Causes of Heart Disease.* Report prepared for the North York Heart Health Network, Toronto, Canada. http://depts.washington.edu/eqhlth/paperA15.html.

Rigauer, B. (1969) *Sport and Work.* New York: Columbia University Press.

Scott, J. (1971) *The Athletic Revolution.* New York: Free Press.

Thompson, K. and Tunstall, J. (eds) (1975) *Sociological Perspectives.* Harmondsworth: Penguin.

Vinnai, G. (1973) *Football Mania.* London: Orbach & Chambers.

Wacquant, L. (1992) 'The social logic of boxing in black Chicago: toward a sociology of pugilism', *Sociology of Sport Journal*, 9: 221–54.

Williams, R. (1977) *Marxism and Literature.* Oxford: Oxford University Press.

2

Politics, Power, Policy and Sport

BARRIE HOULIHAN

OVERVIEW

- » *The scope of political science*
- » *Definitions of politics*
- » *Example 1: the National Stadium*
- » *Example 2: women's participation in the Olympic Games*
- » *Macro-level perspectives*

The social sciences are differentiated primarily by their substantive concerns but also by their particular methodologies and associated methods. Psychology, for example, is concerned primarily with the study of individual behaviour and has developed methodologies that support the use of experimental methods largely derived from the natural sciences as well as methods more familiar in sociology such as observation. The substantive concern of sociology is the study of group behaviour and social institutions, such as the family and the school, and has developed a wide variety of methods for gathering information ranging from the collection of census data to the study of life histories and participant observation. By contrast the substantive concerns of political science are far less neatly delineated, being focused on the sharply contested concept of power and its use in all its myriad forms. Nor does political science claim a distinctive methodology as it has tended to rely on the adaptation of methodologies developed in other social sciences.

THE SCOPE OF POLITICAL SCIENCE

Part of the difficulty of pinning down the focus of political science and its contribution to the study of sport is the diversity of fields of study that it encompasses. The major substantive fields within the discipline include government/public administration, policy analysis, political theory and international relations, with each raising a distinctive set of questions relevant to the study of sport and politics. In addition, there is a rich diversity of macro-level perspectives and analytical frameworks from which these substantive fields may be studied, which includes Marxism, neo-Marxism, neo-pluralism, behaviourism, feminism and rational choice and a similarly broad range of middle-range/meso-level frameworks associated with the analysis of policy such as advocacy coalitions, policy communities and policy networks. Table 2.1 illustrates both the scope of politics and also the range of issues related to sport that are raised.

As can be seen from Table 2.1, in addition to the concept of power, a further central thread in much political science is a concern with the role of the state either as a focus for policy or as a reference point for the analysis of concepts such as citizenship and civil society. Consequently, for many political scientists, politics is defined primarily in relation to the actions of the state and particularly the role of government and its authoritative use of power to make rules and laws that have precedence over rules from other sources in society (Moodie, 1984: 23). If this definition of politics is accepted, then attention would be directed towards, for example, the use of public funds to support sports policy, the location of responsibility for sport within the structure of government, and the way public policy for sport is determined and executed. Thus the decisions by UK governments to support the bid to host the 2012 Olympic Games, to provide a subsidy of £120m for the construction of a national stadium on the site of Wembley Stadium, and to establish a UK Sports Institute would all be examples consistent with Moodie's definition, as would (a) the decision by the US government to legislate in 1978 to resolve the friction between the American Athletic Union, the National Collegiate Athletic Association and the United States Olympic Committee, (b) the licensing by the French government of sports clubs and coaches, and (c) the decision by the Chinese government to bid for the 2007 women's soccer World Cup.

This conception of politics broadly confines attention to a limited range of institutions and forums such as parliaments, cabinets, ministries and courts. Power is conceptualised as largely a property of political institutions and a resource which enables 'power-holders' to achieve their particular goals. Consequently, the focus for study of sport and politics in the UK would include the decisions of ministers, the activities of the various sports councils, and legislation. However, while state institutions are clearly powerful, a second, more comprehensive and more subtle definition of politics requires that we look beyond the activities and outputs of the formal institutions of the domestic state and acknowledge the power wielded by non-state actors such as media businesses, commercial sponsors of

TABLE 2.1   The scope of political science

Field	Illustrative research topics	Illustrative research questions related to sport
Government/public administration	(a) Allocation of functions between central government departments and between central, local/regional government and semi-independent agencies (b) The influence of public officials on policy (c) The basis for successful policy implementation (d) The processes for protecting citizens' rights	(a) What are the consequences of responsibility for sport being given to a semi-independent agency (such as the various sports councils in the UK) rather than to a central government department? (b) How important are public officials (relative to political parties, ministers, media, sports lobby groups, etc.) in setting the agenda for sport policy making? (c) What administrative/management factors affect the successful implementation of policies designed, for example, to increase participation in sport or the amount of time in the school curriculum devoted to PE and sport? (d) How, and with what impact, are the views of elite athletes, school children and sports fans, for example, conveyed to public administrators?
Policy analysis	(a) The process by which some private concerns become public policy issues and, maybe more importantly, some do not (b) Assessing the effectiveness of different combinations of policy instruments (incentives, sanctions and information) in achieving policy objectives (c) Assessing the impact of policy	(a) By what process did women's participation in sport, disability sport and drug use in sport emerge as public policy concerns in the form that they did and at the time that they did? (b) How effective have incentives such as leisure cards been in encouraging those on low incomes to use leisure facilities? (c) What evidence would be valid in demonstrating that involvement in sport reduces juvenile delinquency or that designation as a specialist sports college raised the self-esteem of pupils?
Political theory	(a) The changing conceptualisation of citizenship and its relationship to civil society (b) The role of the state in promoting individual liberty and social equality (c) The challenge to the division between the public and the private spheres	(a) Should access to sport and leisure be treated as a right and as an essential element of full citizenship? (b) Does state intervention to enhance access to sport (e.g. subsidies to leisure facilities) increase liberty or constrain liberty by influencing/directing the use of 'free time'? (c) To what extent is it the case that male participation in elite sport in the public sphere is only possible because of the exploitation of women in the private sphere of family life?

TABLE 2.1   *(Continued)*

Field	Illustrative research topics	Illustrative research questions related to sport
International relations	(a) Diplomacy between states (b) The development of international policy regimes (c) The role and importance of non-governmental international organisations	(a) Is sport an effective diplomatic resource? (b) What is the character and effectiveness of international policy regimes in dealing with issues such as doping in sport and the recruitment and transfer of players between clubs? (c) Are international sports organisations such as the IOC independent actors in international politics?

sport and international sports federations, and by international governmental bodies such as the European Union and the Council of Europe. As Goodin and Klingemann (1996) suggest, politics is about the *constrained use of power*. 'It is the constraints under which political actors operate, and strategic manoeuvring that they occasion and that occurs within them, that seems to us to constitute the essence of politics.' This conceptualisation leads us away from an overconcentration on the formal institutions of the domestic political process and encourages an acceptance that power has sources not only within those institutions but also elsewhere.

> ## Box 2.1   Definition of 'policy'
>
> There are many competing and overlapping definitions of policy. Hogwood and Gunn (1984) identify 10 different uses of the term, including policy as a set of proposals, the decisions of government, a programme of action, and an aspiration or expression of general purpose. Heclo gives perhaps the most useful definition of policy as applying to 'something "bigger" than particular decisions, but "smaller" than general social movements. Thus, policy, in terms of level of analysis, is a concept placed roughly in the middle range' (1972: 84).

A further implication of this broader view of sport politics is that not all decisions affecting sport will be made formally and publicly: many, even very important decisions are made in an ad hoc and far less explicit manner. For example, the intensity with which a government pursues the objective of drug-free sport may be determined informally and even implicitly as public officials interpret the minister's statements, or lack of comment, on the issue. Similarly, the balance of emphasis between elite achievement and mass participation in government sports policy might be determined by informal lobbying by national governing bodies, the national Olympic Committee and health interests.

However, while these processes may be informal, discreet or implicit and reflect an acknowledgement that power in the political system extends beyond the formal institutions of the state, they are nonetheless still largely centred on recognised state institutions and personnel. A third and significantly different definition is one that treats politics as an activity that takes place wherever there are disputes about objectives and how they might be achieved, and that power is a much more ambivalent and elusive concept than is reflected in conventional political science usage. This view suggests that attempting to maintain a distinction between the public and private spheres is misguided and indeed unsustainable in modern complex societies. Ponton and Gill, for example, argue that politics is about the arrangements for ordering social affairs and as a result the scope of study 'cannot, in principle, exclude the possibility of political activity in any sphere of human life at any level, from the smallest of groups, such as the nuclear family, to the activities of international organisations' (1993: 8). Thus politics is seen as a pervasive feature of modern life, inherent in all organisations whether public or private and common to all areas of human activity including sport.

Box 2.2   Definitions of 'the state' and 'government'

The state refers primarily to a territorial unity and to a collection of institutions. The term 'state' is often used to refer not only to government but also to a range of other distinct institutions including the military, the courts system, the police, the system of local administration and the school system. There is considerable debate about the boundary between the state and civil society with some arguing that even when voluntary organisations receive financial grants from government, they become part of the state. The 'state' as a territorial entity is easier to define as it refers to an area over which the state has unrestricted power. However, unrestricted power in modern global society is unlikely.

The term 'government' refers to the arrangements for making policy decisions that prevail at a particular time. While the state is a long-lasting or permanent entity, governments come and go. A state may therefore move from democracy to dictatorship and, within democracy, from a socialist to a conservative government.

While Moodie's more limited definition of the scope of politics is in marked contrast to that of Ponton and Gill, both share a common focus on institutions and a narrow view of

TABLE 2.2   *(Continued)*

Model	Politics	Power	Focus for analysis	Gender equity as an example of a focus for analysis
		values embedded in society. Power as manipulation and strategy		through a multiplicity of sites including the family, school and media as well as the sports club and the sports governing body

WEMBLEY – THE NATIONAL STADIUM

A Brief Chronology of Events

In the mid-1990s Sport England arranged a competition for the location of a national stadium which would be partly funded by the National Lottery. The Football Association, the Premier League, the Football League, the Rugby Football League and the British Athletic Federation were involved in the development of the project. In late 1996 Wembley was selected by Sport England as its preferred location and £120m was allocated from Lottery funds as a contribution to total costs.

Ownership lay with a trust, English National Stadium Trust (ENST), and a separate trust, Wembley National Stadium Limited (WNSL), was established to raise the necessary finance to complete the project. The Football Association (FA) was the dominant partner in both trusts. By mid-1998 UK Athletics (the successor to the British Athletic Federation) had informed the ENST that none of its annual competitions would fill the stadium and that only two international athletics events would do so, namely the Olympic Games and the World Athletics Championships. Later the British Olympic Association (BOA) admitted that Wembley was not necessarily the centrepiece for any future bid for the Olympic Games. However, in January 2000 UK Athletics submitted a bid to host the 2005 World Athletics Championships in London with the rebuilt Wembley Stadium a clear possibility as the main venue.

Because of the weakness of support for the project from the BOA and UK Athletics, it was clear that it would be the FA that would take the long-term financial risk. By 2000 estimated costs for the project had risen from £136m to £334m. The growing uncertainty over the project was compounded by the government's increasing concern to achieve regeneration benefits for the local area from the national stadium project. In addition, problems were emerging with the design, especially regarding the cost and feasibility of incorporating an international competition standard running track.

By December 2000 the project had run into financial problems with the FA unable to borrow the revised estimate of £410m. By May 2001 the FA had announced that it was pulling out of the project, a decision which prompted the Home Secretary to appoint a working party to review the situation chaired by Patrick Carter. The Carter Report, published in September 2001, favoured Wembley over rival bids from Coventry and Birmingham, but did not make a firm recommendation. In late 2001 the government announced that while Wembley was the preferred option, a final decision was some way in the future. According to Tony Banks, the then Minister for Sport, the development of a national stadium at Wembley was 'a project that we simply cannot allow to go wrong' (1997). Not only did the project 'go wrong' but it did so in spectacular style.

In September 2002 the government provided an additional £20m in order to help WNSL secure a loan of £433m in return for greater, though unspecified, control over the project. Construction of the new stadium began in late 2002 by the Australian company Multiplex which had agreed a fixed price contract with WNSL of £445m. A serious setback for the project occured in August 2004 when a subcontractor responsible for providing the steelwork withdrew and began legal action against Multiplex. Later in November 2005 Multiplex announced an anticipated loss on the contract of around £180m. It was later also announced that the stadium would not be ready in time for the FA Cup Final in May 2006. By the time the stadium opened in 2007 total costs had reached approximately £800m, the FA had narrowly avoided bankruptcy and the planned FA national training centre at Burton upon Trent had been abandoned partially completed. The debacle raised a large number of questions for the political scientist such as:

- **Why was the government so keen to have a national stadium?**
- **Which nation was it to cater for?**
- **Which interests were involved in the decision making?**
- **What was the role of the Department of Culture, Media and Sport?**
- **Why was the government offering a subsidy to the richest sport in the UK?**
- **Why did the project go so badly wrong?**

There is no obligation on a country to have a national stadium: although France has one, Italy, the United States and Germany do not. It is possible that the UK government was motivated simply by populism – a desire to curry favour with the electorate, or at least that large proportion of the electorate who are football supporters. Few politicians, especially in the Labour Party, can resist the opportunity to exploit the publicity that surrounds the 'people's game' and even Margaret Thatcher, who was both uncomprehending and contemptuous of sport, was photographed being given a kiss by Kevin Keegan, then captain of the England football team. While populism was probably one motive, there were certainly others. In recent years governments have become acutely aware of the regeneration potential of major sports infrastructure projects. In the United States, building prestigious stadiums is a well-recognised form of city promotion or what is often referred to as 'civic boosterism'.

The decision to support Manchester's bid to host the 2002 Commonwealth Games was in large part motivated by the urban regeneration potential. With well over £80m of funding from the National Lottery, a cluster of sports venues (stadium, velodrome, indoor tennis centre and squash centre) have been built on the eastern side of the city in the hope that it will lead to a permanent boost to the local economy. The £120m that Sport England allocated to the Wembley national stadium project could be seen as part of a similar regeneration strategy for one of the less affluent London suburbs. According to the local authority, 'The multi-million pound regeneration proposals ... stemming from the new stadium development ... offer the best chance of reversing over two decades of economic decline in the Wembley area ...' (House of Commons, 2000: Appendix 10, para. 1.2). The decision to support Wembley rather than Coventry or Birmingham was also partly due to an assumption that if the UK were to bid to host a major sports event such as the soccer World Cup or the Olympic Games, a London location would be a requirement as the centrepiece for the bid.

The government of Tony Blair had made it clear that one of its objectives was to bring major international sports events to the UK partly because of the substantial contribution to the national economy, largely through tourism income, that can be gained from the hosting of sports events of global significance such as the Olympic Games, the football World Cup or the World Athletics Championships. Recent Olympic host cities, particularly Barcelona and Sydney, obtained substantial and, in the case of Barcelona at least, sustained increases in overseas tourist numbers which have been directly attributed to the publicity value of the Games. In the UK it is estimated that the annual value of sports tourism to the economy is £1.5bn, while it has been estimated that the Sydney Olympics will help reduce Australia's current account deficit by 1.25 per cent. For the city of Sheffield the first-round matches of the Euro '96 football competition generated around £5.8m of expenditure with the 26,000 supporters who visited the city during the 10-day period each spending between £50 and £100 per day. It is estimated by the Australian Tourist Commission that the country attracted an additional 2.1 million visitors between 1994 and the start of the Sydney Olympic Games in 2000 due to the city's raised profile and contributed over A$4bn to an aspect of the economy which already, in 1993, accounted for 11 per cent of Australia's exports. This expectation was based on assessments of Australia's previous experience in bidding for and hosting major sports events. For example, it was estimated that the hosting of the 1987 America's Cup generated expenditure of $464m and the equivalent of 9,500 full-time jobs. Even Brisbane's failed bid for the 1992 Olympic Games provided a significant boost to the local economy as it focused 'world-wide attention on Australia, its tourism potential, its excellent sporting facilities and its professional sports administration' (Department of Sport, 1987). The UK would dearly like to emulate Australia.

In addition to the fairly clear economic motives for supporting the idea of a national stadium, there is the far less specific, but nonetheless important notion of the identity politics of sport. For some countries, the development of a national stadium is an expression of collective identity and a way of asserting the vigour and vitality of the nation and, especially, its economy. Thus national stadiums can be seen as modern monuments fulfilling the same function as palaces in the eighteenth and nineteenth centuries and museums and 'sights' (such as the Eiffel Tower) in the nineteenth and twentieth centuries. Although some cultural monuments may be deemed expensive 'white elephants' at the time (e.g. the Millennium Dome in London) others, such as the Sydney Opera House or the Guggenheim Museum in Bilbao, can fulfil important symbolic functions for an entire community. However, the absence of a national stadium does not necessarily indicate a lack of sensitivity towards identity; rather, it may simply reflect the complexity of identity politics. For example, the absence of national stadiums in Germany, Spain and Italy may well reflect the strong political regionalism in these countries. Consequently, major sports events circulate throughout the country much in the same way that the Spanish monarch and court did in the seventeenth and eighteenth centuries. The absence of a national stadium thus allows symbolic national sporting events to fulfil the role of reinforcing national identity at the same time as acknowledging regional identities. The political dilemma for the UK is to decide which nation the national stadium is to represent. The Welsh have completed a new national stadium (the Cardiff Millennium Stadium), the Scots have long had a national stadium at Hampden Park, while Windsor Park in Northern Ireland fulfilled the same function, at least for the unionist community.

An analysis of governmental motives in relation to the national stadium provides rich opportunities to address a range of issues in sport politics, including how the regeneration potential of sports facilities and major events gained acceptability within government and the impact of the symbolic politics of identity on practical policy decisions. However, for a fuller understanding of the politics of the national stadium, the analysis of motives needs to be supplemented by an analysis of processes of decision making. A series of questions arise regarding how the agenda was set, who was involved and influential, and what were the motives, not just of government, but also of the other key players such as the various governing bodies, the commercial owners of the Wembley site, Brent Borough Council, the Greater London Authority and the BOA. In addition, attention might also be focused on the significance of the series of highly critical reports on aspects of the government's stadium policy by the House of Commons Culture, Media and Sport Select Committee. The analysis would also involve uncovering the sources of influence of key policy actors and the strategies adopted to exert influence.

Table 2.3 lists some of the organisations with an interest in the decision regarding the national stadium, but it is not exhaustive, with the most significant omission being the voice of the sports fan. However, as is routinely the case in many areas of public policy making, the public – whether as patients, tenants or sports fans – are confined to the margins of the policy process. As regards the role of the DCMS and especially of the Secretary of State, the latter seems to have had a potentially determining role, but one that appears to have been squandered, perhaps because of the lack of clarity of

TABLE 2.3 Motives of selected actors involved in the national stadium debate

Interest/organisation	Motives/interests	Resources	Involvement
British Olympic Association	Consideration of a possible London-based bid to host the Olympic Games in 2012. Interested in the Wembley proposals but refused to commit to a Wembley-centred bid possibly due to concern at the influence of the FA. Attracted by the possibility of an East London location and GLA support	(a) Support crucial to any future Olympic bid (b) No financial capacity to support a stadium project	(a) Significant influence over the DCMS Secretary of State regarding the acceptability of the various design options
UK Athletics	Concerned to host World Athletics Championships in either 2003 or 2005. Selected as host for the 2005 Championships by the IAAF	(a) Extremely limited, as predecessor body (British Athletics Federation) went bankrupt in 1997 and there was no possibility of a financial contribution to the cost of the new stadium (b) No regular events that could make the use of an 80,000-seat stadium viable	(a) Increasingly peripheral from mid-1990s to 2000 (b) Sport England offered support for an alternative athletics stadium at Pickett's Lock in London to cater for the 2005 World Athletics Championships, but support was withdrawn due to cost in late 2001 with the result that the Championships were reallocated
Football Association	Seeking a replacement for Wembley, but daunted by the cost. Seeking to offset some of the cost by accepting the idea of a national stadium to cater for more sports than football	(a) The richest sport in England (b) Control major sporting assets, e.g. the England team and the FA Cup (c) The only sport that could guarantee capacity crowds for more than one or two events	(a) Wanted Wembley as the centrepiece of its subsequently unsuccessful bid to host the 2006 World Cup, but the FA will probably bid again for the 2018 finals
Rugby Football League	Keen to retain access to a major venue for its flagship cup and international matches	(a) No financial contribution to the cost of the stadium	
Sport England	Main supporter of the idea of a multi-sport national stadium, but also having to	(a) Controlled access to National Lottery funding	(a) Awarded £120m for the purchase of the Wembley site early in negotiations and

TABLE 2.3 (Continued)

Interest/organisation	Motives/interests	Resources	Involvement
	take account of regeneration potential of any investment Strong supporter of a Wembley-based stadium		consequently had little leverage over the FA in later discussions until costs began to escalate and more public money and government support needed to resolve the dispute with Multiplex
UK Sport	Concerned to attract major sports events to the UK	(a) No access to funding for capital projects (b) Ministerial advice (c) Responsible for attracting major sports championships to the UK	(a) Commissioned an independent review of the various stadium designs
Brent Borough Council	Regeneration in the Brent area	(a) Planning approval powers (b) Some financial capacity to contribute to infrastructure development	(a) Strongly involved in negotiating the 'planning gain', i.e. the regeneration benefits, in return for its support to WNSL
Greater London Authority	Regeneration in London	(a) Limited, but could 'spoil' the Wembley plans by offering the prospect of an East London stadium for a possible bid for the 2012 Olympic Games	(a) Negotiations with the BOA over an East London site for Olympic bid
Potential commercial lenders	Ensuring the security of, and an adequate return on, their investment	(a) Finance of approximately £350m	(a) Reluctant to lend to WNSL as they were not persuaded that the project could make an adequate return on capital
Department of Culture, Media and Sport	(a) Vaguely in favour of Wembley as the location for the national stadium. (b) Became more involved as costs escalated, delays became more protracted and the risk of political embarrassment rose	(a) Strong influence over Sport England decisions (b) Control access to Treasury funding for bids for major events such as the soccer World Cup	(a) Strongly in favour of public/private financial partnerships rather than full public subsidy as was the case in France for the building of the Stade de France (b) A series of uncertain interventions which rarely clarified issues or moved the decision-making process forward

government objectives and indeed the incompatibility of objectives. The desire to construct a multi-sport national stadium as a centrepiece for bids for major international sports events conflicted with the desire to limit the commitment of public expenditure to the project, thus ensuring conflict with the FA which bore the brunt of the financial risk. In addition, the equivocal position of the BOA and the fragile financial position of both UK Athletics and the Rugby Football League left them at the margins of much of the debate. More significant from the standpoint of the DCMS was the loss of any substantial influence with the FA and its trust, WNSL, once the £120m of Lottery funding had been released for the purchase of the site, at least until the dispute between WNSL/FA and Multiplex required the government to play a broker role.

Political scientists, especially those with a particular interest in policy, would find the national stadium episode a rich opportunity to analyse power in British sport policy making. There are important questions raised in each of the four broad fields of political science identified in Table 2.1. For example, the influence of public officials, especially those within the quangos Sport England and UK Sport, is a recurring theme among specialists in public administration. Policy analysts may focus on the interplay between the various interests identified in Table 2.3 and be concerned to examine the resources possessed by each and the effectiveness of the negotiating strategy followed in pursuit of organisational interests. Political theorists might be interested in the implications for democratic accountability of the public/private financial partnership that underpinned the Wembley project. Or they might question spatial equity in relation to the location of a national stadium in London, when one of the three sports it is designed to cater for, rugby league, has only shallow roots in the south and when the main user, football, has roots in the north of England at least as deep as those in the London area. Finally, international relations specialists would focus on the growing influence of international non-governmental organisations such as the IOC and the major international federations, such as FIFA, in shaping, via the BOA and the FA, domestic sports policy objectives.

Not surprisingly, the events surrounding the decision to construct a national stadium gave a prominent place to state institutions and government as well as confirming the centrality of the concept of power – even if it is the power to obfuscate and prevaricate. The second example of sport politics, the participation of women in the Olympic Games, is very different in focus and context but, as will be shown, it is an issue that benefits considerably from political science analysis.

WOMEN'S PARTICIPATION IN THE OLYMPIC GAMES

The founder of the modern Olympics, Pierre de Coubertin, expressed the view in the late nineteenth century that 'the Olympic Games must be reserved for the solemn and

TABLE 2.4 Women's participation in selected Summer Olympic Games

Year	Location	No. of countries represented	No. of sports open to males/females (women's events as % of men's)	No. of male competitors	No. of female competitors	Female competitors as % of male competitors
1908	London	22	50/0 (0%)	1,999	36	2
1932	Los Angeles	47	87/14 (16%)	1,281	127	16
1964	Tokyo	93	115/32 (28%)	4,457	683	15
1980	Moscow	81	146/50 (34%)	4,238	1,088	26
1984	Los Angeles	140	153/73 (48%)	5,458	1,620	30
1988	Seoul	160	165/86 (52%)	7,105	2,476	35
1992	Barcelona	170	171/98 (57%)	7,555	3,008	40
1996	Atlanta	197	170/108 (64%)	6,813	3,506	52
2000	Sydney	199	180/132 (73%)	6,582	4,069	62
2004	Athens	201	176/136 (77%)	6,262	4,306	69

Sources: Coakley (2001); IOC Report of the Sydney Olympic Games (2001); IOC Report on the Athens Olympic Games

periodic exaltation of male athleticism with … female applause as reward' (quoted in Coakley, 2001: 210). De Coubertin's views reflected the then dominant social Darwinist ideology that women possessed a limited quantity of energy for all functions – physical, social and intellectual – and that priority needed to be given to the physical function of reproduction and child rearing. This argument was used to justify not only the exclusion of women from education, but also their exclusion from participation in sport in general and the Olympic Games in particular. As Table 2.4 indicates, progress towards equality of participation in the Olympic Games has been slow and still has some way to go.

A political science analysis of the slow progress of women's participation in the Games would focus on a range of issues and questions including the following:

- the role and significance of ideology in shaping IOC policy and also in shaping the attitudes of governments towards the issue;
- the role and significance of women's pressure groups; and
- the attitude of individual international federations.

Hargreaves (1994) traces the interplay between broader changes in social attitudes towards women and the lobbying by women's organisations and their combined effect on the status of women in sport. In particular, she draws attention to the persistence of gender stereotyping throughout the history of modern Olympic sport which made women's participation in sports such as archery, tennis and figure skating in the early part of the twentieth century more readily acceptable than their participation in athletics. Success in gaining acceptance for women's athletics was more the result of pressure from the Fédération Sportive Féminine Internationale which, in the 1920s, organised an alternative Women's Olympics in 1922 and a series of international competitions throughout the 1920s. The IOC has always been vulnerable to any threat to its self-perception as the organiser of the world's leading multi-sport festival. Consequently, the evidence of the growing popularity of the Women's World Games and the continuing shift in social attitudes resulted in the gradual acceptance by the IOC of women's participation in a steadily broadening range of sports events.

In addition to charting the interplay between changing cultural values and lobbying, Hargreaves also highlights a further recurring issue in the politics of women's sport, namely the choice between separate organisational development or assimilation into the existing male-dominated international federations. As the standard and popularity of women's sport increased, there was an understandable aspiration among many female athletes involved in Olympic sports to gain access to the Games. However, entry to the Games programme would mean losing their organisational independence and coming under the control of the existing male international sports federations. As Hargreaves comments, whereas 'women could more easily insulate themselves from opposition in the separate sphere of their own association; in a mixed association they were rendered weak and vulnerable' (1994: 214). The attitude of sportswomen in the 1920s and 1930s, when these debates were taking place, was split on the question of participation in the Olympics owing to differing attitudes towards the culture of male-dominated elite sport, the impact of commercialism on sport, and class attitudes towards many track and field events which were perceived to be low status. The relationship between women's sports organisations and the IOC and international federations on the one hand, and the internal divisions between different groups of women on the other, demonstrates the importance of appreciating the internal politics of sport: 'power and control were fought over, not just between men and women, but between different groups of women' (Hargreaves, 1994: 215).

The question of assimilation or segregation remains a major current issue for women athletes, where it often appears to be the case that the price paid for increased opportunities for participation at the highest levels is a gradual loss of control over coaching and decision making within governing bodies (Coakley, 2001; Houlihan and White, 2002). While women's participation in the Olympic Games has steadily moved closer to that of men's, their involvement in the decision making of the IOC has increased far less rapidly

TABLE 2.5   Percentage of women coaches in a selection of the 10 most popular women's intercollegiate sports

Sport	1977	1987	1997	2000	% point change 1977–2000
Basketball	79.4	59.9	65.2	63.3	−16.1
Volleyball	86.6	70.2	67.8	59.6	−27.0
Tennis	72.9	54.9	40.9	36.7	−36.2
Track	52.3	20.8	16.4	20.1	−32.2
Field hockey	99.1	96.8	97.6	99.4	+0.3
Soccer	29.4	24.1	33.1	34.0	+4.6

Source: Acosta and Carpenter (2000) quoted in Coakley (2001)

and is still woefully inadequate. Of the 111 members of the IOC, only 14 are women (an increase from 11 in 2002 and 3 in 1972), while of the 15 members of the powerful Executive Board of the IOC, only one is a woman. In the mid-1990s the IOC did adopt a more proactive approach largely as a result of the sustained lobbying by a small group of women in senior positions in sports organisations. In 1995 the IOC set NOCs (National Olympic Committees) and international sports federations a target of 10 percent female membership by 2005. Although the target has proved very difficult to reach for most organisations the issue is now clearly on their agenda. According to White and Henry (2004), not only has the 'establishment of minimum targets ... served to raise consciousness of the issue of women's involvement in [NOC] Executive Committees', but it has also brought 'talented women in to the Olympic family and [improved] Olympic governance by setting an example and providing moral leadership to the world of sport in terms of equity in representation' (2004: 7). However, one of the few longitudinal studies of women's involvement in non-athlete roles in sports organisations does not offer significant grounds for optimism. Acosta and Carpenter (reported in Coakley, 2001), examined the impact of Title IX on women in coaching (Table 2.5). The passage into law of Title IX in 1972, which required that US colleges provide women with equal access to sports resources, resulted in many college athletics departments not only increasing the number of coaches to take account of the increased demand for coaching from female students, but also developing integrated coaching programmes. Both developments had the effect of reducing the proportion of female athletes receiving coaching from a female coach. It is also interesting to note that the two sports, soccer and field hockey, where the proportion of female coaches has remained steady are both sports where male participation is comparatively low.

The slow pace of change is also a reflection of the long-established informal power networks of male sports administrators, which create an informal 'male world' for sport which women find difficult to enter. The informal power network is reinforced by the formal power of sports federations which allocate resources – access to elite coaches, specialist training facilities and sports science expertise, television coverage, funding for travel and training, and competition opportunities – within their sport. The reluctance of boxing authorities to permit women's bouts, the frequent treatment of synchronised swimming and also long-distance swimming as being of secondary importance to diving and pool swimming, and the equivocal attitude of some football federations towards women's football, all attest to the depth and abuse of male organisational power.

Although state power played only a limited role in shaping the early years of the modern Olympics, from about the mid-1960s onwards state sports agencies and governments became much more significant actors on the issue of gender equity and sport. In many developed countries in Europe and North America, legislation was used in an attempt to achieve greater gender equity with not always unequivocally positive results, as the example of the impact of Title IX in the United States demonstrated. However, in a significant number of mainly Islamic countries, state power has had an equally profound effect on women's participation in sport. As recently as 1996, over 30 Islamic countries sent male-only teams to the Atlanta Olympic Games. However, there are clear signs of change, albeit extremely gradual, as a number of Islamic countries, even some of the most traditional, are considering how to provide sports opportunities for their female population. For example, in 1993 Iran hosted the first Islamic Women's Games albeit with only an all-female audience permitted. More recently in 1998 the conservative country of Qatar hosted an IAAF Grand Prix II meeting at which male and female athletes were permitted to take part. These tentative signs of change are of particular interest to political scientists who, in seeking to explain the changed attitude towards women's participation in competitive international sport, might point variously to:

- **the attraction of prestigious international sports events to rich though small states as a way of raising their international profile;**
- **the impact of lobbying groups such as those associated with the Brighton Declaration and Atlanta Plus, which have the aim of raising the issue of the exclusion of women from international sport; and**
- **the globalisation of ideas about universal human rights and their acceptance as an implicit condition of entry to the international political community represented by bodies such as the United Nations and the Olympic Movement.**

This very brief review of one issue in the politics of women's sport shows the opportunities for the application of political science analysis, even vis-à-vis an issue in which state involvement is more recent and generally far less central and in which many of the key policy actors are independent organisations. Despite the less significant role for the state, the concept of power is central to much of the history of women's sport. At one level there is the power arising from the deeply embedded and male-dominated culture, which resisted change on the grounds of a stereotyped view of women as physiologically unsuited to vigorous exercise, of women's sport as vulgar, and more recently of women's sport as dull. Even the Olympic slogan of '*Citius, Altius, Fortius*' (faster, higher, stronger) reflects a male conceptualisation of sport and one that embodies the militaristic and nationalistic context within which the modern Olympic Movement emerged in the late nineteenth century. This concept is constantly reinforced by the modern media with their concern with drama, violence and excitement. How different would elite Olympic sport be if the slogan suggested by Won (2001) of 'More vividly, more harmoniously, more beautifully' were adopted?

Many of the concepts employed to analyse the two cases are drawn from middle-range theories of decision making and policy analysis which tend to emphasise institutional processes, pressure group activity, bargaining and the political behaviour of policy actors. While this level of analysis can be insightful, macro-level theorising not only provides a challenge to middle-level analysis, but also raises analytical issues concerning the fundamental structuring of the social formation, as Table 2.6 indicates. As such, political science offers the student of sport a variety of levels of analysis and also a range of macro-level perspectives, which illuminate different facets of an issue and provide alternative formulations of the issue and alternative avenues of enquiry and scholarship.

CONCLUSION

The two examples of sport politics discussed above illustrate the value and centrality of key political science concepts such as power and the state in developing a comprehensive understanding of the social significance of sport in contemporary society. They also illustrate the range of application of political science analysis, encompassing not just politics *of* sport but also politics *in* sport. The study of the politics *of* sport draws attention to the identification and analysis of the motives for government and broader state involvement in sport and the process by which sports policy is formulated. In democracies attention would focus on the interplay between the institutions of the state (including parliaments, the civil service, the courts and schools) and non-state sports organisations (including governing bodies, media companies and sponsors) in shaping sports policy. By contrast, a concern with politics *in* sport accepts that the capacity to affect the distribution of sports opportunities is not just possessed by the state, but also evident in sports clubs, governing bodies and media businesses. According to this view, the power to 'act politically' is derived from control over a wide variety of resources such as expertise, money, organisational capacity and moral authority. By acknowledging the insights that may be derived from the study of politics of sport and politics in sport, political science offers an important complement to the analyses provided by the other major social sciences.

TABLE 2.6 Macro-level perspectives on sports politics and policy

Key features	Neo-Marxism	Neo-pluralism	Liberal feminist	Radical feminist
Unit of analysis	Economic classes; social movements (ecological, feminist, anti-globalisation, etc.)	Groups, though an acknowledgement that business is a particularly powerful group	Gender	Gender
Social dynamic	Class conflict in the workplace but also conflicts in other areas crucial to capitalist domination such as the media and culture, and also in conflicts over social issues such as the environment, racism and sexism	Competition for influence over policy between groups	Gender relations and the advocacy and pressure group activity of social interests including those of women's organisations	Patriarchy and the resistance to patriarchal oppression by feminist activism
Role of the state	Dominated by the capitalist class but itself a site of class conflict. However, any victory for anti-capitalist interests will only be short term as in the last instance the state will defend capitalist interests	Both an arena for group competition and also an important independent policy actor	An arena for gender equity activism and a target of gender equity lobbying	Both a reflection of the patriarchal nature of society and an important source of the maintenance of patriarchy
Perception of sport	An element of contested cultural terrain may be exemplified by conflicts between fans and corporate interests for control over football clubs	A policy area around which cluster a number of interest groups which compete for the attention and resources of the state	An important arena in which to pursue gender equity	A highly visible reflection of patriarchal hegemony. When women's sport is permitted, it is done on terms dictated by male-dominated governing bodies and in ways that confirm male perceptions of appropriate sport for women

TABLE 2.6 (Continued)

Key features	Neo-Marxism	Neo-pluralism	Liberal feminist	Radical feminist
Case studies: illustrative concerns				
The national stadium	Emphasis on the impact of commercial banking interests in shaping the project and furthering the commodification of sport, but also on the motives of the government in incorporating sport into its management of national identity	Focus on the interplay of competing interests, including those whose main concern is with profit, regeneration benefits, bidding for international sports events and the promotion of national identity	Further evidence of the skewing of resources for sport towards facilities primarily used by sportsmen	The stadium is a monument to male conceptualisations of sport and an important symbolic element in the reproduction of patriarchal hegemony
Women's participation in the Olympic Games	Concerned with the significance of feminist activism as a non-class social movement. Also concerned with the role of the Games in reproducing patriarchal relations that are necessary to the continuing success of capitalism	Focus on the interplay between women's rights campaign groups and the major sports institutions	Assessing progress towards equality of access to all levels of sports competition and to all other functions within sport such as coaching and management	Concerned with the compromises required from women as a condition of participation in the patriarchal hegemony that is contemporary sport

CHAPTER SUMMARY

» Political science offers a number of subfields through which to approach the analysis of sport.
» Power is a central concept in political science whether the focus is on the actions of governments and public agencies or private sports organisations.
» The two contrasting examples of the national stadium and women's participation in the Olympic Games illustrate the range of interests involved in sports decision making and the scope for the application of perspectives in the analysis of the use of power.
» While much political science analysis of sports policy involves the application of middle-range theories and concepts the use of macro-level theories such as neo-Marxism, neo-pluralism and feminism offers valuable additional insights into the source, utilisation and consequences of power.

FURTHER READING

Goodin and Klingemann (1996) provide a clear introduction to the scope and potential of political science, while Hogwood and Gunn (1984) and John (1999) provide a similarly valuable introduction to policy analysis. Coakley (2006) applies, both directly and indirectly, concepts and theories of political science to a range of issues in sport. The volume edited by Sugden and Tomlinson (2002) investigates the concept of power in sport from a number of different perspectives. Hargreaves (1994) uses many concepts from political science in her analysis of women in sport. Houlihan (1994) and Riordan and Krüger (1999) provide political analyses of international sport. Houlihan (1997) provides a comparative analysis of sports policy and Green and Houlihan (2005) provide an analysis of elite sports development policy in three countries.

REFERENCES

Acosta, R.V. and Carpenter, J. (2000) *Women in Intercollegiate Sport: A Longitudinal Study – Twenty-three Year Update, 1977–2000.* Mimeo. Brooklyn, NY.

Banks, T. (1997) *House of Commons* debates, 3 March, col. 500W.

Coakley, J.J. (2001) *Sport in Society: Issues and Controversies.* 7th edn. Boston, MA: Irwin, McGraw-Hill.

Coakley, J.J. (2006) *Sport in Society: Issues and Controversies.* 7th edn. Boston, MA: Irwin, McGraw-Hill.

Dahl, R. (1957) 'The concept of power', *Behavioral Science,* 2: 201–15.

Department of Sport (1987) *Recreation and Tourism,* Annual report 1986–87, p. 49.

Foucault, M. (1978) *The History of Sexuality, Vol. 1.* New York: Pantheon.

Goodin, R.E. and Klingemann, H.-D. (1996) 'Political science: the discipline', in *A New Handbook of Political Science.* Oxford: Oxford University Press.

Green, M. and Houlihan, B. (2005) *Elite Sport Development: Policy Learning and Political Priorities.* London: Routledge.

Hargreaves, J. (1994) *Sporting Females: Critical Issues in the History and Sociology of Women's Sports.* London: Routledge.

Heclo, H. (1972) 'Policy analysis', *British Journal of Political Science,* 2: 83–108.

Hogwood, B. and Gunn, L. (1984) *Policy Analysis for the Real World.* London: Oxford University Press.

Houlihan, B. (1994) *Sport and International Politics.* Hemel Hempstead: Harvester Wheatsheaf.

Houlihan, B. (1997) *Sport, Policy and Politics: a Comparative Analysis.* London: Routledge.

Houlihan, B. and White, A. (2002) *The Politics of Sports Development: Development of Sport or Development through Sport.* London: Routledge.

House of Commons (2000) The Culture, Media and Sport Select Committee, 4th Report, *Wembley National Stadium,* Session 1999–2000, Cm. 4686. London: HMSO.

John, P. (1999) *Analysing Public Policy.* London: Pinter.

Laclau, E. and Mouffe, C. (1985) *Hegemony and Socialist Strategy: Towards a Radical Democratic Politics.* London: Verso.

Lasswell, D.D. (1936) *Politics: Who Gets What, When and How.* New York: McGraw-Hill.

Lukes, S. (1974) *Power: a Radical View.* London: Macmillan.

Moodie, G.C. (1984) 'Politics is about government', in A. Leftwich (ed.), *What is Politics? The Activity and its Study.* Oxford: Basil Blackwell.

Ponton, G. and Gill, P. (1993) *Introduction to Politics.* Oxford: Basil Blackwell.

Riordan, J. and Krüger, A. (1999) *The International Politics of Sport in the Twentieth Century.* London: E & FN Spon.

Sugden, J. and Tomlinson, A. (eds) (2002) *Power Games … a Critical Sociology of Sport.* London: Routledge.

White, A. and Henry, I. (2004) *Women, Leadership and the Olympic Movement.* Loughborough University: Institute of Sport and Leisure Policy.

Won, Young Shin (2001) 'Reconsidering the Olympic motto relating to socio-cultural changes and the variations of the events in the 21st century! More vividly, more harmoniously, more beautifully'. Proceedings of the First World Congress of Sociology of Sport, Yonsei University, Seoul, Korea.

3

History and Sport

MARTIN POLLEY

When J.K. Rowling created Hogwarts Academy as a supernatural version of a private school for her Harry Potter novels, she gave it a distinctive sport: Quidditch, a ball game played by teams on broomsticks. It is used in Hogwarts to teach loyalty and team-work. In recognition of the parallels with real school sports, such as the Eton Wall Game and Rugby football, Rowling created a history for Quidditch, which her characters were meant to know about:

> [Hermione] had ... lent him [Harry] *Quidditch through the Ages*, which turned out to be a very interesting read. Harry learnt that there were seven hundred ways of committing a Quidditch foul and that all of them had happened during a World Cup match in 1473. (Rowling, 1997: 133)

Under a pseudonym, Rowling subsequently wrote *Quidditch through the Ages* as a charity spin-off from her novels (2001). Successful satire always tells us much about the subject being satirised. What Rowling did through Quidditch was to draw attention to an important feature of all sports' cultures: that each sport's distinctive past matters to the people who play and follow it in the present.

Some of the ways in which this can be seen are worth considering before we analyse the ways in which history can contribute to sports studies, as they can shed light on the way in which a sense of the past is deeply engrained in contemporary sport. The related cults of record keeping and record breaking demonstrate a symbiotic relationship between past and present: Matthew Webb's Channel swim in 1875, Roger Bannister's 1954 sub-four-minute mile, and Geoff Hurst's World Cup final hat-trick of 1966, are just a few examples of superlative performances which become learnt by generations of each sport's followers. Rules and styles of play are not reinvented on a daily basis: they are inherited from the past, and adapted when new situations arise. The sporting calendar is heavily based on historical circumstances: the use of Saturday afternoons for team games is linked to the working patterns established in nineteenth-century cities, for example, while longer-term traditions around Christmas and Easter are still evident in the timing of some sports (Brailsford, 1991). The names of many events can be linked to particular moments: the 12th Earl of Derby's patronage of a horse race at Epsom in 1780, and the diffusion of a version of football out of Rugby School during the nineteenth century, are two examples of the roots of sporting names still in use. The ways in which sports are scored are linked to the past: for example, real tennis's traditional usage of a clockface has given us the point sequence in lawn tennis. The use of terminology from certain languages links sports to their roots: the widespread use of French in fencing, or of Japanese in judo, are explicable only historically.

Clubs in many sports also care about the past; and another way of seeing how the past matters in contemporary sport is to look at certain features of their cultures. The practice of naming grounds, or parts of grounds, after famous players is one way in which we can see this, evident, for example, in the Sir Tom Finney Stand at Preston North End FC's Deepdale, or in NEC Harlequins RFC's Stoop Memorial Ground. The erection of statues to significant individuals from a club's or a city's past is another form of this, as evidenced by those of footballer Billy Bremner in Leeds, cyclist Reg Harris in Manchester, and boxer Joe Louis in Detroit. The proliferation of sports museums and halls of fame, and the promotion of sports sites as tourist attractions, also bear witness to this trend. Wimbledon and Lord's include historical elements in their guided tours, for example; while specific sports are catered for by such museums as the River and Rowing Museum at Henley-on-Thames and the National Horseracing Museum at Newmarket (Vamplew, 1998). A sense of the past clearly matters to many sports' and clubs' followers whenever change is debated, whether it be the movement of a club to new premises, or a change in format or timetable. The former can be exemplified by the words of a Reading FC supporter recalling Robert Maxwell's 1983 attempt to merge this club with Oxford United: 'When will these petty despots realise that messing about with a football club is a dangerous business? The locals, wherever they are, will not go quietly' (Kirkpatrick, 2001). Indeed, this attitude can be seen in many Rugby League enthusiasts' resistance to the restructuring of the sport for the

1995–6 season (Kelner, 1996: 146–72). A large part of the sports publishing sector is devoted to non-academic historical materials such as amateur club histories, statistical records and personal histories after *Fever Pitch* (Hornby, 1992). Finally, we can see the way in which the conservation lobby is beginning to take an interest in sport sites, with such buildings as Victorian swimming pools, early modern bowling greens, and 1930s speedway tracks now attracting the attention of English Heritage (Played in Britain, 2006).

Any present-centred analysis of sport needs to remember that the past figures strongly. Moreover, any study of past societies can show that sport has mattered. Sport has taken people's attention, time and money in many historical settings, and has been seen by those playing and watching as a way of expressing community identity. Any history that ignores sport is missing something. With these strands in mind, it is clear that the historical study of sport is an academic exercise that can contribute to the interdisciplinary field of sports studies. By going to the past, we can learn both what sport was in different times and how contemporary sports developed as they did. This chapter aims to explore and analyse some of the ways in which historians can make that contribution.

HISTORIANS AND SPORT

To understand how history can contribute to the study of sport, we need first to consider some general points about what historians do. No sports historian comes to sport without some form of wider historical training. Thus, no sports historian treats sport in isolation, or comes to it without a wider sense of how history can be studied (Polley, 2007).

Historians' approaches to the past vary enormously, but some common disciplinary features unite them: 'history takes an interest in the past in its own right rather than using it as a source to explain the present' (Holt and Mason, 2000: ix). However, there are limitations on what historians can study, which gives us the second common disciplinary feature: they can study only parts of the past that left evidence behind, and for which evidence has survived. The dominant type of evidence has been documentary: government archives, private papers, newspapers and published materials have long been the most consulted forms of sources. The range has recently broadened, and many historians are now happy to use artefacts, buildings, visual evidence, oral testimony and many other non-written sources (Brivati et al., 1996: parts III–VII). However, regardless of the type of evidence, the point is that without some evidence, historians cannot function. So all studies of history are driven by the discovery of evidence from the period being studied, and its analysis and interpretation. Historians aim to be able to describe what happened, explain how and why it happened, and link past events to wider contexts and to the passage of time.

This requirement for evidence from the period being studied has helped to create something of an anti-theoretical strand in some historical writing. Generations of historians have been trained to find evidence, interpret it and then come to a conclusion. In this setting, many practitioners have avoided overtly theoretical approaches in favour of empiricism. In the second half of the twentieth century, uncontested empiricism became less prevalent, particularly under the influence of Marxism, feminism, psychoanalysis, structuralism and postmodernism. Moreover, Collingwood's *The Idea of History* (1994), and Carr's *What Is History?* (1961) and postmodernist texts such as Munslow's *Deconstructing History* (1997) encouraged historians to think critically about the nature of their evidence, the decisions involved in choosing subject matter and sources, and how the historian's autobiography influences the way in which s/he approaches the past (Carr, 1961; Collingwood, 1994; Munslow, 1997). These influences have made many historians critical of the things that their predecessors took for granted. In this setting, 'the removal of "objective truth" as a meaningful goal is counterbalanced by a perceived need for many different accounts of the past – none claiming any special privilege, but each providing some illumination from its own perspective' (Southgate, 1996: 8). A consideration of these issues can help us to understand how historians approach their subject matter.

A final characteristic that we need to note is that historians' approaches to the past change over time. All historians live and work in their own present, and however much a historian may immerse her/himself in the period under investigation, that present will be evident in what gets written. The topics chosen for study vary with time and are influenced by contemporary concerns and personal ideology: for example, very few historians investigated women's history before the growth of feminism (Holloway, 1998). The sources historians use do not remain static, as new materials may be discovered or made available. This is most obvious in the annual release of government archives under the 30-year rule in the British system (Cox, 1996). The methodologies used vary with time and technology, seen most obviously in the recent growth of computer-based projects. Historians are linked to their own time and place through the media in which their work is disseminated: mass-produced books, academic journals, websites and television documentaries are four media in which historians currently work, none of which has been available for all historians who have ever lived. Finally, the historian's vocabulary will link the historian to the time and place of research and publication, a point illustrated in this chapter by the use of subjective pronouns that are not gender specific.

These examples illustrate the observation that the historian's agenda is set by a combination of past and present: the events and issues that mattered at the time being studied meet the attitudes, ideologies, techniques, language and hindsight of the historian's own day. Historians can work around these constraints by avoiding anachronistic treatment of their periods. Holt and Mason's model is one to aspire to here. Writing in the late 1990s about British sport in the period immediately following the Second World War, they justified the themes covered in their book in historical rather than contemporary terms:

> We have tried to piece together what mattered *then* rather than what matters now. Women, ethnic minorities and the disabled are more important in the 1990s than they

were in the 1950s and we try to explain this. But the 1950s cannot be understood simply in terms of the absence of disadvantaged groups. Post-war sport had its own agenda which has to be understood in its own terms. (Holt and Mason, 2000: ix; emphasis in original)

However, despite historians using these criteria as part of their basic approach, the links between the past and the historian's present are ultimately unavoidable. We can see this very clearly in Collins's *Rugby's Great Split*, his 1998 monograph on the development of Rugby League. He starts by asking 'Why are there two forms of rugby?': 'given the profound changes which both rugby league and rugby union are currently undergoing, the question now has an importance which transcends mere historical curiosity' (1998: xi). For our purposes, the keywords here are 'currently' and 'now'. Only a historian writing in the late 1990s, who had witnessed the development of professionalism in Rugby Union and the league code's restructuring, could have approached the subject in this way. We must keep this relationship between the time of writing and the historiography in mind if we are to understand the ways in which historians have approached sport.

Once we accept this relationship, then we can put sports history into a disciplinary context. Historians have not always been interested in sport as an area of analysis. Up until the late 1960s, sport was largely ignored, despite the fact that history by that time encompassed many political, social, economic and cultural subjects. In 1963, James highlighted the anomalies involved in historians' ignorance of sport when he argued in favour of cricket's inclusion in social history books:

A famous Liberal historian [Trevelyan] can write the social history of England in the nineteenth century, and two famous Socialists [Postgate and Cole] can write what they declared to be the history of the common people of England, and between them never once mention the man who was the best-known Englishman of his time. I can no longer accept the system of values which could not find in these books a place for W.G. Grace. (1963: 157)

By the end of the 1960s, as Baker (1983) has shown, only a few books had attempted to bring sport into academic history, most notably Brailsford's *Sport and Society* (1969). This pioneering work, driven by the assumption that sport was related to the society in which it took place, was expanded in the 1970s and 1980s by a new generation of sports historians, including Holt, Mangan, Mason and Vamplew. By the late 1980s, the subject was being taught at universities, while new research was being fostered by journals (such as *The International Journal of the History of Sport*), monograph series (such as that by Manchester University Press) and by the British Society of Sports History (BSSH) (Cox, 2000; Holt, 1996; Polley, 1998: 166–71; Vamplew, 2000). The expansion of the subject matter was acknowledged by Holt in 1989 in the introduction to *Sport and the British*. His attempt to 'explain the nature of sport in modern Britain in terms of change in society, politics, and culture' had been made possible by the changing academic climate: 'It is only as a result of the appearance of a substantial body of new research in the history of sport itself and in the wider realm of social history that such a survey can be attempted at all' (1989: vii). Holt's declaration was a clear sign that an academic historiography of sport had emerged.

These trends continued since the late 1980s, but with some notable developments helping to establish sports history as a branch of historical study. Higher education institutions' willingness to support postgraduate studies in the field has created a training structure for sports historians. Undergraduate courses have also proliferated. These developments helped to create markets for more books, for which academic publishers such as Frank Cass have catered. Cass's series 'Sport in the Global Society', subsequently taken over by Routledge, showed history's place in the mainstream of the socio-cultural study of sport. Alongside works rooted in sociology (such as Finn and Giulianotti, 2000), the law (such as Greenfield and Osborn, 2000) and politics (e.g. Booth, 1998) were books based firmly in history, notably Beck's *Scoring for Britain* (1999) and Williams's *Cricket and England* (1999). The BSSH continued to grow, broadening its constituency in the late 1990s by promoting both non-British and postgraduate research (BSSH, 2001). British sports historiography's coming of age was neatly summarised by Beck. When comparing an unpublished early 1980s version of his research on football with his 1999 monograph, he noted that 'whereas previously I included a whole chapter justifying the historical study of sport, today such a rationale seems superfluous' (1999: vii). So, despite the 'suspicions of those who drift slowly along what is left of the old historical mainstream' (Lowerson, 1998: 201), British sports history has now become a vital and dynamic area of historiography. It has an increasingly diverse gaze, taking in the global and the local, the general and the specific, and the paradigms of class, gender, ethnicity and physical ability. Moreover, British sports historians have established good links with colleagues in many other disciplines, and with sports historians working in other parts of the world, particularly through such organisations as the North American Society for Sport History (NASSH) and the International Society for the History of Physical Education and Sport (ISHPES). These characteristics enable it to make a distinctive contribution to the wider study of sport in society, one that complements and supplements the approaches of the present-centred disciplines.

WHAT HISTORY CAN CONTRIBUTE

What, then, has sports history told us about sport? What can sports studies gain from a consideration of historiography? Any attempt to synthesise the historiography is bound to be selective, so we shall concentrate on a number of areas in which historians' insights can benefit any other social science or humanities-based enquiry into sport.

The first theme that has emerged is an obvious one: that sport has been played differently in different settings across time. From this starting point a great deal of analysis of the nature of sport, and of the nature of its relationship with its contexts, has flowed. It is easy to assume that the models on which our sports are based embody eternal values. As Guttmann noted after introducing classical sport to his sociology students, the fact that 'the sports festivals of the ancient Greeks took place without significant quantification and without the modern obsession with the sport record is … a great surprise' (1990: 239). Sports history can help us to refine our vocabulary and our assumptions beyond the kind of common-sense approach criticised by Guttmann. To begin with, the term 'sport' itself is shown up as historically variable and relative. Up until the mid-nineteenth century, 'sport' was usually taken to entail hunting, shooting and fishing. The term was appropriated for team games and individual physical activities after that; and it is now fluid, as activities as wide ranging as Building, Antennae, Span, Earth (BASE) jumping, extreme ironing and ballroom dancing bid for categorisation as sports, while older activities such as shin-kicking also contend for recognition. Historical study can allow us to get above emotive and absolute positions in such debates, and recognise that meanings change in relation to social change.

Beyond semantics, historical study shows us that the use of current sports' names can be misleading if they are applied uncritically to past physical activities. Records of activities called 'football' exist from at least the fourteenth century (Russell, 1997: 5), but none of the games played under that name in the early twenty-first century can claim a simple linear relationship over 700 years. Association, Australian Rules, Gridiron, Rugby League, Rugby Union, for example, all have structural features in common with the many local and regional versions of the pre-industrial period. They are all invasion games involving varying amounts of handling, kicking and running.

To trace lineage is far harder than noting basic similarities, however, as the diffusion routes are extremely complicated. This can be illustrated through the example of Rugby Union in Wales. The Rugby School version of football was introduced to Wales by old Rugbeans through Llandovery College and St David's College, Lampeter. The Rugby version itself drew on various local traditions, while the areas in West and South Wales exposed to the Rugby/Lampeter/Llandovery version had their own traditions. By the 1870s, the modern form had emerged under the name of rugby football, which went on to become the major male team sport of the area (Smith and Williams, 1980). Counter this complicated route, which has come to light through historical research, against a simplistic account of how 'football' in Welsh villages in the sixteenth and seventeenth centuries was a direct forerunner of modern Rugby Union. So, instead of approaching the development of sport from the present, and looking for patterns in the obvious folk games appearing in all sports' genealogies, sports history encourages us to judge the past by its own standards. It may be convenient to claim that 'ancient Central and South American civilizations played a form of basketball, which they called pok-tapok', but it cannot be accurate: the people playing pok-tapok could not have conceptualised their activity as 'a form of basketball' (Cox and Physick, 2000: 31). So the first point to emerge from sports historiography – that sports have been played in different ways at different times – can teach us to avoid anachronism.

The second theme that we can isolate is linked to a basic concept in the present-centred study of sport: that all sports are linked to the contexts in which they are played. If we are to understand how sports have developed, and how sport in the present inherits features from the past, then we need to think about the wider contexts in which sports are played. Historians of the British Isles have tended to divide that area's history into three broad periods: pre-industrial, industrial and post-industrial, with the first running approximately to the mid-eighteenth century, the second running into the twentieth century and the last emerging from approximately the 1930s. These models are problematic. In particular, applying the points about anachronism made above should stop us from using the phrase 'pre-industrial', since the people living then could not have known what was coming next. However, the periodisation does work as a useful model for examinations of social, economic and cultural activity. This three-part model has been attractive to many historians who have wanted to contextualise sport.

The assumption at work here is that the predominant characteristics and 'core features' (Horne et al., 1999: 2) of the given society will be evident in the sports that it played. There are two linked elements to this. First, that the contexts within which sport is played provide historically relative opportunities and constraints for those involved; and second, that the form the play itself takes – its level of physicality, its degree of regulation, its timespan and so on – is linked to shared characteristics of the people playing at that moment in time.

The opportunities and constraints model has proved useful for historians wanting to understand the relationship of any sport with its society. Much of the analysis in this area has concentrated on social class, a detail which we can link to the early academic sports historians' research agendas, influenced as they were by 'history from below' (Lowerson, 1998: 201; Wiggins and Mason, 2005: 40–3). Malcolmson's *Popular Recreations in English Society 1700–1850* (1973), Mason's *Association Football and English Society, 1863–1915* (1980) and Bailey's *Leisure and Class in Victorian England* (1978) set an agenda which has remained relevant in sports history (Collins, 1998; Holt, 1989; Holt and Mason, 2000; Jones, 1986; Polley, 1998). While the bulk of this work has been on working-class sport, Lowerson (1993), Holt (1989, 1996) and others have shifted attention to the middle classes. Subsequent work has kept class in focus, but has also taken other contexts into account: gender, ethnicity, politics and group identities have all been brought in as important contextual issues.

A few examples will suffice here. Brailsford's work (1969) on leisure in the early modern period showed how educational precepts and religious beliefs set limitations on the amount of sport that could be played, and on its timing. The Puritans' objections to recreational Sabbath-breaking, for example, and their suppression of sports and games that were redolent of Catholicism, placed constraints on what could be played. For the nineteenth century, Bailey (1978) and others have shown how the provision of sport in various areas was linked to wider socio-economic settings, and to the political and social concerns of the providers. Hargreaves's *Sporting Females* (1994) brought together much of the pioneering work on women's sport, and showed how contexts based in gender relations influenced which sports could be played by women; while Vertinsky's work has explored the cultural representation of gender in various sporting locations (Vertinsky, 1990; Vertinsky and Mckay, 2004) The influence of political contexts on sporting opportunities and constraints can be seen in Beck's work (1999) on the relationships between sport and British diplomacy. Domestic political contexts were explored in Jones's work (1988) on the role of trade unions and the Labour Party in lobbying for more time and sports facilities during the interwar period, and the role of communist and socialist organisations in promoting alternative sporting events. The influence of wider senses of identity on sport can be seen in Cronin's work on Ireland (1999), where widespread discourses of nationalism, republicanism and unionism have all influenced people's access to sport. It has also been explored through many regional and local studies of sport, of which Hill and Williams's collection of essays on *Sport and Identity in the North of England* (1996) and Metcalfe's *Leisure and Recreation in a Victorian Mining Community* (2006) are excellent examples. These are illustrations of the wealth of work that has been done in this area. The contexts outlined here show that we need to look beyond the basic model of a sport's socio-economic setting. It is only through a holistic approach to contexts that we can get a clear picture of why certain sports flourished in certain settings.

When we come to the relationship between the historical context and the form that sports have taken, historians have been particularly influenced by two models, developed by Guttmann (1978) and by Dunning and Sheard (1979). Guttmann developed his model by defining 'seven characteristics of modern sports': secularism; equality; specialisation; rationalisation; bureaucracy; quantification; and records (1978: 54). These were 'likely to be taken for granted and to be thought of as self-evidently "natural"' (1978: 15). His model became historical in its exploration of the sports of different periods, from primitive to modern. He checked off his seven characteristics against the sports of these settings. For example, he found that classical Roman sport had much in common with modern sport, with only the importance of religion, limited equality of access and limited quantification marking it as different. His analysis of how sports were performed in different settings established a useful model. However, it can be problematic because of its apparently present-centred approach: it appears to account for change over time by showing what sport was moving towards (i.e. the modern model), rather than what players in the past were 'moving away from' (Struna, 2001). Nevertheless, his sociological and anthropological insights did much to focus historians' attention on how the forms of sport embody wider values, best illustrated in his overarching model of how the rise in the quantification of sports performance ('record') has been related over time to the decline of sport's religious significance ('ritual'):

> When we can no longer distinguish the sacred from the profane or even the good from the bad, we content ourselves with minute discriminations between the batting average of the .308 hitter and the .307 hitter. Once the gods have vanished from Mount Olympus or Dante's paradise, we can no longer run to appease them or to save our souls, but we can set a new record. It is a uniquely modern form of immortality. (Guttmann, 1978: 55)

Because of Guttmann's wide-ranging periodisation, and the fact that British sport was not central to his work, his model for explaining the forms of sports in historical context has been less influential in British sports historiography than Dunning and Sheard's more specific model. Working within figurational sociology, they developed a schema for understanding sport in historical context for their study of rugby football, *Barbarians, Gentlemen and Players* (1979). They took the basic periodisation of 'premodern' and 'modern', which they linked to socio-economic and cultural characteristics, and identified certain features that were present in the team games of each period. Their table, 'The structural properties of folk games and modern sports', listed 15 characteristics common to each type of game, paired in oppositional terms to allow comparison over time. For example, the lack of 'fixed limits on territory, duration, or numbers of participants' of folk games was placed alongside the 'spatially limited pitch with clearly defined boundaries, within fixed time limits and with a fixed number of participants' of modern sports (Dunning and Sheard, 1979: 33–4). This scheme synthesised historians' findings on how pre-industrial and industrial Britain had played, and fitted into figurational sociology's wider interest in uncovering cultural aspects of the 'civilising process'.

This approach has been very influential in all British sports historiography, and has been widely assimilated as a framework for understanding the dramatic changes that occurred in sport during the nineteenth century. Its influence is still evident, as seen in Horne et al.'s reproduction of the table in their *Understanding Sport* (1999: 9). Moreover, Dunning and Sheard recognised that folk games sometimes survived the modernisation process in relatively unchanged forms, exemplified by them in the Ashbourne version of folk football and the specific forms of football played at Eton (Dunning and Sheard, 1979: 4–5). Other historians have developed the theme of survival of old forms alongside the development of new forms, exemplified by Holt's cameo of Jerry Dawson to illustrate this. In the early twentieth century, Dawson played one of the modernised versions of football – Association Football – to a high standard, playing in goal for Burnley and England. Alongside this, he was 'a champion at knur-and-spell', a traditional sport played on moorland in Lancashire and Yorkshire. Similarly, this trend has also been shown in Murfin's coverage of football in Workington. A traditional form of football, matching all of Dunning and Sheard's characteristics as a folk game, was played from at least 1775. It involved teams of unequal sizes playing across meadows, streets, the beach and the river, with the 'goals' a mile apart. This game increased in frequency to three times a year in the late nineteenth century, at a time when such sports were supposed to be dying out. Alongside this, Workington also developed a number of organised Association Football teams. The most successful one, Workington Town FC, was formed in 1884, two years after the third Easter match was probably instituted. The club and the folk game coexisted, suggesting that both versions were meaningful to their players and followers regardless of the changing context (Murfin, 1990: 110–15).

However, putting too much emphasis on modernisation as a specifically industrial development can disguise the fact that some sports became highly organised before industrialisation. Horse racing, cricket and golf had widely accepted rules, decision-making bodies and high levels of national organisation by the mid-eighteenth century. Indeed some of the clubs involved – the Jockey Club, Marylebone Cricket Club and the Royal and Ancient Golf Club at St Andrews – remain influential. Evidence also exists of multi-sport events, requiring high levels of organisation, which took place in various parts of the British Isles in the seventeenth and eighteenth centuries. Furthermore, the modernisation model clearly cannot be applied to all parts of the British Isles at the same time. It may work for the ports, textile and mining towns of the industrial period, which became the heartlands of the large-scale male team sports of football and Rugby League; however, it had far later relevance for such areas as mid-Wales, rural Scotland, the bulk of Ireland and south-western England. Beyond these historical examples, the survival of such a blatantly premodern sport as fox hunting into the twenty-first century also shows up the model's limitations beyond team sports. The model of premodern and modern sports has thus been an influential one in focusing historians' attention on how, when and why sports change in relation to wider socio-economic change, but its limitations need to be recognised. However, the ways in which many historians have attempted to apply it critically serve as a neat illustration of the theory/empiricism clash evident in much historical work. Despite these debates, the key point remains that work on the history of sport has shown up ways in which sports in the past have been linked to wider contexts, both through the opportunities and constraints that fenced the events, and through the exact forms that sports took. We cannot hope to understand sports in the present unless we explore this aspect of their past.

Our third theme – that of origins – is linked to the wider issue of contexts, but is worth studying on its own. This is because it is an area of the past which, if left to individual sport's apologists, would remain mythologised. It is difficult to ascribe a precise moment of origin to any sport. Organised forms tended to evolve out of various local and regional versions, with diffusion routes and wider contexts of technology, patronage and the media playing their parts in shaping the new versions. However, the quest for origins is one that interests historians in many areas. In researching sport and play, historians have encountered many problems in their attempts to identify the first recognisable form of a particular sport. Young, in his *History of British Football*, noted that 'a historian knows that to speak of any phenomenon as being the first of its kind is either impossible, or impolitic, or both' (1968: 3). The evidence of forms of organised play from all societies for which we have records bears this out. However, many sports establishments have worked hard to promote a straightforward heritage for their sports, a heritage designed to stress both antiquity and legitimacy. MacLennan gives us an extreme example of this in his work on shinty (*Camanachd*). He quotes from *The Book of the Club of True Highlanders* of 1881, which notes:

> [I]t is said, and, no doubt, with great truth, that the game of *Camanachd*, or club playing, was introduced into the Green Isle [Great Britain] by the immediate descendants

of Noah. On such authority we may rationally conclude that it was played by Noah himself; and if by Noah, in all probability by Adam and his sons. (Quoted in MacLennan, 1998: 4)

While no one would dispute that ancient peoples played games, the attempt to trace a linear history from biblical to modern times needs to be treated critically.

The quest for origins has not gone exclusively to the ancient world: in many sports specific 'origin myths' have been located in the modern period. Dunning et al. (1993) have drawn attention to two such events that are often cited as specific moments of birth: the 'Doubleday myth' of 1839 in baseball, and the 'Webb Ellis story' from 1823 in Rugby Union. Claiming that belief in these myths is 'a kind of sports equivalent of the belief in the tooth fairy or Father Christmas', the authors draw our attention instead to the political and social reasons why certain groups wanted to promote such specific myths (1993: 1). Going beyond this, historians have confirmed the truth of Young's comments, and accepted that games based on invasion principles, or striking/fielding principles, cannot be simplistically linked to modern sports with those structural similarities. Indeed, the wide variety of modern sports which do share such similarities – such as cricket, baseball, rounders and stoolball, or the many versions of football – warns us against any belief in linearity. The specific 'origin' of any one of them needs to be linked to local and regional issues, and to the power relations of the individual game's promoters, rather than any moment of invention.

It is this type of origin, rather than mythical moments of birth, that has exercised historians, who have been involved in studying how specific sports emerged by name, and under some kind of control, at different points in history. It is the attention to the organised and standardised nature of these events for which primary evidence is available that has been evident in the historiography. Collins (1998) has done this in an exemplary way in his account of the splits within rugby football in the 1880s and 1890s that led to the formation of the northern rugby union, which, in 1922, took on the name of Rugby League. Similarly, Mason (1980) examined the gradual formalisation of rules and practices between different football clubs in the 1850s and 1860s which led to the formation of the Football Association in 1863, while Harvey and Dunning have conducted a fascinating debate about the relative roles of different schools and clubs in the early years of English football (Dunning, 2001; Harvey, 2001, 2005). So, while the subject of origins has rightly occupied many historians, they have tended to approach it critically and empirically rather than tracing any sport's pedigree back to Genesis. Here we can see the historian's insistence on evidence shaping the way in which s/he approaches the past, and the attendant scepticism towards mythologised views of the past.

These are some of the key themes that have emerged from sports historiography. Taken together, they show up the richness and complexity of sport in the past, while also demonstrating the problems involved in taking too narrow an approach to how sport developed. While sports historians recognise the value of looking at sport in the past as a way of understanding sport in the present, their work shows that sport in the past needs to be understood on its terms.

LINKS WITH OTHER DISCIPLINES

Academic sports historians have not been the only people to explore sport's past. Non-academic historians, who have come to the subject out of enthusiasm and interest, have also worked in this area. These historians, typically devoted to individual clubs or institutions, 'often deal with their topic without reference to the wider issues' (Vamplew, 2000: 179). Holt noted that the historiography they produced was 'little more than the book of Chronicles or the book of Numbers' (1989: 2). However, the particular contribution that this literature makes is becoming recognised by academics: Vamplew, for example, has praised the way in which such work can provide 'empirical evidence needed to test academic hypotheses' (2000: 179).

Another group to have made a contribution to the understanding of sport in the past has been sports sociologists, particularly those working within the tradition of developmental or figurational sociology after Elias. Dunning, Maguire, Jarvie and others have gone to sport's pasts in order to trace the development of forms over time, always linking change and continuity in sport to 'structured processes that occur over time and space. Emphasis is placed on probing how the present has emerged out of the past' (Jarvie and Maguire, 1994: 132). Under this academic flag, useful work has been done which has illuminated how sports have emerged. As we have seen, concepts and models from this approach have influenced the approaches of many historians. Indeed, many of the individuals involved work comfortably in both history and sociology camps, exemplified best by Grant Jarvie. A sociologist by training, Jarvie was the Chairman of the BSSH from 1997 until 2001, while his publications range from an analysis of the development of Highland Games through to a co-authored survey of the main issues in sports sociology and a book on the global role of sport (Jarvie, 1991; Jarvie and Maguire, 1994; Jarvie, 2005). Hargreaves's work also illustrates this linkage, most obviously in her seminal *Sporting Females* of 1994. However, it is worth noting that there are some genuine differences between the approaches of historians and sociologists, despite the success with which some individuals have balanced the disciplines:

> Sociologists frequently complain that historians lack a conceptual framework for their research, whilst historians tend to feel social theorists require them to compress the diversity of the past into artificially rigid categories and dispense with empirical verification of their theories. (Holt, 1989: 357)

The debates that this can lead sports analysis into are neatly summarised and exemplified by Horne et al. (1999: 73–94). Their claim that 'history without adequate conceptualisation or theorisation can be little more than a form of antiquarianism' (1999: 77) is a useful rejoinder to some historians' anti-theoretical stances.

Sociology has also been influential in getting historians to interview people who took part in the events being analysed. The development of oral history in the 1960s borrowed from qualitative sociology the idea that ordinary participants' accounts could contribute to our understanding of an event or phenomenon. It clearly has limitations for any historian: the survival of witnesses, the reliability of their memory and the role of hindsight all influence the process. However, many historians have been happy to use it as a way of getting factual information about events that may not have been recorded in other sources, and as a way of bringing to life the culture that surrounded these events. These aspects have been obvious in, for example, Duval's work (2001) on women's athletics, in which interviewees talked not just about participation, but also about the social life that surrounded the sport, and in the Oral History Society's 2006 annual conference on 'Passion, Play and the Everyday'. This approach is now becoming commonplace.

While sociology may be the most obvious discipline to complement sports history, it is not the only one. A few examples must suffice. Whannel's work on sport and the media, particularly *Fields in Vision* (1992), includes coverage of television's historical relationship with sport, as well as models for analysis of media texts that historians can use. In cultural studies, Blake's work on sport, alongside his work on literature and pop music, has analysed sport's cultural place over time, with an emphasis on such aspects as its language, and on the ways in which the sporting body has been displayed (1996). The influence of cultural studies on sports historians is becoming notable as a number of them apply models from linguistic theory to their primary sources (Oriard, 2005). Hill (1998) has been influential here. His reading of the 'legend' of footballer and cricketer Denis Compton is characterised by an emphasis on narratives and mythologies within the texts written about him. Through this approach, we can learn not just what happened, but what sport meant to its players, followers and administrators, and how it fitted into their world views. Geography is another discipline with some links to sports history, best seen in Bale's work on sporting landscapes and townscapes, notably in *Landscapes of Modern Sport* (1994). In all of these areas, and many more, a fascinating cross-fertilisation has gone on between sports historians and sports analysts based in other disciplines.

CONCLUSION

This chapter has outlined some of the approaches taken by sports historians to provide us with a detailed picture of how sports were in the past. Sports historians, and their colleagues in other disciplines, have demonstrated and exemplified the links between sports and their various contexts, and have shown how both continuity and change across time have given us the sports we play in the present. As sports history has developed into a subdiscipline of history, it has attracted more academics, many with new questions to ask of old material, or with wholly new research agendas. This is also demonstrated by the growth of works of synthesis, which is always evidence of the health of a discipline. The fact that mainstream historians writing general texts on periods of British history now routinely include some sporting material is another sign of the discipline's importance, as seen in Marwick's *British Society since 1945* (1996). Moreover, while academic journals catering exclusively for sports history develop and thrive, notably *The International Journal of the History of Sport* and *The Sports Historian*, other journals continue to pick up on the subject: the *Journal of Contemporary History* and *History Today* are among those that have encouraged research on sport.

This suggests that the discipline of history is now taking sports history seriously. Sports studies is also taking sports history seriously. The inclusion of historical chapters in many key texts in the field stresses the fact that sports studies students need to know about the past: Cashmore (2000), Coakley (1998) and Horne et al. (1999) all deploy history as a necessary area for any understanding of the subject, while methodological guides aimed at sport students are also providing historical guidance, such as Polley's book on sports history (2007), and the chapters on historical research in Andrews et al. (2005) and Thomas et al. (2005). It is within this tradition that this essay has been offered. While it has been acknowledged that a knowledge of sports history is an important part of any study of sport, emphasis has also been placed on how to deal with the material that historians write. Without engaging with the culture within which historians work, and without looking at the common interests and themes running through much of the diverse historiography, it is easy to use historians' writings simply as a storehouse for factual information. While sports historiography must fulfil this purpose, it is about more than this: it is about our interest in roots and origins, and our desire to know what happened and why.

CHAPTER SUMMARY

» Historians aim to describe what happened, explain why it happened, and link past events to wider contexts and to the passage of time.

» Although largely ignored by social historians until the late 1960s, sports history is now a vital and dynamic area of historiography.

» Sports history encourages us to judge the past by its own standards and to understand sport in the context in which it is played. In particular, sports history highlights the effect of political and social context on what sport is played, by whom and in what way.

» There has been a mutually enriching dialogue especially between historians and sociologists, but also with geographers and students of the media.

FURTHER READING

Brailsford's 1969 text remains a key introduction to the scope, methods and potential of sports history. Guttmann (1978) and Dunning and Sheard (1979, revised edition 2005) also provide contrasting, but highly stimulating and wide-ranging historical analyses of sport. Jarvie's 1991 study of the Highland Games, Whannel's 1992 study of sport and the media, and Hargreaves's 1994 study of women's sport all demonstrate the insight that can be derived from sports history in the study of particular aspects of sport. Struna (2001) and Vamplew (2000) discuss some of the methodological issues that sports historians face, while large-scale works of synthesis that link sport to wider contexts include those by Hill (2002), Holt and Mason (2000), Jarvie (2005) and Polley (1998).

REFERENCES

Andrews, David, Mason, Daniel and Silk, Michael (eds) (2005) *Qualitative Methods in Sports Studies.* Oxford: Berg.

Bailey, Peter (1978) *Leisure and Class in Victorian England: Rational Recreation and the Contest for Control, 1830–1885.* London: Routledge & Kegan Paul.

Baker, William (1983) 'The state of British sport history', *Journal of Sport History*, 10 (1): 53–66.

Bale, John (1994) *Landscapes of Modern Sport.* Leicester: Leicester University Press.

Beck, Peter (1999) *Scoring for Britain: International Football and International Politics, 1900–1939.* London: Frank Cass.

Blake, Andrew (1996) *The Body Language: the Meaning of Modern Sport.* London: Lawrence & Wishart.

Booth, Douglas (1998) *The Race Game: Sport and Politics in South Africa.* London: Frank Cass.

Brailsford, Dennis (1969) *Sport and Society: Elizabeth to Anne.* London: Routledge & Kegan Paul.

Brailsford, Dennis (1991) *Sport, Time, and Society: the British at Play.* London: Routledge.

British Society of Sports History (BSSH), official website http://www.umist.ac.uk/sport/index2.htm

Brivati, B., Buxton, J. and Seldon, A. (eds) (1996) *The Contemporary History Handbook.* Manchester: Manchester University Press.

Carr, E.H. (1961) *What Is History?* London: Penguin.

Cashmore, Ellis (2000) *Making Sense of Sports.* 3rd edn. London: Routledge.

Coakley, Jay (1998) *Sport in Society: Issues and Controversies.* 6th edn. Boston, MA: Irwin McGraw-Hill.

Collingwood, R.G. (1994) *The Idea of History.* Revised edn. Oxford: Oxford University Press.

Collins, Tony (1998) *Rugby's Great Split: Class, Culture and the Origins of Rugby League Football.* London: Frank Cass.

Cox, Nicholas (1996) 'National British archives: public records', in B. Brivati, J. Buxton and A. Seldon (eds), *The Contemporary History Handbook.* Manchester: Manchester University Press, pp. 253–71.

Cox, Richard (2000) 'British Society of Sports History', in Richard Cox, Grant Jarvie and Wray Vamplew (eds), *Encyclopedia of British Sport.* Oxford: ABC-Clio, pp. 48–9.

Cox, Richard and Physick, Ray (2000) 'Basketball', in Richard Cox, Grant Jarvie and Wray Vamplew (eds), *Encyclopedia of British Sport.* Oxford: ABC-Clio, pp. 31–3.

Cronin, Mike (1999) *Sport and Nationalism in Ireland.* Dublin: Four Courts Press.

Dunning, Eric (2001) 'Something of a curate's egg: comments on Adrian Harvey's "An Epoch in the Annals of National Sport"', *International Journal of the History of Sport,* 18(4): 88–94.

Dunning, Eric and Sheard, Kenneth (1979) *Barbarians, Gentlemen and Players: a Sociological Study of the Development of Rugby Football.* Oxford: Martin Robertson.

Dunning, E., Maguire, J. and Pearton, R. (1993) 'Introduction: sports in comparative and developmental perspective', in E. Dunning, J. Maguire and R. Pearton (eds), *The Sports Process: a Comparative and Developmental Approach.* Champaign, IL: Human Kinetics, pp. 1–18.

Duval, Lynne (2001) 'The development of women's track and field in England: the role of the athletic clubs, 1920s–1950s', *The Sports Historian,* 21 (1): 1–34.

Finn, Gerry P.T. and Giulianotti, Richard (eds) (2000) *Football Cultures: Local Contests, Global Visions.* London: Frank Cass.

Greenfield, Steve and Osborn, Guy (eds) (2000) *Law and Sport in Contemporary Society.* London: Frank Cass.

Guttmann, Allen (1978) *From Ritual to Record: the Nature of Modern Sports.* New York: Columbia University Press.

Guttmann, Allen (1990) 'Teaching "sport and society"', in D.L. Vanderwerken (ed.), *Sport in the Classroom: Teaching Sport-Related Courses in the Humanities.* London: Associated University Press, pp. 237–47.

Hargreaves, Jennifer (1994) *Sporting Females: Critical Issues in the History and Sociology of Women's Sport.* London: Routledge.

Harvey, Adrian (2001) 'An epoch in the annals of national sport: football in Sheffield and the creation of modern soccer and rugby', *International Journal of the History of Sport,* 18(4): 53–87.

Harvey, Adrian (2005) *Football: the First Hundred Years: the untold story.* London: Routledge.

Hill, Jeffrey (1998) 'The legend of Denis Compton', *The Sports Historian,* 18 (2): 19–33.

Hill, Jeffrey (2002) *Sport, Leisure and Culture in Twentieth-Century Britain*. Basingstoke: Palgrave.

Hill, Jeff and Williams, Jack (eds) (1996) *Sport and Identity in the North of England*. Keele: Keele University Press.

Holloway, Gerry (1998) 'Writing women in: the development of feminist approaches to women's history', in William Lamont (ed.), *Historical Controversies and Historians*. London: UCL Press.

Holt, Richard (1989) *Sport and the British: a Modern History*. Oxford: Oxford University Press.

Holt, Richard (1996) 'Sport and history: the state of the subject in Britain', *Twentieth Century British History*, 7(2): 231–52.

Holt, Richard and Mason, Tony (2000) *Sport in Britain 1945–2000*. Oxford: Blackwell.

Hornby, Nick (1992) *Fever Pitch: a Fan's Life*. London: Victor Gollancz.

Horne, John, Tomlinson, Alan and Whannel, Garry (1999) *Understanding Sport: an Introduction to the Sociological and Cultural Analysis of Sport*. London: E & FN Spon.

James, C.L.R. (1963) *Beyond a Boundary*. London: Stanley Paul.

Jarvie, Grant (1991) *Highland Games: the Making of the Myth*. Edinburgh: Edinburgh University Press.

Jarvie, Grant (2005) *Sport, Culture and Society: An Introduction*. London: Routledge.

Jarvie, Grant and Maguire, Joseph (1994) *Sport and Leisure in Social Thought*. London: Routledge.

Jones, Stephen (1986) *Workers at Play: a Social and Economic History of Leisure 1918–1939*. London: Routledge & Kegan Paul.

Jones, Stephen (1988) *Sport, Politics and the Working Class: Organised Labour and Sport in Interwar Britain*. Manchester: Manchester University Press.

Kelner, Simon (1996) *To Jerusalem and Back*. London: Macmillan.

Kirkpatrick, Jeff (2001) 'Reading', *Guardian Unlimited*, 21 February 2001. http://football.guardian.co.uk/fanzines/story/0,8507,441097,00.html (accessed April 2001).

Lowerson, John (1993) *Sport and the English Middle Classes*. Manchester: Manchester University Press.

Lowerson, John (1998) 'Opiate of the people and stimulant of the historian? Some issues in sports history', in W. Lamont (ed.), *Historical Controversies and Historians*. London: UCL Press, pp. 201–14.

MacLennan, Hugh Dan (1998) 'Shinty's place and space in the world', *The Sports Historian*, 18 (1): 1–23.

Malcolmson, R.W. (1973) *Popular Recreations in English Society 1700–1850*. Cambridge: Cambridge University Press.

Marwick, Arthur (1996) *British Society since 1945*. 3rd edn. Harmondsworth: Penguin.

Mason, Tony (1980) *Association Football and English Society, 1863–1915*. Hassocks: Harvester.

Metcalfe, Alun (2006) *Leisure and Recreation in a Victorian Mining Community: the Social Economy of Leisure in North-East England, 1820–1914*. London: Routledge.

Munslow, Alun (1997) *Deconstructing History*. London: Routledge.

Murfin, Lyn (1990) *Popular Leisure in the Lake Counties*. Manchester: Manchester University Press.

Oriard, Michael (2005) 'A linguistic turn into sport history', in M. Phillips (ed.), *Deconstructing Sport History: a Postmodern Analysis*. Albany, NY: State University of New York Press.

Played in Britain (2006) http://www.playedinbritain.co.yk/index.html (accessed January 2007).

Polley, Martin (1998) *Moving the Goalposts: a History of Sport and Society since 1945*. London: Routledge.

Polley, Martin (2007) *Sports History: a Practical Guide*. Basingstoke: Palgrave.

Rowling, J.K. (1997) *Harry Potter and the Philosopher's Stone*. London: Bloomsbury.

Rowling J.K. (as Kennilworthy Whisp) (2001) *Quidditch Through the Ages*. London: Bloomsbury.

Russell, Dave (1997) *Football and the English: a Social History of Association Football in England, 1863–1995*. Preston: Carnegie.

Smith, Dai and Williams, Gareth (1980) *Fields of Praise: the Official History of the Welsh Rugby Union 1881–1981*. Cardiff: University of Wales Press.

Southgate, Beverley (1996) *History: What and Why? Ancient, Modern, and Postmodern Perspectives*. London: Routledge.

Struna, Nancy (2001) 'Reframing the direction of change in the history of sport', *International Journal of the History of Sport*, 18(4): 1–15.

Thomas, Jerry, Nelson, Jack and silverman, Stephen (2005) *Research Methods in Physical Activity*. 5th edn. Champaign, IL: Human Kinetics.

Vamplew, Wray (1998) 'Facts and artefacts: sports historians and sports museums', *Journal of Sports History*, 24(2): 268–82.

Vamplew, Wray (2000) 'History', in Richard Cox, Grant Jarvie and Wray Vamplew (eds), *Encyclopedia of British Sport*. Oxford: ABC-Clio, pp. 178–80.

Vertinsky, Patricia (1990) *The Eternally Wounded Woman: Doctors, Woman and Exercise in the Late Nineteenth Century*. Manchester: Manchester University Press.

Vertinsky, Patricia and Mckay, Sherry (2004) *Disciplining Bodies in the Gymnasium: Memory, Monument and Modernism*. London: Routledge.

Whannel, Garry (1992) *Fields in Vision: Television Sport and Cultural Transformation*. London: Routledge.

Wiggins, David and Mason, Daniel (2005) 'The social-historical process in sports studies', in David Andrews, Daniel Mason and Michael Silk (eds), *Qualitative Methods in Sports Studies*. Oxford: Berg, pp. 39–64.

Williams, Jack (1999) *Cricket and England: a Cultural and Social History of the Inter-war Years*. London: Frank Cass.

Young, Percy (1968) *A History of British Football*. London: Stanley Paul.

Part Two

Structuring Opportunities in Sport

4

Social Exclusion from Sport and Leisure

MICHAEL F. COLLINS

Jesus is recorded as saying *the poor you will have among you always, and you can help them whenever you like.* (Mark 14:7, *Revised English Bible*)

OVERVIEW

» *Introduction: What is social exclusion?*
» *Citizenship, class and social capital*
» *Class differences in sport and how they exacerbate other factors*
» *Sports participation and race, gender, disability, age, geography and sexuality*
» *Case studies: combating poverty and exclusion in sport and leisure*
» *The costly parameters of social inclusion via sport*

INTRODUCTION: WHAT IS SOCIAL EXCLUSION?

Rowntree in York and Booth in London undertook the first serious studies of poverty in nineteenth-century England. They described, as did Dickens, '*absolute poverty*' – people 'on the breadline'. These were people without the basics of life: adequate, warm shelter, nutritious food, education and life-supporting work. However, by the mid-twentieth century, life was seen as more than survival, and included aspects of enjoyment and involvement in society, encompassing culture, art and sport. The absolute definition was gradually replaced by a relative definition of poverty measured in relation to what was customary for the standard of living and style of life in the country. This definition was adopted in the 1990s by the European Union (now defined as below 60 per cent of contemporary median income).

But social exclusion is a process, and is described much more widely in terms of access, or lack of it, to four basic social systems, namely democracy, welfare, the labour market, and family and community (Commins, 1993). The term 'social exclusion' was first used by a French welfare minister in 1974, but is now everyday EU-speak. With the return of the New Labour government in 1997, tackling social exclusion became a high priority and a 'cross-cutting' theme of first central and soon local government. The new Social Exclusion Unit (1998) in the Cabinet Office used a description, rather than a definition in *Bringing Britain Together,* as

> a shorthand label for what can happen when individuals or areas suffer a combination of linked problems such as unemployment, poor skills, low incomes, poor housing, high crime environments, bad health and family breakdown. (Cabinet Office, *www.open. gov.uk/co/seu/more.html*)

The EU's, and indeed Tony Blair's, main weapon against exclusion and in support of social insertion has been to fit people for work and encourage the economy to produce jobs. As I shall point out, this will not meet everyone's needs.

Exclusion and Poverty, and Sport and Leisure

I argue elsewhere (Collins et al., 1999; Collins, 2003) that poverty is the core of exclusion: a few people who are not poor may be affected by other dimensions in which exclusion can be expressed (such as sexuality, gender, age, ethnicity, disability or location, as discussed below), but few poor people are not excluded in some way. So, who is poor in the UK? Before the 1970s the post-war welfare state had ensured that the poor fell overwhelmingly into two overlapping groups: the elderly who had no personal pension provision and the chronically sick. But now the poor are more heterogeneous. Tony Blair's manifesto was to halve child poverty inside a decade and eliminate it in 20 years, a huge task given that in 1997, 24 per cent of adults and 30 per cent of children were officially poor.

Bradshaw (2004) brilliantly summarised the state of poverty and social policy (Box 4.1).

Box 4.1 Poverty in the UK

How are we doing on poverty in the UK? (below 60% of contemporary median income 1998–9 and 2003–4)

- *Child poverty* fell by 15% after housing costs to 28% (i.e. two-thirds of the government's target), not taking into account £3.68bn of new Child Tax credits budgeted for in 2003–5; but 3.9 million were still poor in 2001
- *Adult poverty* did not decrease from 14% despite record levels of employment; but 12.9 million people were still poor in 2001
- *Pensioner poverty* fell from 27% to 21% thanks to modest growth in state pensions and Pensioner Credit
- *Income inequality* fell only in 2002–3 (but it had grown in all previous periods of economic growth)

How is UK doing compared with 14 EU partner states?

- Child poverty showed the greatest fall, but took the UK from top to only 11th place

Who is likely to be poor and why?

- low-earning families with inadequate state benefits
- pensioners with no/small occupational pensions (nearly 1 million of whom fail to claim benefits to which they are eligible)
- many disabled people (benefit levels and means testing result in 75% of disabled being poor)
- lone-parent households, especially if headed by women
- households of Bangladeshi, Pakistani and black ethnic origin
- households renting social housing
- certain regions (notably Wales and London), neighbourhoods and streets, based on housing choices, whose outcome is 'to segregate the better off from poorer groups' (Fitzpatrick, 2004: 19)
- households headed by young mothers, people with low educational attainment and people with numerous children

Sources: Bradshaw (2004); Palmer et al. (2002)

In his *Theory of justice*, the philosopher Rawls (1971) argued that societies should be by how they treated the less well off; similarly, Bradshaw (2004) argued that poverty is a moral imperative, because it:

- May be seen as a moral or religious duty to remedy
- Is an intolerable unfairness and injustice, for example that a baby born into a family with three other children should be three times more likely to be poor than if it had been born first, and
- Is inefficient and a waste, because poor people are unlikely to thrive physically, mentally, and cognitively, thus harming society and all citizens (first in being linked to poor adult outcomes – 'poor wellbeing leading to poor becoming'; second by being associated with numerous social problems; and third being associated with most types of social exclusion, 'from normal social and leisure activities'). (2004: 13)

He concluded by assessing the policy gaps and size of challenges remaining:

1 with employment high and stable, and the bulk of gains having been related to work, future progress depends on welfare for those who can't work
2 benefits need to be re-linked to earnings rather than prices if gaps are not to widen perversely; Nelson (2004) concurred – there are far greater benefits in states like Sweden whose non-means tested benefits are more universal and generous, and
3 the state provides a greater support to low earnings than any other EU state, much in subsidizing low paying employers.

Hills and Stewart's (2005) and Toynbee and Walker's (2005) analyses are similar, the former's final chapter being pithily entitled 'a tide turned but mountains left to climb.'

Poverty restricts leisure spending, and disparities between the richer and poorer become marked as shown in Table 4.1, but which also shows a slow creep in the importance of spending on leisure (and also motoring and travel illustrating similar patterns) in modern society.

CITIZENSHIP, CLASS AND SOCIAL CAPITAL

If, following Commins (1993), citizenship is defined as the ability to take part fully in all aspects of society, then the cultural sphere including sport must be included. Taking part for the individual requires confidence, skills, knowledge, ability to manage time and relationships, and having a group of supportive friends and companions, including some who share the same desire to take part. This is what Bourdieu called social capital, and which I call personal social capital, to distinguish it from the communal sort discussed below. Bourdieu (1985) argued that the social capital of different strata of society varied according to the *habitus*, or social, economic, environmental and psychological milieu in which they were brought up and lived, and the associated values and meanings. Surveys show that social groups ABC1 – middle- and upper-class people with higher incomes,

TABLE 4.1   Leisure expenditure in different groups of household

Leisure goods and services (L), and total spending (T) by household type		Real total spending (£/wk Sept 2003 prices equivalised)			Share of total spending		
		1996–7 mean	2000-1 mean	% change	1996-7 mean	2000-1 mean	% change
House-holds with youngest child aged 0–4	Low income						
	L	21.0	28.0	33.6		10.6	1.5
	T	212.5	235.3	10.7	9.1		
	Middle income						
	L	40.7	52.0	8.4	12.1	14.1	2.0
	T	321.0	356.7	11.1			
	High income						
	L	95.1	106.9	12.4	16.3	17.3	0.9
	T	?	?	?			
All households with children <16 years	Low income						
	L	23.6	30.9	31.3	9.8	11.7	1.9
	T	220.2	240.8	9.3			
	Middle income						
	L	48.5	64.7	33.3	13.8	16.6	2.8
	T	333.6	365.0	9.4			
	High income						
	L	99.0	105.2	15.4	17.4	19.1	1.7
	T	?	?	?			

Source: Analysis by Gregg et al. (2005)

higher educational attainment, their own cars (often personal rather than one shared by the household) and a wide-ranging social network – spend more on sport and leisure and have a wider range of interests.

The second form of social capital is a shared one; this I call communal capital. Putnam (2000), studying American society, defined this as: shared values; social control and order; reduced financial inequalities; confidence in institutions and leaders in society; participation in political, social and cultural networks (including playing sport and belonging to sports clubs); and trust in and support from one's friends, neighbours and close kin – the social glue, as it has been called. In *Bowling Alone* (Putnam, 2000), he reported finding that in the contemporary United States all these forms of social involvement and commitment were in steep decline, with more and more individualised, consumerised activity, relying on others to provide high-quality goods and services, but with no commitment in the transaction other than ephemeral customer satisfaction.

Others have made similar claims regarding the decline in social cohesion. Fukuyama (1992), for example, argued that since the fall of European communism, one form or another of liberalism has become the dominant political ideology. This analysis led him to assert 'the end of history' insofar as history lies in active political contention about how society should be ordered. From a different perspective, Beck (1992) argued that in a postmodern, individualised society, the concept of class is terminally crumbling, and will be replaced by individual values and behaviours centred around consumption. How an individual country defines the boundaries of individual classes lies in its own social history, though the UK has been held up as the epitome of a strongly socially stratified society, from elite and aristocracy to meanest labourer. Roberts concurred with Beck's view, arguing that 'money is now at the root of the main differences between the use of leisure in different social strata, and the leisure differences between them are basically and blatantly inequalities rather than alternative ways of life' (Roberts, 1999: 87).

Others contend that this view is mistaken. Adonis and Pollard argued strongly that 'Britain's class system separates its people as clinically today as it did half a century ago – far from diminishing, class divisions are intensifying as the distance between the top and bottom widens and the classes at both extremes grow in size and identity' (1997: ix) and that 'far from leisure being in the vanguard of the classless society, the way we live our lives is a daily, hourly testament to our place in Britain's class structure' (1997: 244). Kew (1997: 149) agreed, and wrote of Bourdieu providing 'compelling evidence for the saliency of social class in structuring if not determining a person's choice and preferences in sport'. Horne et al. (1999), Jarvie and Maguire (1994) and Sugden and Tomlinson (2000) also concur, the last summarising Bourdieu's perspective that:

> Sport acts as a kind of badge of social exclusivity and cultural distinctiveness for the dominant classes; it operates as a means of control or containment of the working or popular classes; it is represented as a source of escape and mobility for talented working class performers ... it articulates the fractional status distinctions that exist within the ranks of larger class grouping. (Sugden and Tomlinson, 2000: 319)

Sport has been seen in different ways as part of citizenship. In 1975 a Labour government White Paper, *Sport and Recreation*, called it part of the fabric of the social services, which Coalter et al. (1986) termed *recreation as welfare* (of participants). Thereafter it became an instrument of economic policy (in job creation and regeneration), youth control (as a result of rising youth crime, unemployment and urban unrest) and health promotion (as much by the commercial fitness industry as by government), which the same authors labelled *recreation for welfare*. The widening poverty gap, and attempts to increase efficiency in public leisure services under Mrs Thatcher, especially through Compulsory Competitive Tendering, led to 'good', middle-class citizens being able to access such services and being effectively subsidised by poorer taxpayers (Audit Commission, 1989). As Ravenscroft noted, the 'politics of choice' had been replaced by the 'politics of means' (1993: 42). Glyptis (1989: 42) and Coalter both commented on the dualism of policies for welfare and for promoting participation, the latter arguing that there was a 'lack of a coherent philosophy or politics of "recreational welfare" with which to resist consumerist definitions and managerialist practices' (1989: 127). Of course, in a post-industrial society, consumption is necessary to sustain employment – Tony Blair encouraged people to go on spending to avoid the depression afflicting Japan, the United

TABLE 4.2   The effect of gender, disability, ethnicity and class in sports participation

Adult (16+) index for (once a month or more, excluding walking)	1B (casual participation*)		3B (frequent participation+)	Young people's (6–16) index	1E (at least ten times a year outside school)		2E(3 sports at least 10 times a year excl.walking)	
Benchmark	av. 43%		av. 14.4%	**Benchmark**	av. 85%		av. 64%	
	2002	1996	2002		2002	1999	2002	1999
Male, professional/managerial	140	123	164	Key stage 2 (aged 7–11)	104	102	108	109
Female, professional/managerial	111	104	95	Male	102	103	106	109
Black/ethnic minority male	101	108	129	White	102	101	102	102
Benchmark, all adults	**100**	**100**	**100**	**Benchmark, all young people**	**100**	**100**	**100**	**100**
Male, semi-unskilled	86	99	68	Key stage 4 (aged 14–16)	99	97	92	93
Black/ethnic minority female	60	69	51	Key Stage 1 (aged 5–7)	97	101	98	106
Female, semi-unskilled	56	60	50	Female	98	97	91	91
Black/ethnic minority disabled	40	66	40	Key Stage 3 (aged 11–14)	95	97	93	90
Disabled	38	46	M54, F42	Black/ethnic minority	83	90	72	82
				Disabled	67	60	39	37

*once a month or more often; + three times a week
Source: Sport England (2005a)

States and Germany in 2001–2. Coalter (2000) accused leisure students of neglecting and despising consumption as shallow, passive and meaningless in contrast to active participation (especially in 'serious' leisure) which they value as deep in meaning and constructive for the individual and society.

CLASS DIFFERENCES IN SPORT AND HOW THEY EXACERBATE OTHER FACTORS

Poverty exacerbates other forms of exclusion mentioned above, and one group thus affected that has become a policy target is at-risk disaffected youth. This can be demonstrated by Sport England's (2001a) Sport Equity Index of participation, which benchmarks participation for each subgroup against the group with the highest participation (e.g. for adult index 1B males have a participation rate of 43 per cent = 100). Thus in Table 4.2 the separate effect of gender, disability and ethnicity can be seen, and the additional effect of being in the semi- or unskilled groups. It is clear that the gaps between the high and average and lower participant groups have opened between 1996 and 2002, when overall participation dropped by 4 per cent. The differentials for young people (indexes 1E, 2E) are generally smaller, except for those with a disability. For both adults and children, gaps widen for frequent participation.

How does this affect sport? Box 4.2 identifies the impact of class on different levels of participation ranging from children's to that of the elite squads of selected sports:

- *Item 1* shows the great difference in take-up of starter and performer schemes between affluent and deprived areas of Nottinghamshire, reflecting the national gaps.
- *Item 2A* shows that the gap in adult participation seems to have closed recently but socio-economic definitions have changed. It had started to do so in the early 1990s but in the recent recession, the leisure expenditure of poorer people was cut and the gap began to widen to 1996.
- *Item 2B* shows that over the last generation, visiting leisure centres has become much more concentrated among upper social strata, in part the result of above-average price increases and the marketing policies pursued in the public sector due to budget pressures and CCT (Compulsory Competitive Tendering).
- *Item 3* makes it equally clear that there continues to be a strong gradient in joining sports and fitness clubs, the latter in particular with a strong gap in quality and price between budget and premium brands. It also shows the combined advantage enjoyed by full-time students who had access to facilities and clubs which are often subsidised and who come disproportionately from social groups ABC1.
- *Item 4* shows that the class gap carries through into elite sport. The AB social groups were over-represented by 100 per cent while the DE social groups were 60 per cent under-represented. Only Rugby League was near to the average. The cost of supporting elite participants is such that even swimming, Rugby Union and cycling have 83 per cent, 69 per cent and 50 per cent respectively in AB groups.

Box 4.2   Social gradients in forms of sports participation

1   Children's take-up in youth sports schemes, Nottinghamshire

	% less deprived areas	% deprived areas
Champion Coaching beginners	87	13
Go for Gold beginners	92	8
Performance Resources squads	92	8
Notts population	71	29

Source: Collins and Buller (2000)

2A   *Adult (aged 16+) participation, at least once a month excluding walking (%)*

	1996	2002
Professional	63	58–61
Unskilled	24	29
Difference	39	29–31

Sources: Sport England (1999); Sport England (2005b); note changes in classification between dates

2B   *Adult visits to sport and leisure centres (%)*

	1960s	1990s
Professional	20	40
Unskilled	7	8
Difference	13	32

Source: UK Sport/Sport England (1999)

3   *Adult membership of sports clubs, 1996 and 2002 (%)*

		Health/fitness	Sport
	1996	2002	1996–2002
Professional	6	69.9–13.4	16 10.9–11.1
Unskilled	1	1 2.4	4 3.5
Difference	5	5 7.5–11.0	12 7.4–7.6
Student	4	n/a	n/a

Sources: Sport England (1999); Sport England (2005b)

4   *Adult participation in 12 elite national squads (%)*

	National squads	GB population	Difference
Professional/managerial AB	38	19	19
Low/unskilled DE	10	25	15
Difference	28	6	

Source: English Sports Council (1998)

The classic argument for the value and operation of the unfettered market and of those less convinced of structural class differentials is that these non-sporting folks are choosing something else from the wide leisure menu available. This is just not so, as Table 4.3 shows – generally the same groups show high and lower participation.

TABLE 4.3   Social inequalities in participation across the leisure spectrum

%	GB	Abroad	Air char.	Coach	Advent.	Pub	Library	Theatre	Pop music	Gall.	Books Buy	Books Read	Cinema	Day vis.	Tourist	GB pop.
AB	76	65	31	7	63	24	79	34	26	47	32	69	17	23	32	22
C1	73	51	36	10	59	29	75	33	34	31	31	61	19	30	33	27
C2	70	41	40	9	54	38	51	18	22	23	18	44	11	21	20	23
D	69	36	47	8	49	34	57					41	10			
E	60	26	37	9	33	24	49	16	18	15	19	46	2	26	15	28
Diff. AB–DE	16	35	+2	+2	30	0	30	18	8	32	13	23	15	−3	17	n/a

Source: Collins (2003)

Large differences in participation as measured by social groups exist in relation to foreign and adventure holidays, visiting libraries, museums and galleries, and reading books. Smaller, but still significant gaps in participation exist in relation to domestic holiday-taking, visiting theatres, cinemas and countryside, and in buying books. Only in going to pop concerts, pubs and coach holidays does the gap narrow. Slightly more people from social groups D and E make day visits to the countryside than ABs, but this includes going to the coast and village pubs and shops. This is not evidence of a different leisure lifestyle, only of a much narrower one. Smith (2001) graphically showed how some 40 per cent still do not take a holiday, most for cost, health and social reasons rather than choice, and highlighted how the then English Tourism Council believed it could not promote inclusion policies in a too-fragmented market.

Finally, is the same strength of class differences exhibited in other countries? De Knop and Elling (2001) found a similar pattern of social difference in Flanders and The Netherlands, as did Nagel and Nagel (2001) in Germany, and Van der Meulen et al. (2001) in performance sport in The Netherlands. More (1999) explained exclusion of lower-income groups from outdoor recreation in US state and national parks in terms of the same financial pressures on authorities as in the UK, which led to increasing prices to users to raise income.

EXCLUSION IN SPORT AND RACE, GENDER, DISABILITY, AGE, GEOGRAPHY AND SEXUALITY

Other authors in this volume deal with three factors traditionally associated with exclusion through societal/structural effects, namely gender, race and disability. Tess Kay suggests that 'the history of women's involvement in sport is one of substantial exclusion', on medical, aesthetic and social grounds – that most forms of sport are unsuited or even especially hazardous to women's bodies, unpleasing in presenting women as athletes, or inappropriate to women's roles in society (see also Kay's chapter 6 in Collins, 2003). This structural and limiting masculinity is evidenced clearly from primary school onwards (Sport England, 2000) to the international boardroom and medal podium, in playing, coaching, administering and making policy in sport. Only recently, after hard lobbying and the lonely efforts of pioneers, under the umbrella of the Brighton Declaration (Sports Council, 1994a), are these attitudes changing. But Kay shows that change will only come when the institutions become less male dominated and move to empower women. The slowness to do this, from the IOC to local clubs, is testimony to the fact that the importance of change is only grudgingly accepted.

Carrington and McDonald deal with race in sport as part of wider social and political discourses, and show how the 1970s saw the Labour government adopt affirmative action through programmes like Action Sport, but allied it with images of urban decay and criminality. This set up what they call a *racialised discourse* through the 1980s which problematised cultural differences. This was partly redressed by the Sports Council's (1994b) policy paper and English Sports Council's (1997) guide for local authorities. However, concurrently the Major government's policy priority in *Sport: Raising the Game* (DNH, 1995) shifted to excellence, and did not mention ethnic issues. Action was left to the governing bodies of professionalised team games, notably in soccer (*Kick It* [racism] *Out*), Rugby League (*Tackling Racism*) and cricket (*Hit Racism for Six*). The Blair government has shown more sensitivity to the issue with two Social Exclusion Unit reports on ethnicity in urban renewal and labour markets (Cabinet Office, 2000, 2001).

Carrington and McDonald criticise the DCMS, however, for ignoring the issues of unequal power in institutions, even after the establishment of the organisation Sporting Equals. A catalyst for addressing this issue might be the publication of the Cantle Report on community cohesion in the wake of the 2001 riots in Bradford, Oldham and Blackburn, which commented that fragmentation and segregation had developed to the point where 'many communities operate on the basis of parallel lives [that] do not seem to touch at any point, let alone overlap and promote any meaningful interchanges' (Home Office, 2002a: 9). Despite little evidence, a parallel report by MPs (Home Office, 2002a: 28) asserted that 'sporting and cultural opportunities can play an important part in re-engaging disaffected sections of the community, building shared social capital and grassroots leadership through improved cross-cultural interaction', a mantra much repeated since by DCMS (2004a, 2004b) and Sport England (2005e, 2005f), despite little more evidence than further anecdotes. Both the Local Government Association (LGA, 2001) and ODPM (2005b, 2005c, 2005d) have produced guidance on implementation.

Box 4.3 Variations in sports participation by gender, race and disability

Gender

1a   Sport at school (no. of sports played 10 or more times a year)

	Boys	Girls	Difference
Played in primary school	3.3	3.5	+0.2
Played outside primary school	10.1	9.5	−0.6
'I am a sporty person' (%)	60	47	13
Played in secondary school	3.7	4.0	+0.3
Played outside secondary school	4.8	3.6	−1.2
'I am a sporty person' (%)	52	28	22

Source: Sport England (2000)

2a   Adults participating in sport once a month or more (%) (excl. walking)

	Men	Women	Difference
1987	57	34	−23
1990	58	39	−19
1993	57	39	−18
1996	54	39	−16
2002	51	37	−14

Sources: Sport England (2005c); UK Sport/Sport England (1999)

2b   Club membership in the last 4 weeks, 1996 and 2002

	Men		Women		Difference	
	1996	2002	1996	2002	1996	2002
Health/fitness club	3	5.8	4	7.1	+1	+1.3
Sports club	13	10.6	4	2.6	−9	+4

Sources: Sport England (2005b); UK Sport/Sport England (1999)

2c   Visiting sport and leisure centres

	Men	Women	Difference
1960s	71	29	−42
1970s	68	33	−36
1980s	55	45	10
1990s	42	58	+16

Source: Sport England (1999)

Ethnicity

3 Participating in one or more activities in the last 4 weeks (% excl. walking)

	White	Minority groups	Difference
1990	48	43	−5
1993	48	38	−10
1996	46	41	−5
2002	44	35	−6

	White	Caribbean	African	Indian	Pakistani	Bangladeshi
1999–2000	46	39	44	39	31	30
Difference		7	2	7	15	16

Sources: Rowe and Champion (2000); Sport England (2005b); UK Sport/Sport England (1999)

4 Disability and children

	Disabled, 2000	All, 1999	Difference
Not playing any sport 10+ times a year	26	6	20
Less than 3 hours a week secondary PE	20	53	23
1 hour or none in summer holiday	32	10	22

Source: Sport England (2001b)

5 Disability and adults

% participation in at least one activity excluding walking

	Once a month	Once a week	Three times a week
Limiting longstanding illness or disability	26.3	17.9	7.7
non-limiting longstanding illness or disability	41.6	30.6	13.7
no limiting longstanding illness or disability	50.7	36.9	17.8

Source: Sport England (2005c)

Recent Sport England national statistics (Rowe and Champion, 2000) confirmed that people of South Asian origin have markedly lower participation rates than other minorities or the indigenous population. *The Cantle Report* remarked on the notably poor provision of leisure for youth in most multicultural areas. Of course it has to be remembered that first-generation minorities settling into a new land and new communities worry first about obtaining employment and housing; the second generation strive to achieve a good education for their children; often it is only the third generation who seek to adopt or adapt in cultural terms. Many of the South Asian groups settled later than others and may not have passed through these transitions.

Thomas describes how the medical model of disability prevailed for many decades, individualising the problem and blaming the victim (Barnes et al., 1999), especially in terms of their ability to undertake paid work – 75 per cent of disabled people depend on welfare, and by definition are poor, which limits their ability to afford transport and sport and leisure activities. In the last decade and a half the social model suggests that disability in society (and in sport) is socially constructed by common values and by institutions. I suggest elsewhere (Collins, 2003) that recent events demand a further model – of empowerment – to be offered. A new broad 1995 Act of Parliament makes any form of discrimination illegal, and Thomas describes how establishing a new (1998) English Federation of Disability Sport is an attempt to weave together two disparate threads of organisations (of provision by form of disability and by type of sport) into a stronger, unified institutional fabric.

How these factors produce differences in sports participation is summarised in Box 4.3. Gender role differences are evident at primary school level and become more pronounced in secondary school (Item 1). Although the gap in overall adult participation is closing, it is doing so very slowly and a gap still exists in sports club membership with its competitions, though women have become more avid than men in joining fitness clubs (Items 2a and 2b). However, the growth of aerobics, dance, aquarobics and general fitness activities has led to women becoming the noticeable majority of sports centre users (Item 2c). So far as ethnic differences are concerned (Item 3), only the African group comes close to the level of participation of indigenous whites. The participation rate of South Asian minorities is notably low, and particularly so amongst the women. So far as disability is concerned, Sport England national survey data were due in 2002, but those published already for children clearly show them to be markedly disadvantaged, even when many are enrolled/'mainstreamed' in ordinary schools.

After the publication of *Game Plan* (DCMS, 2002), and a report by the Chairman Lord Carter (2005), Sport England (2004) made a new commitment to contribute to improving the fitness and health of the population with a major population survey and Everyday Sport campaign, while the Department of Health (2004, 2005a, 2005b; Chief Medical Officer, 2004) recognised the significance of sport and physical activity in maintaining and improving health. The 2002 General Household Survey also showed the role of limiting illness or disability in reducing participation (Item 5), and it is clear that there is a huge overlap of policy interest between those with low participation in sport, with poor health and who are socially excluded, including coincident spatial inequalities (Bailey, 2005; Shaw et al., 2001). Sport England has taken on fitness in the workplace, a wholly new area of work, but despite much rhetoric there is no evidence of major budgetary commitment by the DoH nationally or the Primary Care Teams locally nor any community of interest such as has grown between sport and education.

Discrimination by gender, race and disability has resulted in anti-discrimination legislation, the allocation of public expenditure and the establishment of promotional/lobbying organisations. These types of discrimination have also attracted significant media attention, as reflected in the coverage of the London Marathon and the Sydney Olympics and Paralympics which raised the level of public awareness.

Other forms of exclusion have received much less coverage and attention. Ageism, for example, has received far less attention in Europe (Collins, 2003) than in North America, where greater affluence and consumer confidence among older people have perhaps made it a higher-profile issue. There was a flurry of activity in the UK in the 1970s with Bernard's (1988) and Midwinter's (1992) studies on leisure and age and the Sports Council's '50 and All to Play For' campaign. Despite the ageing of the population in the UK, the proven benefits of physical activity in maintaining body functions in older people, and the potential savings on health and social budgets of sustained mobility and independence, Sport England and DCMS have remained steadfastly silent on the issue. Other European countries as in Belgium and Scandinavia (see UK Sport, 1999) have achieved greater participation of people over 50.

As regards the geography of exclusion, far more attention has been directed towards issues of access in urban than in rural areas, despite the levels of poverty being almost the same (see Coalter et al., 2000). More area-based initiatives for urban renewal and sports promotion have been focused on inner cities than the countryside despite evidence of only modest benefits, as shown by Robinson (n.d.), for example, in his assessment of the City Challenge programme over five years on Tyneside. The small number of programmes designed to overcome rural exclusion have, arguably, to address a more daunting series of barriers to participation including greater distance, poor and costly transport, and also the problems of meeting capital costs or providing a threshold population to support services and facilities in sparsely populated areas (Countryside Agency, 2005; Slee et al., 2001).

Perhaps the least understood and acknowledged aspect of exclusion is that of sexuality. It is clear that the masculine ethos of most sport has created an aura of homophobia, and homosexuals and lesbians have for years kept quiet rather than risk homophobic stereotyping and abuse. Recently homosexual and lesbian sportspeople have 'come out'; homosexual clubs and teams have appeared; and Gay Games have been launched (Clarke, 1998). Few governments or national sports bodies have tackled this issue: the Dutch Ministry of Welfare, Public Health and Culture had Hekma (1998) undertake a review, and its national Olympic Committee has included sexuality in its anti-discrimination code since 1994.

Now we look at two case studies of attempts to break the barriers of cost and access: the first concerns the use of leisure cards and the second a local project, the Nottinghamshire's Sports Training Scheme, designed to widen access to youth sport.

CASE STUDIES: COMBATING POVERTY AND EXCLUSION IN SPORT AND LEISURE

Anti-poverty Strategies and Leisure Cards

In the 1980s local authorities, especially those that were Labour controlled and in large cities, became concerned to combat the growth in poverty. By 1995 a third had developed formal anti-poverty strategies and some had also begun producing leisure passports or cards, which offered discounts for a broad range of services rather than discounts limited to particular locations or activity. Collins and Kennett (1999) described them as a tool that enabled improved targeted marketing without the problem of 'free riders', while aiming at social and specifically inclusionary objectives. This made them acceptable to Tory managerialists as well as welfarist or egalitarian Liberal and Labour politicians. Collins and Kennett discovered 50 per cent adoption in their national survey in 1996–7, but aspirations for this increased to 80 per cent in 3–5 years. Authorities with corporate anti-poverty strategies were three times as likely to have a leisure card scheme. Some schemes offered a standard discount to targeted populations while others had two tiers, with one tier offering a discount to all citizens and a second tier offering more substantial discounts to target groups. The most recent data on the adoption of leisure cards are shown in Table 4.4.

With several relaunches the total number of cards has increased by 25 per cent to over 9 out of 10 authorities, but there are still only 2.2 million holders across England and Wales, and only 600,000 in low-income groups compared with the 16 million who are poor. Patently, the offers are either inappropriate in nature or price, or poorly marketed. Only the 13 authorities listed in the notes to Table 4.4 have more than 40,000 holders, and 56 authorities served fewer than 2,000 holders with their scheme, and 102 in the low-income/benefit tier. Only 30 per cent of authorities have extended the leisure card scheme to arts and commercial offers, a sure way of limiting take-up, since it will miss a large number of children, women and men who do not see themselves as sporty (about 38 per cent according to the Allied Dunbar National Fitness Survey, 1991), and most older people. A Leicester City officer said that to be attractive cards should provide 'from veg to Verdi'.

Despite the widespread adoption of the card scheme, the evidence – which is admittedly fragmented – of its success in overcoming social exclusion is weak:

- **Apart from a few authorities that reach 25–30 per cent of their target groups, many have low take-ups of between 5 and 15 per cent.**
- **Owing to financial pressures, many local authorities reduced the discounts they offered to levels that were unattractive to people with little disposable income.**

TABLE 4.4   Local authorities with leisure and loyalty cards, 1999

Authority 1999(2005–6)	Total	Total	Incl sport	Incl arts	Incl Commercial	Average membership 000	Average low income/benefit membership 000
London Boroughs[1]	20	27	27	5	7	17.2 (13.7)	3.9 (3.3)
Metropolitan Boroughs[2]	27	39	30	12	12	15.6 (9.0)	9.4 (6.8)
Unitary authorities[3]	30	36	34	15	15	15.6 (12.6)	2.9 (4.2)
Non Met authorities[4]	108	127	124	39	35	7.7 (6.5)	1.9 (1.8)
Welsh authorities[5]	8	12	12	2	2	12.6 (7.9)	1.0 –
Total	193	241	217 (90%)	73 (30%)	71 (29%)	2,239.60	606.7

[1] Average figures in brackets exclude Greenwich, Westminster and Waltham Forest.
[2] Average figures in brackets exclude Wigan, Liverpool, Birmingham and Leeds.
[3] Average figures in brackets exclude Nottingham, Peterborough and Plymouth.
[4] Average figures in brackets exclude Derbyshire Dales, Rushcliffe.
[5] Average figures in brackets exclude Conwy.
Sources: Chartered Institute of Public Finance and Accountancy (1999; 2005)

- Most schemes were severely under-resourced, with a third having no budget, and a quarter having no staff dedicated to marketing/managing their cards. Leicester City Council, a pioneer whose card reached 30,000 citizens and incorporated many arts, retail and other commercial services, recently cut its marketing staff and lost 10,000 holders in two years until a relaunch and better marketing more than restored the losses.
- Only a minority of local authorities had active outreach marketing (roadshows/ sessions in job centres, ethnic/women's/disabled/senior citizens' clubs, etc.); the rest depended on passive/shotgun methods of marketing (e.g. posters, on-site leaflets, leaflet drops) which had very low success rates of only 1–2 per cent.

For most local authorities, the judgement must be that as a contribution to combating social exclusion, leisure/loyalty cards are an act of tokenism. There seem to be three major areas of weakness, the first of which is the clear underinvestment in the management of the card schemes, particularly to enable the exploitation of new swipe/smart card technology. Second, too few schemes are public/private partnerships. Leisure/loyalty cards must be a public/private partnership otherwise more and more private sector initiatives will erode the more attractive parts of the package. One very successful scheme is in the City of Nottingham which has 64,000 leisure card-holding residents, and 6,600 with concessions to use a wide range of public and private outlets. Likewise, Westminster's new card has been successful with 66,000 holders. Third, card schemes need professional marketing, of both business and social types. Put simply, most local authorities have not invested sufficiently in knowing, serving and retaining their customers by comparison with companies such as the David Lloyd chain of fitness clubs. Under the new (2005–6) Audit Commission's system of Comprehensive Performance Assessment with benchmarks relating to the representativeness of use of public facilities, authorities may have to answer questions about their cards, and smarten up their acts.

Starting Young in Sport: Nottinghamshire Sports Training Scheme (NSTS)

Most European countries have specialist primary PE teachers, the UK does not; similarly, many countries provide two hours a week or more of PE and sport, whereas the UK does not. Furthermore, there was no professional and co-ordinated training of coaches until the National Coaching Foundation (NCF) started work in the 1980s. By 2003 this had changed, with 1 million people in England involved in coaching, 41 per cent qualified, 30 per cent licensed by their sport's governing body, and 20 per cent paid (MORI, 2004). The weakness of primary school PE teaching and the lack of well-qualified coaches were frequently cited as explanations for the poor foundation of sports skills among the young and the large post-school drop in sports participation. In response to these problems, Nottinghamshire County Council, which had often pioneered developments in sport, decided in 1989 to promote a county-wide Nottinghamshire Sports Training Scheme (NSTS) to encourage more youngsters to participate. Using clubs and governing bodies linked to PE teachers, NSTS provided starter courses which led to improver and advanced courses. The NCF's nationwide Champion Coaching scheme, introduced in 1991, was incorporated into the NSTS, as was a performance and excellence element (later called Performance Resources), to provide links to county squads or higher-level competitive clubs. Champion Coaching was organised through the governing bodies of sport. From 1993 the County Council organised, in conjunction with the district councils, a pre-Champion Coaching course called 'Go for Gold'.

The city and southern county have enjoyed a buoyant economy, but coal mining in north Nottinghamshire has almost disappeared, and textiles and other industries have suffered cuts in jobs. Collins and Buller (2000, 2003) used postal, telephone and interview surveys to examine children's take-up of Champion Coaching and relate it to indicators of deprivation, levels of satisfaction with the programme, and the children's involvement in sport. The surveys showed a high degree of enjoyment and satisfaction of both children and parents with the organisation and delivery of the coaching courses (around 90 per cent). Between a

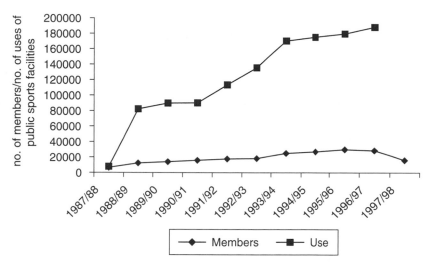

FIGURE 4.1   Use of Leicester leisure pass compared to membership totals

quarter and a third had joined local sports clubs, and found those helpful and supportive. There were two big caveats to this success. First, two in five of the children claimed that they were not told about 'exit routes' into clubs and squads, and second, the take-up of all three sets of courses was socially selective. As the figures in Box 4.3 and Figure 4.1 show, affluent areas produced a disproportionate number of entrants. There is no obvious explanation for the low take-up of places on Champion Coaching by children from poorer areas. The NSTS, of which Champion Coaching was a part, was well publicised and cheap (fees were waived on request if they were problematic for families). There still seemed to be a fear, on the part of parents on low incomes, of not being able to keep up even the low payments. It is less easy to explain why teachers in schools in such areas were not proposing their interested or gifted pupils to the NSTS.

This case study shows that even in a well-resourced and managed scheme, there is as much reproduction of existing structural disadvantage as there is breaking of barriers. Sport England has demonstrated considerable awareness of exclusion issues, as indicated by its high-profile Active Sports programmes in schools, clubs and communities, through 45 County Sports Partnerships and over 200 School Sport Partnerships, and through schemes targeted at places of concentrated deprivation via Sport Action Zones and Priority Areas. However, there is not much evidence of a detailed strategy for implementation to ensure the breaking of these powerful and persistent social barriers to participation. Although there is guidance for national governing bodies of sport on tackling social exclusion due to race, gender and disability, there is little guidance regarding the more pervasive factor of poverty (Sport England, 2001c).

TABLE 4.5   Multiple constraints and exclusion in sport and leisure

Group Excluded			Youth					
Constraint/ exclusion	I Children	Young people	Young delinq.	Poor/ unemployed	Women	Poor people	Ethnic factor minorities	People with disabilities/ learning difficulties
Structural factors								
Poor phys./soc. environ.	+	+	++	++	+	+	++	+
Poor facilities/ community capacity	+	+	++	++	+	+	+	++
Poor support network	+	+	++	++	+	+	+	++
Poor transport	++	++	++	++	++	++	+	++
Mediating factors								
Managers' policies/attitudes	+	+	++	++	+	+	++	++
Labelling by society	+	++	+++	+	+	+	+++	++
Lack of time structure	+	+	++	+++		+		+
Lack of income	+	+	++	+++	+	++	++	++
Personal factors								
Lack of skills/personal social capital	+	+	+++	+++	+	+	++	++
Fears of safety	++	++	++	++	+++	++++	++	++
Powerlessness	++	++	+++	+++	++	++	++++	++
Poor self/body image	+	+	++	++	+	+	++	++

Key: The number of + shows the severity of constraints for particular groups

THE (COSTLY) PRINCIPLES OF EFFECTIVE INCLUSION POLICY

Everyone is looking for good practice with which to respond to the government's concern for social inclusion. Nonetheless there is hardly any serious research or evaluation of schemes (Collins et al., 1999), and while some schemes seem to have good short-term effects (DCMS, 1999; Coalter, 2001), it is too soon to say if these are lasting or significant outcomes as it is estimated that programmes need to operate for between 5 and 10 years in order to overcome such strong long-term barriers (Brodie and Roberts, 1992).

If successful social inclusion policy is to be developed, a number of factors need to be acknowledged and issues addressed, including the following.

Excluded People Face Multiple Constraints

Some constraints are societal and can rarely be overcome by the agency of an individual; some are personal and can only be overcome by good self-image, self-confidence and set-tled values; other constraints, mediating between these two groups, need the action of intermediaries, such as managers and policy makers. Table 4.5, synthesised by the author from a large number of studies, indicates the strength of different types of constraints. Particularly in relation to the unemployed, disabled, ethnic minorities and young delinquent groups, the removal of one constraint leaves a number of others firmly in place. As can be seen from the rows of the table, some constraints affect several groups, like poor transport systems and all non-car owners, which is patently difficult to grapple with now privatisation has dispersed control of provision on rail or buses. Attention to such constraints therefore helps many people in several groups like aids to mobility for the physically disabled, which also benefit the frail and elderly, parents with children in prams and shoppers laden with bags and bundles (SEU, 2004).

Joined-Up Policies

The multiplicity of constraints is what justifies the Blair government in advocating proper linkage between the separate policies and departments of central and local government when they affect the same people and areas. It is not easy to overcome political *amour-propre*, bureaucratic empire building, or different priorities, timescales, styles and philosophies of delivery between departments responsible for education, environment, housing, transport, leisure services, community education and sometimes social services. The 'brigading' together of services in both town hall and Whitehall into large, multi-service administrative units may simply mean higher walls and deeper ditches between larger ministries.

Partnerships

A corollary of joined-up policies is that of establishing partnerships for delivery (ODPM, 2004c, 2005a) which cut across the public, commercial and voluntary sectors. Sport England is trying to make this the basis of its Active Sports development system, with local authorities, county governing bodies of sport and their clubs, and education authorities and their schools having to co-operate before they can have Exchequer funding for a partnership manager or apply for Lottery funding for facilities and programmes. Sport cannot 'go it alone', but it has to be recognised that partnerships are sometimes difficult to arrange and costly to run, and partners are not always yoked equally in resources or power (sport often is a minor partner in redevelopment projects, for example), and can be fragile (Balloch and Taylor, 2001). One of the new Sport England showcase projects has 39 partners; satisfying so many can be a managerial nightmare, if not an impossibility.

Sustained Policies and Longer Timespans

Every new politician or chief executive feels the pressure to do and *be seen to do* something new; consequently there is in sport and leisure, from Sport England and DCMS in particular, a constant stream of new programmes and new or changed grant conditions. This 'initiativitis' is compounded by a reliance on short-term programmes, often of three years' duration, which is nowhere near long enough to yield outcomes of significant social change. The PAT 10 report (DCMS, 1999) advocated that programmes should last at least five years, and more programmes of this length are being established.

Tighter Focus of Both People and Place Policies

There is a political temptation when drawing up policies targeted at places to take in as many people as possible. However, given that even in the most deprived areas the major-ity of people are not poor and excluded, it is not easy to ensure that benefits get to those who need them most. One of the strengths of leisure card schemes was the capacity to reach target groups efficiently and effectively, and with no outward stigma. The new Sport Action Zones range in size from 1,100 people in south Leicester through 88,000 living in Lambeth and Southwark to 480,000 in the whole of Cornwall, and 852,000 in South Yorkshire. Given that each receives the same modest budgets and has one professional manager, it is difficult to see how work in such large areas as the latter two can be more than token in the face of the problems that they face.

Involving the Citizens and Building Social Capital

Giddens (1994) foresaw the development of a more active, clever, individualised citizenry, with each citizen seeking his/her own networks, which Ellison described as 'new solidar-ities across a range of putative "communities" as a form of defence against social changes which continually threaten to frustrate such ambitions' (1997: 714). Sports clubs as a form of social capital are a classic example of self-help, and their voluntary work has been crucial to sport in every country in the world. Indeed no country, even those with the most *dirigiste* command economy, has been able to manage without them. The particu-lar contribution of voluntary organisations has been clearly recognised by the Blair gov-ernment which would like to see community organisations taking a greater role in shaping society. Many departmental and lottery grants are predicated on voluntary organisations, including sports clubs, being partners in, and agents of, change. Yet the pressures of time, the demands for coaches and administrators to be as knowledgeable and skilled as those who are paid, combine with the attractions of playing until a greater age and a myriad of other leisure interests to threaten their future. A recent international survey found that in all the countries studied, the volunteer force was ageing and strug-gling to meet new demands (Heinemann, 1999).

Unfortunately, we know very little about the UK's approximately 150,000 sports clubs except that, with on average 43 members, they are much smaller than their European coun-terparts. The small size of clubs intensifies the pressures on volunteers, yet requires the duplication of roles like chair, secretary, treasurer, etc., for small numbers of members. Thus they constitute a fragile resource base for preparing capital funding bids, and for meeting the needs of target population groups such as disabled people or ethnic minorities. Yet the small scale of many clubs often indicates that they have deep local roots and strong social ties. The government, Sport England and the Central Council of Physical Recreation need to know much more about these clubs (as the Germans do with their quadrennial survey, e.g. Heinemann and Schubert, 1994) before adding to the tasks and challenges already thrown out to them in Active Sports, World Class programmes, Sport Action Zones, flagship schemes and other programmes. For all that, communal social capital in the form of sports clubs seems in a stronger state in the UK (Hall, 1999) than found by Putnam in the United States, but still not as strong as in Norway (Rothstein, 2001).

A final point under this heading is that on the whole it is better to bolster and revive existing sports clubs than to let struggling ones die and then to have to create successors. For example, the Coal Industry Welfare clubs in villages and suburbs whose mining industry disappeared between the 1970s and 1990s often provided the best, if not the only, sports facilities in their communities. Despite urging from the Sports Council, many CISWO clubs were lost, leaving many communities with few sports facilities. Currently, the government is using Lottery funding to support sports development officers to work in these ex-mining communities with one of their key tasks being to encourage community development and club formation – a task that is proving extremely slow and difficult. Sport England is seeking to establish several multi-sport, multi-activity hub clubs in every region (Moore, 2005) but even if these are successful they will not change the overall single-sport culture in which it is highly desirable that networks of clubs in the same or different sports be devised in each locality (Collins, 2005).

CONCLUSIONS

The Blair strategy for tackling poverty and exclusion is based on a principle that everyone has a right to participate in society and the opportunity to reach their full potential (DSS, 1999) through:

- **tackling the main cause of poverty – worklessness, and providing security for those for whom work is not always an option;**
- **providing support at all points in the life cycle through improving housing, education, health facilities, obtaining work skills, reducing discrimination, and removing the 'benefits traps' that discourage working; and**
- **investing in individuals and communities, getting away from the old single-policy, top-down approaches, to delivering policies in a way that is relevant to people's lives. (DSS, 1999: 30–1).**

What is quite clear is that a good proportion of the socially excluded from sport and other aspects of a good society will not be able to be helped by training and work (e.g. those too old, too sick or too disabled). However, they *will* require social investment (Bradshaw, 2004; Hills and Stewart, 2005). Some of all excluded groups will require affirmative and concentrated action to overcome their doubts, based on past experience, about the truth of the promises and the reality of the help offered by politicians and managers: 'we've heard it all before' is a litany that kills social policy all too often.

The lessons from this chapter are that the three-sector (public, commercial and voluntary) sports system is evolving, but that the public and voluntary sectors, despite the plethora of policy statements and initiatives, are struggling. They have made and could yet make substantial contributions to the deeply rooted issue of social exclusion, independent of other services such as social housing, economic development or welfare: after all, *mankind shall not live by bread alone* (Matthew 4: 4). However, to release the potential of sport as a vehicle for achieving greater social inclusion, we need to know more than the relatively scattered and small-scale existing research tells us about both sport and social exclusion (Carter, 2005), otherwise much of our scarce and hard-won investment of both money and ideas will benefit the already well supplied or will wither on the vine; the new surveys of motivation and satisfaction, and participation and the reviews on the Value of Sport database (www.sportengland.org), should help

---

CHAPTER SUMMARY

» Social exclusion may be defined as the lack of access to one or more of four basic social systems, namely democracy, welfare, the labour market, and family and community networks of support.

» While sport has increasingly been used as a tool of social engineering, it is generally acknowledged as an important element of welfare.

» Social class is at the heart of social exclusion from sport, with those in social classes D and E having markedly lower levels of participation, as in most other forms of active leisure.

» Inequalities in terms of social class are often compounded by other social characteristics such as race, ethnicity, gender, (dis)ability, age, geography and sexuality.

» Public agencies have introduced policies, such as discount cards, aimed at overcoming social exclusion from sport. Successful schemes need to take account of a number of factors, including the multiple nature of constraints and the need for a precise focus on target groups.

» Despite a new recognition of the role of sport and physical activity in promoting health, there is no policy concord, linkage and delivery system between the sport and health policy communities as there is between sport and education.

FURTHER READING

The Social Exclusion Unit (1998, 2004) provides a description of the conditions that contribute to social exclusion and Adonis and Pollard (1997) explore the relationship between social class and opportunity. Collins (2003) explores social exclusion in more detail in relation to sport.

There are many studies which examine the impact of particular factors affecting participation in sport: Glyptis (1989) looked at the relationship between unemployment and leisure; Hekma (1998) explored sexuality and sports participation; Slee et al. (2001) examined social exclusion from countryside recreation; Bailey (2005) looked at links with health.

REFERENCES

Adonis, A. and Pollard, S. (1997) *A Class Act: the Myth of a Classless Society.* London: Hamish Hamilton.

Audit Commission (1989) *Sport for Whom?* London: The Audit Commission.

Bailey, R. (2005) 'Evaluating the relationship between physical education, sport and social inclusion', *Educational Review,* 57 (1): 71–90.

Balloch, S. and Taylor, M. (2001) *Partnership working: Policy and Practice.* Bristol: Policy Press.

Barnes, C., Mercer, G. and Shakespeare, T. (1999) *Exploring Disability: a Sociological Reader.* Oxford: Polity Press.

Beck, U. (1992) *Risk Society: Towards a New Modernity.* London: Sage.

Bernard, M. (ed.) (1988) *Positive Approaches to Ageing: Leisure and Lifestyle in Older Age.* Stoke on Trent: Beth Johnson Foundation.

Bourdieu, P. (1985) *Distinction: A Social Critique of the Judgement of Taste.* London: Routledge.

Bradshaw, J. (2004) 'Understanding and overcoming poverty', Paper presented to Joseph Rowntree Centenary Conference York, 13 December, www.jrf.org.uk (accessed 15 May 2005).

Brodie, D. and Roberts, K. (1992) *Inner City Sport: Who Plays, What are the Benefits?* Culembourg: Giordano Bruno.

Cabinet Office (2000) *Minority Ethnic Issues in Social Exclusion and Neighbourhood Renewal.* London: Cabinet Office.

Cabinet Office (2001) *Improving Labour Market Achievements for Ethnic Minorities in British Society: a Scoping Note.* www.cabinetoffice.gov.uk/info/2001/ethnicity/scope.shtml (accessed 13 August 2001).

Carter, Lord (2005) *Review of National Sport Effort and Resources.* London: Department of Culture Media and Sport.

Chief Medical Officer (2004) *At Least Five a Week.* London: Department of Health.

Clarke, G. (1998) 'Queering the pitch and coming out to play: lesbians in physical education and sport', Sport, Education and Society, 3 (2): 145–60.

Coalter, F. (1989) 'Leisure policy: an unresolvable dualism?', in C. Rojek (ed.), *Leisure for Leisure.* Basingstoke: Macmillan, pp. 115–29.

Coalter, F. (2000) 'Public and commercial leisure provision: active citizens and passive consumers?', *Leisure Studies,* 19: 163–81.

Coalter, F. (2001) *Realising the Potential of Cultural Services: the Case for Sport.* London: Local Government Association.

Coalter, F., Duffield, B. and Long, J. (1986) *The Rationale for Public Sector Investment in Sport.* London: Sports Council/ESRC.

Coalter, A., Allison, M. and Taylor, J. (2000) *The Role of Sport in Regenerating Deprived Urban Areas.* Edinburgh: Scottish Central Research Unit.

Collins, M.F. (2003) *Sport and Social Exclusion.* London: Routledge.

Collins, M.F. (2005) 'Sports clubs and social capital', in G. Nichols and M.F. Collins (eds), *Volunteers and Sports Clubs.* Publication 85. Eastbourne: Leisure Studies Association.

Collins, M.F. and Buller, J.R. (2000) 'Bridging the post-school institutional gap: Champion Coaching in Nottinghamshire', *Managing Leisure,* 5: 200–21.

Collins, M.F. and Buller, J.R. (2003) 'Social exclusion from high performance sport: are all talented young people being given an equal opportunity of reaching the Olympic podium', *Journal of Sport and Social Issues (US),* 27 (4.1): 420–2.

Collins, M.F. and Kennett, C. (1999) 'Leisure, poverty and social exclusion: the growing role of passports in leisure in Great Britain', *European Journal for Sports Management,* 6 (1): 19–30.

Collins, M.F., Henry, I. and Houlihan, B. (1999) *Sport and Social Exclusion.* Report to Policy Action Team 10, DCMS. London: DCMS.

Commins, P. (ed.) (1993) *Combating Social Exclusion in Ireland 1990–94: a Midway Report.* Brussels: European Commission.

Countryside Agency (2005) *The State of the Countryside 2005.* Cheltenham: The Countryside Agency.

De Knop, P. and Elling, A. (eds) (2001) *Values and Norms in Sport.* Aachen: Meyer & Meyer Sport.

Department of Culture, Media and Sport (DCMS) (1999) *Policy Action Team 10 Report: Sport, Arts and Social Exclusion.* London: DCMS.

Department of Culture, Media and Sport (DCMS) (2002) *Game Plan: a Strategy for Delivering Government's Sport & Physical Activity Objectives.* London: DCMS.

Department of Culture, Media and Sport (DCMS) (2004a) *Government and the Value of Culture.* London: DCMS.

Department of Culture, Media and Sport (DCMS) (2004b) *Bringing Communities Together Through Sport and Culture.* London: DCMS.

Department of Health (2004) *Choosing Health.* London: DoH.

Department of Health (2005a) *Delivering Choosing Health.* London: DoH.

Department of Health (2005b) *Choosing Activity.* London: DoH.

Department of National Heritage (DNH) (1995) *Sport: Raising the Game.* London: DNH.

Department of Social Security (DSS) (1999) *Opportunity for All: Tackling Poverty and Exclusion.* DSS 1st Annual Report. London: DSS.

Ellison, N. (1997) 'Towards a new social politics; citizenship and reflexivity in late modernity', *Sociology,* 31 (4): 697–717.

English Sports Council (1997) *Working Towards Racial Equality – a Good Practice Guide for Local Authorities.* London: ESC.

English Sports Council (1998) *The Development of Sporting Talent, 1997.* London: ESC.

Fitzpatrick, S. (2004) 'Poverty of place' paper to Joseph Rowntree Centenary Conference, York, 14 December, www.jrf.org.uk (accessed 16 May 2005).

Fukuyama, F. (1992) *The End of History and the Last Man.* New York: Free Press.

Giddens, A. (1994) *Beyond Left and Right: the Future of Radical Politics.* Oxford: Polity Press.

Glyptis, S. (1989) Leisure and Unemployment. Milton Keynes: Open University Press.

Gregg, P., Waldfogel, J. and Washbrook, E. (2005) 'That's the way the money goes: expenditure patterns as incomes rise for the poorest families with children', in J. Hills and K. Stewart (eds), *A More Equal Society? New Labour, Poverty, Inequality and Social Exclusion.* Bristol: Policy Press, pp. 251–76.

Hall, P.A. (1999) 'Social capital in Britain', *British Journal of Politics,* 29: 417–61.

Heinemann, K. (ed.) (1999) *Sports Clubs in Various European Countries.* Cologne: Club of Cologne.

Heinemann, K. and Schubert, M. (1994) *Der Sportverein* [The sports club]. Schorndorf: Verlag Karl Hofmann.

Hekma, G. (1998) '"As long as they don't make an issue of it" ... gay men and lesbians in organised sports in the Netherlands', *Journal of Homosexuality,* 35 (1): 1–23.

Hills, J. and Stewart, K. (eds), (2005) *A More Equal Society? New Labour, Poverty, Inequality and Social Exclusion,* Bristol: Policy Press.

Home Office (2002a) *Community Cohesion: Report of the Review Team chaired by Ted Cantle.* London: Home Office.

Horne, J., Tomlinson, A. and Whannel, G. (1999) *Understanding Sport: An Introduction to the Sociological and Cultural Analysis of Sport.* London: E & FN Spon.

Institute of Public Finance (1999, 2005) *Charges for Leisure Services Statistics, 1999–2000, 2005–6.* London: IPF.

Jarvie, G. and Maguire, J. (1994) *Sport and Leisure in Social Thought.* London: Routledge.

Kew, F. (1997) *Sport: Social Problems and Issues.* Oxford: Butterworth–Heinemann.

Local Government Association (2001) *Tackling Poverty and Social Inclusion Through Cultural Services: a Toolkit for Local Authorities.* London: LGA.

Midwinter, E. (1992) Leisure: *New Opportunities in the Third Age*. Dunfermline: Carnegie UK Trust.

Moore, N. (2005) 'At the hub', *Leisure Manager*, 23 (12): 16–17.

More, T.A. (1999) 'Reconceiving recreation policy in an era of growing social inequality', *Proceedings of NE Recreation Research Symposium*, US Forest Service, pp. 415–19.

MORI (2004) *Sports coaching in the UK*. Leeds: SportscoachUK.

Nagel, M. and Nagel, S. (2001) *Social Background and Top Performance Sports*. Paper presented to ECSS Congress, 24–28 July, Cologne.

Nelson, K. (2004) 'Mechanisms of poverty alleviation: antipoverty effects of non-means-tested and means-tested benefits in five welfare states', *Journal of European Social Policy*, 14 (4): 371–90.

Office of the Deputy Prime Minister (2004c) *Joint working in sport and neighbourhood renewal*. London: Neighbourhood Renewal Unit, ODPM.

Office of the Deputy Prime Minister (2005a) *Sport and physical activity partnerships*. www.renewal.net (accessed 10 September 2005).

Office of the Deputy Prime Minister (2005b) *Sport, physical activity and renewal*. www.renewal.net (accessed 10 September 2005).

Office of the Deputy Prime Minister (2005c) *Sport, physical activity and educational attainment*. www.renewal.net (accessed 10 September 2005).

Office of the Deputy Prime Minister (2005d) *Sport, physical activity and health*. www.renewal.net (accessed 10 September 2005).

Palmer, G., Rahman, M. and Kenway, P. (2002) *Monitoring Poverty and Social Exclusion*. York: Joseph Rowntree Foundation.

Putnam, R.D. (2000) *Bowling Alone*. New York: Simon & Schuster.

Ravenscroft, N. (1993) 'Public leisure provision and the good citizen', *Leisure Studies*, 12: 33–44.

Rawls, J. (1971) *A Theory of Justice*. Cambridge, MA: Harvard University Press.

Roberts, K. (1999) *Leisure in Contemporary Society*. Wallingford: CABI Publishing.

Robinson, T. (n.d.) *The City Challenge Programme in South Newcastle*. Newcastle upon Tyne: Newcastle University Press.

Rothstein, B. (2001) 'Social capital in the social democratic welfare state', *Politics and Society*, 29 (2): 207–41.

Rowe, N. and Champion, R. (2000) *Sports Participation and Ethnicity in England – National Survey 1999–2000. Headline Findings*. London: Sport England.

Shaw, M., Dorling, D., Gordon, D. and Davey Smith, G. (2001) 'Putting time, person and place together: the temporal, social and spatial accumulation of health inequalities', *Critical Public Health*, 11 (4): 298–304.

Slee, W., Curry, N. and Joseph, D. (2001) *Removing Barriers, Creating Opportunities: Social Exclusion in the Countryside Leisure in the UK*. Cardiff: Countryside Recreation Network.

Smith, R. (2001) 'Including the forty per cent: social exclusion and tourism policy', in G. McPherson and M. Reid (eds), *Leisure and Social Exclusion: Challenges to Policy and Practice*. Publication 73. Eastbourne: Leisure Studies Association.

Social Exclusion Unit (1998) *Bringing Britain Together*. London: Cabinet Office.

Social Exclusion Unit (2004) *Transport and Social Exclusion*. London: SEU, Cabinet Office.

Sports Council (1994a) *The Brighton Declaration on Women and Sport*. London: Sports Council.

Sports Council (1994b) *Black and Ethnic Minorities in Sport: Policy and Objectives*. London: Sports Council.

Sport England (1999) *Survey of Sports Halls and Swimming Pools in England*. London: Sport England.

Sport England (2000) *Young People and Sport in England, 1999*. London: MORI, for Sport England.

Sport England (2001a) *Sports Equity Index*. www.sportengland.org.uk.

Sport England (2001b) *Young People with a Disability and Sport: Headline Findings*. London: Sport England.

Sport England (2001c) *Making English Sport Inclusive: Equity Guidelines for Governing Bodies*. London: Sport England.

Sport England (2004) *The Framework for Sport in England: a Vision for 2020*. London: Sport England.

Sport England (2005a) *Participation in Sport in England: Sports Equity Index 2002*. London: Sport England.

Sport England (2005b) *Participation in Sport in England: Participation in Sport in England 2002*. London: Sport England.

Sport England (2005c) *Participation in Sport in England: Trends 1987–2002*. London: Sport England.

Sport England (2005e) *Sport Playing its Part: the Contribution of Sport to Building Safe, Strong and Sustainable Communities*. London: Sport England.

Sport England (2005f) *Sport Paying its Part: the Contribution of Sport to Healthier Communities*. London: Sport England.

Sugden, J. and Tomlinson, A. (2000) 'Theorising sport and social class', in J. Coakley and E. Dunning (eds), *Handbook of Sports Studies*. London: Sage, pp. 309–21.

Toynbee, P. and Walker, D. (2005) *Better or Worse?* London: Bloomsbury.

UK Sport (1999) Compass 1999: Sports Participation in Europe. London: UK Sport.

Van der Meulen, R., Kraylaar, G. and Utlee, W. (2001) *Lifelong on the Move: an Event Analysis of Attrition in Non-elite Sport*. Paper presented to ECSS Congress, 24–28 July, Cologne.

5

The Human Rights of Young Athletes

PAULO DAVID

OVERVIEW

» *Is youth sport only positive?*
» *International human rights law and sport*
» *Abuse, neglect, violence and exploitation in youth sport*
» *Child labour and economic exploitation*
» *Empowering young athletes*
» *Accountability of states, sport authorities and adults*
» *Conclusion*

IS YOUTH SPORT ONLY POSITIVE?

Over many decades, the involvement of children and adolescents in competitive sports was overwhelmingly perceived solely as positive. A majority of observers systematically affirmed that sport was the best school of life; it would provide life-skills for young people, strengthen their self-confidence, improve mental and physical health, support cognitive and social development as well as generate a broad variety of opportunities. The assumption of the positive impact of sport remained for long unchallenged, especially by sport authorities. Even today, there is much resistance in the sports circle to accept a more critical, nuanced and balanced analysis, despite growing evidence of serious side effects for young athletes involved in competitive sports. Evidence increasingly demonstrates that young athletes can become vulnerable to various forms of abuse, neglect, violence and exploitation through their involvement in sports (David, 2005).

Roughly, it can be estimated that 70 per cent of young athletes benefit from their sport activity, 20 per cent are at risk of having their rights challenged and 10 per cent have them violated (obviously the nature and severity of these violations can vary drastically). This chapter aims at reviewing how children's rights are respected in the context of competitive sports. It will also look at the potential contribution human rights can offer to improve the protection of the rights of young athletes.

INTERNATIONAL HUMAN RIGHTS LAW AND SPORT

For most of its history, the majority of sports organisations and authorities believed that they were free from legal obligations – or even above the law (Grayson, 2000). The sporting movement grew and matured under the principles of self-organisation and self-regulation. This was perfectly acceptable as long as sports associations' internal rules, policies and practice were defined and applied in conformity with domestic and international law.

Despite persistent resistance, it is today nevertheless increasingly accepted that the rule of law also applies to the sport field. Therefore, international human rights law, which is usually incorporated into domestic legislation, also directly applies to athletes. International human rights law consists essentially of nine core international treaties, including the UN Convention on the Rights of the Child (CRC), adopted by the UN General Assembly in 1989 and since ratified by all but two states of the world (193 states parties, only the United States and Somalia have not ratified this treaty). The CRC defines a child as 'every human being below the age of eighteen years unless under the law applicable to the child, majority is attained earlier' (article 1). The other eight international human rights treaties also implicitly apply to persons below 18 years of age.

The CRC does not explicitly refer to the concept of 'sports'; nevertheless it clearly suggests links with practically all provisions of the treaty. Of its 42 substantive provisions, 37 are of *direct* relevance to child athletes. They include:

- **the right to non-discrimination (article 2);**
- **the principle of the best interests of the child (article 3);**
- **the right to be provided appropriate direction and guidance (article 5);**
- **the right to development (article 6);**
- **the right to an identity and nationality (article 7);**
- **the right not to be separated from their parents (article 9);**
- **the right to have their views taken into account (article 12);**
- **freedom of expression and association (articles 13 and 15);**
- **protection of privacy (article 16);**

- the right to access appropriate information (article 17);
- protection from abuse and neglect and other forms of violence (article 19);
- the right to health (article 24);
- the right to education (articles 28 and 29);
- the right to rest, leisure, recreation and cultural activities (article 31);
- the right to be protected from economic exploitation (article 32), illegal drugs (article 33), sexual exploitation (article 34), abduction, trafficking and sale (article 35), and other forms of exploitation (article 36);
- the right to benefit from rehabilitative care (article 39); and
- the right to due and fair process (article 40).

Ratification by a state of an international human rights treaty is undertaken on a voluntary basis, but once ratified the treaty implies *legal obligations* for states' branches: the executive, the legislative and the judiciary. States which are party to the CRC are accepting, *inter alia*, the legal obligation to ensure comprehensive legislative review of their laws to guarantee their full compatibility with the requirements of the treaty; they also commit to improve their policies and programmes as well as to reform their institutions in order to implement the provisions of the treaty. The judiciary is bound to take into account human rights provisions in all legal processes and in the design and formulation of its decisions. Consequently, children's rights – as defined in the CRC – need to be guaranteed and protected in 193 countries, including when young athletes are involved in sports.

A UN human rights expert body distinguishes three fundamental types of obligations under international human rights law: the obligation to *respect* rights requires states to *refrain* from interfering directly or indirectly with people's enjoyment of their human rights; the obligation to *protect* requires states to take *measures that prevent* third parties (such as parents, coaches or sports organisations or authorities) from interfering with human rights; and the obligation to *fulfil* requires states to adopt appropriate legislative, administrative, budgetary, judicial, promotional and other measures towards the full realisation of human rights (UN Committee on Economic, Social and Cultural Rights, 2000).

Evolution from a Needs Approach to a Rights Perspective

Recognition by the international community in 1989 of the human rights of persons below 18 was a remarkable breakthrough. It moved children and adolescents away from old-fashioned welfare and charity policies by turning needs into legal rights (see Table 5.1), to which all children are entitled by law irrespective of their social or other status (Cantwell, 1998; Freeman, 1992; Verhellen, 1992).

Fundamentally, the CRC suggests a new status and role for society's youngest members. The child is recognised as a *fully fledged subject of rights* to whom public authorities

TABLE 5.1   Different implications between a needs approach and a rights-based perspective

	Needs-based approach	Right-based approach
Objective	Meeting needs	Realising rights
Nature and process	Reactive: based on charity and paternalistically motivated goodwill, and political decisions Potential space for arbitrary decisions	Preventive: legal obligations under domestic law Non-discriminatory and equality guarantees
Status of the child	Passive object	Subject of rights Exercise rights, according to age and maturity Recognition of the child evolving capacities
Universal definitions	No guarantee Definition of needs can vary arbitrarily due to socio-cultural factors and considerations	Universally recognised rights under international law (Convention on the Rights of the Child and other international human rights treaties)
Scope of action	Focuses narrowly on specific needs when problems are identified Addresses restrictively child protection issues by addressing situations identified as problematic	Wide range of human rights Holistic and multi-sectoral interdependence and indivisibility of social, economic, cultural, civil and political rights Addresses rights linked to child protection, child participation and empowerment and all other child-related situations in society
Focus	Superficial – emphasises the social and emergency context	Structural – emphasises the legal, institutional and policy context
Accountability	Political and moral (at best) No clear identification between duty-holders (obligations) and claim-holders (entitlements)	Political and legal Clear identification under law between duty-holders (obligations) and claim-holders (entitlements)
Empowerment	Needs can be meet without empowering Unchallenged power relations	Realising rights empowers Strives towards equal power sharing
Redress and remedy	Arbitrary (no legal basis guaranteed)	Access to judicial or non-judicial redress guaranteed under law

are accountable (David, 2002; Newell, 1998; Verhellen, 1992), rather than as a vulnerable individual solely in need of protection. The CRC is articulated around three concepts: the traditional one of child protection and the new ones of the right to access provisions and the right to participation. Children are not seen only as passive vulnerable human beings; according to their age and maturity, they are also perceived through their capacities to participate in all decision-making processes. The right of children to express their opinions freely and have them taken into account (article 12) is obviously one of the most innovative and challenging rights recognised by the treaty (Freeman, 1992).

This evolution from a needs approach to a rights-based perspective provides some advantages to improve the situation of children and ensure their most optimal development. These added values can be identified as follows:

- *Accountability.* The CRC sets *legally binding obligations* on public authorities (and their agents). The child's care, needs and interests do not, therefore, merely rely on generosity and political will, but are a right and an obligation established under law. It provides clear identification between *duty-bearers* (the state and its agents, and indirectly those caring for the child) and *rights-holders* (children).
- *Normative clarity and detail.* The CRC provides a full set of *universally recognised norms* and *standards* that can be applied in any situation and in all social-cultural environments and are agreed upon by the international community.
- *Empowerment, ownership and participation.* According to their *evolving capacities*, children are *progressively empowered* and recognised as actors with their own rights instead of being simply perceived as powerless and passive objects in the hands of adults.
- *Comprehensive and holistic analytical tool.* Traditional research on children is usually fragmented, being rarely undertaken from a *multi-sectoral* angle. By covering the most essential developmental rights of children, the CRC frames analysis within a holistic dimension of the child. In general, the child is examined from a medical, psychological, sociological, legal or pedagogical angle, rather than from a holistic approach covering the child from a multi-disciplinary angle.
- *Remedy.* When guaranteed rights are not respected, children, or their legal representative, have a legal basis to complain and claim for redress in or outside the formal judicial setting.
- *International scrutiny.* In 1991, the CRC established the UN Committee on the Rights of the Child, an international and independent expert body, which *monitors the progress* achieved by all state parties in their efforts to implement the treaty's provisions and principles. By ratifying the CRC, states accept the obligation to report to the Committee periodically and thereby to be under *international scrutiny*.

ABUSE, NEGLECT, VIOLENCE AND EXPLOITATION IN YOUTH SPORT

Absence of Debate, Research and Data

Critical debate within the sport world on issues relating to the potential harmful side effects of competitive sport on children have often been taboo and perceived as being formulated by anti-sport lobbies. The sport community has been historically very protective of its activities, trying to keep them immune from critical analysis. Only the academic world has, since the 1960s (mainly), developed in several countries critical knowledge about the implications of involving children and adolescents in sport. This knowledge has mainly developed in research fields such as medicine, psychology, pedagogy and sociology. But so far only very little and fragmented research has been undertaken on the links between human rights and the sport world, especially regarding the way athletes enjoy their human rights.

In addition to providing the capacity to identify emerging issues, human rights analysis also provides a different angle on well-known issues. For example, one should not confuse an examination of the education status with the right to education. The education community might be satisfied to see that in a given country 96 per cent of children have access to primary education. Human rights analysis will try to go beyond this statistic to understand the quality of education, whether violence is used as a means of discipline and how the group which constitutes the remaining 4 per cent of children is composed. If 91 per cent of the latter are girls from an indigenous community, a pattern of discrimination might be identified and will have to be addressed. The same rationale applies to competitive sports. We can find out how many children join football academies or elite training centres in a given country, and perhaps the percentage of young athletes who reach the top and make an adequate living from the sport. We cannot determine, however, the quality of the training and supervision in sports clubs and how they comply with international child rights standards, nor what happens to those – the majority in this case – who drop out of the system.

Rainer Martens, the American sports psychologist, was probably the first to address child athletes issues in his book *Joy and Sadness in Children's Sports*, a key compilation of 36 articles, published in 1978. Although none of the articles explicitly discussed athletes' human rights, the publication was the first to present a wide range of emerging issues, such as fanatical behaviour by parents, coaches and sports officials; racism and violence; excessive pressure; young athletes' opinions about competitive sports; and the influence of the media. The book ends with a remarkable and visionary 'Bill of Rights of Young Athletes': 10 rights to protect the physical, social and psychological health of young athletes. Drafted more than 10 years before the adoption of the CRC, the document recognised fundamental human rights principles such as non-discrimination, human dignity, protection from physical abuse, freedom of choice and of opinion, and the specific status of children.

Abuse, Neglect and Violence

We are not yet properly equipped to understand fully whether children involved in competitive sports are as much, more or less vulnerable to abuse, neglect or violence than children that are not involved. Some research and anecdotal information, though, assist in identifying a large spectrum of child rights violations that can affect young athletes,

TABLE 5.2   Typology of main forms of abuse, neglect and violence in competitive sports

Physical	Excessive intensive training
	Systematic insufficient rest
	Corporal punishment
	Severe food diets
	Peer violence, including 'hazing' or 'ragging'
	Encouragement of 'play hard' or 'play hurt' attitudes
	Imposed usage of doping products
	Imposed practice and competition on injured athletes
Sexual	Verbal comments
	Physical advances
	Abusive touching
	Forced intercourse and rape
Psychological	Excessive pressure
	Verbal violence
	Emotional abuse
Neglect	Failure to provide proper care and attention
	Deliberate negligence
	Imposed isolation

including from physical, psychological and sexual abuse and violence as well as various forms of neglect (see Table 5.2). Article 19 of the CRC obliges states to:

> take all appropriate legislative, administrative, social and educational measures to protect the child from all forms of physical or mental violence, injury or abuse, neglect or negligent treatment, maltreatment or exploitation, including sexual abuse, while in the care of parent(s), legal guardian(s) or any other person who has the care of the child.

It is argued by an increasing number of specialist bodies, including the World Health Organization (WHO), that excessive intensive training regimes can amount to child abuse:

> Organization of children's sports activity by adults does have a potential for abuses to occur if those who set the amount of sports participation and the training regimen are inexperienced and use adult models. (WHO, 1998)

In a position statement on intensive training, the American Academy of Pediatrics (2000) stated that:

> To be competitive at a high level requires training regimens that could be considered extreme for adults. The ever-increasing requirements for success create a constant pressure for athletes to train longer, harder, more intelligently, and in some cases, at an

earlier age. The unending efforts to outdo predecessors and outperform contemporaries are the nature of competitive sports.

In extremely demanding competitive sports such as tennis, gymnastics, figure skating, diving, ice hockey, basketball or football, children as young as 4 years old may have already been pushed by adults to train frequently and some, at around the age of 6, may be starting systematic intensive training programmes and competition (Maffuli, 1998: 298). Children might potentially lose control over their destiny by being pressured by parents, coaches, sport managers or other interested parties into intensive training schemes that can negatively affect their holistic development, including their capacity to complete basic education. In an article published in the *New England Journal of Medicine* in 1996, four leading child health specialists stated that:

> The development of gymnastics champions involves hard training, stringent coaching, and often parental pressure, ostensibly in the best interest of the child. Over-training, injuries, and psychological damage are common consequences. Parents and coaches, in collusion with the young athlete, may seek to experience vicariously the success of the child, a behavior that could be called 'achievement by proxy' ... Its hallmark is strong parental encouragement of a potentially dangerous endeavor for the purpose of gaining fame and financial reward. We suggest that in its extreme form 'achievement by proxy' may be a sort of child abuse. (Tofler et al., 1996: 281)

Children starting intensive training and competition too early run the risk of becoming victims of the burn-out syndrome and might drop out of sport at some early stage of their career. Over-training has been identified as a leading cause of stress and burn-out, to which children are far more vulnerable than adults (Holander et al., 1995). The right of children to rest, as recognised in article 31.1 of the CRC, is fundamental to ensure proper child development and needs to be carefully addressed in the context of competitive sports, especially those involved at an early age in intensive training programmes. Systematic deprivation of rest is a form of child abuse.

Excessively high expectations, financial interests and search for fame can make children vulnerable to emotional abuse and violence. The demands of high-level competition can become overwhelming for some athletes who might be unable to cope with the related pressure, despite children's proven capacity of resilience. Emotional abuse can also translate in the form of verbal abuse by parents or coaches when they are not satisfied with results obtained or pushing athletes to their limits. Coakley (1998: 503) notes that:

> In coach-athlete relationships, it is generally accepted that coaches can humiliate, shame and derogate athletes to push them to be the best they can be. Athletes are expected to respond to humiliation by being tougher competitors willing to give even more of themselves in their quest for excellence.

Pressure on young athletes to conform to a strict diet in order to increase their chance of winning is a relatively frequent pattern in high-level sports. At a stage of life – adolescence – where athletes are naturally vulnerable to identity crises and major biological changes, imposed diets can have a very harmful consequence as it is generally acknowledged that athletes are a population group with higher levels of eating disorders (Sundgot-Borgen, 1999). Nevertheless, it remains debatable whether this is a direct result of the sporting environment or whether some athletes presented the pathology before taking up elite sport (Khan et al., 2002; Nativ et al., 1997).

Though little research exists, some pieces of evidence show that young athletes can be victims of various forms of physical abuse and violence (Klein and Palzkill, 1998; Kohler, 2000). Corporal punishment is sometimes used by coaches to discipline their athletes, but also to push them to their limits or to punish them in case of disappointing results or insufficient performance during training sessions or competition. Athletes can also be pushed into 'play hard' mentality by coaches that encourage harsh behaviour and even intentional injury of opponents. One scholar believes that:

> Young players are taught that violence is an acceptable and successful method of achieving victory. (Clarke, 2000)

Very little research exists also on the occurrence of hazing in sports, but anecdotal information tends to show that is an existing phenomenon in several countries. A rare study undertaken by the Alfred University (New York) in 2000 on hazing in high schools revealed that 48 per cent of the 20,000 students surveyed (aged 15 to 17) reported being subjected to activities that they considered hazing, half of them in the sporting context; 22 per cent qualified their hazing experience as 'dangerous' (Hoover and Pollard, 2000).

One issue that has received slightly more attention by academics and the media is the one of sexual abuse in sports. However, it remains still debatable whether children are more or less vulnerable to this form of abuse in the context of sport; this is mainly due to insufficient research and knowledge (Brackenridge, 2001: 4). Only one study so far compared prevalence of sexual abuse within and outside sports and the results raised serious concern: twice as many athletes have experienced sexual harassment from authority figures (Brackenridge, 2000; Council of Europe, 2000a: 6). Generally, most studies tend to show that between 1 and 10 per cent of young athletes experience some form of sexual abuse. But it is also believed that sexual abuse is still widely under-reported owing to the fear of many victims to reveal these abuses and the perceived (or true) incapacity of the sports system to deal with them, confidentially and fairly. The fear of ruining one's sporting career by speaking out is also often reported. Only a handful of renowned adult champions have had the courage to speak out as victims of sexual abuse, such as Australian Olympic champion Cathy Freeman and Canadian NHL ice hockey player Sheldon Kennedy.

Some characteristics of sports can increase vulnerability of children to sexual offences (see Box 5.1). Sport is by nature a physical activity in which corporal contacts can be easily justified; it is also an activity that requires changing clothes. Sports also carries traditional values, such as paternalism, that do not encourage empowerment and favours hierarchy, obedience and dependence. Athletes in general, especially the young ones, are rarely empowered individuals. Their entire careers depend on the goodwill of coaches, sports administrators, managers, and therefore they might be made more vulnerable to abuse.

Box 5.1   Characteristics of sports systems that potentially increase the vulnerability of young athletes to sexual abuse

Young athletes:

- are frequently in close physical contact with coaches, masseurs, physiotherapists, etc.
- undress and shower with others;
- are isolated from their families, their natural support and protection system.

Sport:

- is a male-driven activity, run on strictly paternalistic and hierarchal systems;
- offers easy access to volunteer and professionals with the wrong intentions;
- is not open to independent monitoring and investigation;
- has a very positive image that might generate excessive confidence in the system.

Coaches:

- feel a great ownership of their athletes;
- are authority figures, upon whom athletes are dependent.

Intensive training:

- requires such an investment of time and energy that it limits and slows social development and the learning of coping strategies and life-skills;
- offers ample opportunity for abuse to take place, for example during closed practices, travel, unsupervised team trips and overnight.

Doping

For long, both the specialist and the public at large believed that the use of illicit performance-enhancing products was a phenomenon uniquely affecting adults. In fact, in ancient Greece, child athletes aged about 12 years were selected and sent to sports schools to become professional athletes, where they were offered drugs to increase their performances (Vanoyeke, 1992). The first recorded case in modern sport goes probably back to 1959 when a Texan doctor allegedly administered an illegal substance (Dianobal) to a high school football team (Yesalis et al., 1993). Today, the media reveal increasingly cases of youth doping, such as 15-year-old (at the time) Bulgarian tennis prospect Sesil Karatantcheva who was caught in 2005 using nandrolone, a banned substance. Some experts even predict the end of traditional medical doping with the appearances of bio-genetics (Miah, 2001: 37).

The use of doping by young athletes is not surprising as many societal factors would tend to push them into this practice. Today, children, especially those living in the Western world, grow up in a heavily 'medicalised' society, sometimes referred to as the 'pill-popping' culture about which the UN International Narcotic Control Board raised serious concern (INCB, 2000). Any problem or challenge is often expected to be solved through a medical means. Children are also strongly influenced by the behaviour of their idols who act as role models. This is significant in sports; famous sport figures who use doping may legitimise to some extent this activity for the youngest. Finally, child athletes might give in to the wishes of those who want them to win at all costs: parents, coaches, sport officials, managers, etc.

With passive and sometimes even complaisant sport authorities doping in general did not receive the political attention it deserved until the 1990s, despite the fact that, along with sexual abuse, doping is the other child rights issue that received considerable consideration from the academic world. A relatively important body of research has existed on youth and doping since the mid-1980s. It tends to demonstrate that between 1 and 10 per cent of young people under 18 – and not just athletes – (3 to 5 per cent as an average) take illegal performance-enhancing drugs, with some studies quoting figures as high as 18 per cent in specific situations (Tanner et al., 1995: 109). Girls are also affected by this phenomenon, though to a lesser extent than boys.

When discussing the use of doping by young athletes from a human rights perspective, it is fundamental to address the issue of responsibility. It is considered that the average age of use of doping by young athletes is between 14 and 16 years old. Can such a young person be made fully accountable when resorting to doping? If an adult is usually considered as being able to make informed choices freely, young people may be less equipped to understand fully the implications of their decisions and actions and can be more easily manipulated, influenced or pressured. The risk of their being coerced into drug use is therefore considerable, and depends on their age, maturity and capacity of discernment.

Young athletes can obtain doping products through different means: legally through medical doctors, or illegally through, for example, their parents, teachers, coaches and peers, or directly from dealers. Studies tend to show that the main groups of providers are peers (44 per cent); the remaining 56 per cent are divided between parents, coaches and physicians (Tanner et al., 1995: 112). In all cases, it is important to note that the doping substances are initially given by adults, even if they might transit through peers. Therefore, judging that athletes below 18 act with full responsibility when they use doping is a fragile position. Considering that doped youth athletes are partially responsible for their actions is more consistent with human rights law, the same way partial responsibility is usually applied as a principle under penal law. The CRC requires that persons below 18 having infringed the law be considered *specifically* and not in the same way as adults (article 40.3). International law also requires that children be treated with dignity and takes into account the *child's age* and the desirability of promoting the *child's reintegration* (article 40.1). Children using doping should be perceived and treated more as *victims* than as criminals or cheats. Adults offering or pushing children into doping should also be sanctioned, on the basis of protection from abuse (article 19), right to health (article 24) and protection from all forms of exploitation (article 36). France and Italy have legislation sanctioning not only the doped athlete, but also the person(s) offering the products.

In almost all cases of doping of young athletes brought before sport or judicial authorities, including the Court of Arbitration for Sports (CAS), these instances have not (yet) recognised children as different cases as adults. When caught using illicit substances, in an overwhelming number of cases, child athletes are sanctioned the same way as adults, despite the requirements of the CRC. For example, Bulgarian tennis player Sesil Karatantcheva, caught aged only 15, was sanctioned by the CAS in 2005 with a suspension of two years, which is exactly the same sanction applied to adults. The same position was taken by CAS when 16-year-old Romanian gymnast Andrea Raducan tested positive for 'drugs' (given by the team's physician) and was stripped of her gold medal during the 2000 Sydney Olympics.

CHILD LABOUR AND ECONOMIC EXPLOITATION

Sport as Child Labour

Since the 1970s, sport has increasingly been commercialised and in parallel its development has moved in many countries from being a limited and private activity to a mass phenomenon. Today, it is usually considered that in Western societies (but also in others) between 20 and as high as 60 per cent of persons below 18 are involved in an organised sport activity! The commercialisation of sport has had at least four types of impact on young athletes:

- **Young athletes are generating job creation.**
- **Young athletes are advertising mediums.**
- **Young athletes can be commodities.**
- **Young athletes, at least the ones involved in intensive training, should be recognised as workers.**

Article 32 of the CRC protects children from all forms of economic exploitation:

1. States Parties recognize the right of the child to be protected from economic exploitation and from performing any work that is likely to be hazardous or to interfere with the child's education, or to be harmful to the child's health or physical, mental, spiritual, moral or social development.
2. States Parties shall take legislative, administrative, social and educational measures to ensure the implementation of the present article. To this end, and having regard to the relevant provisions of other international instruments, States Parties shall in particular:

   (a) Provide for a minimum age or minimum ages for admission to employment;
   (b) Provide for appropriate regulation of the hours and conditions of employment;
   (c) Provide for appropriate penalties or other sanctions to ensure the effective enforcement of the present article.

The treaty (which implicitly refers to the International Labour Organization treaties in article 32.2) does not outlaw labour per se for persons under 18: it regulates the age of admission and strictly prohibits all forms of abusive and exploitative labour. ILO Convention No. 138 sets different minimum age limits: article 2 prohibits work for children under 15 years (14 years for developing countries), but article 7 tolerates 'light work' for children aged 13 (12 in developing countries). It also prohibits hazardous work for all children under 18 (article 3). In addition, it defines a number of conditions that qualify child labour: any activity 'likely to jeopardise the health, safety or morals of young persons' (article 3) and any activity that does not 'prejudice [their] attendance at school' (article 7).

Children and adolescents who train intensively in a sport should be considered as workers and be provided related legal protection. Quality (including safety) and quantity (in terms of hours and efforts) should be regulated and impact on schooling should be constantly assessed. The concept of 'child athletic workers' has only been recognised by one academic (Donnelly, 1997: 390), but is totally rejected both by the public and sport authorities, even in cases where children spend more time training and competing (sometimes for money) than doing anything else. In case of intensive involvement in sport, one cannot consider the activity to be 'light work', as it is the main occupation of the child and can jeopardise their education and health. In some situations, intensive training can be considered hazardous work and should be prohibited to persons below 18, especially when:

- **average training exceeds 25 to 30 hours a week (in some countries, the legal working week for adults is 32 or 35 hours);**
- **physical efforts are comparable with those undertaken by adults and therefore excessive;**
- **insufficient time is allowed for rest and recuperation;**

- working conditions are dangerous and risk of injuries and accidents much higher than normally accepted (this is sometimes the case in sports such as gymnastics, boxing, football, American football, etc.); and
- competitive stress is excessive and therefore jeopardises the mental health of athletes.

No country in the world has enacted comprehensive labour legislation covering young athletes, despite the fact that many have similar laws to regulate the work of children involved in the entertainment industry and that many young athletes train and compete for over 20 hours a week (some in sport centres even train 30 to 40 hours a week). These laws generally do not cover young athletes so the latter are in a loophole, despite the fact that at a young age they might already be involved in training and competition along with adults. Considering young athletes as labourers would benefit them in many ways and would protect them from being abused or exploited, including limiting the number of hours spent training and defining their conditions, as required in article 32, which engages states to 'provide for appropriate regulation of the hours and conditions of employment' (article 32.2.b).

Trafficking and Sale of Young Athletes

One of the most shocking and blunt violations of child rights in sport is the trafficking and sale of young athletes. Trafficking and sale are considered by the UN as a modern form of slavery and strictly prohibited under international law, including by article 35 of the CRC. Though due to its illegal and clandestine nature it remains difficult to know the number of children trafficked yearly for the purpose of sport, conservative estimates indicate several hundreds. Unscrupulous agents recruit by all means (using sometimes deception, lies, blackmail, ruse, fake or illegal contracts, etc.) young prospects in poor countries to try them out in wealthy European or North American teams. These agents hope that their investment can be increased a hundred or even a thousand times in case one of the trafficked player succeeds in signing a significant contract.

The first reported cases of trafficked young athletes came about in Belgium in an official governmental report in 1998 (Centre pour l'égalité des chances et la lutte contre le racisme). Young footballers (aged between 15 and 17), believed to be talented, were brought illegally from Latin America and Africa to be tested by local football clubs. According to the report, only a minority succeeded in getting a professional contract – though for a very low salary and short time. The majority were abandoned by their 'managers', living underground and left to their own devices, with no money to return to their home country. A similar official French report that was leaked in 2000 revealed the same phenomenon, but on an even larger scale. During the 1998–9 football season, 58 young African players came (usually on tourist visas) to France for try-outs, many of whom were under 15 years old. One year later 108 non-European players migrated to France, among them 96 Africans (Government of France, 1999). Today, it is recognised that young football players are smuggled to the major European football countries by unscrupulous agents, though FIFA adopted in 2001 new transfer regulations that provide improved protection to players under 18. The same phenomenon also exists in baseball between Central America (mainly the Dominican Republic) and North America. It is estimated that between 500 and 700 baseball players under 18 (usually 17) are brought illegally to the United States every year (Breton and Villegas, 1999: 83).

The trafficking and sale of children to be exploited as camel jockeys was first denounced in 1986 a newspaper article in Pakistan (David, 2005: 175). Since then international attention has slowly but steadily intensified on this unique form of child exploitation. Children from very poor backgrounds are bought, usually from South Asian and African countries, and illegally transferred to Gulf States were they are forced to train and compete in camel races as child jockeys. Their added value over adults is clearly their light weight and their obedience. Camels can run up to 45 kilometres an hour and races are extremely dangerous for jockeys. Despite the fact that jockeys are strongly strapped on the camel, falls are common and can lead to serious, and sometimes even fatal, injuries. The most conservative estimates believe that a few hundreds (maybe thousands) of children are forced into this trade every year.

After over a decade of criticism by non-governmental organisations and the UN (UN Special Rapporteur on trafficking and sale of children, International Labour Organization and UN Committee on the Rights of the Child), Gulf States authorities finally started to acknowledge the very serious problem. Qatar and the United Arab Emirates (UAE) recently took some measures to prohibit racing for children below 15. Nevertheless, today this child rights violation still occurs in the some states of the Gulf region.

EMPOWERING YOUNG ATHLETES

One of the underlying principles of human rights is the empowerment of individuals and groups, especially the marginalised ones. Empowering human beings, including the youngest ones, is also providing them with tools to better protect their own rights. Empowerment of athletes in sports has almost no history or tradition (Duquin, 1984). Sports have grown around traditional values such as paternalism, military organisation, strict discipline, authoritarianism, hierarchy and masculinity that are not necessarily conducive to empowerment of individuals, whether young or old.

Promoting and protecting child rights requires providing this group a chance to participate in decision-making processes. Article 12 of the CRC guarantees that:

1. States Parties shall assure to the child who is capable of forming his or her own views the right to express those views freely *in all matters affecting the child, the views of the child being given due weight in accordance with the age and maturity of the child.*
2. For this purpose, the child shall in particular be provided the opportunity to be heard in any judicial and administrative proceedings affecting the child, either directly, or through a representative or an appropriate body, in a manner consistent with the procedural rules of national law. (Emphasis added)

This provision is particularly challenging for adults and children alike, as for long children have been treated as simple objects of protection and not as active subjects of rights. Involving children in decision making in sports means that their voice should be heard and that their opinions can impact decisions affecting them. Commenting on this evolution, Van Bueren says (1995: xxii):

> the central issue is not one of law, but of respect, and of recognition that children as human beings are entitled not only to care and protection, but also to participate in decisions involving their own destinies to a greater extent than is generally recognised.

When involved in decision making, young athletes might feel a stronger ownership of their destiny.

Right to Education

In the context of empowerment, the right to education (articles 28 and 29 of the CRC) are fundamental. Empowerment requires individual and collective skills that can be learnt at best through formal and informal education channels.

Athletes involved in early intensive training programmes can have their right to education challenged. The requirements of elite training and competing are nowadays so high that they potentially are incompatible with the school ones. The risk is significant that young athletes, trying to combine both, drop out of school and are not sufficiently talented to make a living through sport. Johan Cruyff, former world top footballer and coach, warned (Coadic 1998: 112):

> Today, football and sports in general destroy many adolescents. At 16, a footballer, a swimmer or a track and field athlete has to make a choice. For 90 per cent it will be sports, with the risk of failure.

The sports system feeds the illusion that a potential sport career is a better option than completing the school system. The problem is not that 'baby' sports champions, such as Swiss Martina Hingis (tennis) or American Tara Lipinski (figure skating), left the education system early; they were the exception to the rule. But when these exceptions become role models (the 'get-rich-quick' myth) and are perceived by the general public as the norm, the message sent to parents and other adults involved in youth sports is wrong and undermines the right to education of every child.

Civil Rights

In addition to their rights to education and to express their views freely and have them taken into account, young athletes are recognised as having the same civil rights as all children: rights to freedom of expression, association, thought, movement and privacy (articles 13–17 of the CRC). The right to freedom of association is important in the context of sports and can be of three dimensions for children: if they wish to participate in the governing process of their sport club; when they wish to change club or association; and if they wish to join labour unions.

Freedom of association can be breached in cases when a young talented player wishes to change club and the club managers try to keep him or her by requesting from the other club an excessively high compensation fee. Similarly, young athletes can be transferred to another club against their will when their club wants to make a profit through selling its players. These types of conflict situations have been brought to courts in Belgium and Luxembourg during the 1990s in cases where the wishes of young football and basketball players to move or not to move to another club were not respected by club managers. The courts' decisions made jurisprudence and the national federations of these two sports were required to amend their transfer rules to respect the right to freedom of association of young athletes (David, 2005: 197–9).

Potentially, young professional athletes should be permitted to join labour unions and bargain collectively as of the age of 15 (international legal age for admission to work). Few adult athletes are unionised; this is mainly due to their historical lack of political empowerment. Athletes' labour rights are usually poorly protected, with the great exception of the most famous, and they are often handled by third parties.

Protection from discrimination is also key to ensure empowerment of children. Article 2.1 of the CRC guarantees:

1. States Parties shall respect and ensure the rights set forth in the present Convention to each child within their jurisdiction without discrimination of any kind, irrespective of the child's or his or her parent's or legal guardian's race, colour, sex, language, religion, political or other opinion, national, ethnic or social origin, property, disability, birth or other status.

Children experience various forms of discrimination worldwide, including through their sporting activity. Racial and gender-based discrimination are common in sports; children with light disabilities can also be discriminated by being excluded from mainstream sport, though the nature of their disability would permit them to compete with so-called valid athletes. HIV/AIDS status and the political or other opinions of parents have also been grounds for discrimination against young athletes (David, 2005: 202–9).

ACCOUNTABILITY OF STATES, SPORT AUTHORITIES AND ADULTS

Towards a Child-Centred Sport System

One of the particularities and strengths of human rights law is that it defines clear accountability lines between duty-bearers and rights-holders. In the case of children and sport, responsibility lies mainly in the hands of the state, and indirectly with sport authorities, parents and other adults involved. Indeed, article 19 of the CRC extends the state obligation to protect children from all forms of abuse, neglect, violence, injury and exploitation, 'while in the care of parent(s), legal guardian(s) or any other person who has the care of the child'. The CRC also recognises 'the responsibilities, rights and duties of parents ... to provide ... appropriate direction and guidance in the exercise by the child of the rights recognized in the present Convention' (article 5) and parents' 'primary responsibilities for the upbringing and development of the child' (article 18.1). In other words, adults, especially parents, have the obligation to provide proper guidance and advice to their child athletes that truly strives towards their best interests and dignity, and not to any other selfish, abusive or exploitative considerations. Excessive ambitions of adults can typically generate violation of children's rights. Top American gymnast Amy Jackson felt overwhelmed by her father's ambitions:

> I was kind of worried that my father was so excited about it. I was scared, scared of learn-
> ing new things, scared I wasn't going to be good enough, that I wouldn't be able to do
> anything to please him. I was already thinking of quitting. I always did what I was told. I
> was scared of what my dad would say if I said anything (Ryan, 1995: 163).

Today youth sport is generally not very child sensitive. It is overwhelmingly managed by adults who set the rules, nurture their own ambitions and keep unchallenged monopoly over decision making. The main participants – children themselves – are rarely given the chance to express their views, ideas, feelings and wishes about the activity they undertake. There are many ways of integrating children's rights in the sport world. One is to adopt a certain number of principles that would ensure that youth sports policies are child centred (see Table 5.3).

Human rights law is certainly not the only tool that can be used to safeguards children's rights in sport, but it is potentially one of the most effective. This is mainly due to the *legally binding* nature of the CRC in 192 countries of the world. The main obstacle for

TABLE 5.3   A child centred sport system: 10 fundamental principles

1	Equity, non-discrimination, fairness
2	Best interests of the child: children first
3	Evolving capacities of the child
4	Subject of rights; exercise of rights
5	Consultation, the child's opinion, informed participation
6	Appropriate direction and guidance
7	Mutual respect, support and responsibility
8	Highest attainable standard of health
9	Transparency, accountability, monitoring
10	Excellence

implementing child rights in sport lies at best in the lack of awareness about child rights and, at worst, in the obsessive resistance of the sport world to accept that the rule of law also applies to the sport sphere. So far, the International Olympic Committee (IOC) has been very passive in looking at children's rights implications of involving children in amateur and professional sports; it leaves the responsibility to the international sports federations. But the IOC could potentially use its significant moral authority to advance child rights protection in sports. International sports federations have only taken targeted reactive measures when they felt threatened by negative publicity for their sports. Only when major criticism developed in the public domain and the media did the international federations governing tennis, figure skating and gymnastics increase the age of admission to professional events or the Olympic Games. The same applies to sexual abuse: when a few cases involving children were suddenly highly profiled in the British and American media, they generated public hysteria and a moral panic among parents. Again, some measures were taken by sports federations, even at a later stage by the IOC and some of its national affiliates, as a *reaction* to the crisis, and not as *preventive* policies.

Grass-roots non-governmental organizations (NGOs) and some states, such as France, the Nordic countries, Belgium, The Netherlands and in some regions of Germany, started during the 1990s to implement child protection measures in sport. The case of the Child Protection Unit, established in 2001 by the main child protection NGO of the United Kingdom (NSPCC), demonstrates a major advance in tackling child protection issues in sport. Institutional responses were mainly focusing on the following measures but were usually a response to sexual abuse, and in a few cases doping and fair-play-related issues:

- **adoption of child protection policies and ethical charters;**
- **criminal record checks (of trainers or coaches);**
- **awareness raising and training of athletes, parents, coaches and other officials;**
- **appointment of child protection officers in sports clubs and federations;**

- establishment of telephone helplines;
- establishment of conflict resolution and litigation mechanisms;
- quality control management and labelling; and
- research on child protection in sport issues.

Though these initiatives are commendable, they still focus more on the relatively limited area of *child protection* (and essentially on sexual abuse), and not on the broader field of *child rights* which also deals with participation rights and empowerment.

The UN and its various agencies have stayed very silent on the issue of children's rights and sports. Neither UNICEF, the Office of the UN High Commissioner for Human Rights, the ILO nor the Special Adviser to the UN Secretary-General on Sport for Development and Peace have ever addressed a single issue relating to the topic. The WHO has tackled doping, but not with a specific youth angle. Only UNESCO adopted a significant statement, in 2003, but one that, so far, has received no follow-up:

> The protection of young athletes should be understood in the perspective of the principles stated in the UN Convention on the Rights of the Child. That is why protection should not be understood solely in terms of health as well as physical and psychological integrity. It also involves quality education that facilitates long-term personal and professional development. To this end, flexible modalities of educational provisions should be provided which meet the educational needs of young athletes. Protection also includes safeguarding against such dangers such as child labour, violence, doping, early specialization, over-training, and exploitative forms of commercialization as well as less visible threats and deprivations, such as the premature severance of family bonds and the loss of sporting, social and cultural ties (UNESCO, 2003: 2).

It is the Council of Europe that has proved since the early 1990s to be the most active regional or international political body on the issue, adopting many strong recommendations to its member states as well as engaging in awareness-raising campaigns and activities.

A remarkable and so far unique initiative was the decision of the Irish Sports Council and the Sports Council for Northern Ireland (the highest domestic sport authorities) in 2001 to unite and adopt a 'Code of Ethics and Good Practice for Children's Sport in Ireland' (2001: 4), which affirms that:

> As citizens, adults have a responsibility to protect children from harm and to abide by government guidelines in responding to and reporting child protection concerns. This responsibility exists wherever such concerns might arise, whether inside or outside sport. Guidelines contained in the Code of Ethics and Good Practice for Children's Sport in Ireland *took account of the UN Convention on the Rights of the Child* and are in accordance with government guidelines. (Emphasis added)

CONCLUSION

Despite increasing attention given to many traditional issues relating to the involvement of children in sports since the 1970s, their human rights implication – as defined under domestic and international law – has still been neglected. There are at least two global arguments considering more seriously the human rights of young athletes:

- *Respect for the rule of law.* **The sporting world, like any other, is bound by human rights laws and policies and can no longer remain an entirely closed and hermetic system.**
- *Elimination of harmful side effects.* **In order to ensure that competitive sport remains a largely positive experience for young people, its potentially harmful side effects must be addressed, so that the number of athletes whose holistic development is irreversibly affected is kept to a minimum. Therefore, applying the rule of law to the sport sphere can potentially be a powerful tool.**

The challenge in the future is the following one: will the IOC, international sports federations, and international, regional and national public authorities take effective measures to integrate human rights law and policies in sport regulations, by-laws, jurisprudential decisions, policies, programmes and practice? Will the most powerful sport decision makers one day take the rule of law seriously in order to promote and guarantee the rights of young athletes as recognised in the most universally ratified international treaty in the world's history, the UN Convention on the Rights of the Child?

CHAPTER SUMMARY

- » International human rights law needs to be applied to the sport sphere in order to guarantee improved promotion and protection of the human rights of young athletes.
- » The downsides of youth competitive sports have to be acknowledged by both public and sporting authorities in order to address these issues properly.
- » International child rights norms and standards represent a powerful tool to address issues such as physical, emotional and sexual abuse, doping, trafficking and sale of athletes, etc.
- » Young athletes involved in intensive training programmes should be granted the status of workers in order to have increased protection.
- » Through the UN Convention on the Rights of the Child, national and local public authorities are accountable worldwide to ensure that sport authorities and other actors involved respect the human rights of young athletes.

FURTHER READING

So far the only comprehensive book on the issue of the respect of children's rights in sport is David (2005). Brackenridge (2001) wrote a very thorough book on the issue of sexual exploitation in sport. Martens (1978) was the first to identify emerging child rights issues in sport during the late 1970s and his book is still relevant today. Finally, Donnelly's (1997) study compared young athletes to child workers.

REFERENCES

American Academy of Pediatrics (2000) 'Intensive training and sports specialization in young athletes', *Pediatrics*, 106 (1): 154–7.

Brackenridge, C. (2000) 'Harrassment, sexual abuse and safety of the female athlete', *Clinics in Sport Medicine*, 19.2, 187–198.

Brackenridge, C. (2001) *Spoilsports: Understanding and Preventing Sexual Exploitation in Sport*. London: Routledge.

Breton, M. and Villegas, J.-L. (1999) *Away games: the Life and Times of a Latin Ball*. Albuquerque, NM: University of New Mexico Press.

Cantwell, N. (1998) 'The history, content and impact of the Convention on the Rights of the Child', in Verhellen, E. (ed.), *Understanding Children's Rights*. Ghent: University of Ghent.

Centre pour l'égalité des chances et la lutte contre le racisme (1998) *Rapport annuel d'évaluation sur l'évolution et les résultats de la lutte contre la traite des êtres humains* [Annual evaluation report on the evolution and the results of the fight against trafficking in human beings], Brussels.

Clarke, J. (2000) 'Anabolic steroids – a growing problem', *Network Northwest*, no.10. Liverpool: Healthwise Liverpool.

Coadic, L. (1998) 'Le Sportif est une victime', *L'Equipe Magazine*, number 858, 19th September.

Coakley, J. (1998) *Sport in Society, Issues and Controversies*. Boston: WCB McGraw-Hill.

Council of Europe (2000a) *Background Studies on the Problem of Sexual Harrassment in Sport, Especially with Regard to Women and Children*. Brackenridge, C. and Footing, K. 9th Council of Europe Conference for Ministers responsible for Sport. Bratislava, Slovakia, 30–31 May.

David, P. (2002) 'Implementing the rights of the child: six reasons why the human rights of children remain a constant challenge', *International Review of Education*, 48 (3–4): 259–63.

David, P. (2005) *Human Rights in Youth Sport. A critical review of children's rights in competitive sports.* London: Routledge.

Donnelly, P. (1997) 'Child labour, sport labour. Applying child labour laws to sport', *International Review for Sociology of Sport*, 32 (4): 389–406.

Duquin, M.E. (1984) 'Power and authority: moral consensus and conformity in sport', *International Review for the Sociology of Sport*, 19 (3–4): 295–303.

Freeman, M. (1992) 'Introduction: rights, ideology and children', in M. Freeman and P. Veerman (eds), *The Ideologies of Children's Rights.* The Hague: Martinus Nijhoff.

Government of France (1999) *Le recruitement, l'accueil et le suivi des jeunes étrangers (hors Union Européenne) dans les centres de formation des clubs de football professionnels en France* [The recruitment, reception and follow-up of young foreigners (ex-European Union) in the training centres run by professional football clubs in France]. Paris: Ministère de la Jeunesse et des Sports, unofficial translation.

Grayson, E. (2000) 'The historical development of sport and law', in S. Greenfield and G. Osborn, *Law and Sport in Contemporary Society.* London: Frank Cass.

Holander, D.B., Meyers, M.C. and LeUnes, A. (1995) 'Psychological factors associated with overtraining: implications for youth sport coaches', *Journal of Sport Behavior*, 18 (1): 3–20.

Hoover, N.C. and Pollard, N.J. (2000) *Initiation in American High Schools: A National Survey, Final Report.* Alfred, NY: Alfred University.

Irish Sports Council and Sports Council for Northern Ireland (2001) *Code of Ethics and Good Practice for Children's Sport in Ireland.* Dublin. Irish Sports Council.

Khan, K.M., Liu-Ambrose, T., Saran, M., Ashe, M.C., Donaldson, M.G. and Wark, J.D. (2002) 'New criteria for female triad syndrome?', *British Journal of Sports Medicine*, 36: 10–13.

Klein, M. and Palzkill, B. (1998) *Gewalt gegen Mädchen und Frauen im Sport.* Studie, Dokumente und Berichte 46. Dusseldorf: Ministry for Women, Young People and Family, Nordrhein-Westfalen.

Kohler, I (2000) *Quand on fait du sport, les contacts physiques sont courants...* [When you practise sports, physical contact is frequent...]. Berne: Association Suisse pour la protection de l'enfant.

Maffuli, N. (1998) 'At what age should a child begin regular continuous exercise at moderate or high intensity?', *British Journal of Sports Medicine*, 32: 298.

Martens, R. (ed.) (1978) *Joy and Sadness in Children's Sport.* Champaign, IL: Human Kinetics.

Miah, A. (2001) 'Genetic technologies and sport: the new ethical issue', *Journal of the Philosophy of Sport*, 28: 32–52.

Nativ, A., Agostini, R. and Drinkwater, A.R.B. (1997) 'The female athlete triad. The interrelatedness of disordered eating, amenorrhoea, and osteoporosis', *Clinical Sports Medicine and Exercise*, 29: 1–4.

Newell, P. (1998) 'Children's active participation as a role of government', in E. Verhellen (ed.), *Monitoring Children's Rights*. The Hague: Martinus Nijhoff.

Ryan, J. (1995) *Little Girls in Pretty Boxes: the Making and Breaking of Elite Gymnasts and Figure Skaters*. New York: Doubleday.

Sundgot-Borgen, J. (1999) 'Eating disorders among male and female athletes', *British Journal of Sports Medicine*, 33 (4): 434.

Tanner, S.M., Miller, C.A. and Alongi, C. (1995) 'Anabolic steroid use by adolescents: prevalence, motives and knowledge or risks', *Clinical Journal of Sport*, 5: 108–115.

Tofler, I.R., Stryer, B.K., Micheli, L.J. and Herman, L.R. (1996) 'Physical and emotional problems of elite gymnasts', *New England Journal of Medicine*, 335 (4).

UN Committee on Economic, Social and Cultural Rights (2000) *The right to the highest attainable standard of health, article 12 of the International Covenant on Economic, Social and Cultural Rights*. General Comment No. 14, E/C.12/2000/4. Geneva: UN.

UN Educational, Social and Cultural Organization (UNESCO) (2003) *Final Communiqué of the Round Table of Ministers and Senior Officials Responsible for Physical Education and Sport, 10 January*. Paris: UNESCO.

UN International Narcotic Control Board (2000) *INCB Annual Report*, E/INCB/1999/1. Vienna: UN.

United Nations Convention on the Rights of the Child, UN General Assembly resolution 44/25, 20 November 1989, http://www.ohchr.org/english/law/crc.htm.

Van Bueren, G. (1995) *The International Law on the Rights of the Child*. The Hague: Martinus Nijhoff.

Vanoyeke, V. (1992) *La Naissance des Jeux Olympiques et le Sport dans l'Antiquité* [The birth of the Olympic Games and sport during Antiquity]. Paris: Les Belles Lettres.

Verhellen, E. (1992) 'Changes in the image of the child', in M. Freeman, and P. Veerman (eds), *The Ideologies of Children's Rights*. The Hague: Martinus Nijhoff.

World Health Organization (1998) 'Sports and children: consensus statement on organized sports for children', FIMS/WHO ad hoc Committee on Sports and Children, in *Bulletin of the World Health Organization*, no. 76(5). Geneva: WHO.

Yesalis, C.E., Vicary, J.R. and Buckley, W.E. (1993) 'History of anabolic steroid use in sport and exercise', in C.E. Yesalis (ed.), *Anabolic Steroid in Sport and Exercise*. Champaign, IL: Human Kinetics, pp. 35–47.

6

Women, Sport and Gender Inequity

TESS KAY AND RUTH JEANES

OVERVIEW

» *The female experience of sport: a history of exclusion*
» *Gender and sports research: the development of feminism*
» *The female experience of sport: the contemporary picture*
» *Choice or constraint? Explanations for female under-representation in sport*
» *Gender inequity in the production of sport*
» *Gender and the sports media*
» *Resistance and empowerment: female use of sport to challenge gender expectations*
» *Conclusion*

Contemporary sport is a truly global phenomenon, bringing shared experiences to a worldwide audience – yet sport is not universally inclusive. It can also be a powerful mechanism for delivering a divisive version of society – one that promotes white above black, male above female, physical prowess above alternative qualities, certain body types above others. And because of its pervasive presence, the divisions that arise through sport carry a social significance that reach far beyond sport itself. The very fact that sport appears to be outside the bounds of 'real life', and thus outside real social relations, heightens its power in constructing an extreme notion of the social order as a hierarchy based on difference.

Sport is considered an arena where traditional gender identities are constructed, reinforced and contested (Humberstone, 2002). This chapter examines the relationship between sport and gender. Its focus is on the significance of sport in contributing to the gender order – that is, the social relations between males and females. Here we are concerned with three things – how gender relations are evident within contemporary sport, how sport itself influences contemporary gender relations and also how sport can be used as a vehicle to challenge contemporary gender relations.

The scale and visibility of modern sport make it an extraordinarily significant social institution, and one that is well positioned to transmit its values and ideologies. A core value within sport is its construction of a form of masculinity that elevates male experience over female. A wide range of scholars have depicted sport as a particularly powerful setting for the construction of masculinity (e.g. Birrell and Theberge, 1994a, 1994b; Bryson, 1987, 1990; Connell, 1987; Hall, 1993; Hargreaves, 1994; Messner and Sabo, 1990; Willis, 1982). Whitson (1990) described sport as one of the central sites in the social production of masculinity, while Connell (1987) considered it to be the institution that most systematically promotes images of ideal masculinity. The close identification of sport with masculinity places 'non-masculine' groups at the margins of sport and, in doing so, undermines their position in a society in which sport is highly valued. The increasing prominence of women in other areas of society, such as within the labour force, leaves sport as one of the few areas left in the public domain where force and intimidation and other constructs of masculinity are acceptable. Men can use the sporting arena to celebrate their toughness and superiority without question and as such can be unwilling to allow sport to become a further area where women's presence is viewed as acceptable (Whitson, 2002).

THE FEMALE EXPERIENCE OF SPORT: A HISTORY OF EXCLUSION

This section explores the rationales for women's exclusion from sport; the history of opposition to women's sports participation; how gender discrimination is embedded in the structures of sport; and the contemporary significance of this historical legacy.

Throughout the world, there is a lengthy history of sport being seen as incompatible with feminine qualities. Three rationales have been given for opposing women's participation:

1   *the medical rationale*, **that women are physiologically unsuited to sporting activity and may be damaged by it;**
2   *the aesthetic rationale*, **that women engaging in sport are an unattractive spectacle; and**
3   *the social rationale*, **that the qualities and behaviours associated with sport are contrary to 'real' femininity.**

The history of women's involvement in sport is therefore one of substantial exclusion: through formal or informal means, women have been debarred from equitable access to sports experiences.

Change has clearly taken place: few people would today argue that it is 'unnatural' for women to take part in sport. In the UK the slow acceptance of women into sporting activity became evident from the late nineteenth century, when the development of sport within educational institutions lent impetus to women's participation in sport and physical recreation. By the outbreak of the First World War, there was scarcely a sport that women had not tried; nonetheless, participation was still considerably limited by prevailing definitions of femininity, and sport remained an unusual, almost extraordinary activity for women to engage in (Theberge, 1990).

Progress came slowly in the face of opposition both within and beyond sport. In France, the churches formally opposed women taking part: 'Even the Pope spoke against women's participation in some competitive sports events' (McPherson et al., 1989: 227). The sports establishment itself displayed substantial resistance to women's involvement. Pierre de Coubertin, founder of the modern Olympics and influential in international sport, publicly opposed women's participation in competitive sport well into the 1930s, arguing that women should be expelled from the Olympic Games, and even claiming that their Olympic participation was illegal (McPherson et al., 1989). Opposition to women's participation in the Olympics was not helped by some unfortunate displays when women participated in the Games in events in which they appeared to have little experience. The inaugural Olympic women's 800 metre race in 1928 was a debacle:

> Both of Canada's entries in that 800 metres event finished the race, and this in itself was quite an achievement. It was the first time that such an event had been held for women, and most of the entrants were not prepared for the gruelling distance. Of the eleven starters, only six finished, and most of those collapsed at the end of the race. (Schrodt, 1976: 40)

De Coubertin's efforts to remove women from the Olympics more than 20 years after they had been admitted give some indication of the strength of feeling on the issue. Although primarily concerned with women's exclusion from public competitive sport, de Coubertin's argument that their participation was unaesthetic and contrary to the laws of nature went further. His ultimate view was that women's function within sport was not to compete themselves, but to applaud the male competitor: 'At the Olympic Games their primary role should be, as in the ancient tournaments, to crown the victor with laurels' (de Coubertin, 1935; in McPherson et al., 1989: 227).

Attitudes to women's involvement in sport have become more receptive as expectations about their position in society have become less restrictive, but traditional notions of what is 'appropriate' are still influential. Sports have become divided into appropriate forms to reflect the diverse binaries associated with masculinity and femininity. Many sports continue to be seen as less suitable for women than men, and female participation in the types of activities in which women have traditionally participated (e.g. tennis, netball, gymnastics) is generally seen as more compatible with femininity than their participation in 'male' sports (e.g. football, rugby, cricket). Women's sports often are associated with balance, flexibility and grace rather than strength, speed and stamina and, it may be argued, that participation in these sports does not necessarily challenge traditional gender notions. As Treagus points out, 'The discipline and restraint required of the netball player reflects the restraint required of feminine girls and women through much of the twentieth century' (2005: 102).

The masculinity of sport is a product of the way in which sport has been institutionalised and developed, rather than a reflection of the intrinsic qualities of sporting activity. In itself, sport is no more ideally suited to men than to women (Coakley, 1990), but has been comprehensively masculinised through its history of male control. Throughout history men have controlled sport, used it for their purposes, and shaped it to fit their abilities. The simple legacy of this is that gender inequities are inherent in sports structures today. They are most evident on the international stage, where women not only still compete in smaller numbers than men, but face specific restrictions on the events in which they are allowed to take part. The sports establishment's reluctance to remove increasingly anomalous restrictions on women's competitive sport has shown just how resistant sport can be to the supposed attitudinal shift of the late twentieth century.

In comparison with earlier times, women's involvement in sport has undoubtedly increased – but historical comparisons can be flattering. What is at issue today is not how women's sports involvement compares with that of previous generations of females, but how it contrasts with that of the contemporary male. The current situation certainly demonstrates 'improvement' vis-à-vis earlier eras, but pro-feminist analyses of sport of the 1980s and 1990s suggested that 'the female in sport is still considered a woman in a man's territory' (Birrell, cited in Boutilier and San Giovanni, 1983: 80).

GENDER AND SPORTS RESEARCH: THE DEVELOPMENT OF FEMINIST ANALYSIS

Over the last three decades the growing recognition of women's marginalisation in the sporting arena and men's continued dominance has led to an abundance of research focusing on this issue. Following the realisation that most research into sport was produced by men and focused on the experiences of men, pro-feminist researchers responded by applying feminist theory, which was already receiving widespread use in mainstream sociology, to examine female experience in sport. Feminism is concerned with ensuring the female voice is at the centre of the research process and is heard within the public domain. As the position of women in sport has changed so too has the type of feminist analysis that has been considered appropriate for examining women's experience. This section briefly examines the key strands of feminist theory that have been used and their applications to sports research.

The starting point for reviewing the various theoretical frameworks deployed in feminist research is liberal feminism. Founded on the principle that females are disadvantaged because they do not have equality of access and opportunities with men, liberal feminism views sport and its structure as offering a potentially positive experience if women have the opportunity to participate. Early work undertaken using this perspective (e.g. Dyer, 1982; Ferris, 1981) was valuable for rejecting biological explanations of women's lack of participation and highlighting the extent of gender inequalities, by demonstrating the lack of provision for female sport and the more limited opportunities for them to participate. Liberal feminism, however, failed to demonstrate how the complexities of gender interaction influenced women's sports participation and how and why women are perceived as unequal to men. Researchers switched focus, using radical feminism to enable these inequalities to be addressed in greater depth by highlighting the oppression women experience through patriarchal power. Sport, using a radical feminist approach, is viewed as a continuing site where female oppression occurs (Cahn, 1994; Clarke, 1998; Griffin, 1998; Lenskyj, 1995).

Whilst increasing our understanding of how gender inequalities develop, radical feminism in turn received criticism for focusing solely on patriarchy as the source of oppression for women and failing to explore fully divisions created between women by class, race and ethnicity (Scraton and Flintoff, 2002). Marxist feminism, by contrast, attempts to explain how gender inequalities derive from capitalism, class and economic exploitation. Research directed by Marxist feminist traditions maintains that men control the means of production and are also likely to control systems that create dominant ideologies and maintain them (Wearing, 1998). Using this approach researchers in the Marxist feminist tradition have highlighted how women have less financial capacity to engage in sport due to being lower earners and often having less time due to domestic and family requirements which are considered a 'woman's responsibility' (Deem, 1986; Griffin et al., 1982).

Although significant macro frameworks, these approaches failed to provide a theoretical analysis which enabled a synthesis between class, gender and cultural power. Socialist feminism was subsequently developed as a combination of the theorising used in Marxist and radical feminism. This theory has been applied to examine how women's dual role in paid and domestic labour affects their time and interest available for sport (Green et al., 1987; Wearing, 1990; Wimbush, 1988). Nonetheless, while these attempts to theorise class and gender provided a more complete framework than previously available, they were not completely successful, with critics claiming class issues still gained precedent over ones concerning patriarchy. Feminist analysis was continually developing and beginning to focus on resistance to gender expectation which the previous macro frameworks failed to address adequately. This led to cultural studies frameworks being developed which offer feminist research the flexibility to examine social life and cultural practices. Utilising Gramsci's concept of hegemony, which works through the construction of common-sense beliefs, the theory assists with understanding the complex relationship between freedom and constraint in sport and the potential for women to use sport as a means of breaking down the dominant hegemony or male patriarchal power (Birrell and Theberge, 1994b; Hall, 1996; Scraton et al., 1999). The theory acknowledges that cultural belief is responsible for teaching males that sport is a significant part of manliness and the subsequent exclusion and distancing of women from this domain, but maintains that women are still able to challenge and contest this dominant assumption (Connell, 1995).

Post-structural theorisations provide the final approach used in feminist analysis. In contrast to previous macro analyses, post-structural feminist approaches suggest that not all women are the same and that it is possible for individual women to have multiple experiences within sport. This means, for example, that women may be aggressive and competitive within the sports arena and challenge the gender order, but also be concerned with appearance and body shape away from it, thus not experiencing a complete trans-formation of dominant gender ideologies. Using the work of Foucault (1980, 1983) to offer alternative definitions of power as plural and productive, rather than simply top down as the previous theories suggest, post-structural theory has been used to challenge the dichotomy of masculinity and femininity and argues that multiple femininities exist. Analyses using this approach to examine sport have focused on how it maintains binary opposites and gender relations but also offers potential for participants to transgress gen-der expectations and deconstruct these binaries (Caudwell, 1999; Obel, 1996; Pronger, 1990, 1998). However, post-structuralism also has its critics and users of this theory have been accused of focusing too much on diversity and in doing so dissolving the political power of the collective female voice.

It must be recognised therefore that none of these theories offer a complete framework for understanding women's experiences and positions within sport or the use of sport to maintain and challenge the gender order. Each new wave has built on the ideas and assumptions provided by the previous framework. All approaches have their critics and flaws, but all have also deepened understanding of women's experiences of sport. We now turn our attention to the evidence of women and girls' current relationship to sport, and the issues that arise from it.

THE FEMALE EXPERIENCE OF SPORT: THE CONTEMPORARY PICTURE

Sports participation by women and girls is lower than participation by men and boys in virtually every country in the world. The differential between the sexes varies from country to country, and there are now a handful of countries in which the differences are only marginal. In most, however, they are marked and, in some cases, quite extreme. The overall pattern is unequivocal: females do not participate in sport on the same scale as males, and in most countries there is a wide gap between the sexes.

In the UK, differences in sports participation between the sexes begin to emerge in secondary school years. Initially the differences are not great – young people in the UK generally have high levels of sports participation, and during school years the gap between the sexes is only about 3 per cent. However, school sport appears artificially to inflate girls' 'natural' sports participation levels: outside school, girls are much less likely to take part in sport than are boys. Girls are less likely than boys to be frequent participants in sport, more likely than them to be non-participants, and more likely to give up sport when they leave school.

These and other differences lay a pattern that becomes even more marked in adulthood. Throughout their lives, women are less likely than men to take part in sport; women who do participate, on average participate less frequently than men, and the range of sports in which women engage is narrower than that for men. There are also qualitative differences in the type of sports participation, for girls and women show a preference for less structured forms of sport, and are less likely than males to take part in competitive sports – especially 'traditional' team sports. The areas that do attract women, and have shown marked increases in the last 20 years, are exercise and keep-fit activities with a strong body-shaping component.

It is therefore unsurprising that taking part in sport on a regular basis is not particularly widespread among British women. Despite universal exposure to sport during their school years, in 2002 only a slight majority (53 per cent) of women (aged 16+) participated in at least one sports activity in the four weeks before interview, compared with almost two-thirds (65 per cent) of men (the General Household Survey, 2002). More women had participated once in the previous 12 months (70 per cent), but still fewer than men (80 per cent). Women's sports participation also declines more quickly with age than does that of men, and is much more susceptible to the impact of family and household responsibilities than men's. There is a particularly strong impact on women's sports participation when their household contains a child under the age of 5, while men's participation is much less affected. Women's social class also appears more significant for their sports participation than for men's: the gap between male and female participation rates widens going down the socio-economic scale; among manual workers, women's participation rate is only three-quarters of men's (Table 6.1). Overall, women's sports participation is more sensitive than men's to the impact of other social structural constraints, including age, social class, ethnicity and disability. It is only women who are relatively favourably positioned within the social structure who come close to closing the sports participation gap with men.

This pattern of female under-representation is even more acute in elite sport. Although female involvement at the top level of performance has been transformed over the last hundred years, stark inequalities remain. The number of sports in which women can compete

TABLE 6.1   Sports participation rates by sex and occupational group, 2002: % participation four weeks before interview

Occupational group	Men aged 16	Women aged 16
Large employers and high managerial	76	73
Higher professional	79	71
Lower managerial and professional	74	66
Intermediate	69	52
Small employers and own account	61	54
Lower supervisory and technical	60	48
Semi-routine	53	42
Routine	51	38
Never worked and long-term unemployed	51	30

Source: General Household Survey (2002)

is still lower than for men, and there are fewer single-sex sports for females. Overall, women continue to be a small minority of participants at the major international games, and there are still many countries which participate with no female representatives at all.

Women's relationship to contemporary sport is therefore a mixed picture. Comparisons with males appear discouraging, for there is little question that sport plays a smaller part in women's lives than in men's, and appears less accessible to them. Seen over time, however, there is little doubt that this situation is changing. In the UK, absolute levels of female sports participation have been rising since the 1970s, especially in health and fitness activities. There have also been rises in female participation in the sports that have traditionally been the preserves of males. Yet by most measures, women's participation remains low in absolute as well as relative terms: for example, despite the increased participation in fitness activities, most have physical activity levels below the threshold required for health benefits. We now move on to examine the barriers that appear to inhibit full access to sport by females.

CHOICE OR CONSTRAINT? EXPLANATIONS FOR FEMALE UNDER-REPRESENTATION IN SPORT

It has long been recognised that women and girls are under-represented in sport – but it was not until the late twentieth century that the assumption that sport is 'naturally' more suited to men came under sustained attack. Since then, the processes through which sport has been constructed as a determinedly masculine sphere have been subject to increasing scrutiny. The result has been a wealth of analyses of how women and girls are marginalised in sport; these address factors both within sport itself and in the broader pattern of social relations in which sport is situated. In this section we examine both types of explanation and the interrelationship between them. We start with the broad picture – the social context of sport, and the societal pressures that contemporary patterns of gender relations exert on females.

Gender differentiation in social relations is a universal phenomenon which takes place within the contemporary patriarchy. In the public and private spheres, women can lack the power, resources, autonomy and sense of self that males possess. This imbalance is a product of the gender relations between the sexes and strongly influences the sexes' differing experience of sport. As we have seen, women participate in sport less than men. Moreover they participate in different types of sport to men, although the range of sports in which women take part is broadening. However, for the most part, women participate in those that conform to conventional notions of femininity. Furthermore, the areas of greatest growth in women's participation (i.e. fitness and exercise activities) are those which most obviously directly contribute to the attainment of the idealised female body image. The sports that females participate in therefore affirm popular images of femininity. Female athletes who are heavily muscled and do not use their bodies within the usual limits of conventional femininity face criticism and insinuations of de-feminisation. Issues surrounding the heterosexual female have been prevalent in maintaining the social control of women's participation in sport. Society has been able to maintain a great deal of control over women by perpetuating the belief that female sports participants equate to lesbians (Lenskyj, 1998). By discrediting all women in sport as lesbians, men can be assured that they are not 'real' women and are therefore not offering any genuine threats to the masculine sports world (Birrell and Theberge, 1994a). The predominant pattern of female participation is therefore very much in line with traditional views on appropriate 'feminine' behaviour, suggesting that the female socialisation process continues to promote attitudes and values that influence women and girls' relationship to sport.

Gendered expectations are instilled in children at a very early age. Parents, as a result of their own sex-role socialisation, transmit gendered values to their children that reproduce gender stereotypes (Greendorfer, 1983). The differences start almost from birth, when baby girls are more frequently touched, handled and talked to by their parents than baby boys, and are generally treated more protectively. Boys are allowed to be more adventurous and are more often allowed to explore their environment without intervention from their parents. This contributes to girls becoming less independent in their behaviour than boys, and as children's play behaviour develops, this sex typing becomes more marked. By the time they have reached school age, many children have learnt that physically active play is appropriate for boys, but less so for girls. A close association has been established between sport and masculinity, which also places it in opposition to supposedly 'feminine' behaviour.

In the UK it is during secondary school and adolescence that girls appear to turn away decisively from sport and to develop quite negative attitudes to it. There is a drastic decline in the proportion of girls who enjoy PE in school, which drops from 74 per cent at primary school age to less than a third (29 per cent) by school-leaving age (Rowe, 1995). Some of the blame for this has been laid at the door of secondary school experiences of PE, which are notably less successful at instilling a long-term interest in sport in girls than in boys (Evans et al., 1987; Penney, 2002; Scraton, 1986; Wright, 1999, 2000). However, school experiences are only a part of a broader set of influences that affect adolescents. Many teenage girls simply do not associate sports activity with the femininity to which they aspire; in fact, sport and physical activity are more commonly seen as a distinguishing trademark of the 'unfeminine' girl.

Girls' dismissal of sport is in strong contrast to boys' affinity with it. The link between masculinity and sport is a close and enduring one: although most adult males give up active participation in sport as they grow older, they remain within the sports culture. The sports in which boys participate at school are those that are replicated and exalted in later life as major, prestigious, national and international institutions. Indeed, continued involvement in the world of sport is part of a rite of passage into a communal masculine adulthood. In contrast, girls' school experiences of sport tend to lack relevance to adult life: the activities traditionally offered to schoolgirls do not enjoy either the mass participation or elite status of boys' football, cricket and rugby, and role models are few. Sport is barely visible as a component of womanhood, and the transition to female adulthood is more likely to be seen as a time to leave sport behind than to continue with it. This is reinforced as women reach adulthood and encounter widespread exposure to attitudes about their expected role. The need or wish to establish a heterosexual partnership as a central aspect of 'being female' encourages women to adopt behaviour deemed appropriate to attracting a male partner, combining 'good girl' behaviour with feminine sexuality expressed through an attractive appearance. The emphasis on female bodies as decorative and passive, rather than active and vigorous, draws women to leisure forms that reproduce these qualities and away from those, such as sport, that appear to contradict them.

To a considerable extent, however, sporting qualities continue to be classed as 'masculine', with 'femininity' seen as the antithesis of sport. The influence of traditional notions of 'real' womanhood as heterosexual femininity thus remains very strong. Kay (2000) has suggested that it is especially influential on women's experiences of sport in countries and cultures where gender roles are most strongly differentiated. Kay drew on European sports participation data and analyses of international family-related social policy to explore the relationship between the two. She found substantial correlation: countries where social policy promoted strong gender differentiation in adult roles had the highest differentiation in sports participation, while those that made little distinction between the sexes exhibited much smaller differentials in male–female sports participation rates (see Box 6.1).

Box 6.1   Case study: How gender ideology influences sport

'Gender ideology' is a powerful, diverse, complex and pervasive phenomenon – but it is also remarkably hard to pin down. One way of doing this is to borrow the approaches that social policy analysts use to address gender issues.

Social policies are implemented by governments to respond to and influence social behaviour. For example, government legislation can make it relatively easy or hard for couples to divorce, depending on how much importance is attached to upholding 'traditional' families. Policies take account of public (electoral) opinion, and are therefore a broad indication of a nation's current consensus on its social institutions.

Family-related social policies contain assumptions about adult men and women's roles, and can be used as a yardstick of a country's gender ideology. A key issue for policy analysts is the extent to which such policies encourage mothers either to stay at home to care for their children when they are young ('traditional' gender relations, with strong male–female differentiation) or to combine parenting with employment ('modern' gender relations: low male–female differentiation). We can use analyses that categorise countries on this basis, to see whether patterns of male–female sports participation seem to be related to broader gender differentiation in society.

The data in Table 6.2 show us that countries that support 'modern' gender roles, with relatively low gender differentiation, are also those where sports participation is most

TABLE 6.2   Gender differentiation in social policy and sports participation

A Gender differentiation in family-related policy		B Female sports participation rates (%)		C Female sports participation rates: difference over male (%)		D Female sports participation rates as % of male rate	
		All	Regular	All	Regular	All	Regular
Low	Finland	78	72	−5	+2	94	103
	Sweden	70	59	0	+1	100	102
Medium	Netherlands	61	27	−2	−9	97	75
High	Italy	15	9	−17	−4	47	69
	UK	60	21	−12	−13	83	62

Notes:
(a) The categorisation of countries' social policies (column A) is based on Gornick et al. (1997). The data used in columns B, C and D are based on Gratton (1999).
(b) The Compass project devised seven categories of sports participation. Here, 'regular' sports participation excludes 'irregular', 'occasional' and 'non-participant' participation.
(c) In column C, a positive figure (e.g. +2) indicates that the female participation rate is higher than the male; a negative figure (e.g. -5) indicates that the female participation rate is lower than the male.

equal between the sexes. Countries that encourage mothers' employment have much smaller differentials in male–female sports participation rates than countries in which policy encourages mothers to remain at home to care for their children. In Finland and Sweden, low gender differentiation in social policy is reflected in sports participation: 'overall' sports participation rates are much less differentiated between men and women than in all of the 'high' countries, while 'regular' participation rates are marginally higher for women than men. At the other extreme, the two countries with the highest gender differentiation in social policy (Italy and the UK) also have the biggest differentials in overall participation rates for males and females, although not so markedly for regular participation. Overall, these patterns indicate a broad if imprecise correspondence between gender differentiation in sports participation and broader gender differentiation in a country.

Broad societal pressures are not the only factors that inhibit female presence in sport. We now examine the evidence that sport itself is a strongly masculine institution, and explore the implications this has for women and girls' involvement.

GENDER INEQUITY IN THE PRODUCTION OF SPORT

Women's under-representation in the organisational and administrative structures of sport is a worldwide phenomenon. In comparison with men, women hold fewer positions of power in sport, and they hold positions of less power. In the UK they are under-represented across the full spectrum of sports provision, including the PE profession, local government leisure services, sports governance, regional and national policy-making organisations, and as representatives in international sports organisations. In this section we look at the gender bias in the structure of sport, and efforts to counter it through gender equity policies.

The Sports Structure

Whannel's (1983) suggestion that male dominance was built into the structure of British sport, in lasting form, fits well with the evidence of women's under-representation in sports organisations. Until the 1990s no woman had been appointed to direct any of the Sports Council's national sports centres, only one had headed a Sports Council regional office, and only 2 out of the 14 senior positions at Sports Council headquarters had been held by women. The exception at national level was the National Coaching

Foundation, whose Director was a woman. However, in coaching as a whole, women were greatly under-represented, especially at higher levels of responsibility. (White and Brackenridge, 1985). Women were even less visible in the sports media, particularly at management level, and were very much in the minority in sports-related research, where the use of concepts that did not incorporate the experiences of females risked judging females as marginal, deviant or comparative (Talbot, 1986). The one area where women were better represented was sports development. However, this has been attributed by men in some sports organisations to development work being associated with nurturing and is therefore 'women's work' and not appealing to men who should be at the 'sharp end' of the organisation (Shaw and Slack, 2002).

Female under-representation in the structure of sport is not only inequitable in its own right but has far-reaching consequences for women's involvement in sport as participants. This has been particularly evident at elite level, where women still face formal restrictions on their participation. Towards the end of the twentieth century, it looked as if these were disappearing: when the marathon became available to women in the 1984 Olympics, the argument that women's sport was limited by physiology appeared to have been laid to rest. Yet well into the 1990s, women continued to be excluded in the Olympics from the 3000 m steeplechase, 20 km walk, the 50 km walk and the pole vault, by a male sports hierarchy claiming to be acting protectively with women's best interests at heart (Coakley, 2001). It has also been suggested that women's involvement in the marathon did not necessarily challenge dominant gender relations so much as help women to conform to gender expectation through elite female marathon runners selling the sport as an ideal way to maintain a feminine body shape (Jutel, 2003). Alongside these changes has been the introduction of specific female sports into the Olympic such as 'beach volleyball' with participants being instructed not to wear briefs with the sides longer than 6 inches (15 cm). There is no practical justification for this other than to feminise the sport and ensure the players are viewed as sexual objects rather than athletes. By the end of the twentieth century it was clear that a male-dominated sports structure had failed to provide women with an equal basis for involvement. The advancement allowed to women had too often been grudging and piecemeal, coming only as a result of confrontation and struggle (Hargreaves, 1994), rather than fundamental attitudinal shifts within sport.

Rather perversely for an age of supposed gender awareness, the male stranglehold on sport seemed to be increasing. Although women's sports participation has risen, women's involvement in sport as providers has dropped (Sports Council, 1992). In the UK, there has been a long-term decline in women's influence in physical education (Talbot, 1986), and considerable deterioration in women's representation elsewhere, for example on national governing bodies. Those positions developed to promote female participation within certain sports which have been filled by women are often marginalised and kept on the periphery in terms of importance in the organisations (Shaw and Slack, 2002). Few women are able to obtain central managerial positions in sports organisations that are not related to either the promotion of female participation or development of sport more generally.

The overall pattern of women's involvement in sports production is therefore clear: women are under-represented in all areas, and their under-representation is most acute at higher levels of responsibility, including those for higher levels of performance. The resulting lack of female presence has not only been a disincentive to other women to become involved in sports production, but also led to isolation and relative powerlessness of those already involved. The lack of women involved in the provision of sport is regarded by feminist analysts as contributing to the 'maleness' of sport as a whole which alienates many females. It is this, rather than technical issues such as poor facilities and inappropriate programming, which most fully contributes to women's invisibility in sport. The institutional and organisational characteristics of sport are therefore central to the women and sport 'problem', and imply that women's access to sport requires their increased representation in all aspects of its provision.

Gender Equity Policies in Sport

Many countries have now tried to address women's under-representation in sport by adopting formal policies to enhance their position. The United States predated most other nations in addressing female under-representation in sport through the use of Title IX of the 1972 Education Amendments Act. By the mid-1990s, Canada had implemented federal and provincial legislation to build gender equity into all levels of the structure of the Canadian Sport Coalition, established in 1992; while in Australia, programmes for promoting women's sports were operating in every state and territory by the early 1990s (Hargreaves, 1994). In Europe, the work of transnational institutions such as the European Sports Conference and the Council of Europe has supported and encouraged gender equity efforts within individual nation states.

Over this period there has been significant development in the policy approaches adopted. Early policies tended to concentrate on the participation aspect of involvement, and came under criticism from feminist critics who argued that these were a superficial response to a deeply embedded problem. In the UK, 'top-down' policies that tried to 'get women into sport' were criticised by authors such as Green et al. (1990) as failing to recognise let alone address the fundamental issues affecting women. Above all, critics stressed that policies that focused on practical barriers to participation did little to challenge the underlying assumption that sport was an intrinsically masculine activity. They argued that the only effective strategy for addressing the root causes of women's alienation was to lessen sport's 'maleness' by giving women power within sport structures and organisations.

This was the approach underpinning the first formal British policy for Women and Sport, introduced in the early 1990s. The policy explicitly recognised female under-representation in sports organisations as a fundamental barrier to gender equity, and advocated women's equal involvement in all aspects and at all levels of sports participation, provision and management. It set detailed aims and objectives for major improvement in women's access to power and influence in the structure of sport, and was an explicit challenge to male power in the existing organisational and administrative structure of UK sport. The policy's successful implementation would result in far-reaching change within the sports establishment; however, it was dependent on voluntary action by the very organisations in which change is sought, and here it became evident that progress might be slow.

It is increasingly evident that in sport, as elsewhere, formal policies do not guarantee effective action. The problem is well illustrated by the experience in the United States in the 1970s, when Title IX triggered a rapid professionalisation in women's sport that led to many men taking posts that had previously been held in an amateur capacity by women. Although female sports participation rates rose significantly, women's power within the sports establishment weakened rather than strengthened. Fasting (1993) reported another mixed picture when she reviewed European countries' progress towards the 'women and sport' goals adopted by the European Sports Conference in 1991. Although there was evidence of a generally receptive response, there was a considerable gap between intent and achievement: most countries (14 out of 24) had made progress in less than half of the agreed areas. McKay's (1997) in-depth analysis of resistance to 'affirmative action' initiatives in sports organisations in Australia, Canada and New Zealand confirmed these difficulties.

To date, policies to promote gender equity have too often foundered in the face of organisational and societal cultures in which gender differentiation was entrenched. The advent of the National Lottery in the UK has done much to raise the profile of female sports participation, alongside lobbying groups such as the Women's Sports Foundation, although these can struggle to have an impact, other than advising and raising awareness within women's sport, due to lack of funding. The lottery funding has, however, ensured that women and girls are cemented as a target group within organisations responsible for promoting, developing and facilitating sports involvement in both administration and participation. Groups seeking lottery funding are required to demonstrate that they are attempting to improve provision for at least one target group resulting in better funding for female participation opportunities and for women to undertake coaching and administration courses.

GENDER AND THE SPORTS MEDIA

The way in which sport is portrayed is influential in limiting its appeal to women. Media coverage has been a major contributor to perceptions of sport's limited relevance to women. Masculine and feminine ideologies are culturally accepted because alternative images are rarely presented in the media. Inequality in the quantity and quality of coverage of male and female sport appears to have a long history.

Both the media and women's involvement in sport have undergone profound changes in the last century; however, contemporary coverage of sport remains discriminatory and contains overwhelming masculine bias. Once again, the growing professionalisation and commercialisation of sport have encouraged this, fostering a portrayal of sport most likely to appeal to mass audiences. More coverage has been given to men's sport than to women's; there has been a general emphasis on sport's masculine characteristics; and coverage of women's sport has been highly selective, focusing on its most obviously feminine forms (Hargreaves, 1994; Theberge and Birrell, 1994; Wright and Clarke, 1999). As a result, women commonly receive less than 10 per cent of sports coverage, and often less than 5 per cent, with women's sport usually only being reported at the very highest levels of performance. Coverage of men's sport not only is more plentiful, but covers a wider range of performance levels and a wider range of sports. There are also differences in the tone of coverage: men's performance is more likely to be described in terms of 'strength', while women receive more attributions of weakness. In Duncan and Hasbrook's (2002) study of television commentary of female sport in the United States they found commentators discussing a female basketball game focused on how the players were 'very pretty', 'nice' and 'so fun to watch'. It was concluded this style of reporting only denigrated female athletes' performances and suggested they are incapable of playing sport in the same way as men. News stories about women's sport also often focus on titillation and human interest rather than on performance and achievement. Wright and Clarke (1999) found the media often discuss female athletes' families, husbands or children rather than focusing on their sporting achievements as they do with men. This emphasises the sexuality of the female athletes and importantly that they are heterosexual and therefore acceptable.

A marked trend of recent years has been the increased coverage of non-sporting attributes of the more obviously attractive sportswomen, through features that focus exclusively on their appearance and personal life. One of the issues that arises from this is the extent to which female performers collude with, exploit and/or actively seek out coverage that capitalises on their non-playing attributes. As leading sports personalities of both sexes assume greater status as general media 'personalities' and derive a growing proportion of their earnings from their non-sporting activities, the attribution of responsibility for stereotypical coverage of sportswomen becomes more complex. The implications for women's sport as a whole are also hard to assess. On the one hand, these developments have increased the potential earning power of a select band of elite sportswomen. Set against this is the negative impact of coverage that many feel degrades and trivialises women's sport, and reinforces the very notions of restrictive femininity that involvement in sport can help women to challenge.

Media influence on sport is not confined to its sports-specific reportage. A wide range of media products contribute to the portrayal of sport as an element of men's and women's lifestyles and identities. Kay's (1999) study of the 'sport-related' content of 'general' magazines for men and women showed that sport was deeply embedded in the construction of maleness promoted in men's magazines, but had a minimal presence in the representation of femaleness in magazines for women. Where sport was presented to women, there was an overwhelming emphasis on body-shaping exercise activities which concurred with stereotypical notions of decorative femininity. There were also differences in the extent to which men and women's magazines featured sport as a cultural product for mass consumption. Men's magazines gave extensive exposure to the internationalised professional sports that dominate sports broadcasting and newspaper reportage; magazine coverage for women did not feature these sports at all. In some cases articles on fitness exercises went so far as to offer women 'sport-substitute' physical activities, to allow them to gain the benefits of sport without actually having to take part in it (Curry et al., 2002). The overriding message was that even in the late 1990s, 'real' sport was not for women.

The media play a significant part in the construction of the ideology of women's sport, and are a major contributor to perceptions of sport as a marginal activity for women. Harris and Clayton discuss that the 'sports worlds, but particularly the sports media, emit a message that female sexuality is of greater importance that athletic ability' (2002: 408). This reinforces notions that women's sport has less intrinsic value than men's, and that taking part in sport is only 'natural' for women when it involves activities that concur with conventional female gender-role images. The lack of coverage of women's sport at performance and excellence levels not only undermines women competing at these levels, but deprives all females of role models to counter these views.

RESISTANCE AND EMPOWERMENT: FEMALE USE OF SPORT TO CHALLENGE GENDER STEREOTYPES

The view that sport is contradictory to femininity has proved very persistent but is at odds with studies of women who do participate. Far from detracting from their personal development, sport appears to offer women substantial benefits. Those who take part in it experience little role conflict and report positive changes including increased self-esteem, personal development, physical power and well-being. More recent theorising has recognised the potential of sport as a site for women to challenge and contest dominant stereotypes rather than solely being a site where these are reproduced (Scraton et al., 1999; Whitson, 2002).

Colwell (1999) argues that simply participating in sport challenges 'patriarchal definitions' of submissiveness, passivity and dependence. Contemporary female sporting achievement has dramatically surpassed what would be considered their 'limits'. They use their bodies as skilled and forceful subjects and challenge fundamental sources of male physical power (Whitson, 2002). Some women are clearly not passive in their sporting endeavours or in any aspects of their lives.

Sport has been demonstrated to help some women achieve empowerment and use their bodies to challenge sexual stereotypes and patriarchal control of women's bodies (Theberge and Birrell, 1994). As Talbot (1989) suggests, participating in sport can be a liberating experience for female athletes. It acts as a subculture that challenges traditional expectations that women should take responsibility for 'female tasks'. Aerobics has been criticised as an activity that maintains dominant ideology, contributes to women's lack of power and is a sexual commodity designed to sell an 'appropriate' exercise form to women (Haravon Collins, 2002). However, it has been demonstrated that aerobics can provide some women with the means and space to empower their bodies and thus contest gender expectation, albeit in a subtle and somewhat limited way.

The freedom and strength women have been shown to experience through sport has been linked to redefining previous boundaries of their body. This may be discovering new capabilities and ways of using the body through pursuing new, more challenging goals or taking part in different activities. Thorpe considered that snowboarding assisted females with developing 'strong individual women who were unafraid to challenge their male counterparts' and lead to personal empowerment (2005: 95) The majority of women in Wright and Dewar's (1997) study of sports experience at an amateur level described how they set themselves challenges or personal goals in the sports arena. Achieving these goals evoked a deep sense of pride, while others felt it contributed to their sense of identity by providing an area over which they had some control.

Sport is not always an area of restriction for women or even an activity that they can benefit from as men do. It can be a motivating force which helps them structure their experiences and control their activities on their own terms and in their own ways (Talbot, 1989). Empowerment through sport does not always have to encompass images of strength. For women sports participants, empowerment has been redefined as the pleasure that is derived from the sense of accomplishment. Women feel empowered by the confidence they gain from learning how to execute complex sport skills, rather than the physical enjoyment of dominating others in a competitive sports situation. This suggests any exercise which increases women's activity levels will go some way to confronting male hegemony. However, resistance and challenge is an individual process. What one woman considers as opposition to gender stereotypes may be considered compliance by another.

Female participation in male-dominated sports indicates a change in the power relationship between men and women (Colwell, 1999). Although traditional male sports continue to be male dominated, the increasing number of female participants (as illustrated in football in the UK) alone constitutes a change in power. Female football players generally reported a sense of joy and empowerment from mastering a sport that personifies masculinity (Cox and Thompson, 2000; Scraton et al., 1999). However, for many of the female athletes engaging in male sports it would seem that transgressing gender boundaries is acceptable for the duration of the game, so long as they can prove they are feminine afterwards. Mennesson's (2000) study of female boxers indicated the pleasure they obtained from competing and being accepted in one of the most aggressive male arenas. However, both in and out of the ring they still felt compelled to behave in 'feminine' ways.

Women do contest, but do not completely change gender expectations through sport. Instead participation represents a complex mix of compliance and contestation rather than complete transformation. Some elements are successfully challenged, with the body being a central component in enabling women to achieve this. Women clearly gain a great deal of pleasure from sports participation, but their activities continue to be modified by feminine ideology. Women's entry into male sport is now tolerated, but only if it is accompanied by attitudes and behaviour that serve to normalise this deviant action and do not challenge male superiority within the sport. However, the mere entry is enough to redefine femininity and allow women to empower their bodies in what has previously been viewed as an exclusively male practice.

CONCLUSION

Sport is fundamental to the contemporary construction of gender differentiation. In an era when sport is established as a global phenomenon with a global audience, the impact of co-opting sport for males and excluding women from full sports citizenship is all the greater. The particular significance of sport, however, is not that it is per se a site for gender difference, but that it is uniquely positioned to foster arguments that such difference is natural.

The significance of sport in naturalising gender difference, and thus legitimising gender relations that privilege men over women, lies in the extent to which sport reinforces widely held assumptions that relationships of power between the sexes are based on 'natural' or biological factors (Birrell and Theberge, 1994a). Men's measurably superior performance in sports trials of strength and speed, and the construction of sports protocol around their physical aptitudes in more complex game-codes, 'prove' female inferiority. Sport therefore delivers 'apparently incontrovertible' evidence of men's superior command of highly valued and visible skills, and by implication depicts females as less skilful, less capable and of lesser value (Bryson, 1987). Women's social inferiority is seen not as a product of social processes such as gender stereotyping, but as a natural extension of women's traditional physical inferiority (Birrell and Theberge, 1994a). The cultural origins of patriarchal hegemony are thus obscured: 'An ideological view comes to be deposited in our culture as a commonsense assumption – of course women are different and inferior' (Willis, 1982: 130).

The particular power of sport in upholding gendered power relations lies in the closeness of sport to issues of men and women's embodiment and physicality. During the 1990s, theories of women's oppression have increasingly recognised how physicality and the control of women through the control of their bodies underpin the reproduction of inequitable gender relations (Birrell and Theberge, 1994b). Control of women's bodies, through the promotion of idealised standards of physical beauty and compulsory heterosexuality, is one of the primary mechanisms for control of women in patriarchal societies. However, the significance of gendered influences on men and women's relationship with their own physicality often goes unrecognised: 'everyone has difficulty acknowledging the extent to which the body is a social construction' (Holmlund, 1994: 300). Bodies are, however, central to our sense of who we are and how we relate to the world (Whitson, 1990), and masculinising and feminising practices associated with the body lie at the heart of the social construction of masculinity and femininity. The maintenance of gender differentiation in sport is therefore instrumental in reinforcing the established structure of inequitable gender relations which sustains hegemony.

Theorists believe that sporting practices reinforce hegemony in the rest of society in a number of ways. Sport upholds the primacy of heterosexual men by linking maleness with highly valued and visible skills, and by sanctioning the male's use of aggression, force and/or violence (Bryson, 1987). The paradox is that the exaggerated patterns of sex differentiation that occur within sport 'have a deceptive aura of common sense and naturalness' (Lenskyj, 1986: 144), and are more commonly recognised and accepted than contested and rejected. Sport is 'what boys and men naturally do, and what girls and women do not do, or do at peril to their own identities' (Birrell and Theberge, 1994b: 344). Sport therefore defines maleness as being in contrast to femaleness, and in this way makes a fundamental contribution to the construction of gender identities and gender relations that are based on assumptions of difference, which in turn perpetuate structures of disadvantage and exclusion.

CHAPTER SUMMARY

» Women's under-representation in sport has a long history and is closely associated with traditional views of gender relations. Historically women have faced formal and informal restrictions on their sports participation, and have played little role in the production of sport.

» Although social attitudes to men and women have become less restrictive, the modern female socialisation process continues to emphasise a form of femininity that gives little value to sport. At the start of the twenty-first century, women still occupy a marginal position in sport in virtually every country in the world.

» Societal disincentives for females to be involved in sport are reinforced by resistance within the sports establishment. Men dominate all areas of sports provision including the sports media, creating a masculine ethos that pervades sport. Policies that promote gender equity within sport can face considerable resistance, and may be negated by the stronger forces of professionalisation which characterise modern sport.

(Cont'd)

Foucault, M. (1983) *This is Not a Pipe*. Los Angeles, London: University of California Press.

Gornick, J.C., Meyers, M.K. and Ross, K.E. (1997) 'Supporting the employment of mothers: policy variation across fourteen welfare states', *Journal of European Social Policy*, 7 (1): 45–70.

Gratton, C. (1999) *Compass 1999: a Project Seeking the Co-ordinated Monitoring of Participation in Sports in Europe*. London: UK Sports Council.

Green, E., Hebron, S. and Woodward, D. (1987) *Leisure and Gender: A Study of Sheffield Women's Leisure Experience*. The Sports Council/Economic and Social Research Council, Sheffield.

Green, E., Hebron, S. and Woodward, D. (1990) *Women's Leisure, What Leisure?* London: Macmillan.

Greendorfer, S. (1983) 'Shaping the female athlete: the impact of the family', in M.A. Boutilier and L. San Giovanni (eds), *The Sporting Woman*. Champaign, IL: Human Kinetics, pp. 135–56.

Griffin, P. (1998) *Strong Women, Deep Closets: Lesbians and Homophobia in Sport*. Champaign, IL: Human Kinetics.

Griffin, C., Hobson, D., McIntosh, S. and McCabe, T. (1982) *Women and Leisure*. New York and London: Routledge.

Hall, M.A. (1993) 'Gender and sport in the 1990s: feminism, culture, and politics', *Sports Science Review*, 2: 48–68.

Hall, M.A. (1996) *Feminism and Sporting Bodies: Essays on Theory and Practice*. Champaign, IL: Human Kinetics.

Haravon Collins, L. (2002) 'Working out the contradictions: feminism and aerobics', *Journal of Sport & Social Issues*, 26 (1): 85–109.

Hargreaves, J. (1994) *Sporting Females: Critical Issues in the History and Sociology of Women's Sports*. London and New York: Routledge.

Hargreaves, J. (2000) *Heroines of Sport: the Politics of Difference and Identity*. London: Routledge.

Harris, J. and Clayton, B. (2002) 'Femininity, masculinity, physicality and the English tabloid press', *International Review for the Sociology of Sport*, 37 (3): 397–413.

Holmlund, C.A. (1994) 'Visible difference and flex appeal: the body, sex, sexuality and race in the Pumping Iron films', in S. Birrell and C.L. Cole (eds), *Women, Sport and Culture*. Champaign, IL: Human Kinetics, pp. 299–315.

Humberstone, B. (2002) 'Femininity, masculinity and difference: what's wrong with a sarong?', in A. Laker (ed.), *The Sociology of Sport and Physical Education: an Introductory Reader*. Routledge: London and New York, pp. 58–77.

Jutel, A. (2003) '"Thou dost run as in flotation": femininity, reassurance and the emergence of the women's marathon', *International Journal of the History of Sport*, 20 (3): 17–36.

Kay, T.A. (1999) 'Gender ideologies in magazine portrayal of sport: King Eric v. the Billion $ Babe', *Journal of European Area Studies*, 7 (2): 157–76.

Kay, T.A. (2000) 'Leisure, gender and the family: the influence of social policy context', *Leisure Studies*, 19 (4): 247–65.

Lenskyj, H. (1986) *Out of Bounds.* Toronto: Women's Press.

Lenskyj, H. (1987) 'Canadian women and physical activity 1890–1930: media views', in J.A. Mangan and R. Park (eds), *From 'Fair Sex' to Feminism: Sport and the Socialisation of Women in the Industrial and Post-industrial Eras.* London: Frank Cass.

Lenskyj, H.J. (1995) 'Sport and the threat to gender boundaries', *Sporting Traditions,* 12 (1): 47–60.

Lenskyj, H.J. (1998) '"INSIDE SPORT" OR "ON THE MARGINS?" Australian Women and the Sport Media', *International Review for the Sociology of Sport,* 33 (1): 19–32.

McKay, J. (1997) *Managing Gender: Affirmative Action and Organizational Power in Australian, Canadian and New Zealand Sport.* Albany, NY: State University of New York.

McPherson, B.D., Curtis, J.E. and Loy, J.W. (1989) *The Social Significance of Sport.* Champaign, IL: Human Kinetics.

Mennesson, C. (2000) 'Hard women and soft women: the social construction of identities among female boxers', *International Review for the Sociology of Sport,* 35 (1): 21–33.

Messner, M.A. and Sabo, D.F. (eds) (1990) *Sport, Men and the Gender Order.* Champaign, IL: Human Kinetics.

Obel, C. (1996) 'Collapsing gender in competitive body building: Researching contradictions and ambiguity in sport', *International Review for the Sociology of Sport,* 31: 185–202.

Pronger, B. (1990) *The Arena of Masculinity: Sports, Homosexuality and the Meaning of Sex.* New York: St. Martin's.

Pronger, B. (1998) 'Post-Sport: Transgressing Boundaries in Physical Culture', in G. Rail (ed.) *Sport and Postmodern Times.* Albany, NY: State University of New York Press, pp. 277–300.

Penney, D. (2002) 'Equality, equity and inclusion in physical education and school sport', in A. Laker (ed.), *The Sociology of Sport and Physical Education. an Introductory Reader.* Routledge: London and New York, pp. 110–28.

Rowe, N.F. (1995) 'Young people and sport', Internal Sports Council Discussion Paper (unpublished).

Schrodt, B. (1976) 'Canadian women at the Olympic Games 1924–1972', *Canadian Association for Health, Physical Education and Recreation Journal,* 42 (4): 34–42.

Scraton, S. (1986) 'Gender and girls' physical education', *British Journal of Physical Education,* 17 (4): 145–47.

Scraton, S. and Flintoff, A. (2002) 'Sports feminism: The contribution of feminist thought to our understanding of gender and sport', in S. Scraton and A. Flintoff (eds) *Gender and Sport: a Reader.* London and New York: Routledge, pp. 30–45.

Scraton, S., Fasting, K., Pfister, G. and Bunuel, A. (1999) '"It's still a man's game?" The experiences of top level European women footballers', *International Review for the Sociology of Sport,* 34 (2), pp. 99–113.

Shaw, S. and Slack, T. (2002) 'It's been like that for donkey's years: the construction of gender relations and the cultures of sport organisations', *Culture, Sport, Society,* 5 (1): 86–106.

Sports Council (1992) *Women and Sport: A Consultation Document.* London: Sports Council.

Talbot, M. (1986) 'Gender and physical education', *British Journal of Physical Education,* 17: 120–2.

Talbot, M. (1989) 'Being herself through sport', Paper presented to the Leisure Studies Association Conference 'Leisure, Health and Wellbeing', Leeds.

Theberge, N. (1990) 'Women and the Olympics: a consideration of gender, sport and social change', Paper presented to the International Symposium 'Sport – The Third Millennium', Quebec, Canada.

Theberge, N. and Birrell, S. (1994) 'The sociological study of women and sport', in D.M. Costa and S.R. Guthrie (eds), *Women and Sport – Interdisciplinary Perspectives.* Champaign, IL: Human Kinetics.

Thorpe, H. (2005) 'Jibing the gender order: females in the snowboarding culture', *Sport in Society,* 8 (1): 76–100.

Treagus, M. (2005) 'Playing like ladies: basketball, netball and feminine restraint', *International Journal of the History of Sport,* 22 (1): 88–105.

Wearing, B. (1990) 'Beyond the ideology of motherhood: leisure as resistance', *Australian and New Zealand Journal of Sociology,* 26 (1): 36–58.

Wearing, B. (1998) *Leisure and Feminist Theory.* London: Sage.

Whannel, G. (1983) *Blowing the Whistle: the Politics of Sport.* London: Pluto.

White, A. and Brackenridge, C. (1985) 'Who rules sport? Gender divisions in the power structure of British Sport', *International Review for the Sociology of Sport,* 20 (1–2): 95–107.

Whitson, D. (1990) 'Sport in the social construction of masculinity', in M.A. Messner and D.F. Sabo (eds), *Sport, Men and the Gender Order.* Champaign, IL: Human Kinetics, pp. 19–30.

Whitson, D. (2002) 'The embodiment of gender: discipline, domination and empowerment', in S. Scraton and A. Flintoff (eds), *Gender and Sport: a Reader.* London: Routledge, pp. 227–39.

Willis, P. (1982) 'Women in sport and ideology', in J.A. Hargreaves (ed.), *Sport, Culture and Ideology.* London: Routledge & Kegan Paul, pp. 117–35.

Wimbush, E. (1988) 'Mothers meeting', in E. Wimbush and M. Talbot, *Relative Freedoms: Women and Leisure.* Milton Keynes: Open University Press, pp. 66–74.

Wright, J. (1999) 'Changing gendered practice in physical education: working with teachers', European Physical Education Review, 5 (3): 181–97.

Wright, J. (2000) 'Reconstructing gender in sport and physical education', in C. Hickey, L. Fitzclarence and R. Matthews (eds) *Where the Boys Are: Masculinity, Sport and Education.* Geelong, Vic: Deakin University Press, pp. 13–26.

Wright, J. and Clarke, G. (1999) 'Sport, the media and the construction of compulsary heterosexuality: a case study of women's rugby union', *International Review for the Sociology of Sport,* 24 (3): 227–43.

Wright, J. and Dewar, A. (1997) 'On pleasure and pain: women speak out about physical activity', in G. Clarke and B. Humberstone (eds), *Researching Women and Sport.* London: Macmillan, pp. 80–95.

7

Sport and Health

PARISSA SAFAI

> ### OVERVIEW
>
> » *Problematising the assumption that 'sport is good for one's health'*
> » *Distinguishing the benefits of physical activity*
> » *The risks of sport*
> » *Sports medicine and the provision of health care to athletes*
> » *Conclusion*

In 2003, the United Nations General Assembly adopted 'Resolution 58/5: Sport as a Means to Promote Education, Health, Development and Peace' and designated 2005 as the International Year of Sport and Physical Education (IYSPE) in its recognition of sport's ability to contribute positively to healthy human, and in particular childhood, development. In promotional materials about the IYSPE, the United Nations General Assembly (International Year of Sport and Physical Education, 2005) repeatedly drew links between sport and health, arguing that:

> Sport and physical education play an important role at the individual, community, national and global levels. For the individual, sport enhances one's personal abilities, general health and self-knowledge. On the national level, sport and physical education contribute to economic and social growth, improve public health, and bring different communities together. On the global level, if used consistently, sport and physical education can have a long-lasting positive impact on development, public health, peace and the environment. (5)

The glowing and affirmative descriptions of the relationship between sport and health continued:

> Sport and play improve health and well-being, extend life expectancy and reduce the likelihood of several non-communicable diseases including heart disease. Regular physical activity and play are essential for physical, mental, psychological and social development. Good habits start early: the important role of physical education is demonstrated by the fact that children who exercise are more likely to stay physically active as adults. Sport also plays a major positive role in one's emotional health, and allows … valuable social connections, often offering opportunities for play and self-expression. (7)

Such positive comments resonate with our commonplace assumptions about sport's power to improve our health. However, a closer examination and analysis of these statements in light of existing research in the socio-cultural study of sport on the relationship between sport and health reveal a number of concerns that problematise the conventional wisdom that 'sport is good for one's health'. This chapter explores the relationship between sport and health and, in particular, focuses on the ways in which participation in sport contributes to increased rates of morbidity and mortality. The central argument here is that while sport may have the potential to enhance and augment health, it is currently structured in ways that foster the production and reproduction of health-compromising norms and behaviours. Divided into three parts, this chapter first draws attention to some of the positive health associations that accompany increased participation in non-sport forms of physical activity. The second section focuses on the negative associations between sport and health in an attempt to demonstrate how the structure and production of sport can facilitate ill health, while the last section of this chapter explores the provision of therapeutic care to athletes and, in particular, the development and implications of the medical/paramedical field of practice known as sports medicine.

DISTINGUISHING THE BENEFITS OF PHYSICAL ACTIVITY

One of the most significant challenges to our understanding of the negative relationship between sport and health resides in the ways in which sport is often discursively wrapped up with and within other types of physical activities. In the United Nations description of sport cited above, 'sport', 'physical activity', 'physical education', 'exercise' and 'play' are blended together in the excerpts without consideration of the differences between each form of activity. Sport is a physical activity; sport is often used in physical education curricula; it incorporates exercise; and may even involve an element of play. However, this does mean that sport is the same as physical education, exercise or play. Sports are 'institutionalized and competitive activities that involve rigorous physical exertion or the use of complex physical skills by participants motivated by personal enjoyment and external rewards' (Coakley and Donnelly, 2004: 5), and the conflation of sport with physical education, exercise and play obscures its differences in intensity, frequency and duration of participation from other forms of physical activity. We must be cognisant of these differences since the institutionalised, competitive, rigorous and complex nature of sport has markedly different consequences for health than physical education, exercise or play. As Waddington (2000: 20) fittingly notes:

> In short, to suggest that a 30-minute gentle swim three times a week is good for one's health does not mean that running 70 miles a week as a means of preparing for running marathons is good for one's health in an equally simple or unproblematic way.

The IYSPE and the UN commitment to the promotion of physical activity is admirable and welcomed; however, the loose use of sport in the whole-scale promotion of the positive health benefits of physical activity is problematic. In order to better understand the relationship between sport and health, we must firmly distinguish between sport and other forms of physical activity.

In our effort to examine critically the consensus that 'sport is good for one's health', we cannot overlook the positive health benefits associated with some, specifically mild to moderate, forms of physical activity. A cursory survey of press releases, publications and policy documents from such organisations as the World Health Organization, Health Canada, the Public Health Agency of Canada, the United Kingdom's Department of Health, and the United States Centers for Disease Control and Prevention highlights the ways in which many national and international organisations (and initiatives) echo one another in their support and promotion of 30–60 minutes of moderate physical activity most, if not all, days. There is compelling evidence from all over the world that supports the physiological and psychological benefits of regular rhythmic exercise and physical activity for people of all ages (Bouchard et al., 1990; Department of Health, 2004; Donnelly and Harvey, 1996; Health Canada, 2004; Health Education Authority, 1995; Intersectoral Healthy Living Network, 2005; Kesaniemi et al., 2001; Pate et al., 1995; Quinney et al., 1994; US Department of Health and Human Services, 1996; World Health Organization, 2002, 2004). Such health gains include improved quality of life, improved self-esteem, increased strength and flexibility, increased energy, improved mental health and reduction in stress, and continued independent living in later life. There is also significant evidence supporting the risks associated with physical inactivity such as increased risk for cardiovascular diseases including stroke and hypertension/high blood pressure, osteoporosis, depression, adult-onset diabetes, some forms of cancer, and premature death and disability. The 2002 World Health Report (World Health Organization, 2002) noted that such chronic/non-communicable diseases accounted for 60 per cent of all deaths and 47 per cent of the global burden of disease in 2001 and estimated that

Based on available research, 'a 30-minute gentle swim three times a week' can contribute to reduced absenteeism, turnover and injury but this does not mean that 'running 70 miles a week as a means of preparing for running marathons [can do so] in an equally simple or unproblematic way' (Waddington, 2000: 20). And yet sport, and its 'significant economic benefits for business, communities, and nations', is uncritically and problematically conflated with other forms of physical activity (see Bloom et al., 2005). The following section will take a closer look at the negative associations between sport and health and the ways in which sport can facilitate pain, injury and ill health.

THE RISKS OF SPORT

Despite the conventional wisdom that greater participation in sport enhances health and the quality of life for many individuals, researchers from a number of academic disciplines are beginning to identify and investigate the ways in which the health benefits of intense participation in sport are questionable and the ways in which intense sport participation may in fact contribute to increased rates of morbidity and mortality (Waddington, 2000; White and Young, 1999). Epidemiological research into the costs of injury from sport is slowly getting off the ground (e.g. McCutcheon et al., 1997; Young, 2004; see White, 2004, for a comprehensive overview of research in this area); however, this area remains in its infancy and empirical and methodological inconsistencies and deficits plague the existing literature:

> Although there are statistics for incidence of injury for most sports and active pursuits, it is more difficult to find data on the numbers of people who take part in those activities and how frequently. Secondly, there is a lack of prospective studies on this topic. Thirdly, it is difficult to identify rates of injury accurately. (Department of Health, 2004: 73–4)

For example, admission records at doctors' office and emergency wards are a primary way of tracking the number of sport-related injuries per year, but not everyone who twists their ankle while participating in a sport goes to see a physician for treatment. Even with these limitations, the available data provide some insights into the patterns and costs of sport-related injury that support the argument that 'sports injuries are not uncommon, [they] affect a large number of people and make considerable demands on the nation's health services' (Nicholl et al., 1993: foreword). Large-scale surveys from Australia, Canada, the United Kingdom and the United States support arguments that injuries sustained in sports present a serious public health problem; that the greatest risks are associated with vigorous competitive (in particular, contact/collision) sport and those who do 'excessive' amounts of exercise; and that there are gender differences in patterns of sport injury (Finch and McGrath, 1997; Hume and Marshall, 1994; Marshall and Guskiewicz,

2003; Nicholl et al., 1995; Shepard, 2003; Sport and Recreation Research Communiqué, 1996; Tator et al., 1993; White and Young, 1999). Economically, estimates of direct treatment (e.g. medications, medical/dental/paramedical professional services, supplies, rehabilitation services) and indirect (e.g. reduced worker productivity, increased morbidity, increased mortality) costs of sports injury are astonishing. Nicholl et al. (1993, 1995) estimated the annual cost of sport injuries in the UK at £997 million, whereas, in Canada, the cost of sport injuries was estimated at C$637 million (at 1996 prices) for the province of Ontario alone (Sport and Recreation Research Communiqué, 1996). In a cost–benefit analysis of injuries associated with sport and exercise, Nicholl et al. (1994) offer what may be one of the most interesting conclusions about the costs and benefits of sport. They argue that while there are clear economic benefits associated with exercise for adults aged 45 years and older, the medical costs from participation in sports by younger adults between the ages of 15 to 44 years greatly exceed the costs avoided by the disease-prevention benefits of participation. In other words, 'there are strong economic arguments in favour of exercise in adults aged 45 or over, but not in younger adults' (Nicholl et al., 1994: 109).

Nowhere is the argument against the health benefits of sport more evident than for athletes participating at the extreme end of vigorous competitive physical activity – high-performance sport (e.g. see Pipe, 2001). The ideology of excellence within high-performance sport demands the instrumentally rationalised and calculated pursuit of the linear record on the world sporting stage which in turn demands, on the part of the athlete, the development of levels of disregard for the body in the pursuit of sporting excellence (Beamish and Ritchie, 2004; Kidd, 1988). Given the intense and rigorous training and competition regimens involved in the production of high-performance sport, it is somewhat ironic that while athletes are often seen as symbols of strength and vitality, they often sacrifice their health and well-being in the pursuit of success and idealised athleticism (Hoberman, 1992; Hughes and Coakley, 1991; Young and White, 1995; Young et al., 1994). Simply put, as athletes move up the competitive ladder, they often wear down their bodies through a variety of health-compromising behaviours such as the uncritical tolerance of pain/injury, dangerous dieting practices, or the use and abuse of drugs. Athletes' immersion in, what is referred to as, sport's 'culture of risk' (Nixon, 1992) sees their often unquestioned acceptance and re/production of norms and behaviours that endanger health. The concept of the 'culture of risk' has great utility in examining the relationship between sport and health, but it is important to recognise that while there is widespread acceptance and tolerance of health-compromising norms and behaviours in competitive sport, researchers also acknowledge the varied and complex ways in which athletes and other sport participants (e.g. coaches, administrators) produce and respond to this culture (e.g. Howe, 2004; Pike, 2005; Roderick et al., 2000; Safai, 2003; Walk, 1997). Bearing in mind Donnelly's (2004) caution about the loose use of the term 'culture of risk' in the socio-cultural study of sport, the term is used in this chapter as shorthand for the negative consequences of risk taking in sport, and while this chapter focuses on sport-related pain and injury, athletes' immersion in the 'culture of risk' applies in many ways to other health-endangering practices such as disordered eating (Johns, 2004).

Many athletes come to understand pain and injury as physical and symbolic cues of identity, such that pain tolerance and the disregard of bodily limits are often seen as reflections of strength of character. The pervasiveness of this ideology extends into the lives of male and female athletes (White and Young, 1999) and becomes part of the construction of athletic identity for many of these individuals. In short, it becomes part of their 'sport ethic' (Hughes and Coakley, 1991). In their seminal study, Hughes and Coakley (1991: 308) characterise the acceptance of pain and injury in sport as 'positive deviance', which they suggest is 'caused by an unqualified acceptance of, and unquestioned commitment to a value system framed by ... the sport ethic'. Positive deviance refers to a form of overconformity that goes so far in 'following commonly accepted rules or standards that it interferes with the wellbeing of self or others' (310). Much of the positive deviance in sport involves an unqualified acceptance of and overconformity to the value system embodied in the sport ethic, as defined by Coakley and Donnelly (2004: 157) as 'a cluster of norms that many people in power and performance sports have accepted and reaffirmed as the dominant criteria for defining what it means, in their social worlds, to be an athlete and to successfully claim an identity as an athlete'. Hughes and Coakley (1991) identify four beliefs that make up the sport ethic: (1) being an athlete involves making sacrifices for 'the game'; (2) being an athlete involves striving for distinction; (3) being an athlete involves accepting risks and playing through pain; and (4) being an athlete involves refusing to accept limits in the pursuit of possibilities. Not all athletes overconform to this ethic, but these norms make up the mindset and culture of many athletes in competitive sports. It is in this framework that athletes learn to expect, accept, minimise and/or ignore pain and injury as a normal part of the game, and even take pride in their pain threshold as proof of their character as athletes and their dedication to the team (Nixon, 1992). As Hughes and Coakley (1991: 316) stress, 'it [should be] emphasized that the norms of the sport ethic are positive norms; it is under the condition of uncritical acceptance and extreme overconformity that they are associated with dangerous and destructive behaviour'. Overconformity to the sport ethic becomes part of the overall participation experience, and although it varies between sports and athletes, it appears to be both common across sport and emphasised in particular sport cultures (White and Young, 1999).

Immersion in the 'culture of risk', overconformity to the sport ethic, and the uncritical tolerance of pain and injury, have become the purview of both male and female athletes. Much of the early socio-cultural research in this area focused on men and pointed to, as noted above, gender differences in patterns of sports-related pain and injury (see Box 7.1).

Box 7.1   Men and sports-related pain and injury

White and Young (1999: 74) highlight a wide range of literature to support their arguments that:

[There] is something about the ways in which boys and men experience and play sport that exposes them to greater risk of injury than their female counterparts ... the greater incidence of injury among males is explained by a number of factors, including the fact that more boys and men play sport than women and girls, that males play sports that are more conducive to injury, and that males play in ways that pay insufficient attention to physical self-preservation.

Sport remains one of the most important sites for the construction of hegemonic forms of masculinity, within which the use of violence and force, as well as the practice of tolerating pain, become part of the masculinising process (Young, 1993; Young et al., 1994). In short, men have championed the physical basis of gender difference through the paradoxical identification of the male body as a weapon to cause harm and to be harmed (see Messner, 1990; Sabo and Panepinto, 1990). But, a growing body of research on women's experiences of sport-related pain and injury shows that girls and women are beginning to adopt similar norms and patterns of behaviour with regard to overconformity to the sport ethic and the 'culture of risk', such that Young and White (1995: 51) suggest, 'if there is a difference between the way male and female athletes ... appear to understand pain and injury, it is only a matter of degree' (see also Charlesworth and Young, 2004; Pike and Maguire, 2003; Theberge, 1997). The evidence suggests that as women intensify their participation in sport and 'colonize "new" sport territory' (Young and White, 1995: 96) – for example, the increased number of women participating in such sports as ice hockey, rugby and wrestling; what Theberge (1997: 70) describes as the 'flag carriers of masculinity' – they adopt and reproduce the underlying masculinist meanings of sport structures and 'appear to [contribute] to an already defined sport process replete with violence, excessive and compromising health behaviour' (Young and White, 1995: 56). As Young and White (1995) show, some of the very strategies that women use in discussing the tolerance of pain and injury represent 'the cornerstones of the dominant male model of sport, and are adopted for a number of reasons: to show courage or character; to consolidate membership or kudos in a group; to avoid being benched; [or] to help make sense of compromised health in a lifestyle that reveres health and fitness' (53). This discussion of the role of pain and injury in the construction of gender and athletic identity leads us back to the paradox of competitive sport described above. Many people see sport (often overlapped with non-sport forms of physical activity) as building, enhancing and improving the body, but it also hurts and damages the body. This destructive process implicates other participants in the sport system such as coaches, administrators and, given our focus on the relationship between sport and health, medical and paramedical health care practitioners.

SPORTS MEDICINE AND THE PROVISION OF HEALTH CARE TO ATHLETES

In Canada, as in many other nation states competing in the world's high-performance sporting arena, the provision of clinical/therapeutic support to athletes has become naturalised and institutionalised as part of the high-performance sport system and sports medicine has come to assume expertise and authority on the health of the sporting body. The Canadian Olympic Committee (COC) acknowledges this in its recognition that: 'Health care practitioners play an increasingly significant role in the performance of Canadian athletes and are an essential component in the preparation and performance of Canadian athletes for high performance competitions' (COC, personal communication, August 2004). Such a statement is not unique to the COC, but rather a telling marker of the built-in assumption that high-performance athletes train and compete to the physiological (and psychological) limit at all times in the pursuit of excellence. As Donnelly (1999) and Young (2004) note, critical analysis of the provision of health care to athletes, specifically sports medicine, has been relatively absent (Box 7.2) in the socio-cultural study of sport (exceptions to this include the foundational works of such scholars as Berryman and Park, 1992; Hoberman, 1992; Nixon, 1992; Waddington, 1996).

Box 7.2 Why does the high rate of sports-related injuries receive so little attention?

The rates of injury in many sports are quite astonishing, but do not seem to have attracted the type of social criticism necessary to bring them to the forefront of public attention. If a similar rate of injury, and even death, existed in other areas of social life (e.g., in schools, factories, or the fast-food industry) it would warrant major legal and policy attention. Imagine a fast-food industry where there are regular accidents such as burns from the hot fat fryer, or falls on grease-covered kitchen floors; where there is a whole sub-specialty of medicine ('fast-food medicine') which included designated clinics, and therapists and specialists in the treatment of such injuries; and where particularly dangerous restaurants have a clinician attached to the workplace. While this may seem absurd with regard to fast-food, it is normal practice in sport. (Donnelly, 2004: 33)

This last section of the chapter will explore in greater depth the provision of therapeutic health care to athletes and, in particular, the development, role and practices of sports medicine and sports medicine occupational groups (e.g. sports medicine physicians, athletic therapists, sport physiotherapists, sport chiropractors, sport massage therapists) in mediating the relationship between competitive sport and health.[1]

Sports medicine, as we know of it today, emerged in Germany in the early 1900s (Hoberman, 1992; Riordan, 1987) at a time when the athletic body was seen mainly as a tool in the pursuit of scientific knowledge. By the early twentieth century, technological advances in science and medicine were enlisted in the pursuit of athletic success and while it is important to acknowledge the ways in which the development of sports medicine was intertwined with the broader growth and development of physical education and sport sciences, it cannot be emphasised enough that the care, treatment and rehabilitation of athletes are decidedly a phenomenon of the mid-twentieth century (Berryman and Park, 1992). One of the main reasons for this has to do with the transformation of the production of sport, specifically high-performance sport, following World War II, since a number of scholars acknowledge the strong connections that exist between high-performance sport and the growth and development of sports medicine (e.g. Hoberman, 1992; Waddington, 1996). A rapidly changing international socio-cultural, political and economic climate post-war, both within and outside of sport, saw the adoption of an ideology of excellence in sport in many nation states (cf. Beamish and Ritchie, 2004). This ideological shift transformed the nature and culture of high-performance sport – privileging the professionalised, commercialised, bureaucratised and instrumentally rationalised production of sport and fostering, as Hoberman (1992: 25) puts it, the 'promise of limitless performances'. The single-minded and focused pursuit of sporting success as espoused by this ideology has come to define how high-performance sport should be produced and conducted (Kidd, 1988). But, the promise of 'limitless performance' does have its limits. Athletes, in subscribing to the ideology of excellence and in uncritically accepting and overconforming to the 'sport ethic', regularly train and compete at the borders of physical breakdown (Theberge, 2005; Young and White, 1995; Young et al., 1994).

Another reason for the accelerated development of sports medicine since the 1950s has to do with the broader medicalisation of life, including sport (Waddington, 1996). Medicalisation refers to the process whereby a larger number and broader range of human conditions are brought under the medical 'gaze', such that both medical intervention and the emergence of medical specialties ready to intervene are justified. In a provocative statement, Waddington suggests that 'one can see here the development of the idea, now very widespread, that athletes require routine medical supervision, not because they necessarily have any clearly defined pathology but, in this case, simply because they are athletes' (1996: 179). We must approach this statement cautiously since there is simply not enough empirical research on the extent and nature of medical supervision of athletes in competitive sport contexts. In fact, in light of the above discussion on the 'culture of risk', one could argue that athletes may avoid medical supervision and intervention because it goes against their sport ethic. Existing research demonstrates that there is a continuum of ways in which athletes negotiate with clinicians when such help is available and accessible and that context is a key determinant of how negotiations can and do proceed (see Roderick et al., 2000; Safai, 2003; Walk, 1997; Young, 2004). The medicalisation of sport is not definite or all encompassing but has been facilitated by a number of factors including the broader medicalisation of life and the professionalisation of the production of high-performance sport such that athletes may actively turn to clinicians for ways of improving performance.

It is against this socio-cultural, political, economic and ideological backdrop that contemporary sports medicine developed. In Canada, discussion of the care, treatment and rehabilitation of athletes did not gain focused attention until the late 1960s and since that time the therapeutic aspect of sports medicine, including the occupational groups that comprise the field of sports medicine, has enjoyed accelerated, uncritical and unquestioned development in the high-performance sport system. Banks (1983: 860) writes:

> During the 60's and 70's we … saw a huge increase in sports participation at all levels. The so-called 'fitness explosion' caused a complete change in our way of life – more leisure time and recreation, more exercising, a rapid development of organized sports, tougher competitions and more rigorous and sophisticated training techniques. And, of course, more injuries and health problems. From out of this time frame has emerged an athlete who is better educated and at least somewhat more knowledgeable of the medical care he needs and deserves. It's obvious that each country must provide superb health care for its athletes – before, during, and after – major games.

The obviousness of the need for sports medicine is problematic here. The ideological transformation of the high-performance sport system in this period of time and the shift towards 'tougher competitions and more rigorous and sophisticated training techniques' supported and welcomed the unquestioned proliferation of various sport experts, including sports medicine clinicians. But the transformation of the high-performance sport system, specifically the production of high-performance sport, also supported 'more injuries and health problems'. In many countries around the world, this rise in injuries and health problems was not met with critique but rather with support for the professional development of the field of sports medicine and its various disciplines. In the late 1970s, the Canadian government created and funded the Sport Medicine Council of Canada (later known as the Sport Medicine and Science Council of Canada) in response to these changing dynamics. This Council was a platform on which sports medicine and science occupational groups boosted and accelerated their professional development, but its mandate was fairly limited to the provision of care to athletes at major games – in order to maintain peak performance (cf. Theberge, 2005) – rather than the prevention of injury in high-performance sport (Safai, 2005). There *was* genuine concern about athletes' health and well-being – it would be inappropriate to suggest that there was not a real desire to help athletes with their pain and injuries. However, a more critical reading highlights a greater concern over the poor performance in relation to and the risk of defeat at the hands of athletes from other nation states (see Safai, 2005). If success in high-performance sport was seen as a way in which to bolster pan-Canadian identity and nationalism in the international arena, thus legitimating increased state intervention in sport (Kidd, 1988), then state support and subsidisation of sports medicine was a way in which to ensure that success by minimising the risks to the athletes' 'limitless performances'. See Box 7.3 for a brief discussion of sports medicine outside the context of high-performance sport.

Box 7.3 Sports medicine beyond high-performance sport

Whereas the naturalisation of sports medicine within the high-performance sport system, from the late 1960s onwards, helped in legitimating state intervention into sport, the current field of sports medicine extends well beyond the elite athlete. There is a significant, and significantly under-researched, sports medicine industry (including clinics, medications and orthopaedic products) that operates, conservatively, in the hundreds of millions of dollars annually in North America alone (see Donnelly, 1999). There is a cyclical relationship here in that as the need for sports medicine is stimulated (i.e. the need for 'expert' knowledge to manage the negative risks of sport), the institutionalisation of sports medicine is legitimated. In other words, sports medicine stimulates a need for its services, provides the means with which to meet the needs of patients who have to come to accept sports medicine's expertise, and in turn further secures its authoritative position on the health of the athletic body. For non-high-performance athletes, sports medicine is a body of knowledge and area of expertise for sale and people – albeit only those with disposable income and a particular cultural capital that recognises the specialised expertise of sports medicine as somehow better – are buying. In this light, it is not far-fetched to suggest that the profitable economic aspect of sports medicine supports injury treatment and rehabilitation, but not necessarily prevention (cf. Donnelly, 2004).

CONCLUSION

This chapter has been concerned with exploring the relationship between sport and health and, in particular, focused on the ways in which sport contributes to pain, injury and ill health. One of the challenges to our better understanding of this relationship remains the continued conflation of the positive benefits of mild to moderate forms of physical activity with organised, competitive sport. The empirical evidence for the positive benefits of sport is tenuous, and yet many people, including health and sport policy makers, continue to tout the commonplace assumption that 'sport is good for one's health' (cf. Waddington, 2000). There are a number of positive health associations that accompany increased participation in non-sport forms of physical activity, but the increased intensity, frequency and duration of participation involved in competitive sport often negate those benefits and produce risks of their own in the form of health-compromising norms and behaviours. It would be wrong to paint a completely bleak picture of the health benefits of sport – participation in sport can and does have a positive transformative health effect for many people. However, the structure of sport – its 'culture of risk', its dependence on aggression and violence in the construction of gender and athletic identity, its commitment to an ideology of excellence – makes these positive health effects the exception and not the rule. The structure and production of competitive sport facilitate ill health, and this implicates the ways in which health care is provided to athletes. Sports medicine and the occupational groups that comprise the field of sports medicine have come to assume expertise and authority on the sporting body and have created a niche for themselves in the sport and health care systems of many countries. However, we must question how much of a role they have played in the prevention and reduction of sport injury and the implications of their more curative role in the treatment and care of sport injury. Much more research is needed in this area in order to ensure the good health of sport participants and to give credence to the belief that 'sport is good for one's health'.

CHAPTER SUMMARY

» There is compelling evidence supporting the health benefits of mild to moderate forms of physical activity but despite the conventional wisdom that 'sport is good for one's health', research on the negative health benefits of sport is growing.

» A challenge to our understanding of the negative relationship between sport and health resides in the ways in which sport is often conflated with non-sport forms of physical activity.

» In overconforming to the sport ethic, athletes are often immersed in a 'culture of risk' that fosters the uncritical acceptance and tolerance of health-compromising norms and behaviours.

» Sports medicine has become naturalised and institutionalised in high-performance sport and supports, directly and indirectly, the ideology of excellence and the dedicated pursuit of success. This is problematic since the dedicated and focused pursuit of success demands that athletes train and compete at the physiological and psychological limit, the edge of pain and injury, at all times.

» While there remain a number of research gaps in the critical study of sports medicine in high-performance sport, even less is known about sports medicine beyond the high-performance sport arena.

FURTHER READING

Young's (2004) edited volume, *Sporting Bodies, Damaged Selves*, provides a strong overview of the state of knowledge in the socio-cultural study of sport on sport-related pain and injury. With regard to sports medicine, Berryman and Park (1992), Hoberman (1992) and Waddington (2000) provide important foundational readings on the socio-historical development of sports medicine from the nineteenth century onwards in parts of Europe and North America.

NOTE

1 An exploration of the sociological debates around professions and professionalisation falls beyond the scope of this chapter, but the term 'occupational group' is used quite intentionally here as a type of 'neutral' terminology for all clinician groups, since the word 'profession' is loaded with signifiers of status, prestige and social closure.

REFERENCES

Banks, M. (1983) 'Providing the product: the sport medicine council of Canada', in S. Kereliuk (ed.), *The University's Role in the Development of Modern Sport: Past, Present and Future*. Edmonton: FISU Conference – Universiade '83, pp. 860–3.

Beamish, R. and Ritchie, I. (2004) 'From chivalrous "brothers-in-arms" to the eligible athlete: changed principles and the IOC's banned substance list', *International Review for the Sociology of Sport*, 39 (4): 355–71.

Bercovitz, K. (2000) 'A critical analysis of Canada's "Active Living": science or politics', *Critical Public Health*, 10 (1): 19–39.

Berryman, J. and Park, R. (1992) *Sport and Exercise science: Essays in the History of Sports Medicine*. Urbana, IL: University of Illinois Press.

Bloom, M., Grant, M. and Watt, D. (2005) *Strengthening Canada: the Socio-economic Benefits of Sport Participation in Canada*. Ottawa: Conference Board of Canada.

Booth, F.W. and Chakravarthy, M.V. (2002) 'Cost and consequences of sedentary living: new battleground for an old enemy', *President's Council on Physical Fitness and Sports research Digest*, Series 3 (16): 1–8.

Bouchard, C., Shepard, R., Stephens, T., Sutton, J. and McPherson, B. (1990) *Exercise, Fitness and Health: a Consensus of Current Knowledge*, Champaign, IL: Human Kinetics.

Canadian Population Health Initiative (2002) *Charting the Course: a Pan Canadian Consultation on Population and Public Health Priorities*. http://secure.cihi.ca/cihiweb/en/downloads/cphi-charting-jun2002-e.pdf (accessed 24 September 2007).

Centers for Disease Control and Prevention (2005) *The importance of physical activity and good nutrition: Essential elements to prevent chronic diseases and obesity*. http://www.cdc.gov/nccdphp/publications/aag/dnpa.htm (accessed 24 September 2007).

Charlesworth, H. and Young, K. (2004) 'Why English female university athletes play with pain: motivations and rationalisations', in K. Young (ed.), *Sporting Bodies, Damaged Selves: Sociological Studies of Sport-related Injury*. Oxford: Elsevier, pp. 163–80.

Coakley, J. and Donnelly, P. (2004) *Sports in Society: Issues and Controversies*. 1st Canadian edn. Toronto: McGraw-Hill Ryerson.

Colditz, G.A. (1999) 'Economic costs of obesity and inactivity', *Medicine and Science in Sports and Exercise*, 31: S663–7.

Conference Board of Canada (1996) *Physical activity and the cost of treating illness*. Special Report Series (No. 944S010). Ottawa: Canada Fitness and Lifestyle Research Institute.

Department of Health (2004) *At least five a week: Evidence on the impact of physical activity and its relationship to health*. A report from the Chief Medical Officer. London: Department of Health.

Donnelly, P. (1999) 'Gulliver's travels: a sport sociologist among the labcoats', *Journal of Sport & Social Issues*, 23 (4): 455–8.

Donnelly, P. (2004) 'Sport and risk culture', in K. Young (ed.), *Sporting Bodies, Damaged Selves: Sociological Studies of Sports-related Injury*. Oxford: Elsevier, pp. 29–58.

Donnelly, P. and Harvey, J. (1996) *Overcoming Systemic Barriers to Access in Active Living*. Report presented to Fitness Branch, Health Canada and Active Living Canada.

Evans, R.G., Barer, M.L. and Marmor, T.R. (eds) (1994) *Why Are Some People Healthy and Others Not? The Determinants of Health of Populations*. New York: Aldine de Gruyter.

Federal/Provincial/Territorial Advisory Committee on Population Health (1999) *Toward a Healthy Future: Second Report on the Health of Canadians*. Ottawa, ON: Health Canada.

Finch, C. and McGrath, A. (1997) *Sportsafe Australia: a National Sports Safety Network*. Report prepared for the Australian Sports Injury Prevention Taskforce. Canberra: Australian Sports Commission.

Gard, M. and Wright, J. (2005) *The Obesity Epidemic: Science, Morality and Ideology*. London: Routledge.

Health Canada (2004) *Healthy Living: Canada's Guide to Healthy Eating and Physical Activity*. Ottawa: Health Canada.

Health Education Authority (HEA) (1995) *Moving On: a Summary*. London: HEA.

Hoberman, J. (1992) *Mortal Engines: the Science of Performance and the Dehumanization of Sport*. New York: Free Press.

Howe, P.D. (2004) *Sport, Professionalism and Pain: Ethnographics of Injury and Risk*. London: Routledge.

Hughes, R. and Coakley, J. (1991) 'Positive deviance among athletes: the implications of the sport ethic', *Sociology of Sport Journal*, 8: 307–25.

Hume, P. and Marshall, S. (1994) 'Sports injuries in New Zealand: exploratory analyses', *New Zealand Journal of Sports Medicine*, 22: 18–22.

International Year of Sport and Physical Education (IYSPE) (2005) http://www.un.org/sport2005 (accessed 24 September 2007).

Intersectoral Healthy Living Network (2005) *Integrated Pan-Canadian Healthy Living Strategy*. In partnership with the Federal/Provincial/Territorial Healthy Living Task Group and the Federal/Provincial/Territorial Advisory Committee on Population Health and Health Security (ACPHHS). Ottawa: Public Health Agency of Canada.

Johns, D.P. (2004) 'Weight management as sport injury: deconstructing disciplinary power in the sport ethic', in K. Young (ed.), *Sporting Bodies, Damaged Selves: Sociological Studies of Sport-related Injury*. Oxford: Elsevier, pp. 117–33.

Katzmaryk, P.T. and Janssen, I. (2004) 'The economic costs of physical inactivity and obesity in Canada: an update', *Canadian Journal of Applied Physiology*, 29 (1): 90–115.

Katzmarzyk, P.T., Gledhill, N. and Shepard, R.J. (2000) 'The economic burden of physical inactivity in Canada', *Canadian Medical Association Journal*, 163 (11): 1435–40.

Kesaniemi, Y.K., Danforth, E., Jensen, M.D., Kopelman, P.G., Lefebvre, P. and Reeder, B.A. (2001) 'Dose-response issues concerning physical activity and health: an evidence-based symposium', *Medicine and Science in Sports and Exercise*, 33(6 Suppl.): S351–8.

Kidd, B. (1988) 'The philosophy of excellence: Olympic performances, class power, and the Canadian state', in P. Galasso (ed.), *Philosophy of Sport and Physical Activity*. Toronto: Canadian Scholars' Press, pp. 11–31.

Marmot, M. (2004) 'Creating healthier societies', *Bulletin of the World Health Organization*, 82 (5): 320–1.

Marshall, S.W. and Guskiewicz, K.M. (2003) 'Sports and recreational injury: the hidden cost of a healthy lifestyle', *Injury Prevention*, 9: 100–2.

McCutcheon, T., Curtis, J.E. and White, P.G. (1997) 'The socioeconomic distribution of sport injuries: multivariate analyses using Canadian national data', *Sociology of Sport Journal*, 14 (1): 57–72.

Messner, M.A. (1990) 'When bodies are weapons: masculinity and violence in sport', *International Review for the Sociology of Sport*, 25 (3): 203–19.

Mills Report (1998) The Standing Committee on Canadian Heritage and the Sub-Committee on the Study of Sport in Canada. *Sport in Canada: Leadership, Partnership and Accountability – Everyone's Business*. Ottawa: Public Works and Government Services of Canada.

Mirolla, M. (2004) *The Cost of Chronic Disease in Canada*. Ottawa: Chronic Disease Prevention Alliance of Canada (CDPAC).

Mokdad, A.H., Bowman, B.A., Ford, E.S., Vinicor, F., Marks, J.S. and Koplan, J.P. (2001) 'The continuing epidemic of obesity and diabetes in the United States', *Journal of the American Medical Association*, 270: 2207–12.

Nicholl, J.P., Coleman, P. and Williams, B.T. (1993) *Injuries in Exercise and Sport: Main Report*. London: Report to the Sports Council.

Nicholl, J.P., Coleman, O. and Brazier, J. (1994) 'Health and health care costs and the benefits of exercise', *Pharmaco Economics*, 5: 109–22.

Nicholl, J.P., Coleman, P. and Williams, B.T. (1995) 'The epidemiology of sports and exercise-related injury in the United Kingdom', *British Journal of Sports Medicine*, 29: 232–8.

Nixon, H. (1992) 'A social network analysis of influences on athletes to play with pain and injuries', *Journal of Sport & Social Issues*, 16 (2): 127–35.

Pate, R.R., Pratt, M., Blair, S.N., Haskell, W.L., Macera, C.A., Bouchard, C., Buchner, D., Ettinger, W., Heath, G.W., King, A.C. et al. (1995) 'Physical activity and public health: a recommendation from the Centers for Disease Control and Prevention and the American College of Sports Medicine', *Journal of the American Medical Association*, 273: 402–7.

Pike, E. (2005) 'Doctors just say "Rest and take Ibuprofen": a critical examination of the role of "non-orthodox" health care in women's sport', *International Review for the Sociology of Sport*, 40 (2): 201–19.

Pike, E. and Maguire, J. (2003) 'Injury in women's sport: classifying key elements of "risk encounters"', *Sociology of Sport Journal*, 20: 232–51.

Pipe, A. (2001) 'Adverse effects of elite competition on health and wellbeing', *Canadian Journal of Applied Physiology*, 26 (Suppl.): S192–201.

Pratt, M., Macera, C.A. and Wang, G. (2000) 'Higher direct medical costs associated with physical inactivity', *The Physician and Sportsmedicine*, 28 (10): 63–70.

Quinney, Q., Gauvin, L. and Wall, A. (eds) (1994) *Toward Active Living*. Proceedings of the International Conference on Physical Activity, Fitness and Health. Champaign, IL: Human Kinetics.

Report from the United Nations Inter-Agency Task Force on Sport for Development and Peace (2003) *Sport for Development and Peace: Towards Achieving the Millennium Development Goals*.

Riordan, J. (1987) 'Sports medicine in the Soviet Union and German Democratic Republic', *Social Science and Medicine*, 25 (1): 19–28.

Roderick, M., Waddington, I. and Parker, G. (2000) 'Playing hurt: managing injuries in English professional football', *International Review for the Sociology of Sport*, 35 (2): 165–80.

Sabo, D. and Panepinto, J. (1990) 'Football ritual and the social reproduction of masculinity', in M.A. Messner and D. Sabo (eds), *Sport, Men and the Gender Order: Critical Feminist Perspectives*. Champaign, IL: Human Kinetics, pp. 115–26.

Safai, P. (2003) 'Healing the body in the "culture of risk": examining the negotiation of treatment between sport medicine clinicians and injured athletes in Canadian intercollegiate sport', *Sociology of Sport Journal*, 20 (2): 127–46.

Safai, P. (2005) 'The demise of the Sport Medicine and Science Council of Canada', *Sport History Review*, 36: 91–114.

Shepard, R.J. (2003) 'Can we afford to exercise, given current injury rates?', *Injury Prevention*, 9: 99–100.

Smith, A., Green, K. and Roberts, K. (2004) 'Sports participation and the "obesity/health" crisis', *International Review for the Sociology of Sport*, 39 (4): 457–64.

Sport and Recreation Research Communiqué (1996) *Injuries incurred by Ontario residents during participation in sport and other recreational activities.* Ottawa: Ministry of Citizenship, Culture and Recreation.

Tator, G., Edmonds, V. and Lapczak, L. (1993) *Serious and catastrophic sport/recreational injuries.* Ottawa: Ministry of Culture, Tourism and Recreation.

Theberge, N. (1997) ' "It's part of the game": physicality and the production of gender in women's hockey', *Gender and Society*, 11 (1): 69–87.

Theberge, N. (2005) ' "This is really about performance": the provision of health care in the context of high performance sport', Paper presented at the 26th Annual Conference of the North American Society for the Sociology of Sport, Winston-Salem, NC.

US Department of Health and Human Services (1996) *Surgeon General's report on physical activity and health.* Washington, DC.

Waddington, I. (1996) 'The development of sports medicine', *Sociology of Sport Journal*, 13: 176–96.

Waddington, I. (2000) *Sport, Health and Drugs: a Critical Sociological Perspective.* London and New York: E & FN Spon.

Walk, S. (1997) 'Peers in pain: the experience of student athletic trainers', *Sociology of Sport Journal*, 14: 22–56.

White, P. (2004) 'The costs of injury from sport, exercise and physical activity: a review of the evidence', in K. Young (ed.), *Sporting Bodies, Damaged Selves.* Oxford: Elsevier, pp. 309–31.

White, P.G. and Young, K. (1999) 'Is sport injury gendered?', in P.G. White and K. Young (eds), *Sport and Gender in Canada.* Toronto: Oxford University Press, pp. 68–84.

Wilkinson, R. and Marmot, M. (2003) *The Social Determinants of Health: The Solid Facts.* 2nd edn. Copenhagen: WHO Regional Office of Europe.

World Health Organization (2002) *The world health report 2002: Reducing risks, promoting healthy life.* Geneva: WHO.

World Health Organization (2003) *Annual global move for health initiative: A concept paper.* Geneva: WHO.

World Health Organization (2004) *Global strategy on diet, physical activity and health.* Geneva: WHO. http://www.who.int/gb/ebwha/pdf_files/WHA57/A57_R17-en.pdf (accessed 24 September 2007).

Young, K. (1993) 'Violence, risk and liability in male sports culture', *Sociology of Sport Journal*, 19: 373–96.

Young, K. (ed.) (2004) *Sporting Bodies, Damaged Selves: Sociological Studies of Sport-related Injury.* Oxford: Elsevier.

Young, K. and White, P. (1995) 'Sport, physical danger and injury: the experience of elite women athletes', *Journal of Sport & Social Issues*, 19 (1): 45–61.

Young, K., White, P. and McTeer, J. (1994) 'Body talk: male athletes reflect on sport, injury and pain', *Sociology of Sport Journal*, 11: 175–94.

landscape of harmful and/or abusive behaviours. However, the fact that the bulk of the existing research has so far focused on the first two cells is reflected in the relative weight of the discussions that follow. Shorter summaries of the remaining 16 cells are designed to provide the reader with a sense of the aforementioned 'broader landscape' of SRV, and the research that has been committed to it to date.

Crowd Violence

Crowd violence is best understood as direct or indirect acts of physical violence by sports spectators, at or away from the sports arena, that result in injury to persons or damage to property. It may also include forms of racism, or racially motivated threats and attacks. Unlike acts of violence among players, violence among fans has tended to elicit anxious responses from the authorities and often is closely policed. The recurrence of injurious, and sometimes deadly, crowd episodes in several countries has sensitised the public and social controllers to the need for careful regulation of sports crowds. Indeed, in many settings, fan violence is seen as a serious social problem, and strict measures, including new laws, have been introduced (Young, 2000, 2002a). Fans of English and European soccer have certainly gained notoriety for their violent rituals and practices but, in fact, violent crowd disturbances at soccer occur regularly worldwide – so much so that Dunning and his colleagues (2002) have referred to the problem as a 'world phenomenon'. Many other sports have also been affected, some more consistently than others. It is equally apparent that sports crowd violence has a long history (Guttmann, 1986).

Undeniably, in terms of overall work produced, most sociological attention paid to sports violence has focused on forms and causes of English soccer hooliganism. In step with a popular, but not necessarily accurate (Dunning et al., 1988), perception that hooliganism began in the 1960s and 1970s, and with several tragic episodes resulting in multiple injuries and deaths at soccer games, especially in the 1980s (see Box 8.1), the literature expanded rapidly during this period, though it has diminished somewhat of late. The debates between scholars on this issue have been complex and occasionally fractious, but certain strands within the research are well known.

> **Box 8.1 The 1980s: a crisis period in English soccer violence?**
>
> The mid to late 1980s are widely considered to represent a pivotal crisis period in the history of English soccer. On 11 May 1985, as Bradford City played at home against Lincoln City, a fire broke out in a wooden-framed stadium built almost a century earlier.

The section of the stadium burned to the ground in less than 10 minutes, and 57 people were burned to death trying to escape the fire. The horrific scenes were displayed on television and in the print media. Eighteen days later, on 29 May, the European Champion's Cup was due to be played between Liverpool of England and Juventus of Turin, Italy. Approximately one hour before kick-off, and following a period of mutual taunting between rival groups of fans, a charge by the Liverpool fans into the Juventus 'end' resulted in a retainer wall collapsing and the injuring of hundreds of fans. Far worse, 39 mostly Italian fans died in the ensuing crush (Taylor, 1987; Young, 1986). Again, the scenes were broadcast live on television. Finally, on 15 April 1989, Liverpool fans were once more involved in a tragic incident prior to a domestic cup game against Nottingham Forrest played at Hillsborough Stadium, Sheffield, although in contrast to Turin this time the incident was not hooligan related. After the police opened a gate to accommodate latecomers, as many as 4,000 Liverpool fans were channelled into the stadium, unaware that hundreds of fans inside the stadium were being crushed against a high steel control fence. At least 94 fans were killed, over 200 injured (Scraton et al., 1995; Taylor, 1989). Once again, the grizzly scenes were broadcast live to the world. A subsequent inquiry led by Lord Justice Taylor was heavily critical of the decisions made by, and responses of, the police on duty.

One of the initial explanations of hooliganism was social psychological. Building on Tiger's (1969) controversial study of aggression among *Men in Groups*, and on presumptions of the 'need' for male bonding, Marsh et al. (1978) developed the 'Ritual of Soccer Violence Thesis' following observations at Oxford United Football Club. Employing a so-called 'ethogenic method' to explore the organisation and motives of hooligan fans from an insider's point of view, Marsh et al. conceptualised aggression as a means of controlling the social world in the process of achieving certain outcomes. Therefore, fan violence at soccer matches was viewed as a cultural adaptation to the working-class environment for male English adolescents – a 'ritual of teenage aggro'. The contention that hooliganism is largely a ritualistic 'fantasy' of violence has been heavily criticised, especially for failing to explain the regularity of serious injuries at soccer games, and for offering superficial explanations of the social class background of participants. There are ritualistic elements to soccer 'aggro' in England and elsewhere (for instance, many of the crowd chants and gestures, and even aspects of intergroup provocation, are certainly ritualistic), but to argue that the essence of hooliganism is ritualistic, and that actual violence seldom occurs, raises doubts about the potential of this approach, particularly when hooligan encounters have been widely reported, routinely injurious and occasionally fatal.

In the 1970s and 1980s, the Marxist criminologist Ian Taylor (1971, 1987) offered a more macro-sociological and class-sensitive account of soccer hooliganism. For him, hooliganism was associated with two different phases in the development of the English game and of British society more generally. First, Taylor looked historically to the emergence of soccer in working-class communities, and to the disruptive effects of commercialisation on the game. Commercialisation, he argued, fractured a formerly rich 'soccer subculture' that weaved its way through such communities. Practices such as the invasion of playing fields and vandalism were interpreted as attempts by the remnants of this subculture to reclaim a game that had become increasingly removed from its control. In the 1980s, and clearly moved by the tragic events of the 1985 Bradford Stadium fire and Heysel Stadium riot, as well as the 1989 Hillsborough Stadium crush, Taylor revised portions of his earlier thesis to argue that contemporary manifestations of soccer hooliganism could better be understood if placed against crises of the British state. Specifically, he argued that increasing dislocation within working-class communities and the development of an 'upper' working-class jingoism (or 'Little Englanderism') during Margaret Thatcher's Conservative rule exacerbated England's hooliganism problem, and helped fuel a long sequence of xenophobically violent exchanges between fans of English club teams and fans of the English national team and those of rival countries.

While sensitive to questions of history and social class, Taylor's work has been criticised for 'romanticising' any real 'control' working-class fans may ever have exerted over the game during its early phases, for ignoring very early 'hooligan' encounters (during, for instance, the early twentieth century and alleged 'soccer consciousness' phase), and for misidentifying the majority of hooligan fans as 'upper' (and thus more affluent and resourceful) working-class. The fact that Taylor's ideas, while provocative, were never based on any acknowledged empirical protocol has not helped their durability, though his attempts to offer a form of 'social deprivation thesis' has certainly influenced subsequent North American accounts of fan violence (cf. Young, 2002a).

Taylor's Marxist views on dynamic class culture and on the development of the English game were echoed at approximately the same time by several writers at the Centre for Contemporary Cultural Studies at Birmingham University, England, where, once again, soccer hooliganism was viewed as a reaction by working-class males to commercialising processes, such as the increasing presentation of soccer as a market commodity, emerging in what had traditionally been construed as 'the people's game'. Examining deep structural changes in working-class communities, Clarke (1978) and others added a strong subcultural/ ethnographic component to their class analysis, allowing them to explain the presence in the 1960s and 1970s of hooligan 'phases' of flamboyant skinhead groups combining traditional working-class values (such as the fierce defence of local and national identities, and a passion for soccer) with interests in commercial youth style. Relating soccer hooliganism to the context of a culture in flux is a helpful framework of analysis, and the socio-historical approaches of Taylor, Clarke and others certainly offer considerably more explanatory insight into a complex social problem than the micro-sociological ventures of Marsh et al. However, as with Taylor's early work, Clarke and colleagues actually produced little concrete evidence to support the argument that hooliganism was a response to changing working-class traditions and values. Stability of working-class social relations in an allegedly 'hooligan-free' past (i.e. in the pre-1960 era) is a view that both parties tended to assume too uncritically. This, again, has not gone unnoticed by critics.

A group of sociologists (formerly based) at the University of Leicester have been interested to examine the 'social roots' of English soccer hooliganism (cf. Dunning et al., 1988; Murphy et al., 1990; Williams et al., 1984). Unlike Marsh and Taylor, however, the Eliasian/figurational work of the Leicester group is grounded in extensive comparisons of the phenomenon in its past and present contexts. Principally, Eric Dunning and his colleagues (Patrick Murphy, Ivan Waddington and John Williams) argue that aggressive standards of behaviour displayed by soccer hooligans are directly influenced by the social conditions and values inherent in the class–cultural background of those involved.

A predominant theme of their work, and one which represents a direct counterpoint to Taylor's 'Little England' thesis, is that hooligan groups are largely comprised of individuals from the roughest and lowest (rather than 'upper') sectors of the working classes. They argue that the hooligan's relatively deprived social condition is instrumental in the production and reproduction of normative modes of behaviour, including strong emphases on notions of territory, male dominance and physicality. It is precisely the reproduction of this social condition that is seen to lead to the development of a specific violent masculine style manifested regularly in the context of soccer. Notions of dynamic territoriality are also offered which allow the Leicester researchers to account for the shifting allegiances of fan support (and thus shifting expressions of fan violence) at local, regional and international levels. There are several unique features to the ideas of the Leicester 'School', perhaps the most important of which is the adoption of a long-term Eliasian view regarding the development of soccer hooliganism, which allows them to demonstrate that forms of spectator disorder have existed for over a century. The Leicester research has been heavily influential in the UK and internationally, both within the academy and with policy makers.

As comprehensive as these four approaches are, they do not represent the full spectrum of work available on fan violence in the UK. Other studies which have contributed to the 'hooligan debate' include, but are not limited to, Murray's (1984) social history of religious sectarianism in Scottish football, Robins's (1984) accounts of the intersections between soccer violence and the popular cultural interests of young British men, Armstrong's (1998) and Giulianotti's (1994) ethnographic and qualitative studies of English and Scottish hooliganism, and studies of soccer, violence and gender in Ireland (Bairner, 1995).

This impressive volume of research on soccer hooliganism has not been matched elsewhere, despite the known existence of problems with violence among sports crowds. In North America, for instance, where there is clear evidence of fan disorders, remarkably little sociological work has been tendered. The work that does exist is neither as thorough nor as theorised as the British work. Notwithstanding several notable attempts (cf. Smith, 1983; Young, 2002a) to explain North American fan violence in terms of its social causes, there seems to be a general reluctance on the part of researchers to take the phenomenon seriously, and far more work is needed. Indeed, despite the fact that the bulk of the research on violence among fans relates to transatlantic contexts and experiences, many countries where organised sport is played and prized have recorded problems with fan violence at one time or another. Regrettably, however, the research, and especially that portion of it written in, or translated into, English, remains slim, and there are no clear ways of classifying or categorising this work into thematic 'schools' or coherent bodies of theory.

Lever's (1983) work on fan violence associated with Brazilian soccer set an early marker for the international research. Using a structural functionalist approach, Lever sought to show how sport in South America can represent both unifying and divisive properties – unifying in the sense that it may enhance community awareness and loyalty, but divisive because it underlines social class distinctions. Fan violence, she argues, is but one side effect of failed attempts by the Brazilian authorities to deal with poverty and such class distinctions. Soccer stadiums have often been used as a venue for the expression of class conflict such as missile throwing from the 'poorer' stadium sections into the 'richer' sections. Arguably, Lever's functionalist approach cannot easily account for these tensions and her study is now outdated, but it nevertheless represents ground-breaking sociological work on fan violence in South America. A more contemporary account of fan violence in this context may be found in Archetti and Romero (1994).

By now, most serious students of sports violence understand that the argument that soccer hooliganism is a British or English 'Disease' is a myth. In their early figurational studies, Williams et al. (1984) unearthed over 70 media reports of fan violence at soccer games in 30 different countries in which English fans were not involved between 1904 and 1983. Slightly later, Williams and Goldberg (1989: 7) identified numerous cases of hooliganism where English fans were, in fact, the 'victims of foreign hooliganism' rather than the assailants. Today, cases of fan violence in diverse international contexts are routinely reported in the popular media and over the Internet, and organised hooliganism has become a problem for the authorities in many countries.

Notwithstanding cultural variance in the nature and extent of fan violence, evidence indicates that soccer hooliganism expanded throughout the 1980s in a number of European countries. A considerable European research literature also emerged at this time. Greece, France, Spain, Belgium, Austria, Sweden, The Netherlands, Germany and Italy are among countries known to have experienced significant problems with soccer hooliganism (Young, 2000: 389). In many of these locations, fan violence has been shown to intersect with far-right-wing politics and racist ideologies (see cell 16), demonstrating a clear sociological link between problems in sport and those in the wider society.

Crowd violence is a multi-dimensional and complex topic that has generated a huge volume of research on matters such as causes, manifestations and responses, as well as media coverage, but this research shows serious imbalances. For example, while there seems little doubt that the most substantial and rigorously theorised body of work in this area has examined forms and causes of British soccer hooliganism, relatively little is known about fan violence in other parts of the world. Again, this is true of North America, for instance, where the phenomenon is acknowledged by sports organisations and authorities alike, but where, with only a few exceptions, much of what we know comes from descriptive and often less than reliable media accounts (Young, 2002a).

Player Violence

Player violence, involving behaviours encompassed within the rules as well as outside the rules of sport, has traditionally been condoned in many settings as 'part of the game'. This is witnessed in the way that aggressive, high-risk or injurious practices that would be socially and/or legally intolerable apart from sports are encouraged and expected to occur in connection with sports. Further, in many countries, sport is immersed in fervent cultures of aggression that may serve to compromise participant safety and limit the possibility of change. Such cultures may also have influenced research on sport, since sociologists have paid far less attention to player violence than to crowd violence.

Most sociologists agree that while there is no single cause of player violence, understanding the phenomenon requires examining socialisation processes associated with many sports and, indeed, with the institution of sport in general, where athletes learn from an early age that behaviours such as hitting and being hit, and conceiving of violence as a vehicle to resolve conflicts (Coakley, 1989; Coakley and Donnelly, 2004), are acceptable and easily rationalised. Combined with an emphasis in many commercialised sports on heroic values, physical dominance and winning at all costs, thinking and behaving aggressively are simply part of the learning that individuals and groups undertake in sport. Player violence is one outgrowth of this learning.

Several typologies of player violence exist, but one of the most popular and useful comes from Canadian sociologist Michael Smith (1983), who classified violence among athletes into four categories, the first two being relatively legitimate and the last two relatively illegitimate in the eyes of sports organisations and the authorities. *Brutal body contact* includes ordinary occurrences such as tackles, blocks and body checks – acts that can be found within the official rules of many sports, and to which most would agree that consent is given or implied. *Borderline violence* involves acts prohibited by the official rules of a given sport but occur routinely and are more or less accepted by persons connected with the game (e.g. the fist fight in ice hockey). These actions carry potential for causing injury as well as prompting further violence between players – such as, in ice hockey, the bench-clearing brawl. Historically speaking, sanctions imposed by sports leagues and administrators for borderline violence have been light and often tokenistic. *Quasi-criminal violence* violates the formal rules of a given sport, the law of the land and, to a significant degree, the informal norms of players. This type of violence usually results in serious injury and precipitates considerable official and public attention. Quasi-criminal violence in ice hockey, for instance, may include practices such as dangerous stick work, which can cause severe injury, and which often elicits in-house suspensions and fines. Finally, *criminal violence* includes behaviours so seriously and obviously outside the boundaries of acceptability for sport and the wider community that they are handled as exceptional, and possibly unlawful, from the outset. Consequently, it becomes possible to conceive of violence among athletes as sports 'crime' (Young, 2002b, 2004b). In-depth assessments of how sports violence and sports injury cases are adjudicated by the courts, and the sorts of legal defences available to prosecuted athletes, have been advanced in a number of countries (e.g. United States – Horrow, 1980; UK – Gardiner et al., 1998; Canada – Young, 2004b).

Smith's socio-legal approach is useful, but it has two serious limitations. First, prompted by shifting scales of public and legal tolerance since approximately the 1970s, there has been some 'collapsing' of his categories. For example, incidents considered just a decade ago as 'quasi-criminal' or even 'borderline' violence may today be brought before the courts and scrutinised seriously under law as 'criminal' sports violence. In this connection, while Smith's typology addresses the important sociological question of the 'legitimacy of violence' – that is, the legitimation/de-legitimation process with regard to what is perceived as acceptable violence and what is not (Ball-Rokeach, 1971) – it requires updating to fit a dynamic socio-legal climate (Young, 2004b).

Second, Smith's typology overlooks the way in which aspects of violence among athletes may result from wider social influences, such as gender processes. Feminist work on sport and gender (e.g. Bryson, 1987; Theberge, 1997) allows us to understand male tolerance of risk and injury linked to aggression and violence in sport as a constituting process enhancing masculine or subcultural identity. In this respect, playing sport in a hyper-aggressive way and causing or incurring injury are means of establishing positive status and career success in the form of reputational and/or material benefits. How strongly dominant codes of masculinity insert themselves into different sports and sports cultures varies, but it is clear that numerous sports contain 'patriarchal dividends' (Connell, 1995: 79; Messner and Sabo, 1994; Young and White, 2000; Young et al., 1994; see cell 5) for males who are willing to 'sacrifice their body' in violent ways in order to win. However, research on the masculinisation of player violence is complicated by the fact that studies demonstrate that many female athletes also revere risk and the use of aggression (Cove, 2006; Rail, 1992; Theberge, 1997; Young and White, 1995; see cell 6). Female involvement in high-risk, aggressive and violent sport values thus suggests that sport socialisation may be more important than gender socialisation but, on this important question, far more research is needed.

The literature on player violence is not new, but it remains limited. Perhaps most importantly, sociologists have not exercised sufficient care in definitional and conceptual matters. 'Aggression', which most people would accept is a normative (though not necessarily agreeable) feature of many sports, is not the same thing as 'violence' itself, which is often vaguely conceived of as the 'unwanted' version of the sorts of aggressive behaviours and attitudes many sports simply require. Unravelling such definitional quandaries is important, though this is admittedly complicated by varied sport-specific traditions where the definition of 'wanted' and 'unwanted' behaviour is concerned.

Individualised Fan–Player Violence

With some justification, crowd violence has normally been approached in terms of collective episodes of spectator disorder. For example, soccer hooliganism in England and post-event riots in North America have been shown to be enacted, for the most part, by large groups of fans behaving in a disorderly, threatening or violent manner. Indeed, as noted above, much of the early literature on sports violence explained fan violence as a form of 'collective behaviour' using principles of group dynamics such as 'emergent norm' theory, 'value-added' theory and 'contagion' theory (Lewis, 1982; Smith, 1983). However, not all crowd violence is perpetrated in groups (the precise ratio of individualised–collective fan violence is both difficult to measure and rarely recorded as such), and not all fan violence involves other fans. Athletes themselves may also be the targets of attack. Well-known examples include the 1995 case of female professional tennis player, Monica Seles, who was stabbed in the neck by a fan (Gunther Parche) obsessed with, and stalking, her opponent (Steffi Graf) during a tennis match played in front of thousands of people in Hamburg, Germany (*Sports Illustrated*, 17 July 1995: 18–26), and the killing of Colombian soccer player, Andres Escobar. During the 1994 USA World Cup, Colombian defender Escobar accidentally scored an 'own goal' causing his team to lose 2–1 to the United States, and thus to be eliminated from the competition. On his return to Colombia, Escobar was confronted in a parking lot by gunmen who shot the player multiple times, allegedly shouting 'goal' for each bullet fired.

Player Violence away from the Game

It is also the case that the existing research has restricted its examination of player violence to incidents occurring within the context of the game itself. Ironically, despite the fact that Smith's (1983) widely used early typology of (what he called) 'sports violence' underlined the possibility of player violence occurring away from the field of play and/or outside the arena in its fourth and final category ('criminal violence'), most researchers have limited their examination of player violence to conduct taking place during the game and inside the stadium. From one point of view, this is understandable – statistically speaking, this is clearly the locus of most player violence 'action'. However, player violence occurring away from the game has certainly concerned sport organisations and the authorities. One of the most shocking episodes in recent memory emanated from an unlikely sport – figure skating. It involved a planned attack upon American skater, and favourite to win the women's US Figure Skating Championship, Nancy Kerrigan, by acquaintances of her direct rival, Tonya Harding, in the build-up to the Lillehammer Winter Olympics (*Time*, 24 January 1994: 34–8). The off-ice assault on Kerrigan following a practice session held in Detroit, and perpetrated with a length of lead pipe striking her right knee, resulted in criminal charges being laid against the assailant, and Harding being temporarily suspended by the governing body of her sport.

Dangerous Masculinities/Street Crimes

There is abundant evidence from a number of countries that athletes behaving badly, and even criminally, have been given preferential treatment by sport and legal authorities. Critical questions, almost always surrounding the behaviours of men, have been asked regarding the cultural significance of sport which seems to provide (especially elite and high-profile) male athletes in trouble with sports bodies and the law a certain amount of leniency to what otherwise may be serious charges and repercussions. The sorts of gendered lessons that male athletes learn in sport settings have been highlighted in this respect (Messner and Sabo, 1994), as have the rather compliant reactions of the (again largely male) authorities (Young and Wamsley, 1996; Young, 2004b). Questions have also been raised regarding the apparently disproportionate involvement of professional male athletes in common street crimes (Coakley and Donnelly, 2004), particularly in the United States, where male athletes in conflict with the law is a news item of almost daily frequency. Research on this sub-strand of violence includes examinations of the intersections between sex, violence and sport (Lenskyj, 1990; Messner and Sabo, 1994), studies of male athletes and sexual assault (Benedict and Klein, 1997; Crosset et al., 1995; Melnick, 1992), and accounts of fraternal bonding and rape cultures in sport (Curry, 1991). One of the common threads in this body of research concerns the cultivation in many sports cultures of what pro-feminist scholar Connell (1995) calls 'hegemonic masculinity', where values such as privileging force/aggressivity/physical strength and the ability to dominate others physically intersect with patriarchal and misogynist values also present in those same cultures, culminating often in forms of violence against women. Further, North American sociologists have underlined the link between race, poverty, gender and sport, which also offers a partial explanation for why so many high-level African American (and African Canadian) athletes find themselves in conflict with the law (Coakley and Donnelly, 2004).

Women, Aggression and Violence

While there is no evidence that females have participated in aggressive and violent sports-related behaviours or cultures in anything like the numbers, or to the degree, of their male counterparts – either as athletes or as fans – there is a growing body of literature that unambiguously demonstrates that behaving aggressively in sport settings does resonate with female players (e.g. Cove, 2006; Mennesson, 2000; Rail, 1992; Theberge, 1997; Young, 1997; Young and White, 1995). As opportunities for female athletes have increased in traditional 'male preserves' such as rugby, ice hockey, boxing and martial arts, actions such as playing ultra-aggressively, hitting, being hit, becoming injured and injuring others are assuming an increasingly central place in female sport and sport cultures. Earlier interview-based research with colleague Philip White (Young and White, 1995) on the meanings elicited from involvement in aggressive and high-risk sport led us to reflect on the sport 'spaces' that were increasingly being occupied by female athletes in the following way: 'many such spaces are being occupied by women who … appear to be contributing to a male-defined sports process replete with its violent, macho and health-compromising aspects' (45). While, as with men's sport, this is not an exhaustive or exclusive process, and while there is the possibility that female athletes may be newly defining the meanings of aggressive sport for themselves (Young and White, 1995), the trend towards women's involvement in aggressive and sometimes violent sport behaviours, on and off the pitch, cannot be denied. Nor can their debilitating outcomes. Predictably, as opportunities for women to 'play rough' have grown, so have their experiences with injury. A new research literature on this topic is growing rapidly (e.g. Charlesworth and Young, 2004, 2006; King, 2000; Pike, 2004; Safai, 2004; Theberge, 1997).

Violence Against the Self

It has rarely been viewed as such, but the range of forms of violence that occur in sport clearly involves types of harm perpetrated against the self, especially visible in behaviours such as sports-related eating disorders and chronic drug use, which can reach serious and occasionally life-threatening proportions. For instance, American journalist Joan Ryan (1995) and Canadian social scientist Caroline Davis (1999) have written compellingly on the dangers of anorexia nervosa and bulimia, especially in the so-called 'appearance' sports such as gymnastics and figure skating where so much emphasis is placed (particularly on young females) on weight control, though this may also be problematic for female *and* male competitors in a range of other sports including horse racing (where jockeys must conform to strict weight expectations), boxing, wrestling and synchronised swimming. Conversely, it is equally clear that so many of our most popular sports encourage and even necessitate, in their current format at least, huge body mass and musculature. It comes as no great surprise, then, that sports such as gridiron football, rugby, ice hockey, throwing and sprint events in track and field, and bodybuilding, with their ever-increasing emphasis on size and strength, have had long and persistent problems with anabolic steroids (cf. Courson, 1991; Waddington, 2000; Young, 1993) and other performance-enhancing drugs. Doing unnatural and dangerous things to the body may also be found in a cluster of other sports, such as those requiring excessive endurance, for which the body is not naturally suited (Atkinson, 2005; Young et al., 1994). The link between the expectations of sport and forms of risk and violence done to the self seems clear. As American sociologist Michael Messner (1990) has argued, the injured athlete (including the *self*-injured athlete) represents the ultimate paradox of sport – the use of the body as a weapon against others, or as a vehicle to push back physical and athletic 'frontiers' (Young, 1993: 376), seems almost inevitably to result in violence *against* one's body. Once again, burgeoning literatures on risk, pain and injury in sport, and on health and sport, emphasise this point austerely (cf. Roderick, 2006; Waddington, 2000; Young, 2004a).

Athlete Hazing/Initiation

Hazing – or the required performance by neophyte athletes of often traumatic initiation rituals in the pursuit of a new group identity and induction into a new team setting – is one of the worst kept secrets in all of sport. It has been traced back centuries and located in a number of social institutions, notably education and the military (Bryshun and Young, 1999, 2007). Not all athletes are 'hazed', but many are in many countries, and almost every athlete knows another who has been. In North American, British or Australian sport, for instance, initiation is simply part of the language of sport, though its often abusive and deviant elements, and a growing trend towards policing and anti-hazing policy, such as on school and college and campuses, has changed its articulation somewhat as well as consolidated codes of silence around the practice. There is clear evidence on both sides of the Atlantic that neophyte athletes are sometimes coerced into embarrassing, degrading and often high-risk initiation practices (Bryshun and Young, 1999, 2007; Johnson and Holman, 2004; King, 2000; see case study Box 8.2), and there is increasing concern with the complicity of coaches, administrators, parents and social institutions in allowing hazing to take place. The research on hazing is growing slowly but, at this time, relatively little is work has actually been produced. With the frequency of troubling episodes reported in the popular media, with concern over matters such as the hazing of child athletes, and with questions of institutional complicity being raised more and more, it is likely that hazing research will continue to expand.

Box 8.2   Hazing in Canadian sport

Sports-related hazing has probably been as systematically researched in Canada as in any other country, and one obvious reason for this is 'need'. A host of Canadian sports have been affected over the years, and Bryshun and Young (1999, 2007) have reported in-depth cases from numerous sports, many of which have received widespread attention in the media. From the sport of ice hockey, they cite the following cases:

- In 1994, four members of a male hockey team in Chatham, Ontario, reported that they were forced to masturbate publicly. Thirteen people were charged with over 100 sexual offences in the case.
- In 1996, three University of Guelph students were cut from the men's Gryphons hockey team for refusing to participate in an initiation party in the team dressing room. The event allegedly involved drinking volumes of alcohol through funnels and games that included nude players eating faeces-contaminated marshmallows (*Fifth Estate*, 29 October 1997; *Toronto Sun*, 28 February 1996: 5).
- In 2005, the coach of the Windsor Spitfires of the Ontario Hockey League (OHL) was suspended for 40 games and his team was fined $35,000 (the league maximum) following a hazing incident held on a team bus during which rookie players were stripped and crowded into the bathroom for up to 10 minutes at a time.

Harassment, Stalking and Threat

There is also compelling evidence to suggest that sport is replete with a range of unwelcome conventions and behaviours that represent, at best, a 'chilly climate' for many participants and, at worst, a locus of exploitation and abuse for others (Kirby et al., 2000). These behaviours range from persons in positions of authority and power (often but not always men), taking advantage of young, impressionable athletes (often but not always females), to 'superstar' athletes being hounded and/or threatened by fans obsessed with obtaining their attention. Canadian sociologist Peter Donnelly has examined the causes, manifestations and outcomes of harassment (1999, 2007) and summarises a number of well-known cases, but sociologists have in general been very slow in acknowledging the need for research on forms of stalking and threat – despite their known existence. For instance, widespread cases of stalking and threat throughout the world of sport have spawned a thriving muscle-for-hire security industry for both male and female athletes (*USA Today*, 14 July 1995: 3C). Among a long list of recognised male and female athletes from a range of sports who report being stalked, harassed or threatened is figure skater Katarina Witt. In 1992, an obsessed fan was charged on seven counts of sending obscene and threatening mail, and was sentenced to three years in a US psychiatric centre. In the case it was revealed that Harry Veltman II had, among other things, followed Witt around the world attempting to distract her as she skated in competition (*USA Today*, 14 July 1995: 3C). More recently, a belligerent fan following golf star Tiger Woods at a 1999 Professional Golf Association (PGA) event was found by security personnel to have a loaded semi-automatic hand-gun in his waist pack (Bonk, 1999). Threats against, and excessive intrusions into, the lives of professional athletes, coaches, administrators and other officials are far from uncommon.

Sexual Assault Against Adults and Children

The extent to which athletes and other sports personnel are involved in forms of sexual assault against adults and children is not known precisely but, again, that behaviours such as assault, sexual assault, rape and gang rape occur in the world of sport and have become highly publicised cannot be denied. Some research is available (Benedict and Klein, 1997; Benedict and Yaeger, 1998; Crosset et al., 1995; Curry, 1991) but, while researchers have, on the whole, been appropriately cautious with respect to matters such as root causes and generalisability, it is very difficult to assess whether the involvement of male athletes in cases of, for instance, sexual assault is similar or disproportional to the general popula-tion (cf. Coakley and Donnelly, 2004). Most researchers agree, however, that sexual assault by athletes is bound up with wider social structures of gender and power and, in particular, with the acting out of codes of hegemonic masculinity and sexism – which, again, are far from rare in the often hyper-'masculinist' setting of sport (Curry, 1991; Messner and Sabo, 1994; Young, 1993).

Where sexual assault against children is concerned, Canadian sport has been in the news of late. Specifically, there have been scandals throughout many levels of Canadian ice hockey regarding the sexual abuse of young boys, some of whom, now as adults, are beginning to 'go public' with their histories of victimisation. For example, in early 1997, the world of Canadian ice hockey was stunned by claims made by National Hockey League (NHL) player Sheldon Kennedy that his junior coach had sexually abused him on over 300 occasions. After a short trial, in which the complicity of others, including some high-profile names within the hockey community, was revealed or implied, hockey coach Graham James was sentenced to three years in jail.

Partner Abuse

Since publicised cases of female athletes assaulting their partners or being involved in rape, gang rape or other such crimes of violence are extremely rare, and since most offending athletes appear in most of the evidence that we have available to be men, the values and behaviours reported in cells 5 and 10 intersect with the issue in focus here. The involvement of many male athletes in partner abuse, or what *Sports Illustrated* provocatively termed 'sport's dirty little secret' (31 July 1995: 62), is highly controversial because no one really knows, to cite the oldest of criminological quandaries, whether the information we receive through such means as media coverage is an outcome of actual incidence or of reporting and perception. Certainly, just a glance at British or North American newspapers is sufficient to suggest a problem with partner abuse among male athletes, and the list of known athletes in trouble with the law for assaulting their female partners is again depressingly long, but media reportage is hardly scientific fact and far more work is needed. Some of the most in-depth and challenging work conducted on this topic may again be found in the US-based studies of Messner and Sabo (1994), Crosset (1999) and Benedict and Yaeger (1998), all of which suggest that the problem with male athletes and partner abuse is real. However, as Crosset notes, it is important that caution is exercised in making comparisons with other social groups, or with the general population, until such time as far more reliable information on the nature and extent of athlete-related partner abuse becomes available.

Offences by Coaches/Administrators

Coaches and persons holding administrative responsibilities in sport occupy important and trusted positions in the lives of athletes, especially child athletes. In the same way that they may positively shape a player's athletic experience, so, too, may the responsibility entrusted in the coach be taken advantage of, often in the context of an athlete–coach power relationship, much of which is acted out in private (such as the Graham James case cited above). Coaches are also central in the legitimation of aggression and the teaching of violent practices. From a social learning point of view, they represent one principal means of learning how to 'do' violence, and how to rationalise it. In the same way, coaches learn from and imitate other coaches, many of whom have achieved fame and respect through their reputations for aggression. Anyone familiar with high-level and professional sport knows that the world of sport is replete with examples of players being verbally assaulted by angry, tyrannical or otherwise hostile coaches. But this is just one dimension of coaching abuse. Perhaps more important and far more common are the lessons regarding how to 'do' violence to rival opponents that players glean from coaches and coaching staff. For instance, through codes of learning and positive reinforcement, ice hockey 'enforcers' not only learn how to ply their trade; they are also rewarded financially, subculturally/reputationally and occupationally for their particular brand of violence, and some of the most revered coaches in North American history have become revered precisely because of their commitment to a belligerent style of play and applying a 'winning at all costs' ethos (Gillett et al., 1996; Young, 1993). In these ways, the pro-violent norms, conventions and rhythms of sport are reproduced over time.

Where the law is concerned, a changing socio-legal climate has relatively recently begun to affect the legal implications of player violence for the coach/team/league, and now, more than ever before, coaches may be held 'vicariously liable' for the conduct of their players. In a number of locations (cf. 1993, 2002b, 2004b), Young underlines the expanding role of the courts in player violence.

Parental Abuse

Oddly, there are numerous disturbing practices which occur in the world of sport that even casual observers know something about and regular participants know all too well, but on which there is very little research. Parental abuse is one such topic. From an informal glance at the North American media, and using anecdotal 'evidence', many sports have been affected, and there have been numerous cases of violence in the form of harassment of coaches (both verbal and physical), fighting among parents, the encouragement of aggressive behaviour in child athletes by parents (i.e. shouting, abusing, rewarding rough or injurious play, etc.) and even, in extreme cases, homicidal behaviour by parents. For instance, in 2005, a 47-year-old Toronto man was criminally charged after choking the coach of his 9-year-old son's minor ice hockey team and was banned from attending arenas for 5 years, the harshest penalty ever levied by the Greater Toronto Hockey League (http://www.ctv.ca/servlet/ArticleNews/story/CTVNews/1106308011832_81/?hub=Top Stories). Three years earlier, in the United States, a Massachusetts judge sentenced Thomas Junta to 6–10 years in state prison for the fatal beating of another father, Michael Costin, 40, after a youth hockey practice in which the sons of both men participated (http://archives.cnn.com/2002/LAW/01/25/hockey.death.verdict/index.html). The latter cases are, to this point, statistically rare, but they may be understood as extensions of parent behaviours which regularly accompany many sports at many levels in many countries. So concerned have Canadian authorities become of late that the government has introduced several initiatives, such as the 'Relax! It's Just a Game' television campaign released in 2003, to combat the disorderly and sometimes violent actions of parents attending minor league hockey games. Indeed, many sports have found the introduction of such 'fair play' initiatives necessary in the face of what appears, observationally at least, to be an enduring problem with sports-based 'parent-rage'.

'Blood' and Animal Sports

Considerable attention has been paid to brutal contact and combat sports involving humans, and to sport involving animals and/or which routinely culminate in blood or even death, but relatively little of this has been proffered by sociologists. Perhaps the best known scholarly research on animal sports was offered by the anthropologist Clifford

Geertz (1972) whose study of the cultural meanings of Balinese cockfighting is well known and widely cited, as is Eric Dunning's figurational work on the social class origins of fox hunting in the UK (Dunning, 1999; Elias and Dunning, 1986). Information in varying degrees of detail is also available on a range of activities including bull fighting, dog fighting and bear baiting, as well as on human-based events such as boxing, martial arts, street fighting, backyard fighting, 'ultimate' fighting, and the development of underground 'fight clubs' – practices which appear to have grown in popularity of late, despite their often extremely injurious consequences.

The focus of such studies revolves around what sociologist Erving Goffman (1959) would call the 'front' and 'back' regions of these activities. Examples of the 'front' regions might include the graphically bloody way that a boxer is punched into submission, a fox or a hare is torn to pieces by converging hounds, or the torture imposed upon a bull by repeated bull ring 'workers', culminating, almost always, in its public death. On the other hand, the 'back regions' of such blood and animal sports would include practices related to such things as the preparation of the event or the manner in which the participants are treated. Here, the focus shifts to the lesser known, and often hidden, dimensions of these sports, such as the often debilitating and sometimes deadly injuries sustained by boxers, the ways in which a bull is 'prepared' for death (for instance, by being antagonised behind the scenes or by having petroleum jelly rubbed in its eyes), whether a racing horse sustains injuries that necessitate its euthanisation, or the ways in which racing dogs are sometimes kept, housed and/or discarded under the most cruel of circumstances (Atkinson and Young, 2005a; see case study Box 8.3). Again, notwithstanding differences in the cultural meanings and significance of these sorts of 'sports', the common thread in this body of work concerns what should and should not be considered as 'appropriate' brutality and violence in the lives of these human and animal participants – both at and away from the arena of participation.

Box 8.3   Violence against greyhounds

From 'overuse' and the intensity of the races themselves, pain and injury inevitably occur. Like human athletes, some greyhounds live through pain on a daily basis ... broken bones, torn ligaments or muscles, back and neck injuries, lacerations, and facial abrasions caused by muzzling are common ... As part of their daily training maintenance, greyhounds require a substantial amount of food. Rather than feeding the dogs a high calibre diet, some 'low budget' tracks utilize what has been termed '4-D' (dead, dying, downed, diseased) meat to temporarily sustain the greyhounds' athletic bodies. This meat is often rife with E-coli toxins and may not be sold commercially according to USDA

(Cont'd)

standards. It is illegally purchased for pennies per pound, and its consumption may lead to a skin condition in the dogs referred to disconcertingly by handlers as 'Alabama rot' (open lesions and ulcers) or an intestinal problem referred to as 'blow-out' (chronic vomiting and diarrhea leading to death from dehydration) … The housing of greyhounds at some racetracks often reflects a cost-cutting low overhead mentality, and further objectifies the dogs in order to justify brutally inhumane care methods. A greyhound track, at any given time, may house up to 1,000 dogs through a series of kennels. A kennel operator is in charge of all dogs in a specific kennel (anywhere from 10–100 plus dogs). The dogs are often kept in rows of stacked cages (sometimes, a cage may be only 24 inches [60 cm] in width), being housed and muzzled up to 22 hours per day … Without opportunity to adequately socialize, the dogs are literally 'left alone together'. They are 'turned out' several (1–4) times per day to urinate/defecate, and usually once to eat and receive water. Due to the stacking approach to kennelling, the wire mesh nature of the kennels, and lack of proper flooring in each, greyhounds at the bottom rows are showered with the waste of others. At some of the more disreputable tracks, music is blasted in the kennels to drown out the perpetual barking or whining of the dogs. (Excerpted from Atkinson and Young, 2005a)

Political Violence and Terrorism

This cell embodies aspects of violence threatened or perpetrated at sports events in the pursuit of political or ideological goals. Even before the September 11 attacks on the United States in 2001 (including the destruction of the 'twin towers' of New York's World Trade Center), preparations for international sports events such as the FIFA World Cup, the Commonwealth Games and the Olympic Games had long involved the international exchange of policing and security information on possible problems and probable offenders. But it is unlikely that any sport event has been plagued for as long with international political tensions as the Olympics. Atkinson and Young (2003, 2005b) provide a detailed summary of such tensions, such as those occurring at: the 1908 Summer Games in London, where tensions bubbled between English Protestants and Irish Catholics; the 1936 or so-called 'Nazi Games', held in Berlin, and used by Hitler to showcase German military might to the world; the 1968 Mexico City Games, remembered more for the 'Black Power' salute of two African American sprinters than for the deaths of hundreds of young protesters at the hands of a government seeking to quell student protests; the 1972 Munich Games, where members of the Palestinian 'Black September' group killed 11 members of the Israeli team; the 'Cold War' Games in Moscow and Los Angeles in 1980 and 1984 remembered for their boycotts; and the Atlanta Games in 1996 where a pipe bomb exploded and killed 2 people and injured over 100 others. The sharing of international criminal intelligence in advance of large-scale sports events is clearly not new, but since the events of '9/11', security preparations guarding against the threat of political violence and terrorism have been significantly stepped up, and the mere suggestion that a host city may be politically or militarily vulnerable to an attack is now enough to squash a bid. Consequently, many of the larger sports events, of which the Olympics is but one instance, now take on more of the appearance of an armed military camp (replete with fighter jets, armed guards, machine guns, razor wire, electronic scanners and the like) than a festive public spectacle.

Racism

Available research shows that racism – or the expression of systems of racially motivated intolerance and xenophobia – and violence intersect in the world of sport in a number of disturbing ways. These include, but are not restricted to: fans of soccer teams, sometimes associated with far-right political parties, using racist chants, songs and threats against players of colour in a number of countries (e.g. black English players such as Sol Campbell and Emile Heskey claim to have frequently been harassed both at home and abroad over the years, and Celtic midfielder Neil Lennon has reported being the victim of sectarian attacks); hooligan fan groups, again sometimes linked with organised right-wing politics, abusing immigrants and ethnic minorities in the context of soccer (see e.g. Murphy et al., 1990); television commentators offering stereotypical and jingoistic assessments of national 'character' in the context of game reporting (such as the case of the notorious Canadian ice hockey personality Don Cherry, who makes no effort to disguise his derogatory views on Swedes and Russians discussed in Gillett et al., 1996); and media personnel making flagrantly racist claims and slurs during sports events (e.g. in North American sports television, this has over the years led to the instant removal of numerous high-profile commentators such as CBS reporter Jimmy 'The Greek' Snyder, fired after publicly stating that African Americans were naturally superior athletes because they had been bred to produce stronger offspring during slavery: 'During the slave period, the slave owner would breed his big black with his big woman so that he would have a big black kid–that's where it all started' (http://en.wikipedia.org/wiki/Jimmy_Snyder). In response to sports-related racism, many groups have 'fought back', as may be witnessed in the work of associations such as 'Foxes Against Racism' at Leicester City Football Club in England (http://www.le.ac.uk/far/), and in the attempts by FIFA to emblazon the centre of 2006 World Cup soccer pitches on match days with huge banners appealing to the public to 'Say No to Racism'.

Crimes Against Workers and the Public

Crimes against workers and the public include harmful (physical and sexual) forms of human rights violations of often under-age workers in sports-related 'sweatshop' industries of the poorer nations of the world, such as Malaysia and Indonesia. Recently, there has been a growth in international campaigns against the use of exploitative labour in developing countries where sports merchandise, such as running shoes, is produced for very little by workers who are often very young, very poor, underpaid, and working in atrocious labour conditions. Worse, and as Donnelly (2003, 2007) indicates, such workers may suffer further forms of abuse at the hands of their more powerful bosses, whom they may fear. A modest but growing body of research has been produced on the ways in which the production of sport, and sport paraphernalia, interfaces with the violation of human justices for workers and the public (cf. Sage, 1999; see also Kidd and Donnelly, 2000). Notable also are human rights movements which have sprung up in opposition to these sorts of 'violences' and abuses, such as the US student-led anti-Nike movement (Eitzen and Sage, 2003: 201).

Crimes Against the Environment

Long-standing public concerns that sports events and venues may have negative ecological and environmental effects have recently prompted some research in the sociology of sport. For example, Lenskyj (2000) has investigated the negative impact on the environment of hosting large-scale sports events, such as the Olympic Games, that require the development of huge areas of land and that may produce 'degraded environments' (155) and even threaten animal and wildlife extinction. Similarly, critics have decried the development of golf courses in untouched and pristine wilderness where wildlife and natural habitat may be damaged or lost altogether. Social and political opposition to sport venue development is such that proposed plans for even medium-sized sports facilities (such as golf courses), and certainly so-called 'mega' sports events (such as the Olympic Games), now require compelling evidence that construction will not unduly compromise, or do violence to, the environment. For instance, careful environmental statements have now become a staple of all successful Olympic bids.

THINKING SOCIOLOGICALLY ABOUT FORMATIONS OF SRV

Not all of the practices encapsulated in this matrix of cells are normally thought of as 'sports violence', but they are all clearly intentionally abusive or potentially harmful acts that cannot easily be separated from the sports process and that only begin to make sense when the social significance of sport is closely examined. That is to say, they all fall within the jurisdiction of the definition of SRV offered at the outset of this chapter. On a scale of social legitimacy, and echoing Smith's (1983: 9) earlier typology, some of the cells represent behaviours which are *relatively* legitimate and, while considered 'deviant' in the eyes of some observers, occur frequently and may be widely acknowledged and accepted within the world and culture of sport. However, other cells represent behaviours that are entirely less acceptable on a number of levels, including the official rules of a given sport, the informal norms and values of players, the general public, as well as the law of the land. Needless to say, in both cases, what is considered as 'legitimate' and 'illegitimate' depends on who is doing the defining, and it is on this exact matter (i.e. the matter of how we understand violence in sport and what we propose to do about it) that people and groups disagree, and where violence in sport intersects with questions of culture, power and ideology (Coakley and Donnelly, 2004; Donnelly and Young, 2004).

All of the cells demonstrate dynamism: that is to say, they have not remained static over time, and many have significantly changed in their form. For instance, as most British researchers have acknowledged, soccer hooliganism has become far more organised and 'global' over the past two decades, and its local and domestic manifestations also changed considerably in concert with widely implemented policing modifications in the 1970s and 1980s. Specifically, at this time, one unintended effect of increases in policing mechanisms *inside* soccer stadiums was to displace the problem to *outside* stadiums and also to affect the timing of hooligan encounters (Dunning et al., 1988; Murphy et al., 1990). In this way, it is important to note the *changing and processual* nature of SRV. Some behaviours are deeply grounded in culture, tradition and ritual and, while faced with organised opposition, show no signs of disappearing any time soon. Boxing, bull fighting, dog racing, ice hockey and golf are all sports which have been forced to counter resistance to their 'violent' outcomes – whether injured 'parties' be human, animal or environmental. Fox hunting in the UK represents an exceptional recent case as a blood sport which has been both prohibited at the level of government and marginalised at the level of cultural meaning and acceptability, though such is the strength of its place in British society that it currently endures, despite an outright ban. Further, other types of SRV, though hardly new, have taken on entirely more sinister trappings in a changed and changing global community, as Atkinson and Young demonstrate in their study of political violence and terrorism at the Olympic Games (2005b). In this particular case, the threat of political violence has now significantly changed the way that sport is played, funded, policed and insured. Again, the ripple effects on what a 'secure' Olympic Games both costs and 'looks like' are enormous.

Each of the cells has received a certain amount of scholarly attention, though some (soccer hooliganism and fist fighting in ice hockey in particular) have been far more comprehensively studied than others, and some have been curiously under-studied (e.g. cruelty in animal and 'blood' sports, and environmental offences and political violence related to sport). Taken individually, the cells have certainly been approached as forms of aggression, violence or abuse that may threaten, hurt or victimise, but scholars have fallen short of interpreting them as dimensions of 'sports violence' per se. Very little is known about the links that they may share. In this sense, a sociological assessment is important because it both acknowledges differences and underscores common threads and overlaps.

A number of points can be made in this regard. First, and perhaps most importantly, the cells demonstrate one critical feature in common: they all unite violent practices *through* sport – that is to say, *sport* (rather than, for instance, other social institutions such as the workplace, the family, the church, or education, etc.) is the context and locus of these activities. In order to both understand SRV phenomena and to react responsibly to them, acknowledging that they are centrally connected to the sports process is very important. Second, all of the cells represent the attempt by one group or individual to exert control over others. In this respect, all dimensions of SRV may be understood in terms of themes of power, dominance and control, or what Donnelly and Young (borrowing from sociologist David Garland) call 'cultures of control' (2004). Third, in terms of who 'does' the behaviour, who supports and funds the behaviour, and who consumes and watches it, most, if not all, of the cells display strongly gendered underpinnings. Unsurprisingly, given the male preserve that sport has traditionally represented, men and masculinity feature centrally, and rarely flatteringly. It may be, for instance, that cell 5 is not a specific case at all, but rather a condition prevalent in many of the cells. Critics might argue that, since all violence is done by men and women, cells 5 and 6 should be collapsed into the other cells. However, this approach recognises neither the fact that most violence is done by men, nor the variance in forms and brands of 'masculinity' itself that express themselves in such varied ways in the matrix. Nor does it adequately capture the role of gender in certain articulations of SRV which deserve far closer inspection and justify cells 5 and 6 as 'standalone' entities. However, cell 6 also demonstrates the uses of aggression and violence by females in sport, which the research strongly suggests is increasing as opportunities for female involvement in sport have opened up. This raises important questions as to whether aggressive and violent conduct is best understood as part of socialisation into gendered roles and identities in sport, or socialisation into sport per se.

Crucially, it is when one delves into the question of such commonalities and interconnections between the various dimensions of SRV that its sociological underpinnings become clear. While genes and impulses and individualised pathologies likely play some role in violence in sport, the fundamentally sociological underpinnings of SRV are evident.

Importantly, the cells are meant to be understood as interactive rather than exclusive or isolated components of SRV. Indeed, around particular behaviours, and in certain cases, many of them coalesce and overlap. For instance, and using real cases of SRV as examples:

- a college hazing incident involving male wrestlers in acts of sexual or physical abuse in a public bar links cells 5 ('Dangerous masculinities/street crimes'), 8 ('Athlete hazing/initiation'), 10 ('Sexual assault against adults and children'), 17 ('Crimes against workers and the public') and, since coaches may be complicit in the act, possibly cell 12 ('Offences by coaches/administrators');

- a female fan stalking a male star athlete connects cells 6 ('Women, aggression and violence') and 9 ('Harassment, stalking and threat');
- a young female gymnast starving herself due to repeated criticism for being 'too fat', and eventually dying from anorexia, links cells 7 ('Violence against the self'), 12 ('Offences by coaches/administrators') and 13 ('Parental abuse').

Further, each individual cell should be examined for its sociological underpinnings, and its association with factors such as age, gender, social class, regionality, race and ethnicity, on its own accord, as well as for the links it may share with other cells along these axes. For instance, soccer hooliganism and fox hunting clearly demonstrate strong social class attachments and, once again, gender is a common thread throughout most, if not all, of the cells in the matrix.

CONCLUSION

Whether one prefers to adhere to traditional lines of thinking and conceive of 'sports violence' primarily in terms of crowd violence and player violence, or to accept the wider notion of SRV, it is clear that violence in sport assumes a variety of forms and expressions. Emphasising the latter line of thinking, this chapter has attempted to expand the way that we think about violence *related to* sport. The matrix of cells representing varied formations of SRV offers one way that we might usefully broaden our understanding of behaviours that threaten, harm and victimise *in and through* sport.

Arguably, this sort of approach to a more inclusive notion of SRV is needed because, far from existing in a vacuum, violent practices related to sport grow out of, and exist relationally with, other aspects of the social process, such as relations of power, as well as social stratifiers such as social class, ethnicity and gender. In this respect, this SRV approach contains a number of potential strengths. It provides, for example, a useful tool and a fresh lens through which we may consider the subject matter in a broader social and sociological light, and a model in which the dynamic connections between SRV and other social issues can be identified and analysed. Additionally, rather than seeing the formations of SRV as mutually exclusive, the cells can be used in conjunction with one another to account for the genesis, manifestation and ramification of sport cultures in many settings.

The vast majority of existing sociological studies of SRV is limited to the behaviour of fans and players in quite specific contexts. Of course, this is both understandable and useful. However, if the sociological and, indeed, social purpose of sports violence research is to understand better not only direct acts of physical violence that may result in personal injury, but also harmful acts perpetrated in the context of sport that threaten or produce injury or in some other way compromise human justice and civil liberty, then perhaps we need to widen the focus of what we consider 'violence' and to change the type of sociological lens we are using?

Arguably, with very few exceptions (cf. Dunning, 1999), conventional approaches to sports violence have produced sociologically and socially isolated snapshots of violence. The empirical moments they represent are, of course, important enough. We need them, and they provide the crucial 'lived experiences' that empirically minded sociologists and anthropologists cherish. But what matters most is that these snapshots are placed in the context of broader *formations* of sports-related and social violence; what matters most is the tracing, in Elias's terms (in Rojek, 1985: 159), of the interdependencies among the many and varied individuals and groups involved.

An excellent empirical example of Elias's suggestion comes from someone with no scholarly interest in sport at all. Writing on formations of political violence in Northern Ireland, Feldman (1991: 1) talks about the importance of seeing violent practices as 'relational sequences of action'. What Feldman means by this is that ostensibly unrelated practices are likely deeply connected and interlaced, and that it is important to uncover these links to truly understand patterns and trends, as well as to enable predictions about future violent phenomena to be made (which may be of practical benefit to policy makers and the authorities). Whether the focus is on practitioners of political terror or acts and actors of SRV, the important sociological point is surely to trace back the behaviour under investigation to the communities that forge it in the first place, and to look for parallels in other, apparently disparate, social behaviours and settings. To do this with respect to violence in sport, we need to consider the landscape of the phenomenon in its *widest* and *fullest* form.

CHAPTER SUMMARY

» While considerable attention has been paid to violence in sport, much of the research has been limited to fairly restrictive notions of crowd and player violence.
» Sports-related violence (SRV) may be defined as: (a) direct acts of physical violence contained within or outside the rules of the game that result in injury to persons, animals or property, and (b) harmful or potentially harmful acts conducted in the context of sport that threaten or produce injury or that violate human justices and civil liberties.
» It is possible to conceive of SRV in terms of a matrix of 18 cells, each representing a different manifestation of the phenomenon.
» Rather than isolated 'standalone' categories, the cells are meant to be understood as interactive and relational in their social construction, manifestation, meaning and outcome.
» Forms of social stratification – social class, gender, age, regionality, race and ethnicity – may be visible in each of the SRV cells.

FURTHER READING

Dunning (1999) offers a comprehensive and deeply sociological interpretation of the place of violence in sport in numerous contexts, specifically the United States and the UK. Messner and Sabo (1994) cover a range of challenging issues relating to sport, sexuality and power in provocative ways. Young's (2004a) edited volume examines the historical and contemporary place of risk, injury, physicality and aggression in sport.

REFERENCES

Archetti, E.P. and Romero, A.C. (1994) 'Death and violence in Argentinian football', in R.Giulianotti, N. Bonney and M. Hepworth (eds), *Football Violence and Social Identity*. London: Routledge, pp. 37–73.

Armstrong, G. (1998) *Football Hooligans: Knowing the Score*. Oxford: Berg.

Atkinson, M. (2005) 'You are what you eat: sports supplementation in endurance athlete figurations', Paper presented at North American Society for the Sociology of Sport, Winston-Salem, NC, 27 October.

Atkinson, M. and Young, K. (2003) 'Terror games: media treatment of security issues at the 2002 Winter Olympic Games', *OLYMPIKA: The International Journal of Olympic Studies*, XI: 53–78.

Atkinson, M. and Young, K. (2005a) 'Reservoir dogs: greyhound racing, mimesis and sports-related violence', *International Review for the Sociology of Sport*, 40 (3): 335–56.

Atkinson, M. and Young, K. (2005b) 'Political violence, terrorism and security at the Olympic Games', in K. Young and K. Wamsley (eds), *Global Olympics: Historical and Sociological Studies of the Modern Games*. Oxford: Elsevier, pp. 269–74.

Bairner, A. (1995) 'Soccer, masculinity and violence in Northern Ireland', Paper presented at the North American Society for the Sociology of Sport, Sacramento, CA, 1–4 November.

Ball-Rokeach, S. (1971) 'The legitimation of violence', in J.F. Short and M.E. Wolfgang (eds), *Collective Violence*. Chicago: Aldine, pp. 100–111.

Benedict, J. and Klein, A. (1997) 'Arrest and conviction rates for athletes accused of sexual assault', *Sociology of Sport Journal*, 14: 86–95.

Benedict, J. and Yaeger, D. (1998) *Pros and Cons: The Criminals who Play in the NFL*. New York: Warner Books.

Bonk, T. (1999) 'A new hazard: fans', *Calgary Herald*, 2 February: C1.

Bryshun, J. and Young, K. (1999) 'Sport-related hazing: an inquiry into male and female involvement', in P. White and K. Young (eds), *Sport and Gender in Canada*. Don Mills, Ontario: Oxford University Press, pp. 269–93.

Bryshun, J. and Young, K. (2007) 'Hazing as a form of sport and gender socialization', in K. Young and P. White (eds), *Sport and Gender in Canada*. 2nd edn. Don Mills, Ontario: Oxford University Press, pp. 302–27.

Bryson, L. (1987) 'Sport and the maintenance of masculine hegemony', *Women's Studies International Forum*, 10: 349–60.

Charlesworth, H. and Young, K. (2004) 'Why female university athletes play with pain: motivations and rationalisations', in K. Young (ed.), *Sporting Bodies, Damaged Selves: Sociological Studies of Sports-Related Injury*. Oxford: Elsevier, pp. 163–80.

Charlesworth, H. and Young, K. (2006) 'Injured female athletes: experiential accounts from England and Canada', in S. Loland, B. Skirstad and I. Waddington (eds), *Pain and Injury in Sport: Social and Ethical Analysis*. London: Routledge, pp. 89–106.

Clarke, J. (1978) 'Football and working class fans: tradition and change', in R. Ingham (ed.), *Football Hooliganism: The Wider Context*. London: Inter-Action Imprint.

Coakley, Jay J. (1989) 'Media coverage of sports and violent behavior: an elusive connection', *Current Psychology: Research and Reviews*, 7 (4): 322–30.

Coakley, J. and Donnelly, P. (2004) *Sports in Society: Issues and Controversies*. Toronto: McGraw-Hill Ryerson.

Connell, R. (1995) *Masculinities*. Berkeley, CA: University of California Press.

Courson, S. (1991) *False Glory*. Stamford, CT: Longmeadow.

Cove, L. (2006) 'Negotiating the ring: reconciling gender in women's boxing', Unpublished MA thesis, Department of Sociology, University of Calgary.

Crosset, T., Benedict, J. and MacDonald, M. (1995) 'Male student-athletes reported for sexual assault: survey of campus police departments and judicial affairs', *Journal of Sport and Social Issues*, 19: 126–40.

Crossett, T. (1999) 'Male Athletes' Violence Against Women: A Critical Assessment of the Athletic Affiliations, Violence Against Women Debate', *Quest*, 51: 224–57.

Curry, T. (1991) 'Fraternal bonding in the locker room: a feminist analysis of talk about competition and women', *Sociology of Sport Journal*, 8: 119–35.

Davis, C. (1999) 'Eating disorders, physical activity, and sport: biological, psychological, and sociological factors', in P. White and K. Young (eds), *Sport and Gender in Canada*. Don Mills, Ontario: Oxford University Press, pp. 85–107.

Donnelly, P (1999) 'Who's fair game? Sport, sexual harassment and abuse', in P. White and K. Young (eds), *Sport and Gender in Canada*. Don Mills, Ontario: Oxford University Press, pp. 107–29.

Donnelly, P. (2003) 'Marching out of step: sport, social order, and the case of child labour', Keynote Address, Second World Congress of the Sociology of Sport, Cologne, Germany, 18–21 June.

Donnelly, P. (2007) 'Who's fair game? Sport, sexual harassment and abuse', in K. Young and P. White (eds), *Sport and Gender in Canada*. 2nd edn. Don Mills, Ontario: Oxford University Press, pp. 279–301.

Donnelly, P. and Young, K. (2004) ' "Sports-related violence" as an outcome of cultures of control in sport', paper presented at the Pre-Olympic Scientific Congress, Thessaloniki, Greece, 6–10 August.

Dunning, E. (1999) *Sport Matters: Sociological Studies of Sport, Violence and Civilization.* London: Routledge.

Dunning, E., Murphy, P. and Williams, J. (1988) *The Roots of Football Hooliganism: An Historical and Sociological Study.* London: Routledge & Kegan Paul.

Dunning, E., Murphy, P., Waddington, I. and Astrinakis, A. (eds) (2002) *Fighting Fans: Football Hooliganism as a World Social Phenomenon.* Dublin: University College Dublin Press.

Eitzen, S. and Sage, G. (2003) *Sociology of North American Sport.* London: McGraw-Hill.

Elias, N. and Dunning, E. (1986) *Quest for Excitement: Sport and Leisure and the Civilizing Process.* New York: Basil Blackwell.

Feldman, A. (1991) *Formations of Violence: The Narrative of the Body and Political Terror in Northern Ireland.* London: University of Chicago Press.

Gardiner, S., Felix, A., James, M., Welch, R. and O'Leary, J. (1998) *Sports Law.* London: Cavendish.

Geertz, C. (1972) 'Deep play: notes on Balinese cockfight', in C. Geertz (ed.), *Interpretation of Cultures.* New York: Basic Books, pp. 412–53.

Gillett, J., White, P. and Young, K. (1996) 'The Prime Minister of Saturday night: Don Cherry, the CBC, and the cultural production of intolerance', in H. Holmes and D. Taras (eds), *Seeing Ourselves in Canada: Media Power and Policy.* 2nd edn. Toronto: Harcourt Brace & Company Canada, pp. 59–72.

Giulianotti, R. (1994) 'Taking liberties: Hibs casuals and Scottish law', in R. Giulianotti, N. Bonney and M. Hepworth (eds), *Football, Violence and Social Identity.* London: Routledge, pp. 229–62.

Goffman, E. (1959) *The Presentation of Self in Everyday Life.* Garden City: Doubleday-Anchor.

Guttmann, A. (1986) *Sports Spectators.* New York: Columbia University Press.

Horrow, R. (1980) *Sports Violence: The Interaction between Private Lawmaking and the Criminal Law.* Arlington, VA: Carrollton Press.

Johnson, J. and Holman, M. (eds) (2004) *Making the Team: Inside the World of Sport Initiations and Hazing.* Toronto: Canadian Scholars Press.

Kidd, B. and Donnelly, P. (2000) 'Human rights in sports', *International Review for the Sociology of Sport*, 35: 131–48.

King, C. (2000) 'Trial by fire: a study of initiation practices in English sport', Unpublished MSc thesis, School of Sport and Exercise Sciences, Loughborough University.

Kirby, S., Greaves, L. and Hankivsky, O. (2000) *The Dome of Silence: Sexual Harassment and Abuse in Sport.* Halifax, Nova Scotia: Fernwood Publishing.

Lenskyj, H. (1990) 'Power and play: gender and sexuality issues in sport and physical activity', *International Review for the Sociology of Sport*, 25: 235–46.

Lenskyj, H. (2000) *Inside the Olympic Industry: Power, Politics and Activism*. New York: SUNY Press.

Leonard, W. (1998) *A Sociological Perspective of Sport*. 5th edn. Boston: Allyn and Bacon.

Lever, J. (1983) *Soccer Madness*. Chicago: University of Chicago Press.

Lewis, J.M. (1982) 'Fan violence: an American social problem', *Research in Social Problems and Public Policy*, 12, 175–206.

Marsh, P., Rosser, E. and Harre, R. (1978) *The Rules of Disorder*. London: Routledge & Kegan Paul.

McPherson, B., Curtis, J. and Loy, J. (eds) (1989) *The Social Significance of Sport: An Introduction to the Sociology of Sport*. Champaign, IL: Human Kinetics.

Melnick, M. (1992) 'Male athletes and sexual assault', *Journal of Physical Education, Recreation and Dance*, May/June: 32–5.

Mennesson, C. (2000) '"Hard" women and "soft" women: the social construction of identities among female boxers', *International Review for the Sociology of Sport*, 35 (1): 21–35.

Messner, M. (1990) 'When bodies are weapons: masculinity and violence in sport', *International Review for the Sociology of Sport*, 25: 203–21.

Messner, M. and Sabo, D. (1994) *Sex, Violence, and Power in Sports: Rethinking Masculinity*. Freedom, CA: The Crossing Press.

Murphy, P., Williams, J. and Dunning, E. (1990) *Football on Trial: Spectator Violence and Development in the Football World*. London: Routledge.

Murray, B. (1984) *The Old Firm: Sectarianism, Sport and Society in Scotland*. Edinburgh: John Donald.

Pike, E.C.J. (2004) 'Risk, pain and injury: "a natural thing in rowing"?', in K.Young (ed.), *Sporting Bodies, Damaged Selves: Sociological Studies of Sports-Related Injury*. Oxford: Elsevier, pp. 151–62.

Rail, G. (1992) 'Physical contact in women's basketball: a phenomenological construction and contextualization', *International Review for the Sociology of Sport*, 27 (1): 1–27.

Robins, D. (1984) *We Hate Humans*. Markham, Ontario: Penguin.

Roderick, M. (2006) *The Work of Professional Football: A Labour of Love?* London: Routledge.

Rojek, C. (1985) *Capitalism and Leisure Theory*. London: Tavistock.

Ryan, J. (1995) *Little Girls in Pretty Boxes: The Making and Breaking of Elite Gymnasts and Figure Skaters*. New York: Doubleday.

Safai, P. (2004) 'Negotiating with risk: exploring the role of the sports medicine clinician', in K. Young (ed.), *Sporting Bodies, Damaged Selves: Sociological Studies of Sports-Related Injury*. Oxford: Elsevier, pp. 269–86.

Sage, G. (1999) 'Justice do it! The Nike transnational advocacy network: organization, collective actions, and outcomes', *Sociology of Sport Journal*, 16: 206–33.

Scraton, P., Jemphrey, A. and Coleman, S. (1995) *No Last Rights: The Denial of Justice and the Promotion of Myth in the Aftermath of the Hillsborough Disaster.* Liverpool: Alden Press.

Smith, M. (1983) *Violence and Sport.* Toronto: Butterworths.

Snyder, E. and Spreitzer, E. (1989) *Social Aspects of Sport:* 3rd edn. Englewood Cliffs, NJ: Prentice Hall.

Taylor, I. (1971) 'Soccer consciousness and soccer hooliganism', in S. Cohen (ed.), *Images of Deviance.* New York: Penguin, pp. 134–65.

Taylor, I. (1987) 'Putting the boot into a working class sport: British soccer after Bradford and Brussels', *Sociology of Sport Journal*, 4: 171–91.

Taylor, I. (1989) 'Hilsborough, 15 April 1989: some personal contemplations', unpublished paper.

Theberge, N. (1997) ' "It's part of the game": physicality and the production of gender in women's hockey', *Gender and Society*, 11: 69–87.

Tiger, L. (1969) *Men in Groups.* London: Thomas Nelson.

Waddington, I. (2000) *Sport, Health and Drugs.* London: E and FN Spon.

Wann, D.L., Melnick, M., Russell, G. and Pease, D. (2001) *Sport Fans: the Psychology and Social Impact of Spectators.* London: Routledge.

Williams, J. and Goldberg, A. (1989) 'Spectator behaviour, media coverage and crowd control at the 1988 European Football Championships: a review of data from Belgium, Denmark, the Federal Republic of Germany, Netherlands, and the United Kingdom', Strasbourg: Council of Europe.

Williams, J., Dunning. E. and Murphy, P. (1984) *Hooligans Abroad: the Behaviour and Control of English Fans in Continental Europe.* London: Routledge & Kegan Paul.

Young, K. (1986) ' "The killing field": themes in mass media responses to the Heysel stadium riot', *International Review for the Sociology of Sport*, 21 (2/3): 253–67.

Young, K. (1993) 'Violence, risk, and liability in male sports culture', *Sociology of Sport Journal*, 10 (4): 373–96.

Young, K. (1997) 'Women, sport, and physicality: preliminary findings from a Canadian study', *International Review for the Sociology of Sport*, 32 (3): 297–305.

Young, K. (2000) 'Sport and violence', in J. Coakley and E. Dunning (eds), *Handbook of Sports Studies.* London: Sage, pp. 382–408.

Young, K. (2002a) 'Standard deviations: an update on North American sports crowd disorder', *Sociology of Sport Journal*, 19 (3): 237–75.

Young, K. (2002b) 'From "sports violence" to "sports crime": aspects of violence, law and gender in the sports process', in M. Gatz, M. Messner and S. Ball-Rokeach (eds), *Paradoxes of Youth and Sport.* New York: SUNY Press, pp. 207–24.

Young, K. (ed.) (2004a) *Sporting Bodies, Damaged Selves: Sociological Studies of Sports-Related Injury.* Oxford: Elsevier.

Young, K. (2004b) 'The role of the courts in sport injury', in K.Young (ed.), *Sporting Bodies, Damaged Selves: Sociological Studies of Sports-Related Injury*. Oxford: Elsevier, pp. 333–53.

Young, K. and Wamsley, K. (1996) 'State complicity in sports assault and the gender order in twentieth century Canada: preliminary observations', *Avante*, 2 (2): 51–69.

Young, K. and White, P. (1995) 'Sport, physical danger, and injury: the experiences of elite women athletes', *Journal of Sport and Social Issues*, 19 (1): 45–61.

Young, K. and White, P. (2000) 'Researching sport injury: reconstructing dangerous masculinities', in J. McKay, M. Messner and D. Sabo (eds), *Masculinities, Gender Relations and Sport*. Thousand Oaks, CA: Sage, pp. 108–26.

Young, K., White, P. and McTeer, W. (1994) 'Body talk: male athletes reflect on sport, injury, and pain', *Sociology of Sport Journal*, 11 (2): 175–95.

9

Sport and Disability

NIGEL THOMAS

OVERVIEW

» *Theorising disability*
» *The emergence of disability sport*
» *Physical education and youth sport*
» *Organisational and policy development in the UK*
» *Elite competition, classification and the Paralympics*
» *Perspectives on disability sport*
» *Conclusion*

The Paralympic Games held in October 2004 provided an illustration of the quality and excitement in elite-level disability sport, and the significant advances in its development. In a short but rich history, disability sport has undergone substantial changes in its organisation, funding and public and political profile. However, there appears to be a paucity of literature that traces and evaluates these developments. This chapter seeks to fill this gap and provides a critical examination of the phenomenon of disability sport.

THEORISING DISABILITY

Those considered different from the physical, sensory or intellectual norm are considered abnormal and thus disabled in almost all societies. Being labelled as disabled has, at different times and in different cultures, led to reverence, pity, mockery, torture or death.

In ancient Greece there was no place for women, non-Greeks and the physically or intellectually inferior; rather there was an obsession with bodily perfection. Greeks and Romans from 500 BC to AD 400 killed children that they considered to be disabled. The early Christians were compassionate to all but those with mental illness, who were considered as sinful and were often killed as a result. On the other hand, in the sixteenth and seventeenth centuries deaf people were deemed godly and superior to the hearing. It was not until the eighteenth century and the emergence of welfare and caring social policies that disabled people were treated with more dignity. However, the ideology of caring in the late eighteenth and early nineteenth centuries marginalised disabled people, as illustrated by the proliferation of segregated institutions such as special schools and asylums for the mentally ill and the 'handicapped' (Barnes, 1997).

Industrialisation in the UK exacerbated this segregation by creating social divisions between those who were deemed to be of use in the workplace and those who were not. Those not up to the physical and mental standards required for the workplace were thus considered useless. This is consistent with the dominant capitalist ideology which values individuals according to their productivity: from this perspective inability to produce results in low or no value. As Oliver suggests, disability is 'culturally produced through the relationship between the mode of production and the central values of the society concerned' (1990: 23). As a result, *disabled people are six times more likely to be out of work than non-disabled people* (DfEE, 2000).

DISABILITY MODELS

The way in which disability is defined helps to explain how sport for disabled people has developed. Definitions of disability generally fall into one of two categories, medical or social.

The medical model or 'personal tragedy theory' perceives disability as an impairment owned by an individual, resulting in a loss or limitation of function. This implies the need for professionals to impose their own priorities on the lifestyles of disabled people, often relegating other personal or social needs to second place. This medicalised perception of disability allows little leeway for the role of society in the construction of disability. Such definitions and understandings of disability are based on notions of normality or function, with little or no recognition of other cultural or personal factors. According to Stone (1995), individualised medical definitions and explanations of disability that ignore the wider aspects of disability are often depersonalised and insulting, treating disabled people as unfortunate, dependent, helpless and pitiable. Indeed, the obsession with bodily perfection, Stone suggests, is oppressive not just to those who are considered as disabled, but also to the non-disabled, as it alienates us all 'from our bodies'. Stone maintains that

Westernised culture treats disability as a condition to be avoided, encouraging us to deny visible difference and aspire to the body perfect.

An alternative model of disability views disability as socially constructed, whereby *the responsibility for the disability lies with society rather than with the individual*. It is argued that society disables people by limiting their worth in society, thus placing an additional burden on their own impairment, and isolating them unnecessarily from the rest of society. The central tenet of this model is that disability is created by non-disabled values, norms and beliefs, reducing it to a medical and individual problem.

There seems to be a general consensus among academics that, despite the acceptance of environmental explanations, the medical model has dominated definitions of disability, and disabled people have been dominated by the medical professions (Drake, 1994; Oliver, 1990). Oliver (1990) argues that the ruling classes were dominant in the professions and acted as social controllers of the impaired. Furthermore, with disabled people under-represented in positions of authority, they have had little control over the organisations meant to serve them. For example, in an analysis of British voluntary organisations, Drake (1994) found that (a) few of the influential positions were held by disabled people; (b) organisations run by non-disabled people had more resources and access to staff than organisations run by disabled people; and (c) organisations run by non-disabled people are more likely to receive financial support from the government.

The Disability Discrimination Act (DDA) was passed in 1996 to reduce the discrimination faced by disabled people. The Act states that disabled people should never be refused services or entry to places where the public can normally go because of their impairment. It has been criticised, however, for being too weak. Furthermore, whilst legislative changes, such as those detailed in the DDA, signify a challenge to the dominant non-disabled culture, typically, disabled people remain in subordinate, powerless positions and continue to be dominated by the predominant able-bodied hegemony.

THE NEED FOR A NEW MODEL

There has been growing support for the social model as it 'under-played the importance of impairment in disabled people's lives, in order to develop a strong argument about social structures and processes' (Shakespeare and Watson, 1997: 298). However, the social model has itself been criticised for failing to provide a definition and understanding of disability which acknowledge impairment and experience.

Hughes and Paterson (1997), for example, suggest that contrary to the beliefs of Shakespeare and Watson a necessary repositioning of the distinction between disability and impairment is required. They argue that both the medical and social models consider bodily impairment in similar ways: that is, as discrete, physical and inert, 'pulled apart' from the social consequences of the impairment. Hughes and Paterson believe that if disabled people are to challenge effectively the political and economic structures that oppress and exclude them, they need to embrace body politics and accept the significance of the individual within the wider socio-political environment. In 2000 the World Health Organization revised the 1980 International Classification of Impairment, Disability and Handicap (ICIDH-2). The ICIDH-2 was an acknowledgement of the criticisms made of the earlier definition, particularly by disabled activists and academics. The ICIDH-2 attempts to incorporate both the individual and the social models of disability by distinguishing between those limitations to activity that are best dealt with by medical intervention and those that are the cause and subject of social and environmental barriers. Bickenbach et al. (1999) claim that this model disabuses people of the notion that impairment is necessarily the prime disabler. Nevertheless the new classification has been criticised for continuing to classify difference in relation to prevailing social norms, thus perpetuating the stigmatising effects of labelling.

The literature indicates that:

1   disability has traditionally been defined as an individual loss or restriction;
2   the contemporary social explanation of disability, whilst perceived as an improvement, fails to embrace the individual experiences of impairment within the broader environmental explanation; and
3   in professional practices such as welfare and education, disabled people have been dominated by non-disabled officers and their medical understanding of disability.

Consequently, people with impairments continue to be disabled by a society dominated by the norms and values set by people without impairments.

THE EMERGENCE OF DISABILITY SPORT IN THE UK

Despite the intensification of debates on disability, relatively little attention has been paid, in the UK at least, by disabled activists to disability sport, perhaps because it provides such an overt and often visual illustration of the significance of impairment. Despite the long association between participation in sport and the development and maintenance of physical and mental health, the marginal status of disabled people has militated against their involvement in the dominant able-bodied sporting culture.

Where disabled people have been encouraged to participate in sport and physical activity, it has often been as a vehicle for physical or psychological therapy. For example, in the twentieth century the war injured were encouraged to use sport and recreational physical activity as a means of rehabilitation back into civilian life. This 'therapeutic recreation' concept became particularly well developed in the United States, where hospitals and schools have continued to use recreation as a form of therapy.

Whilst hospitals in the UK also embraced the American therapeutic recreation model, the concept of sport and competition specifically for disabled people, and in particular those with spinal cord injury, was first realised by Guttmann at Stoke Mandeville Hospital in England. Although the initial rationale for his intervention was to provide therapeutic recreational activities, he soon recognised the wider potential of competitive sport. Consequently, Ludwig Guttmann and the International Stoke Mandeville Games Federation (ISMGF) which he then formed are acknowledged by many as instrumental in the inspiration and early development of disability sport in England. One of the earliest international competitive events for physically disabled people was held in 1948. Sports clubs and hospitals were invited that year to Stoke Mandeville, to coincide with the Olympic Games being held in London. According to Bernard Atha, President of the English Federation of Disability Sport, 'although Guttmann was a most remarkable pioneer, he was a single-minded autocrat and maverick, whose interest was limited to those with spinal cord injury and he would not entertain the involvement of other disabilities which I, as Vice-Chairman of the Sports Council, wished him to do' (interview, June 2000). Indeed, even though sport for blind and deaf people was, according to Bob Price, Chairman of the British Paralympic Association and currently President of the European Paralympic Committee, established long before wheelchair sport, the inclusion of these disabilities was 'far removed from the consciousness of Guttmann' (interview, June 2000). Despite Guttmann's highly personal and distinctive views, few would deny his contribution to giving disability sport its early impetus.

Level of Sports Participation in the UK

There is scant empirical work which clearly demonstrates disabled people's low levels of participation in sport. The few studies that have been carried out tend to reflect similar patterns of participation. The Council for Europe (1987) found that while 30 per cent of non-disabled adults participated in sport, only 3 per cent of disabled people did so. Later studies in the UK found that 2.5 per cent of disabled people participated in sport (Williams and Newman, 1988) compared with 38.4 per cent for non-disabled men and 24.2 per cent for non-disabled women (Sports Council, 1988). Schmidt-Gotz et al. (1994) refer to a study in Germany in which 28 per cent of non-disabled people and 2.5 per cent of disabled people were found to participate in sport. Sport England found from a survey of 2,293 young disabled people in 2000 that whilst the majority of disabled young people participate in sport both in and out of school time, the rate and frequency of participation are significantly lower than for the overall population. Only 14 per cent of disabled young people, compared with 45 per cent of the general population, take part in extracurricular sport and only 12 per cent of disabled young people compared with 46 per cent of the general population were members of a sports club not organised by their school. A survey of disabled adults identified that – excluding walking – 38 per cent of disabled adults compared with 59 per cent of non-disabled adults participated in sport (Sport England, 2002).

As regards the range of sports played, Elvin (1994) found, in a survey of 137 local authority leisure services, that swimming was the most frequently mentioned programme of activity (94 per cent), weightlifting the most frequently run integrated activity (84 per cent) and short mat bowls the most frequently run segregated activity. Sport England (2002: 7) also identified swimming as the most popular activity and interestingly that 'nine out of the top-ten most popular sports were activities that can be played as an individual', with football as the only popular team sport. While the shortage of data on participation is regrettable, its collection is fraught with practical and ethical problems:

1   It is very difficult to achieve agreement on definitions of impairment and disability.
2   It is difficult to estimate casual participation outside the club and national governing body structure.
3   The collection of such data may necessitate a labelling of 'people with impairment' and consequently perpetuate their social stigma.

Moreover, according to Fitzgerald and Kay (2004), much of the available research has failed to elicit young disabled people's views on their sport participation and has reinforced the perception of disabled people as passive and dependent.

Constraints on Participation

Notwithstanding the paucity of empirical research, available evidence indicates that, however defined, disabled people take part in sport significantly less than their non-disabled peers. According to a Health Education Authority study (1999) involving 40 in-depth interviews and five focus groups, the significant causes of this lower participation in physical activity and sport include:

- lack of motivation and confidence;
- negative school experiences;
- no support from family and friends;
- lack of information on opportunities;
- transport problems;
- a lack of time and money; and
- poor physical access.

This list reflects many of the commonly cited barriers to participation. For example, Sport England (2002) found the most common reasons for not playing any sport were health (60 per cent), money (7 per cent) and lack of time (6 per cent). It also identified that transport was a problem for 32 per cent of young people and that 21 per cent believed that staff at centres and sports clubs were not welcoming. The lack of time others have to supervise and support participation also seems to be a significant constraint, along with a lack of disabled role models (Brittain, 2004). The most common barriers to participation in after-school sport were lack of money, ill health and unsuitability of sports facilities. Whilst the DDA requires sports facility managers to take steps to ensure their facilities are accessible, facility design and the provision of adequate ramps and changing facilities are only a small part of the process of making a venue attractive for general use by disabled people (ISRM, 1999). A further factor which may contribute to low levels of participation is the poor media coverage of disability sport. Notwithstanding what may be perceived as the BBC's positive coverage of the 2004 Paralympic Games, the general coverage of disabled people in the mass media – and in particular in the print media – continues either to ignore or medicalise, patronise and dehumanise disabled people, reinforcing stereotypes which 'form the bedrock on which the attitudes towards, assumptions about and expectations of disabled people are based' (Barnes, 1992: 39). In a study of British newspaper coverage of the 2000 Paralympic Games, articles commonly referred to athletes as 'brave' or 'courageous', regularly focused on their impairment, and only recognised Paralympians' sporting achievements by comparing them with non-disabled Olympians (Thomas and Smith, 2003).

The socialisation process suggests that young people, influenced by socialising agents such as the media, family, peers, grow up adopting the values of their own society. Typically, these agents perpetuate and reinforce negative perceptions of disabled people in society and in sport. Thus, in society's system of social stratification, whereby individuals are ranked according to their contribution to society, disabled people are placed low in the social hierarchy and are therefore denied the power, prestige and life chances enjoyed by their 'superiors'. The lack of opportunity to take part in organised sport is just one consequence of this low status.

Compounding their low status in sport and in wider society is the homogeneous treatment disabled people are accorded, which assumes that they have similar lifestyles and experiences. For example, poor transport, unemployment and low self-esteem may be the key barriers for one group of disabled people, while for another group the most significant constraint might be the lack of local sports provision. This heterogeneity of experience has consequently made it difficult for disabled people to form effective lobby groups. Indeed, it could be suggested that whilst many disability sport organisations have been formed since 1940, their multiplicity and differing concerns have made sustained and effective lobbying difficult.

PHYSICAL EDUCATION AND YOUTH SPORT

Special Educational Needs and Integration

After the 1944 Education Act, pupils with disabilities were assigned to medically defined categories, including: the physically handicapped, blind, epileptic or educationally subnormal. Placement into special education was often a response to a medical or psychological assessment which placed pupils in predetermined categories of impairment and which did not, according to Halliday (1993), consider individual needs and competencies. The Warnock Report of 1978 abolished the previous set of medical categories and introduced the concept of special educational needs. One of the main reasons for this was to prevent the sharp distinction between two groups of children – the handicapped and the non-handicapped. The 1981 Education Act accepted the recommendations of the Warnock Report and defined a child as having a special educational need (SEN) if 'he has a significantly greater difficulty in learning than the majority of children of his age; or he has a disability which either prevents or hinders him from making use of the educational facilities of a kind generally provided in schools' (DES, 1981: 1).

The 1981 Education Act indicated that as many as 20 per cent of children have special educational needs, of which only 2 per cent are in special schools. It was also recognised that some children might not be deemed to have a special need in many curriculum areas, but might have such a need in physical education. Conversely, some children who have special educational needs in other academic subjects may not have a special need in physical education.

The Act encouraged what has been a gradual and partial transference of pupils from special to mainstream schools and thus to mainstream physical education. It has been partial inasmuch as the pupils mainstreamed into ordinary schools typically are those with less severe disabilities. Special schools still remain the traditional establishment for those with more severe disabilities.

PHYSICAL EDUCATION

Disabled children are typically considered to have a special educational need and their specific needs and types of provision are identified in a Statement. Despite the obligation on schools to meet these needs, disabled children regularly miss out on the range of physical education opportunities available to their non-disabled peers. In 1987 the Sports Council funded the Everybody Active Project in the North-East of England (as one of the

National Demonstration Projects) to investigate how to improve the physical education experiences and sporting opportunities of disabled young people (Stafford, 1989). Results of the study revealed that 96 per cent of the 51 mainstream schools in the survey excluded disabled pupils from specific activities. This massive structural inequality facing disabled people in sport was due to a low level of awareness of disability sport issues among leisure providers, poor knowledge of provision for disabled children among PE teachers, and poor PE training for teachers in special schools.

In 1992, the National Curriculum for Physical Education (NCPE) was introduced providing, for the first time, all pupils with an entitlement to a broad and balanced curriculum. Encouraging teachers to modify and adapt activities to suit pupils with special educational needs, the interim reports provided substantive support and advice on the planning and delivery of an accessible curriculum. However, a survey of 38 mainstreamed schools attended by disabled pupils found that despite 79 per cent of the PE department heads claiming to provide suitable PE activities, pupils with SEN, and in particular physically disabled pupils, did not have access to the full range of activities (Penney and Evans, 1995). For example, only 42 per cent provided dance and 56 per cent provided games for physically disabled pupils, although not always integrated with their peers. Games has been highlighted as the activity area in which it may be most difficult to provide an appropriate experience for pupils with a disability in mainstream education. Furthermore, as Penney and Evans warn, since the publication of *Sport: Raising the Game* (DNH, 1995), the PE curriculum has emphasised competitive team games, which, coupled with the lack of flexibility in the guidelines, was unlikely to lend itself to a broad and balanced curriculum for pupils with SEN.

In its survey, Sport England found that 53 per cent of primary-aged disabled children and 41 per cent of 11–16-year-old disabled children spent less than one hour in PE lessons and only 20 per cent of young disabled people spent two or more hours in PE lessons compared with 33 per cent of the overall school population. Moreover, the proportion of young disabled people taking part in after-school sport was 40 per cent compared with 79 per cent of the general school population.

In any case, according to Barton (1993) and Smith and Thomas (2004), PE for a disabled person is normally an adapted version of that originally designed for non-disabled people. Consequently, a pupil with SEN is likely to receive, at best, an inappropriate programme of activities, as it was originally intended for his/her able-bodied peers and has been adapted or amended in an attempt to meet his/her needs, taking no account of individual circumstances and after-school choices. According to a study by Fitzgerald and Kay (2004), when PE activities are adapted for disabled young people in ways which emphasise their 'difference', it can have an adverse affect on enjoyment. It has been argued that these early experiences in PE will have a profound effect on children's sporting careers.

ORGANISATIONAL AND POLICY DEVELOPMENT IN THE UK

The Legacy of Ludwig Guttmann

The history of disability sport organisations in the UK has been short but turbulent. As well as the ISMGF, the British Paraplegic Sports Society (BPSS) was also established in 1948 as a result of the Stoke Mandeville Games, initially to serve the sporting interests of those with spinal cord injury and, much later (when renamed the British Wheelchair Sports Foundation), to serve the sporting interests of other wheelchair users. In 1961 Guttmann inaugurated the British Sports Association for the Disabled (BSAD) which promoted itself as the national body with responsibility for providing, developing and co-ordinating sport and recreation opportunities for all people with disabilities. BSAD, supported by the Sports Council, sought to co-ordinate the plethora of organisations that were emerging to develop sport for disability groups other than those catered for by BPSS.

By the mid-1980s the Sports Council was playing a significant role in the policy development of sport for disabled people. In 1982 the Sports Council published *Sport in the Community: the Next Ten Years*, which recognised that for some groups, its vision of 'Sport for All' had not become a reality, and groups such as those with a physical or learning disability had substantial barriers 'to overcome' (Sports Council, 1982: 29). The promotion of sport for disabled people was acknowledged, but it formed no part of the national strategy, despite eight out of the nine regional sports councils identifying disability as a priority area within their regional strategies (1982: 31). However, during the 1980s the British Sports Council began to develop policy in the area of disability sport, although this rarely amounted to more than funding other organisations that were pursuing a more innovative and inclusionary vision of 'Sport for All'.

In 1988 the Sports Council published *Sport in the Community: Into the 90's* in which local authorities such as Northamptonshire, and governing bodies such as the Amateur Rowing Association, were cited as examples of organisations using innovative schemes to promote mass participation opportunities for disabled people. More significantly, by 1988 the Sports Council was providing BSAD with a grant of £100,000 a year. However, despite substantial Sports Council and commercial funding, it was perceived that BSAD failed to provide either the effective unified voice for disability sport or an efficient organisational infrastructure for competition.

The 1989 Government Review

Despite BSAD's decision in 1987 to switch from being an umbrella to a membership organisation, dissatisfaction with it led to a gradual decline in BSAD membership and a weakening of the credibility of its claim to be the primary advocate on behalf of other disability sport organisations. According to Price:

TABLE 9.1   Examples of national disability sports organisations (1948–98)

Founded	Organisation
1930	British Deaf Sports Council*
1948	British Paraplegic Sports Association (later British Wheelchair Sports Association*)
1961	British Sports Association for the Disabled (later Disability Sport England*)
1976	British Blind Sport*
1978	British Amputee Sports Association (BASA)
1981	United Kingdom Sports Association for the People with Mental Handicap* (later, in 1995, the English Sports Association for People with Learning Disability*)
1981	Cerebral Palsy Sport*
1982	British Les Autres Sports Association (BLASA)
1989	British Paralympic Association
1990	British Les Autres and Amputee Sports Association* (merger of BASA and BLASA)
1998	English Federation of Disability Sport
2001	English Sports Association for People with Learning Disability integrated in Mencap (learning disability charity)

*National disability sports organisations recognised by the Sports Council.

the dual responsibility for membership (through BSAD's network of clubs) and national co-ordination (acting as an umbrella over all the NDSOs) had always been over-ambitious and misguided. As BSAD could not and did not claim exclusive responsibility for all disability groups, it could never adequately represent their interests vis à vis the Sports Council, but nor could it ignore that responsibility and invest its limited resources exclusively in its membership services. (Interview, 2000)

In 1989 Colin Moynihan, then Minister for Sport, initiated a review prompted in large part by criticisms aimed at BSAD by the other disability sport organisations and mainstream governing bodies. The disability sport organisations were accused of creating confusion and duplication by the Minister for Sport Review Group (1989). A key recommendation of the review called on governing bodies and other mainstream agencies to afford disabled people the benefits currently enjoyed by the non-disabled, as it was perceived that segregated disability sport organisations did not have the resources to support their athletes adequately.

As a result of the perceived failure of BSAD to be an effective representative body, numerous organisations had been established, some with a remit to improve the range and quality of opportunities for one disability group in all sports, such as Cerebral Palsy Sport, and others to meet the sporting needs of all disability groups in one particular sport, such as the British Table Tennis Association for Disabled People. Table 9.1 shows that by 1989 there was a vast array of disparate autonomous organisations representing a range of disability and sporting interests.

Whilst at an international level disability-specific organisations liaised with their own equivalent disability-specific international federations (e.g. British Blind Sport with the

International Blind Sport Association), it was at the local, regional and national levels that BSAD was perceived as failing to develop competition and sports development structures to meet the specific needs of the disability groups in its remit. Whilst recognising the invaluable role BSAD played in the early development of disability sport, it failed to represent the breadth of disability sport interests (see box 9.1). This failure became more pronounced as more disability-specific organisations were established and began to impose higher expectations for policy action and lobbying on BSAD. Notwithstanding these organisational shortcomings, Price claimed that the smaller NDSOs (National Disability Sport Organisation) at times seemed envious of BSAD's position. 'They didn't have then, and haven't developed since, the network of grassroots clubs and regional organisations that even come close to BSAD's, nor did they enjoy the financial support of the Sports Council' (interview, 2000).

Box 9.1   The British Sports Association for
the Disabled (BSAD)

In 1961 Ludwig Guttmann inaugurated the British Sports Association for the Disabled (BSAD). BSAD, supported by the Sports Council, sought to co-ordinate the plethora of organisations that were emerging to develop sport for disability groups. The untenable dual responsibility of promoting participation for other organisations, as well as developing its own sports club and event infrastructure, led to a gradual decline in BSAD membership and a weakening of the credibility of its claim to be the primary advocate on behalf of other disability sport organisations.

The Mainstreaming of Disability Sport

As consequence of the publication of *Building on Ability* by the Minister for Sport Review Group in 1989, there occurred during the 1990s a gradual policy shift by the Sports Council towards the mainstreaming of disability sport. In 1993 the Sports Council published a policy statement, *People with Disabilities and Sport*, in which it recommended that sport for disabled people was at a stage where 'having developed its own structures, [it should] move from a target approach to the mainstream' (Sports Council, 1993: 5). In other words, the Sports Council was recommending a gradual shift of responsibility for the organisation and provision of sport for disabled people, to move away from the NDSOs towards the mainstream, sports-specific national governing bodies. In doing so it highlighted those mainstream and disability sport agencies that were involved in the network of disability sport. However, whilst the NDSOs, regional sports forums, facility managers and teachers were all identified as being potential partners, no clarification was offered regarding the precise role of these groups. Elvin (1994), in an attempt to map the 'complex variety' of agencies involved in the provision of opportunities, found that despite the similarity in their objectives, many of the public and private sector organisations worked independently of one another. The NDSOs had, he believed, an important part to play but 'often lacked the resources and the facilities' to deliver programmes (1994: 325), and thus needed the co-operation of other agencies.

A New Start

In recognition of the continued poor co-ordination between these agencies together with the wider political trend towards integration, the Sports Council convened a National Disability Sports Conference in 1996 to consider the future of disability sport in England. As a result of the conference, the Sports Council established a task force with the remit to 'facilitate the mainstreaming of disability sport in England by the year 2000' (Collins, 1997). In June 1997 the National Disability Sports Conference was reconvened to receive the task force recommendations and the results of the consultation exercise. Collins (1997: 1) reported that in contrast to earlier attempts at reform, there was now a unity of opinion on the future of disability sport policy, the main recommendation of which was the creation of an English Federation of Disability Sport (EFDS). The EFDS was established in 1998 and plays a pivotal role in the co-ordination of opportunities provided and developed by disability sport organisations and continues to work closely with the national disability sport organisations. Its mission is to be the united voice of disability sport seeking to promote inclusion and achieve equality of sporting opportunities for disabled people. Following a review of the EFDS is 2003, it has recently published its four-year strategy 'Count Me In', which identifies as its targets:

- To develop and enhance the inclusion of disabled people in community-based sport and physical activity opportunities.
- To develop sporting pathways for disabled people.
- To improve skills, knowledge and understanding of the community to effectively deliver sport for disabled people.
- To improve the quality and quantity of PE and school sport for young disabled people in special and mainstream education.
- To empower disabled people to take a full and active role within sport.
- To increase awareness and understanding of sport for disabled people.

Atha (President of the EFDS) suggested in 1999 that the EFDS provided 'a much needed united voice for disability sport in England' which combines the 'specialist expertise of the NDSOs', thus enabling the EFDS 'powerfully [to] demonstrate that disabled people have a right to access sport as a matter of common practice' (EFDS, 1999). While applauding the contribution of the NDSOs and re-emphasising their importance to disability sport, in 2004 Atha expressed concern over the limited funding received by the NDSOs. The success of the EFDS will depend upon a diverse range of factors, including its capacity to retain the respect of disability sport organisations. Whilst the ability of the EFDS to represent the interests of the regions and the NDSOs is largely within the control of the EFDS, government funding of sport, government and local authority policies on sport and school PE and the media coverage of disability sport, for example, are all factors outside its control but which may be crucial to its success.

The establishment of the EFDS provided a sharp insight into the policy environment within which disability sport organisations operate. It can be argued that the slow progress towards the development of an effective organisational lobbying focus for disability sport was due in part to two factors: first, the reluctance of mainstream sports governing bodies to acknowledge disability sport as a significant issue and, second, the unwillingness of the non-disabled administrators in existing disability organisations to relinquish what Price suggests had become for many a personal crusade. Indeed Derek Casey, former Chief Executive of Sport England, Price and Atha concur that the attractions of working in elite disability sport had encouraged the retention of roles better served by different and possibly mainstream organisations. Price claims that a significant opportunity to improve sport for disabled people has been missed and is disappointed by the current organisational arrangements. The relationship between Sport England and the EFDS seems reminiscent of that between BSAD and the former Sports Council, with Sport England, like the Sports Council before it, seeming to prefer a single outlet for all disability needs and interests. This is not to ignore the gradual, and welcome, increase in the involvement of NGBs (National Governing Bodies) and others in the mainstream of sport at the elite end of the spectrum; simply to express disappointment with the slow pace of movement in that direction and apparent lack of emphasis on the involvement of mainstream providers closer to the grass roots (Price, personal communication). Atha is generally more optimistic and contends that the disability sport organisations, currently under the direction of the EFDS, should retain control and power, as the mainstream NGBs 'will never take on disability fully so we will need disability sports organisations well into the foreseeable future and quite possibly always' (Atha, interview June 2000). A recent study of mainstreaming in seven sports, reflected the diverse values of, and commitment towards, mainstreaming, by governing bodies of sport and disability sport organisations (Thomas, 2004).

ELITE COMPETITION, CLASSIFICATION AND THE PARALYMPIC MOVEMENT

The Paralympic Movement

The first Paralympic Games were held in 1960 immediately after the Olympic Games in Rome. However, as Doll-Tepper (1999) highlights, the term 'Paralympic' is a recent title replacing the previous disability or organisationally defined nomenclature such as the Paraplegic Games. Advocates within the Paralympic Movement emphasise that whilst the Paralympics were once exclusively for paraplegics, the word 'Paralympic' is derived from the Greek preposition *para* (beside or alongside) and is so called to reflect its 'para-llel' status to the Olympics. It should also be noted that the deaf are not a part of the Paralympic Movement, instead providing elite competition in a Deaflympics (previously named 'World Games for the Deaf').

The Paralympic Games are now significantly larger than they were in 1960, in terms of the number of athletes, administrators and countries represented. In Athens 2004, 3,806 athletes from 136 countries competed in 19 sports, 15 of which are shared with the Olympics, and the other four are exclusively Paralympic (i.e. boccia, goalball, powerlifting and wheelchair rugby). Although the Paralympic Games were initially developed for the spinally injured only, they now include amputees, people with cerebral palsy, people with an intellectual disability, the visually impaired, wheelchair users and les autres (the term used to cater for those with other forms of physical impairment). Table 9.2 summarises the development and expansion of the Paralympic Games.

The increase in links between the Olympics and the Paralympics is mirrored by the increase in standards, events, spectators, hospitality, technology and sports science. The link between the Olympics and Paralympics was reinforced on 19th June 2001, when an agreement was signed between the IOC and the IPC (International Paralympic Committee) to ensure that, from the 2012 games onwards, the host city chosen to host the Olympic Games will be obliged also to host the Paralympics.

The increase in standards is often exemplified by the diminishing divide between Olympic and Paralympic world records. For example, Nigerian amputee Ajibola Adoeye set a Paralympic record of 10.72 seconds for the 100 m, less than 1 second slower than the Olympic record.

The Great Britain team has achieved significant success in the Paralympic Games. Recent performances earned them third position in 1992 at Barcelona and fourth position at Atlanta in 1996. However, the success in Barcelona, at least according to the Sports Council (1993), was in spite of the 'minimal support' offered by the formal organisational structures. Notwithstanding what the Minister for Sport described, in 1989, as a 'long history of fragmentation and dissatisfaction within the UK disability sports organisational

TABLE 9.2   The Summer Paralympics, 1952–2004

Year	Olympics venue	Paralympics venue	No. of countries	No. of athletes	Disability groups	GB position
1952	London, UK	Aylesbury, UK	2	130	SCI	n/a
1960	Rome, Italy	Rome, Italy	23	400	SCI	n/a
1964	Tokyo, Japan	Tokyo, Japan	22	390	SCI	2nd
1968	Mexico City, Mexico	Tel Aviv, Israel	29	750	SCI	n/a
1972	Munich, Germany	Heidelberg, Germany	44	1,000	SCI	4th
1976	Montreal, Canada	Toronto, Canada	42	1,600	SCI, VI, LA	5th
1980	Moscow, USSR	Arnhem, Netherlands	42	2,550	SCI, VI, AMP, CP	5th
1984	Los Angeles, USA	New York, USA Aylesbury, UK	42	4,080	SCI, VI, AMP, CP	2nd 6th
1988	Seoul, Korea	Seoul, Korea	61	3,053	SCI, VI, AMP, CP, LA	3rd
1992	Barcelona, Spain	Barcelona, Spain	82	3,020	SCI, VI, AMP, CP, LA	3rd
1996	Atlanta, USA	Atlanta, USA	103	3,195	SCI, VI, AMP, CP, LA	4th
2000	Sydney, Australia	Sydney, Australia	127	4,500	SCI, VI, AMP, CP, LA, LD	2nd
2004	Athens, Greece	Athens, Greece	136	3,806	SCI, VI, AMP, CP, LA	2nd

Key:

SCI	spinal cord injury	CP	cerebral palsy
LD	learning disability	LA	les autres (the others)
AMP	amputees	VI	visually impaired and blind

structure', recent changes to the funding for both Olympic and Paralympic development have significantly enhanced the opportunities for athletes and their coaches. In particular, the formation of the British Paralympic Association (the first national Paralympic Committee) and the introduction of the National Lottery World Class Performance Plans have provided athletes with a higher quality of training and event preparation. The result of this support is illustrated by the success of the 2000 Games in Sydney, where Great Britain finished in second position, with a total of 131 medals, only 18 less than the triumphant host nation, and in Athens in 2004 where Great Britain won 94 medals and finished in second position to China.

In 2005, the first Paralympic World Cup was held in Manchester; 334 competitors from 44 countries competed in athletics, cycling (track), swimming and wheelchair basketball. The organisation of the World Cup was deemed a significant success by Sir Phil Craven

(President of the IPC) and Richard Caborn (Minister for Sport), and a useful illustration of the UK's ability to host the 2012 Olympic and Paralympic Games. Notwithstanding the UK's ability to organise another World Cup in 2006 and the Paralympics in 2012, the difficulties in identifying young talented disabled people, inadequate sport-specific structures and quality coaching offer significant challenges to securing similarly high positions in the medal table.

Classification

Classification is a central characteristic of competitive disability sport, as it is the method that groups athletes into the categories which enable 'fair' competition. Initially athletes were classified in groups according to their impairment, for example: eight classes for CP athletes, three for VI athletes, seven for wheelchair athletes, nine for AMP, six for LA and one for LD. Since 1992, at the Paralympic Games in Barcelona, sport-specific classification systems have been introduced in which individuals are grouped according to their functional ability in the sport rather than their clinical impairment, which reduces the number of classes and improves the standard of competition. Athletes are classified many times prior to Paralympic competition and further checks are carried out by international classifiers during the event. However, whilst classification is central to disability sport, as it provides the vehicle by which disabled people compete fairly, concerns surrounding the fairness of classification systems have abounded. The difficulty in providing suitably robust classification systems was demonstrated when some of the Spanish basketball team from the 2000 Games were found to be fraudulently claiming to have a learning disability. As a consequence – and to the outrage of many key administrators such as Bernhard Atha – the IPC took the decision to ban learning disabled athletes from the 2004 Games and encouraged the International Sports Federation for Persons with an Intellectual Disability (INAS-FID) to develop a new eligibility system.

Integration and the Paralympics

As standards of performance have increased, it is argued that the original rehabilitation purpose through sport has given way to sport for sport's sake and competition for competition's sake. Furthermore, as part of the IPC's commitment to increase the integration of disabled athletes into mainstream sporting structures, demonstration Paralympic events have been held within the Olympic schedule, and full-medal-status events within the Commonwealth Games, a primary rationale for which is to provide athletes with sports science support and afford elite-level athletes a similar status to that enjoyed by their Olympic counterparts. The Commonwealth Games in 2002 became known as the 'inclusive games' as they were the first international competition in which events for 'elite athletes with a disability' were included in the overall medal tally. However, according to Smith and Thomas (2005), because the events combined classification groups so those who finished first did not necessarily receive a medal, television coverage of the events was often confusing and newspaper coverage indicated that the 'inclusive games' was not received as positively as the IPC intended. Tim Marshall (a recent member of the board of Sport England), for example, holds the view that the IPC should stop trying to gain access to the Olympic Games but should continue to encourage the IOC to provide the Paralympic Games with similar services to those provided to the Olympic Games.

PERSPECTIVES ON DISABILITY SPORT

Dominant Perspective: Sport as a Form of Therapy/Socialisation

Sport is a phenomenon that reflects wider cultural values within society; thus in a similar way to women, blacks and homosexuals, disabled people have been excluded from both mainstream society and sport. Whilst there is rich discourse on sport as a predominantly white, male, middle-class hegemony, discussions on disabled people's marginalisation in sport are not so common. Administrators and athletes in disability sport have striven, however, for greater recognition and in doing so have tended to emphasise the extent to which sport can be of physical and psychological benefit, and a vehicle for social acceptance. This approach supports the notion that sport is a form of therapy, used to rehabilitate individuals into mainstream society. This is illustrated by Steadward's suggestion that the Paralympic Movement 'provides a tremendous inspiration for people around the world to overcome adversity' (1996).

The Health Education Authority (1999) found that the existence of disability sport clubs in the UK provided a motivation for disabled people to be involved in regular physical activity. However, others believed that the emphasis by disability sport organisations on competition may serve to discourage rather than encourage participation. Nonetheless, it seems reasonable for those considering themselves as disabled to seek the benefits of sport in a similar way to their non-disabled peers; that is, to develop friendships, release stress, and improve health and fitness. Guttmann believed that sport was:

> invaluable in restoring the disabled person's physical fitness, i.e. his strength, co-ordination, speed and endurance ... restoring that passion for playful activity and the desire to experience joy and pleasure in life ... promoting that psychological equilibrium which enables the disabled to come to terms with his physical defect, to develop activity of mind, self-confidence, self-dignity, self-discipline, competitive spirit, and comradeship, mental attitudes ... to facilitate and accelerate his social re-integration and integration. (1976: 12–13)

According to Brasile et al. (1994), disabled people's motives for participation are similar to those of non-disabled people: for example, using after-sport social activities to seek acceptance from others. Whilst Taub and Greer (1998) concur, their interviews with disabled athletes revealed that the non-disabled respond to disabled people's participation in sport with disbelief about their physicality and with a clear lack of knowledge about their physical capability. One interviewee with cerebral palsy said, 'they [non-disabled people] want to be so nice to people, but they don't really know what they're doing. So they give you the wrong kind of support, either paternalistic or the wrong type of information' (Taub and Greer, 1998: 290). They found that disabled athletes did not internalise these negative responses, believing that sport made them feel (a) more capable and (b) that they had not yet reached their full physical potential.

In summary, disability sport may simply provide the opportunity for acceptance and normalisation, maintaining society's equilibrium by providing positive opportunities and rehabilitative benefits for those whose impairment has disrupted society's balance. A wheelchair user, for example, may be disabled by the steps and kerbs of a shopping centre but the same individual may enjoy the benefits of, and not be disabled by, a game of wheelchair basketball in an accessible sports centre. Whilst recognising the sporting excellence of disabled athletes, and the potential for shifting perceptions away from a therapeutic to a recreative model, disabled people's participation in sport may still be as much about therapy as it was in the 1950s.

Challenging the Dominant Perspective

Emulating Able-bodiedness

The overall treatment of sport and disability has been largely descriptive, atheoretical and uncritical (Barton, 1993; Williams, 1994) and policy and practice have been dominated by a medical, individualised approach to disability. Consequently, Oliver (1990) argues that the dominant perspectives of policy makers and researchers perpetuate disabled people's subordination. Using Gramsci's analysis of culture, the following section offers alternative explanations to the functionalist positions implicit in much of the literature concerning the involvement of disabled people in sport.

The relationship between disability and sport has been described by Steadward (1996) as 'contradictory and complex', as disability is associated with individual weakness, whereas sport is associated with strength, aggression and power over an opponent – characteristics rarely attributed to disabled people. This perspective helps to explain Hahn's (1984) suggestion that disabled people's participation in sport is an attempt to emulate non-disabled values and an example of disabled people's struggle for acceptance in a predominantly able-bodied world.

Concurring with this argument, Barton (1993) asserts that disability sport is merely an imitation of non-disabled sport in which disabled people are encouraged to accept a set of non-disabled values. Hahn (1984) suggests that much of the literature surrounding the study of sport for disabled people has focused on the attempts to adapt non-disabled people's activities for individuals with impairments. It seems that PE and sport for a disabled person are normally adapted versions of those originally designed for non-disabled people. However, to start from the premise that sport should be adapted and made appropriate for the disabled individuals confirms and reinforces the hegemony of able-bodied sport.

High Cost – Low Gain

A second reason for questioning the dominant perspective on sport for disabled people lies with the disproportionate efforts and costs that disabled people have to make to achieve what may be perceived as equality in sport. As Hahn suggests, disabled men and women seemingly can seek to approximate equality only through 'the exertion of almost superhuman effort' (1984: 6). This concept of equality is consistent with the experiences of other minority groups and ignores the additional economic, physical and emotional price that disabled people may need to pay in order to reap the same benefits as their non-disabled peers.

Moreover, there is little evidence to suggest that disabled people's participation in sport, however successful, has made any impact upon the broader social, political and economic environment in which disabled people live. For example, disabled people are still less likely to be in paid employment. That is not to say that participation in sport by disabled people may not produce many personal benefits, indeed for some it may now be a career. However, for the majority of the disabled population, it seems that sport has done little to challenge the dominant able-bodied hegemony and advantage the wider disabled community. Furthermore, it seems that disabled people are traditionally offered opportunities in special or separate settings segregated from the mainstream community, thus reducing any impact such performances may have on non-disabled people, and detracting from the important social, economic and environmental barriers facing disabled people. For example, an unintended consequence of the Paralympic Games could be that the exclusively able-bodied culture of the Olympics remains unchallenged, thus maintaining and perpetuating disabled people's inequality.

The oppression and marginalisation of disadvantaged groups through the medium of sport are well documented. According to Hahn (1984), similar to blacks in the ghettos of the United States, disabled people by participating in sport are encouraged to strive for goals that are both unattainable and less important than the wider and more important political, social and occupational goals.

Exclusivity of Able-bodied Sport

It is accepted that sport is a valued cultural practice and, as such, is significant in the lives of disabled people. Sport has the capacity therefore to play what Hahn (1984) calls a gate-keeping role, whereby those who are able to participate in the commonly recognised sports will be accepted into wider society and those who do not possess these physical capabilities may be denied the benefits of this membership. Even participation in adapted versions of recognised sports does not ensure acceptance into wider society. Furthermore, society's increasing concern with physicality, health, fitness and the 'body beautiful' provides the disabled population with the opportunity to challenge and clarify the values that these preoccupations project. Greek males were expected to compete both individually and collectively in the pursuit of physical and intellectual excellence in gymnasiums, amphitheatres and of course the Olympic Games (Barnes, 1997). It could be argued that the most significant gatekeeping role that sport plays is in the context of the aesthetic screening for physicality, with only some movements deemed as graceful and only some types of sporting bodies as attractive. The institution of sport gives priority to certain able-bodied forms of human movement (Barton, 1993); this means that the sports disabled people may wish to play, and the way they participate, may not be deemed attractive according to non-disabled values. Moreover, even within the disability sport and Paralympic sport movements, there appear to be some impairments that are considered less acceptable than others.

CONCLUSION

Despite considerable change since the formation of BSAD in 1961, it is clear that the organisational structure of sport for disabled people is still in a state of transition. Over the last 40 years or so a wide range of disability-generic, sport-specific and local organisations have developed sport at all levels but have worked predominantly in isolation from the mainstream sports bodies. Now enjoying better financial and political support, some disability sport organisations, encouraged by Sport England, are striving to co-ordinate their efforts, provide a united voice for disability sport, and build relations with mainstream sporting agencies. Unfortunately, the level of organisational coherence among disability sport organisations is still poor and the links between disability sport organisations and mainstream governing bodies are weak.

In recent years mainstream governing bodies of sport have begun to consider issues related to disability sport, often stimulated by Sport England funding. However, the response has been varied. While some national governing bodies of sport have embraced disabled people's needs within their existing national and regional structures, others have allied themselves to new disability, sport-specific governing bodies, and others have encouraged the traditional generic disability sport organisations to retain responsibility. The pattern of response reflects the varying levels of expertise, confidence and commitment within mainstream governing bodies of sport.

The current emphasis within Sport England on mainstreaming is problematic. The rationale for mainstreaming, that is providing access to services typically provided by, and generally only available to, able-bodied people, seems to be (a) that resources controlled by mainstream sport organisations are greater, and (b) that able-bodied sport is the norm to which disabled athletes should aspire. With regard to the latter, it seems that the policy and practice of sport for disabled people are primarily concerned with the extent to which we can, or should, integrate groups or individuals who are considered as outside of the main body of society into the mainstream. In most cases the discussions of main-streaming are based on an implicit assumption that integration is necessarily desirable. This perspective is logical in so far as it is mainstream non-disabled society that has con-structed definitions and public perceptions of disability. However, if integration is about equality, it can be argued that integration can only be achieved by deconstructing what is considered as 'normal'. That is, rather than categorising people into normal and abnor-mal groups, and then seeking to integrate the disabled or abnormal in with the non-disabled or normal, perceptions of what is 'normal' may need to change.

CHAPTER SUMMARY

» Competing models of disability – the medical and the socially constructed – shape the way in which disability sport has developed and shape the nature of current policy debates.
» Disability sport developed substantially within a medical model of disability that treated sport primarily as a vehicle for physical and/or psychological therapy.
» Low levels of participation by disabled people have been explained with reference to a variety of factors, including negative school experience, lack of motivation and confidence, lack of support from family and friends, transport problems and poor physical access.
» The UK has a complex pattern of organisations providing sports opportunities for the disabled, some defined by sport and others by type of disability.
» A key and highly controversial debate within British sport is whether disability sport should be organised separately from mainstream governing bodies.

FURTHER READING

Barnes (1997), Oliver (1990) and Hughes and Paterson (1997) provide rich points of entry to the politics of disability in general. Stone (1995) provides a challenging critique of 'body politics' and disability. For an examination of the development, current context and politics of disability sport, Doll-Tepper (1999) provides a European perspective. Steadward (1996) explores the politics of integration within the Paralympic Movement and Barton examines the provision for children with disabilities within the PE curriculum and schools.

REFERENCES

Barnes, C. (1992) *Disabling Imagery and the Media. An Exploration of the Principles for Media Representations of Disabled People.* Halifax: The British Council of Disabled People and Ryman Publishing.

Barnes, C. (1997) 'A legacy of oppression: a history of disability in western culture', in L. Barton and M. Oliver (eds), *Disability Studies, Past, Present and Future.* Leeds: The Disability Press, pp. 45–61.

Barton, L. (1993) 'Disability, empowerment and physical education', in J. Evans (ed.), *Equality, Education and Physical Education.* London: Falmer Press, pp. 43–54.

Bickenbach, J.E., Chatterji, S., Badley, E.M. and Ustun, T.B. (1999) 'Models of disablement, universalism and international classification of impairments, disabilities and handicaps', *Social Science and Medicine*, 48: 1173–87.

Brasile, F.M., Kleiber, D.A. and Harnisch, D. (1994) 'Analysis of participation incentives among athletes with and without disabilities', *Therapeutic Recreation Journal*, January–March: 18–33.

Brittain, I. (2004) 'Perceptions of disability and their impact upon involvement in sport for people with disabilities at all levels', *Journal of Sport and Social Issues*, 28: 429–52.

Collins, D. (1997) *Conference Report.* National Disability Sport Conference, King's Fund Centre, London.

Council for Europe (1987) *European Charter for Sport for All: Disabled Persons.* Strasbourg: Council for Europe.

Department for Education and Employment (DfEE) (2000) *Key Facts and Figures Feb. 2000 Disability Briefing.* Labour Force Survey Autumn 1999 Great Britain. www.disability.gov.uk (accessed 14 March 2000).

Department for Education and Science (DES) (1981) *The Education Act.* London: HMSO.

Department of National Heritage (DNH) (1995) *Sport: Raising the Game.* London: DNH.

Doll-Tepper, G. (1999) 'Disability sport', in J. Riordan and A. Kruger (eds), *The International Politics of Sport in the Twentieth Century.* London and New York: E & FN Spon, pp. 177–90.

Drake, R.F. (1994) 'The exclusion of disabled people from positions of power in British voluntary organisations', *Disability and Society*, 9: 461–90.

Elvin, I.T. (1994) 'A UK perspective in the development and management of sport for people with a disability', in H.V. Coppenolle, Y. Vanlanderwijck, J. Simons, P. Van de Vliet and E. Neerinckx (eds), *First European Conference on Adapted Physical Activity and Sports: a White Paper on Research and Practice.* Leuven, Belgium: ACCO.

English Federation of Disability Sport (EFDS) (1999) *Building a Fairer Sporting Society.* Sport for Disabled People in England. A Four Year Development Plan 2000–2004. Crewe: EFDS.

Fitzgerald, H. and Kay, T. (2004) *Sports Participation by Disabled Young People in Derbyshire.* Loughborough: Institute of Youth Sport.

Guttmann, L. (1976) *Textbook of Sport for the Disabled.* Oxford: HM & M.

Hahn, H. (1984) 'Sport and the political movement of disabled persons examining non-disabled social values', *Arena Review,* 8 (1): 1–15.

Halliday, P. (1993) 'Physical education within special education provision – equality and entitlement', in J. Evans (ed.), *Equality, Education and Physical Education.* London: Falmer Press.

Health Education Authority (1999) *Physical Activity in Our Lives. Qualitative Research among Disabled People.* London: Health Education Authority.

Hughes, B. and Paterson, K. (1997) 'The social model of disability and the disappearing body: towards a sociology of impairment', *Disability and Society,* 12 (3): 325–40.

Institute of Sport and Recreation Management (ISRM) (1999) *Disability in Sport: the Legal Framework. The Disability Discrimination Act 1995.* Melton Mowbray: ISRM. Ref. 188: 12/99.

Minister for Sport Review Group (1989) *Building on Ability.* Leeds: HMSO for Department of Education, the Ministers' Review Group.

Oliver, M. (1990) *The Politics of Disablement.* Basingstoke: Macmillan.

Penney, D. and Evans, J. (1995) 'The National Curriculum for physical education: entitlement for all?', *British Journal of Physical Education,* Winter: 6–13.

Schmidt-Gotz, E., Doll-Tepper, G. and Lienert, C. (1994) 'Attitudes of university students and teachers towards integrating students with disabilities into regular physical education classes', *Physical Education Review,* 17 (1): 45–57.

Shakespeare, T. and Watson, N. (1997) 'Defending the social model', *Disability and Society,* 12 (2): 293–300.

Smith, A. and Thomas, N. (2004) 'Inclusion, special educational needs, disability and physical education', in K. Green and K. Hardman (eds), *Physical Education: Essential Issues.* London: Sage.

Smith, A. and Thomas, N. (2005) 'The "inclusion" of elite athletes with disabilities in the 2002 Manchester Commonwealth Games: an exploratory analysis of British newspaper coverage', *Sport, Education and Society,* 10 (1): 49–67.

Sport England (2000) *Young People with a Disability and Sport.* London: Sport England.

Sport England (2002) *Adults with a Disability and Sport: National Survey 2000–2001.* London: Sport England.

Sports Council (1982) *Sport in the Community: the Next Ten Years.* London: Sports Council.

Sports Council (1988) *Sport in the Community: Into the 90's. A Strategy for Sport 1988–1993.* London: Sports Council.

Sports Council (1993) *People with Disabilities and Sport. Policy and Current/Planned Action.* London: Sports Council.

Stafford, I. (1989) 'Everybody active. A Sports Council national demonstration project in England', *Adapted Physical Activity Quarterly*, 6: 100–8.

Steadward, R. (1996) 'Integration and sport in the Paralympic movement', *Sports Science Review*, 5 (1): 26–41.

Stone, S. (1995) 'The myth of bodily perfection', *Disability and Society*, 10 (4): 413–24.

Taub, D.E. and Greer, K.R. (1998) 'Sociology of acceptance revisited: males with physical disabilities participating in sport and physical fitness activity', *Deviant Behaviour*, 19: 279–302.

Thomas, N. (2004) 'An examination of the disability sport policy network in England: a case study of the English Federation of Disability Sport and Mainstreaming in Seven Sport', Unpublished PhD. thesis, Loughborough University.

Thomas, N. and Smith, A. (2003) '"Pre-occupied with able-bodiedness?": an analysis of the British media coverage of the 2000 Paralympic Games', *Adapted Physical Activity Quarterly*, 20 (2): 166–81.

Williams, T. (1994) 'Sociological perspectives on sport and disability: structural-functionalism', *Adapted Physical Activity Quarterly*, 17 (1): 14–24.

Williams, T. and Newman, I. (1988) 'Initial research on integration and involvement in community sport and recreation', *Working Papers of the Everybody Active Demonstration Project No. 4*, Sunderland Polytechnic.

10

The Politics of 'Race' and Sports Policy in the United Kingdom

BEN CARRINGTON AND IAN MCDONALD

OVERVIEW

» *The emergence and development of sports policy and 'race'*
» *Sports policy, community and multiculturalism*
» *From anti-racism to managing racial inequalities*
» *Contemporary developments and issues in sports policy and 'race'*
» *From racial equality towards human rights*
» *Bureaucratic managerialism: the new discourse of anti-racism?*
» *Conclusion*

On 6 July 2005, in a hotel in downtown Singapore, Jacques Rogge, the President of the International Olympic Committee (IOC), announced that London had been awarded the right to host the 2012 Olympic Games. The initial commentary within the British print media on why London had beaten the other cities (including the likes of Madrid, New York, Moscow and Paris) focused on the decision to include 30 'inner-city' children from London's East End amongst the 100 representatives each city was allowed in the voting hall. Compared with the slick film produced for Paris by the renowned filmmaker Luc Besson, the London bid chose, instead, to focus on London's racial and ethnic diversity. It was the ordinary, everyday, lived multiculturalism of contemporary London that was seen to have swayed the IOC voting members. The immediate news coverage thus praised

London's (and the UK's) successful multiculturalism and the role that sport had played in producing both social cohesion and community integration whilst respecting cultural and ethnic diversity. As the leader in *The Independent* put it:

> The final video presentation to IOC delegates yesterday made great play of the city's ethnic diversity. This was a masterstroke. London is a true world city, with inhabitants from every nation on Earth and citizens from a huge number of backgrounds. It is hard to think of a city more firmly in the tradition of the Olympic movement, which seeks to bring together all nations under the common banner of sporting excellence. (2005: 36)

The following morning, on 7 July 2005, four separate explosions took place in central London in what turned out to be a series of linked bombings. The resulting carnage led to over 700 people being injured, many seriously, and 56 deaths, including the four 'suicide bombers'. Once it became clear that the bombers were in fact British and these were 'home-grown' terrorists, the public debate quickly shifted to examining the role of multiculturalism itself in 'fanning the flames' of terrorism. Many right-wing, as well as some liberal, commentators suggested that multiculturalism had 'gone too far' in promoting separate, segregated communities. Rather than assimilating into British values and mores 'ethnic communities' were allowed, if not encouraged, to celebrate their difference. According to such arguments, this had led to a breakdown in the normative order, a lack of respect on the part of ethnic minorities towards the institutions of 'Britishness', and the spread of extremism and radical Islamism. For some pundits London (and by extension the UK as a whole) was now *Londonistan* (Phillips, 2006), a seething, amoral place where relativism and political correctness prevented honest discussion about the 'fifth-column' infiltration of Islamist fascists into the heart of the nation. Thus, in the space of 24 hours, 'multiculturalism' had shifted from a sign that embodied all that was great and strong about the UK, to all that was wrong and weak with contemporary British society. Further, the embrace of multiculturalism was so dangerous that it could, if left unchecked, result in the end of liberal democracy in the UK itself.

In the midst of these discussions, sport was once again invoked as a signifier that could help to guide the nation through the tumultuous events of '7/7'. It emerged that one of the suicide bombers, Shazad Tanweer, was an avid cricket player and had actually studied sport science at university. Newspaper headlines drew upon this apparent contradiction of what they termed the 'cricket-loving suicide bomber' (Laville and Cobain, 2005). The implicit and somewhat simplistic suggestion seemed to be: how could someone who loved a sport as quintessentially English as cricket, and whose father reportedly owned a 'fish and chip' shop, commit such a (non-British) heinous act? Sports supposed integrative function was asserted again when Trevor Phillips, then Chair of the UK's Commission for Racial Equality (CRE), wrote in *The Observer* that the Olympics should act as a catalyst for social cohesion, not just for the city, or even the country, but the entire world too; the unity in diversity that won us the Games and that saw us through last week's dreadful carnage will be at the heart of the 2012 Games. By the time London is finished, everyone on Earth should want to know how we created the diverse, integrated society we have. The 2012 Olympic flame will illuminate some wonderful sport. But it should also light the path ahead for the future of our common humanity. (Phillips, 2005: 5)

As we demonstrate in this chapter, questions of identity, nationalism, and race, as well as concerns over social cohesion and inclusion, have been central to British governments' sports policies for over 30 years. Current discussions concerning whether or not the UK is and should be a multicultural society, the extent to which understandings of 'race' and racial difference structure this debate, and the place of sport within this, need to be set within this broader historical framework.

Writing about the growing body of literature on racism and ethnicity in critical studies of social policy, Law noted that although 'issues of racism and ethnicity remain topical and there is a steady growth in research and writing which engages with these issues across the varied fields of social policy, there is a noticeable underdevelopment in areas such as health and sport and leisure' (1996: x). A decade later, sport and leisure theorists in the UK have finally begun to address these key issues (see e.g. Long et al., 2005; Spracklen et al., 2006; Swinney and Horne, 2005). As a contribution to this emergent body of work, this chapter will, first, give a chronological and thematic overview of key developments in government sports policy and 'race' in the UK since the 1970s and, second, provide a social and political analysis of these developments. Although sports policy has its own set of concerns and has a degree of autonomy from other social fields, it does not exist within a social and political vacuum. It is not only the national context that is crucial in this regard, but also, and increasingly, the European and global contexts (Henry, 2001). Furthermore, it is important to pay particular attention to how the specific concerns and issues within sports policy are refracted through other policy agendas. Our approach is to locate the analysis of 'race' and ethnicity in sports policy within broader social and political discourses. In this way, we avoid two dangers of policy analysis. We avoid a reduction of the analysis to formal or stated policy commitments by the government and sporting bodies on 'race' and ethnicity. Policy is interpreted processually as a complex and dynamic course of action or inaction involving contingently constructed social networks in which particular goals may be as much implicit and unintended as explicit and intended. In short, the policy *text* is decentred and the policy *context* prioritised. In this way, we can talk of a *de facto* government sports policy for 'race' and ethnicity that both precedes and transcends the formal and stated aim of policy. The substantive significance of particular policy interventions is derived from their constitutive role as part of broader social and political discourses. This guards against the second danger of policy analysis, namely of overplaying the fecundity of policy statements and underplaying the political meaning of policy implementation.

THE EMERGENCE AND DEVELOPMENT OF SPORTS POLICY AND 'RACE'

The Racialisation of Sports Policy Discourse

The first UK sports policy intervention on 'race' and ethnicity was framed within a discourse of equality, expressed in the slogan of 'Sport for All'. Although always more an aspiration than a specific policy goal, 'Sport for All' signalled a belief amongst an incipient sports policy community in the early 1970s that access to participation opportunities in sport was a right of citizenship in developed European liberal democracies.

The early to mid-1970s was a propitious time for the development of sporting opportunities with two factors in particular being important in raising the levels of participation. First, the formation of an executive Great Britain (GB) Sports Council in 1972 meant that a strategic approach to the development of sport was possible. Second, the restructuring of local authority administrative boundaries in 1974 resulted in the creation of discrete and often large leisure and recreation departments with a higher political profile and dedicated budgets (Houlihan, 1991). In 1973–4 alone, 137 sports centres and 190 swimming pools were built (Henry, 1993: 117). Coalter et al. (1988) refer to this period as 'recreational welfare', reflecting the consensus that sport and recreation played a legitimate function in terms of an expansive welfare state improving the quality of life for those unable to access opportunities in the private sector. During this period, 'race' and ethnicity were not identified as areas requiring specific intervention. It was considered evident that levels of participation amongst all under-represented groups would benefit from the general expansion in facilities. This was a viewpoint that was proven later to be naive and unrealistic.

No sooner had the concept of 'recreational welfare' been established than it was subjected to a series of initially subtle but, over a period of time, fundamental changes. 'Recreational welfare' was a philosophy that depended on a buoyant economy with generous levels of public spending on sports facilities. Yet the mid-1970s saw the UK enter a period of profound economic crisis. Recreational welfare was, according to Coalter et al., 'conceived in affluence, born in uncertainty and ended in austerity' (1988: 22). Faced with a severe economic crisis, the Labour government (1974–9) abandoned its Keynesian approach to economic management, and embraced a monetarist position. This resulted in cuts in public expenditure, hastening a reduction in the levels of welfare services available to the most needy and vulnerable in society, and inevitably feeding into the increasing levels of poverty and alienation in many parts of the country (Cliff and Gluckstein, 1988; Solomos and Back, 1996). The deteriorating social fabric of the inner cities increasingly became a central policy concern of government and a source of wider public anxiety.

The slide into economic crisis provided the backdrop for the racialisation of political debates about urban policy and social policy that developed from the late 1960s, with black youths being linked in popular and political discourse to social instability and crime. As Solomos notes, it was during the 1970s that 'the imagery of violence and decay became synonymous with those inner-city localities in which black migrants had settled and established themselves' (2003: 130). An important influence on the process of criminalisation was the media-produced moral panic about 'mugging' in the early 1970s. This was constructed as a new 'black juvenile' crime, and perceived by the public as constituting a major social problem that required an authoritarian and populist 'law and order' solution in order to discipline young black people in particular into more productive citizens (Hall et al., 1978). However, in response, there was a growing sense of frustration within black communities, and an increasingly antagonistic relationship between black youths and the police (Witte, 1996: 59). These tensions would eventually explode in the summer of 1981, with the riots in Brixton, Toxteth, Moss Side and many other cities and towns across the UK. Although white and black youth were involved in the riots, they were construed in popular and political discourse as 'race riots', thus feeding the imagery of inner cities as havens of black criminality.

Unwilling to address the structural nature of the problems caused by mass unemployment and reduced welfare spending, the Labour government had already laid the basis for sport to be used as one of its more affordable and politically expedient options. A number of official government reports, including the White Papers on *Sport and Recreation* (DOE, 1975), *A Policy for the Inner Cities* (DOE, 1977a) and the *Recreation and Deprivation in Urban Areas* (DOE, 1977b) document, had delineated the role of sport as a tool of urban social control. It meant, in effect, a racialisation of sports policy discourse as 'equality of opportunity was ... abandoned and resources were henceforth concentrated more on the problems of "deprived areas", that is, on preventing vandalism and delinquency, dealing with the consequences of unemployment and doing something about the plight of ethnic minorities' (Hargreaves, 1986: 187).

At the same time as the Labour government was pressing for a shift in sports policy towards targeting deprived areas, a consensus was emerging in the sports policy community that a facility-based strategy for reducing the unequal patterns of sport participation was ineffective. As Henry noted:

> While 'sport for all' might be the avowed goal of sports policy, with a particular emphasis on reaching disadvantaged groups, research evidence throughout the latter half of the 1970s increasingly indicated a failure on the part of the public sector services to attract ethnic minorities, the unemployed, the elderly, women, the disabled, and low-income groups. (1990: 46)

Accordingly, the Sports Council encouraged local authorities to move away from the building of large prestigious sports centres and towards the development of locally accessible centres (Henry, 1993: 118). The paternalism of traditional facility-based management approaches thus gave way to a community-development approach based on the principle of 'empowering' disadvantaged members of the local community. This new emphasis in Sports Council strategy was confirmed with the publication of its strategic document in 1982, *Sport in the Community: the Next Ten Years,* which argued for the need to 'target' recreationally disadvantaged groups, such as women, the disabled, the elderly and ethnic minorities. However, which groups would actually be targeted was to be dictated by the pressing political concern with the perceived social breakdown in the inner cities. So while Houlihan (1991: 99) noted that 'Sport For All slowly became "sport for the disadvantaged" and "sport for inner-city youth"', Hargreaves argued that in practice this meant a preoccupation with youth, especially black youth: 'It is clear that the main concern is with the potentially troublesome – the unemployed, young white working-class males, and young working-class blacks' (1986: 189). The first significant programme to use the new target-group approach was the 15 Action Sport projects that were piloted in inner-city locales in London and Birmingham from 1982 to 1985 (Rigg, 1986). Action Sport was a project-based initiative that revolved around a sports worker going into particular communities to set up activity sessions and programmes. These first Action Sport programmes can be interpreted partly as a result of deliberations within the sports policy community, and partly as a response to the riots of the early 1980s. So, despite the long list of Sports Council target groups, Action Sport focused predominantly on the perceived protagonists of social disorder, namely urban black youth and young working-class males.

Thus, the specific intervention to increase the opportunities for participation by ethnic minority groups was ambiguous. It was 'positive' to the extent that those in the sports policy community recognised that, in effect, affirmative action was required to redress the structural imbalances in participation. However, the racialisation of political discourse with its constructions of black criminality and inner-city decay ensured that the implementation of Sports Council policy agendas reinforced stereotypes about black physicality and intellectual deficiency, therefore performing 'ideological work at reproducing blacks' subordinate position' (Hargreaves, 1986: 197). If the riots of 1981 elicited a physical response by the state to regain social control of the inner cities, then there is an argument for interpreting the role of sports policy as a form of 'soft' policing, ensuring in Foucauldian terms the maintenance of social control by involving perceived problematic groups in sporting activities.

SPORTS POLICY, COMMUNITY AND MULTICULTURALISM

Although, predictably, there was strong condemnation of the riots in 1981 from the Thatcher government (1979–90), there was also acknowledgement in subsequent state-sponsored investigations that racism in the police, along with problems of social deprivation and alienation, were contributory factors in producing such disorder (Solomos,

2003; Witte, 1996). The Scarman Report (1981) referred to the importance of sport and leisure provision as a means to alleviate social tensions, paving the way for a growth of racial equality strategies mainly from local rather than central government, where anti-racist policies based on the concept of multiculturalism were most vigorously pursued. Multiculturalism was welcomed by many people as an advance on assimilationist models of 'race relations' in the embrace rather than the denial of cultural diversity. However, the doctrine of official multiculturalism is problematic as it often fails to break out of the discourse of 'race'. In the context of what Barker (1981) called the New Racism – which shifted the discourse of racism from biology to ethnicity and culture – a new form of racial stratification emerged based on stereotypical notions of absolute ethnic difference. Ethnicity was intended by advocates of multiculturalism to be conceived of as a dynamic and fluid process of cultural self-identification and conceptually distinct from the objectifying and static category of 'race' (cf. Hesse, 2000). However, under the new racism, multiculturalism and ethnicity often rearticulated the old meanings of 'race' within a new socio-political discourse of inherent difference. Ethnicity became an imposed, fixed and immutable category, a cultural prison from which those it embraced could rarely escape – what Gilroy (1987) called ethnic absolutism.

Much of the focus for the Sports Council during the 1980s lay with working alongside local authorities in promoting sport in the community. As we have seen, its strategic document *Sport in the Community: the Next Ten Years* identified a number of target groups requiring specific policy interventions. However, the political climate of the early part of the decade dictated that black (male) urban youth were prioritised. However, as the memory of the riots faded, so the Action Sport projects incorporated other designated target groups, in particular Asian women. Though many of these projects were worthy and well intended, they tended to conform to an ethnic absolutist discourse of multiculturalism. For example, a number of projects in Manchester based on swimming, badminton and keep-fit, which were set up in 1987–8 and targeted at South Asian women (and cited as an example of good practice by the Sports Council), reveal a tendency to view 'Asian women' as a culturally homogeneous 'other': 'Unlike the men, many Asian women living in Old Trafford had no social life outside the family. The strict constraints on young women, which they readily accepted, had to be understood and respected by project workers' (Sports Council, n.d.). Stereotypical perceptions of South Asian women as socially isolated and passive, colluding in their subordination to a patriarchal domesticity, abound in the evaluative project report.

The problem with adopting the target-group approach is that it tended not to recognise the cause of the estrangement felt by many black and South Asian people towards sport. The emphasis on 'cultural constraint' or 'difference' led policy makers and sport development officers to problematise the target groups in question. In asking what it was about 'their culture' or 'their religion' that needed to be understood in order for opportunities in sport to be made available, it allowed 'our sports' and 'our structures' to be left unexamined. Therefore, the persistent 'problem' of relatively low levels of participation amongst many ethnic minority groups is inadvertently blamed on 'them', whilst at the same time legitimating a presumed 'normal' level of sporting participation based on unacknowledged sporting practices of white middle-class males. Fleming, whose research among South Asian male youths showed that sport could be used as a tool by the white ethnic majority for excluding minority South Asian communities, argued that 'the pre-occupation with cultural difference is a diversion and a distraction from the most fundamental issue – the pervasive impact of racism in all its guises' (1994: 172).

So the early Action Sport projects were geared towards black youth, but were located within a problematic law and order framework, whilst the attempt to relate to other ethnic minority groups was premised on the notion of cultural disadvantage and otherness. Furthermore, there was little evidence that such policies were succeeding in 'evening out' the differential levels of sport participation. Black and ethnic minority groups were still less likely to participate in sport than their white counterparts (McIntosh and Charlton, 1985; Verma and Darby, 1994). Such stubborn patterns of inequality in levels of participation demanded a different strategic focus, from one that treated 'race' and ethnicity as static variables that had to be overcome by sport *animateurs,* to one that saw 'race' and ethnicity as relations of power.

FROM ANTI-RACISM TO MANAGING RACIAL INEQUALITIES

The development of policy should not be seen exclusively through the prism of governmental action (or inaction) in responding to political crises. Other non-state actors, including voluntary associations and social movements, have been instrumental in effecting policy changes. For example, during the early 1990s, fan-based football groups became increasingly successful at challenging popular images of all football fans as racist hooligans. They argued that although crude and overt forms of racism were still a problem on the terraces, they were restricted to a minority of fans who, in the absence of an anti-racist initiative, could attract much larger numbers behind them. They succeeded in persuading a number of bodies to come together to launch the 'Let's Kick Racism Out of Football' campaign in 1993. Sponsored initially by the Commission for Racial Equality (CRE) and the Professional Footballers' Association (PFA), with support from the Football Trust, the campaign soon gained the backing of all the main football bodies. It aimed to ensure that all those who go to see or play football could do so without fear of racial abuse or harassment. After the initial focus on fan racism in the professional game, it has since broadened its priorities to include amateur football, the dearth of professional South Asian players, the issue of racism in European football, and the continuing forms of discrimination from the boardrooms and managerial positions off the field of play (Asians in Football Forum, 2005; Back et al., 1996, 2001; Bains and Johal, 1998; Burdsey,

2007; Garland and Rowe, 2001; King, 2004). The significance of this campaign is that it has shifted the debate about 'race' and ethnicity away from the 'cultural peculiarities' of ethnic minorities towards the perpetrators of racism, whilst developing a more complex understanding of the articulation of racism beyond forms of 'race hate', and placed the responsibility for action on the relevant authorities.

The Sports Council accepted this shift of emphasis at a seminar organised in 1992, which was confirmed in its 1994 policy document on *Black and Ethnic Minorities and Sport*. It recognised that disadvantage and discrimination caused racial inequality and that positive action was required to address the causes of racism, rather than just its effects. It stated:

> The Sports Council recognises that racism is present in sport and can appear in many forms. We define racism to be all actions (or inactions), policies and practices of individuals or organisations, whether deliberate or not, which create or sustain racial inequality ... Because many people in sport have understood racism to consist only of overt and deliberate forms of discrimination, more subtle and unintentional racism is often not even detected. (Sports Council, 1994: 17)

The authors of the document argued that a combination of, and complex interplay between, socio-economic status, cultural lifestyle and racism accounted for the position of black and ethnic minorities in sport. It recognised the failings of previous approaches that did little:

> to challenge the underlying causes of this inequity ... A majority of decision-makers have little understanding of the sporting needs and aspirations of black and ethnic minorities. They are not aware of how disadvantage and discrimination restrict access to sport. (Sports Council, 1994: 18)

The report recommended that sports organisations inspect their own procedures and practices, and develop proactive policies to ensure equity within their own structures. In addition, it advocated community development interventions to support and develop not only levels of participation but also self-management of projects.

Black and Ethnic Minorities and Sport was an analytically sound, realistic and constructive document. Its publication suggested that a more progressive approach to sport and racial inequality might be adopted. However, no sooner had the document been published than John Major's Conservative government (1990–7) launched a major new policy for sport in 1995 which privileged the development of excellence in the UK's traditional team sports. Outlined in the policy document, *Sport: Raising the Game* (DNH, 1995), the new policy not only omitted any discussion of racism, but embraced a wholly traditionalist approach to sport that completely erased equality as a serious or central issue (McDonald, 2000). Furthermore, the strategic emphasis on top-level sport, with its evidence of black athletic success, had the effect of denying the existence of racial barriers to progression in sport. In addition, in rejecting its responsibility towards sport in the community, it could also ignore the problems of racism in non-elite sport.

The ease with which the analyses and recommendations contained in *Black and Ethnic Minorities and Sport* could be marginalised by the Sports Council – and sport governing bodies – so soon after its publication, suggests that a commitment to anti-racism had yet to be cemented in the organisation, and that the nuanced understanding of 'race' and ethnicity was probably restricted to those responsible for producing the report.

The campaign for racial equality in sport continued in football, and on a smaller scale in other sports, as evidence of racist practices intermittently emerged, leading to varied attempts to address the problem. For example, in cricket, in 1995, issues of racism in sport hit the headlines when the reputable *Wisden Cricket Monthly* magazine published an article arguing that black and other foreign-born players should not play for England as they apparently would not try as hard as their white team-mates, referred to as 'unequivocal Englishmen'. The article went on to suggest that the England Test Team's decline in world standings at the time was directly related to the increase in the number of black and foreign-born players representing England (Henderson, 1995). The spurious evidence provided for these claims owed more to nationalistic prejudices against 'non-white' cricketers than it did to any serious discussion about nationality and sport (Marqusee, 2001). In the wake of this and other evidence of racism in cricket, the campaign to 'Hit Racism for Six' (1996) was established to lobby the England and Wales Cricket Board (ECB) to address racism in the game.

Similarly in 1996, the launch of the 'Tackle It – Tackle Racism in Rugby League' campaign – a joint venture from the CRE and the Rugby Football League (RFL) – was a response to research that demonstrated that racism was 'a small but significant' issue in the sport (Long et al., 1995; see also Long et al., 1997a). The campaign aimed to make Rugby League clubs take positive action to eradicate all racist abuse from their grounds, and to develop the game among ethnic minority communities in the clubs' local areas.

CONTEMPORARY DEVELOPMENTS AND ISSUES IN SPORTS POLICY AND 'RACE'

Social Exclusion and Racial Equality under New Labour

It was expected that the election of a Labour government (1997–) would herald a broader approach to sports policy – one that would be as concerned with increasing mass participation as raising levels of excellence (English Sports Council, 1997; Labour Party, 1997). However, as Houlihan argues, in office Labour have enthusiastically embraced the quest for international sporting success as evidenced by the government's successful bid to host the 2012 Olympic Games in London:

> Despite rhetorical flourishes about reinvigorating the concept of Sport for All, it is the extent of continuity between the in-coming Labour government and its predecessors that has been most striking over the last two years ... in many ways the Labour Party sought to outshine the Conservatives in its commitment to competition and elite achievement. (Houlihan, 2000: 175)

Notwithstanding Houlihan's comments, within their shared commitment to national success, there are important policy distinctions between the two governments. Unlike *Sport: Raising the Game*, the publication of Sport England's National Lottery Strategy, *Investing for Our Sporting Future* (1999) and the subsequent government policy documents *A Sporting Future for All* (DCMS, 2000), *The Government's Plan for Sport* (DCMS, 2001) and *Game Plan: A strategy for delivering Government's sport and physical activity objectives* (DCMS, 2002) contain significant references to the issue of equality. Sensitive to charges of favouring the elite levelled at their predecessors, Labour have emphasised that they are as much concerned with developing opportunities for a broader range of the population. This is expressed in policy commitments that see sport as a regenerative resource in deprived urban areas, and in the belief that diverse social groups should not be discriminated against and disenfranchised in the sporting sphere (DCMS, 2000). New Labour's use of sport to press its claims for a more just society is framed within the concept of 'social exclusion' (Long et al., 2002). In political discourse, social exclusion and social inclusion are seen as binary opposites, so that in tackling social exclusion, the desired political goal of social inclusion will be achieved (Giddens, 1998). Although often used this way within sports policy (Collins, 2003), it is important to recognise that Sport England refers to social inclusion in an additional way; that is, as the conceptual framework to promote equality in terms of gender, 'race' and disability in sport. Social inclusion is the *principle* under which all sports organisations are asked to ensure that no barriers exist towards the increased participation of disabled people, women and ethnic minorities in sport. When used in this sense it is distinct from the use of social exclusion/inclusion in political discourses of poverty and lack of opportunities within deprived communities. Social exclusion has been very precisely operationalised in policy discourse: it occurs as a consequence of high unemployment, high rates of crime, poor health and low educational achievement. Where sport is part of this discourse, the concern is with how sports – along with other activities such as the arts, community projects and regeneration programmes – can be used to tackle social problems and thereby assist in the process of developing social cohesion (DCMS, 1999).

Sport England's Active Communities programme, which is aimed at providing participation and coaching opportunities in areas of social deprivation, has perhaps most relevance to the social exclusion agenda. In referring to the regenerative remit of sport, the social exclusion agenda at best implicitly relates to ethnic minorities inasmuch as they are part of the designated deprived communities. However, if the critics are correct that absent from the discourse of exclusion is the determining effect of structural relations of power, then the impact of racism in perpetuating discriminatory treatment will not be recognised. So, while 'race' is recognised as a social factor in patterns of social exclusion, the significance of *racism* is rarely treated as a contributory factor. Hargreaves's (1986: 198) prescient remark that 'the social structure is conjured away and what is left are individuals with their problems' remains as pertinent to New Labour's approach in the first decade of the twenty-first century, as it was about the individualistic neo-liberal ideology of the Conservative government throughout the 1980s and early 1990s.

Whereas the social exclusion agenda disavows the significance of racism, Sport England's principle of social inclusion leaves open the possibility for a discourse of racial discrimination and therefore of anti-racism. Indeed, there has been a flurry of activity, predominantly at the level of policy formulation, in recent years around the issue of social inclusion, racial equality and sport. A number of political factors coalesced to put racial equality on the political and sporting agenda. Not least of these were the high-profile inquiries and court cases relating to the murder of the black teenager Stephen Lawrence, and the subsequent Macpherson Report published in February 1999. The definition of institutional racism contained in the report was taken up as the benchmark against which all public organisations should measure themselves. It defined institutional racism as:

> The collective failure of an organisation to provide an appropriate and professional service to people because of their colour, culture or ethnic origin. It can be seen or detected in processes, attitudes and behaviour which amount to discrimination through unwitting prejudice, ignorance, thoughtlessness and racist stereotyping which disadvantage minority ethnic people. (Macpherson, 1999)

The changing political climate was reflected in the legislative amendments to the 1976 Race Relations Act. The Act was changed to make it unlawful for any public authority (private or voluntary bodies as well as statutory bodies) to discriminate on racial grounds when it is carrying out public functions. Further, and of greater significance for sports policy, it is now a duty of all public authorities to work towards eliminating racial discrimination and promoting racial equality in carrying out their functions. The second of these changes has potentially huge implications for sports governing bodies and clubs in placing the responsibility on them to be proactive in eliminating racial inequalities. *The Future of Multi-Ethnic Britain – The Parekh Report,* an influential and widely debated report defending the virtues of multiculturalism in promoting a progressive and cohesive society, was published in 2000. It acknowledged the contribution of anti-racist campaigns in sport, especially in football, in promoting social cohesion (Runnymede Trust, 2000: 159–75). It is the political space opened up by the Parekh and Macpherson Reports, the legislative changes made in the latter's wake, and the campaigns by various sports anti-racist groups (aided by academic research in this area) that have allowed significant policy developments to occur.

FROM RACIAL EQUALITY TOWARDS HUMAN RIGHTS

Until recently, the analysis of patterns of racial inequality in sports participation has relied on small-scale and localised surveys, or information derived from the General Household Survey. The results of the first ever large-scale quantitative survey into the relationship between sports participation and ethnicity conducted by the Office for National Statistics on behalf of Sport England is therefore of particular interest in that it confirms the existence of racial inequalities (Sport England, 2000). The survey found that the overall participation rate for ethnic minority groups in sport was 40 per cent compared with a national average of 46 per cent. Clearly, there are significant differences in rates of participation when the figures are broken down by gender and ethnicity. For example, black African men have a higher participation rate than the national average for all men, while Bangladeshi women had participation rates well below the national average for women.

The survey revealed that a large proportion of individuals from all ethnic groups say they would like to take part in a sport in which they currently do not participate, demonstrating a positive attitude to sport. However, also revealed was the fact that the main reasons for individuals not participating in sport were related to home and family responsibilities, work demands and lack of local facilities. The report concluded that while there is clear evidence of racial inequality in sport, this appears to have little to do with racism. Such a conclusion has to be treated with caution and may be largely a function of the quantitative methodology employed. As we have argued, racism works in increasingly complex and subtle ways: racial inequalities are often achieved and maintained while eschewing a language of 'race' and racism. It may be that more qualitatively inclined methodologies are better suited to eliciting the dynamics of racial ideologies buried beneath alternative explanations. In reflecting on his experience of conducting research into racism in sport with South Asian and black athletes, Long concluded that 'had we not been doing qualitative interviews, we may not have uncovered their experiences of racism' (2000: 129).

While uncovering levels of participation in sport lends itself to a quantitative approach, understanding the subjective experiences of individuals in sport demands a theoretically informed interpretative approach. It will be necessary for Sporting Equals, a body created by Sport England and the CRE in 1998, to work with governing bodies to develop policies for racial equality and to achieve a sophisticated understanding of the dynamics of racism in sport if it is to make progress. The evidence from a survey by Sporting Equals in 1999 to gauge the approach of governing bodies to racial equality indicated a general resistance to discuss these issues. Of 62 national governing bodies surveyed, half did not respond, while 50 per cent of those that did claimed that racial discrimination was not a problem in their sport (Sporting Equals, 2000).

In producing a Racial Equality Charter for Sport (see Box 10.1), Sporting Equals appears to recognise that patterns of racial inequality in terms of participation, management and support are intimately related to a culture of racism that permeates British sporting establishments. As Box 10.1 reveals, racial inequality is not seen as being divorced from racial discrimination and, in a novel departure for policy makers, representation in aspects of sport apart from participation is recognised.

Box 10.1 The Racial Equality Charter for Sport

Governing bodies and sports organisations will:

- Make a public commitment to challenge and remove racial discrimination and to achieve racial equality in sport.
- Encourage people from all communities to become involved in sport.
- Welcome employees and spectators from all communities, and protect all employees and spectators from racial abuse and harassment.
- Encourage skilled and talented individuals from all communities to become involved at all levels of sports administration, management and coaching.
- Develop the best possible racial equality policies and practices, and to review and update them regularly.
- Celebrate cultural diversity in sport. (Sporting Equals, 2000)

The first signatories to the Charter included the Chief Executives of Rugby Football League, Rugby Football Union, UK Athletics, England and Wales Cricket Board, English Basketball, Amateur Swimming Association and the National Coaching Foundation (Sporting Equals, 2000). In December 2000, Sporting Equals published *Achieving Racial Equality: A Standard for Sport* (2000). It encouraged governing bodies and organisations to provide evidence that they were working towards race equality objectives by developing Race Equality Action Plans and by monitoring the people who are taking part in the sport by age, gender, disability and ethnic origin. It also provided a means to measure the outcomes of its policies and action plans. Sporting Equals has devised a four-tier 'quality mark' scheme – foundation, preliminary, intermediate and advanced – which indicates the level of achievement by the organisation. This *Standard* is intended to be incorporated in Sport England's criteria for National Lottery funds and evidence suggests that this mechanism has been at least partially successful in 'pushing' sports organisations to develop policies on racial discrimination. As Long et al. note, despite its shortcomings, 'the *Standard* has encouraged activity. In many cases, it has been the process of applying for the award itself that has promoted work on racial discrimination that would otherwise not have happened or else would have been addressed to a lesser extent' (2005: 49).

It is apparent then that racial equality is increasingly accepted at the level of policy formulation, although the situation is far more uneven amongst particular governing bodies. The chief mechanism for encouraging national governing bodies and sports organisations to integrate racial equality objectives into their strategic development plans is to link it to National Lottery funding criteria (DCMS, 2000). Yet, despite this, a report for Sporting Equals concluded that although there is now a greater recognition of the importance of racial equality, such policies are not given a high priority within sports organisations and often lose out when faced with competing demands, being particularly vulnerable to staff changes (Long et al., 2003). Mapping the effectiveness of such policies will be further complicated by the decision in 2004 to replace the Racial Equality Standard with a broader Equality Standard that includes issues of gender and disability as well as 'race' and ethnicity. This shift in emphasis reflects broader changes that have resulted following the Equality Act (2006) which established the Commission for Equality and Human Rights (CEHR) in October 2007. The CEHR integrated the duties previously carried out by the Disability Rights Commission, the Equal Opportunities Commission as well as the CRE. Quite how the change in the legislative framework will affect the ongoing policy initiatives for racial equality in sport is open to question. Indeed, what may emerge over the next few years as the policy framework matures is a recognition by policy makers and others that a progressive policy framework for eradicating racial abuse and inequalities in sport represents the start of the process rather than being an end in itself. If the commitment to racial equality is to be more than a form of paying lip-service, then it is also necessary to engage with the deep-rooted cultural relations of power that sustain racially exclusive practices. Without such a shift, then the danger is that the campaign for racial equality in sport may become little more than a managerial response by bureaucratic organisations like sport governing bodies compelled by law to show they have policies on equity in place, but understanding little and doing less about the entrenched cultures of racial exclusion. The experience of the campaign for racial equality in English cricket is instructive in this regard.

BUREAUCRATIC MANAGERIALISM: THE NEW DISCOURSE OF ANTI-RACISM?

Arguably, the sport that has made the most progress in developing a strategy for racial equality is cricket. The first half of the 1990s saw cricket officials and commentators promoting an inward-looking and racially exclusive form of nationalism (Marqusee, 2005). This invoked an imperial conception of Englishness prevalent in political discourse in the 1980s and 1990s, which actively sought to exclude 'non-white' citizens from the national imagined community (Carrington, 1998). However, by the end of the 1990s, the main debate centred on the need for cricket to tackle racism and to embrace its 'non-white' players, especially those from the Asian communities.

Such a dramatic shift can be seen as the result of a number of factors:

- **the combination of anti-racist lobbying (Hit Racism for Six, 1996) and research (Long et al., 1997b; McDonald and Ugra, 1998);**
- **a recognition that traditional notions of Englishness may be detrimental to the performance of the national team (Engel, 1999; Hughes, 1999);**
- **the pressure to respond to the challenges set out by the Macpherson Report;**
- **the vigour with which Sport England promoted equity; and**
- **the contribution of the Asian communities to ensuring that the Cricket World Cup in 1999 was a commercial and sporting triumph (Crabbe and Wagg, 2000).**

In 1998 the ECB created a Racism Study Group to compile a report that would outline the extent of racism in the game, based mainly on a quantitative survey of players and officials, and to produce a set of recommendations on how to tackle racism and ensure racial equality. The report was published in the autumn of 1999 and, according to Terry Bates of the ECB, was 'comprehensive and conclusive' (ECB, 1999: 5). After the racial controversies that had embroiled cricket for much of the 1990s, the report was widely received as a welcome step forward for this most tradition bound of sports.

Unfortunately, the report failed to address the most fundamental issue on whether and how racism exists in cricket. It would only go as far as saying that the survey revealed that 58 per cent of respondents (of whom only a minority were 'non-white') *believed* that racism exists in English cricket. Accordingly, the report recommended 'that the ECB accepts and acknowledges ... that there is definitely, at least, *perceived racism* in cricket' (ECB, 1999: 43; emphasis in the original). However, in formulating the recommendation in this way, it allowed the ECB to sidestep the question of whether it accepted that racism was a real, rather than just a perceived, problem in the game. If the problem was one of perception, then it was that, rather than structural change, that needed to be managed. Furthermore, the report also stated that 'this survey did not establish that there is institutional racism in English cricket, as only 12 per cent thought that racism was ingrained in English cricket' (ECB, 1999: 43). This is a *non sequitur* as the measurement of institutional racism is not dependent purely on the beliefs of individuals covered by the survey. The report was silent on whether it accepted the conclusions of two separate academic reports based on Yorkshire (Long et al., 1997b) and Essex and East London (McDonald and Ugra, 1998) that a culture of racial exclusion is endemic within the structure of cricket.

If the report was weak analytically, then at least it came up with some measured and practical proposals to tackle racism and embrace the black and South Asian cricket communities. However, a decade later, many of the most significant proposals have not been implemented. For example, in the wake of the carnival atmosphere brought to the 1999 World Cup by many South Asian fans, it was recommended that the ban on banners, flags, placards and musical instruments in One Day Internationals and Test matches be lifted for sections of the stands. The ban remains in force at certain grounds. It was recommended in the report that a number of tickets for these matches be reserved for sale on match days at affordable prices, which would give better access to more people from the black and South Asian community. This was rejected on 'commercial' grounds. The report also recommended the establishment of a national forum to discuss the progress of anti-racism policies and the development of black and South Asian cricket. This forum has yet to be created. Marqusee dismissed the report as 'an empty, cynical document, offering little more than lofty declarations and skirting all the difficult questions' (2000; for a more optimistic reading of the report see Williams, 2001).

The document illustrated how a governing body can be compelled to address the issue of 'race' and investigate issues of racial inequality, but will tread far more circumspectly around the issue of racism, especially where it might be implicated as a perpetrator. While the publication of *Clean Bowl Racism* illustrated how the ECB may appreciate the importance of 'race' as an issue, and while it is clearly sensitive to widespread perceptions of racism in the game, there is no evidence in the report that it accepts that these perceptions may be reflecting the reality of racism in cricket. The problems facing black and South Asian cricket teams is, according to the ECB, more a question of poor facilities and lack of coaching opportunities than racial discrimination. Yet, even on the question of investment in inner-city cricket, which would have a dramatic effect in widening the participation base of the group amongst all ethnic groups, the report had little of import to say. During the same period as the publication of *Clean Bowl Racism,* the ECB launched its Inner-city Community Cricket Project, amidst much publicity and government support. However, in an evaluation of the projects in East London, Miller found that they were insufficiently funded and planned, and, after the initial publicity, poorly supported by the ECB. He concluded that the commitment from the ECB to developing cricket in the inner cities 'represents little more than rhetoric' (Miller, 2001: 58).

The report can be seen as a bureaucratic managerialist response by the ECB. That is, on paper, the ECB now has a clear anti-racism strategy and a commitment to improve the opportunities for ethnic minority cricket communities, which are predominantly located in inner-city areas. The ECB is also one of the signatories to the Sporting Equals' Racial Equality Charter for Sport. However, in practice, as we have outlined, the policy declarations have had little impact in affecting the culture of cricket or the relations of power with regard to control of the game. As Long et al. have noted, 'If the *Charter* project is to be a success, more than just the written procedures stipulated by the preliminary award are necessary. The organization has to act decisively to promote the interests of under-represented groups and be outward looking' (2005: 53). The general point is that unless policy documents are supported by analytical rigour, political commitment, financial support and systematic development, they will have little impact in reducing racism in sport and they will continue to have a negligible effect on the social exclusion of ethnic minority groups.

CONCLUSION

In this chapter we have provided a critique of the relationship between 'race' and ethnicity and the development of sports policy since the 1970s. Our approach has been to locate sports policy within its social and political context in order to elicit a fuller understanding of how 'race', ethnicity and anti-racism are implicated in the policy process. We have argued that a concern with 'race' has been a constituent, if complex and ever-shifting feature of national sports policy since the 1970s. We have been guided in providing a critique by the advice of Hill (1997: 22) to be: 'wary of taking policy-makers too seriously [*or too literally – text added*]. Policies may be intended to improve social conditions, but examining whether this is the case should be part of the object of enquiry rather than the assumption of research.'

A critical perspective is especially pertinent in the area of 'race' and ethnicity as governments in liberal democratic regimes rarely declare that their intention is to worsen or maintain poor social conditions, or contain the anger and disaffection of disadvantaged ethnic minorities. Yet despite the plethora of policy documents produced over the past 20 years, which have declared their intention to improve the opportunities for black and ethnic minorities in sport, patterns of racial inequality persist in participation, while many sports governing bodies still obstinately refuse to discuss 'race' issues *within* their own organisations. Those governing bodies that do, as we have illustrated with the case of cricket, prefer a managerialist approach that permits a discussion of 'race', encourages the signing of charters, and embraces policy pledges. Unfortunately, they are often reluctant to pursue policies that require significant investment of resources or that threaten entrenched interests. As Spracklen et al. note, 'if the Racial Equality Standard coerced sports managers into a reactive engagement with equality and diversity, then the new Equality Standard may well end up being gestural unless there is a clear framework in place that balances intervention, encouragement and support' (2006: 301). In this context we would argue that it is necessary for *all* governing bodies to take proactive steps in seeing the policy process as a framework that enables intervention and change both within their sports and within their own structures (see Table 10.1).

TABLE 10.1   Racialisation in sport: a framework for policy intervention

Arena	Context	Forms of racialisation	Policy response
Sporting institutions	• Administration, ruling bodies and decision making • Players' associations • Club ownership and committee control	• Racial inequality in terms of access to decision-making forums • Racial exclusion in relation to membership	• Increasing access and representation of Asian and black people within the administrative and ruling bodies of the sport • Challenging the normalised nature of whiteness in sport environments, representation through the media and the economics of ownership
Sporting practices	• Scouting and patterns of recruitment • Players' culture • Management and coaching • Administration and marketing • Representation/ experiences of black and Asian fans	• Connection between racialised attributes, sporting capacity and professional competence • Racialised forms of abuse within the playing/coaching/ spectating arenas	• Awareness within sport of racial • stereotyping • Building a consensus against racialised common sense • Tighter adherence to codes of practice for players and coaches • Priority to developing Asian and black coaches/scouts • Where appropriate, action against racist activity

Source: Adapted from Back et al. (2001: 214)

Meanwhile, the opportunity to develop sport in disadvantaged and deprived communities (a strong policy theme over the last 30 years) has been compromised by its justification within a problematic social control and empowerment rationale. While it may be overstating the case to assert that the conditions of black and ethnic minority communities in sport have not improved as a result of policy initiatives over the past 30 years, we cannot simply accept the underlying premise of these initiatives that sport improves 'race relations'. A more critical understanding of the changing nature of the politics of 'race' and sport would be aided if social policy analysts who have examined 'race' and racism began to take sport more seriously than they have up until now, and similarly if sports policy theorists paid greater attention to the centrality of 'race' and racism within their own analyses of the politics of sport and leisure.

We have argued elsewhere that inequalities and discrimination continue to structure the reality of sport for black and ethnic minorities in the UK in complex and often contradictory ways (Carrington and McDonald, 2001). Nonetheless, it is important to recognise the progress that has been made within sports policy, at least in terms of defining the problem. For example, the discussion in the sports policy community has shifted away from problematising minority groups and towards adopting a reflexive positioning regarding their structures of provision. Furthermore, the legitimacy of tackling racism and working towards racial equality is increasingly accepted, if not necessarily adequately understood, within the higher echelons of the sports policy community, notably the Department of Culture, Media and Sport, Sport England and Sporting Equals. Although a deep culture of racism may permeate sport in the UK, it is a still a contested cultural space. As such, the goal of creating a socially inclusive sporting world, which is both necessary and realistic, cannot be solely a matter of the right policy. If racism and racial inequality in all aspects of sport are to cease to be of significance, and if the promise of Sport for All is to be realised, then the analysis of policy needs to be related to broader relations of power in the culture of sport and society.

CHAPTER SUMMARY

» Policy on 'race' and ethnicity and sport needs to be analysed within the context of broader changes in social policy, not just within the UK but within Europe too.

» 'Sport For All' reflected the discourse of equality dominant in the 1970s and early 1980s and which was replaced in the 1980s with a discourse that targeted potentially disruptive social groups such as black (male) urban youth.

» The policy of targeting problematised the target group rather than focusing on structural barriers and constraints on participation in sport.

» In the 1990s there was a move away from the policy of focusing on the 'cultural peculiarities' of ethnic minorities towards a concern with the perpetrators of racism.

» The impact on sport of changes in social policy has been to support a series of initiatives aimed at overcoming barriers to participation, and challenging racism at sports events and in sports organisations.

» Sporting Equals has had a positive effect in encouraging governing bodies to develop racial equality plans, though it is less clear whether this has resulted in actually challenging white privilege and racial discrimination.

» While recognising the progress that has been made, it is still the case that inequalities and discrimination continue to structure the reality of sport for blacks and ethnic minorities.

FURTHER READING

Law (1996) provides an introduction to the interrelationship between 'race' and ethnicity and the evolution of social policy, while Solomos (2003) provides a comprehensive socio-logical account of the issue of 'race' and racism in the UK. There are a number of studies that explore racism in particular sports such as soccer (Back et al., 2001; Garland and Rowe, 2001; King 2004,) cricket (Williams, 2001) and Rugby League (Long et al., 1997a). There are also studies (e.g. Bains and Johal, 1998; Burdsey, 2007; Ismond, 2003) that focus on racism as experienced by particular ethnic groups. Collins (2003) has a useful chapter on sport policy, social exclusion and 'race', while Carrington and McDonald (2001) provide a comprehensive examination of 'race' and sport in the UK.

REFERENCES

Asians in Football Forum (2005) *Asians Can Play Football: Another Wasted Decade.* London: Asians in Football Forum.

Back, L., Crabbe, T. and Solomos, J. (1996) *Alive and Still Kicking:* London: Advisory Group Against Racism and Intimidation and the Commission for Racial Equality.

Back, L., Crabbe, T. and Solomos, J. (2001) *The Changing Face of Football: Racism, Identity and Multiculture in the English Game.* Oxford: Berg.

Bains, J. and Johal, S. (1998) *Corner Flags and Corner Shops – the Asian Football Experience.* London: Victor Gollancz.

Barker, M. (1981) *The New Racism.* London: Junction Books.

Burdsey, D. (2007) *British Asians and Football: Culture, Identity and Exclusion.* London: Routledge.

Carrington, B. (1998) '"Football's coming home" But whose home? And do we really want it? Nation, football and the politics of exclusion', in A. Brown (ed.), *Fanatics! Power, Identity and Fandom in Football.* London: Routledge, pp. 101–23.

Carrington, B. and McDonald, I. (eds) (2001) *'Race', Sport and British Society.* London: Routledge.

Cliff, T. and Gluckstein, D. (1988) *The Labour Party: a Marxist History.* London: Bookmarks.

Coalter, F., with Long, J. and Duffield, B. (1988) *Recreational Welfare: The Rationale for Public Leisure Policy.* Aldershot: Avebury.

Collins, M., with Kay, T. (2003) *Sport and Social Exclusion*. London: Routledge.

Crabbe, T. and Wagg, S. (2000) 'A carnival of cricket? The cricket world cup, 'race' and the politics of carnival', *Culture, Sport and Society*, 3 (2): 70–88.

Department of Culture, Media and Sport (DCMS) (1999) *Policy Action Team 10. A Report to the Social Exclusion Unit*. London: DCMS.

Department of Culture, Media and Sport (2000) *A Sporting Future for All*. London: DCMS.

Department of Culture, Media and Sport (2001) *The Government's Plan for Sport*. London: DCMS.

Department of Culture, Media and Sport (2002) *Game Plan: a Strategy for Delivering Government's Sport and Physical Activity Objectives*. London: DCMS.

Department of the Environment (DOE) (1975) *Sport and Recreation*. London: HMSO.

Department of the Environment (1977a) *A Policy for the Inner Cities*. London: HMSO.

Department of the Environment (1977b) *Recreation and Deprivation in Urban Areas*. London: HMSO.

Department of National Heritage (DNH) (1995) *Sport: Raising the Game*. London: HMSO.

Engel, M. (ed.) (1999) *Wisden Cricketer's Almanack*. Guildford: John Wisden.

England and Wales Cricket Board (ECB) (1999) *Clean Bowl Racism: 'Going Forward Together': a Report on Racial Equality in Cricket*. London: ECB.

English Sports Council (1997) *England, the Sporting Nation: a Strategy*. London: English Sports Council.

Fleming, S. (1994) 'Sport and South Asian youth: the perils of false universalism and stereotyping', *Leisure Studies*, 13: 159–77.

Garland, J. and Rowe, M. (2001) *Racism and Anti-racism in Football*. Basingstoke: Palgrave.

Giddens, A. (1998) *The Third Way: the Renewal of Social Democracy*. London: Polity Press.

Gilroy, P. (1987) *There Ain't No Black in the Union Jack*. London: Hutchinson.

Hall, S., Critcher, C., Jefferson, T., Clarke, J. and Roberts, B. (1978) *Policing the Crisis: Mugging, the State, and Law and Order*. London: Macmillan.

Hargreaves, J. (1986) *Sport, Power and Culture*. London: Polity Press.

Henderson, R. (1995) 'Is it in the blood?', *Wisden Cricket Monthly*, July: 9–10.

Henry, I. (1990) 'Sport and the state: the development of sports policy in post-war Britain', in F. Kew (ed.), *Social Scientific Perspectives on Sport*. Leeds: BASES/NCF.

Henry, I. (1993) *The Politics of Leisure Policy*. Basingstoke: Macmillan.

Henry, I. (2001) *The Politics of Leisure Policy*. 2nd edn. Basingstoke: Macmillan.

Hesse, B. (ed.) (2000) *Un/Settled Multiculturalisms: Diasporas, Entanglements, Transruptions*. London: Zed Press.

Hill, M. (1997) *The Policy Process in the Modern State*. 3rd edn. London: Harvester Wheatsheaf.

Hit Racism for Six (1996) *Hit Racism for Six: Race and Cricket in England Today*. London: Wernham Press.

Houlihan, B. (1991) *The Government and Politics of Sport*. London: Routledge.

Houlihan, B. (2000) 'Sporting excellence, schools and sports development: the politics of crowded policy spaces', *European Physical Education Review*, 6 (2): 171–93.

Hughes, S. (1999) 'Talking cricket: ethnic minorities in search of a level playing field', in *Electronic Telegraph*, 28 August 1999. http:// www.telegraph.co.uk/.html

Ismond, P. (2003) *Black and Asian Athletes in British Sport and Society: a Sporting Chance?* Basingstoke: Palgrave.

King, C. (2004) *Offside Racism: Playing the White Man*. Oxford: Berg.

Labour Party (1997) *Labour's Sporting Nation*. London: Labour Party.

Laville, S. and Cobain, I. (2005) 'From student and cricket-lover to terror suspect', *Guardian*. 13 July: 1.

Law, I. (1996) *Racism, Ethnicity and Social Policy*. London: Prentice Hall.

Long, J. (2000) 'No racism here? A preliminary examination of sporting innocence', *Managing Leisure*, 5 (3): 121–33.

Long, J., Tongue, N., Spracklen, K. and Carrington, B. (1995) *What's the Difference? A Study into the Nature and Extent of Racism within Rugby League*. Leeds: Leeds Metropolitan University/The Rugby Football League/Leeds City Council.

Long, J., Carrington, B. and Spracklen, K. (1997a) '"Asians cannot wear turbans in the scrum": explorations of racist discourse within professional rugby league', *Leisure Studies*, 16: 249–60.

Long, J., Nesti, M., Carrington, B. and Gilson, N. (1997b) *Crossing the Boundary: the Nature and Extent of Racism in Local League Cricket*. Leeds: Leeds Metropolitan University.

Long, J., Welch, M., Bramham, P., Butterfield, J., Hylton, K. and Lloyd, E. (2002) *Count Me In: The Dimension of Social Inclusion through Culture and Sport*. Leeds: Leeds Metropolitan University.

Long, J., Robinson, P. and Welch, M. (2003) *Raising the Standard: an Evaluation of Progress*. Leeds: Coachwise.

Long, J., Robinson, P. and Spracklen, K. (2005) 'Promoting racial equality within sports organizations', *Journal of Sport & Social Issues*, 29 (1): 41–59.

Macpherson, Sir W. (1999) *The Stephen Lawrence Inquiry: Report on the Inquiry by Sir William Macpherson of Cluny*. Cm. 4262. London: HMSO.

Marqusee, M. (1996) *War Minus the Shooting: a Journey through South Asia during Cricket's World Cup*. London: Heinemann.

Marqusee, M. (2000) 'English fans priced out as ECB sidesteps race equality', http://thewicket. com/2000_08_01/sub_story3.asp (accessed 4 July 2002).

Marqusee, M. (2001) 'In search of the unequivocal Englishman: the conundrum of race and nation in English cricket', in B. Carrington and I. McDonald (eds), *'Race', Sport and British Society*. London: Routledge.

Marqusee, M. (2005) *Anyone but England: An Outsider Looks at English Cricket*. London: Aurum Press.

McDonald, I. (2000) 'Excellence and expedience? Olympism, power and contemporary sports policy in England', in M. Keech and G. McFee (eds), *Issues and Values in Sports and Leisure Cultures*. Oxford: Meyer and Meyer, pp. 83–100.

McDonald, I. and Ugra, S. (1998) *Anyone for Cricket? Equal Opportunities and Changing Cricket Cultures in Essex and East London*. London: University of East London Press.

McIntosh, P. and Charlton, V. (1985) *The Impact of Sport for All Policy, 1966–1984, and a Way Forward*. London: Sports Council.

Miller, N. (2001) 'Cricket, racism and identity: a critical analysis of English cricket in the 1990s', Unpublished MA dissertation, University of Surrey, Roehampton.

Phillips, M. (2006) *Londonistan: How Britain is Creating a Terror State Within*. London: Gibson Square Books.

Phillips, T. (2005) 'Let's show the world its future', *Observer: Olympics 2012*, 10th July: 4–5.

Rigg, M. (1986) *Action Sport: an Evaluation*. London: Sports Council.

Runnymede Trust (2000) *The Future of Multi-Ethnic Britain – The Parekh Report*. London: Profile Books.

Scarman, L.G. (1981) *The Brixton disorders 10–12 April: report of an inquiry*. Cmnd 8427. London: HMSO.

Solomos, J. (2003) *Race and Racism in Britain*. 3rd edn. London: Palgrave Macmillan.

Solomos, J. and Back, L. (1996) *Racism and Society*. Basingstoke: Macmillan.

Sport England (1999) *Investing for Our Sporting Future: Sport England Lottery Fund Strategy 1999–2009*. London: Sport England.

Sport England (2000) *Sports Participation and Ethnicity in England: National Survey 1999–2000*. London: Sport England.

Sporting Equals (1999) *Findings from the racial equality survey of national governing bodies*. Leeds.

Sporting Equals (2000) *Achieving Racial Equality: a Standard for Sport*. London: Sport England/CRE.

Sports Council (n.d.) *Action Sport: Selected Case Studies*. London: Sports Council.

Sports Council (1982) *Sport in the Community: the Next Ten Years*. London: Sports Council.

Sports Council (1994) *Black and Ethnic Minorities and Sport*. London: Sports Council.

Spracklen, K., Hylton, K. and Long, J. (2006) 'Managing and monitoring equality and diversity in UK sport: an evaluation of the Sporting Equals Racial Equality Standard and its impact on organizational change', *Journal of Sport & Social Issues*, 30 (3): 289–305.

Swinney, A. and Horne, J. (2005) 'Race equality and leisure policy discourses in Scottish local authorties', *Leisure Studies*, 24: 271–89.

The Independent (2005) 'A moment for Britain to glory in the Olympic spirit', 7 July: 36.

Verma, G. and Darby, D. (1994) *Winners and Losers: Ethnic Minorities in Sport and Recreation*. London: Falmer Press.

Williams, J. (2001) *Cricket and Race*. Oxford: Berg.

Witte, R. (1996) *Racist Violence and the State*. London: Longman.

11

Physical Education and School Sport

KATHLEEN M. ARMOUR AND DAVID KIRK

OVERVIEW

» *The development of physical education as a school subject*
» *Responses to the marginal status of physical education within education*
» *The relationship between physical education and sport*
» *Attempts to bridge the gap between physical education and sport*
» *Gender inequalities and physical education*
» *A critical review of the benefits of physical education*

INTRODUCTION

Most readers of this book have at least one life experience in common: taking part in some form of physical education at school. For many of you, physical education was the first place you encountered a variety of organised sports and you might even be able to trace your current interest in sport to a dedicated physical education teacher. Some of you, on the other hand, might argue that you have sustained your interest in sport *in spite of* your physical education experiences, and still others would probably define those experiences as irrelevant. Whichever group you fall into, there are three important points to remember as you read this chapter. First, you have extensive personal experience of schools and physical education, so you have a strong knowledge base upon which to draw. Second, physical education and sport are not the same; they share enough common ground to make them appear similar, yet the differences have been bitterly contested throughout history. Third, several of the issues covered in other chapters in this book manifest themselves in physical education. For example, a recent text entitled *Physical Education: Essential Issues* includes such topics as policy, politics and power, gender, social class, race and inclusion (Green and Hardman, 2005). It might be useful, therefore, to view physical education as a case study of the ways in which social issues converge, and are enmeshed, constructed and enacted in one social context.

HISTORICAL OVERVIEW OF THE DEVELOPMENT OF PHYSICAL EDUCATION AS A SCHOOL SUBJECT

The earliest forms of physical education to appear in government schools in the UK, somewhere between the 1860s and 1880s, were commonly referred to as drill. Drill involved a combination of marching and other military manoeuvres and exercises drawn from one or more of the many systems of gymnastics that existed at the time. Although not easily related to physical education as we now understand it, the significance of drill in establishing the principle that children should take exercise as part of their schooling should be recognised.

It is important to note the strength of the military influence upon schools at the time. For example, recruits to the army for the Boer War were found to be in poor physical condition, leading the Board of Education in conjunction with the War Office to create a course of physical training. Schools were encouraged to employ army instructors to teach the course; however, many of these instructors were drawn from the ranks of NCOs, they were often ill-educated and they were accorded low status within schools. It could be argued that physical education's enduring status concerns within education originated here. Even when it became clear that military exercises were unnecessary, inappropriate and in some cases harmful for young children, the militarists from all sectors of society were set against any change and believed military drill to be essential for the maintenance of law and order in schools and in society more broadly (Penn, 1999). However, by the time of the publication in 1909 of the official government syllabus for schools, a system of free-standing exercises devised by the Swede Per Henrick Ling had largely replaced earlier military versions of drilling and exercising. The adoption of the Ling system was viewed as progressive at this time since it was based on a therapeutic rationale despite being delivered in a militaristic way. Nonetheless, the new Ling system was implemented against a backdrop of ferocious debate and much acrimony.

The choice of a military form of drilling and exercising for young primary school children in the 1880s was based, in large part, on the view that working-class children had to be controlled and disciplined (Kirk, 1998). The legal requirement that all children attend school was new in the 1880s, and school authorities were keen to extract the maximum benefits from the state's investment in education for the masses. They saw military drilling and exercising to be ideal for controlling the behaviour of allegedly unruly and undisciplined working-class children (Smith, 1974). On the other hand, public (i.e. private) schools were exempt from government syllabi. So whereas working-class pupils in state schools were taught drill, exercises and some games in order to instil discipline and obedience, pupils in private schools played sports and games so they could learn discipline, 'good' character and leadership skills. The hegemony of games and sports in public schools has prevailed throughout history.

The publication in 1933 of a new physical education syllabus marked an important shift in government policy. In this syllabus, which endured for nearly 20 years, the term 'physical education' was used in addition to 'physical training', the importance of daily exercise was stressed, and the links between exercise and health were endorsed. At this time, physical education was viewed as part of the physical welfare services in education, and was located within the medical department of the Board of Education. Moreover, the British Medical Association had a specific committee for physical education and, in 1936, the committee affirmed the importance of exercise, pronouncing that divorcing mind and body in education was 'unscientific' (BMA, 1936: 1). These early links to health were lost in later years, and are only now being re-established in light of the perceived 'obesity crisis' among young people.

In government schools, the period between 1950 and 1980 saw several important changes, and some of these can still be recognised as influences on physical education practice today. For example, in 1952 a new form of syllabus for state schools was produced, introducing the notion that physical education could be viewed as a 'release' from the restraints and rigours of classroom lessons. The physical education profession has since, however, fought against this view, feeling that it undermines the educational value of their subject. The syllabus also allowed head teachers to decide upon the time allocation for physical education based on their assessment of the 'needs' of their pupils. It is interesting to note that time allocations for physical education soon fell, and that it is only in the last three years that the government has set meaningful targets to increase curriculum time (see the section on PESS below). It was also during the 1950s that girls and boys were first taught the main national games separately. Football and cricket were viewed as suitable activities for boys, and hockey was regarded as particularly suitable for girls. By 1967, this notion was expressed even more strongly in the government's Plowden Report (para 708):

> Girls and boys at the top of the primary school will be acquainted with the rudiments of the main national games – netball, hockey and tennis for the girls, football and cricket for the boys.

Early attempts to reverse this sex segregation met with fierce resistance. As one education inspector argued:

There are social and moral and quasi-legal reasons [for segregated physical education]. I am thinking particularly of the man teacher who maybe at risk from an unscrupulous girl, especially in educational gymnastics. (Schools Council, 1971: 33)

In many schools, this sex segregation has endured and you may recognise it from your own experience of physical education.

The next major event in the history of physical education was the Education Reform Act of 1988 and the advent of the National Curriculum in England and Wales. Evans and his colleagues (1996) have focused much of their research since the late 1980s on the effects of the Act on the provision of physical education in schools and on the implementation of a National Curriculum for physical education (NCPE). Essentially, this research has analysed the ideological forces shaping the government's positioning of physical education within the school curriculum. It documents, for example, the debates between those in the government who held traditional views of physical education and wished to see a curriculum organised around a focal point of competitive team sport, and those in the physical education profession who argued for a more innovative and inclusive form of physical education (Evans, 1990). What we now know is that the traditionalists won, and Penney and Evans (1999) argue that this has meant that children are denied access to a broad and balanced experience of physical education. In essence the development of the NCPE (Box 11.1) did not result in the emergence of new or diverse practices in physical education but, these researchers argue, consolidated marginality and the reinforcement of established discourses in both 'policy' and 'practice'.

Box 11.1   The National Curriculum for physical education

The NCPE has been revised twice in 1995 and 1999 since its first appearance following the Educational Reform Act of 1988. In its current form, the NCPE requires schools to use six categories of activities: games, gymnastics, athletics, dance, outdoor and adventurous activities, and swimming and water safety, to facilitate learning in the following four key aspects: acquiring and developing skills; selecting and applying skills, tactics and compositional ideas; evaluating and improving performance; knowledge and understanding of fitness and health. Requirements for what activities must be offered vary for each key stage, with the latest revision streamlining the number of activities to be offered at KS 1 and 2.

What this brief tour of history demonstrates is that the form of physical education that is practised in schools at any point in history is a product of competing social and political pressures. Physical education is, therefore, an essentially contested concept, and some of the fiercest contests have been over the marginal status of physical education in schools and, linked to that, the relationship between physical education and sport. Before examining the current policy context, therefore, it is worth considering these issues in a little more depth.

THE MARGINAL EDUCATIONAL STATUS OF PHYSICAL EDUCATION

For those who believe that schools should be concerned primarily with teaching 'academic' subjects, the role of subjects on the curriculum that are primarily practical in nature is problematic. The roots of this issue can be traced to beliefs in an essential separation of mind and body, a belief known as Cartesian dualism. For some influential educational theorists (e.g. Hirst, 1974; Peters, 1966; White, 1973) education was centrally about the development of the mind, thus reinforcing prejudices against physical education that already existed within the educational policy and teaching communities. For example, Hirst (1974) argued that cognitive development was the key function of schools, and that practical activities could not result in cognitive development. Yet, Ryle (1949) had earlier argued persuasively for a 'monist' view of education where knowing how to do things (rather than simply knowing something in theory) was an important form of knowledge. Ryle pointed out that 'we learn how by practice ... often quite unaided by any lesson in the theory' (41) and he argued that this was an important learning process that could not be explained by some form of mindless repetition:

> It is of the essence of merely habitual practices that one performance is a replica of its predecessors. It is of the essence of intelligent practices that one performance is modified by its predecessors. The agent is still learning. (42)

In another dimension to this issue, Aspin (1976) made a strong case for the 'logically primitive' concept of the person: 'The idea of 'person' precedes the idea of mind and body: a person is both' (112). In terms of the curriculum, therefore, Pring (1976) argued:

> Important though it is to know *that* certain statements are true, knowing *how* to do things (to play a piece of music, to enjoy a concert, to make a sketch, to appreciate a poem, to climb skillfully) is equally a cognitive achievement, a development of the mind, which is not reducible to 'knowing that' or to the kinds of knowledge that can be stated in propositions. (79)

The issue at the heart of status concerns for physical education is, therefore, one of differing views about the purposes of education and the educational benefits to be gained from participation in physical education activities. An idea developed from Jacks's (1937) book *The Education of the Whole Man* was that physical education could claim a place in the curriculum on the grounds that it complemented, rather than contributed to, the academic and intellectual development of pupils. Carr (1983) refuted an instrumentalist view, arguing instead that sports and games should be valued for themselves, being seen as 'expressions of important human aims, purposes and interests of a social, cultural and individual nature' (8). The educational benefits claimed for physical education are explored in more detail in the penultimate section of this chapter. At this point, it is interesting to consider two claims that, it is argued, can provide partial support for the place of physical education on the curriculum: making physical education an examinable subject with a strong theoretical component, and linking physical education to improvements in children's health.

Status Solutions: Examinations in Physical Education

Morgan (1974) argued that 'it is well to make the point that physical education is not, in any fundamental sense, a theoretical subject' (96). For those of you who have recently taken public examinations in physical education/sports studies this will come as something of a surprise. The dramatic growth in examinations in physical education in countries such as England, Wales and Australia has presaged a much stronger theoretical focus in physical education. For some teachers, the inclusion of examinations has been an essential step towards addressing status concerns. For example, teachers in Armour and Jones's (1998) research in England argued that 'academically, we've proved that we're a subject to be reckoned with' and 'we have got into examinations because it seems to justify our place a little more' (100). Similarly, O'Sullivan et al. (1994) found that for teachers in Australia and New Zealand:

> the cognitive emphases of these new courses of study have provided a 'certain legitimacy' for physical education in schools that had been lacking for most teachers during their careers. (428)

Certainly it can be argued that the advent of examinations in physical education has been, generally, a positive development, particularly when taking into account their popularity amongst young people. Nonetheless, whether the rush to include theoretical components in these exams was justified is a moot point. Indeed, looking back to some of the earlier epistemological arguments about mind/body and theory/practice, it could be argued that seeking status within education through the inclusion of theory simply reinforces the marginal status of much of the physical education curriculum, i.e. that which is practical.

Status Solutions: Improving Health

There is no doubt that for some in the physical education profession, the answer to concerns about marginal status within education lies in exploiting links to health. The health-related exercise (HRE) movement that began in the UK in the early 1980s seemed to some physical educators to offer solid arguments for physical education's place in the curriculum. Indeed, it could be argued that locating the value of physical education in a health context has two clear advantages: it re-establishes historical links to what is regarded as a higher-status medical profession; and it presents physical education as the solution to a topical social and cultural concern: obesity.

Keddie (1971) argued that for any subject on the curriculum, 'we can only learn what they are by learning what teachers and pupils who are involved in defining that knowledge claim to be doing; subjects are what practitioners do with them' (44). For teachers, research over many years has shown that the role of physical education in promoting physical activity and, therefore, health is attractive. For example, teachers in the Armour and Jones (1998) study were committed to a health role:

> Jane … saw her role as educating pupils for life after school, hoping her pupils would 'see that they really have got fitness for life' … Grant wants pupils in physical education to be 'fit and healthy' … Pete saw health and fitness as important based on his personal belief in 'the importance of staying fit and consequently healthy'. (97)

Furthermore, in a recent study of young people's views of physical education, Smith and Parr (2007) found strong support for the notion that physical education had a role to play in health promotion, for example:

> Susie: It keeps you fit and active.
> Jenna: It's, like exercise isn't it? Well it's exercise and every other lesson you're not doing much … it's active so it will keep you healthy and stuff …
> Rebecca: Well yeah, if you didn't do any exercise, then you would just be fat wouldn't you?
> Susie: Yeah, I think it's for obesity and trying to combat it. (45)

However, the links between physical education and health are fraught with difficulties. For example, Smith and Parr's (2007) study recognised, like Biddle et al. (2004), that the time allocated to physical education is often insufficient to result in major health impacts. Moreover, just as Harris found in her research in 1994, the young people in Smith and Parr's research offered health justifications for physical education that were superficial, rarely going beyond what they had gleaned from the media. Tinning and Glasby (2002) offer some explanation for this. They question whether physical education teachers are equipped to offer young people a critical understanding of health issues:

> they are not equipped with the skills of cultural critique. In addition, many have heavy investments in the 'cult' of the body … and this can render them blind (or at least myopic) to the possible cultural 'side-effects' of their physical education practices. (110)

This critique is similar to some of the early critiques of a health-based rationale for physical education. For example, Sparkes (1989) argued against the individualism inherent in health-related exercise, suggesting that it reinforced a view of health as largely a matter of personal choice, diverting attention away from the impacts of environmental pollution and 'from the inequalities that exist in relation to health in terms of social class, gender and race' (61) (see the section below on social construction). Moreover, in reviewing the role of schools in promoting health and physical activity, Cale and Harris (2006) concluded that whereas there is evidence to suggest that school-based physical education programmes can be effective in increasing young people's activity levels during physical education, 'there is less evidence that they are as effective in improving out-of-school physical activity levels' (405). It could be argued, therefore, that what is required is to develop young people's critical understanding of physical activity and health within a broader critical and cultural framework. Undoubtedly, such a critical framework would have to embrace the wider world of sport, with which physical education has a tense but necessary relationship.

THE RELATIONSHIP BETWEEN PHYSICAL EDUCATION AND SPORT

Physical educators often become agitated when sport is used in place of physical education as a label for their subject. They point out that the aims of physical education are different from the aims of sport and to confuse the two fails to do justice to the educational mission of physical education. Yet, to an outsider, the relationship between physical education and sport is very straightforward: physical education teachers teach pupils how to play and understand a range of sports and physical activities, including dance. Furthermore, many physical education teachers are also accomplished sports participants and coaches (Chelladurai and Kuga, 1996). One could be forgiven, therefore, for seeing physical education and sport as being, at the very least, closely related. In Armour and Jones's (1998) study, one teacher summarised the difference between physical education and sport as follows:

> Well, there's a link between the two, but I think when we're talking about physical education we're really talking about education – acquisition of knowledge, understanding … give them the *feel* behind something and not *necessarily* that they can do it but at least they know about their bodies and they've got a clear understanding of how to get fit even if they're not. But sport is just *doing* it.

Perhaps what this issue really demonstrates is the lack of a clear and widely accepted definition of physical education. Kirk (1994) argued that without such a definition, or at least one upon which most of the profession can agree, it is very difficult to have a clear understanding of the physically educated pupil, and researchers in both Australia and

United States of America pointed to similar difficulties (Brooker and Macdonald, 1995; Siedentop, 1987). In England, attempts were made during the formulation of the NCPE to make a working distinction between sport and physical education:

1.1   In *physical education* the emphasis is on learning in a mainly physical context. The purpose of the learning is to develop specific knowledge, skills and understanding and to promote physical development and competence. The learning promotes participation in sport.
1.2   *Sport* is the term applied to a range of physical activities where emphasis is on participation and competition. Different sporting activities can and do contribute to learning. (DES, 1992)

Yet, although this distinction was the outcome of a working party of committed individuals, it seems to offer very little real clarity. Perhaps the real question to be addressed is why seek to make the distinction at all?

Reference to earlier sections of this chapter, and the struggles physical education has had to establish itself as a valued subject on the school curriculum, provide the answer. Physical educationalists have sought to align their work with the broader field of education, emphasising the educational value of their subject. However, Peters (1966) argued that curriculum subjects should be justified on their own worth, and Arnold (1985) cautioned against justifying physical education in terms of its 'spin-offs' such as health or social and moral development, although this has often been done (see e.g. the penultimate section of this chapter). The reasons probably lie in educationists' views about sport. Links to sport have been shunned in the past because sport was deemed to be too visibly practical (undermining claims to theory) and too closely identifiable with what is viewed, by some physical educators, as the highly competitive, elitist and exploitative world of professional sport. Furthermore, if physical education mainly involves teaching (or coaching) sport, then it could be suggested that coaches are required in schools rather than expensively trained physical education teachers. In order to preserve the professional status of physical educators, therefore, it may be the case that reaffirming these distinctions was necessary. Yet, provision for youth sport has developed dramatically since the 1980s, and some coaches would argue that they, too, are 'professional' (Chelladurai and Kuga, 1996). Moreover, as ever younger children have been drawn into adult forms of organised sport, such sports have begun to adopt more pedagogically sound, developmentally appropriate and ethically defensible practices (e.g. Australian Sports Commission, 1994). In other words, for at least the last decade it has been increasingly recognised that sport for young people needs to be underpinned by most of the same principles that inform school physical education.

Undoubtedly it can be argued that not all of what is taught in physical education can be categorised as sport. For example, the curriculum includes dance, outdoor adventure activities and other non-competitive activities such as exercise for health. These activities have tended to be devalued, however, where physical education is viewed primarily as the foundation of a sport development continuum where the sports stars of the future are introduced to sport skills (Kirk and Gorely, 2000). While schools certainly can play a role in sport development, it is too restricting of school programmes and too limiting of the opportunities offered to young people for this to be the primary purpose of school physical education. This is simply because not all young people will become sports performers beyond school. Indeed, it has been argued that the pyramid structure that underpins thinking about sport development, where increasing numbers of people are excluded as performers ascend to higher and higher levels, actually works against lifelong sports participation (Box 11.2).

Box 11.2 The relationship between physical education and sports performance

Kirk and Gorely (2000) examine the relationship between school physical education and sports performance. They criticise traditional ways of thinking about this relationship (e.g. pyramids, foundation stones and trickle-down effects). They suggest that these ways of thinking are problematic in their logic, their exclusionary nature and their positioning of physical education. They present a more inclusive way of thinking about the relationship. The alternative model is based on four components: clearly articulated pathways, the use of modified games and sports, teacher and coach education, and policy development. The researchers argue that this alternative model brings physical education and sport performance into a sensible and productive relationship which meets the needs of the general population for quality physical education while at the same time meeting the needs of sport performance across the lifespan.

So, some key challenges remain for physical educators in their relationship with sport and the sports development community. For physical educators to deny their intimate relationship with sport has perhaps been unwise given the massive appeal sport has for the general public. At the same time, physical educators have never wanted to be cast in the role of working solely to produce elite sports performers. In this context, the advent of 'sport education' is a particularly interesting development.

Sport Education

The increasing popularity of 'sport education' (Box 11.3) in schools is a significant development for physical education and its relationship with the wider world of sport.

According to Siedentop (1994), sport education models competitive sport including the allocation of roles such as player, coach, administrator and reporter and competitions between teams and leagues played within seasons. This model of sport education has now been trialled extensively. Research and development projects have been carried out in the United States mainly in primary schools (Siedentop, 1994) and in New Zealand in secondary schools (Alexander et al., 1996; Grant et al., 1992).

Box 11.3   Sport education

Siedentop (1994) identifies six features of sport education that resemble the forms of sport practised in the community. Seasons are one key characteristic of Siedentop's model and represent the macro unit of time around which sport is organised. Seasons include periods of practice and competition. A second key feature is affiliation. Affiliation relates to players' identification with their team, to their sense of membership and belonging. In sport education, individuals usually remain in the same team throughout the season. Formal competition is a third, and defining, characteristic of sport. As such, it must be present in sport education, even though the nature of the competitive experience for children is carefully regulated according to their developmental levels and the teachers' intended educational outcomes. A fourth feature, the culminating event, provides a focus for the season and a motivator for players to work hard. A fifth feature, record keeping, provides feedback and incentives for individuals and teams. Finally, festivity adds an important social element to sport for its participants. The development of sport education as a way of teaching sport as part of physical education may be one possible resolution to this conflict between physical education and sport issue, since sport is presented in an explicitly educational form and mirrors the real world of sport more closely than most multi-activity physical education programmes.

These studies and others that followed have reported findings in relation to student learning outcomes and teacher professional development. They have shown that sport education provides a more meaningful experience of physical education for young people than the traditional, multi-activity model, and higher levels of identification with school physical education (e.g. Alexander et al., 1993; Bennet and Hastie, 1997; Grant, 1992). Hastie (1998) has shown that sport education delivers improvements both in the development of techniques and in tactical decision making, and also improves young people's understanding of games through their participation in a range of roles such as umpire, manager, score keeper, and so on (Hastie, 1996). Grant et al. (1992) and Carlson and Hastie (1997) suggest that sport education provides opportunities to develop the student social system in classes, such as higher levels of peer support, while other researchers have shown that it enhances learning experiences for all categories of students, including 'lower-skilled' young people (Alexander and Luckman, 1998; Carlson, 1995; Hastie, 1998). Studies suggest this model provides teachers with more opportunities to interact with students on a one-to-one basis (Hastie, 1998), delivers quality professional development opportunities to teachers (Alexander et al., 1996) and in primary schools provides opportunities for curriculum integration (Alexander and Luckman, 1998).

What is clear about the introduction of sport education is that it is an initiative that was developed from *within* the physical education profession. It has since spread widely and is having a real impact on practice in some schools. However, another interesting attempt to bridge the physical education–sport gap in England has been generated from outside the physical education profession. This initiative is supported and funded by central government and it has had a dramatic impact on the structure of physical education in schools: the Physical Education, School Sport and Club Links (PESSCL) strategy.

PHYSICAL EDUCATION AND SCHOOL SPORT (PESS)

There is no doubt that the physical education landscape in England has changed dramatically in recent years. The national PESSCL strategy was launched in October 2002 and, running up to 2008, the government is investing over £1.5 billion in delivering the strategy and providing additional facilities for physical education and school sport. The overarching target for the PESSCL strategy is to increase the percentage of school children who spend a minimum of two hours a week on high-quality physical education and school sport (within and beyond the curriculum) to 75 per cent by 2006 and then 85 per cent by 2008, the so-called 'minutes' target. The ambitious target for 2010 is to increase this to a minimum of four hours per week. As was noted earlier in this chapter, this is the first sustained attempt by the government to reverse the decline in time spent on physical education in state schools since the 1950s. Almost uniquely in the field of physical education, funding has been allocated to ensure that both the PESSCL strategy and some elements of the new facility funding are being evaluated by independent researchers. Why did this happen?

It could be argued that there were three factors that created an enabling climate for this change to happen:

1   **General concerns about children's health, obesity and reported low levels of physical activity.**
2   **The political influence of one individual. Sue Campbell established a charitable organisation known as the Youth Sport Trust and managed to persuade key government departments that physical education and school sport could help them to achieve some of *their* targets for schools and pupils; for example, raising aspirations,**

improving motivation and addressing disaffection ('spin-offs' in Arnold's (1985) terms).

3   The introduction of the title 'Physical Education and School Sport' (PESS) for what was previously known as 'Physical Education'. This was not just a matter of semantics. Use of this title was designed to send a clear signal to government ministers and the world of sport that the historical 'war' between physical education and sport was effectively over. Moreover, the addition of 'Club Links' to the title of the strategy signalled that physical educators were not expected to deliver elite performers to the world of adult sport. Instead, a smooth passage from school to club-level sport was to be facilitated.

The Youth Sport Trust became, very quickly, a high-profile, dynamic and politically astute organisation. In contrast, the physical education professional associations appeared to be low profile and stagnant. Being politically astute, the Youth Sport Trust recognised that in order to persuade government to invest in PESS, there needed to be some clear and (deceptively) simple targets that PESS would meet in return for any new investment. Moreover, it was necessary to fund independent research to report on progress made towards meeting the targets, for example the 'minutes' target.

The qualifier 'high-quality' PESS was added more recently to signal that merely getting children active was not sufficient to meet the target. Thus, 'high-quality' physical education was defined in terms of outcomes (i.e. 'this is what high-quality physical education looks like'). Schools are now expected to work towards providing 'high-quality' physical education and to report their 'minutes' to government in an annual return. Within this framework, links to health promotion have been retained. From a PESSCL perspective, the role of PESS in health promotion is clear: it is about getting children physically active in meaningful activity where they are learning; creating sustainable opportunities by signposting physical activity opportunities outside and beyond school (and making sure the routeways are open); and ensuring that no groups are excluded

The national PESSCL strategy is being delivered through nine interlinked work-strands. The two main strands are:

*   **The establishment of sports colleges. These are secondary schools that have a special focus on sport, on raising the standard of PESS provision for primary and secondary schools in their local area, and in making an impact on whole-school improvement as a result.**
*   **The creation of school sports partnerships. These are families of schools that receive additional funding from the government to come together to enhance sports opportunities for all pupils within a locality. Each partnership is individual in character within a national partnership model. By 2006, all schools and all pupils were in a partnership.**

The remaining seven work-strands include professional development for teachers and a programme for gifted and talented pupils. These are the tools that schools and partnerships draw on to enable children to take up their two-hour entitlement and move towards the 2010 ambition of four hours. There is also additional funding for more sports coaches and competition managers to work across the network of school sport partnerships.

In order to deliver the strategy and meet the targets, the new structure that has been created for schools has also resulted in new salaried posts and career opportunities for physical education professionals. For example, school sports partnerships (often hosted in sports colleges) require a partnership development manager (a relatively highly paid post); school sport coordinators and primary link teachers. The outcome of all this is that PESS has become an important focus of work for schools and those involved in PESS have a new sense of worth. For example, a National Specialist Sports Colleges Conference is held each year. The venue is always of high quality, the tone is professional and so the delegates feel respected. Head teachers attend – voluntarily – to keep abreast of new developments and to learn what PESS can do for their schools and pupils. That is quite a shift and it represents progress in the status problems that physical education has faced over the years.

The PESSCL strategy has not resolved all the issues facing physical education. For example, finding sufficient, well-qualified staff to fill all the new roles, especially in inner-city areas, is challenging; definitions of 'high-quality' PESS can be disputed; and there is a real danger that complacency will set in, with the government assuming that this investment has 'solved' the problems of physical education and promoting physical activity for young people. Nonetheless, the evaluation evidence to date does suggest that increasing numbers of young people are engaged in a wider range of physical activities for longer periods of time than before the advent of the PESSCL strategy. Moreover, within the strands of PESSCL is the imperative to engage those young people who, historically, have had low levels of engagement in physical education and sport. One example is girls, particularly adolescent girls, whose engagement in physical activity has long been regarded as a 'problem'. The question is: where is the source of the problem? Do girls have a problem or is the problem a reflection of wider social issues? The earlier historical overview of the development of physical education hinted at some key structural issues facing girls in physical education. Indeed, Hargreaves (1986) drew on a post-Marxist framework to argue that physical education and sport in schools was a key site for the production of unequal relations of class, race and sex and that it remained instrumental in reproducing power and culture through practices of schooling bodies. From a sociological perspective, therefore, it is interesting to analyse the ways in which inequalities are created or reproduced through different layers of social policy and practice. What follows is an illustration of this process using gender inequality as an example.

THE SOCIAL CONSTRUCTION OF GENDER IN PHYSICAL EDUCATION

As a professional body of physical educators began to emerge in the first half of the twentieth century, they were strictly segregated in their training according to 'the sex of the individual' (Kirk, 1992). Owing to this single-sex training, gendered forms of physical education have vied with each other for a dominant place in school programmes. In the last 30 years, a form of physical education sponsored principally by male physical educators with competitive team games at its core has come to dominate school programs in Australia, the UK and parts of North America. In this historical context, a significant research programme has developed around the topic of the social construction of gender in and through physical education, focusing particularly on girls' and women's experiences of physical education and physical education teacher education.

There is a long history of sex segregation in the institutions that train physical education teachers. This, clearly, set an important precedent for different kinds of physical education to be made available to boys and girls. Whereas men focused on competitive sports and fitness, women were keen to promote a more generic form of movement education with dance and educational gymnastics at its core. Research by Flintoff (1993) and Dewar (1990) examined the social construction of gender and the reproduction of gender inequalities at a time when legislation required teacher education institutions to change to co-educational provision in both Europe and North America. In both studies, the researchers found that female teacher training students were forced to negotiate forms of gender and sexual identity that were regarded as appropriate to the dominant masculinist ethos of the institutions. In Dewar's study, for example, women negotiated identities within their student peer group such as a 'prissy' ultra-feminine identity, a 'jock' identity that involved women displaying strongly masculine behaviours, and a 'dyke' identity of lesbian students. Flintoff's and Dewar's studies hold important implications for school physical education and suggest that teacher education programmes face serious challenges in addressing the ingrained social construction of gender in physical education.

Wright's study of teacher talk and its contribution to the construction of gendered subjectivity in physical education is one of the few sociological studies of physical education to employ the analytical tools of social semiotics utilising audio and video recordings of lessons in addition to standard ethnographic methods (Wright, 1993, 1997; Wright and King, 1991). Her findings supported earlier research to the extent that girls were represented through teacher talk as being in deficit of qualities physical education teachers valued, such as skilfulness, perseverance, application and toughness. The language teachers used to communicate with students revealed deeply entrenched expectations of appropriate gendered behaviour of girls and boys, lending support to Martinek's (1981) earlier research on the Pygmalion effect.

What seems clear is that the problem of girls' declining interest in physical education can be located not so much in girls themselves, as in the social construction of gender. In order to attain societal standards of femininity, many girls (particularly at adolescence) choose not to participate in activities offered in physical education programmes since too many of these activities emphasise masculine qualities such as physicality, aggression and strength. A key issue for physical education is to offer forms of physical activity that are acceptable to girls and that equip them to lead active and healthy lives.

It is also important to remember that a sizeable proportion of boys fail to thrive in the dominant culture of physical education. While boys have been included in some studies of gender, their participation in physical education tended not to be conceptualised as a 'problem'. Yet, the construction of masculinities, and the dominance and subordination of particular forms of masculinity, are clearly evident within physical education. Not all boys enjoy traditional masculine sports and their attendant macho cultures and an emerging line of research has now begun to examine boys' experiences of physical education and sport (Connell, 1989; Fitzclarence, 1995; Gard and Meyenn, 2000; Walker, 1988; Wright, 2000) and outdoor adventure activities (Humberstone, 1990).

Perhaps the key message from all the research on the social construction of gender through physical education is that physical educators need to develop anti-sexist pedagogies that challenge hyper-masculine practices. Physical education has been rooted in gender difference for over 150 years and, as one researcher observed, sport has been a 'male preserve' for much of this time (Theberge, 1985). There is a view among some physical educators that gender inequalities in sport and physical education have been largely removed; however, the multi-layered nature of the problem indicates that whereas progress has been made, the ingrained issues are not so easily resolved.

THE EDUCATIONAL VALUE OF PHYSICAL EDUCATION AND SCHOOL SPORT

Looking back on this chapter so far, it is clear that physical education has had a somewhat chequered history. It could be argued that with the advent of the PESSCL strategy the current period, in England at least, is a time of unprecedented growth and development. In addition, 2004 was designated the European Year of Education through Sport, and 2005 was named the United Nations' International Year of Physical Education and Sport. Implicit within these policies and initiatives is a view that, in some way, PESS has significant and distinctive contributions to make to children, to schools and to wider society. The precise nature of these contributions is not always clear, however, nor is the physical education profession often held accountable for delivering them. For example, the International Council for Physical Education and Sport Science claims that PESS helps children to develop respect for the body – their own and others' – contributes towards the integrated development of mind and body, develops an understanding of the role of aerobic and anaerobic physical activity in health, positively enhances self-confidence and self-esteem, and enhances social and cognitive development and academic achievement (ICSSPE, 2001). In a similar vein, a Council of Europe report suggests that PESS provides opportunities to meet and communicate with other people, to take different social roles, to learn particular social skills (such as tolerance and respect for others), and to adjust to team/collective objectives (such as co-operation and cohesion), and that it provides experience of emotions that are not available in the rest of life (Svoboda, 1994). The question is: can PESS really deliver all these things?

In 2005–6, the British Educational Research Association commissioned an academic review of 'The Educational Benefits Claimed for Physical Education & School Sport'. The purpose of the review was to seek research evidence to support or challenge the claims that are widely made by, or on behalf of, the physical education profession. The review was undertaken in four broad domains – physical, social, affective and cognitive – reflecting the domains in which the benefits of physical education are traditionally claimed. The review was undertaken by a group of physical education and sport pedagogy researchers in the UK, and it also drew upon international expertise. What follows are some excerpts from that review, the outcomes of which are interesting given the prominence of PESS in social policy in England today, and some questions about accountability.

Physical Benefits

Without doubt, there is a broad understanding that the distinctive contribution PESS makes to a child's education is within the physical domain. It has been noted in earlier sections of this chapter that the nature of the physical focus of PESS has shifted over time, moving from an initial health-related rationale in the first half of the twentieth century to more performance-related considerations following the Second World War, to concerns about the health impact of sedentary behaviours more recently. In the mid-1990s, a series of robust longitudinal studies identified the importance of regular physical activity across the lifespan (US Department of Health and Human Services, 1996). Physical activity emerged as an important public health issue and has remained in the political spotlight ever since (HEA, 1998; Scottish Executive, 2003). Moreover, with adult physical inactivity continuing to be a concern and attempts to rectify this situation being at best equivocal (King et al., 1998; Sevick et al., 2000), the role of PESS in promoting engagement in lifelong physical activity has become widely accepted (Green, 2002; Penney and Jess, 2004).

At one level, this is surprising because the evidence of significant physical benefits for young people from physical activity is limited (Biddle et al., 2004; Cale and Harris, 2005). For example, there is evidence of a clear link between childhood physical activity and bone strength, with its potential impact on osteoporosis later in life (Bass, 2000).

However, the relationship with cardiovascular disease risk factors is less apparent, with physical activity seemingly having little impact on children's blood pressure (Tolfrey et al., 2000) or blood lipid levels (Despres et al., 1990). It has been suggested that this may, in part, be due to the fact that many young people are already healthy and that most disease end points appear later in life (Biddle et al., 2004). In addition, the role PESS can play in combating the well-documented increase in childhood obesity (Baur, 2001; Reilly and Dorotsky, 1999) is unclear. There is some cross-sectional evidence that physical inactivity is linked to the development of obesity (Steinbeck, 2001) but, as yet, studies investigating the role of physical activity in childhood obesity have been 'uninspiring' (Biddle et al., 2004).

Social Benefits

It is claimed that purposeful engagement in PESS has the potential to engender in young people positive social behaviours (such as co-operation, personal responsibility and empathy) and to address a number of contemporary social issues relating to problematic youth behaviour, such as depression, crime, truancy and alcohol or drug abuse (Burt, 1998; DCMS, 1999; Hellison et al., 2000; Lawson, 1999; QCA, 2001). Thus, it is argued, the value of PESS lies in the acquisition and accumulation of various personal, social and socio-moral skills which, in turn, can act as social capital to enable young people to function successfully (and acceptably) in a broad range of social situations (Bailey, 2005).

Discussion on the claimed social benefits of engagement in PESS is founded largely on the belief that the nature of physical activity renders it a suitable vehicle for the promotion of personal and social responsibility and the development of pro-social skills (Martinek and Hellison, 1997; Miller et al., 1997; Parker and Stiehl, 2005). The social element of participation and, more specifically, the need for individuals to work collaboratively, cohesively and constructively are believed to encourage (and necessitate) the development of a number of skills such as trust (Priest, 1998), a sense of community (Ennis, 1999), empathy (Moore, 2002), personal and corporate responsibility (Priest and Gass, 1997) and co-operation (Miller et al., 1997). It is important to note, however, that the role of the PESS teacher is recognised as central to the social learning process. It has been suggested, for example, that teachers and leaders who are respectful, fair and honest are particularly well placed to act as positive role models (and models of positive behaviour) for the young people with whom they work (Martinek and Hellison, 1997; Nichols, 1997; Parker and Stiehl, 2005).

The increasing levels of interest in the youth development potential of PESS programmes have led to questions about the nature of the evidence supporting such claims. However, while the findings of evaluation research are generally positive, researchers have generally found that inconclusive evidence usually prevents firm conclusions from being drawn about the precise impact of youth development programmes (e.g. Morris et al., 2003; Nichols, 1997; Sandford et al., 2006). Researchers have also commented on the difficulties of determining causal relationships between participation in a programme and positive impact, noting that it is not always possible to know what other intermediate processes have been at work (Coalter, 2002; Maxwell, 2004).

Affective Benefits

The affective domain is difficult to define, owing to its subjective, imprecise and personal nature (Pope, 2005). 'Affective' is generally seen as synonymous with psychological and emotional well-being and encompassing a range of assets that include mental health, positive self-regard, coping skills, conflict resolution skills, mastery motivation, a sense of autonomy, moral character and confidence. Components of the affective domain also include dimensions such as emotion, preference, choice and feeling, beliefs, aspirations, attitudes and appreciations (Beane, 1990), providing wide scope for philosophical and psychological research to investigate associations between physical activity and psychological well-being (Biddle and Mutrie, 2001).

There is strong evidence for the enhancement of children's self-esteem through participation in sport and physical activity (Fox, 2000; Fox and Biddle 1988). Structured play and specific PESS programmes also appear to contribute to the development of self-esteem in children (Gruber, 1985), although physical self-constructs, rather than a 'global' self-esteem, are thought to be the most likely benefits (Anshel et al., 1986; Blackman et al., 1988). It has been suggested that self-esteem is influenced by an individual's perception of competence or adequacy to achieve (Harter, 1987). Enjoyment experienced during physical activity and sport can reinforce self-esteem, which, in turn, can lead to enhanced motivation to participate further (Sonstroem, 1997; Williams and Gill, 1995). Kimiecik and Harris (1996) suggested that enjoyment allows for the development of intrinsic motivation, a notion supported by Deci and Ryan (1985) who argued that a high level of intrinsic motivation follows from feelings of enjoyment and low levels of anxiety. Some, however, feel that fun is counterproductive to the cause of PESS (Whitehead, 1988) and that it trivialises physical activity. It should also be said that children who do not choose to take part in physical activity outside school are not necessarily those for whom PESS is not fun; reasons such as peer and family influences or lack of opportunities to participate may be the overriding factors at work (Brennan and Bleakley, 1997).

It is clear, however, that not all pupils enjoy PESS activities, at least when presented in particular ways (Ennis, 1999; Jirasek, 2003; Williams and Bedward, 2001). Learned helplessness, development of a negative self-concept and ensuing avoidance of an activity are perceived by some to be negative outcomes of poor experiences in PESS (Biddle, 1999; Fox, 1992; Hellison, 1973).

Cognitive Benefits

Studies of cognitive benefits focus on the development of learning skills and academic performance associated with participation in PESS. As such, they could be said to test the frequently made claims that a 'healthy body leads to a healthy mind', and that PESS can support intellectual development in children (Snyder and Sprietzer, 1977). Classical writers on education, such as Plato and Aristotle, and Rousseau, writing in the eighteenth century, have all asserted a view to the effect that the development of the mind needs to be balanced by the development of the body (Hills, 1998). More recently, numerous authors have argued for transfer effects of PESS to other areas of the school curriculum (Pirie, 1995), while others have suggested that physical activity stimulates the development of generic cognitive or learning skills (Barr and Lewin, 1994).

Such claims ought to be understood within the context of an increasing concern by some parents that, whilst PESS has its place, it should not interfere with the real business of schooling, which many still believe to be academic achievement and examination results (Lau et al., 2004; Lindner, 1999). Thus, it is not surprising that some of the most strenuous advocates of a link between PESS and cognitive outcomes are professional associations and advocacy groups, who claim that quality PESS helps improve a child's mental alertness, academic performance, readiness to learn and enthusiasm for learning.

A classic study of the relationship between PESS and general school performance was carried out in France between 1951 and 1961 (Hervet, 1952). Researchers reduced 'academic' curriculum time by 26 per cent, replacing it with PESS, yet academic results did not worsen and there were fewer discipline problems, greater attentiveness and less absenteeism.

More recent studies have found small improvements for some children in academic performance when time for PESS is increased in their school day (Sallis et al., 1999). A review of three large-scale studies found that academic performance is maintained and occasionally enhanced by an increase in a student's levels of PESS, despite a reduction in the time for the study of academic material (Shephard, 1997). It has also been found that PESS and physical activity levels are higher in relatively high-performing than low-performing schools (Lindner, 1999). These findings should, however, be taken with some caution, as other studies found no relationship, or a trivial one, between participation in PESS and educational achievement (Melnick et al., 1988, 1992; Tremblay et al., 2000).

CONCLUSION

The task of this chapter was to demonstrate the contested and complex character of physical education and, drawing upon research, to overview what we know about its practices.

It was also suggested in the introduction that physical education could be viewed as a case study of the ways in which social issues converge, and are enmeshed, constructed and enacted in one social context. As a young person engaged in physical education at school, it is likely that you were unaware of many of the issues raised in this chapter. However, looking back on those school experiences now, it is interesting to consider whether some of them become more apparent. Physical education today reflects its historical legacy in a number of ways: the early historical links between physical education and physical 'fitness' are being re-established; debates are ongoing about the value of 'theory' in an essentially practical subject; gender difference and inequality in participation are readily apparent; and claims are still being made about social and moral development through physical education and sport. Looking back with a critical eye, therefore, may help to explain why physical education was – or was not – an educative experience for you and your peers.

CHAPTER SUMMARY

» The form of physical education that is practised in schools at any point in history is a product of competing social and political pressures.

» It could be argued that seeking status within education through the inclusion of theory simply reinforces the marginal status of much of the physical education curriculum, i.e. that which is practical.

» What is required is to develop young people's critical understanding of physical activity and health within a broader critical critique and cultural framework.

» The relationship between physical education and sport, especially sports talent development, remains strongly contested.

» The development of sport education as a way of teaching sport as part of physical education may be one possible resolution of the tension between physical education and sport, since sport is presented in an explicitly educational form and mirrors the real world of sport more closely than most multi-activity physical education programmes.

» The evaluation evidence to date suggests that increasing numbers of young people are engaged in a wider range of physical activities for longer periods of time than before the advent of the PESSCL strategy.

» There is a view among some physical educators that gender inequalities in sport and physical education have been largely removed; however, the multi-layered nature of the problem indicates that whereas progress has been made, the ingrained issues are not so easily resolved.

NOTE

1 This section of the chapter is a summary of an academic review that was commissioned by the British Educational Research Association (BERA) in 2006. BERA is organised around a number of special interest groups (SIGs), one of which is the Physical Education and Sport Pedagogy SIG. The purpose of such a review is to provide an overview of a key topic within the field that could be of interest to those within the field of physical education but also to the wider BERA community. The authors of the review are: Richard Bailey, Roehampton University, Kathleen Armour, Loughborough University, David Kirk, Leeds Metropolitan University, Mike Jess, Edinburgh University, Ian Pickup, Roehampton University, Rachel Sandford, Loughborough University, and the BERA Physical Education and Sport Pedagogy SIG.

FURTHER READING

Kirk, D., MacDonald, D., and O'Sullivan, M. (2006) *The Handbook of Physical Education.* London: Sage.

REFERENCES

Alexander, K. and Luckman, J. (1998) 'Teacher's perceptions and uses of the sport education curriculum model in Australian schools', Paper presented to the British Sports Council's Seminar on Sport Education, Loughborough University, November.

Alexander, K., Taggart, A. and Medland, A. (1993) 'Sport education in physical education: try before you buy', *The ACHPER National Journal,* 40 (4), 16–23.

Alexander, K., Taggart, A. and Thorpe, S. (1996) 'A spring in their steps? Possibilities for professional renewal through Sport Education in Australian schools', *Sport, Education and Society,* 1 (1): 23–46.

Anshel, M.H., Muller, D. and Owens, V.L. (1986) 'Effects of a sports camp experience on the multidimensional self-concepts of boys', *Perceptual and Motor Skills,* 61, 1275–9.

Armour, K.M. and Jones, R.L. (1998) *Physical Education: Teachers' Lives and Careers.* London: Falmer Press.

Arnold, P.J. (1985) 'Rational planning by objectives of the movement curriculum', *Physical Education Review,* 8 (1): 50–61.

Aspin, D. (1976) '"Knowing How" and "Knowing That" and physical education', *Journal of Philosophy of Sport,* 3: 97–117.

Australian Sports Commission (1994) *National Junior Sport Policy.* Canberra: Australian Sports Commission.

Bailey, R.P (2005) 'Evaluating the relationship between physical education, sport and social inclusion', *Education Review*, 57 (1): 71–90.

Barr, S. and Lewin, P. (1994) 'Learning movement: integrating kinesthetic sense with cognitive skills', *Journal of Aesthetic Education*, 28 (1): 83–94.

Bass, S. (2000) 'The pubertal years: a unique opportune stage of growth when the skeleton is most responsive to exercise?', *Sports Medicine*, 30: 73–8.

Baur, L.A. (2001) 'Child and adolescent obesity in the 21st century: an Australian perspective', *Asia Pacific Journal of Clinical Nutrition*, 11: S524–8.

Beane, J.A. (1990) *Affect in the Curriculum: Toward Democracy, Dignity, and Diversity.* New York: Teachers College Press.

Bennet, G. and Hastie, P. (1997) 'A sport education curriculum model for a collegiate physical activity course', *Journal of Physical Education, Recreation and Dance*, 68 (1): 39–44.

Biddle, S. (1999) 'The motivation of pupils in physical education', in C.A. Hardy and M. Mawer (eds), *Learning and Teaching in Physical Education.* London: Falmer Routledge.

Biddle, S.J.H. and Mutrie, N. (2001) *Psychology of Physical Activity: Determinants, Well-being and Interventions.* London: Routledge.

Biddle, S.J.H., Gorely, T. and Stensel, D. (2004) 'Health-enhancing physical activity and sedentary behaviour in children and adolescents', *Journal of Sports Sciences*, 22: 679–701.

Blackman, L., Hunet, G., Hilyer, J. and Harrison, P. (1988) 'The effects of dance team participation on female adolescent physical fitness and self-concept', *Adolescence*, 23: 437–48.

Brennan, D. and Bleakley, E.W. (1997) 'Predictors, problems and policies for post school participation', in J. Kremer, K. Trew and S. Ogle (eds), *Young People's Involvement in Sport.* London: Routledge.

British Medical Association (BMA) (1936) *Report of the Physical Education Committee.* London: BMA Office.

Brooker, R. and Macdonald, D. (1995) 'Mapping physical education in the reform agenda for Australian education: tensions and contradictions', *European Physical Education Review*, 1 (2): 101–10.

Burt, J.J. (1998) 'The role of kinesiology in elevating modern society', *Quest*, 50: 80–95.

Cale, L.A. and Harris, J. (eds) (2005) *Exercise and Young people: Issues, Implications and Initiative.* Basingstoke: Palgrave Macmillan.

Cale, L. and Harris, J. (2006) 'School-based physical activity interventions: effectiveness, trends, issues, implications and recommendations for practice', *Sport, Education and Society*, 11 (4): 401–20.

Carlson, T.B. (1995) 'We hate gym: student alienation from physical education', *Journal of Teaching in Physical Education*, 14: 467–77.

Carlson, T.B. and Hastie, P.A. (1997) 'The student social system within sport education', *Journal of Teaching in Physical Education*, 16 (2): 176–95.

Carr, D. (1983) 'On physical education and educational significance', *Momentum*, 8 (1): 2–9.

Chelladurai, P. and Kuga, D.J. (1996) 'Teaching and coaching: group and task differences', *Quest*, 48 (4): 470–85.

Coalter, F. (2002) *Sport and Community Development: a Manual.* Research Report No. 86. Edinburgh: Sport Scotland.

Connell, R.W. (1989) 'Cool guys, swots and wimps: the interplay of masculinity and education', *Oxford Review of Education*, 15 (3): 291–303.

DCMS (1999) *Policy Action Team 10: Report to the Social Exclusion Unit – Arts and Sport.* London: HMSO.

Deci, E.L. and Ryan, R.M. (1985) *Intrinsic Motivation and Self-Determination in Human Behaviour.* New York: Plenum Press.

Department of Education & Science (DES) (1992) *Physical Education in the National Curriculum.* London: HMSO.

Despres, J.P., Bouchard, C. and Malina, R.M. (1990) 'Physical activity and coronary heart disease risk factors during childhood and adolescence', *Exercise and Sport Sciences Reviews*, 18: 243–61.

Dewar, A. (1990) 'Oppression and privilege in physical education: struggles in the negotiation of gender in a university programme', in D. Kirk and R. Tinning (eds), *Physical Education, Curriculum and Culture.* Lewes: Falmer Press, pp. 67–100.

Ennis, C.D. (1999) 'Creating a culturally relevant curriculum for disengaged girls', *Sport, Education and Society*, 4 (1): 31–49.

Evans, J. (1990) 'Defining the subject: the rise and rise of the New PE', *British Journal of Sociology of Education*, 11 (2): 155–69.

Evans, J., Penney, D., Bryant, A. and Hennick, M. (1996) 'All things bright and beautiful? PE in primary schools post the 1988 ERA', *Educational Review*, 48 (1): 29–40.

Flintoff, A. (1993) 'Gender, physical education and initial teacher education', In J. Evans (ed.), *Equality, Education and Physical Education.* London: Falmer Press, pp. 184–204.

Fox, K. (1992) 'Physical Education and the development of self-esteem in children', in N. Armstrong (ed.) *New Directions in Physical Education*, 2: 33–54, Leeds: Human Kinetics.

Fox, K. (2000) 'The effects of exercise on self-perceptions and self-esteem', in S. Biddle, K. Fox and S. Boutcher (eds), *Physical Activity and Psychological Well-being.* London: Routledge.

Fox, K. and Biddle, S. (1988) 'The child's perspective in physical education part 2: children's participation motives', *British Journal of Physical Education*, 19 (2): 17–82.

Gard, M. and Meyenn, R. (2000) 'Boys, bodies, pleasure and pain: interrogating contact sport in schools', *Sport, Education and Society*, 5 (1): 19–34.

Grant, B.C. (1992) 'Integrating sport into the physical education curriculum in New Zealand secondary schools', *Quest*, 44: 304–16.

Grant, B., Tredinnick, P. and Hodge, K. (1992) 'Sport education in physical education', *New Zealand Journal of Health, Physical Education and Recreation*, 25 (3): 3–6.

Green, K. (2002) 'Lifelong participation, physical education and the work of Ken Roberts', *Sport, Education and Society*, 7 (2): 167–82.

Green, K. and Hardman, K. (eds) (2005) *Physical Education: Essential Issues.* London: Sage.

Gruber, J.J. (1985) 'Physical activity and self-esteem development in children: a meta-analysis', *Academy Papers,* 19: 330–48.

Hargreaves, J. (1986) *Sport, Power and Culture.* Cambridge: Polity Press.

Harris, J. (1994) 'Young people's perceptions of health, fitness and exercise: implications for the teaching of health related exercise', *Physical Education Review,* 17: 143–51.

Harter, S. (1987) 'The determinants and mediational role of global self-worth in children', in N. Eisenberg (ed.), *Contemporary Topics in Developmental Psychology.* New York: Wiley.

Hastie, P. (1996) 'Student role involvement during a unit of sport education', *Journal of Teaching in Physical Education,* 16: 88–103.

Hastie, P.A. (1998) 'Skill and tactical development during a sport education season', *Research Quarterly for Exercise and Sport,* 69 (4): 368–79.

Health Education Authority (HEA) (1998) *Young and Active? Policy Framework for Young People and Health-enhancing Physical Activity.* London: HEA.

Hellison, D., Cutforth, N., Kallusky, J., Martinek, T., Parker, M. and Stiel, J. (2000) *Youth Development and Physical Activity: Linking Universities and Communities.* Champaign, IL: Human Kinetics.

Hellison, D.R. (1973) *Humanistic Physical Education.* London: Prentice Hall.

Hervet, R. (1952) 'Vanves, son experience, ses perspectives', *Revue Institut Sports,* 24: 4–6.

Hickey, C. and Fitzclarence, L. (1999) 'Educating boys in sport and physical education: Using narrative methods to develop pedagogies of responsibility', *Sport Education and Society,* 4(1): 51–62.

Hills, A. (1998) 'Scholastic and intellectual development and sport', in K.-M. Chan and L. Micheli (eds), *Sports and Children.* Champaign, IL: Human Kinetics.

Hirst, P.H. (1974) *Knowledge and the Curriculum.* London: Routledge & Kegan Paul.

Humberstone, B. (1990) 'Warriors or wimps? Creating alternative forms of PE', in M. Messner and D. Sabo (eds), *Sport, Men and the Gender Order.* Champaign, IL: Human Kinetics, pp. 201–10.

ICSSPE (2001) *World Summit on Physical Education.* Berlin: International Council for Physical Education and Sport Science.

Jacks, L.P. (1937) *The Education of the Whole Man.* London: University of London Press.

Jirasek, I. (2003) 'Philosophy of sport, or philosophy of physical culture: an experience from the Czech Republic: philosophical kinanthropology, *Sport, Education and Society,* 8 (1): 105–17.

Keddie, N. (1971) 'Classroom knowledge', in M.F.D. Young (ed.), *Knowledge and Control.* London: Collier Macmillan, pp. 133–60.

Kimiecik, J.C. and Harris, A.T. (1996) 'What is enjoyment? A conceptual/definitional analysis with implications for sport and exercise psychology', *Journal of Sport and Exercise Psychology,* 14: 192–206.

King, A., Rejeski, W. and Buchner, D. (1998) 'Physical activity interventions targeting older adults: a critical review and recommendations', *American Journal of Preventative Medicine*, 15: 316–33.

Kirk, D. (1992) *Defining Physical Education: The Social Construction of a School Subject in Postwar Britain*. London: Falmer Press.

Kirk, D. (1994) 'Making the present strange: sources of the present crisis in physical education', *Discourse*, 15 (1): 46–53.

Kirk, D. (1998) *Schooling Bodies: School Practice and Public Discourse, 1880–1950*. London: Leicester University Press.

Kirk, D. and Gorely, T. (2000) 'Challenging thinking about the relationship between school physical education and sports performance', *European Physical Education Review*, 6 (2): 119–33.

Lau, P., Yu, C., Lee, A., So, R. and Sung, R. (2004) 'The relationship among physical fitness, physical education, conduct and academic performance of Chinese primary school children', *International Journal of Physical Education*, 12: 17–26.

Lawson, H.A. (1999) 'Education for social responsibility: preconditions in retrospect and prospect', *Quest*, 51: 116–49.

Lindner, K. (1999) 'Sport participation and perceived academic performance of school children and youth', *Pediatric Exercise Science*, 11: 129–44.

Martinek, T. (1981) 'Pygmalion in the gym: a model for the communication of teacher expectations in physical education', *Research Quarterly for Exercise and Sport*, 52: 58–67.

Martinek, T.J. and Hellison, D.R. (1997) 'Fostering resiliency in underserved youth through physical activity', *Quest*, 49 (1): 34–49.

Maxwell, J.A. (2004) 'Causal explanation, qualitative research, and scientific enquiry in education', *Educational Researcher*, 33 (2): 3–11.

Melnick, M., Sabo, D. and VanFossen, B. (1992) 'Educational effects of interscholastic athletic participation on African, American and Hispanic Youth', *Adolescence*, 27: 295–308.

Melnick, M., Vanfossen, B. and Sabo, D. (1988) 'Developmental effects of athletic participation among high school girls', *Sociology of Sport Journal*, 5: 22–36.

Miller, S.C., Bredemeier, B.J.L. and Shields, D.L.L. (1997) 'Sociomoral education through physical education with at-risk children', *Quest*, 49: 114–29.

Morgan, R.E. (1974) *Concerns and Values in Physical Education*. London: G. Bell & Sons.

Moore, G. (2002) 'In our hands: the future is in the hands of those who give our young people hope and reason to live', *British Journal of Teaching in Physical Education*, 33 (2): 26–7.

Morris, L., Sallybanks, J., Willis, K. and Makkai, T. (2003) 'Sport, physical activity and antisocial behaviour in youth', *Trends and Issues in Crime and Criminal Justice online*, 249. http://www.aic.gov.au/publications/tandi/tandi249.html (accessed 10 February 2007).

Nichols, G. (1997) 'A consideration of why active participation in sport and leisure might reduce criminal behaviour', *Sport, Education and Society*, 2 (2): 181–90.

O'Sullivan, M., Siedentop, D. and Tannehill, D. (1994) 'Breaking out: co-dependency of high school physical education', *Journal of Teaching in Physical Education*, 13: 421–8.

Parker, M. and Stiehl, J. (2005) 'Personal and social responsibility', in J. Lund and D. Tannehill (eds), *Standards-based Physical Education Curriculum Development*. Boston, MA: Jones and Bartlett, pp. 130–53.

Penn, A. (1999) *Targeting Schools: Drill, Militarism and Imperialism*. London: Woburn Press.

Penney, D. and Evans, J. (1999) *Politics, Policy and Practice in Physical Education*. London: E & FN Spon.

Penney, D. and Jess, M. (2004) 'Physical education and physically active lives: a lifelong approach to curriculum development', *Sport Education and Society*, 9 (2): 269–87.

Peters, R.S. (1966) *Ethics and Education*. London: Allen & Unwin.

Pirie, B. (1995) 'Meaning through movement: kinesthetic English', *English Journal*, December: 46–51.

Plowden Report (1967) *Children and their Primary Schools*. Department of Education and Science. London: HMSO.

Pope, S. (2005) 'Once more with feeling: affect and playing with the TGfU model', *Physical Education and Sport Pedagogy*, 10 (3): 271–86.

Priest, S. (1998) 'Physical challenge and the development of trust through corporate adventure training', *Journal of Experiential Learning*, 21: 31–4.

Priest, S. and Gass, M.A. (1997) *Effective Leadership in Adventure Programming*. Champaign, IL: Human Kinetics.

Pring, R. (1976) *Knowledge and Schooling*. London: Open Books.

Qualifications and Curriculum Authority (QCA) (2001) *PE and School Sports Project*. www.qca.org.uk/ca/subjects/pe/pess.asp (accessed 10 February 2007).

Reilly, J. and Dorotsky, A. (1999) 'Epidemic of obesity in UK children', *Lancet*, 354: 1874–5.

Ryle, G. (1949) *The Concept of Mind*. London: Hutchinson.

Sallis, J., McKenzie, J., Kolody, B., Lewis, M., Marshall, S. and Rosengard, P. (1999) 'Effects of health-related physical education on academic achievement: Project SPARK', *Research Quarterly for Exercise and Sport*, 70: 127–34.

Schools Council (1971) *Physical Education 8–13*. Working Paper 37.

Scottish Executive (2003) *Let's Make Scotland More Active: a Strategy for Physical Activity*. Edinburgh: HMSO.

Sevick, M.A., Bradham, D.D., Muender, M., Chen, G.J., Enarson, C., Daiely, M. and Ettinger, W. (2000) 'Cost-effectiveness of aerobic and resistance exercise in seniors with knee osteoarthritis', *Medicine and Science in Sports and Exercise*, 32 (9): 1534–40.

Shephard, R. (1997) 'Curricular physical activity and academic performance', *Pediatric Exercise Science*, 9: 113–26.

Siedentop, D. (1987) 'The theory and practice of sport education', in G.T. Barette, R.S. Feingold, C. Roger Rees and M. Pieron (eds), *Myths, Models and Methods in Sport*

Pedagogy. Proceedings of the Adelphi-AIESEP World Sport Conference, 19–22 August, New York. Champaign, IL: Human Kinetics.

Siedentop, D. (ed.) (1994) *Sport Education: Quality PE Through Positive Sport Experiences.* Champaign, IL: Human Kinetics.

Smith, A. and Parr, M. (2007) 'Young people's views on the nature and purposes of physical education: a sociological analysis', *Sport, Education and Society*, 12 (1): 37–58.

Smith, W.D. (1974) *Stretching Their Bodies: The History of Physical Education.* London: David & Charles.

Snyder, E. and Sprietzer, E. (1977) 'Sport education and schools', in G. Lueschen and G. Sage (eds), *Handbook of Social Science of Sport.* Champaign, IL: Stipes.

Sonstroem, R.J. (1997) 'Physical activity and self-esteem', in W.P. Morgan (ed.), *Physical Activity and Mental Health.* Washington, DC: Taylor & Francis.

Sparkes, A.C. (1989) 'Health related fitness: a case of innovation without change', *British Journal of Physical Education*, 20 (2): 60–2.

Steinbeck, K.S. (2001) 'The importance of physical activity in the prevention of overweight and obesity in childhood: a review and an opinion', *Obesity Reviews*, 2: 117–30.

Svoboda, B. (1994) *Sport and Physical Activity as a Socialisation Environment: Scientific Review part 1.* Strasbourg: Council of Europe.

Theberge, N. (1985) 'Towards a feminist alternative to sport as a male preserve', *Quest*, 37: 193–202.

Tinning, R. and Glasby, T. (2002) 'Pedagogical work and the "cult" of the body: considering the role of HPE in the context of the "new public health"', *Sport, Education and Society*, 7 (2): 109–19.

Tolfrey, K., Jones, A.M. and Campbell, I.G. (2000) 'The effect of aerobic exercise training on the lipid-lipoprotein profile of children and adolescents', *Sports Medicine*, 29: 99–112.

Tremblay, M., Inman, J. and Willms, J. (2000) 'The relationship between physical activity, self-esteem, and academic achievement in 12-year-old children', *Pediatric Exercise Science*, 12: 312–24.

USDHHS (1996) *Physical Activity and Health: a Report of the Surgeon General.* Atlanta: US Department of Health and Human Services.

Walker, J.C. (1988) *Louts and Legends.* Sydney: Allen & Unwin.

White, J.P. (1973) *Towards a Compulsory Curriculum.* London: Routledge & Kegan Paul.

Whitehead, J. (1988) 'Why children take part', *Isis Journal*, 1: 23–31.

Williams, A. and Bedward, J. (2001) 'Gender, culture and the generation gap: student and teacher perceptions of aspects of National Curriculum Physical Education', *Sport, Education and Society*, 6 (1): 53–66.

Williams, L. and Gill, D.L. (1995) 'The role of perceived competence in the motivation of physical activity', *Journal of Sport and Exercise Psychology*, 17: 363–78.

Wright, J. (1993) 'Regulation and resistance: the physical education lesson as speech genre', *Social Semiotics*, 3: 23–56.

Wright, J. (1997) 'A feminist poststructuralist methodology for the study of gender construction in physical education: description of a study', *Journal of Teaching in Physical Education*, 15 (1): 1–24.

Wright, J. (2000) 'Bodies, meanings and movement: a comparison of the language of a physical education lesson and a Feldenkrais movement class', *Sport, Education and Society*, 5 (1): 35–50.

Wright, J. and King, R.C. (1991) '"I say what I mean", said Alice: an analysis of gendered discourse in physical education', *Journal of Teaching in Physical Education*, 10: 210–25.

12

Physical Culture and the Polarised American Metropolis

DAVID L. ANDREWS, MICHAEL SILK AND ROBERT PITTER

Race is the modality in which class is lived. (Hall et al., 1979: 394)

OVERVIEW

» *Contextualising the contemporary city*
» *The (ill) health of the urban United States*
» *Suburban soccer and embodied privilege*

Our aim within this chapter is to illustrate how painfully explicit, and all too predictable, patterns of socio-spatial ordering and arrangement within the contemporary American metropolis are tied to distinct provisions, expectations and experiences of physical health, fitness and activity. In doing so we engage the city as a complex and contradictory space, fragmented by pervasive, and indeed intersecting, class and racial divisions. Such socio-spatial cleavages are neither natural nor inevitable; they are historically entrenched within, and bounded by, particular power struggles and associated political and economic trajectories. Soja (2000) described American cities as an archipelago of fortressed enclosures that share little (socially, culturally and economically) in common with adjacent neighbourhoods: the material contrast between such divergent private worlds helping to constitute effective social and psychic barriers that allow for the unquestionably tense – but in many respects, surprisingly insouciant – coexistence of such disparate communities. Hence, both voluntarily and involuntarily, individuals, and indeed entire communities, become barricaded 'in visible and not-so-visible urban islands, overseen by restructured forms of public power and private authority' (Soja, 2000: 299). Thus, we focus on cities as highly differentiated and complex spaces (Merrifield, 2000; Walks, 2001) which incorporate markedly different physical cultural experiences (Ingham, 1997) for those differentially located, and equally complex, (sub)urban populations.

Following an overview of the race- and class-based polarisation of the contemporary American metropolis, we examine the (ill) health of the urban United States addressing how, within the context of particular governmental regimes, those marginalised by class and race are subject to astounding levels of disease, restricted health care provision, and negligible access to health and well-being resources. From this juncture, we turn to the antithesis of urban health and physical disinvestment: the suburban cultures of sporting privilege within which suburban middle-class bodies deploy sport as an agent of social distinction and differentiation. Finally, in our concluding comments, we problematise the material and symbolic return to the city: the new patterns of urban regeneration in select parcels of the North American downtown that serve to marginalise further those not included in the dominant economic and political processes restructuring the city.

CONTEXTUALISING THE CONTEMPORARY CITY

While the archetypal North American city has long been marked by a distinct social morphology defined in, and through, interconnected class and racial relations (see Riess, 1991), this process of metropolitan polarisation intensified in the period immediately following the end of the Second World War. It was at this juncture that 'decentralization of population from the cities' (Savage and Warde, 1994: 76) – the suburbanisation of North America – experienced its most startling growth. Earlier phases in the history of North American suburbanisation were engineered in order to accentuate very definite class and race divisions; however, the sheer scale of post-war suburbanisation wrought the most profound influence on differentiating the collective experiences of class and race in (sub)urban North America. There are, of course, numerous intersecting reasons for the post-war reformation of American metropolitan space. First, the massive out migration (colloquially referred to as 'white flight') of mainly middle-income white inhabitants from the urban cores of midwest and north-eastern cities, combined with large-scale inmigration of predominantly poor African Americans from the rural south into the evacuated urban centres, conclusively established residential racial segregation as the defining characteristic of the late twentieth century (McKay, 1977). This pattern of racial segregation was reinforced through ill-conceived and implemented public housing policies, and the race-based discriminatory practices within the private housing industry (Wit, 1993). Further fracturing of the post-war American city was the criminal disinvestment and therefore collapse of the urban low-wage labour market, in favour of service-oriented suburban employment centres (Jacobs, 1992). In addition, over the last 20 years, and in the face of crippling post-industrial poverty, the American populace has had to contend with the massive retrenchment of social welfare sensibilities and programmes wrought by the emergence of a neo-liberal hegemony that has come to frame all aspects of American life (Giroux, 2005; Neisser and Schramm, 1994).

As Grossberg (2005) indicated, urban poverty, and the widespread hopelessness and alienation it produces, is the result of targeted political and economic initiatives, not some cultural inevitability or social pathology. Following an unprecedented period of consumer prosperity and confidence during the 1950s and into the 1960s, the political and economic troubles of the late 1960s and early 1970s were, somewhat prematurely, construed as evidence of deep-rooted problems in the US socio-political order. Thus, from the 1970s onwards, and increasingly with the onset of the Reagan Revolution, a *perfect storm* (or more appropriately, the *perfect nightmare*) of reactionary and regressive political (the denial of continued race-based inequality, justifying the programmatic disassembling of the social welfare system), economic (widespread corporate and civic disinvestment in the American city's traditional industrial cores) and legal (aggressive and egregious policing tactics and judicial targeting) trajectories conspired to exacerbate the social injustices and inequalities that had historically plagued the urban African American populace. Exploding the welfare consensus instantiated through New Deal and Great Society reforms, the US government has shifted away from its role as an economic and social 'safety net' keying on stabilising national productivity, and ensuring the provision of societal needs manifest in welfare, education and health care services (Clarke, 1991). Instead, and in the name of cutting taxes and dismantling 'big government', successive administrations in the latter decades of the twentieth century have reformulated the role of government within the United States. This involved the aggressive diminution of state influence over major industries, public services and social welfare, in favour of an approach centred on enhancing capital accumulation by bolstering the scope and 'logics' of the free market (Brenner and Theodore, 2002; Peck, 2003; Peck and Tickell, 2002; Sheller and Urry, 2003). While the doses vary, the basic prescription for this new 'neo-liberal' governance is the same: purge the system of obstacles to the functioning of free markets; celebrate the virtues of individualism (recast social problems as individual problems, such as drug use, obesity, inadequate health insurance) and competitiveness; foster economic self-sufficiency; abolish or weaken social programmes; include those marginalised (often by this shift in the role of government) or the poor into the labour market, on the market's terms (such as through the workfare scheme); and criminalise the homeless and the urban poor (subject this population to curfew orders, increased surveillance, or 'zero-tolerance' policing) (Giroux, 2005; Peck, 2003; Rose, 1999, 2000).

This ideology of neo-liberalism has found its material expression in an all-out attack on democratic values and on the very notion of the public sphere, particularly, if by no means exclusively, within the city. As Giroux (2005) points out, the discourse of neo-liberalism devalues the collective or public good (as was manifest in, for example, welfare and health care provision) in favour of a wider rationale for a handful of private interests to control as much of social life as possible in order to maximise their personal profit: public services such as health care, child care, public assistance, education and transportation are no different and are subject to the rules of the market (Giroux, 2005). With specific regard to health, a diversity of traditionally public issues and concerns have thus become incorporated into the reach of the private sector: disease prevention, health promotion, 'latch-key' children, personal and public health, juvenile curfews, medical services, day care, nutrition, substance abuse prevention, mental health and family counselling, teen pregnancy, services for the homeless, family and community revitilisation, family abuse, arts and cultural awareness, education, recreation, career structures, improvement of infrastructures and economic revitalisation (Pitter and Andrews, 1997). In this sense, the existing neo-liberalism produces, legitimates and exacerbates the existence of persistent poverty, the absence of employment opportunities, inadequate health care, substandard housing and education: an extant racial apartheid created by ever-increasing 'problems of social dislocation in the inner city' (Wilson, 1987: 22), leading to growing inequalities between the rich and the poor (Giroux, 2005: 46). Grossberg (2005), for example, talking of children within the United States, paints a grim picture: the wealthiest nation in the world, it seems, is 'willing to allow between one-fifth and two-fifths of its kids to live in or close to the abysmal conditions of poverty, many with no shelter and no access to medical care' (62).

The cumulative result of this concerted post-war neglect has been most visibly and catastrophically manifest in polarised patterns and experiences of post-industrial suburban socio-economic growth and urban socio-economic decline (Andrews et al., 2003; Kleinburg, 1995; Wacquant, 1993, 1994; Wacquant and Wilson, 1989). As a result of these socio-economic and political processes the contemporary American city evolved into two starkly contrasting spaces: the predominantly white and smugly affluent distending 'technoburbs' (Lemann, 1989) and the largely black (and increasingly Hispanic) 'hyper-ghettos' crippled by the ravages of federal and corporate disinvestment (Wacquant, 1994). As such, and pointing to the intersections of class and race, the bulk of the population living in the low-density, relatively affluent, suburban peripheries of the nation's 320 metropolitan areas is white – 79 per cent of non-Hispanic whites lived outside metropolitan areas while 52 per cent of all Blacks lived in a central city within a metropolitan area in 2002 (US Census Bureau, 2003) – the nation's inner urban environments having become the site of highly concentrated black and Hispanic poverty (Jacobs, 1992).

By 2001, the US Census Bureau (2003) reported that 12 per cent of the US population lived in poverty; this rate, however, differs by race: 23 per cent of blacks and 8 per cent of non-Hispanic whites live at or below the poverty line. Further, as Squires and Kubrin (2005) proposes, these figures are spatialised: the dominant features of metropolitan development in the post-war years in North America are suburban sprawl, concentrated poverty and segregation (if not hypersegregation). This (hyper)segregation is manifest in increased and concentrated poverty. Within the city poverty grew between 1970 and 1995 from below 13 per cent to 20 per cent, while, between 1970 and 1990, the number of census tracts in which at least 40 per cent of the population was poor increased from under 1,500 to more than 3,400 and the number of people living in those tracts grew from 4.1 million to more than 8 million. (Squires and Kubrin, 2005; US Department of Housing and Urban Development, 1997). The urban centres of North American cities are thus often places of poverty and despair: low-wage work, insecurity, poor living conditions and dejected isolation for the many at the bottom of the social ladder daily sucked into them. These are often polluted spaces that are tiring, overwhelming, confusing and alienating (Amin, 2006). They are places of ill health that 'hum with the fear and anxiety linked to crime, helplessness and the close juxtaposition of strangers. They symbolize the isolation of people trapped in ghettos, segregated areas and distant dormitories, and they express the frustration and ill-temper of those locked into long hours of work or travel' (Amin, 2006: 1011).

Within this context, unsurprisingly, Squires and Kubrin (2005) identified that racial segregation persists as a dominant feature of metropolitan areas. Cities in the United States are disproportionately non-white with over 52 per cent of blacks and 21 per cent of whites residing in central-city neighbourhoods, while suburbs are disproportionately white where 57 per cent of whites but just 36 per cent of blacks reside (McKinnon, 2003; Squires and Kubrin, 2005). Racism and racial inequality are far from a thing of the past and, in terms of concentrated poverty and racial segregation, are the fruits of previous waves of urban policy and planning – *pace* the racially skewed death toll of Hurricane Katrina, particularly with regard to the loss of life in New Orleans (Gibson, 2006; see also Denzin, 2006; Molotch, 2006) – that are particularly pronounced within the city as an 'actually existing spaces of neoliberalism' (Brenner and Theodore, 2002). Indeed, in 2003, 30–34 per cent of Hispanic and black children were poor compared with 10–13 per cent of Asian and non-Hispanic white children, figures that are predicted to rise in the foreseeable future due to record levels of immigration (US Department of Health & Human Services, Center for Disease Control & Prevention, 2005). It seems that the internal, domestic war against the poor, youth, women and the elderly, especially those further marginalised by class and colour (Giroux, 2003a, 2003b, 2005), continues unabated within the contemporary neo-liberal city – the intersections between race, poverty and urban youth becoming fixed and undisputed as a 'problem' that government or other socio-political apparatus needs to 'look into' or 'resolve' (Zylinska, 2005). Indeed, these historically rooted patterns are not just statistical or demographic curiosities, they are spatial and racial inequalities directly associated with access to virtually all products and services associated with the 'good life' (Squires and Kubrin, 2005). While there are multiple manifestations of inequality – such as high levels of racial discrimination in the housing market, the fear of crime, increased surveillance, the violent crime victimisation rate (35.1 per 1,000 in urban areas, 25.8 in suburban areas, figures that are higher for black residents), home-ownership rates, job opportunities, access to retail and commercial businesses, family life (Squires and Kubrin, 2005; US Department of Justice, 2001) – it is the institutionalised patterns of health inequality with which we are most interested within this current chapter.

THE (ILL) HEALTH OF THE URBAN UNITED STATES

As Giroux (2005) has pointed out, while the United States ranks 1st in military technology, military exports, defence expenditures and the number of millionaires and billionaires, it ranks 18th among advanced industrial nations in the gap between rich and poor children, 12th in the percentage of children in poverty, 17th in efforts to lift children out of poverty, and 23rd in infant mortality (Giroux, 2005: 87). Thus, in the richest democracy in the world, and in figures marked by race: 12.2 million children live below the poverty line, more than 16 million are at the low end of the income scale, and 9.2 million, nearly 90 per cent of which belong to working families, lack health insurance (Giroux, 2005). These figures, however, become even more horrific when considering the concentrated poverty and racial segregation within the inner city (Frazier et al., 2003; Massey, 2001; Massey and Denton, 1993; Sampson et al., 2002; Squires and Kubrin, 2005). In 2000, for example, the poverty rate for African Americans was 22 per cent, double that of the entire nation, while the poverty rate for black children was 29.4 per cent compared with 8.4 for white children (Street, 2001, in Giroux, 2005).

It appears that health disparities may constitute the most concrete disadvantages associated with the spatial and racial divide in urban areas (Squires and Kubrin, 2005), given poverty causes poor health by its connection with inadequate nutrition, substandard housing, exposure to environmental hazards, unhealthy lifestyles and decreased access to and use of health care services (US Department of Health & Human Services, Center for Disease Control & Prevention, 2005) (see also Box 12.1). Even more perturbing, these disparities manifest themselves quite early in life. The black infant mortality rate in 1995 was 14.3 per 1,000 live births compared with 6.3 for whites and Hispanics and 5.3 for Asians. Further, and perhaps an indicator of the shift of the role of government away from social provision, the ratio of black to white infant mortality increased from 1.6 to 2.4 between 1950 and the 1990s (Kingston and Nickens, 2001, in Squires and Kubrin, 2005). The spatial inequalities inherent within the inner city clearly contribute to the long-established disparities in health and wellness of those populations disadvantaged by class, race and social location. For example, access to clean air and water, exposure to lead paint, stress, obesity, smoking habits, diet, social isolation, availability of public spaces (such as parks and recreation facilities), proximity to hospitals and other medical treatment facilities, and availability of health insurance are all determined by spatial location (Bullard, 1996; Dreier et al., 2001; Kingston and Nickens, 2001; Klinenberg, 2002; Squires and Kubrin, 2005: 52). For example, while the hospital admission rate for asthma in the state of New York is 1.8 per 1,000, it is three times higher in the Mott Haven area of the South Bronx (Dreier et al., 2001; Squires and Kubrin, 2005).

The magnitude of the crisis is exacerbated by evidence that in some cities, such as the District of Columbia, the child poverty rate is as high as 45 per cent (Giroux, 2005). Indeed, and as a telling exemplar, within the Washington, DC area, the affluent and predominantly white suburb of Bethesda, Maryland, has one paediatrician for every 400 children, while the poor and predominantly black neighbourhoods in the District's south-east side have one paediatrician for every 3,700 children (Squires, 2005). These figures are not just a localised occurrence. According to Eberhardt et al. (2001), overall mortality was one-third higher for black Americans than for white Americans. In 2003 age-adjusted death rates for the black population exceeded those for the white population by 43 per cent for stroke, 31 per cent for heart disease, 23 per cent for cancer, and almost 750 per cent for HIV disease (US Department of Health & Human Services, Center for Disease Control & Prevention, 2005: 11). Further, preliminary age-adjusted death rates for the black population exceeded those for the white population by 38 per cent for stroke, 28 per cent for heart disease, 27 per cent for cancer, and more than 700 per cent for HIV disease (Eberhardt et al., 2001: 6). These horrific imbalances are also manifest in the leading cause of death: young black males aged 15–24 years old are most likely to die through homicide, which is also the second leading cause for young Hispanic males. Indeed, this homicide rate for young black males in 1999 was 17 times the rate for young non-Hispanic white males, and the rate for young Hispanic males was 7 times the rate for young non-Hispanic white males (Eberhardt et al., 2001: 6). The US Department of Health and Human Services, Office of Minority Health's (OMH's) own figures do not reveal any more of a progressive picture. The OMH reported in 2001 that African American men were 1.5 times as likely to have new cases of lung and prostate cancer, 1.8 times as likely to have new cases of stomach cancer, had lower 5-year cancer survival rates for lung, prostate and pancreatic cancer, compared with non-Hispanic white men. African American women were 20 per cent less likely to have been diagnosed with breast cancer; however, they were 30 per cent more likely to die from breast cancer, compared with non-Hispanic white women, they were 2.6 times as likely to have been diagnosed with stomach cancer, and they were 2.3 times as likely to die from stomach cancer, compared with non-Hispanic white women (OMH, 2006). These figures are even more astonishing for diabetes and heart disease with African American adults 2.4 times as likely to be diabetic that non-Hispanic whites and 20 per cent more likely to suffer from heart disease. Further, most astoundingly, and a clear indicator of health as a spatialised and racialised condition within the contemporary United States, while African Americans make up 13 per cent of the total US population, they accounted for 50 per cent of HIV/AIDS cases in 2003.

Box 12.1   Spatialised and racialised health-based inequities in Baltimore

While cautious not to map the experiences of one particular city with those of the remainder of the nation (see e.g. Massey, 1997, 2000), we would like to offer a very brief sketch of one particular city – Baltimore. Indeed, Harvey (2001) suggests that Baltimore is emblematic of the political and economic conditions that have moulded cities within our present moment, thus we offer this exemplar as telling with regard to the spatialised and racialised health-based inequities of the distinct geographic morphology of urban life. While a small or select portion of the city has been subject to intense regeneration and capital investment, – especially apparent in the Inner Harbor 'tourist bubble', 24 per cent of the city's residents live in poverty (compared with 14% nationally) as Baltimore's per capita income level fell to 57 per cent of Maryland's average (Johns Hopkins Institute for Policy Studies, 2000), life expectancies are 14 years under national averages, teen pregnancy was the highest among the nation's 50 largest cities in 1999, and 34 per cent of children under 18 in the city live below the poverty level (nationally, this figure is 10 per cent) (Hagerty and Dunham, 2005; Harvey, 2000; Johns Hopkins Institute for Policy Studies, 2000; Siegel and Smith, 2001; Silk and Andrews, 2006; US Census Bureau, 2004). Homicide rates in the city average around 300 per year (around seven times higher than the national rate, six times higher than New York City, and three times higher than Los Angeles) in the last decade – the majority of homicides are endemic to drug- and gang-related violence (Dao, 2005). Furthermore, large parcels of the city are characterised by block after block of vacant row houses, the city has led the nation in violent crime, juvenile homicide, heroin, cocaine and syphilis rates, and a higher percentage of the city's population tested positive for heroin than in any other US city, with some 59,000 addicts in a city of 675,000, nearly 1 in 10 of the population (Cannon, 1999). Put simply, although there has been a recent stabilisation in murder rates and violent crime, Baltimore is, as with many cities whose civic administration operates less in the interests of citizens and more in the interests of bolstering the 'logics' of the marketplace (see e.g. Sheller and Urry, 2003), the 'home of the comfortable and the prison of the choice-less' (Johns Hopkins Institute for Policy Studies, 2000: 48).

The relationships between community infrastructure and health have a long and detailed history (see e.g. Dalgard and Tambs, 1997; Halpern, 1995; Sampson et al., 1999; Witten et al., 2003). With regard to leisure-time physical activity, not surprisingly, lack of infrastructure and poorer (in economic terms) school districts mean that those living below or near poverty are less likely to have regular leisure-time physical activity and more likely to be inactive. Indeed, in 2003 about one-half of adults who were poor or near poor were inactive in leisure time compared with about one-third of adults living in families with income more than twice the poverty level (US Department of Health & Human Services, Center for Disease Control & Prevention, 2005: 40). Yet, the pathways said to overcome such concentrated inequalities – enhanced opportunities for physical activity associated with access and satisfaction with parks and recreational facilities (Sharp et al., 1999), the direct health effect of close proximity to amenities such as health services and public transport (Dalgard and Tambs, 1997; Taylor et al., 1997), the opportunities community amenities provide for social connections (Warin et al., 2000; Witten et al., 2003) – seem to be those very social programmes discarded by power blocs centred on securing the logics of the marketplace. The provision of public amenities such as parks, recreational facilities and social and cultural services – venues that provide opportunities for health-promoting activity, well-being, as well as informal meeting places, outside home and work, where social relationships can be formed and maintained (Oldenburg, 1997; Warin et al., 2000; Witten et al., 2003) – are those venues subject either to 'development' or increased surveillance (see e.g. Flusty, 2001; Rose, 2000). Within such spaces of catastrophic social, psychological and physical ill health, the potential for organised sporting activities to be used as a fulcrum for improving general public wellness has been overlooked. Instead, and as woefully underfunded urban public school systems struggle to provide even the most basic physical education programming, representative sport teams and interschool competition, sport has become an important facet of the politically reactionary 'social problems industry' (Hartmann and Depro, 2006; Pitter and Andrews, 1997). Under such auspices, recreation-based sport initiatives (such as the vanguard Midnight Basketball League) have become agents of social surveillance and control designed to ameliorate elevated crime and delinquency rates, impoverished urban populations thus being pathologised as problems in need of redress, rather than as woefully underprivileged and underserved swathes of humanity deserving of significant social, economic and indeed health-related programmatic intervention.

SUBURBAN SOCCER AND EMBODIED PRIVILEGE

Within this section of the chapter, we focus upon the prevalence and significance of soccer within the contemporary American suburb as a means of illustrating the contrasting position, and indeed influence, of physical culture within a socio-spatial context considerably different from the urban dystopia previously described. Thus, our aim is to demonstrate how, whereas the unhealthy nature of contemporary urban spaces has become one of the 'afflictions of inequality' (Wilkinson, 1996), the contrasting health-oriented sensibilities and orientations (such as seemingly obligatory youth soccer participation) associated with suburban American culture have become the expected and unacknowledged *corollaries of privilege*, as manifest in very different health provisions, practices and outcomes. Despite their overbearing cultural, economic and political presence (the suburban American populace grew from 41 million or 27 per cent of the total population in 1950 to 76 million or 37 per cent in 1970: by the 1990s suburbanites became the absolute majority of the national populace: see Kleinberg, 1995; Lemann, 1989; Thomas, 1998), American suburbs are by no means homogeneous bastions of upper middle-class affluence (Zwick and Andrews, 1999). We nonetheless focus on the experience and vision of the American suburb that dominates popular perception: those affluent, largely white, metropolitan peripheries and populations dominated by aesthetically driven cultures of lifestyle consumption (Andrews, 1999). Out of this fundamentally competitive socio-spatial context, the American suburban soccer phenomenon was to emerge.

Whilst not envisioned as part of the suburban American dream (see Jackson, 1985), soccer, like the detached family home, the reliance on the automobile, the shopping mall, and a preoccupation with material consumption, has become an emblematic constituent of suburban American reality:

> What has happened is that soccer was viewed by the general populous (*sic*) as ethnic, urban and very blue collar. What we find, however, is that while there is still a base of ethnic and urban supporters, the reality is that soccer today is mom and dad, two kids, two lawn chairs, Saturday afternoon with the family dog, watching the kids play, $40,000 income, mini van. (Hank Steinbrecher, Executive Director and General Secretary of the United States Soccer Federation, quoted in Pesky, 1993: 31)

Thus, in recent decades, soccer's ethnically differentiated, hyphenated-American identity (see Hayes-Bautista and Rodriguez, 1994; Malone, 1994) has comfortably coexisted with the game's emergence as perhaps *the* sporting practice and symbol of the *fin-de-millennium* suburban United States, the two populations combining to form 'America's silent sporting revolution' (Anon., 1996: 27) mobilized by the 45 million 'soccer Americans' who either played or watched the game on a regular basis (Steinbrecher, 1996).

Soccer does not possess any innate, essential, qualities that can explain its seeming affinity with the status-driven suburban middle-class habitus. However, more than the simple act of 'playing the game', the entire *soccer field* has been incorporated into the complex universe of 'practices and consumptions' (Bourdieu, 1990) which structure and constitute the suburban cultural system. As heretofore 'noncommodifiable phenomena' (Gephart, 1996: 33) youth soccer has, in a Bourdieuian sense, been discursively constructed as a highly exclusive asset in the field of cultural production, whose scarcity makes it a prized activity in the cultural marketplace and puts those with access to it in a position of cultural privilege. Access to economic capital is probably the single most critical determinant of participation in suburban youth soccer (Andrews, 1999).

Not that formal barriers are erected to preclude participation in competitive soccer programmes, yet the significant financial outlay demanded by participation effectively precludes many less economically secure middle-class families (Andrews et al., 2003). That individual players are able to apportion considerable amounts of their time to soccer also speaks to more than their evident commitment to the game: it also illustrates the extent to which their lives encompass an 'absence of necessity' (Bourdieu, 1984, 1986) that is pointedly missing from the lives of children from less privileged populations. Unlike many US adolescents, the offspring of the affluent suburban middle class certainly did not face pressures to enter the part-time labour force in order to augment their family's income. Rather, their parents' financial stability afforded them a wholly unfettered out-of-school time, without which they simply could not have been a member of the soccer team. As with other trappings of their existence, the privilege of 'spare time' often passes as unrecognised, its being viewed as a taken-for-granted condition of being a teenager, rather than an expression of membership of a dominant class (Shilling, 1993).

Part of soccer's ability to appeal to contemporary suburban values lies in its obtuse relationship with more established elements of American sporting culture. Specifically, both American football and basketball did not rest easily with the superficially progressive mores of the maturing suburban hegemony of the United States. The exaggerated hypermasculinity and female marginalisation celebrated by American football became increasing incongruous with a new generation of post-Civil-Rights parents, many of whom strove for a semblance of gender equality in their children's lives, if not their own. Within this climate of increased gender awareness and activity in the realm of sport – and emerging as it was in the shadow of American football's physical and symbolic chauvinism – soccer assumed the mantle of the gender-inclusive American sport *par excellence*. Interestingly, the same rationale that made soccer a suitable physical activity for girls – its perceived encouragement of non-aggressive behaviour, sociability and the all important *fun* – similarly made it attractive to parents seeking an alternative to American football for their sons. According to Wagg, 'soccer' appeals to liberal and/or Democratic families concerned to promote equal opportunities but deterred by the aggressive masculinity' embodied within American football (1995: 182). As Hornung noted, soccer is 'a sport preferred by middle- and upper-middle class parents who want to protect their kids from the savagery of American football' (Hornung, 1994: 39). Soccer was thus popularised because it appeared to offer the *right* type of aerobic and corporeal benefits for boys *and* girls (Bondy, 1992; Pesky, 1993), as dictated by the health and aesthetic norms of the suburban middle-class habitus.

Soccer has also been cast as the appropriate activity for the *normal* suburban athlete, whose *innate* intelligence was counterpoised, even *in absentia*, by the *natural* athletic ability of the black urbanite. According to a 1977 article in *US News & World Report*, 'Another possible reason for the growth of soccer in some suburbs - one that the game's proponents do not discuss publicly, but a few say privately – is that some white youths and their parents want a sport not as dominated by blacks as football and basketball' (1977: 100). Over the last three decades a racially charged 'national fantasy' (Berlant, 1991) has enveloped basketball. This centred upon the popular fears and fascinations associated with the perceived natural physicality of the urban African American athlete, who, were it not for sport, would unerringly be involving his body in more deviant, promiscuous and irresponsible pursuits (see Cole, 1996; Cole and Andrews, 1996; McCarthy et al., 1996; Reeves and Campbell, 1994). Unquestionably, the racial signifiers contained within popular basketball (and to a lesser extent American football) discourse have, in opposition, influenced soccer's symbolic location within the contemporary popular imaginary. In spatial (suburban/urban), racial (white/black) and corporal (cerebral/physical) senses, soccer became the antithesis of basketball. There also appears to be a widespread assumption that the standard of US soccer is hampered by the *type* of athlete (i.e. white/suburban/cerebral) who is presently dominating the game, and that soccer in the United States would undoubtedly improve if the *right* populations (i.e. black/urban/physical) were encouraged to take up the sport. Accordingly, a *Chicago Sun-Times* columnist noted, 'soccer will never take off in America until the talent that still resides within our cities is fully tapped and discovered ... Somewhere in the Robert Taylor Homes are a handful of Peles' (Hornung, 1994: 39).

The particular class location of soccer in the United States engenders a specific health-oriented relation to the body, which is itself related to the suburban middle-class habitus – the system of dispositions, tastes and preferences – which forms the basis of the suburban middle-class lifestyle (see Bourdieu, 1978, 1980, 1984, 1990). The economic stability proffered by membership of the relatively privileged middle class allows for the development of relationships with the body based upon sport's ability to further the interrelated health and aesthetic dimensions of physical existence. Thus, bodies are invested in, through health/fitness-inducing predilections, practices and programmes, for future life benefits, and contemporaneous social approval. For, within the American suburban context, the bodies of the middle classes and indeed those of their children are markers of upward social mobility, status and achievement that are self-actualised through involvement in the right healthy lifestyle practices, leading to the assemblage of the appropriately formed healthy bodies (Howell, 1991). Soccer provides the suburban middle class with an opportunity for distancing itself from the instrumental relation to the body exemplified by the pragmatic habitus of the black urban working class. Soccer is implicitly performed as a symbolic site for reaffirming the ascendant position of the suburban middle-class lifestyle; involvement in the soccer ritual effectively sustains the normalised suburban community, thereby advancing notions of the moral and cultural superiority of (white) suburban practices, institutions and individuals in relation to their (black) urban counterparts. Soccer is part of a middle-class lifestyle 'that separates those who live in the suburbs from urban others. Those who are different ... perceived as dangerous' (Dumm, 1993: 189). Youth soccer participation has thus become an important part of a normalised culture that marks a fetishised suburban affluence and productivity as the antithesis of a pathologised urban deprivation and indolence.

In many respects, suburban soccer culture represents the sporting version of the gated residential community: an artificial space and population protected by exorbitant property values from the perils and unease created by the proximity of social undesirables and economic subordinates. Thus, soccer is ascribed an exclusivity, or rarefied symbolic value, through which the ever status-conscious suburban middle class is able to nonchalantly 'distinguish itself from the less fortunate' (Ehrenreich, 1989: 39). Moreover, the economics of suburban soccer participation effectively denies the urban and suburban poor, the working class, and even many of the lower middle class from access to the game in its bourgeois incarnation. This class division is explicitly racialised, since socio-spatial apartheid in the United States has resulted in the nation's affluent suburbs – and thereby soccer as a field of suburban cultural production – continuing to be the domain of the white middle class (see Jackson, 1985; McCarthy et al., 1996). As Hersh noted, 'soccer in the U.S. is essentially a white, middle-class, suburban sport, just the opposite of the game's demographics in most of the world' (1990: 1).

CONCLUSION

Within this social autopsy of health and physical culture within the North American urban landscape, we addressed how the urban poor – those increasingly categorised as degenerate or unproductive – have become subject to elevated levels of ill health and disease, continued restricted access to heath care, well-being resources and to physical culture. We contrasted these horrific lived experiences, the afflictions of inequality (Wilkinson, 1996), with their suburban corollary, the contrasting health-oriented sensibilities and orientations of the American suburb. Unlike the very real and sadly tangible ill health and poverty of the American inner city, we suggested normalised suburban existence is manifest through soccer as a racially coded, embodied performance of the cultural values and ideals espoused by the suburban middle class. Characterised by the *right* interrelated health, corporeal and aesthetic norms for suburban boys and girls, soccer is experienced and advanced as a compelling popular euphemism for spatial, class and racial superiority. In this way, the spatialised and racialised inequities of urban life become mapped onto the material and symbolic constitution of health; differently put, and somewhat rearticulating the quote with which we opened this chapter, health becomes the modality through which race, and by extension class, is lived.

This contention is only strengthened when one considers that in our contemporary moment there has been a perceptible economic and emotional (r)eturn to North America's urban landscapes. That is, select parcels of the downtown cores of numerous US cities have become, are in the process of becoming, or aspire to be, spectacular consumptive environments predicated on capital leisure spaces: urban governments have sought to (re)capitalise upon the economic landscapes of their cities (through shopping malls, themed restaurants, bars, theme parks, mega-complexes for professional sport franchises, gentrified housing, conference complexes and waterfront pleasure domes) (Brenner and Theodore, 2002; Gottdiener, 2000; MacLeod, 2002; MacLeod et al., 2003; Silk and Andrews, 2006; Waitt, 1999; Wilcox and Andrews, 2003). These 'tourist bubbles' (Judd, 1999) are the paragons of urban regeneration and form part of the processes of reclaiming the city as a middle-class space for a newly gentrified, domiciled, tourist class (Florida, 2002). Fully supporting the market logics of urban entrepreneurialism, health or, more accurately, a pervasive *healthy lifestyle* discourse provides a symbolic accoutrement to the reimaged cityscape. As distinct and unimaginable from the sketch we proffered earlier of the decay of the urban environment, the urban core is recast through physical culture. Indeed, these spaces are evaluated and ranked on these very criteria. *Men's Fitness* magazine, for example, which annually evaluates US cities (using such criteria as: the number of fitness facilities, such as gyms, for the new urban residents; diet patterns; reactions to public health 'emergencies' such as obesity; the role of civic legislation and leadership in creating fitness and health education directives, including requiring developers to build open spaces and trails, and in enacting fitness-promotion initiatives (Lucia, 2006)) recently ranked Baltimore as the 'fittest city in America' (Silk and Andrews, 2006). Baltimore achieved this place of honour for apparently having 'one of the healthiest diets around' with 'half the average number of junk-food places per capita of all the cities in our survey', for a 'citizenry who has taken to exercise', for 'excellent air quality', for 'top-notch health-care', and for the efforts of Mayor Martin O'Malley to make 'his populace more active' (Lucia, 2006).

Within such delusional rhetoric, the city becomes represented as a healthy, safe and sanitised urban space that could not be further differentiated from the experiences, lifestyles, health care and access of those within the fortified enclosures on the urban fringes of the phantasmagorical – to borrow from Benjamin (2002) – zones of commercial investment and revitalisation within remodelled, spectacular US cityscapes. Rather, the 'healthy body politic' is mapped onto the inner city, and along with those in the suburb becomes the legitimate public populace. The *right* corporatised, healthy, aesthetic thus becomes the *body proper* (Zylinska, 2004) that fulfils the 'obligations' of participatory democratic citizenship (in this sense through the *right* rates and acts of fitness consumption), and thereby further marks the (ill) health of the corpus, those constitutive socially, morally and economically pathologised *outsiders*, who exist outside of the 'legitimate' North American urban morphology.

CHAPTER SUMMARY

Within the contemporary American context a history of discriminatory housing policies and the more recent neo-liberal policy agenda have combined to create socio-spatial disparities that demarcate two distinct American social worlds, one white and one black. This bifurcated world incorporates frightening discrepancies in infrastructure that contribute to declining health and wellness among the black population of the United States. Equally, the recent surge of soccer within the suburban American context is further manifestation of the distance between poor blacks and middle-class whites, specifically in terms of the relationship between space, culture, economics and health. Recent urban regeneration has borne 'healthy' tourist bubbles which legitimize the lifestyles enjoyed by those productive urbanites, while further pathologizing those who exist outside (both physically and symbolically) the 'legitimate' North American metropolis.

FURTHER READING

Amin, A. (2006) 'The good city', *Urban Studies*, 43 (5/6): 1009–23.

Fainstein, S. and Judd, D. (eds) (1999) *The Tourist City*. New Haven, CT: Yale University Press, pp. 35–53.

Friedman, M.T., Andrews, D.L. and Silk, M.L. (2004) 'Sport and the facade of redevelopment in the postindustrial city', *Sociology of Sport Journal*, 21 (2): 119–39.

Massey, D. (2000) 'Understanding cities', *City*, 4: 135–44.

Schimmel, K.S. (2001) 'Sport matters: urban regime theory and urban regeneration in the late-capitalist era', in C. Gratton and I.P. Henry (eds), *Sport in the city: the Role of Sport in Economic and Social Regeneration*. London: Routledge, pp. 259–77.

REFERENCES

Amin, A. (2006) 'The good city', *Urban Studies*, 43 (5/6): 1009–23.

Andrews, D.L. (1999) 'Contextualizing suburban soccer: consumer culture, lifestyle differentiation, and suburban America', *Culture, Sport, Society*, 2 (3): 31–53.

Andrews, D.L., Pitter, R., Zwick, D. and Ambrose, D. (2003) 'Soccer, race, and suburban space', in R.C. Wilcox, D.L. Andrews, R. Pitter and R.L. Irwin (eds), *Sporting Dystopias: the Making and Meanings of Urban Sport Cultures*. Albany, NY: State University of New York Press, pp. 197–220.

Anon. (1996) 'Major league soccer: growing stars', *The Economist*, 13 April: 27.

Benjamin, W. (2002) *The Arcades Project*. Trans. H. Eiland and K. Kevin McLaughlin. Cambridge, MA: Belknap Press.

Berlant, L. (1991) *The Anatomy of National Fantasy: Hawthorne, Utopia, and Everyday Life*. Chicago: University of Chicago Press.

Bondy, F. (1992) 'Soccer: now kids, that's the way to use your heads!', *New York Times*, 24 December: B9.

Bourdieu, P. (1978) 'Sport and social class', *Social Science Information*, 17 (6): 819–40.

Bourdieu, P. (1980) 'A diagram of social position and lifestyle', *Media, Culture and Society*, 2: 255–9.

Bourdieu, P. (1984) *Distinction: A Social Critique of the Judgement of Taste*. Cambridge, MA: Harvard University Press.

Bourdieu, P. (1986) 'The forms of capital', in J.G. Richardson (ed.), *Handbook of Theory and Research for the Sociology of Education*. Westport, CT: Greenwood Press, pp. 241–58.

Bourdieu, P. (1990). 'Programme for a sociology of sport', in *In Other Words: Essays toward a Reflexive Sociology*. Stanford, CA: Stanford University Press, pp. 156–67.

Brenner, N. and Theodore, N. (2002) 'Cities and the geographies of "actually existing neoliberalism"', *Antipode*, 349–79.

Bullard, R.D. (1996) *Unequal Protection: Environmental Justice and Communities of Color*. San Francisco: Sierra Club Books.

Cannon, A. (1999) 'The charm city blues', *US News & World Report*, 126 (1): 24–6.

Clarke, J. (1991) *New Times and Old Enemies: Essays on Cultural Studies and America*. London: Harper Collins.

Cole, C.L. (1996) 'American Jordan: P.L.A.Y., consensus, and punishment', *Sociology of Sport Journal*, 13 (4): 366–97.

Cole, C.L. and Andrews, D.L. (1996) '"Look – It's NBA ShowTime!": visions of race in the popular imaginary', in N.K. Denzin (ed.), *Cultural Studies: a Research Volume*. London: Elservier Vol. 1, pp. 141–81.

Dalgard, O.S. and Tambs, K. (1997) 'Urban environment and mental health: a longitudinal study', *British Journal of Psychiatry*, 171: 530–6.

Dao, J. (2005) 'Baltimore street meaner, but message is mixed', *New York Times*, 9 February: A1.

Denzin, N. (2006) 'Katrina and the collapse of civil society in New Orleans', *Space and Culture*, 9 (1): 95–9.

de Wit, W. (1993) 'The rise of public housing in Chicago, 1930–1960', in J. Zukowsky (ed.) *Chicago Architecture and Design 1923–1993: Reconfiguration of an American Metropolis*. London: Prestel.

Dreier, P., Mollenkopf, J. and Swanstrom, T. (2001) *Place Matters: Metropolitics for the Twenty-first Century*. Lawrence, KS: University Press of Kansas.

Dumm, T.L. (1993) 'The new enclosures: racism in the normalized community', in R. Gooding-Williams (ed.), *Reading Rodney King: Reading Urban Uprising.* New York: Routledge, pp. 178–95.

Eberhardt, M.S., Ingram, D.D., Makuc, D.M. (2001) *Urban and Rural Health Chartbook. Health, United States, 2001.* Hyattsville, M: National Center for Health Statistics.

Ehrenreich, B. (1989) *Fear of Falling: the Inner Life of the Middle Class.* New York: Harper Collins.

Florida, R. (2002) *The Rise of the Creative Class.* New York: Basic Books.

Flusty, S. (2001) 'The banality of interdiction: surveillance, control and the displacement of diversity', *International Journal of Urban and Regional Research*, 25 (3): 658–64.

Frazier, J.W., Margai, F.M. and Tetty-Fi, O.E. (2003) *Race and Place: Equity Issues in Urban America.* Boulder, CO: Westview Press.

Gephart, R.P. (1996) 'Management, social issues, and the postmodern era', in D.M. Boje, R.P. Gephart and T.J. Thatchenkery (eds), *Postmodern Management and Organization Theory.* London: Sage, pp. 21–44.

Gibson, T. (2006) 'New Orleans and the wisdom of lived space', *Space & Culture*, 9 (1): 45–47.

Giroux, H. (2003a) *Public Spaces, Private Lives: Democracy beyond 9/11.* New York and London: Rowman & Littlefield.

Giroux, H. (2003b) *The Abandoned Generation: Democracy Beyond the Culture of Fear.* New York: Palgrave.

Giroux, H. (2005) *The Terror of Neoliberalism.* New York: Palgrave.

Gottdiener, M. (2000) 'Lefebvre and the bias of academic urbanism: what can we learn from the new urban analysis?', *City*, 4: 93–100.

Grossberg, L. (2005) *Caught in the Crossfire: Kids, Politics and America's Future.* Boulder, CO and London: Paradigm.

Hagerty, J. and Dunham, K. (2005) 'After long decline, Baltimore sees new investors rush into poor neighborhoods', *Wall Street Journal*, 25 May: A1.

Hall, S., Critcher, C., Jefferson, T., Clarke, J. and Roberts, B. (1979) *Policing the Crisis: Mugging, the State, and the Law and Order.* London: Macmillan.

Halpern, D. (1995) *Mental Health and the Built Environment: More than Bricks and Mortar?* London: Taylor & Francis.

Hartmann, D. and Depro, B. (2006) 'Rethinking sports-based community crime prevention: A preliminary analysis of the relationship between midnight basketball and urban crime rates', *Journal of Sport and Social Issues.* 30.2, 180–196.

Harvey, D. (2000) *Spaces of Hope.* Boulder, CO: University of Colorado Press.

Harvey, D. (2001) *Spaces of Capital: Towards a Critical Geography.* London and New York: Routledge.

Hayes-Bautista, D.E. and Rodriguez, G. (1994) 'L.A. story: Los Angeles, CA, soccer and society', *New Republic*, 4 July: 19.

Hersh, P. (1990) 'Soccer in U.S. at crossroads: World Cup seen as last resort to stir fan sport', *Chicago Tribune*, 3 June: C1.

Hornung, M.N. (1994) '3 billion people can't be wrong', *Chicago Sun-Times*, 17 June: 39.

Howell, J.W. (1991) '"A revolution in motion": advertising and the politics of nostalgia', *Sociology of Sport Journal*, 8 (3): 258–71.

Ingham, A.G. (1997) 'Toward a department of physical cultural studies and an end to tribal warfare', in J. Fernandez-Balboa (ed.), *Critical Postmodernism in Human Movement, Physical Education, and Sport*. Albany, NY: SUNY Press, pp. 157–182.

Jackson, K.T. (1985) *Crabgrass Frontier: the Suburbanization of the United States*. New York: Oxford University Press.

Jacobs, B. D. (1992) *Fractured Cities: Capitalism, Community and Empowerment in Britain and America*. London: Routledge.

Johns Hopkins Institute for Policy Studies (2000) 'Baltimore in transition: how do we move from decline to revival?'. http://www.jhu.edu/~ips/newsroom/transition.pdf (accessed 17 October 2003).

Judd, D. (1999) 'Constructing the tourist bubble', in S. Fainstein and D. Judd (eds), *The Tourist City*. New Haven, CT: Yale University Press, pp. 35–53.

Kingston, R.S. and Nickens, H.W. (2001) 'Racial and ethnic differences in health: recent trends, current patterns, future directions', in N.J. Smelser, W. J. Wilson and F. Mitchell (eds), *America Becoming: Racial Trends and Their Consequences*, Vol. II. Washington, DC: National Academy Press, pp. 253–310.

Kleinberg, B. (1995) *Urban America in Transformation: Perspectives on Urban Policy and Development*. Thousand Oaks, CA: Sage.

Klinenberg, E. (2002) *Heat Wave: A Social Autopsy of Disaster in Chicago*. Chicago: University of Chicago Press.

Lemann, N. (1989) 'Stressed out in suburbia: a generation after the postwar boom, life in the suburbs has changed, even if our picture of it hasn't', *Atlantic*, November: 34.

Lucia, J. (2006) 'How fit is America?', *Men's Fitness*, February. http://www.findarticles.com/p/articles/mi_m1608/is_1_22/ai_n16031448 (accessed 12 February 2006).

MacLeod, G. (2002) 'From urban entrepreneurialism to a "Revanchist City"? On the spatial injustices of Glasgow's renaissance', *Antipode*, 602–24.

MacLeod, G., Raco, M. and Ward, K. (2003) 'Negotiating the contemporary city', *Urban Studies*, 40 (9): 1655–71.

Malone, M. (1994) 'Soccer's greatest goal: cultural harmony through sports', *Americas*, May–June: 64.

Massey, D. (1997) 'Problems with globalization', *Soundings*, 7–12.

Massey, D. (2000) 'Understanding cities', *City*, 4: 135–44.

Massey, D.S. (2001) 'Residential segregation and neighborhood conditions in U.S. metropolitan areas', in N.J. Smelser, W.J. Wilson and F. Mitchell (eds), *America Becoming: Racial Trends and Their Consequences*. Washington, DC: National Academy Press, pp. 391–434.

Massey, D.S. and Denton, N. (1993) *American Apartheid: Segregation and the Making of the Underclass*. Cambridge, MA: Harvard University Press.

McCarthy, C., Rodriguez, A., Meacham, S., David, S., Wilson-Brown, C., Godina, H., Supriya, K.E. and Bueudia, E. (1996) 'Race, suburban resentment and the representation of the inner city in contemporary film and television', in N.K. Denzin (ed.), *Cultural Studies: a Research Volume*, Vol. 1. Greenwich, CT: JAI Press, pp. 121–40.

McKay, D.H. (1977) *Housing and Race in Industrial Society: Civil Rights and Urban Policy in Britain and the United States.* London: Croom Helm.

McKinnon, J. (2003) *The Black Population in the United States: March 2002.* Washington, DC: US Census Bureau.

Merrifield, A. (2000) 'The dialectics of dystopia: disorder and zero tolerance in the city', *International Journal of Urban and Regional Research*, 24 (2): 473–89.

Molotch, H. (2006) 'Death on the roof: race and bureaucratic failure', *Space and Culture*, 9 (1): 31–4.

Neisser, P.T. and Schram, S. F. (1994) 'Redoubling denial: Industrial welfare policy meets postindustrial poverty.' *Social Text*, (41): 41–60.

Oldenburg, R. (1997) *The Great Good Place.* New York: Marlowe.

OMH (2006) http://www.omhrc.gov/templates/browse.aspx?lvl=2&lvlID=51 (accessed 25 April 2007).

Peck, J. (2003) 'Geography and public policy: mapping the penal state', *Progress in Human Geography*, 27 (2): 222–32.

Peck, J. and Tickell, A. (2002) 'Neoliberalizing space', *Antipode*, 380–403.

Pesky, G. (1993) 'On the attack: the growth of soccer in the United States', *Sporting Goods Business*, April: 31.

Pitter, R. and Andrews, D.L. (1997) 'Serving America's underserved youth: reflections on sport and recreation in an emerging social problems industry', *Quest*, 49 (1): 85–99.

Reeves, J.L. and Campbell, R. (1994) *Cracked Coverage: Television News, the Anti-Cocaine Crusade, and the Reagan Legacy.* Durham, NC: Duke University Press.

Riess, S.A. (1991) *City Games: the Evolution of American Urban Society and the Rise of Sports.* Urbana, IL: University of Illinois Press.

Rose, N. (1999) 'Community, citizenship, and the third way', *American Behavioral Scientist*, 43 (9): 1395–411.

Rose, N. (2000) 'Government and control', *British Journal of Criminology*, 40: 321–39.

Sampson, R.J., Morenoff, J.D. and Earls, F. (1999) 'Beyond social capital: spatial dynamics of collective efficacy for children', *American Sociological Review*, 64: 633–60.

Sampson, R.J., Morenoff, J.D. and Gannon-Rowley, T. (2002) 'Assessing "neighborhood effects": social processes and new directions in research', *Annual Review of Sociology*, 28: 443–78.

Savage, M. and Warde, A. (1994) *Urban Sociology, Capitalism and Modernity.* Basingstoke: Palgrave.

Sharp, I., Maryon-Davis, A. and Godfrey, C. (1999) 'Preventing coronary heart disease: population policies', in I. Sharp (ed.), *Looking to the Future: Making Coronary Heart Disease an Epidemic of the Past*, pp. 63–95. London: The Stationery Office, pp. 1863–75.

Sheller, M. and Urry, J. (2003) 'Mobile transformations of public and private life', *Theory, Culture & Society*, 20 (3): 107–25.

Shilling, C. (1993) 'The body and physical capital', in C. Shilling *The Body and Social Theory*. London: Sage, pp. 127–204.

Siegel, F. and Smith, V. (2001) 'Can Mayor O'Malley save ailing Baltimore?', *City Journal*, 11 (1): 64–75.

Silk, M. and Andrews, D. (2006) 'The fittest city in America', *Journal of Sport & Social Issues*, 30 (3): 315–27.

Soja, E. (2000) *Postmetropolis: Critical Studies of Cities and Regions*. Oxford: Blackwell.

Squires, G. and Kubrin, C. (2005) 'Privileged places: race, uneven development and the geography of opportunity in urban America', *Urban Studies*, 42 (1): 47–68.

Steinbrecher, H. (1996) 'Getting in on soccer: the hottest sport to reach international markets', Paper presented at the Marketing with Sports Entities, Swissotel, Atlanta, GA, 26–27 February.

Taylor, S.E., Repetti, R.L. and Seeman, T. (1997) 'What is an unhealthy environment and how does it get under the skin?', *Annual Review of Psychology*, 48: 411–47.

Thomas, G.S. (1998) *The United States of Suburbia: How the Suburbs Took Control of America and What They Plan To Do With It*. New York: Prometheus Books.

US Census Bureau (2003) 'The black population in the United States: March 2002'. http://www.census.gov/prod/2003pubs/p20-541.pdf (accessed 25 April 2007).

US Census Bureau (2004) 'Population and housing narrative profile'. http://factfinder. census.gov/servlet/NPTable?_ame=ACS_2004_EST_G00_NPO1 (accessed 29 December 2005).

US Department of Health & Human Services, Center for Disease Control & Prevention (2005) *Chartbook on Trends in the Health of Americans Health, National Center for Health Statistics, United States*, Hyattsville, MD. http://www.cdc.gov/nchs/data/hus/ hus05.pdf (accessed 25 April 2007).

US Department of Housing and Urban Development (1997) *The State of the Cities*. Washington, DC: US Department of Housing and Urban Development.

US Department of Justice (2001) *Criminal Victimization 2000: Changes 1999–2000 with Trends 1993–2000*. Washington, DC: US Department of Justice.

Wacquant, L. (1993) Urban Outcasts: 'Stigma divisions in the Black American ghetto and the French urban periphery' *International Journal of Urban and Regional Research*. 17.3, 366–83.

Wacquant, L. (1994) 'The new urban colour line: The State and fate of the ghetto in post fordist America', in C.J. Calhoun (ed.) *Social Theory and the Politics of Identity*. Oxford: Blackwell.

Wacquant, L.J.D. and Wilson, W.J. (1989) 'Poverty, joblessness, and the social transformation of the inner city', in P.H. Cottingham and D.T. Ellwood (eds) *Welfare Policy for the 1990s.* Cambridge, MA: Harvard University Press, pp. 70–122.

Wagg, S. (1995) 'The business of America: reflections on World Cup '94', in S. Wagg (ed.), *Giving the Game Away: Football, Politics and Culture on Five Continents.* Leicester: Leicester University Press, pp. 179–200.

Waitt, E. (1999) 'Playing games with Sydney: marketing Sydney for the 2000 Olympics', *Urban Studies,* 36 (7): 1062–73.

Walks, R. (2001) 'The social ecology of the post-Fordist/global city? Economic restructuring and socio-spatial polarisation in the Toronto urban region', *Urban Studies,* 38 (3): 407–47.

Warin, M., Baum, F. and Kalucy, E. (2000) 'The power of place: space and time in women's and community health centres in South Australia', *Social Science and Medicine,* 50: 1863–75.

Wilcox, R. and Andrews, D. (2003) 'Sport in the city: cultural, economic and political portraits', in R. Wilcox, D. Andrews, R. Pitter and R. Irwin (eds), *Sporting Dystopias: the Making and Meanings of Urban Sport Cultures.* New York: SUNY Press, pp. 1–16.

Wilkinson, R.G. (1996) *Unhealthy Societies: the Afflictions of Inequality.* London: Routledge.

Wilson, W.J. (1987) *The Truly Disadvantaged: the Inner City, the Underclass, and Public Policy.* Chicago: University of Chicago Press.

Witten, K., Exeter, D. and Field, A. (2003) 'The quality of urban environments: mapping variation in access to community resources', *Urban Studies,* 40 (1): 161–77.

Zwick, D. and Andrews. D.L. (1999) 'The suburban soccer field: the culture of privilege in contemporary America', in G. Armstrong and R. Giulianotti (eds), *Football in the Making: Developments in the World Game.* London: Macmillan.

Zylinska, J. (2004) 'The universal acts: Judith Butler and the biopolitics of immigration', *Cultural Studies,* 18 (4): 523–37.

Zylinska, J. (2005) *The Ethics of Cultural Studies.* London and New York: Continuum.

Part Three

The Impact of Commercialisation

13

The Business of Sport

LEIGH ROBINSON

OVERVIEW

» *The commercialisation of sport*
» *A trend towards sport spectating*
» *Changing technologies, increasing competition and the professionalisation of sports management*
» *The structure of the sport industry*
» *Sports sponsorship and sports betting*
» *Conclusion*

In 2006 tennis player Maria Sharapova was expected to earn $20m in marketing activities alone. Her deals with TAG Heuer, Motorola, Canon, Parlux Fragrances, Nike, Prince and Speedminton are likely to make her the richest female athlete in the world. In 2005, sportswear giant Adidas-Salomon signed a deal with FIFA for $351m that gives it rights to all FIFA events from 2007 to 2014. Leicester Tigers Rugby Club increased profits by 28 per cent on a turnover of $22m. Research carried out by Davies (2000) in Sheffield in the UK provided evidence of revenue from sport amounting to nearly 5 per cent of the city's GDP.

The Olympic Games are perhaps the clearest example of the direction that sport has taken in the last few decades. A fundamentally different event from their amateur beginnings, the Athens 2004 Olympics accommodated over 11,000 athletes from 201 nations; hosted 12,000 media personnel and co-ordinated a workforce of more than 57,000 volunteers. The total surplus from staging the Games was $155m, although this reduced to $8m when government subsidies were repaid. Domestic sponsorship raised over $600m, more than 3.5 million tickets were sold, generating $228m. An estimated 3.9 billion people watched the Games and each viewer watched on average 12 hours of coverage. The television rights from the Games generated $1,476,911,634. Clearly, sport is a big business.

It is not, however, only the major events and professional sports that have been affected. National governing bodies, the organisations that run sport, are required to produce business plans to ensure continued state funding; in turn, they expect the same from affiliated clubs and associations. There are an increasing number of paid professionals employed to develop and promote sport, such as sports managers, sports agents and development workers. It is obvious that sport is no longer a pastime, organised and run by amateurs. It is a business that competes for scarce consumer resources, requiring a 'business' approach to its management, utilising professional management techniques. This chapter considers the reasons why sport has become a business and then goes on to discuss three of the key sectors of the industry: professional sport, sports sponsorship and sports betting.

THE COMMERCIALISATION OF SPORT

In the past two decades, sport has moved from being a pastime to a business as a result of the process of commercialisation, which has led sports managers and organisations to become concerned with business principles. This commercialisation process has led sports organisations to be described as 'business-like' as they become market orientated, pursue operational strategies that maximise profit or revenue, and become responsive to the needs of customers.

This commercialisation of sport has two aspects. The first has been an increase in the truly commercial operations of sport. Sports organisations have become focused on maximising revenue, using this principle as the underlying rationale for decision making and strategy development. As a result, expenditure on sponsorship, television rights, players' salaries and sports betting has risen markedly in the past few decades as sports organisations have sought to optimise their opportunities to generate revenue by adopting a business approach to the management of sport. For example, Fox Television Company's 2004 deal with the NFL will cost it $712m a year, which is 30 per cent more than its previous deal (Fry, 2005). The second aspect of commercialisation has occurred within not-for-profit or state sports organisations. These organisations have undergone substantial cultural and operational change within the last decade, as managers have moved towards a business-like approach in the management of their organisations. This now means that decision making in these organisations reflects that of commercial organisations, and has led to the introduction of strategic planning, performance management and quality management systems.

The increase in the commercial operations of sport has primarily been caused by a growth in the number of professional sports and sports teams. For example, the number of professional football clubs in Germany increased 128 per cent in the 1990s (Zimmerman, 1997), Rugby Union turned professional, and swimmers, cyclists, sailors and athletes are now paid to train. The true value of sport, however, as a business is perhaps most obvious in those spectator sports with a worldwide audience, such as football or Formula One (see Box 13.1).

Box 13.1   The business of car racing

Today's Formula One car is at the cutting edge of technology. The sport is often likened to a 'miniature space programme', and for this reason Formula One consumes large amounts of capital. Sponsors pay the teams between $16m and $60m per year, for their company's livery to appear on the cars. Companies are prepared to pay such large amounts because of the enormous television audience that Formula One attracts worldwide. Billions of viewers tune in to watch the FIA Formula One Championship and those involved in Formula One are becoming richer. In 2004, Bernie Ecclestone, the man primarily credited with the commercial development of Formula One, in particular the worldwide audience, was worth over $4bn and the Formula One Administration increased profits by 78 per cent to $280m.

The commercialisation of the not-for-profit or state sports organisations has been primarily a result of a push towards efficiency, effectiveness and quality and this, alongside the increasingly competitive sports market (discussed below), led these organisations to adopt the same strategies and techniques as profit-orientated organisations. The most obvious example of this is the International Olympic Committee (IOC), ostensibly a not-for-profit organisation that manages one of the most desirable sports 'products' in the world. In the recent past, staging the Olympic Games was guaranteed to cost the host city millions, making countries reluctant to host the Games. As a result of the efforts of Juan Antonio Samaranch, President of the IOC and strong advocate of commercialisation, the Olympic Games are much sought-after product and subject to intense competition between sponsors. This has made the IOC an extremely lucrative organisation and for the 2001–4 Olympic quadrennial the IOC and the Olympic Games Organising Committees generated approximately $4.13bn. Around 8 per cent of this was retained for the running of the IOC, while the remainder was distributed throughout the Olympic Movement (IOC, 2006).

Even at a local level, Robinson (2004) has provided evidence of a substantial culture shift in the management of UK public sports facilities, highlighting how the use of commercial management techniques and practices is now commonplace within this sector of the sports industry. Similarly, in the voluntary sector, the organisation and management of national governing bodies, or national sports organisations, have evolved to reflect the principles of good governance promoted in the commercial sector. Thus, the commercialism of the sport industry has not just been confined to commercial organisations; indeed it could be argued that there is little difference in the management techniques used to run sports organisations, whether commercial, state or not-for-profit in many Western industrialised countries. Robinson's (1999) research certainly suggests that the traditional differences in management between the commercial, state and voluntary sectors of the sport industry are no longer obvious.

The commercialisation of sport has been condemned as an undesirable process, as it has been argued that commercialism takes away from the 'essence' of sport. Robinson (1999) has argued that professionalism and specialism have undermined the community and recreational focus of sport, and it is apparent that the commercialism of today's sport has encouraged doping, match fixing, gambling and violence. However, the money made by professional players and teams, the trend towards professionalisation of traditionally amateur sports, such as Rugby Union, and the increasing amount of money being paid for the right to televise sport suggest that while the *desirability* of the commercialisation of sport can be contested, the actual process of commercialisation cannot be debated.

It is apparent that commercialisation has been the driving force behind the development of sport as a business, resulting in an industry that provides revenue for national and local economies through event revenue, taxes, employment, tourism and sponsorship. This commercialisation has been brought about primarily by the actions and interactions of the following four factors: a trend towards sport spectating; changing technologies; increasing competition; and the professionalisation of sports management.

A TREND TOWARDS SPORT SPECTATING

There is evidence of a growing trend towards sport spectating. In the UK, crowds attending Coca-Cola Football League games reached a 45-year high in 2004–5. Mintel (2005) found that three-quarters of British adults had watched or listened to live sport in 2004, which is considerably more than those who claimed to have taken part. Mintel (2003) also found that more than 25 per cent of adults cite a preference for watching sport as the main reason for non-participation.

The value of spectator sport is perhaps most clearly demonstrated by the cost of the television rights for the Summer Olympic Games. In 1960, broadcast revenue for the Summer Olympics was $1.178m. Twenty years later, it was $87.98m and in 1984, it increased significantly to $286.9m. Athens 2004 raised $1,496m and broadcasting revenue is expected to increase at Beijing 2008 (IOC, 2006).

This trend towards spectator sport has commercialised sport in two main ways. First, given the sums of money involved in sponsorship, gate receipts and television rights, sport needs to be managed as a business venture. Second, in return for revenue, spectators and sponsors have high expectations of the occasion that sport provides. When discussing the reasons for the trend towards sport spectating, Chelladurai (2005) noted that it is not enough simply to play the game; there needs to be opening and half-time entertainment, additional commentary, match analysis, catering facilities and merchandising. Spectator sport is entertainment and needs to be managed as such.

CHANGING TECHNOLOGIES

In the last few decades, technological changes have radically altered the face of sport and the most significant of these technologies has been television. Wilson (1988) argued that television has transformed the lives of all of those who play, organise and promote sport, as television has provided greater income for established sports and an opportunity for exposure for minority sports. He outlined how:

> Nothing was too much to ask of sports desperate to catch television's eye. Traditions, even rules, were tossed aside at the merest hint that by doing so they would please the one-eyed god they had come to worship. Cricket created a new one-day competition for it, and played in pink shirts with a yellow ball under floodlights. Tennis introduced the tie-breaker into its scoring system and moved Wimbledon's men's final to a Sunday. Golf dropped its random draw, and the International Olympic Committee moved the cycle of Winter Olympics by two years. Squash even rebuilt its courts in glass and painted yellow stripes on its ball. (Wilson, 1988: 9)

The impact of television on sport has been significant and has forced the commercialisation of sport by requiring sports providers to develop the business practices necessary to deal with the demands placed on their sport by spectators requiring entertainment. It is, however, a two-way relationship. Although sport has changed to suit the needs of television, television has recognised this and it has accommodated the trend towards spectating by increasing televised sport, as outlined earlier. The potential this offers for additional viewing rights, sponsorship and thus more revenue for sport is enormous. The television market is also highly competitive. The advent of satellite, cable and digital TV, alongside increases in the number of terrestrial channels, has had the consequence of further increasing the value of sport, as major broadcasting organisations compete to televise popular events. This is evident in the deal worth $5bn that the NFL struck with US free-to-air networks CBS, Fox and DirecTV (Fry, 2005). In addition, the advent of 'pay as you view' television technology, where television companies can charge viewers to watch particular events, means that the relationship between sport and television will become even stronger, reinforcing the need for a business approach to the management of sport.

Although television will continue to have a major impact on sport, other technological changes are beginning to have a significant effect. Internet technology has also become increasingly important, particularly broadband. Wireless is becoming increasingly important for English Premier League football clubs as it allows journalists and staff fast wire-free access to the Internet, and may provide an additional revenue stream if the media and fans want to access email or surf the Web while at matches (*SportBusiness*, 2005a). Away from stadiums, 3G is set to become a major method of watching sport, receiving sports results and downloading customised content from the Internet (Britcher, 2005). In the United States, sports leagues are using the new media to create a greater affinity with fans, as the technology allows more personal communication. For example, NFL fans voted for the 'greatest all-time player' via a TXT/SMS, which allowed the TXT company to build up fan profiles (*SportBusiness*, 2005b).

Advances in ticketing software have allowed clubs to develop a relationship with their fans and tackle concerns about security. Rugby referees wear microphones, so that spectators can listen to their comments, and the sport makes use of a video referee to make decisions about difficult tries. The use of video referees to assist officials in Rugby League is commonplace, as is the technology used in tennis to detect faults. Electronic timekeeping has long been part of athletics and swimming. Cricket umpires are told, via technology, when there is not enough light to continue play and in 2006 the use of video umpires in leg before wicket decisions was trialled. The use of such technologies has been introduced into sport as the subjective nature of human decision making is no longer considered appropriate for such a profitable and professional business as sport.

INCREASING COMPETITION

Although sport is still considered one of the biggest links between people, it is clear that sports organisations are operating in an increasingly competitive market, with competition coming from other sports and leisure providers, both at home and abroad. Luker (2000: 48), in his analysis of the sports industry, stated that

> a changing marketplace, new technology and fresh competition for the public leisure time and dollars means that old assumptions have to be challenged ... It's no longer about getting people to say yes to your sport – it's about getting people not to say no.

The increasingly competitive market for sports business is primarily due to improvements in technology. First, technological advances in means of travel have made customers of sports events far more mobile, allowing them to buy sports services in other cities, countries or even hemispheres. Second, modern communications have shrunk the sports world to little more than a village. It is possible for people to view events all over the world, place bets on the outcome and have as their 'local' team a sports team in another country.

Competitiveness becomes even more prominent when one considers that sports organisations compete for discretionary expenditure. Thus, managers are not only competing within the industry, but also competing with other ways of using discretionary income. This requires a business approach to the delivery of sports in order to ensure business survival in an increasingly competitive industry.

PROFESSIONALISATION OF SPORTS MANAGEMENT

One of the main consequences of the commercialism that has occurred in sport over the past few decades has been the increasing professionalisation of those who have been and are involved in managing sports organisations. The presence of strategic planning, human resource strategies and marketing plans in sports organisations has led to improvements in professional practice (Beech and Chadwick, 2004; Chelladurai, 2005; Robinson, 2004). This professionalisation has been brought about by two main factors. First, there has been a growing programme of education and training for those who wish to become sport managers. Over 200 universities in North America offer degree programmes in sports management and it is one of the fastest-growing areas of study in American universities (Chelladurai, 2005). The picture is the same in the UK, where there are over 1,000 higher education courses offered that contain 'sport' or 'leisure' in the title. Professional bodies have also had a role to play: Japan has two organisations catering for professionals and academics, as does the UK. There is a European Association for Sport Management, the North American Society for Sport Management and the Sport Management Association of Australia and New Zealand. All of these organisations have contributed to the increasing professionalism of those involved in sports management.

Second, the academic study of sports management has initiated and carried out research aimed at analysing and evaluating the management of sports organisations, in order to establish best practice. Research in this area has considered all aspects of management, such as organisational design, marketing, sponsorship, the management of people, quality management, ethics and equity. There are several scholarly and trade journals, such as the *Journal of Sport Management* and *SportBusiness* which disseminate the findings of such research to an international audience.

The main consequence of these two factors has been the emergence of a management culture based on the belief that good management practice is the solution to organisational survival. Inherent in this culture is the belief that good management reflects business-like management, which has driven the commercialisation of sport management, and thus sport, in all industry sectors. Beech and Chadwick (2004), Chelladurai (2005) and Robinson (2004) have all provided evidence of professionals using techniques such as performance management, quality management and tighter financial controls. They have also identified the importance of personal and people skills and good generic management skills. It is therefore clear that the professionalisation of sports managers has contributed to the increased commercialisation of the sports industry.

THE STRUCTURE OF THE SPORTS INDUSTRY

The sports industry is arguably one of the most complex to be found as it incorporates the voluntary, public and private sectors and can be broken down into manufacturing, retailing, entertainment and service segments, each containing specialised subfields. Chelladurai (2005) and Parks et al. (2003) have argued that the sports industry should be segmented along the lines of the products (goods and services) that are produced by the sports organisation. Chelladurai (2005) has suggested that sport can be divided into several key segments, which have further subsegments. He believes that the main segments are the provision of sport for participation and spectating, and also considers sponsorship services to be one of the fastest-growing segments of the sports industry. Participation services can be subdivided on the basis of participants' motives, which could be the pursuit of pleasure, excellence, skill or for curative, sustenance or health and fitness reasons. Spectator services are primarily offered by team sports which provide either commercial entertainment (professional sport) or non-commercial entertainment (sport promoting excellence, such as intercollegiate sport). Alternatively, Parks et al. (2007) divide the sports industry into three key parts: settings, types and segments. It is clear from both of these proposed structures that the sports industry is fragmented and complex, made up of a variety of products. In addition, each segment contains organisations from the public, voluntary and private sectors, highlighting the complex structure of the sports industry, as can be seen in Figure 13.1.

This chapter goes on to consider the three aspects of the sports industry which are considered to exemplify the dynamism, breadth and diversity of the business of sport. The first of these is professional sport, which has the primary purpose of making a profit for teams and leagues and which generates income for players. The second of these is sports sponsorship, which is arguably the fastest-growing sector in the business of sport. The sports betting industry is the final sector to be considered: not only is it purely commercial in its operations, but it has also raised public awareness of the management of some sports.

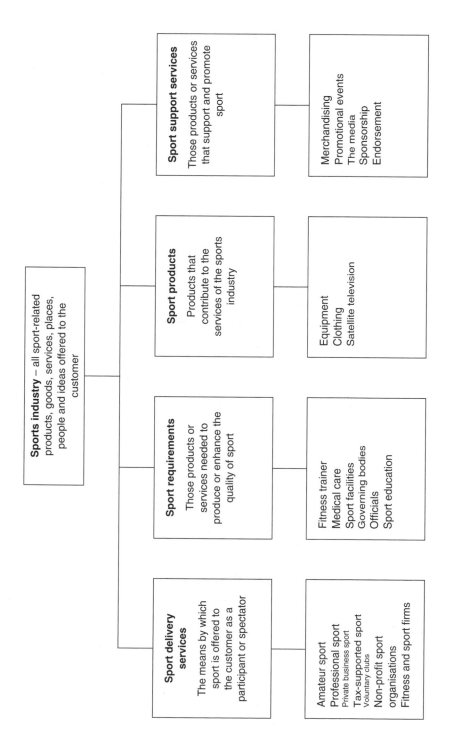

FIGURE 13.1 Sports industry
Source: Adapted from Parks et al. (1998)

PROFESSIONAL SPORT

Professional sports, as packaged events, provide considerable entertainment and pleasure for spectators as well as providing revenue for players and owners. The main purpose of professional sport leagues is to make a profit through the provision of sport as entertainment, while the primary purpose of a professional sportsperson is to make a living from playing sport. As a result, professional sports are the most obvious example of business in sport.

Professional sport has its origins in ancient Greece, where a class of professional sportsmen known as *athletai* existed. These men were well paid, recruited from mercenary armies and trained exclusively for brutal competition. Having said this, it was not until the nineteenth century that professional sport began to develop in earnest, with boxers, jockeys and runners being routinely paid for their efforts. Baseball was the first team to employ professionals and formed the first professional league in 1871. In the UK, football began to pay players illicitly in the mid-1880s and in 1885 the Football Association legitimised professionalism, which led to the multi-million-pound business that football is today, at the beginning of the twenty-first century.

Chelladurai (2005) has suggested that professional sports can be considered as entertainment, which is why they make money. He also suggests that there are three main aspects to sport as entertainment. First is the notion of 'the contest', where competition and the unpredictability of results are considered to be key elements in sporting entertainment. He argues that an essential ingredient in the 'contest' is the level of excellence achieved by the contestants – the higher the excellence, the greater the entertainment value. This is why professional sport is more attractive to watch than amateur sport. Second, professional sport is a 'spectacle'. Although the contest is the core of the event, there is usually a spectacle associated with the event, such as the opening and closing ceremonies of the Olympic Games or the parades and half-time shows associated with rugby, football and basketball. For some, these are more important than the contest itself, as demonstrated by the opening and closing ceremonies of the Athens Olympics having the highest television viewing figures of the Games. Finally, sport as entertainment offers a social venue where people can come together, not only for the contest and spectacle, but also for social purposes. This is particularly obvious in team sports that encourage fan identity, such as football, baseball, basketball and rugby, where watching the spectacle often forms an important social occasion for spectators.

THE UNIQUE NATURE OF PROFESSIONAL SPORT

It is apparent therefore that the package associated with professional sport is paramount for its continued commercial success and as such requires professional management.

However, although professional sport is a commercial enterprise, sport is not simply another business. Smith and Stewart (1999) have outlined the following eight features as making sport distinctive from other forms of business:

- *Irrational passions.* Sport and typical businesses operate within different behavioural parameters. The major concerns of profit-centred businesses are efficiency, productivity and responding quickly to changing market conditions. Sport, on the other hand, is typified by strong emotional attachments that are linked to the past by nostalgia and tradition. For example, a proposal to change training or playing venues may fail simply because of an attachment to a traditional venue. In addition, predictability and certainty – valued in business – are not always valued by sports fans. Fans are more attracted to a game where the result is problematic, than to one where the winner is virtually known in advance.

- *Profits or premierships.* The most significant difference between professional sporting organisations and private business is the way in which they measure performance. The main objective of typical businesses is to optimise profits; however, while this is increasingly important to professional clubs, profits are usually less important than their position in competitive leagues. This is clearly demonstrated by the poor financial performance of some of the English Premier League football clubs, whose expenditure on players to assist with winning the Premiership has caused financial losses.

- *Designing a level playing field.* Business success is often measured by market domination; however, continued domination of a sporting event or league may be self-defeating. Highly predictable outcomes often lead to reduced attendances and waning interest. In order to combat this, some sports have introduced rules to distribute playing talent equally between teams. For example, in an attempt to make teams more evenly matched, in the United States, Major League Baseball has a complex set of rules which regulates the draft or purchase of players based on the previous year's performance and strict eligibility criteria.

- *Variable quality.* Sport is one of the few products or services that depend on unpredictability for their success. With this unpredictability, however, comes variable quality, brought about by many factors such as the weather, injuries, the quality of the opponents or even the crowd. For example, spectators attending an Olympic swimming session may see several close races or even new Olympic records, or they may see a number of races which contain neither of these qualities. The price of the session remains the same no matter what the quality of the performances. This makes sport very different from other businesses, where consistency and reliability are highly valued.

- *Collaboration and cartels.* Team sports depend upon the continued commercial viability of their opponents. Indeed, there is little incentive to see rivals fail as this would reduce the number of clubs or teams involved in competition and thus the number of games and associated gate receipts. In addition, at the most basic level, opponents must co-operate with their rivals in order to deliver an attractive sporting experience to fans or customers. This collaboration can take several forms, such as the cross-subsidising of less successful teams, as occurs in the European Six Nations Rugby Tournament, where a proportion of income from television is divided equally among the countries who participate. In this respect, the sports business is fundamentally different from other businesses, where collaboration is relatively rare.
- *Product and brand loyalty.* On the whole, sport engenders a high degree of loyalty at both the product (sporting competition) level and the brand (team) level. At the product level, there is a low degree of substitutability between sports: that is, the satisfaction that comes from one sport will not easily transfer to another. For example, if a supporter's rugby team was playing away and the match was not televised, it is unlikely that the supporter would watch a hockey match as an alternative. At the brand level, club affiliation is very strong. Fans invest an enormous amount of personal energy in their chosen team and this can create lifelong attachments. For example, 83 per cent of English Premier League supporters have always supported their chosen club. In contrast, if a consumer purchases electronic equipment and is dissatisfied with it, they are likely to change providers.
- *Vicarious identification.* The identification that fans have with sports and teams often spins off into their relationships with family and friends, into the choice of sporting heroes and sporting behaviour, and the wearing of team uniform is one way that people identify with their chosen sporting team. In addition, identification with sporting heroes will lead many supporters to emulate their behaviour in clothing, a fact recognised by Nike and its sponsorship of Tiger Woods. It is difficult to imagine such vicarious identification occurring among consumers of electrical goods.
- *Fixed supply schedules.* Although most typical businesses can usually increase production to meet increased demand, sports clubs have fixed or highly inelastic production curves for their products (excluding the sale of membership and memorabilia). Clubs can only play a certain number of times during a competition or season and although the venue can be changed to allow increased attendances, the organising body cannot usually decide to play the game twice.

Sports managers, spectators and players must appreciate these special features of sport. Viewing sport simply as a commercial enterprise loses sight of the key qualities that give sport its identity – the passion and emotional support of spectators. At the same time, because of its special features, it requires the use of professional management techniques in order to ensure that it is an effective business. In support of this, Smith and Stewart (1999: 21) concluded their discussion of the unique features of sport by arguing that 'anyone who intends to manage sport as if it is somehow culturally privileged and immune from business influences is destined to fail'.

SPORTS SPONSORSHIP

Between 1981 and 2001 the UK sports sponsorship market increased by over 80 per cent. In 2004, expenditure on sports sponsorship was estimated at $695m (Mintel, 2004), with football receiving the greatest amount of sponsorship by far. Meenaghan (1991) attributed the growth in sponsorship to the following reasons:

- *Government policies on tobacco and alcohol.* Changing government policies on the advertising of alcohol and tobacco have caused manufacturers of such products to seek alternative promotional media. Continued sponsorship by such companies is, however, debatable with many governments having banned tobacco sponsorship of sporting events. For example, the European Union Directive imposing a ban on all tobacco advertising and sponsorship achieved full coverage in 2006. Although snooker and Formula One have negotiated limited exemptions to the ban, other sports have had to seek new sponsors as a result.
- *Escalating costs of advertising media.* Part of the attraction of sponsorship is the belief that it provides a highly cost-effective marketing communications tool, compared with traditional advertising. This is particularly the case when a brand becomes associated with an event, such as the Whitbread Round the World Race and the Flora London Marathon.
- *The proven value of sponsorship.* It is often difficult to be certain about the benefits of sponsorship; however, there is increasing evidence of the success of sponsorship in raising the profile of a business and generating sales. One such example is the $14m invested in the 1989–90 Whitbread Round the World Race by Lion Nathan Breweries of New Zealand. Its yacht *Steinlager 2* won the race and gained an estimated $70m in free advertising around the globe. Sales of Steinlager went up by 24 per cent in the United States and by 21 per cent internationally.
- *New opportunities due to increased leisure activity.* The range of activities being pursued in leisure time is greater now than it has ever been, thus providing increased opportunities for sponsorship involvement. Extreme sports have become

popular for sponsors seeking the youth market, and sponsorship of online activities is an increasing source of revenue for many sports.

- *Greater media coverage of sponsored events.* Media coverage of sporting events has extended greatly, increasing the opportunity for sponsorship. Not only has television coverage of sport increased markedly, but also new technologies, such as broadband, wireless and 3G, have increased the types of media outlets available.
- *Inefficiencies in traditional media.* A large part of the attraction of sponsorship has been its potential role in overcoming the inefficiencies of traditional advertising media. For example, many viewers tend to switch channels during advertisements, decreasing the actual audience for television advertising, and sponsorship is seen as a way of gaining more television time.

THE BENEFITS OF SPONSORSHIP TO SPORT

Sponsorship is a marketing strategy that pursues commercial and/or corporate objectives, exploiting the direct association between an organisation, a brand or a product with another organisation's brand or personality. It implies a commercial transaction between the various parties involved. This transaction can involve the exchange of funds, but more commonly it involves an exchange of good or services as value in kind (VIK) (Ferrand, 2006). Arguably, anything is available for sponsorship, providing it has linkages with the sponsor's objectives. Nevertheless, the following six categories can be considered the main areas of sport sponsorship.

- *Event specific*, e.g. Whitbread Round the World Race.
- *Individual specific*, e.g. Nike's sponsorship of Tiger Woods.
- *Team specific*, e.g. adidas's sponsorship of the All Blacks rugby team.
- *Competition specific*, e.g. BMW European PGA Championships.
- *Ground specific*, e.g. The Walker Stadium – Leicester Football Club.
- *Coaching scheme specific*, e.g. Kellogg's sponsorship of swimming development in the UK.

The benefits of sponsorship to sport are two-fold. First, sport requires financing and even those sports and events that can be considered to be commercial welcome the additional income generated by sponsorship activity. Sponsorship has become the second most important source of revenue for the Olympic Games; it has provided a lifeline for governing bodies and has allowed elite players to earn salaries that are the envy of most other occupations.

Second, sport seeks media exposure and publicity. As this is also what sponsoring companies seek, they are likely to take steps to improve publicity for the sponsored event and thus increase awareness of both the event and the company. An example of this is outlined by Gratton and Taylor (2000), who described how the joint publicity of sport and sponsors led snooker from being a low-interest sport with little media coverage, to becoming the fourth most televised sport in the UK.

It is not, however, all positive and Gratton and Taylor have outlined two important costs of sponsorship to sport. First, as sponsorship is essentially a commercial activity, sponsors expect a commercial return on their investment, often leading to their requiring some control over the events and competitors whom they sponsor. For example, top competitors are often subject to excessively crowded schedules in order to meet the demands of the sponsors. Second, Gratton and Taylor (2000) have argued that sponsors are normally only interested in major events and elite performers, which creates several problems. First, conflict can arise between sponsors and the rules of sport federations on the amateur status of competitors, such as occurred in Rugby Union in the early 1990s. Second, there is often a lack of continuity to much sponsorship activity. Sponsors often withdraw from a sport with little notice, leaving sports with a shortfall of income. Finally, the focus on elite events and participants creates a division between sports. For example, the relationship between television and sport determines the attraction of a sport to sponsors. The major sports with their guaranteed television coverage have no difficulty in finding sponsors – it is the minor sports, potential elite athletes and youth schemes that have problems. In addition, this division is occasionally seen within sports. Sponsorship of men's football is phenomenal; sponsorship of women's football is practically non-existent.

THE BENEFITS OF SPORT TO SPONSORS

Shank (2005) has suggested that there are five reasons why organisations sponsor sport. The first of these is image enhancement. Sport creates a positive image and business organisations, identifying the value of this image to their brands or products, have increasingly sought to build an association with sporting activity. By associating elite performers with the product, the aim is to create an elite image for the company. A second reason for sponsorship is to increase awareness of the company and/or of a product. A third reason for sponsorship is the potential for establishing long-term relationships with clients via hospitality opportunities and many organisations regard these opportunities for entertainment as a key motive for sponsorship. This is particularly the case for blue-chip events such as Formula One, golf championships, tennis Grand Slam tournaments and Rugby Union internationals. Not only do these events provide an opportunity to entertain clients, but they also suggest that the company is a major player in industry as it has access to such events (see Box 13.2). Fourth, sponsorship has the potential to increase sales, not only through raised awareness, but also by providing the opportunity to trial products or to make sales opportunities. Sport events, leagues and competitions provide product sampling opportunities, while the sale of sponsors' merchandise is commonplace at sporting events. Finally, sponsorship allows organisations to be competitive.

Box 13.2 RBS Group and Rugby Union's Six Nations Championship

The 2003 Six Nations Championship was sponsored by the RBS Group for the first time. The banking and finance company invested an estimated $40m in the Six Nations Championship. From the RBS perspective, there were two reasons for the sponsorship deal. First, the group wanted to use the Six Nations as a platform to drive brand awareness and prestige in order to position itself as one of the key players in Rugby Union. Second, it wanted to promote the company to key clients through the hospitality rights that accompanied the deal. Its aim of increasing exposure for the brand was achieved in the first year of the sponsorship, particularly through television. The cumulative European televised audience reached 93 million, which was up 22% on 2002. In the UK 47.9 million people watched BBC coverage, which was an increase of 28%.

Source: Mintel (2004)

Sponsorship of sport has reached such levels that those sports and athletes fortunate to attract sponsorship are now receiving unprecedented levels of income. Many sports would not survive without it, a situation also facing many professional athletes. Although the positive impact of sponsorship on sport is undeniable, a major problem is its volatility and unpredictability, as sponsors are quick to change sports if results are not forthcoming. In addition, Mintel (2004) has suggested a decline in the sports sponsorship market since 2002. This requires sports managers and participants to adopt a business-like approach to their sport, as sponsors have, in effect, become employers in the business of sport.

SPORTS BETTING

The sports betting market, originally developed out of a passion for horse racing, has expanded in recent years to take account of a growing demand for the opportunity to gamble on the outcome of a wide range of sports events. Beech and Chadwick (2004) have suggested that the UK gambling market may be worth in excess of $12bn. In recent years, the online betting market has taken off, with the online betting and gaming industry estimated as being worth $11bn (Glendinning, 2005). The online revolution began with Gibraltar-based Victor Chandler's betting operation in May 1999, and in 2000, William Hill, UK bookmakers, became the first major player to offer duty-free betting. In 2000, the first dedicated worldwide football betting Internet service was launched. VIPsoccer.com offered tax-free betting and accepted bets from anywhere in the world on games in leagues across the world. In the UK, the Hilton Group committed $201m to provide betting on the Internet, through interactive television and mobile telephones. The US betting company Autotote aligned itself with Arena Leisure, operators of six UK racecourses, to create an international Web-based betting business founded on horse racing.

Online betting was able to gain market share quickly, by offering tax-free or reduced tax betting to punters, as operators either absorbed the cost of the tax deduction or based their operations offshore. In response to this, the UK government abolished betting tax, replacing it with the requirement for bookmakers to pay 15 per cent of their gross profits directly to the government.

Although sports betting realises little legitimate income for professional sport teams and athletes (with the exception of funding via national lotteries), the sports betting industry impacts on professional sport in two ways. The first of these is arguably positive, encouraging increased spectating and following of sport via the opportunity to make money on outcomes.

The second impact of sports betting on professional sport is much less positive, as the opportunity to earn large sums of money from gambling has raised many concerns among other sectors of the industry. Sports gambling has always been justified on the basis of the revenue it supplies to governments through taxation and in the UK the betting levy raised more than $122m in 1999. It is, however, impossible to ignore the ethical issues surrounding sports betting, with the following being key concerns.

Sports betting is likely to:

- **increase attempts by players and coaches to influence the outcome of scores;**
- **create suspicion by fans who feel that the outcome was influenced;**
- **increase costs spent on monitoring and policing the league to preclude game fixing and point shaving;**
- **change the nature of sport, focusing not on the beauty of competition, but on the 'points spread';**
- **encourage and promote gambling;**
- **increase personal health problems associated with gambling. (Davis, 1994)**

Although all of these concerns are clearly important, it is the first three that are of greatest concern to those who run the business of sport. Marco Pantani, 1998 winner of the Tour de France, was, in 2000, the first sportsperson to be found guilty under civil law of trying to manipulate the result of a sporting event by the use of banned drugs. In the UK, the government has recently established the Independent Football Commission to watch over the game. More obviously, events in cricket, outlined in Box 13.3, demonstrate how sports betting can undermine sport and sporting events. Football, tennis and Rugby League have faced similar problems, with UEFA having expressed concerns about betting syndicates that have infiltrated the sport (Glendinning, 2005b).

Box 13.3   The scandal of cricket

The year 2000 was a bad one for cricket. Allegations of match 'fixing', which originated in India, spread throughout the cricketing world, resulting in lifetime bans for Pakistan's Salim Malik and South Africa's Hansie Cronje. In addition, the investigative report released by India's Central Bureau of Investigations implicated other key past and present players from Sri Lanka, New Zealand, Australia, England and the West Indies in the scandal. These players were accused of accepting sums of money either for 'information' about pitch conditions, tactics or team morale, or, more serious, for 'fixing matches by underperforming in batting and fielding'.

The scale of the match-fixing allegations was so widespread that it was argued that

> the integrity of the game, so accepted that it is a figure of speech, has been dealt a heavy blow. The revelations have undermined the enjoyment of a generation of cricket fans. Every unexpected result, each thrilling comeback against impossible odds, now looks suspect. (*Independent*, 2000)

Betting on cricket, on a major scale, started after India won the World Cup in 1983 and increased when live telecasts of cricket matches started on a regular basis and spread throughout the country. The use of computers and mobile phones promoted and supported the spread of betting until betting on cricket became to be considered to be the biggest organised racket in India, in terms of monetary turnover and volume of transactions.

As the investigation of the named players was carried out, by the anti-corruption unit that was established in the wake of the India scandal, it became clear that it was not just international matches that had been affected. In 2004, the English Cricket Board investigated claims of alleged gambling in county cricket matches. Although the ICCB claims to have 'match fixing' under control, the damage to the reputation of cricket is indubitably enormous and provides a clear example of the problems associated with sports betting.

CONCLUSION

Commercialism has been apparent in sport since the expansion of professional sport in the nineteenth century. What makes the contemporary sports industry so different is that all sectors of the industry are concerned with a business approach to sport. The emergence of sport as a business has been the result of the actions and interactions of a number of factors. Increasing customer expectations of service quality, value for money and entertainment have forced managers of sports organisations to become increasingly innovative, efficient and customer focused. This, alongside increasing competition and advances in technology, has led to a commercial approach to the management of all types of sports organisations – sport managers have become business-like in their operations. It is the money to be made from sport, though, which above all makes it a business. Income from sales of sports clothes, equipment and merchandising, gate receipts and concessions make sport a commercial viability. Income from sponsorship and broadcasting rights makes sport an attractive business.

Sport is a key sector of the national economy. Indeed, sport has become so significant in the economy that it is becoming subject to the same legislation and operating principles as all other industries. This is apparent in the European Union's decision not to consider football as a 'special case', ruling against it remaining exempt from the employment legislation affecting other EU businesses. This also underlies FINA's decision to rule that costumes are to be considered a swimmer's technical equipment, thus allowing swimmers to choose the best tools for their 'job'. Both of these decisions suggest that sport is to compete on the same basis as other industries – recognition indeed of the extent and strength of the business of sport.

CHAPTER SUMMARY

» Sport is no longer a pastime, run and organised by amateurs: it is a business that competes for scarce resources and uses professional management techniques.
» The commercialisation of sport has been driven by the search for profit and, among state-funded not-for-profit sports organisations, the push towards efficiency, effectiveness and value for money.
» A number of factors make professional sports a distinctive form of business including the irrational passions generated, the tension between making a profit and winning a competition or league, and the existence and general tolerance of cartels.
» Sports sponsorship has grown dramatically in recent years, bringing both additional revenue and greater publicity, although it has recently begun to decline.
» Online betting is one of the fastest-growing sectors of the sports business, but raises significant ethical concerns.

FURTHER READING

Chelladurai (2005) provides an excellent introduction to the field of sports management, while Beech and Chadwick (2004) and Torkildsen (2005) are both comprehensive reviews of the focus of sports management and the techniques employed. *SportBusiness* provides a comprehensive review of the issues faced by the business of sport.

REFERENCES

Beech, J. and Chadwick, S. (eds) (2004) *The Business of Sport Management.* Harlow: Pearson Education.

Britcher, C. (2005) 'Can new market entrants boost UK 3G?', *SportBusiness*, December/January: 27.

Chelladurai, P. (2005) *Managing Organizations for Sport and Physical Activity.* 2nd edn. Scottsdale, AZ: Holcomb Hathaway.

Davies, L.E. (2000) 'The economic impact of sport in Sheffield', PhD thesis, Sheffield Hallam University.

Davis, K.A. (1994) *Sport Management: Successful Private Sector Business Strategies.* Madison, WI: Brown & Benchmark.

Ferrand, A. (2006) 'Chapter five: Marketing', in J. Camy and L. Robinson, *Managing Olympic Sport Organizations.* Champaign, IL: Human Kinetics.

Fry, A (2005) 'Has NFL left the rights market high and dry?', *SportBusiness*, December/January: 25.

Glendinning, M. (2005) 'Organized crime alarms UEFA', *SportBusiness*, September: 14.

Gratton, C. and Taylor, P. (2000) *Economics of Sport and Recreation.* London: E & FN Spon.

Independent (2000) 'The integrity of sport has been dealt a heavy blow', *Independent*, 4 November.

International Olympic Committee (2006) 'Revenue generation and distribution', www.olympic.org (accessed 28 February 2006).

Luker, R. (2000) 'US sports sector slips from the summit', *SportBusiness*, March: 48–9.

Meenghan, T. (1991) 'Sponsorship – Legitimising the Medium', *European Journal of Marketing.* 25 (11), 5–10.

Mintel (2003) *The Sports Market.* London: Mintel International Group.

Mintel (2004) *Sponsorship.* London: Mintel International Group.

Mintel (2005) *Spectator Sports.* London: Mintel International Group.

Parks, B.R.K., Quarterman, J. and Thibault, L. (eds) (2007) *Contemporary Sport Management.* 3rd edn. Champaign: IL: Human Kinetics.

Robinson, L. (1999) 'Following the quality strategy – the rationale for the use of quality programmes', *Managing Leisure: An International Journal*, 4 (4): 201–17.

Robinson, L. (2004) *Managing public sport and leisure services.* London: Routledge.

Shank, M.D (2005) *Sports Marketing: a Strategic Perspective.* 3rd edn. Upper Saddle River, NJ: Prentice Hall.

Smith, A. and Stewart, B. (1999) *Sports Management: a Guide to Professional Practice.* St Leonards: Allen & Unwin.

SportBusiness (2005a) 'Leagues go wireless under the cloud', *SportBusiness*, December/January: 30.

SportBusiness (2005b) 'New TXT experience for NFL fans', *SportBusiness*, September: 8.

Torkildsen, G. (2005) *Leisure and Recreation Management.* London: Routledge.

Wilson, N. (1988) *The Sports Business.* London: Piatkus.

Zimmerman, M. (1997) 'Sport management: past, present, future', *The Sport Manager of the Future.* 5th Sport Management Committee European Seminar Proceedings, University of Northumbria at Newcastle.

14

Sport and the Media

DAVID STEAD

OVERVIEW

- » *Context and key issues*
- » *The sport–media partnership*
- » *The media sport product: characteristics, influences and outcomes*
- » *The media sport audience*
- » *Media sport: where to now?*

CONTEXT AND KEY ISSUES

In many ways, both today's sport and the media are classic outcomes and, indeed, icons of the far-reaching social, economic and technological change that characterised the twentieth century. Each has developed extensively and rapidly as a major global industry. Each plays a significant part in structuring and informing people's lives. Each has a global as well as more local scope of operation and has the structures and practices to reflect this. Importantly, they are two industries tied together in complex networks of relationships. Their respective histories of development have been fuelled and influenced by the dynamics of this partnership. The evidence of the partnership is all too apparent. The well-being of particular sports or, indeed, sport as whole has become linked to income generated directly or indirectly from the media. The way in which sport fills newspaper pages and television and radio schedules bears testimony to the influence it has on the structure and extent of media activity.

However, partnerships are not always equal, stable or constructive for those involved. In this chapter, consideration will be given to a number of themes and issues that characterise the link between sport and the media. Difficulties and tensions exist but ultimately a media sports product emerges whether it is, for example, a live television broadcast of the Olympic Games or a newspaper report on a local rugby match. This raises a series of issues about the nature of the product. Does the media presentation of sport mirror reality or is it a representation and a construction reflecting the media's objectives and the influences and practices of the professionals working in it? Such questions will also be considered later but they in turn introduce the part played by the audience for media sport. For example, is the viewer knowledgeable about the sports products on offer to them and do they exercise choice about what they view and how they receive the messages and influences inherent in the programmes? The chapter will conclude by addressing this conundrum. Questions about the genesis and content of media products and the influences impacting on them figure prominently in what is a growing sociology of sport literature on media sport (see in particular Bernstein and Blain, 2003; Kinkema and Harris, 1998; Maguire, 1999; Rowe, 1999, 2003; Wenner, 1998; Whannel, 1992, 2002).

The mass media entered the twentieth century with the emphasis on the printed word. Today, in the early years of the twenty-first century, it is television, radio and the Internet that are to the fore. Satellite-based multinational companies like BSkyB TV have appeared on the scene and are now major players in the global sport media marketplace. There are new developments like third-generation mobile phones which have further extended media activities. Sport has long been an important aspect of media output but more recently there has been a growth in specialist media sports products. Dedicated sports-only television channels (e.g. Sky Sports 1), radio stations (e.g. TalkSport) and publications (e.g. *Sport First*) have appeared in ever-increasing numbers.

The exposure to and consumption of media products, including those concerned with sport, have increased dramatically. A Henley Centre report has gone as far as to suggest that people in the UK spend nine hours a day consuming media in their various forms, with television viewing occupying the equivalent of a day a week (*Financial Mail on Sunday*, 31 January 1999: 38). Television has, indeed, become a principal leisure activity and source of information. Through it we gather our knowledge not only of our immediate world, but also of the complex global village in which we now live. It acts as a key socialisation agent and is integral to framing, determining and influencing our picture of reality. Our experience of sport has become increasingly constructed and ordered through television output.

Sport has become 'big business'. It is now a well-established global industry with international organising bodies, like the International Olympic Committee (IOC), eager to promote and structure its further development. Sport, but not necessarily in all its forms, has something to sell. It has its events, leagues, clubs and elite performers. Sport can make money but the costs involved, not least the large rewards paid to the top performers in some sports and the capital and revenue expense of increasingly spectacular sports stadiums, have left it with an insatiable appetite for more and more funding. The world of sport is a competitive one, in terms of not just which team tops the league or who wins the gold medal, but also which sports are able to attract the greatest financial resources. The relationship with the media is central to the political economy of sport. Traditionally, it was the medium through which key information like schedules of events/matches, venues and times were transmitted to the public. Today, the media, primarily television, offer sport added attractions in terms of finance from broadcasting fees and exposure to advertisers, sponsors and a wider audience. Hence there is the all too apparent readiness of sports organisations to get involved with the media. However, alongside the obvious benefits come some possible costs to sport. To link with the media has meant sport losing a degree of control over its own activities and destiny. The promise of media attention and the wide-ranging spin-offs (in terms of increased profile, status and finance, greater numbers of participants and spectators and enhanced attractiveness to sponsors and advertisers) make such loss of control something sports organisations appear willing to accept (Goldlust, 1987). The ability to appreciate and deal with the full extent of the consequences of its partnership with the media is a major challenge confronting sport in the twenty-first century.

THE SPORT–MEDIA PARTNERSHIP

The Media: Competition and Control

The media sport production process involves the sports organisations, for example the Fédération Internationale de Football Association (FIFA), the governing body of world football, working with the media companies. The sports bodies may do this directly or through intermediary marketing and promotional agencies operating on their behalf. They may engage with the media as individual companies or in partnership with others. The media organisation concerned may be a quasi-governmental body, like the British Broadcasting Corporation, or a multinational global commercial one such as BSkyB. A sport has something to sell, such as the television and radio broadcasting rights to cover its world championships, and it is up to the media companies to submit bids. The competition to become the agreed lead broadcaster can be intense, although the sheer size of the financial undertaking can lead to fierce media rivals working together on a bid. In the example of FIFA selling the rights to its World Cup, the sums involved are considerable and the bidding and decision-making processes are complex and sensitive. Competition for broadcasting rights and the prominence of sport in media schedules have had a dramatic inflationary effect on the fees paid to some sports. An early globally televised Olympics, such as the 1964 Tokyo Games, cost the lead broadcaster around £1m. More recently, it has been reported that the US broadcaster NBC has paid the IOC $3.5bn for the rights to the Winter Olympics of 2002 (Salt Lake City) and 2006 (Turin) and the Summer Olympics of 2004 (Athens) and 2008 (Beijing). These massive sums of money have to be balanced out by the very considerable amount of airtime that can be filled by such events. Indeed, sports broadcasting can be seen as a relatively cheap way to fill schedules. Sports events can also be particularly useful for the all-important audience ratings by attracting large numbers of viewers and listeners. For example, ITV in the UK attracted 23.2 million viewers, some 80 per cent of the available television public, for the England versus Argentina football match at the 1998 World Cup finals. The number of viewers peaked to almost 27 million during the penalty shoot-out! (*Sport First*, 3 January 1999: 16).

A successful bidder's production costs for a major global sporting event will involve the expense incurred in securing the broadcasting rights plus a heavy investment in people, accommodation, travel and equipment. It is not surprising therefore that a media company will endeavour to exercise considerable control over the event. If the sporting event concerned is not one that is deemed to be particularly attractive, then to get the media on board may involve the sports organisation accepting an especially weak bargaining and control position. Even when the sports organisation involved is powerful, such as the IOC or FIFA, there is still a trade-off in terms of a loss of control. This can lead to significant changes in sport, for example to dates, times and venues. The actual structure and presentational style of an event may be strongly reflective of the media's interests. Football's World Cup competition is an example of a particularly large-scale and well-established sport event but it is still not immune from media preferences. Indeed, loss of control needs to be considered whenever a sports organisation, however local and small, gets involved with the media. Many more sports and events are vying for media money and, to an extent, the media, notably television with its schedules to fill, are not averse to encouraging sports bodies to approach them.

The rise in the numbers and influence of the private media companies has had a number of important consequences. The private sector is characterised by the existence of some large-scale monopolistic groupings. Global media entrepreneurs like Rupert Murdoch, Alan Bond, Kerry Packer and Silvio Berlusconi have recognised the value of media sport and each has, to a varying degree, made a significant impact on the world of sport. BSkyB in the UK, FoxTV in North America and Channel Seven in Australia form just part of Murdoch's extensive News Corporation media empire. Each has won major sports contracts and invested heavily in sports-related programming. Murdoch's activities cover radio, television and newspapers and have put him in a powerful position to direct media sport developments. In some cases, these multinational media companies have gone further and strengthened their controlling opportunities by actually moving into sport's ownership through investing in clubs. BSkyB's ambitious, but eventually thwarted, attempt to take a controlling stake in Manchester United is a telling case in point.

Another important control aspect of global media sport is the power exercised by the North American media market. The upward explosion in certain broadcasting fees has been fuelled largely by US media money. Sport on television is particularly popular in the United States and the advertising revenue the media companies can obtain on the back of sports coverage can be enormous. For example, advertising slots around television coverage of the American Football's Superbowl can cost many thousands of dollars per second.

In the UK, the private satellite-based companies have put themselves in a powerful position with regard to their terrestrial and, sometimes, public sector competitors. BSkyB started buying up the right to cover events and sports as soon as it appeared in the UK. Sport was seen as a particularly useful product through which to sell subscriptions to its service. There had always been competition to broadcast some sports. However, the emergence of BSkyB injected new dynamism into the media sport marketplace and highlighted the differential abilities of media organisations to compete financially.

The licence-fee-funded BBC, which for so long had enjoyed a high reputation for its sports programming, has struggled to match the sports resources available in the private sector, principally the satellite companies. It has lost out on the rights to cover many major sports or particular events and is now criticised for what appears to be a lack of commitment to sport. Flagship BBC programmes like *Grandstand,* for decades the UK's leading media sport product, was progressively marginalised as it sought to fill its time with an increasingly limited diet of available events. The programme was finally cut from the schedules in January 2007. From the 2001–2 season, another symbol of the BBC's long-standing contribution to sport (i.e. its Saturday evening football highlights programme) was lost to another terrestrial channel, ITV, working in partnership with BSkyB, although the BBC won back the broadcasting rights from the 2004–5 season. Whilst the BBC may be marginalised in the media sport marketplace, other UK media organisations like ITV and Channel 4 have looked to increase their involvement. The latter has wide sporting interests and invested in motor racing, Italian football, WWF (wrestling) and cricket. To a degree, competition for sports to cover has extended the choice for the television viewer but the question of access is a somewhat more complex question.

Issues of Access and Equity

As media sport has risen in prominence, so questions have to be asked about whether this represents sport for all or only for some. The extensive involvement of satellite companies and their array of dedicated sports-only channels have clearly led to a major extension of the range and number of sports choices available to viewers. However, this has come at a financial cost to the viewer in terms of the equipment (e.g. satellite dishes) and regular subscriptions that are required. These kinds of financial factors, allied to the satellite companies' growing domination of broadcasting rights, highlight the issue of equity in the sense of media sport becoming primarily the preserve of those people who can afford it.

Interestingly, the greater involvement, indeed in some ways the re-emergence, of ITV in the media sport marketplace has been through the introduction of a subscription-based channel. The financial implications for the viewer are likely to become even more problematic as the private companies offer more sport on a 'pay-to-view' basis. This involves events (e.g. boxing championships and selected English Premier League football matches), which require the viewer to make a one-off payment on top of their subscription. The introduction of BSkyB's 'pay-to-view' facility (i.e. Sky Box Office) is representative of what may be the greatest challenge to wide access to media sport.

Governments, particularly in the European Union, have been encouraged to respond to this equity concern, particularly when it is access to major national sporting events that is coming under threat. In 1996, ironically one media form (newspapers) led a 'Save our Sport' campaign in the UK which opposed the movement of sporting events to the satellite companies. Government intervention was called for. The campaign arose in response to Sky buying up, and attempting to monopolise, the media coverage of top sporting events. An example of Sky's success was the obtaining of the rights to golf's Ryder Cup. The significance and concerns at the time can be summed up in the following quote from a disgruntled BBC producer: 'They've sold it to a station nobody watches. It's like buying *Gone with the Wind* and showing it at the bottom of a coalmine' (*Mail on Sunday*, 14 January 1996: 86). In the UK, there are a number of 'jewels in the sporting calendar', like the Football Association's Cup Final and the Wimbledon tennis championships, which are on a special government list requiring them to be broadcast on terrestrial TV. This list has protected opportunities for the media sport consumer but it is a safeguard constantly under threat as the satellite media companies see a valuable and popular commodity beyond their grasp and the sports organisations involved see potentially lucrative events being kept out of the broadcasting rights marketplace.

Interestingly, both FIFA and the IOC have resisted approaches from BSkyB on the grounds that a satellite-based broadcaster did not offer access to the highest possible audience. This is not to say that FIFA and the IOC have not gone some way towards appeasing the media. Both these world bodies have extended the number and the scale of their international flagship events. In doing so they have provided even more broadcasting opportunities. The FIFA World Cup finals now involve more teams than previously and the event extends over a longer time period. Such specific changes in sport are now, to a large extent, often part of a deliberate response to the pressures and promises of being part of the media sport partnership.

The Media Involvement in the Changing Face of Sport

Media's increasing involvement in, and control over, sport and sports organisations have put it in a powerful position to dictate the characteristics of events or, indeed, even to change fundamental aspects of a sport (e.g. its rules). Sport's sovereignty over its own destiny has weakened. In essence, the media have come to play an increasingly influential part in both the construction and destruction of sporting structures and practices. The media have been influential in the genesis and development of new competitions, events and leagues. New sport forms have appeared and old ones have become marginalised. Rules have been changed and playing conditions revised so as to enhance media coverage. Even the clothes athletes wear and the equipment they use have come to reflect media-related interests. The colours and designs can add to the spectacle and the drama. Names on the players' kit help the viewer. Sponsors' logos proliferate. Opportunities to link media, sport and commerce are all too readily available. For example, the increasingly spectacular sports stadiums provide backdrops 'wallpapered' with advertising hoardings. Sport has become more of a product that is manufactured, bought and sold. The sports organisations have gone along with this and, increasingly, have used agents and marketing companies to get their particular products into the media sport marketplace. Thus further complexity to the web of interdependencies that characterises media sport has been introduced. The media/sport production complex that has emerged today comprises the sports organisations, the media marketing organisations and the media personnel (Wenner, 1998).

Sometimes a sport jumps before it is pushed and, in a quest to make itself attractive as a media product, has been keen to introduce changes itself. Highly traditional aspects of the sporting experience disappear or are diluted. English football was once a Saturday afternoon ritual: today it has become almost a daily event as the television companies endeavour to fill their schedules and, importantly, maximise the return on the considerable sums they have invested in the game. Not only can the sporting day change, but so too can the season. English Rugby League, traditionally a winter sport, has now developed a seemingly made-for-television summer Super League characterised by a quest for entertainment and impact (Falcous, 1998). Clubs have changed their names (e.g. to the Bradford 'Bulls'), so as to enhance the spectacle and to offer potentially more commercial spin-offs. Rugby League in England has come under increasing competition for funding and exposure; the newly professional Rugby Union game has emerged as one notable threat. The media-inspired Super League has offered salvation, even though the trade-off has involved the loss of traditions and even the disappearance or downgrading of long-established and famous clubs. There are numerous examples where sports with a record of limited or reducing attraction to media companies have tried to encourage interest. It is not always easy to establish the extent to which the push originated from the media companies. Night games and coloured clothing and many other changes in cricket, tighter 'figure hugging' clothing in a number of female sports (e.g. netball), and rule changes to speed up play (e.g. hockey), are just a few examples of sports trying to add to the glamour and spectacle and thus make them more marketable.

Specific timetabling changes in sports events have been made that are all too clearly about meeting the needs of the media. Events are sometimes held at times that would not appear to be in the best interests of the athletes involved, but which fit in with the viewing habits of the primarily North American television audience. Olympic or World Championship marathons run at the hottest time of the day and a number of high-profile heavyweight boxing championships in the early hours of the morning are cases in point. In the UK, football and rugby matches are not only played on non-traditional days, but lunchtime or early evening kick-offs have become part of the experience. Sports agree to such conditions so as to secure the best broadcasting fees. However, whether such deci-sions benefit the spectator or are consistent with the well-being of the athletes concerned is questionable. The commercial media gain much of their income from advertising, hence the introduction of more or longer breaks in sports events. North American sport, in so many ways the exemplar of the practical realisation of media influence, is charac-terised by action frequently and deliberately punctuated by the 'timeouts' or other breaks in proceedings. Association Football has a '15-minute' half-time break which apparently ends when the referee receives the signal that the TV advertising has been completed.

Another area of sports development particularly reflective of media involvement has been the growth in the 'big event'. The proliferation of high-profile and spectacular events, notably global championships and competitions (e.g. Rugby Union World Cup), has given the media access to larger and more varied audiences and hence greater poten-tial in terms of recruiting advertisers. The media can also be seen as a central factor in the emergence of new sports (e.g. beach volleyball and beach football). Attention has also been focused on the way in which media companies have attempted to extend the wider global diffusion of sports. The initiatives taken by a partnership of the NFL, its sponsors and media companies to make American football a global game are prime examples (Maguire, 1990). A somewhat less far-reaching but nevertheless revealing initiative has been the coverage of Japanese sumo wrestling, which has appeared on European televi-sion schedules.

Sports, large and small, are vying for media attention, exposure and money but the experience of the media sport partnership is by no means the same for all of them.

Who Are the Winners and Losers?

The greater penetration of the media into the world of sport has had an impact on the relative status of particular sports and also on relationships within sports. Sports that are especially attractive to the media (e.g. football) have gained far greater status, exposure and economic wealth compared with other sports. The more glamorous football clubs in the Premier League, with the wealth of their BSkyB/Setanta contracts to support them, have been able to distance themselves from the rest of the clubs in England. The economic and political distance between sports and between clubs and leagues has widened. The media have helped fuel this in a direct sense by their patronage and contracts, but as sponsors and advertisers gravitate to the more glamorous and high-profile sports, events, leagues and clubs, so the differentials further increase. The introduction of media money and influence has also had an impact in pulling elite sport away from its roots. Elite sport, with its media-supported emphasis on spectacle, personalities and financial rewards, can become a somewhat alien activity for the recreational-level participant, who may have difficulty relating to it as the same sport.

The elite performers in a number of sports have become all too aware of their marketability as part of the media sport package and also of the vast amounts of media money that have flowed into sport. Aided by the emergence of agents working on their behalf, an increasing number of elite athletes have sought and obtained very high salaries or substantial prize money. This has further alienated athletes from the people who watch them on television and who read about them in the newspapers. Whilst all this media attention and money may raise the profile and status of elite athletes, this may also contribute to a more restricted life for them. They are now in the public eye and have become part of the media sport spectacle. Their degree of control over their own lives is brought into question. The media create sporting personalities to help sell their programmes and newspapers and this involves athletes being media commodities in situations that can extend way beyond the direct sporting context.

Media sport is about a production process. As media intrusion into sport continues to grow, it becomes more important to delve more deeply into the actual nature of the media sport product, how it is developed and the objectives behind it. The particular ways in which the media structure, direct and influence the public's experience of sport and with what impact are now key concerns. They are more relevant when one considers the significant degree to which people now gain their sports knowledge and understanding through the media rather than through direct personal involvement in spectating and participation. As implied earlier, the media's objective in engaging with sport is based largely on the profit motive. For the government-supported media bodies there is the responsibility of providing a public service. The production process involves the media professionals using their knowledge and expertise to develop media sport products that reflect their ability and proficiency, and in doing so they are, in part, seeking to enhance their status and reputation, not least amongst their peers. These kinds of objectives impact on what is produced.

THE MEDIA SPORT PRODUCT: CHARACTERISTICS, INFLUENCES AND OUTCOMES

Much of what has been discussed has centred on sport's interrelationship with television due to the heavy injection of money from television companies into sport and their desire to assume a greater degree of control over sport products. However, the media sport products on offer also include the printed word, the traditional mediated way that sports knowledge and understanding have been conveyed to the public at large. This section examines the specific nature of the media sport product and what is influencing this. Therefore much of what is discussed reflects the activities of newspapers and other printed media as well as television and radio.

Meanings and Messages

Reference has been made to the higher profile of elite athletes and how the media have been instrumental in bringing this about. However, personality creation is only one of the ways in which the media influence and direct the sporting experience for their customers. This structuring of knowledge, messages and meanings inherent in media sport products has become an increasingly researched and significant area of interest (Bernstein and Blain, 2003; Lawrence and Rowe, 1986; McKay and Rowe, 1987; Sage, 1990; Whannel, 1992, 2002). It is a field of enquiry that encompasses interest in the ideological content of sports coverage and reporting and, in particular, how this reflects the dominant values and ideology prevalent in society. A principal focus is on the ways in which the media transmit the values and support the political and economic objectives of their owners and controllers. At a different level, there is the interest in the roles played by the media professionals and the nature and impact of their particular production codes and techniques on media sport products. In summary, the challenge is to examine the degree to which what the media audience are exposed, not to a neutral and objective presentation of reality, but rather to a packaged representation and construction imbued with ideological content and reflective of the practical and professional interests of the production staff involved (Gruneau et al., 1988).

Textual Messages and Meanings

Research into the textual messages contained in the media sport output of various countries suggests the heavy influence of such ideological factors as capitalism, nationalism, patriarchy and racism (Gruneau, 1989b; Sage, 1990; Whannel, 1992, 2002). Each of these factors may reflect the ideological biases evident within the ownership and control of the increasingly dominant multinational media companies and, indeed, the dominant values in a particular society.

Capitalism

Media sport is an area of endeavour where capitalist virtues can come to the fore, not least in the prevalence of the profit motive (Lawrence and Rowe, 1986; McKay and Rowe, 1987). The media, a key cultural industry and so much a symbol and vehicle of capitalist interests, have become, through sports pages and programming, a source of support for ownership values and priorities. Media's implicit and explicit support for the dominance of monopoly capitalism has contributed to the resilience of capitalism in society and for the status quo in the way society is stratified. The inculcation and acceptance of the desired characteristics of the 'workplace' are fostered. The value of hard work and the spirit of free enterprise are characteristics to be found in sport that the media may choose to emphasise and describe in noticeably positive terms. An adherence to the work ethic is deemed worthy of particular praise. Core sporting characteristics such as competitiveness and teamwork are highlighted. An athlete's power, aggression and competitiveness are applauded. The Olympic motto, *Citius, Altius, Fortius*, emphasises the challenge of getting 'Faster, Higher and Stronger'. It is not surprising therefore that sport, particularly as it has become increasingly commercialised, has been seen by the media ownership as a site for promulgating capitalist values and interests. The United States can be portrayed as the leader in promoting the role and importance of capitalism. It is also a world leader in media sport. Bring these factors together and it is clear why the Americanisation tendencies found in media sport production can be highlighted and explained in terms of monopoly capitalist domination. American media sport glorifies organisation and leadership. The qualities and ambitions inherent in the Olympic motto are particularly evident in US media and sport. There is also the fascination with sporting statistics to back up such interests.

Nationalism

Sociological research has highlighted the significance of media sport as a site for nationalistic fervour and national stereotyping (Maguire, 1999; Rowe et al., 1998). Nationalities can be promoted or put down. The home country's athletes and teams are portrayed as heroes and their opposition as the villains of the piece. Sporting events can be used as a vehicle for calling for unity within a nation and for a show of allegiance. Media-led national and local campaigns can be established to encourage the public to rally to the cause. Heightened emotional attachment can sell newspapers and recruit viewers and listeners. Nostalgic memories of past triumphs can be evoked as a way of 'rallying the troops'. Whilst victories of a sporting nature (e.g. the 1966 England football World Cup success) can be revisited by the media; it is not unusual for audiences to be reminded of events of a non-sporting nature. For example, during the Euro 96 Football Championship held in England, the British media drew attention to the Spanish Armada and the Second World War as part of the build-up to the host countries' matches against Spain and Germany respectively (Maguire and Poulton, 1999). Newspaper coverage of events can involve the use of photographs and headlines to underline the stances being taken. A proliferation of national flags and colours on the sports pages (and even front pages) and emotive banner headlines may serve to direct the reader's interest and enthusiasm. These kinds of media devices can be used extensively in the coverage of events. Story lines strongly reflective of nationalist interests are developed and presented.

Patriarchy

Gender bias and inequality are evident in both sport and media. It is not unexpected therefore that patriarchy is a characteristic of sport media products. It is an area that has come under close and extensive scrutiny (see e.g. Birrell and Cole, 1994; Duncan and Hasbrook, 1988; Eastman and Billings, 2000; Theberge, 1989; Williams et al., 1986). Media sport ownership and production are male dominated; sport and media sport are important aspects of culture which help to underpin male hegemony in society (Birrell and Theberge, 1994). Of particular attention to researchers has been the way in which the media disregard and marginalise women's sport (Daddario, 1994). Female athletes and sports get little coverage in the media relative to their male counterparts. It is rare to find newspaper column inches and photographs allocated to women's sport. Few female sports are to be found in television schedules and those that are tend to be given a low profile.

Not only is the quantity of the media coverage of women's sport highly limited, but its form and quality have also to be questioned. The media are seen to stereotype, trivialise and sexualise female athletes (Duncan, 1990; Duquin, 1989; MacNeil, 1988). Sportswomen are either put down as not fitting male perceptions of appropriate femininity or they are glamorised. Attention has been drawn to photographic approaches that highlight and emphasise the physical characteristics and attractiveness of some female athletes. The narrative that is attached to the media output is of a similar nature, often with sporting prowess disregarded or played down. There are fewer high-profile female athletes, a fact reflective of the low media attention paid to women's sport in general. Those that do exist usually correspond to stereotypical images which frequently view sporting ability as a seemingly secondary consideration. An example is the extensive media coverage afforded to the Russian tennis player, Anna Kournikova: media interest has focused primarily on her physical attributes rather than her prowess on court.

The connection between gender in media sport extends beyond the treatment of female sport and athletes. There is the interest in how the media report male sport. This can encompass a concern with the treatment of violence in sport (Young and Smith, 1989) and the imagery associated with male bodies and masculinity (Messner et al., 2000; Trujillo, 1995).

Racism

The ownership control of the major global media institutions is dominated by white males. National media reflect dominant racial and ethnic interests (Tudor, 1998). The background, values and practices of the professionals working in the media and in sport are usually consistent with such concerns. The consequence of all these factors is that the sporting achievements of certain groups can be either celebrated or played down in the sports media. In a similar fashion to gender, stereotyping based on racial or ethnic lines may also be evident (Davis and Harris, 1998). For example, black male athletes may well be applauded in the media for their aggression and physicality whilst their hard work and intelligence are disregarded. In contrast, it is the latter attributes that the media assign to the white athletes. On television the performance of black athletes is frequently linked to such stereotypical attributes as natural ability and tactical naivety (Whannel, 1992: 129). Racism in the media can also be seen to reflect a kind of nationalistic prioritisation. International success by black British athletes can get played down in comparison with similar successes achieved by their white counterparts.

The above kinds of ideological influences are important considerations when examining media sport but so too are the particular professional approaches of the people who actually put together the programmes and newspapers.

The Media Professionals

The media professionals (e.g. producers, directors, commentators, reporters and camera operators exist to produce a media sport package that aims to attract, interest and excite their audience. They work in a particularly competitive environment. The emphasis is on making the product attractive and to this end it is sometimes difficult to establish where the sport starts and the media event ends. Selling a televised sports programme is the paramount concern. Often sport is sold as 'showbiz' with similar characteristics to the Hollywood 'thriller' or the weekly 'soap opera'. It is not surprising that what emerges is a distorted and packaged representation of reality rather than a neutral, objective and natural presentation. Neutrality is clearly a debatable point, as the evidence of the ideological content referred to above illustrates. The various professionals working in television and radio attempt to naturalise events for their audience. They bring to bear the skills and technical developments. They endeavour to provide atmosphere and to encourage a feeling of attachment to what is happening. They present the event as being an experience of reality. The media companies may bill sporting programmes as providing a 'ringside seat', but in many ways nothing could be further from the truth. So much is missed by not being present at the event and so much is added by the media professionals. Not all your senses are brought to bear. The media sport experience is not the same as being there live at the event.

Sociological research has suggested a number of key characteristics of the media sport product (Gruneau, 1989a; McKay and Rowe, 1987; Whannel, 1992). Each of these characteristics reflects the way in which media professionals work to a series of codes, conventions, assumptions and approaches. The outcome is to move the audience away from a sporting and towards a media experience. The media interpret happenings and provide their audience with explanations and meanings. They structure our knowledge and understanding for us. What is offered is not inevitable. Decisions are taken for the audience; you are directed what to see and read and how to make sense of it. The media professionals construct and frame the sport experience for their audience. The pre-event advertising and build-up, the nature of the presentation and its placement in the programming schedules help to provide the audience with information and points of reference to help explain what is going to happen and why it is significant. There is often harking back to previous events that are deemed to have a bearing on what is about to take place. Statistics and other historical material are presented to contextualise what is about to happen.

Media Sport Production

The ways in which meanings and messages are organised and influenced are reflected in the narrative, audio-visual and technical and presentational/packaging aspects and objectives of the media sport product. The media personnel involved are the commentators and reporters, photographers, camera operators, sound technicians, producers, editors and directors. These production aspects and individuals are central to what is, in essence, a process of event construction undertaken by the media. Increasingly, media sport programmes are being developed with the following important characteristics to the fore.

There is, first, a growing emphasis on *spectacularisation* (Gruneau, 1989a; Sewart, 1987). Reference has already been made to the growth of the big global sporting occasions. These offer opportunities to add variety, colour and impact, to enhance the entertainment element and to provide a wealth of material for the 'big build-up' to the event. The Olympics have gone far beyond the status of a sporting event. The opening ceremonies have become spectaculars tailor-made for the medium of global television.

> Box 14.1   The choreography of the opening of an Olympics: a made-for-television spectacular
>
> Spectacular stadiums and locations. A confined and defined space. Colour, banners and flags. Parades of athletes. Dancers and music. Nationalism and internationalism. Youthfulness. Oaths and speeches. Nostalgia and vision. Symbolism: a release of doves (peace), the entrance of the Olympic Torch and the lighting of the flame.

A second powerful characteristic of media sport production is that of *dramatisation*. The media professionals set up story lines around the sporting event and the individuals involved. They work to script the event so as to excite. They provide pre-event discussion and analysis. The audience's appetite and anticipation are heightened by the extent and form of the build-up that the media provides. The media endeavour to create or home in on tension, emotion and incidents. Suspense, conflict and confrontation are emphasised so as to add to the dramatic effect. Event creation has already been discussed but the media may go further than just helping in the establishment of a particular competition or the development of new sport; they may create happenings within events. For example, a head-to-head encounter between the top two track and field athletes from a particular discipline can provide the drama and personalisation on which the media thrive. Television and radio seek to heighten the dramatic impact by offering the audience a sense of immediacy. The television sport presentation aims to provide that ringside seat mentioned earlier. The media claim to get their audience as close as possible to the action: replays, camera angles and interviews are employed to enhance this effect. Stump cameras in cricket coverage get you close to the action. You too can see what it is like to face the bowling! Athletes today face a barrage of cameras and microphones the moment their event/match is over. Cameras are now even going into changing rooms.

A third aspect of media construction is the process of *personalisation* that is undertaken. Individual sportspeople are highlighted, built up and examined, often in great detail. Media sport superstars are born. Post-event/match press conferences are now a fact of life for many athletes. Both sporting and non-sporting lives come under the media microscope. Great deeds or misdemeanours of the past are resurrected and inspected. The audience are encouraged to associate with and warm to an individual. Alternatively they may be asked to view an individual in less than favourable terms. Heroes and villains are created. Interpersonal rivalries are highlighted, indeed invented by the media. The media's obsession with the relationship between Sebastian Coe and Steve Ovett is a classic example (Whannel, 1992: 140–8). An interesting example from British media sport is the footballer, Vinnie Jones, labelled by the media as a 'hard man' characterised by his uncompromising way of playing. Reference was frequently made to his past offences and colourful disciplinary record. Ironically and perhaps revealingly, Vinnie was later to find stardom as a stereotypical villain and 'hard man' in another media form, that of films.

Often criticised but much in evidence in the construction of media sport production is the use of expert analysis. The wise head with the penetrating insights to aid the lead commentator and the panel of experts to tell us what is going on and why have now become the norm in so many sports presentations. Love them or hate them, these individuals (usually former players or managers/coaches) are there to take a role in educating the members of the audience, directing them to the salient aspects of what is about to or has happened and, importantly, to structure and influence their opinions.

These various media sport construction characteristics are reinforced and enabled by the actual technical conventions and devices employed in the media world. In newspapers, sports reporting is developed and enhanced through the skills of the editors, headline writers and photo-journalists. Sports reporting lends itself to the emotive and 'catchy' headline and to the dramatic or heart-rending photograph. Often a picture can send a stronger message than words. In television, the programme director is central to making the most of the media opportunities available. They are aided in this task by skilled camera and sound work. A camera angle obtained and then selected by the director can add to the spectacle and drama of the occasion. Event location can help: the coverage of swimming events at the Barcelona Olympics in 1992 will long be remembered for the spectacular backdrop of the city. Similarly sound – imported or at the actual event – can be used to direct the attention and interest of the audience.

THE MEDIA SPORT AUDIENCE

A major question surrounding media sport is the role played by the audience. Are they knowledgeable about the media sport product to which they are exposed? Are they able to make informed choices about what they see, hear and read? One viewpoint maintains that the audience do exercise free choice and are essentially receiving the media sport products that they want. Their wishes are reflected in the output from the media companies and the professionals who work for them. The media are viewed as neutral and pluralist, reflecting the diversity in their audience and respecting the sovereignty of their consumers. A contrary viewpoint sees the media sport audience as one lacking in knowledge and experience.

Despite physical improvements in the many sports venues and the attempts by sports organisations to make the 'live' experience a pleasurable and exciting one, for an increasing number of people, their experience of elite sport is solely through the media. The 'couch spectator' has before them a wealth of media sport products to choose from, together with a growing array of gadgetry to make the involvement more interesting and personal. Interactive television, with the ability to choose highlights, to select camera angles and to have facts and figures at the press of a button, is promoted as superior to being present at the event. It can be argued that one aspect of the changing nature of this engagement with sport is a reduction in first-hand knowledge of what actually goes on at the 'live' event. The sporting knowledge base of the audience is therefore reduced and thus renders them more susceptible to the interpretations provided by the media.

MEDIA SPORT: WHERE TO NOW?

The media set fashions but are also influenced by wider social change. They are conscious of the importance of keeping their viewers, listeners and readership. Ratings and sales and linked advertising revenues are crucial and are monitored carefully. Sport, by engaging with the media, has increasingly linked itself with what is a volatile industry built powerfully on the profit motive. It is also a highly competitive industry with media sport broadcasting rights a sensitive and significant battleground. Media commitment to sport, and more particularly to certain sports or events, can change, leaving an evermore dependent world of sport vulnerable to instability. How elite commercialised sport continues to operate in such an environment will be of particular interest. Further far-reaching changes in some sports and in some events may result. Will the line between what counts as sport entertainment and what counts as media entertainment become even more blurred? The initial inroads made by media companies into direct ownership of sport may well be extended. This would fundamentally alter the balance of power within the media–sport partnership and enhance the likelihood of a growth in 'made-for-television' sport. Is the rise to prominence of WWF wrestling the shape of things to come?

Developments in the forms and technical aspects of media, principally the use of the Internet, may have a profound effect on media sport production. This is yet another unknown factor to take into account. New players in what will become an increasingly global media sport marketplace, perhaps more specialised media sport companies, may further enhance the money flowing into sport, but will the patterning still remain in terms of which sports benefit and which do not? The extension of 'pay-to-view' ways of marketing and receiving media sport products is highly likely and therefore the issues of access and equity are unlikely to disappear in the short term. How the media sport audience react to these kinds of developments will be vital. The media live or die on the success or not of their ratings or circulation. Will media sport still retain massive audiences in the years ahead or will the public discover participation and 'live' spectating to be far more satisfying? In doing so, will the audience come to recognise that what they have been receiving as media sport has moved too far away from what sport should be about? Inevitably the answers lie in the capacity of the public to influence their own media usage habits and the ability of the media, in all its forms, to keep its audiences contented with what is offered.

CHAPTER SUMMARY

» Sport and the media have both a global and a local scope of operation and are bound together in a complex network of relationships.

» Since the 1980s the value of sport to media companies and their investment in sport have grown dramatically.

» The power of the small number of major media companies raises important issues of access and equity, especially with the growth of pay-to-view sporting events.

» While the media have demonstrated a considerable capacity to influence the character and development of sport, it should be noted that there is little evidence of resistance to commodification from sports bodies or athletes.

» Sports media generally promote and reinforce a distinctive set of values associated with capitalism, nationalism, patriarchy and racism.

» The media production process emphasises spectacle, drama and personalisation.

FURTHER READING

Wenner's edited volume (1998), Gruneau et al. (1988) and Rowe (2003) provide sound general introductions to the field. Birrell and Cole (1994), Whannel (2002) and Daddario (1994) explore the relationship between media and gender. Davis and Harris (1998) and Tudor (1998) explore the interrelationship between the media and race and ethnicity, and Rowe et al. (1998) examine the impact of the media on sport and nationalism. As regards the role of the media in relation to particular sports, Maguire (1990) offers an analysis of the role of the media in the promotion of American football in the UK and Lawrence and Rowe (1986) provide a similar analysis of cricket. Finally, Young and Smith (1989) and Theberge (1989) explore the treatment of violence in sport by the media.

REFERENCES

Bernstein, A. and Blain, N. (eds) (2003) *Sport, Media, Culture: Global and Local Dimensions*. London: Frank Cass.

Birrell, S. and Cole, L.C. (eds) (1994) *Women, Sport and Culture*. Champaign, IL: Human Kinetics, pp. 245–322.

Birrell, S. and Theberge, N. (1994) 'Ideological control of women in sport', in D.M. Costa and S.R. Guthrie (eds), *Women in Sport: Interdisciplinary Perspectives*. Champaign, IL: Human Kinetics, pp. 341–60.

Daddario, G. (1994) 'Chilly scenes of the 1992 Winter Games: the mass media and the marginalisation of female athletes', *Sociology of Sport Journal*, 11 (3): 275–88.

Davis, L.R. and Harris, O. (1998) 'Race and ethnicity in US sports media', in L.A. Wenner (ed.), *Mediasport*. London: Routledge, pp. 154–69.

Duncan, M.C. (1990) 'Sports photography and sexual difference. Images of women and men in the 1984 and 1988 Olympic Games', *Sociology of Sport Journal*, 7 (1): 22–43.

Duncan, M.C. and Hasbrook, C. (1988) 'Denial of power in televised women's sport', *Sociology of Sport Journal*, 5: 1–21.

Duquin, M. (1989) 'Fashion and fitness images in women's magazine advertisements', *Arena Review*, 13: 97–109.

Eastman, S.T. and Billings, A.C. (2000) 'Sportscasting and sports reporting. The power of gender bias', *Journal of Sport and Social Issues*, 24 (2): 192–213.

Falcous, M. (1998) 'TV made it all a new game: not again! Rugby league and the case of the "Superleague"', *Occasional Papers in Football Studies*, 4–21.

Goldlust, J. (1987) *Playing for Keeps: Sport, the Media and Society*. Melbourne: Longman.

15

Organisation Theory and the Management of Sport Organisations

JOHN AMIS AND TREVOR SLACK

OVERVIEW

» *Organisation structure and design: complexity, standardisation, centralisation; structural configurations; archetypes*
» *External context: factors in the general and task environments; managing interorganisational relationships*
» *Internal context: power and politics, decision making, organisational culture*
» *Organisational change*

Sport organisations come in a variety of different forms and serve a number of functions. There are small, community-based voluntary organisations, such as local hockey or cricket clubs that play in regional leagues, and large professionally operated organisations, such as the International Olympic Committee or the Fédération Internationale de Football Association (FIFA), that stage major international events. There are football clubs such as Chelsea and Manchester United that are privately owned by immensely wealthy foreign nationals, Tottenham Hotspur that are publicly traded on the London Stock Exchange, and village teams that may be sponsored by a local pub. There are local sports shops that are owned and operated by a single individual, and nationwide chains such as JJB Sports. There are multinational apparel and equipment manufactures such as Nike and adidas, and small, independently owned consultancies. There are national governing bodies that are large and wealthy, such as the English Football Association, and others that are smaller with relatively low incomes, such as the English Surfing

Federation. Whether they are large or small, rich or poor, run by volunteers or owned by institutional shareholders, the managers of all sport organisations have to face common issues. How is the organisation going to be structured? What external groups does the organisation have to deal with? How will the organisation secure key resources? How are decisions made? How can required changes be implemented? In seeking answers to such questions, organisation theorists try to uncover ways in which managers may be able more effectively to design and operate their organisations. Our purpose in this chapter is to highlight some of the issues with which managers in the sport industry have to contend and some of the research that has provided insight into them.

ORGANISATION STRUCTURE AND DESIGN

One of the most important questions that organisation theorists address is why organisations are structured in particular ways. This is because structure will directly influence almost every facet of organisation life, from determining how key resources are obtained to how organisation workers are supervised. When we think of how an organisation is structured, a number of things may spring to mind: an organisational chart depicting the various vertical and horizontal relationships; the breakdown and allocation of different tasks to different departments; or the way in which decisions are made. While none of these is incorrect, each provides only a partial view. A useful way to think about structure is that it comprises the formal and informal interactions that make up organisation life. These interactions may include structured meetings between managers from different departments, direct instructions to a subordinate, or a casual work-related conversation in the canteen. Such interactions are seen as useful in bringing order and stability to the organisation so that it may operate effectively; however, they can also produce conflict and uncertainty.

While this is a useful starting point for helping us to understand the concept of organisation structure, it does not really assist us in trying to learn how and why sport organisations are structured differently. To gain insight into this, we need some way to assess the structures of organisations that will in turn allow us to make comparisons. The most common approach that has been used, in both mainstream organisation theory (e.g. Miller and Dröge, 1986; Pugh et al., 1969) and in the study of sport organisations (e.g. Amis and Slack, 1996; Amis et al., 2004a; Frisby, 1986; Kikulis et al., 1995a; Slack and Hinings, 1994), involves an assessment of the structural dimensions of complexity, formalisation and centralisation.

Complexity

The complexity of an organisation is determined by the degree to which the work that is carried out is broken down and assigned to different subunits or individual specialists. This is a process that is known as differentiation. Differentiation, carried out to improve the efficiency of an organisation, may be horizontal, vertical or spatial. Normally, the greater the level of differentiation, the more complex the organisation is to operate because communication, co-ordination of activities and supervision tend to become more complicated.

Horizontal differentiation may occur through either specialisation or departmentalisation. Specialisation refers to the employment of individual specialists to carry out specific tasks, such as the employment of position coaches to work with the England rugby team's forwards, backs and kickers, while departmentalisation occurs when necessary tasks within an organisation are assigned to specific units, such as marketing, finance and distribution. The degree of vertical differentiation in an organisation is usually indicated by the number of hierarchical levels. Spatial differentiation occurs when different parts of an organisation are located in different geographic areas, as is the case with the 59 David Lloyd Leisure Clubs scattered across the UK. Trying to co-ordinate activities among a group of subunits that may be spread around a country, a continent or, as is often the case in today's global economy, the world, all adds to the complexity of the manager's task.

Formalisation

The degree of formalisation in an organisation refers to the extent to which policies, procedures, rules and regulations stipulate the ways in which organisation members should act. Formalisation is usually directly related to complexity as the more complex an organisation, the greater the need for formalised co-ordinating mechanisms. Formalisation works as a method of control by reducing the need for direct supervision. As well as varying among different organisations, the level of formalisation will also vary by department and hierarchical position. For example, the Nike Category Product Teams that move a new athletic shoe from the initial idea through to the marketing of the final product operate in a much less formalised environment than the production staff that actually manufacture the shoes in Asian factories. Because of the nature of their tasks, the latter's roles will be clearly laid out in company and subcontractor regulations while the former will have little more than broad job descriptions. Similarly, new Nike Chief Executive Officer Mark Parker, required to make unusual or even unique decisions on a day-to-day basis, will have very little formalisation of his role. By contrast, a NikeTown shop assistant will have clearly defined procedures outlining every facet of his/her job, from how to interact with customers to the length of time that can be spent on a lunch break. Determining how formalised different roles should be within the organisation is thus another important management role.

Centralisation

Centralisation refers to the locus of decision making within an organisation. An organisation in which senior executives make most decisions is said to be centralised; one in which decision-making authority is delegated to lower-level staff is thought of as decentralised. Despite the apparent simplicity of this definition, attempts to determine whether or not an organisation is centralised have proved difficult. Consider the case of JJB Sports retail outlets. On the one hand, store managers are given autonomy to run their stores as they see fit; on the other, they must comply with policies and procedures regarding corporate branding and image, store layout and pricing. In other words, despite the appearance of autonomy, the nature and scope of the decisions that a manager can make are quite tightly constrained.

However, this uncertainty should not obscure the basic rationale for operating with a centralised or decentralised decision-making structure. A more centralised operation allows a small group of what are typically the most experienced members of the organisation to make decisions in a way that is co-ordinated and, because it avoids any potential duplication of activities, it can also be more cost effective. By contrast, decentralisation allows decisions to be made more rapidly in response to changes at a local level. It also helps motivate employees who feel that they are having an impact on the success of the organisation, and may help them prepare for management careers of their own. Finally, and perhaps most fundamentally for a large organisation, it prevents senior executives from becoming overwhelmed with information that they are unable to process because of cognitive, time and resource limitations.

Organisational Design

One of the most important decisions that senior managers of any organisation have to make is how the organisation should be designed. Essentially, design refers to the ways in which work activities are grouped together and reporting relationships established. The design of many sport organisations is very straightforward. Consider, for example, the sport shop owned and operated by a single individual with two or three staff members working in the shop, or a village cricket club with an elected committee consisting of the chairperson, secretary, treasurer and club captains running two or three teams. Such a design, termed a *simple structure* by Mintzberg (1979), is characterised by a single individual or small group making decisions with other organisation members performing a variety of tasks as needed. Co-ordination and communication are achieved by *direct supervision.*

As an organisation increases in size, design becomes a more complicated issue as mechanisms need to be put in place that facilitate the effective co-ordination of individuals performing related and unrelated tasks. The *functional design* has traditionally proved very popular with organisations in a wide variety of industries. Here individuals are grouped according to their specialist expertise to create functional departments. For example, the Rugby Football Union (RFU) in England includes commercial, legal, human resource, communications, finance, community rugby, stadium and performance departments. These departments are sometimes differentiated even further – for example, the commercial department has specialist sponsorship, merchandising and licensing, rugby store, rugby museum, ticketing and corporate hospitality subunits (Rugby Football Union, 2005). The collection of specialists in close proximity allows for a development of expertise in the organisation that can lead to innovations and economies of scale in dealing with frequently occurring issues that would otherwise be very difficult to attain. The main downside is that a functional emphasis can hamper communication across departments resulting in delays in identifying and dealing with cross-functional issues, a focus on departmental goals at the expense of broader organisational objectives, and a delayed response to environmental changes and particular market needs. Thus, this design works best in stable, predictable operating contexts.

The *divisional design*, in contrast to the functional design, collects individuals together who are working on particular products or services. This design tends to be prominent among large organisations with multiple product lines, particularly those operating in different countries. For example, Octagon, a company that carries out sport marketing, athlete and entertainment personality representation, television and new media production and rights sales, and music and entertainment management and production, is predominantly organised geographically with 60 offices in 24 countries. There is a senior executive team that determines global strategy and close co-ordination across the activities of different offices to allow for the maximum support of clients – such as Anna Kournikova, Paula Radcliffe, Andrew Murray, the English Premier League and Australian Cricket Board. However, business activities are broken down predominantly by geographic area. Each office offers a specific array of services considered most appropriate for that location, and handles staffing and other management functions (recruitment, client relationships, etc.) accordingly (personal communication, Octagon Associate, 16 July 2003; www.octagon.com). Such a design can be very effective in responding to local requirements in a timely and detailed manner, and is thus often considered to have utility in dynamic environments characterised by local idiosyncratic variations. However, it is often inevitable that inefficiencies occur as functions are duplicated across offices and many of the scale economies offered under the functional design are lost.

The *matrix design* (Box 15.1) is an attempt to realise the advantages of both the functional and divisional forms. Under this arrangement, distinct product or geographic divisions are intersected by functional departments in a lattice-like arrangement. The intent is to allow the collection of individuals working together in specific areas to maximise opportunities for innovation and environmental responsiveness while providing functional support across areas that are required in each division. The dual authority structure can lead to conflict and confusion among organisation members and thus requires strong co-ordination mechanisms and, frequently, much time spent in meetings to clarify areas of responsibility.

Box 15.1   Matrix design

The matrix design is well illustrated by Finnish company Amer Sport, a firm that employs 7,500 people around the world and reported pre-tax profits in 2004 of 100.5 million euros. While you may not have heard of Amer Sport, you will certainly know one or more of its major sporting brands: Wilson – retailers of sporting equipment that includes golf clubs, tennis and squash racquets and basketballs; Atomic – skis and snowboards; Salomon – a range of outdoor sporting gear that includes skis, surfboards and clothing; Precor – fitness equipment; and Suunto – sports watches and navigational equipment. The company is currently organised under a structure that has five divisions that control different product lines: Wilson Sporting Goods, Winter Sports, Fitness, Sports Instruments and Salomon (acquired in 2005 from adidas). These are supported by Business Planning and Control, Treasury and Investor Relations, Supply Chain Development, Human Resources, Legal Affairs and Information Technology Departments. Clearly, given the size of an organisation that operates all over the world, each division has control over many of the functional activities required to operate effectively, but the centralised departments provide an overlay of expertise and consistency of approach that can lead to cost and quality benefits across the company. (Based on information from www.amersports.com, other company websites, and personal communication with Julie Jasieniecki, Wilson Team Sports, 27 January 2006)

As industries have become increasingly competitive (e.g. D'Aveni, 1994), so managers and scholars have searched for other ways of organising that will permit greater levels of innovation and responsiveness. Increasingly popular is the *team-based design*. Rather than emphasis being accorded to vertical organising structures in which, for example, individuals are grouped together in functional silos, the team-based design favours the creation of relatively small teams that consist of members from different functional areas who often assume responsibility for a product from the initial idea through to the final product launch. This flat management structure allows different sources of expertise to be applied to problems throughout the design and production process as they arise in a rapid manner, thus reducing the time taken to launch new products and services, something that is often vital in fast-moving, highly competitive industries. Although part of a larger organisation, the Nike Category Product Teams referred to earlier provide a good example. The need for innovation dictates a flexibility of approach that results in empowered team members, including designers, developers and marketing specialists, having broad access to necessary information and an extensive amount of operational latitude. With no rigid hierarchy, co-ordination is achieved by mutual adjustment (Mintzberg, 2003) whereby individuals in the group try to accommodate each other's needs. While potentially highly productive, the need for frequent meetings and the likelihood of conflict arising between individuals working closely together with low levels of formalisation does require team leaders with exceptional social and facilitation skills if the team is to operate effectively.

While the team-based design typically involves individuals employed by the same company physically meeting together in the same place, technological advancements allowing for straightforward and inexpensive electronic, video and audio communication have allowed for the creation of a *virtual network design*. With this approach, it is possible to bring individuals together to work on a project even though they may be geographically dispersed; the group can then be disbanded when the project ends. One example might be the creation of a team to host a major sporting event. For most of the period leading up to the event, it may be possible to have workers in different specialist areas working remotely and 'meeting' perhaps once or twice a week via audio, video or Internet conferencing. Shortly before the event, it may be necessary to bring people physically to the location to finish the project and run the event. The advantage of the virtual network design is that it allows 'best in the world' experts to be gathered together to work on a project without going to the long-term expense of having to relocate individuals or making permanent appointments. The potential drawback is that there may be little loyalty to the 'organisation' and no development of a common culture to bind members together. Again, there is a heavy emphasis on the team leader to have the social and technical skills required to make the team successful.

In taking an holistic view of organisation design, we are adopting a *configurational* approach. While this approach has been favoured by several researchers (e.g. Meyer et al., 1993; Miller and Friesen, 1984), the work of Mintzberg (1979, 2003) has been particularly influential. In an updating on his original ideas, Mintzberg (2003) argues that organisations can be conceptualised as consisting of six basic parts: the *strategic apex* consists of senior management charged with making key organisational decisions; the *operating core* comprises the individuals who do the work of the organisation; the *middle line* consists of middle managers who connect the operating core with the strategic apex; the *technostructure* is made up of technical staff who ensure that organisational outputs conform to certain desired standards (e.g. engineers and planners); the *support staff* carry out activities not directly related to the output of the organisation, but that are necessary to allow it to function effectively (e.g. cleaning, maintenance and cooking). The sixth component is the organisation's *ideology*, the traditions, values and beliefs that bind the organisation together in pursuit of a common purpose.

Mintzberg (2003) also offers seven configurations that he suggests constitute particular designs to which all types of organisations will likely cohere. It is important to note that these are ideal types, and thus while they will resemble real organisations, they are also unlikely to be found in their pure forms. The *simple structure*, or *entrepreneurial organisation*, as noted above, is widely found in the sport and leisure industries. Here the *strategic apex* is the dominant part of the organisation with co-ordination predominantly carried out through *direct supervision*. The *professional organisation* places a heavy emphasis on the work of a professionally trained *operating core*. Co-ordination arises predominantly from the *standardisation of skills* acquired during professional training. Sport law practices, sport marketing firms and physiotherapy clinics are all examples of this type of design. The *machine organisation* is most commonly associated with large-scale, mass production firms such as the Slazenger factory in Bataan in the Philippines. With a need for highly consistent outputs – every one of Slazenger's tennis balls is, after all, expected to perform in precisely the same way whether used at the Wimbledon Championships or on a school tennis court – co-ordination is achieved by having highly *standardised work processes* that hence place a heavy emphasis on the engineers in the *technostructure* responsible for calibrating and maintaining the mass production machinery.

Mintzberg's (2003) *diversified organisation* is exemplified by David Lloyd Leisure. Although each of the clubs operates somewhat autonomously, they must all deliver a similar experience to club members no matter where the club is located. This consistency of experience is achieved by the primary co-ordination mechanism across the organisation being a well-understood *standardisation of outputs*. The key role here is played by the *middle line* of the organisation, in the case of David Lloyd Leisure the general managers of each individual club who have responsibility for delivering similar facilities, services and atmosphere irrespective of where the club is located. The fifth configuration offered by Mintzberg is the *innovative organisation*. Typically operating in dynamic environments that place a heavy requirement on rapid innovation, this type of organisation is characterised by the coming together of individuals with different but complementary sets of skills who operate in highly flexible teams that co-ordinate their activities through a process of *mutual adjustment*. Although part of a larger organisation, the Nike Category Product Teams in which experts from different functional areas come together in a cross-functional team to take responsibility for a product from the initial idea through design, manufacturing and marketing constitute a good example of this design.

Co-ordination in *missionary organisations* takes place via shared values that underpin a *standardisation of norms*. Such organisations tend to be small with low levels of formalisation and complexity. They usually contain people who care passionately about their organisation, as is the case with some small voluntary sport organisations. Finally, the *political organisation* tends to occur in situations that are highly conflictual, often during periods of transition, and when individuals in different subunits are vying for scarce resources. These organisations tend to be characterised by a great deal of political activity and coalition building; they are frequently temporary configurations with no primary co-ordinating mechanism.

While Mintzberg's configurations are based on conceptual ideal types and constitute a typology, other classifications have been based on empirical data to form taxonomies. Hinings and Greenwood's (1988; Greenwood and Hinings, 1988, 1993) uncovering of archetypes among British local government organisations constitute one such exemplar. Another, by Kikulis et al. (1992, 1995a), delineated three archetypes that featured prominently among Canadian national sport organisations (NSOs): the Kitchen Table, Boardroom and Executive Office. We use this work to illustrate the variations in design that can be found in similar types of sport organisations.

The *Kitchen Table* archetype has been the traditional design of Canada's NSOs, and many others around the world. Run by a group of dedicated volunteers these NSOs receive little government funding, relying instead on membership fees and fund-raising for their financing. Because they are run by volunteers on an almost ad hoc basis, Kitchen Table-type organisations generally have a low level of complexity and low levels of formalisation. Decision making is highly centralised with the volunteer Board of Directors, located at the top of the organisational hierarchy, making virtually all strategic and operational decisions.

Those organisations that adhere to a *Boardroom* archetype place more emphasis on the performances of elite-level athletes, although catering for the development of lower-level athletes who just compete domestically is still seen as a key part of the organisation's role. While volunteers retain control of this type of organisation, complexity is influenced by the presence of professional staff who take care of day-to-day operations. With the need to co-ordinate professional staff and a greater number of activities, Boardroom-type organisations are generally more formalised than those with a Kitchen Table design. They are, however, still highly centralised with decision making continuing to remain almost entirely with the volunteer Board of Directors assisted by professional staff.

Sport organisations that have an *Executive Office* design focus almost exclusively on the preparation of elite-level athletes for international competition. In order to achieve this, these organisations have to engage the services of many more professional coaching and administrative staff, they set up High-Performance Centres, and they take part in more international competitions at various age-group levels. As a result, Executive Office-type organisations are much more complex and formalised than either of the other two archetypes. Although a volunteer Board of Directors is retained, most strategic and operational decisions are devolved to the professional staff in what is a much more decentralised structure.

The work cited above is useful in showing us how and why different sport organisations may have different structures. Whichever design is adopted, it is important for managers to adopt a structure that fits the external and internal contexts within which the organisation has to operate, considerations to which we now turn.

EXTERNAL CONTEXT

The external environment in which sport organisations operate can be broken down into two parts. On the one hand, we can think of characteristics of the *general* (or *distal*) *environment* that may not have an impact on a specific organisation, but will indirectly affect an entire industry, such as the rate of inflation or health and safety legislation. On the other hand, there are factors in the *task* (or *proximal*) *environment* that will have immediate and direct consequences for an individual organisation, such as the actions of a competitor or supplier. It is also easy to forget that recent technological, political, social and economic developments have resulted in all of the factors that we consider are impacted to a greater or lesser extent by our location in a global context. Managers, employees and customers, for example, may have to contend with the outsourcing of jobs to a factory overseas, as exemplified by the closing of the Slazenger tennis ball factory in Barnsley following the decision to shift manufacturing to Bataan in the Philippines (*Guardian*, 2002), the ability to purchase products directly from overseas vendors via the Internet, or direct satellite television feeds that can cross national borders (see the case of Guinness, for example, in Amis, 2003). Thus, while considering each of the environmental aspects below, it is important to consider the variation in their immediate (firm-level) and more general (industry-level) effects, and also the impact that broader global forces will have on each aspect in turn. Again, these will vary by organisation, industry and national context.

When attempting to conceptualise the environmental forces with which an organisation must contend, there are 10 sectors that we can consider (Daft, 2004). Although we address each of these in turn, they are not all discrete: changes in one sector will likely affect some of the others. The *industry sector* comprises the number of competitors, level of competition for customers, and presence of acceptable substitute products or services. The *raw materials sector* can be considered to include any inputs required to deliver a product or service. These might include traditionally considered component constituents (e.g. rubber or leather), but may also be broadened out to consider physical geography (e.g. a mountain range or beach) or weather (e.g. level of snowfall or days of sunshine) depending on the nature of the organisation. The *human resources sector* includes the availability of sufficiently skilled workers, the number of competing employers, and the extent to which workers are unionised. The *financial resources sector* may include the availability of bank loans for an entrepreneurial firm or, as in the case of Chelsea Football Club, the willingness of a private benefactor to support financially a particular strategic plan. Gerrard (2005) provides an assessment of the ways in which the securing of resources – notably human and financial – impacts on sporting and financial performances. Drawing on data from teams playing in the English Premier League between 1998 and 2002, Gerrard develops a resource-utilisation model and examines how differential arrays of resources and strategic approaches affect organisational performances.

The *market sector* comprises current and potential customers. A major outcome of the influences apparent in this sector constitutes the varying bundles of product features and prices that competing companies use to try to attract customers. The *technology sector* may involve advances in electronic communications, manufacturing or basic science that can act radically to alter a firm's operation – consider, for example, the effect of carbon fibre materials on tennis racquet and golf club manufacturing. The *economic sector* concerns broad characteristics such as interest and inflation rates or levels of unemployment. The *legal–political sector* is concerned with the effects on organisations of different political ideologies and legislation. The former may affect corporate regulatory frameworks, levels of taxation and local public investment policies. The latter covers national and European legislation that potentially includes requirements concerning health and safety, child protection (e.g. Brackenridge and Kirby, 1997), stadium safety (e.g. Taylor Report, 1990) and athletes' freedom to work across Europe under the 'Bosman ruling' (e.g. McArdle, 2000). The *socio-cultural sector* captures demographic characteristics, (sporting) trends evident in particular markets, and the prominence of particular values and beliefs (e.g. religion, democracy, sexism). The *international sector* can include the presence of direct competitors from overseas, understanding of local cultural norms, and exchange rates.

The 10 sectors outlined above will have different levels of importance for different organisations in different industrial sectors, and will thus feature differently in the day-to-day (task environment) or more long-term (general environment) strategic planning and operative considerations. For example, the market, human resources and raw materials sectors will likely have a direct impact on day-to-day operations, and can also be somewhat directly affected by managerial decisions, such as the altering of prices, raising of wages or the finding of alternative suppliers. By contrast, the effects of the economic, legal-political and socio-cultural sectors will be more indirect and less susceptible to influence by individual managers.

A feature of all organisations, and an indication of the importance attributed to the sectors described above, concerns a common desire of managers to reduce levels of *environmental uncertainty*. The greater the uncertainty in a situation, the more difficult it is for managers to make decisions such as how to allocate resources, whether to hire additional personnel or what hours a facility should be open. Managers therefore try very hard to minimise the uncertainty that they have to face. One way in which they attempt to do this is through the creation of *interorganisational relationships* (IORs).

Interorganisational Relationships

When one considers the vast field of organisation theory, one quickly encounters a wide variety of perspectives that attempt to explain how and why organisations function in particular ways. Some of these (e.g. structural contingency theory, population ecology theory, institutional theory) are highly *deterministic* and position managers as acting and reacting within constraints imposed by the external environment. Other approaches (e.g. strategic choice theories, network theories, resource dependence theories) are much more *voluntaristic* and hold that managers are in fact able, to some degree, to shape the environments within which they operate. Irrespective of the approach adopted, it is undeniable that organisational survival depends upon being able to secure access to required resources, and that this in turn requires interacting with other organisations. Thus, in this part of the chapter we draw on insights provided by resource dependence and network theories to help us further understand organisational function.

The foundational work in *resource dependence theory* is Pfeffer and Salancik's (1978) *The External Control of Organisations: a Resource Dependence Perspective*. According to Pfeffer and Salancik (1978: 2), 'the key to organizational survival is the ability to acquire and maintain resources'. This must be carried out in an environment that is constantly changing and comprised of other organisations, some of which are hostile. Thus, whether it is the securing of English Premier League (EPL) football rights for Sky Television at a time when Sky was haemorrhaging money and in urgent need of new subscribers, or a contract agreement between a fitness instructor and a leisure centre, at some point an organisation's survival depends upon its senior managers being able to secure an adequate supply of critical resources. This usually requires that an organisation enter into agreements with other organisations that can supply those resources.

However, any agreement to exchange resources results in some form of dependence of one organisation on another. As dependence on other organisations increases, so the focal organisation becomes increasingly vulnerable to the actions of those resource providers, and suffers a corresponding loss of autonomy. Thus, managers seek to reduce, as much as possible, the dependence of their organisation on others, while also attempting to exploit those situations in which other organisations are dependent upon them (Aldrich, 1979; Pfeffer and Salancik, 1978). Such considerations raise the role of power in IORs. Power is directly proportional to a focal organisation's control of scarce resources, the criticality of those resources to other organisations' operation and survival, and the extent to which alternative suppliers are available (Pfeffer and Salancik, 1978). Thus, if, for example, EPL football is seen as vital to the survival of Sky Television, the EPL has a great deal of power in the relationship because the resource is viewed as critical, it is the sole distributor of television rights, and any substitute products (e.g. from lower leagues or abroad) are viewed as markedly inferior. The power of the EPL is further increased if several rival television networks also want to bid for the rights. However, if no other television company emerges as a viable bidder, or if the EPL declines in popularity among Sky's viewers, then the power of the EPL, reflected in the value of the broadcast rights, markedly declines.

Effective managers do not simply sit back and let the environment dictate how they should *react*; instead they will attempt to *enact* (Weick, 1995) their environments; that is, shape them in order to produce more desirable operating conditions. Hillman et al. (2000) demonstrated one way of doing this by noting how the composition of Boards of Directors of airline companies altered following deregulation in order to fit better the changed resource dependence needs of the firms. Kikulis et al. (1992, 1995a) and Amis et al. (2002, 2004b) found evidence of similar-level changes as Canadian NSOs moved towards Executive Office archetypal designs that favoured Boards of Directors comprised of members with specific professional expertise and the ability to link with valued external partners, rather than the previously emphasised time-rich enthusiasts.

What is apparent in the above discussion is that organisations are *open systems* that are integrally connected to other organisations in their environments. Further, different organisations place inconsistent and even competing demands on a focal organisation (Pfeffer & Salancik, 1978). Therefore, as Armstrong-Doherty (1996) demonstrated in her examination of Canadian university athletic departments, the management of relationships with organisations that control scarce resources is a vital managerial skill. While some such relationships can be governed by contracts, there is a convincing body of literature that argues that organisations that develop more extensive relationships, such as in the form of *joint ventures, strategic alliances* or some other form of co-operative venture, can take advantage of otherwise unattainable opportunities. Cousens and Slack (1996; see also Cousens et al., 2001), for example, highlighted the ways in which alliances have developed among professional sport leagues, television companies and sponsors in the United States.

In addition to the formation of alliances and partnerships, organisations exist in social networks that have a major impact on their performance. In other words, it is insufficient to simply consider IORs as simple, standalone agreements; instead, we must understand the location of an organisation in a network of other organisations (Aldrich, 1979; Pfeffer and Salancik, 1978).

Uzzi (1996, 1997) offers a particularly useful insight into the development of networks, their potential utility and also their possible liability. The basic tenet of this approach is that embedded exchanges based on the development of trust and personal ties lead to decreased costs associated with policing the agreement, a greater exchange of tacit and proprietary knowledge, and often a willingness to forgo greater profits in order to improve the strength of the network. These, in turn, can lead to speedier exchanges of information, relaxed transactional monitoring, greater understanding of each other's businesses, and an increased desire to engage in business with network members (Uzzi, 1997). Within the network, two of the most important factors in determining which organisations are most advantaged are the degree of centrality, or strategic importance, to the functioning of the network; and the ability to act as bridges between otherwise poorly connected or disconnected organisations (for a comprehensive discussion of organisational networks, see Gulati et al., 2002). By essentially controlling the flow of knowledge and resources across the network, such organisations are vital to the effective functioning of other network members. For example, Wolfe et al. (2002) map a 'sports network' demonstrating resource flows and dominant positions of power. Their model suggests that satellite television companies are holding a central position because of their ability to control resource flows across the network. In fact, the dominant position that media corporations play in their extended networks (e.g. Thompson, 2003), particularly in the sport industry (e.g. Andrews, 2003; Cousens and Slack, 1996, 2005), is starting to emerge.

While tightly bound networks with members engaged in multiple ventures together can be very effective because of the build-up of trust and mutual understanding, there are also potential vulnerabilities. There can be problems in a well-developed network when a core member leaves (Uzzi, 1997) or when some external shock, such as a supply shortage of a critical resource to a key member, hits the network (Provan and Milward, 1995). A third problem can arise when network partners continually seek to do business with each other, leading to the possibility of a lack of required new information coming into the network (Uzzi, 1997). Thus, those organisations that bring new knowledge into a network through their linkages to other domains are particularly valued.

INTERNAL CONTEXT

While organisational design and the external environment constitute imperatives that are important for managers to understand, it is also necessary to have a good appreciation of issues that arise within the organisational context. We consider three of the most prominent of these here.

Power and Politics

According to Weber (1968), power can be defined as the ability of individuals and groups to affect organisational outcomes despite resistance from disaffected parties. Power arises as a consequence of structural differentiation that results in the creation of different subunits with different roles, objectives and interests. Thus, built into any organisation is a structure of advantage and disadvantage (Walsh et al., 1981). According to Hickson et al. (1971), power arises as a consequence of: (a) a subunit's ability to cope with critical uncertainties or contingencies; (b) the unique or non-substitutable capabilities of a subunit; and (c) the importance of the contingency to the functioning of the organisation. Crucially, power depends on all three aspects occurring simultaneously. In other words, because of their position in the organisation, some groups will have more power than others. Thus, in innovation-intensive industries – such as athletic shoe or video game production – in which competitive advantage depends on the frequent creation of new products, a research and design department might well accrue more power than other organisation subunits ostensibly at the same hierarchical level. Power, in this respect, is thus seen more as a property of the embedded social relationship resulting from the differentiation of labour than as a personal characteristic (Hardy and Clegg, 1999).

While the use of power is often overt and direct, more critical views call for a broader understanding of the use and outcomes of power within organisations. For example, power can be used to set the boundaries within which discussions and decision making take place (Bacharach and Baratz, 1962). Setting and circulating an agenda for a meeting, for example, can shape a context for discussion that renders a particular outcome more likely, and may even prevent consideration of some issues. Lukes (1974) goes further with his identification of the ways in which power can be used to convince others to believe what one wants them to believe. In this respect, power is most effective, and perhaps most insidious, when others are unaware of it being used (Lukes, 1974; Ranson et al., 1980).

In addition to having an insight into the bases of power within an organisation, it is also important that sport managers appreciate the ways in which power is utilised. The process of mobilising power has been described by Pettigrew (1973) as the engagement in political behaviour to achieve otherwise unattainable outcomes. There are a number of techniques that can be engaged in to achieve political ends. Coalitions can be built with influential individuals, outside experts can be brought in to give a supposedly objective assessment of a situation, and attempts can be made to control who has access to what information. Each of these strategies is present in Long et al.'s (2004) investigation of a decision to attempt to secure an exclusive sponsorship deal by the leaders of a Canadian university's athletic department. The employment of an external consultant, feelings of powerlessness among many actors within the department, formation of coalitions in an attempt to influence the decision process, and lack of prior guidelines into how such decisions should be made are all illustrative of how the distribution of power and subsequent use of political behaviour shape organisational functioning.

Hinings and Greenwood (1988) hold that the mobilisation of power depends upon the degree to which it is concentrated or dispersed. A concentrated power structure usually precipitates action while power that is dispersed across a wider range of individuals and/or subunits usually results in inertia because it is much harder to get people with different interests and objectives to agree on a course of action. Amis et al. (2004b) built on this thesis to demonstrate that change in Canadian NSOs required that power be relinquished by the volunteer Board of Directors to professional staff such that power then became concentrated in the hands of professional staff or shared between volunteers and professionals with similar objectives. By contrast, those NSOs in which power remained concentrated in the hands of volunteers were able to resist strong institutional pressures for change. A more general investigation of the ways in which power distributions in voluntary sport organisations (VSOs) influence perceptions of board performance was carried out on Australian VSOs by Hoye and Cuskelly (2003). Hoye and Cuskelly uncovered a wide variety of patterns of power within VSOs, and suggested that distributions of power were strongly correlated with perceptions of effective and ineffective board performance.

While the sources of power outlined above are located within organisation structures, they can be amplified by individual bases of power (Box 15.2). French and Raven (1960) highlighted five of these. *Legitimate power* stems from the formal authority that a manager may have based on his/her position in the organisational hierarchy. *Coercive power* involves using a threat of a negative outcome if an individual refuses to comply. By contrast, the allocation of desired benefits in return for compliance is termed *reward power*. *Expert power* arises when the instructions of an individual are followed because he/she is perceived as having technical expertise in an applicable area. Finally, *referent power* is derived from charismatic appeal.

Box 15.2   The mobilisation of bases of power

Sack and Johnson (1996) provide a useful insight into the ways in which bases of power can be mobilised through political behaviour in their analysis of the process of bringing the Volvo International Tennis Tournament to New Haven, Connecticut. They showed how a coalition between various actors in the New Haven region, including Yale University and the New Haven Downtown Council, was formed, subjected to various stresses and strains, and ultimately overcame vocal opposition from local residents to bring the tournament to New Haven. One of the main outcomes of the study was the way in which the main policy decision to move the tournament to New Haven was made 'by a small group of elites well before the general public became involved'. Thus, through the skilful use of political behaviour, those who favoured bringing the tournament to New Haven were able to manage the decision-making process so effectively as to render the outcome almost a *fait accompli* before any active resistance could be organised.

Decision Making

It is clear from the Volvo International Tennis Tournament case that gaining an understanding of how decisions are made is important for any sport manager. In fact, decision making has been described as 'the most crucial part of managerial work' (Beyer, 1981: 181). The most dominant approach to decision making in the managerial literature, and the most intuitively appealing, is the rational model. Proponents of this approach view decision making as a linear series of steps consisting of a recognition of the need for action, diagnosis of the problem, a search for solutions, evaluation of various alternatives, choice of the optimal solution and implementation of the selected choice (Miller et al., 1999). The apparent logic behind the process has led to a belief that decisions can be represented quantitatively. For example, Boronico and Newbert (1999) developed a stochastic model to determine various probabilities of the likelihood of certain play sequences leading to the scoring of a touchdown in different American football game scenarios. Using six sets each of 50 simulated plays, Boronico and Newbert's model comprehensively outperformed a college football coach.

Despite the intuitive appeal of the rational linear approach, and its apparent utility in closed situations such as the American football example above, it has been widely criticised. The earliest critique, and one of the most comprehensive, was made by Simon (1945) in his classic *Administrative Behavior*. Though dated, the insights that Simon provides are as pertinent today as they were in the 1940s. Simon argued that decision makers are limited by the complexity of the organisations in which they work, by their own cognitive abilities and emotions, and by the time that they are able to devote to any one decision. Issues are often unclear, outcomes frequently cannot be precisely determined, individuals may disagree about what constitutes a successful outcome, and time and resource constraints will often limit the amount of analysis that can go into a particular decision. Consequently, decision makers have to operate under what Simon (1945) called *bounded rationality*. Rather than search for the optimal solution, decision makers select the first available solution that meets certain minimum criteria in a process known as *satisficing*.

Simon (1945) acknowledged that some decisions that occur frequently and conform to established protocols – programmed decisions – may lend themselves to a more rational approach, as exemplified in the work by Boronico and Newbert (1999). However, non-programmed decisions, those that are rare or unique, are frequently the most important strategic decisions that have to be made in an organisation and have few if any guidelines within which decision makers can operate. Furthermore, most decisions are not made in a neutral environment; rather, they are frequently characterised, and determined, not by a logical and reasoned debate but by underlying power distributions in which actors who strive for scarce resources seek to block the objectives of others, and will push for alternatives not necessarily beneficial for the organisation (Miller et al., 1999; Morgan, 1997). The more important and far reaching a decision, the more likely it is that the process will be characterised by the mobilisation and utilisation of power bases. Consequently, there is widespread agreement among theorists that key strategic decisions are not made in a traditional rational manner (e.g. Cohen et al., 1972; Cray et al., 1991; Lindblom, 1959; Quinn, 1980).

Several of the studies on Canadian NSOs have endorsed this view in which the decision-making process is often captured within a larger contest for organisational control between professional staff and volunteers (Amis et al., 2004b; Kikulis et al., 1995a; Thibault et al., 1991). Hill and Kikulis (1999) found that struggle also characterised the way in which decisions were made in western Canadian university athletic departments. In a far cry from the neat rational approach, Hill and Kikulis (1999: 41) observed that decision making was a 'complicated association among the concepts of politicality, complexity, and rules of the game; the actions of interest groups; and the diversity of issues that ... [influence] the direction and pace of the decision process'. In other words, rather than individual decision makers working systematically through a variety of options and selecting the outcome which most benefits the organisation, there are other factors which impact on the decision. These include individual and subunit goals that are frequently accorded greater importance than the success of the organisation as a whole.

Organisational Culture

The culture (or cultures) of an organisation, in much the same way as the culture of a country, region or town, comprises those things that help to provide an organisation with its meaning and identity. Culture can encompass a variety of things: beliefs, language, ideology, traditions, myths, rituals and shared understandings – in short, anything that contributes to the way in which members come to conceive of their organisation.

The interest in organisational culture can be traced back to the 1970s and, in particular, American managers' and theorists' desire to uncover the characteristics of Japanese firms that were making them more successful than their Western rivals. Much of this success was put down to differences between the cultures of Japanese and Western societies and firms. This has led to various views about how culture affects the ways in which organisations function.

Frequently, the origin of an organisation's culture lies in the expression of particular values by an influential founder that ultimately permeate through the organisation. Consider, for example, the influence of Richard Branson at the Virgin Group, Bill Gore at W.L. Gore & Associates, Phil Knight at Nike or Yvon Chouinard at Patagonia. Schein (1990) argues that owners and/or other influential leaders create primary embedding mechanisms for culture. These constitute the issues that leaders pay attention to, their reaction to critical incidents and modelling of particular behaviours, the allocation of rewards and the establishment of criteria for punishment and exclusion. Secondary reinforcement mechanisms can comprise the design and structure of an organisation or sub-unit, the establishment of systems and processes, the physical design of buildings, formal mission statements, and stories, myths, legends and symbols (Schein, 1990).

A number of scholars have emphasised the potential integrating role of organisational culture (see e.g. Meyerson and Martin, 1987; Schein, 1990, 1996). Proponents of this approach have suggested that some leaders, such as those cited above, create strong cultures that reflect their own values and ultimately lead to a harmonious operation. McDonald (1991), in one of the best illustrations of the integrationist approach, described how many of the primary and secondary embedding mechanisms outlined by Schein (1990) were utilised in order to rapidly foster organisational commitment among staff and volunteers working for the Los Angeles Olympic Organising Committee. While McDonald cited evidence of department cultures emerging, these were never really conflictual and were always viewed as subservient to the overall culture of the organisation.

Rather than viewing culture as some kind of monolithic all-embracing concept, and trying to determine what constitutes organisational *culture*, some researchers have argued that organisations are in fact made up of multiple *subcultures*. For example, proponents of the differentiation perspective (e.g. Meyerson and Martin, 1987) have argued for a less ethereal approach that also includes consideration of how more mundane things such as pay, organisational hierarchies, and policies and procedures manuals affect the culture of the organisation (Martin and Frost, 1999). The differentiation perspective embraces difference and acknowledges conflicts of interest. While there has been very little work that has explored the existence of subcultures within sport organisations, there is evidence that they exist. Amis et al. (1995), for example, highlighted the way that distinctive groups emerged in several Canadian NSOs on the basis of their technical and administrative responsibilities, volunteer commitments, preference for particular events, language spoken, and/or location in different parts of the country. Hoye and Cuskelly (2003) made similar observations during their analysis of Australian VSOs. While neither group of researchers used the term subculture, the emergence of such groups, development of strong group affiliations among members, and outcome of intergroup rivalries all point to the existence of competing subcultures. Study of such groups and their effect on organisational functioning constitutes an important gap in sport management research.

While the above approaches have been most popular among cultural scholars, other perspectives have also been suggested. One that appears to have great potential for helping us to understand the development of culture in sport organisations has been termed the fragmentation perspective (Martin, 1992). Proponents of this approach have suggested that rather than being permanent features of organisation life, cultures and subcultures are transitory, ephemeral and based around particular issues (Martin and Frost, 1999). This approach has the potential to offer much to our understanding of culture in sport organisations. The mass popularity of sport, its high public profile and the issue-driven nature of its development mean that we frequently see coalitions formed to contest particular issues. The potential location and design of the English National Stadium, the format of the United Kingdom Sport Institute, and who should take responsibility for athlete drug testing have all been the subject of much contestation over recent years. Understanding how cultures have become manifest in Sport England, UK Sport, the Football Association and the Ministry for Culture, Media and Sport, organisations that frequently appear fractious, would undoubtedly help in the management of these decision-making processes. As yet, however, such work has not been forthcoming.

ORGANISATIONAL CHANGE

The subject of organisational change has become increasingly important for management scholars in recent years. Technological advancements, increased national and international competition, changes to geopolitical boundaries, the creation and extension of various transnational trading blocs, and the introduction of market mechanisms to public sector organisations have all conspired to increase the speed and magnitude of change across many organisations. Indeed, survival for virtually all organisations will be predicated on the accomplishment of some form of large-scale change (Tushman and O'Reilly, 1996). Clearly sport organisations are not immune from some forces, and thus the study of change in sport organisations has also become popular (e.g. Amis et al., 2002, 2004a, 2004b; Cousens and Slack, 2005; Garcia and Rodriguez, 2003; Kikulis, 2000; Kikulis et al., 1992, 1995a, 1995b, 1995c; Koski and Heikkala, 1998; Macintosh and Whitson, 1990; O'Brien and Slack, 1999, 2003, 2004; Skinner et al., 2004; Slack and Hinings, 1987, 1992, 1994; Stevens and Slack, 1998). The geographic focus of this work on North America, Europe and Australia, the consideration of amateur and professional sport, and the utilisation of methods ranging from case studies of individual organisations to assessments of industry or field-level transformations indicate the extent of this research. While space precludes comprehensive assessment, we do encourage the interested reader to explore the full extent of change research that has appeared in recent years, only some of which we touch on above. As exemplars, we draw on three distinct portions of this work, more based on our detailed knowledge of it than any attempt to position it as superior to other work in the field.

When considering change we need to differentiate among those minor alterations made in response to competitive pressures and radical transformations that fundamentally change the structures, systems and values of an organisation (Greenwood and Hinings, 2006). Work on change in Canadian NSOs has been particularly widespread. As we highlight above, perhaps most influential in this body of papers has been that of Kikulis et al. (1992, 1995a) and their uncovering of the Kitchen Table, Boardroom and Executive Office archetypes. The utility and robustness of these archetypes, both practically and theoretically, in helping us to understand how sport organisations change, has been substantial because they enable us to plot the tracks, or paths, that organisations follow on their change journeys. These in turn help us to understand better those factors that directly or indirectly affect the change process. Kikulis and her colleagues (1995a, 1995b), in particular, noted the importance of understanding how changes to decision-making systems affect the change process because of their links, both functionally and symbolically, to organisational power distributions. They also demonstrated how managers within sport organisations, far from being passive recipients of external pressures, do indeed have some degree of *agency* and thus exhibit varied responses to similar external pressures (Kikulis et al., 1995c). This work has had a significant influence on scholars throughout the world.

Readers are also pointed towards the research of O'Brien and Slack (1999, 2003, 2004) on the professionalisation of English Rugby Union. This has demonstrated some of the intricacies, contradictions and points of resistance inherent in pronounced institutional change. One of the major findings was that despite the prospect of substantial increases in funding from new broadcast deals, sponsorship agreements and increased attendances, many volunteers actively resisted the shift to professionalisation because of the radical shift in organising arrangements that undermined the amateurs' power bases.

Finally, Cousens and Slack (2005) adopt a macro-approach to examine change across the institutional field of North American professional sport between 1970 and 1997. Using qualitative and quantitative data, the authors highlight changes in the 'community of actors', notably the increased number and importance of cable broadcasting networks. They also document a shift from a loosely coupled collection of organisations to tightly integrated, dense networks of profit-seeking firms. A third transition, from an era that emphasised the roles of sport leagues in virtually all industry activities to one of 'corporate dominance' characterised by sophisticated strategic alliances involving various partners, is also highlighted. Finally, the transformations observed are all underpinned by a corresponding shift in the dominant institutional logic from one consistent with the operation of traditional sport organisations to another more appropriate for a sophisticated entertainment industry.

CHAPTER SUMMARY

» Deciding on an appropriate organisation design is one of the more important managerial tasks. Depending on its internal and external context, the organisation will be more or less complex, standardised and centralised. Kikulis et al.'s (1992, 1995a) archetypes and Mintzberg's (2003) structural configurations can help us to understand how and why organisations have different designs.

» The external environment is composed of those influences that directly and indirectly affect an organisation. These forces include industry, raw materials, human resources, financial resources, market, technology, political, economic, socio-cultural and international factors.

» The general environment consists of those factors that indirectly affect an organisation.

» The task environment comprises those forces that directly affect an organisation. Managers try to influence the task environment to reduce the amount of uncertainty they face.

» One way in which managers of sport organisations can seek to control uncertainty is through the creation of interorganisational relationships with other influential organisations. Such relationships usually result in the creation of networks of mutually dependent organisations.

» The internal context also has a pronounced affect on the way in which an organisation is designed and operated. Factors that need to be considered include the use of power and political behaviour, the way in which decisions are made and the development of organisational cultures.

» Radical change has become a central imperative with which managers or sport organisations of all types must contend.

Definitions

Archetype: the ideas, beliefs and values combined with structures and systems that shape the design of an organisation

Centralisation: the location of decision-making authority within an organisation

Complexity: the degree to which work in an organisation is broken down and assigned to different specialists or subunits

Configuration: the way in which an organisation is designed

External context: everything outside the boundaries of an organisation that affect its design and operation

Formalisation: the extent to which policies, procedures, rules and regulations govern the way in which individuals within an organisation can act

Internal context: those factors inside the organisation that affect its design and operation

Interorganisational relationship: an agreement made between organisations in which parties agree to the exchange of some resource for their mutual benefit

FURTHER READING

There are several texts that will provide further detail on the topics covered here. Comprehensive theoretical insights can be found in the collections edited by Clegg et al. (2006), an update on the very popular first edition of the *Handbook of Organization Studies*, and Baum (2002). Daft (2004) provides an accessible but comprehensive account of the major organisation theory concepts and their application. Morgan (1997) provides an alternative and informative way of examining organisations using a variety of different perspectives. Slack and Parent (2006) provide a useful analysis of the major theoretical concepts and how they can be applied to sport management settings.

REFERENCES

Aldrich, H.E. (1979) *Organizations and Environments.* Englewood Cliffs, NJ: Prentice Hall.

Amis, J. (2003) '"Good things come to those who wait": the strategic management of image and reputation at Guinness', *European Sport Management Quarterly*, 3: 189–214.

Amis, J. and Slack, T. (1996) 'The size-structure relationship in voluntary sport organiza-tions', *Journal of Sport Management*, 10: 76–86.

Amis, J., Slack, T. and Berrett, T. (1995) 'The structural antecedents of conflict in volun-tary sport organizations', *Leisure Studies*, 14: 1–16.

Amis, J., Slack, T. and Hinings, C.R. (2002) 'Values and organizational change', *Journal of Applied Behavioral Science*, 38: 436–65.

Amis, J., Slack, T. and Hinings, C.R. (2004a) 'The pace, sequence and linearity of radical change', *Academy of Management Journal*, 47: 15–39.

Amis, J., Slack, T. and Hinings, C.R. (2004b) 'The role of interests, power and capacity in strategic change', *Journal of Sport Management*, 18: 158–98.

Andrews, D.L. (2003) 'Sport and the transnationalizing media corporation', *Journal of Media Economics*, 16 (4): 235–51.

Armstrong-Doherty, A.J. (1996) 'Resource dependence-based perceived control: an exami-nation of Canadian interuniversity athletics', *Journal of Sport Management*, 10: 49–64.

Bacharach, P. and Baratz, M.S. (1962) 'Two faces of power', *American Political Science Review*, 56: 947–52.

Baum, J.A.C. (ed.) (2002) *Companion to Organizations*. Oxford: Blackwell.

Beyer, J.M. (1981) 'Ideologies, values, and decision making in organizations', in P.C. Nystrom and W.H. Starbuck (eds), *Handbook of Organizational Design*. London: Oxford University Press, pp. 166–202.

Boronico, J. and Newbert, S. (1999) 'Play calling strategy in American football: a game-theoretic stochastic dynamic programming approach', *Journal of Sport Management*, 13: 114–38.

Brackenridge, C. and Kirby, S. (1997) 'Playing safe', *International Review for the Sociology of Sport*, 32: 407–20.

Clegg, S.R., Hardy, C., Nord, W.R. and Lawrence, T. (eds) (2006) *Handbook of Organization Studies*. 2nd edn. Thousand Oaks, CA: Sage.

Cohen, M.D., March, J.G. and Olsen, J.P. (1972) 'The garbage can model of organizational choice', *Administrative Science Quarterly*, 17: 15–32.

Cousens, L., Babiak, K. and Slack, T. (2001) 'Adopting a relationship marketing paradigm: the case of the National Basketball Association', *International Journal of Sports Marketing & Sponsorship*, 2: 331–55.

Cousens, L. and Slack, T. (1996) 'Emerging patterns of inter-organizational relations: a network perspective of North American professional sport leagues', *European Journal for Sport Management*, 3 (1): 48–69.

Cousens, L. and Slack, T. (2005) 'Field-level change: the case of North American major league professional sport', *Journal of Sport Management*, 19: 13–42.

Cray, D., Mallory, G.R., Butler, R.J., Hickson, D.J. and Wilson, D.C. (1991) 'Explaining decision processes', *Journal of Management Studies*, 28: 227–51.

Daft, R.L. (2004) *Organization Theory and Design*. 8th edn. Mason, OH: Thomson.

D'Aveni, R.A. (1994) *Hypercompetition: Managing the Dynamics of Maneuvering*. New York: Free Press.

French, J.P.R. Jr and Raven, B. (1960) 'The bases of social power', in D. Cartwright and A. Zander (eds), *Group Dynamics*. New York: Harper & Row, pp. 607–23.

Frisby, W. (1986) 'The organizational structure and effectiveness of voluntary organizations: the case of Canadian national sport governing bodies', *Journal of Park and Recreation Administration*, 4: 61–74.

Garcia, J. and Rodriguez, P. (2003) 'From sports clubs to stock companies: the financial structure of football in Spain, 1992–2001', *European Sport Management Quarterly*, 3: 253–69.

Gerrard, B. (2005) 'A resource-utilization model of organizational efficiency in professional sport teams', *Journal of Sport Management*, 19: 143–69.

Greenwood, R. and Hinings, C.R. (1988) 'Organizational design types, tracks and the dynamics of strategic change', *Organization Studies*, 9: 293–316.

Greenwood, R. and Hinings, C.R. (1993) 'Understanding strategic change: the contribution of archetypes', *Academy of Management Journal*, 36: 1052–81.

Greenwood, R. and Hinings, C.R. (2006) 'Radical organizational change', in S. Clegg, C. Hardy, W.W. Nord and T. Lawrence (eds), *Handbook of Organization Studies*. 2nd edn. Thousand Oaks, CA: Sage.

Guardian (2002) 'New balls please', *Guardian*, 24 June. http://www.guardian.co.uk/g2/story/0,,742653,00.html (accessed 6 December 2005).

Gulati, R., Dialdin, D.A. and Wang, L. (2002) 'Organizational networks', in J.A.C. Baum (ed.), *Companion to Organizations*. Oxford: Blackwell, pp. 281–303.

Hardy, C. and Clegg, S.R. (1999) 'Some dare call it power', in S.R. Clegg and C. Hardy (eds), *Studying Organization: Theory and Method*. Thousand Oaks, CA: Sage, pp. 368–87.

Hickson, D.J., Hinings, C.R., Lee, C.A., Schneck, R.E. and Pennings, J.M. (1971) 'A strategic contingencies theory of intraorganizational power', *Administrative Science Quarterly*, 16: 216–29.

Hill, L. and Kikulis, L. (1999) 'Contemplating restructuring: a case study of strategic decision making in interuniversity athletic conferences', *Journal of Sport Management*, 13: 18–44.

Hillman, A.J., Cannella, A.A. and Paetzold, R.L. (2000) 'The resource dependence role of corporate directors: strategic adaptation of board composition in response to environmental change', *Journal of Management Studies*, 37: 235–55.

Hinings, C.R. and Greenwood, R. (1988). *The Dynamics of Strategic Change*. Oxford: Basil Blackwell.

Hoye, R. and Cuskelly, G. (2003) 'Board power and performance within voluntary sport organisations', *European Sport Management Quarterly*, 3: 103–19.

Kikulis, L.M. (2000) 'Continuity and change in governance and decision making in national sport organizations: institutional explanations', *Journal of Sport Management*, 14: 293–320.

Kikulis, L.M., Slack, T. and Hinings, B. (1992) 'Institutionally specific design archetypes: a framework for understanding change in national sport organizations', *International Review for the Sociology of Sport*, 27: 343–70.

Kikulis, L.M., Slack, T. and Hinings, C.R. (1995a) 'Sector-specific patterns of organizational design change', *Journal of Management Studies*, 32: 67–100.

Kikulis, L.M., Slack, T. and Hinings, C.R. (1995b) 'Does decision making make a difference? An analysis of patterns of change within Canadian national sport organizations', *Journal of Sport Management*, 9: 273–99.

Kikulis, L.M., Slack, T. and Hinings, C.R. (1995c) 'Towards an understanding of the role of agency and choice in the changing structure of Canada's national sport organizations', *Journal of Sport Management*, 9: 135–52.

Koski, P. and Heikkala, J. (1998) 'Professionalization and organizations of mixed rationales: the case of Finnish national sport organizations', *European Journal for Sport Management*, 5: 7–29.

Lindblom, C.E. (1959) 'The science of "muddling through"', *Public Administration Review*, 19 (2): 79–88.

Long, J. Thibault, L. and Wolfe, R. (2004) 'A case study of influence over a sponsorship decision in a Canadian university athletic department', *Journal of Sport Management*, 18: 132–57.

Lukes, S. (1974) *Power: A Radical View*. London: Macmillan.

Macintosh, D. and Whitson, D. (1990) *The Game Planners: Transforming Canada's Sport System*. Montreal and Kingston: McGill–Queen's University Press.

Martin, J. (1992) *Cultures in Organizations: Three perspectives*. New York: Oxford University Press.

Martin, J. and Frost, P. (1999) 'The organizational culture war games: a struggle for intellectual dominance', in S.R. Clegg and C. Hardy (eds), *Studying Organization: Theory and Method*. Thousand Oaks, CA: Sage, pp. 345–67.

McArdle, D. (2000) *Football, Society and the Law*. London: Cavendish.

McDonald, P. (1991) 'The Los Angeles Olympic Organizing Committee: developing organizational culture in the short run', in P. Frost, L. Moore, M.R. Louis, C. Lundberg and J. Martin (eds), *Reframing Organizational Culture*. Newbury Park, CA: Sage, pp. 26–38.

Meyer, A.D., Tsui, A.S. and Hinings, C.R. (1993) 'Configurational approaches to organizational analysis', *Academy of Management Journal*, 36: 1175–95.

Meyerson, D. and Martin, J. (1987) 'Cultural change: an integration of three different views', *Journal of Management Studies*, 24: 623–47.

Miller, D. and Dröge, C. (1986) 'Psychological and traditional determinants of structure', *Administrative Science Quarterly*, 31: 539–60.

Miller, D. and Friesen, P.H. (1984) *Organizations: A Quantum View*. Englewood Cliffs, NJ: Prentice Hall.

Miller, S.J., Hickson, D.J. and Wilson, D.C. (1999) 'Decision-making in organizations', in S.R. Clegg, C. Hardy and W.R. Nord (eds), *Managing Organizations: Current Issues*. Thousand Oaks, CA: Sage, pp. 26–42.

Mintzberg, H. (2003) 'The structuring of organizations', in H. Mintzberg, J. Lampel, J.B. Quinn and S. Ghoshal (eds), *The Strategy Process: Concepts, Contexts, Cases*. Global 4th edn. Englewood Cliffs, NJ: Prentice Hall, pp. 209–26.

Mintzberg, H. (1979) *The Structuring of Organizations*. Englewood Cliffs, NJ: Prentice Hall.

Morgan, G. (1997) *Images of Organisation*. 2nd edn. London: Sage.

O'Brien, D. and Slack, T. (1999) 'Deinstitutionalising the amateur ethic: an empirical examination of change in a rugby union football club', *Sport Management Review*, 2: 24–42.

O'Brien, D. and Slack, T. (2003) 'An analysis of change in an organizational field: the professionalization of English rugby union', *Journal of Sport Management*, 17: 417–48.

O'Brien, D. and Slack, T. (2004) 'The emergence of a professional logic in English rugby union: the role of isomorphic and diffusion processes', *Journal of Sport Management*, 18: 13–39.

Pettigrew, A.M. (1973) *The Politics of Organizational Decision-Making*. London: Tavistock.

Pfeffer, J. and Salancik, G.R. (1978) *The External Control of Organizations: A Resource Dependence Perspective*. New York: Harper & Row.

Provan, K.G. and Milward, H.B. (1995) 'A preliminary theory of interorganizational network effectiveness: a comparative study of four community mental health systems', *Administrative Science Quarterly*, 40: 1–33.

Pugh, D., Hickson, D. and Hinings, C.R. (1969) 'An empirical taxonomy of structures of work organizations', *Administrative Science Quarterly*, 14: 115–26.

Quinn, J.B. (1980) *Strategies for Change: Logical Incrementalism*. Homewood, IL: Irwin.

Ranson, S., Hinings, C.R. and Greenwood, R. (1980) 'The structuring of organizational structures', *Administrative Science Quarterly*, 25: 1–17.

Rugby Football Union (2005) *Rugby Football Union Online Handbook*. http://www.rfu.com/microsites/handbooks/index.cfm?fuseaction=handbook.home (accessed 6 December 2005).

Sack, A. and Johnson, A. (1996) 'Politics, economic development and the Volvo International Tennis Tournament', *Journal of Sport Management*, 10: 1–14.

Schein, E.H. (1990) 'Organizational culture', *American Psychologist*, 45 (2): 109–19.

Schein, E.H. (1996) 'Culture: the missing concept in organization studies', *Administrative Science Quarterly*, 41: 229–40.

Simon, H.A. (1945) *Administrative Behavior*. New York: Free Press.

Skinner, J., Stewart, B. and Edwards, A. (2004) 'Interpreting policy language and managing organisational change: the case of Queen'sland Rugby Union', *European Sport Management Quarterly*, 4: 77–94.

Slack, T. and Hinings, B. (1994) 'Institutional pressures and isomorphic change: an empirical test', *Organizational Studies*, 15: 803–27.

Slack, T. and Hinings, C.R. (eds) (1987) *The Organization and Administration of Sport*. London, Ontario: Sport Dynamics.

Slack, T. and Hinings, C.R. (1992) 'Understanding change in national sport organizations: an integration of theoretical perspectives', *Journal of Sport Management*, 6: 114–32.

Slack, T. and Parent, M. (2006) *Understanding Sport Organizations: The Application of Organization Theory*. 2nd edn. Champaign, IL: Human Kinetics.

Stevens, J.A. and Slack, T. (1998) 'Integrating social action and structural constraints', *International Review for the Sociology of Sport*, 33: 143–54.

Taylor, Rt. Hon. Lord Justice (1990) *The Hillsborough Stadium Disaster: Final Report*. London: Her Majesty's Stationery Office.

Thibault, L., Slack, T. and Hinings, C.R. (1991) 'Professionalism, structures and systems: the impact of professional staff on voluntary sport organizations', *International Review for the Sociology of Sport*, 26: 83–99.

Thompson, D.N. (2003) 'AOL Time Warner, Terra Lycos, Vivendi, and the transformation of marketing', *Journal of Business Research*, 56: 861–6.

Tushman, M.L. and O'Reilly, C.A. (1996) 'Ambidextrous organizations: managing evolutionary and revolutionary change', *California Management Review*, 38 (4): 8–30.

Uzzi, B. (1996) 'The sources and consequences of embeddedness for the economic performance of organizations: the network effect', *American Sociological Review*, 61: 674–98.

Uzzi, B. (1997) 'Social structure and competition in interfirm networks: the paradox of embeddedness', *Administrative Science Quarterly*, 42: 35–67.

Walsh, K., Hinings, B., Greenwood, R. and Ranson, S. (1981) 'Power and advantage in organizations', *Organization Studies*, 2: 131–52.

Weber, M. (1968) *Economy and Society: an Interpretive Sociology*. New York: Bedminister Press.

Weick, K.E. (1995) *Sensemaking in Organizations*. Thousands Oaks, CA: Sage.

Wolfe, R., Meenaghan, T. and O'Sullivan, P. (2002) 'The sports network: insights into the shifting balance of power', *Journal of Business Research*, 55: 611–22.

16

Doping and Sport

BARRIE HOULIHAN

OVERVIEW

» *Why oppose doping?*
» *Satisfying the lawyers – defining doping*
» *Progress in establishing an effective anti-doping policy*
» *The development of international co-operation*
» *The 1998 Tour de France and the establishment of the World Anti-Doping Agency*
» *Problems and prospects*

Doping in sport is a problem that just will not go away. One scandal has followed another with a steady regularity: in 1998 the Tour de France came to the point of collapse because of the extent of doping uncovered by the French police and customs authorities; in 2001 three Dutch footballers, Jaap Stam, Edger Davids and Frank de Boer, also tested positive for steroids; in 2005 Victor Conte, founder of BALCO, a food supplement company, began a jail sentence for supplying steroids to a number of elite athletes including Great Britain's Dwain Chambers and world double sprint champion Kelli White; in 2006 Olympic gold medallist, Justin Gatlin tested positive for testosterone; and in the same year Tour de France winner Floyd Landis tested positive for suspiciously high levels of testosterone. Furthermore, there is evidence of the development of drugs, such as THG (tetrahydrogestrinone), designed to be undetectable and the abuse of drugs (see Table 16.1) for which there is currently no reliable test including insulin and human growth hormone. Most worrying of all, there is increasing speculation about the potential of genetic manipulation to build bigger muscles or boost the oxygen-carrying capacity of the blood.

The problems of developing an effective anti-doping policy include:

- establishing a persuasive moral basis for opposing doping;
- devising an acceptable and legally defensible definition of doping (moral justification and actual definition); and
- constructing an effective policy regime (well resourced and politically supported).

WHY OPPOSE DOPING?

Argument 1: 'Doping Is Unfair'

Much of the force of this justification rests on the possibility of sustaining a distinction between a fair and an unfair advantage because so much of sport is about seeking an advantage – an 'edge' over one's opponents.[1] That some athletes start with differing physiological and psychological attributes which give them an advantage over others is rarely questioned and is not seen as unfair. Although some sports take account of factors such as weight (judo) and prior success (handicapping in horse racing and golf), most do not. Perhaps then the important distinction is between a natural and an unnatural advantage. Thus while an advantage gained either at birth (height, balance and reach, etc.) or through rigorous training is acceptable, would an unnatural advantage, such as an ultra-low resistance swimsuit, an ultra-light cycle or an innovative Formula One engine be unacceptable? In all these cases the advantage is, like anabolic steroids, external to the athlete. However, as is clearly the case, technological innovation is an integral and generally accepted part of many sports.

A further possible argument to explore in relation to fairness is not whether the advantage is natural or not, but whether there is an intention to keep the advantage a secret or restricted. Thus innovative design of javelins, poles for pole vaulting or swimsuits are acceptable if they are made widely available as quickly as possible. However, the implication for doping is that just as there is nothing inherently unacceptable in designing a more aerodynamic javelin, so there is nothing inherently unfair about using drugs, providing all athletes have equal access. While this argument may have some plausibility, many would find its rationalisation of drug use unacceptable. Indeed, it would appear that each avenue that is taken in pursuit of a secure basis for banning drugs on the grounds of fairness leads into a cul-de-sac of ambiguity and inconsistency, or worst of all rebounds on the supporters of drug-free sport and is used to challenge current anti-doping efforts.

It may be that the acceptability of an advantage depends less on whether it is natural or unnatural, or whether it is differentially available but rather on a perception of how the advantage was acquired. Advantages that are the result of location (skiers living in Norway rather than Holland), natural endowments (Didier Drogba's power, speed and

TABLE 16.1   *Major drugs and banned practices based on the WADA list: medical uses, benefits in sport and side effects*

Drugs and banned practices	Illustrative medical uses, if any	Claimed benefits for athletes	Selected side effects
Stimulants e.g. amphetamine	Relief of mild depression; eating disorders	Used to increase aggression in sports, e.g. American football; increase energy in endurance sport, e.g. cycling; suppress appetite in weight-related sports, e.g. judo	Addiction; may cause loss of judgement, psychotic behaviour, anorexia and insomnia
Narcotics e.g. cocaine	Powerful painkiller	Painkillers	Addiction and loss of judgement regarding injury
Anabolic agents: anabolic androgenic steroids	The management of male development at puberty; anaemia, renal failure, treatment of burns	Increased strength and size; help athletes recover from training and train more intensively; increase aggression	In males: shrinkage of the testicles and the development of breast tissue. In females: masculinising effects including deepening of the voice and growth of facial hair. For both males and females: increased aggressiveness and depression
Diuretics	Control the retention of fluids and high blood pressure	Used to flush out other drugs and to achieve weight in weight-related events	Dehydration and possible risks of muscle cramps and a reduction in muscle strength
Peptide and glycoprotein hormones and analogues e.g. human growth hormone (hGH)	hGH is used to treat growth-deficient children	Aid growth and muscle development. Depress fat accumulation. Strengthen tendons (and thus overcome one of the problems of steroid use)	Over-growth of bones such as the jaw and forehead. Risk of infection from contaminated needles as drug has to be injected
Prohibited methods: pharmacological, chemical and physical manipulation	This category covers a wide range of activities including the corruption of a urine sample with alcohol; for example, the practice of catheterisation whereby drug-free urine is introduced into the bladder so that a 'clean' sample can be provided, or the inhibition of renal excretion.		

balance), or practice and training (Tiger Woods's putting) are all significant but considered to be fair and to be encouraged. The significance of the process by which an advantage is acquired is easily illustrated if we compare the athlete who lives and trains at altitude, and thus acquires naturally a greater oxygen-carrying capacity of his/her blood, with the athlete who achieves the same effect by using EPO (erythropoietin). The moral arguments become blurred again if the athlete who trains at altitude is able to do so because of personal wealth or state sponsorship while the EPO user is from a poor country.

Argument 2: 'Doping Is Bad for an Athlete's Health'

If arguments based on fairness fail to provide a secure and persuasive basis for opposing doping, then a concern to protect the health of the athlete is an alternative. However, there are a number of difficulties with this rationale, the first of which is lack of scientifically valid evidence regarding the impact on health of drug use. Because of the quantities of drugs, especially steroids, that some drug-abusing athletes take, it is not ethically permissible to replicate their pattern of drug use in clinical trials. Nevertheless there is an accumulation of anecdotal evidence relating to the long-term health effects of some drugs. There has been a high incidence of early death among professional road cyclists, many from liver-related diseases, which might be due to blood doping. If there is evidence of a link between drug use and damage to health, it is only slowly emerging.

A second difficulty in building an anti-doping argument based on the protection of the athlete's health is that there are many sports (e.g. football, cricket and rugby) where competing with injury is normal. The use by athletes of analgesics and anti-inflammatory preparations is routine, and permissible, in almost all sport. There thus seems little difference between the athlete who risks his/her health by competing when injured and the athlete who risks his/her health by taking drugs to improve performance. A third difficulty is that there are a number of aspects of elite athlete preparation that are a potential danger to health. Many training regimes are designed to push athletes to their physical limit. More importantly, as Fost argues, 'sport itself carries per se a substantial risk of death and permanent disability' (1991: 481). Boxing, rugby, American football and mountaineering all carry a significant risk of serious injury and on occasion even death.

A fourth difficulty with health arguments is that they can be reversed and used to justify drug use. Black and Pape (1997) argue that the current anti-doping effort puts athletes' health at risk because it results in many obtaining their drugs illegally, when quality and purity cannot be guaranteed; it leads to athletes administering the drugs themselves and thus without professional expertise and possibly without access to clean needles. It is possible to argue that if our primary concern is with athletes health, we would not drive such potentially dangerous practices underground. The final difficulty concerns the underlying paternalism of arguments based on health. If an athlete wishes to take risks with his/her health, on what basis can society interfere? In Mill's classic statement: 'the only purpose for which power can be rightfully exercised over any member of a civilised community, against his will, is to prevent harm to others. His own good, either physical or moral, is not a sufficient warrant' (1962: 135).

Argument 3: 'Doping Undermines the Integrity of Sport'

This argument is predicated on the belief that sports – collectively and individually – have an essence or set of core values that are undermined by drug use. The rules of each sport attempt to encapsulate the mix of skills and challenges which make for a 'good competition'. One basis for determining whether doping should be prohibited is whether it undermines or invalidates the essential challenge of the sport. Thus, just as adding a motor to a cycle would not be acceptable in the Tour de France, nor should blood doping by cyclists as both undermine the essence of the competition. From a broadly similar starting point, Simon provides an argument that may be applied to most, if not all sports. He suggests that 'competition in athletics is best thought of as a mutual quest for excellence'. An opponent is not an obstacle to winning, to be overcome by whatever means, but a co-worker in a joint undertaking: 'athletic competition, rather than being incompatible with respect for our opponents as persons, actually presupposes it' (Simon, 1984: 10). Though persuasive, Simon's position does have problems, the most significant of which is the vagueness of some of the underlying concepts.

Given the difficulty of establishing an unassailable foundation for opposing doping in sport, it is not surprising that supporters of current anti-doping policy rely on a combination of the above arguments or simply argue that avoiding the use of certain drugs is one of the rules of a sport and should therefore be respected. Many of the rules in sport are arbitrary (playing 18 holes in golf or not picking the ball up in football) and it could be argued that anti-doping rules should be treated as simply an addition to the rules of play. If footballers want to be able to pick the ball up during a match and run with it, they will be penalised; or if they want to use amphetamines to increase their energy levels, they should also be disqualified because they are not playing the sport of football as described in the rule book.

Unfortunately, relying solely on the rule book is not a strong basis for opposing doping and, in practice, anti-doping policy is justified on a mix of grounds selected from those discussed and on the continuing public perception of doping as anathema to sport. As with so many other ambiguous moral issues (divorce, abortion, euthanasia, etc.), policy makers rely on a combination of principle and public support to sustain policy efforts. However, once the hurdle of devising a plausible justification for an anti-doping strategy is overcome, there still remain many other problems, not the least of which is the apparently simple matter of defining what doping is.

SATISFYING THE LAWYERS: DEFINING DOPING

If a successful anti-doping strategy is to be developed, it is important to formulate a clear statement of the nature of the problem. Yet providing a clear, succinct and, most importantly of all in these litigious times, legally secure definition of doping has proved extremely difficult despite attempts at clarification by the World Anti-Doping Agency. Charles Dubin, who chaired the Commission of Inquiry following the positive test result on Ben Johnson at the 1988 Seoul Olympic Games, argued that a definition was 'impossible to achieve' (Dubin, 1990: 77). While many would sympathise with the difficulty facing Dubin, a workable definition of doping is essential, given the frequency of legal challenge to the decisions of domestic and international federations on doping infractions. Many definitions adopted by international federations referred variously to the 'intention to seek an unfair advantage', 'the use of substances damaging to the athlete's health' or 'substances that confer an unfair advantage'. All these phrases are laudable in their desire to clarify the basis for objecting to doping but, as should be clear from the discussion in the previous section, they are all fraught with problems. How might intent rather than accident, chance, ignorance or sabotage be proved? Proving that the drugs taken damage the athlete's health is all but impossible given that many of the drugs are available from any pharmacist and most have well-recognised therapeutic applications. The problems with the concept of an unfair advantage were made clear earlier in this chapter.

One response by some international federations (e.g. the IAAF) has been to adopt a strict liability definition, according to which a doping offence is deemed to have been committed if a prohibited substance is present in an athlete's urine sample, irrespective of whether the drug was taken knowingly or whether the drug was capable of enhancing performance. According to Wise, the strict liability definition means that an athlete can be found guilty of a doping infraction 'without the sports governing body proving culpable intent, knowledge or fault; or without the athlete being allowed to prove he or she was faultless' (1996).

Support for the IAAF definition and for a clearly worded definition came from the British judge who heard the case brought by Sandra Gasser against the IAAF in which she challenged its strict liability definition. The judge referred approvingly to the IAAF representative's concern that 'if a defence of moral innocence were open, the floodgates would be opened and the IAAF's attempts to prevent drug taking by athletes would be rendered futile' (quoted in Gay, n.d.). Writing in 1995 and using the IAAF strict liability definition as the benchmark, Vrijman reviewed the definitions of 33 other international federations and found, first, that all of them had definitions that were potentially vulnerable to legal challenge and, second, that there was very little uniformity between sports. Many sports, such as squash and badminton, did not provide a definition of doping at all, while others included a sentence in their rules that associated them with the IOC rules on doping. Of those that did provide a definition, many were unclear and confused and, as mentioned earlier, vulnerable to legal challenge. By 1999 there had been some progress in amending anti-doping rules to make them less vulnerable to legal challenge. Seven federations, including those for gymnastics and ice hockey, had adopted definitions similar to that used by the IAAF, but the vast majority had left their definitions unrevised.

Despite the strong support provided by Gay and other lawyers, there is some doubt regarding the value of a strict liability definition, particularly in the United States. In 1995 Jessica Foschi, the swimmer, tested positive for the anabolic steroid mesterolone and was penalised under the rules of the international federation (FINA). She appealed against the penalty to the American Arbitration Association (AAA), the body prescribed under the terms of the United States Amateur Sports Act 1978. The AAA was emphatic in its rejection of the FINA decision and the application of the concept of strict liability. The arbitrators argued that:

> Having concluded that the claimant and all those connected with her are innocent and without fault, we unanimously conclude that the imposition of any sanction on the claimant so offends our deeply rooted and historical concepts of fundamental fairness as to be arbitrary and capricious. (Quoted in Wise, 1996: 1161)

Similar rejections of the concept of strict liability have been provided by the Swiss courts and the Legal Committee of the German Track and Field Federation, with the latter arguing that 'the maxim "*nulla poena sine culpa*" (no penalty without fault) has the status of a constitutional principle since the principle of the State Rechtsstaatlichkeit is infringed, the corresponding provision in that case is grossly unfair and thus unenforceable' (quoted in Wise, 1996: 1162). The status of the strict liability definition of doping as the preferred definition of international federations was reinforced with the approval of the World Anti-Doping Code in 2003. The Code defines doping as breeching one or more of eight rules, the first of which is 'The presence of a prohibited substance or its metabolites or markers in an athlete's specimen'. The Code justifies the strict liability rule as being 'a reasonable balance between effective anti-doping enforcement for the benefit of all "clean" athletes and fairness in the exceptional circumstances where a prohibited substance entered an athlete's system through no fault or negligence on the part of the athlete' (WADA, 2007: 11). The noting of exceptional circumstances is an acknowledgement that a rigidly applied strict liability rule was unsustainable. However, the Code also notes that 'the strict liability principle set forth in the Code has been consistently upheld in the decisions of CAS [Court of Arbitration for Sport]' (WADA, 22007: 11).

ESTABLISHING AN EFFECTIVE ANTI-DOPING POLICY

The initial reaction of many federations to evidence of doping by athletes involved in their sports was to ignore the problem in the hope that it would disappear. Most federations in the late 1960s and 1970s (see Table 16.2) variously perceived incidents of doping as exceptions in their sport or as a set of largely unsubstantiated allegations that it was convenient to ignore. For both the Olympic Movement and the major federations, there were strong incentives not to investigate the allegations of doping too closely, first,

382 THE IMPACT OF COMMERCIALISATION

TABLE 16.2   *Milestones in the development of anti-doping policy*

Year(s)	Event
1960	• Death of Knud Jensen at the Rome Olympics
1961	• IOC establishes a Medical Commission
1962	• IOC passes a resolution condemning doping
1963	• Convention of international federations led to the formulation of a definition of doping
mid-1960s	• Union Cycliste International introduce drug testing
1964	• IOC adopts a definition of doping
1965	• France and Belgium are among the first countries to introduce legislation concerning doping in sport
1966	• Five elite cyclists in the world road race championships refuse to provide a urine sample
	• FIFA conducts tests at the World Cup in England
1968	• IOC conducts tests at the Summer and Winter Olympic Games
1971	• IOC produces the first list of banned substances and practices
1972	• IOC conducts over 2,000 tests at the Munich Olympic Games
	• Test for anabolic steroids piloted
	• IAAF establishes a Medical Committee
1976	• First use of test for the detection of anabolic steroids at the Montreal Olympic Games
	• Accreditation of laboratories by the IOC introduced
1977	• First use of out-of-competition tests
1978	• Some harmonisation on penalties between international federations
	• Council of Europe formulates a recommendation to member states' governments on doping
1981	• 11th Olympic Congress at Baden-Baden passed a resolution from athletes endorsing the IOC anti-doping policy
early 1980s	• Development of more sensitive testing methods based on gas chromatography/mass spectrometry (GC/MS)
1983	• A large number of athletes withdraw from the Pan-American Games when the use of GC/MS is announced
1988	• Canadian Ben Johnson, winner of the 100 m Olympic final, tests positive for steroids
1989	• IAAF establishes 'flying squads' of doping control officers to conduct unannounced out-of-competition testing especially for steroids
	• Council of Europe publishes the Anti-Doping Convention
late 1980s	• Series of trials begin in Germany which expose the extent of state-organised doping in former East Germany
1998	• Near collapse of the Tour de France because of the seizure of drugs by customs officials and the subsequent police enquiries
1999	• World Anti-Doping Agency (WADA) formed
2000	• 2,500 tests conducted by WADA in the run-up to the Sydney Olympic Games
2003	• World Anti-Doping Code approved
	• THG, a designer (or structurally modified) anabolic androgenic steroid, identified in USA
2006	• BALCO scandal
2007	• Revisions to the World Anti-Doping Code approved
2007	• UNESCO International Convention against Doping in Sport enters into force in February

because of the likely cost and complexity of any action and, second, because of the potential damage to the image of sport that might result.

Up until the mid-1980s, doping policy was being formulated within a number of largely self-contained forums based on a perception of the problem as one that could be confined to particular sports, competitions or countries. Thus the IOC sought to protect the integrity of the Olympic Games through the use of in-competition testing; the major federations also considered that in-competition testing would ensure the continued probity of their elite events; and governments established legal frameworks and instituted domestic testing regimes on the assumption that the practice of sport within their borders could be isolated from cross-border contamination. As a result there was only minimal contact between sports organisations, governments and international bodies such as the Council of Europe. However, by the mid- to late 1980s, such a view of the nature of the problem was no longer sustainable owing, in very large part, to the rapid globalisation of sport. Not only did the 1980s witness the expansion in the number of world championships and grand prix events but also following the widespread abandonment of amateurism, athletes increasingly moved outside their home country to train. International competition circuits and athlete mobility meant that many athletes spent little time in their home country. This highlights the importance of consistency of regulations between domestic federations and the importance of mutual recognition of jurisdiction across national boundaries. In addition, the weakness of an anti-doping regime based on in-competition testing was increasingly apparent in view of the growing use of anabolic steroids as training aids. However, the introduction of out-of-competition testing involved a level of transnational co-operation and an expenditure of resources that few federations or governments had anticipated.

The end of amateurism brought about one further significant change. As more athletes, particularly in track and field, saw sport not only as their primary source of income, but also as a source of substantial wealth, they were consequently much more willing to use the courts to protect their income if it were threatened by a ban for a doping offence. Well-documented cases involving elite athletes such as the German Katrin Krabbe and the Australian Martin Vinnicombe drew the attention of the domestic federations to the potential cost of defending their decisions in court and also made them aware of just how vulnerable many of their decisions were, owing to the poor drafting of regulations and the failure to ensure compatibility of domestic regulations with those of the international federation and with the domestic federations in other countries.

THE DEVELOPMENT OF INTERNATIONAL CO-OPERATION

By the end of the 1980s it was clear that the attempts to tackle doping as a series of discrete problems were proving ineffective. If doping were to be successfully challenged, there would be a need for a high level of co-operation between the international federations and the IOC and also between sports organisations and governments. The impetus for closer co-operation came from the recognition of the increasing complexity of the problem arising from the greater wealth and mobility of athletes, and also from an awareness that a successful anti-doping programme would be expensive and well beyond the resources of individual federations or the IOC. Co-operation at the political level was therefore a primary requirement.

During the 1970s and 1980s the federations had been highly suspicious of the motives of many governments in the area of doping and were generally sceptical of their commitment. Apart from the small number of governments that were prepared to commit resources to the problem, the majority were inactive and a very small, but highly significant number were subversive. The inactive included those that simply did not possess the necessary resources to support an anti-doping programme, but also included a group of governments whose public condemnation of doping was matched by a determination to ignore the signs of doping among their own athletes. The Dubin Inquiry in Canada following the Ben Johnson incident in 1988 and the Senate Committee's investigation of allegations of doping at the Australian Institute of Sport provided ample evidence of inaction by both governments and sporting authorities (Australian Government, 1989; Dubin, 1990). Most damaging to the claims from governments to policy leadership were the revelations from the series of trials in Germany regarding the extent to which the former government of the GDR had constructed a state co-ordinated and funded doping programme for its Olympic athletes (Franke and Berendonk, 1997).

The state inquiries in Canada and Australia prompted a radical change in attitude and led both countries to establish state-supported anti-doping agencies which are currently among the most respected. However, it was not just the cathartic effect of scandal and public scrutiny that led to an improved climate of co-operation between governments and sports organisations. Of equal significance was the ending of the Cold War and the consequent removal of international sport as a surrogate for the ideological confrontation between communism and capitalism. The capitalist democracies could no longer implicitly rationalise their relative inaction on doping. Furthermore the countries of the former communist bloc were keen to rebuild democracy and its civil institutions, of which sports organisations were an important part, and also distance themselves from the tainted reputation of their previous leaders.

In addition to the much more positive political environment of the early 1990s, there was also an emerging global infrastructure of international organisations and forums concerned with the issue of doping. The Council of Europe enhanced the status of the Recommendation on doping, first to a Charter and then to that of a Convention in 1989 which sought to establish a set of standards and objectives that would reach beyond the Council's European membership by inviting non-member states to express their support. The Council's profile on anti-doping policy was further strengthened by its many new members from the former communist countries of Central and Eastern Europe. The work of the Council was complemented by the series of Permanent World Conferences on doping, which sought to create a global forum for policy discussion largely at a governmental level. There was also considerable activity at the regional level with a number of bilateral and multilateral agreements between governments relating to the exchange of information and agreement on mutual testing arrangements (Houlihan, 1999).

Sports organisations had also sought to establish forums, such as the International Athletic Foundation's symposia, where common problems associated with doping could be discussed and information exchanged. However, action by sports organisations was far from dynamic. Although the IOC remained a key organisation, its role was confined to little more than updating the list of banned substances and practices, advising the Council of Europe on the anti-doping Charter, and the overseeing of testing at its own events. The leading federations, with a small number of exceptions, such as those for swimming (FINA) and track and field events (IAAF), adopted a passive and reactive stance with regard to the issue. Such was the growing disparity between the level of policy activity between governments and sports organisations that the IOC was prompted into action in 1994, when it initiated discussions among the Olympic federations that culminated in the publication of the Lausanne Agreement. While the Agreement was important in bringing together all the key sports bodies, and despite the establishment of a working group on harmonisation which contained representatives from governments and governmental bodies, the Agreement was perceived by many governments as further evidence of a lack of urgency and a failure of policy leadership within sport.

By the mid-1990s policy towards doping was at a watershed and the prospects for further progress were mixed. Optimistically one could point to the vastly improved international political climate. Among the major Olympic nations there was only one, the People's Republic of China, where strong suspicions of state inaction towards doping still remained. Second, there were an increasing number of countries that had established anti-doping agencies which could command widespread respect. Third, more countries were involved in multilateral agreements, such as the International Anti-Doping Arrangement between a small group of countries, including Australia, Canada, The Netherlands and Sweden, which enabled the diffusion of good practice in testing and education and also acted as a lobby within the wider global political and sports community. Fourth, the number of forums available for the exchange of information among sports organisations and between sports and governmental organisations had increased significantly.

A more pessimistic assessment of the state of anti-doping policy in the mid-1990s balanced the evidence of progress against the acknowledged limitations of the current testing regime. Ben Johnson, for example, had been tested over 15 times while using steroids before he tested positive at Seoul. Second, the commitment of some domestic and international federations was being weakened by the increasing frequency of legal challenge. It was not just the fear of bankruptcy should a federation lose a case, as the cost of successfully defending decisions was equally crippling. The overall effect was to fuel the suspicion among governments that federations were being overly cautious in deciding when to determine that a doping positive constituted a doping infraction. Third, there was the growing evidence of the use of drugs that could not be detected with current testing methods. EPO and hGH were two of the drugs that were causing greatest concern and the IOC and the federations were acutely aware of the cost of devising a valid and reliable test.

THE 1998 TOUR DE FRANCE AND THE ESTABLISHMENT OF WADA

As is so often the case in policy making, it was a crisis – in this case one that occurred during the 1998 Tour de France – that prompted a renewed round of policy activity. A number of factors combined to force a renewed effort to increase the momentum behind anti-doping policy:

1 the extent of doping discovered during the Tour and the number of riders and team officials implicated;
2 the global prestige of the Tour;
3 the claims by the international federation for cycling, the UCI, to be a leader in the anti-doping campaign; and
4 the strength and intensity of intervention by the French government.

That one of the world's major sports events should be brought near to collapse by doping was serious enough to warrant a review of policy, but it was the intervention by the French government which caused the greatest concern among international federations and the IOC. The decision to treat the doping allegations as a public matter of law and order rather than a matter best left to the disciplinary processes of the UCI and its French affiliate left sports organisations on the margins, as they were effectively barred from investigating the allegations of doping until the various court cases had reached a conclusion. Sports organisations clearly perceived a need to regain the initiative on policy formation or, at the very least, ensure that their voice was heard in the governmental forums that were discussing the matter. The decision by the IOC to convene a conference on doping in February 1999 was a direct consequence of the events surrounding the Tour. The aims set for the conference were to 'discuss and adopt measures allowing the fight against doping to be intensified' and to consider the specific proposal that a new international organisation be established

> as a foundation under Swiss law ... be headquartered in Lausanne, governed by a Council presided over by the IOC President. (IOC, 1998)

While there was general support for an international agency, there was a broad insistence that it should be completely independent of the IOC. Consequently, the Declaration agreed at the conclusion of the Lausanne Conference was ambiguous about the relationship between the proposed agency and the IOC. It was agreed that an 'independent … Agency shall be established so as to be fully operational in time for the XXVII Olympiad in Sydney in 2000', but the brief of the body was less clear as this would now be determined by a new working group convened by the IOC and with membership drawn from among athletes, governments and the Olympic Movement.

The central issue was not whether there should be an international anti-doping body, but who would control it. The focus and remit of the new agency, the World Anti-Doping Agency, did not differ greatly from the initial IOC proposals:

> The Agency's principal task will be to co-ordinate a comprehensive anti-doping program at international level, developing common, effective, minimum standards for doping control … Among its duties, the new Agency is expected to commission unannounced out-of-competition controls in full agreement with [the] public and private bodies concerned.
>
> The Agency is expected to work with existing authorities to promote the harmonisation of anti-doping policies and procedures, identify a reference laboratory to advise the accredited testing laboratories, and co-ordinate the numerous educational efforts now underway. It also is expected to publish an annual list of prohibited substances. (IOC press release, 9 September 1999)

It was acknowledged that the Agency would not seek responsibility for the determination of doping infractions nor for the imposition of sanctions: both these responsibilities would remain with the international federations. The most significant recommendation, strongly supported by the Council of Europe, the European Union and the United States, was that the Agency would now be far more independent of the IOC. Thus membership of the Agency's board would have equal representation from sports bodies and governments (or international governmental bodies). Responsibility for funding would also be shared equally between governments and sports bodies with the IOC agreeing to fund the Agency for its first two years at US$4m per year until the governments could finalise their funding formula. As regards location, it was agreed that WADA would be located initially in Lausanne, but that a competition be held to find a permanent home for the Agency. It was also agreed that Richard Pound, IOC Vice President, would be the first President. However some, including General McCaffrey, considered that Pound had a conflict of interests by virtue of the fact that he was an IOC Vice President and, more importantly, was responsible for the marketing of the Olympic Games – a product that can only be damaged by revelations of doping.

Although the timescale was tight, WADA made a significant and favourable impression at the Sydney Olympic Games. Not only did the Agency fund some 2,500 additional tests prior to the Games, but it also acted as an independent observer evaluating the doping control procedures during the Games. Following the conclusion of the Sydney Games, WADA concentrated on formalising its internal procedures and finances, and also agreeing its permanent location. By late 2001 the Agency had agreed the basis on which the various regions of the world would be represented and by whom. Agreement had also been reached on the formula for apportioning the 50 per cent financial contribution of the public authorities to WADA and it had been agreed that Montreal would be the Agency's permanent location. In addition to finalising its organisation and finance, WADA has acted quickly to establish an agenda and work programme for the next two to three years with the drafting of a World Anti-Doping Code as the key priority, followed by the development of an accreditation mechanism for laboratories, and the design of a test results management system.

That WADA has clearly developed considerable momentum since its establishment is in part a tribute to the commitment of its members and the support of the Australian government during its early activities at the Sydney Olympic Games. However, the promising start by the Agency is also partially due to significant changes in the policy environment. There have been five changes of particular note: the increasing interest of the European Union; the active involvement of the United States; the formation of the International Intergovernmental Consultative Group on Anti-Doping (IICGAD); the emergence of the Court of Arbitration for Sport; and the development by UNESCO of the International Convention against Doping in Sport.

While it is possible to trace EU interest back to the early 1990s when two declarations against doping in sport were made, it was not until the late 1990s that the EU became more directly involved. In December 1998 the European Council expressed its concern 'at the extent and seriousness of doping in sport, which undermines the sporting ethic and endangers public health' and it encouraged the involvement of the Commission in working with international sports bodies to 'fight against this danger' (European Commission, 1999: 1). The views of the European Council were endorsed by the European Parliament later in 1999 and by a series of informal meetings of EU ministers for sport. With its deepening interest in sport in general and doping in particular, it is not surprising that the EU was closely involved in negotiating the statutes that would define the remit and govern the operation of WADA. From the perspective of the IOC, the EU has a range of existing programmes that could support the work of WADA, particularly in relation to the funding of scientific research, furthering the harmonisation of laws among member states, and the funding and co-ordination of public health campaigns aimed at doping in sport.[2] But while the IOC was doubtless aware of the value of harnessing EU resources to the anti-doping campaign, it was probably more acutely aware of the EU's interventionist and regulatory culture and the threat that posed to the independence of sports organisations. Since the establishment of WADA the EU has provided financial support for a number of initiatives including projects concerning athlete education and scientific research.

Of comparable significance to the increasing involvement of the EU was the new-found enthusiasm for action on doping within the United States. In December 1999 the USOC called for the creation of an independent body to enhance the credibility and effectiveness of US efforts to tackle doping. The US Anti-Doping Agency was duly established in late 2000 with responsibility for sample collection, testing, adjudication, sanctions and research. USADA receives funding from the federal government (approximately 70 per cent) and part from the USOC (approximately 25 per cent), enabling the Agency to increase the number of tests to approximately 7,500 per year as well as fund research. By putting its own house in order in relation to Olympic sport at least, the United States has substantially enhanced its credibility in relation to global anti-doping policy and enabled one of the major world 'sports powers' to be fully involved in the establishment of WADA. However, substantial problems remain with the big four commercial sports namely baseball, ice hockey, football and basketball, where progress has been limited and slow despite consistent pressure from WADA, USADA and the US Congress.

The third development in the context of global anti-doping policy was the formation of the International Intergovernmental Consultative Group on Anti-Doping (IICGAD). IICGAD was established because of the need for a collective voice for the public authorities in relation to the IOC proposal for a new global anti-doping agency and also because of the need for a constituency from which representatives of public authorities could be selected. The governments of Canada and Australia were instrumental in convening the International Summit on Drugs in Sport in November 1999 in Sydney, which led to the formation of IICGAD. This organisation was given a brief to co-ordinate worldwide government participation in WADA and to facilitate the process of harmonisation of policies, especially in areas of exclusive government jurisdiction or responsibility such as customs regulations and the labelling of medicines and supplements. For the first time there now existed a permanent global forum for governments to exchange views on doping issues and to co-ordinate their contribution to WADA.

Fourth, the emergence of the Court of Arbitration for Sport (CAS) as a respected and authoritative court of last appeal in doping cases has helped to give the work of national anti-doping organisations consistency, has inspired confidence among athletes and has given legitimacy to the work of WADA and the Code. The final development of importance is the ratification of the UNESCO Convention against Doping in Sport which came into force in February 2007 and had been ratified by 41 countries by early 2007, making it the quickest UN Convention to be ratified. The Convention is a major step in harmonising anti-doping measures across all countries and places an obligation on countries to align their domestic laws with the Code. It is expected that all those countries that signed the Copenhagen Declaration in support of the Code will eventually ratify the UNESCO Convention which together with the 570 international sports organisations that have adopted the Code would provide an extremely comprehensive and powerful foundation for a global anti-doping policy regime.

PROBLEMS AND PROSPECTS

Identifying the ingredients of an effective policy response to a problem as complex and multi-faceted as doping is difficult, but there appear to be six factors that are necessary for progress:

- a global organisational infrastructure;
- adequate financial resources;
- scientific research capacity;
- genetic engineering;
- political support; and
- public support.

It is generally accepted that the various resources of the IOC (e.g. global leadership and network of accredited laboratories), the international federations (IFs) (links with domestic federations and thus with athletes) and governments (legal, financial and administrative capacity) needed to be combined if a successful global response to doping was to be achieved. There is no doubt that the establishment of WADA, the role of CAS and the involvement of UNESCO have marked major steps in the development of an effective global anti-doping regime. Suspicion of WADA by many international federations and within the IOC has steadily declined. The major organisational challenge is now at the national level where only about 30 countries have a national anti-doping organisation, some of which are seriously under-resourced.

The second problem facing WADA is securing a sufficient resource base. The scale of the funding problem is easily illustrated. According to Dr Don Catlin, one of the most respected authorities on doping in sport, 'the labs' ability to respond to [doping] is restricted by funding because doping has never been a serious priority for sport' (*Salt Lake Tribune*, 20 October 1999). He added that although the USOC had paid US$500,000 for a high-resolution mass spectrometer, his laboratory did not have the funds to employ staff with the necessary qualifications to make the machine fully operational. John Hoberman went further and talked of a strategy of 'calculated underinvestment' by the IOC and the major federations. WADA's budget for 2006 was just under US$24m, 15 per cent of which was spent on out-of-competition tests and 60 per cent on scientific research. The sum is substantial, particularly when added to the amounts already being spent by the IFs and by state anti-doping agencies, but the challenge is to maintain the financial commitment of partner organisations once the initial enthusiasm for the work of WADA has passed, and to meet the ever-increasing costs of scientific research.

The third problem is closely related to financial resources and concerns the capacity to meet the scientific challenges that lie ahead as a result of the continuing experimentation by athletes with new drugs. Although scientists have recently successfully developed a dual urine/blood test to detect rEPO, new drugs continue to be developed and used by athletes thus requiring anti-doping organisations to review and update constantly their analytic procedures. According to Don Catlin 'you have to test for a couple of thousand steroids to stay ahead of the game' (AP interview, 25 January 2007, http://www.msnbc.msn.com/id/16818387/). The discovery of THG was a stark warning to the anti-doping authorities of the relative ease with which steroids can be designed to be undetectable by the current range of testing procedures. Each new generation of drugs tends to require more sophisticated and consequently more expensive laboratories, research teams and clinical trials. Despite the income to WADA, it will rely heavily on research programmes funded directly by sympathetic governments or bodies such as the EU.

Although the development of therapeutic applications of genetic engineering is still in its infancy there has already been debate regarding the implications of genetic modification for sport (Miah, 2001a, 2001b), the fourth problem. One way in which knowledge of the human genome might be used is to modify the genome in specific ways including the use of genetically modified red blood cells or the production of various hormones. For example, genetic therapy offers the prospect of inserting genes into a cell to create a faster 'twitch' muscle in sprinters or a stronger take-off leg for high jumpers. Although the effective exploitation of this type of 'genetic doping' is still some way in the future, the prospect raises significant issues for anti-doping authorities associated with detection and the rights of athletes. First, it is still not clear whether genetic doping will leave an evidence trail in the body, for example from the virus used to transport the gene. Second, it is unclear if gene doping will be detectable from a blood sample or whether a tissue sample (a much more invasive procedure) will be necessary.

Genetic knowledge might also be exploited in sport through modifications being made very early in the life of the human organism to the germ-line cells of the newly fertilised egg with the aim of enhancing athletic performance. Among the issues that are raised by this possibility is the extent to which the athlete can be held responsible for the decisions of his/her parents to genetically modify the embryo. In admittedly loosely equivalent cases involving the doping of minors the young athlete is subject to a period of suspension and the coach/parent, or whoever administered the drug, is also sanctioned. However, unlike steroids the effect of genetic modification at the embryo stage may be permanent and irreversible, thus imposing a *de facto* life ban.

Although WADA and the IOC have both considered the implications of advances in genetic modification for anti-doping policy, the World Anti-Doping Code does not deal with the issue specifically. However, at one level genetic modification is simply one more advance in doping that anti-doping authorities such as WADA have to face and could therefore be treated in much the same way as other manipulative practices such as blood doping through transfusion of blood. At the very least the prospect of genetic modification adds a layer of complexity to existing issues regarding athlete rights, but also adds a series of new and less tractable issues.

The fifth problem concerns the maintenance of political support for anti-doping efforts. It is only just over 10 years ago that the main impediments to tackling doping in sport were a series of subversive governments, most notably East Germany and the Soviet Union, and a further group of apathetic governments which included Canada, Australia and the United States. Although much has changed, there remains an intense scepticism among many sports organisations regarding the depth of commitment of governments. However, there are a number of positive developments which augur well for the future. Most notable is the number of examples of co-operation on anti-doping issues between governmental and sports organisations. At the scientific level, the GH2000 project aimed at developing a test to identify the presence of growth hormones relies on joint funding of £1.8m by the IOC and the EU. The EU was also involved in the joint production of *The Clean Sport Guide* along with the Council of Europe (Council of Europe, 1998).

Finally, perhaps the greatest threat to the anti-doping campaign is the loss of public commitment to an anti-doping policy. The foundation of existing policy is the sustained disapproval of doping by the majority of those involved in sport and the continuing vocal public support for current anti-doping efforts. Possibly the greatest danger at the present time is that the debate on the future direction of policy becomes too esoteric for the public, too much the province of experts, and too dissociated from the sports that the mass of the public play and events that the public enjoy watching.

CHAPTER SUMMARY

» There are a number of justifications for opposing doping in sport, none of which is, on its own, convincing.
» The fundamental question of how to define doping in a way that is not unduly vulnerable to legal challenge remains unanswered.
» Over the last 35 years there has been slow and often erratic progress towards a more coherent and effective response to the problem of doping.
» Scandal (e.g. doping by Ben Johnson at the Seoul Olympics in 1988 or doping at the 1998 Tour de France) has often been the catalyst for renewed efforts to strengthen anti-doping policy.
» The establishment of the World Anti-Doping Agency in 1999 is a major landmark in policy development, although substantial problems remain, including the steady stream of new drugs available to athletes and the high cost of doping control and the associated research.

FURTHER READING

Houlihan (2002) and Waddington (2000) both provide reviews of the topic of doping in sport. Black and Pape (1997), Simon (1984) and Fost (1991) explore the philosophical bases for opposing doping in sport, while Wise (1996) discusses the difficulties in producing a legally sound definition of doping. Franke and Berendonk (1997) provide an important insight into doping in the former East Germany as do Fainaru-Wada and Williams (2006) into professional sport in the United States. Houlihan (1999) evaluates the progress in establishing a global anti-doping policy and achieving closer harmonisation.

NOTES

1 See Houlihan (2002) for a fuller discussion of the basis on which doping might be opposed.
2 See The Helsinki Report on Sport (Commission of the European Communities (1999) Report from the Commission to the European Council) for an indication of the scope of the EU's interest in sport, its general priorities and its specific objectives in relation to doping. The EU's acknowledgement of the importance of sport and its potentially central role is in part due to the pre-eminent role of Europe as the focus for elite-level sport. In 1999 Europe hosted 77 world championships and over 100 European championships.

REFERENCES

Australian Government (1989) *Drugs in Sport.* Interim Report of the Senate Standing Committee on the Environment, Recreation and the Arts. Canberra: Australian Government Publishing Service.

Black, T. and Pape, A. (1997) 'The ban on drugs in sport, the solution or the problem?', *Journal of Sport and Social Issues*, 21 (1): 83–92.

Council of Europe (1998) *The Clean Sport Guide.* Strasbourg: Council of Europe.

Dubin, C.L. (1990) *Commission of Inquiry into the Use of Drugs and Banned Practices Intended to Increase Athletic Performance.* Ottawa: Canadian Government Publishing Centre.

European Commission (1999) *Doping in Sport: the Fight against Doping at Community Level – State of Play.* Brussels: European Commission.

Fainaru-Wada, M. and Williams, L. (2006) *Game of Shadows: Barry Bonds, Balco and the Steroids Scandal that Rocked Professional Sport.* New York: Gotham Books.

Fost, N.C. (1991) 'Ethical and social issues in anti-doping strategies in sport', in F. Landry, M. Landry and M. Yerles (eds), *Sport ... The Third Millennium*. Sainte-Foy: Les Presses de l'Université de Laval.

Franke, W.W. and Berendonk, B. (1997) 'Hormonal doping and androgenization of athletes: a secret program of the German Democratic Republic', *Clinical Chemistry*, 43 (7): 1262–79.

Gay, M. (n.d.) 'Constitutional aspects of testing for prohibited substance'. London: n.p.

Houlihan, B. (1999) 'Policy harmonization: the example of global anti-doping policy', *Journal of Sport Management*, 13 (3): 197–215.

Houlihan, B. (2002) *Dying to Win: Doping in Sport and the Development of Anti-doping Policy.* 2nd edn. Strasbourg: Council of Europe Publishing.

International Olympic Committee (IOC) (1998) *Summary of Conclusion from the Meeting of the Working Group 'Financial Considerations'.* Lausanne: IOC.

Miah, A. (2001a) 'Genetics, privacy and athletes' Rights', *Sports Law Bulletin*, 4: 5.

Miah, A. (2001b) 'The engineered athlete: human rights in the genetic revolution', *Culture, Sport, Society*, 3 (3): 25–40.

Mill, J.S. (1962) 'On liberty', in M. Warnock (ed.), *Utilitarianism: Essays of John Stuart Mill*. London: Fontana.

Simon, R.L. (1984) 'Good competition and drug-enhanced performance', *Journal of the Philosophy of Sport*, XI: 6–13.

Vrijman, E. (1995) *Harmonisation: Can It Ever Really be Achieved?* Strasbourg: Council of Europe.

WADA (World Anti-Doping Agency) (2007) *World Anti-Doping Code*. Code Amendments version 1.0. Montreal: WADA.

Waddington, I. (2000) *Sport, Health and Drugs: a Critical Sociological Perspective*. London: E & FN Spon.

Wise, A.N. (1996) '"Strict liability" drug rules of sports governing bodies', *New Law Journal*, 2 August: 1161.

17

The Relationship Between Sport and Tourism

MIKE WEED AND GUY JACKSON

OVERVIEW

» *Sports tourism demand*
» *Sports tourism supply*
» *Sports tourism impacts*
» *Conclusions and future directions*

In this chapter, we look at the growth and significance of sports-related tourism. While sport and tourism, as two distinct elements of the leisure industry, clearly have great significance in their own right, so-called 'sports tourism' has developed significantly over the last two decades and the interrelationship continues to evolve in both the demand and supply structures of contemporary leisure.

Until relatively recently, this growing interrelationship and its significance to the leisure sector were not matched with substantive research or literature specifically examining the links. Work by Glyptis (1982, 1991) and subsequently the report commissioned by the Sports Council on the interrelationship between sport and tourism (Jackson and Glyptis, 1992) were some of the earliest substantive works in the area. Other valuable reviews of the field were carried out by De Knop (1990), Standeven and Tomlinson (1994) and Gibson (1998). The joint work by Standeven and De Knop (1999) was one of the first dedicated books to provide an introduction to the sports tourism phenomenon. Different facets of the interrelationship between sport and tourism have also been researched (e.g. Collins and Jackson, 1999; Jackson and Reeves, 1996; Redmond, 1991; Reeves, 2000; Vrondou, 1999; Weed, 2005).

A number of commercial leisure analysts have reviewed the volume and value of this emerging sector of the leisure industry (Mintel, 2005, 2007; Sport Business, 2005).

The potential of the linkage between sport and tourism clearly has economic, social and environmental impacts, both positive and negative. These have now increasingly been recognised, particularly by the commercial leisure industry, which very quickly saw the market potential and economic benefits of utilising sport within the development of tourism, and subsequently in its diversification and niche marketing strategies.

Initially slow to develop, but increasingly evident, has been a recognition of the importance of a collaborative approach to sport and tourism among the government agencies charged with development planning, policy administration and resource allocation in these fields. For example, Weed and Bull (1997a) described the lack of integration among regional agencies responsible for sport and tourism in England, suggesting in other work (Weed and Bull, 1997b) that government policy for sport and for tourism in the 1990s unwittingly worked against greater integration of these areas. Weed (2003) also suggested that the historically separate development of these functions, along with their very different cultures, is a substantial obstacle to collaborative policy initiatives. Consequently, both in the UK and in Europe, conscious integration between the bodies responsible for the separate sectors of sport and tourism is still rare, except perhaps where major events are concerned. In this respect, Weed (2006) has suggested that the hosting of the 2012 Olympics in London has considerable potential to 'kick-start' policy partnerships between sport and tourism bodies in the UK. However, there still remains scope for further integration of sports policy and tourism policy in many places in order to produce joint investment strategies, more effective facility development and greater economic and social benefit.

Only the commercial tourism sector has really embraced and benefited economically from a recognition of the contribution of sport to tourism product development, whether this be in widening the appeal of products, or inflating the tariff of tourism facilities, or in producing new and broader types of holiday package to include sports participation and/or spectating tourism. There is, however, far more to the sport–tourism interrelationship than these basic types suggest, as will be demonstrated below via an exploration of sports tourism's demand and supply structures and an examination of its impacts.

SPORTS TOURISM DEMAND

Several typologies of sports tourism *demand* have been attempted (e.g. Glyptis, 1982; Hall, 1992; Standeven and De Knop, 1999), invariably but inconsistently linked to specific types of activity, motivation or forms of supply. One of the most robust typologies, which amply illustrates the breadth of the sports tourism phenomenon, is that by Jackson and Reeves (1996), which was substantiated with empirical work from across the range of types (Jackson and Reeves, 1998; Reeves, 2000). They identify a *sports tourism continuum* which encompasses the complete range of sports tourism participation types, from 'incidental' participation (where sport is carried out as an occasional or very sporadic result of being away from the home environment usually during vacation time), through 'sporadic' and 'occasional' sports activity whilst away from the home area, to 'regular' and 'committed' activity, to 'driven' sports tourism (where the act or level of travel is dictated by, and dedicated to, the conduct of sport on a very regular basis – typically the professional or elite sports performer). Figure 17.1 outlines the findings with a number of significant subtypes of sports tourist, and summarises some of their main behavioural characteristics.

The proposed continuum and the associated cross-sectional study identify the complexity of sports tourism demand. The work is recognised to be far from all-encompassing. For example, the research to date does not clarify the influence of aspects such as the extent to which sports tourism participation changes or develops over time or over the life history, or through other social variables. More work is required and clearly explanations of sports tourism behaviour are multi-dimensional. However, the work does allow us to fit most types of sports tourism (whether sports-interested individuals on holiday, or regular spectator travel, or the travel patterns of professional or otherwise dedicated sports performers) onto a 'scale' that helps us to untangle the complex demand profile of the overall sports tourism market. It also provides empirically identified key types within which researchers may focus future attention and the industry may target.

More recently, Weed and Bull (2004) have developed a more complex and multi-faceted 'Sports Tourism Participation Model', which plots the level of participation in sports tourism against the importance attached to such participation by individuals. Key elements of the demand continuum illustrated here are incorporated, but the Weed and Bull model also considers the role sports tourism plays in constructing individual's perceived identities and works towards establishing behavioural profiles across a range of sports tourism activities. In a broad introductory chapter such as this, a detailed discussion of the Weed and Bull model is neither possible nor appropriate, particularly as the demand continuum illustrated introduces many of the key issues. Those interested in this model should look at Weed and Bull (2004).

These and other studies are beginning to provide a demand profile of sports tourists that differs from that of more 'traditional' tourism subsectors. Sports tourists are (unsurprisingly) more activity oriented than most tourists. Sports tourism is more commonly undertaken during 'short' holidays or weekend breaks/trips than much tourism, but is also increasingly significant within longer holidays. Sports tourism tends to be more evenly spread throughout the year, is less focused on coastal destinations, and is more likely to be taken by childless (often young adult) age groups and those with above-average incomes.

What emerges from such an analysis is that sport is significant to, for example, the generation of day-visit tourism. Whilst some analysts do not consider that this should be included within tourism, because no overnight stay is involved, the industry makes no such distinction and day-visit tourism is now a hugely significant element of overall tourism volume (and to a lesser extent its value), and one that continues to grow. Few studies have

SPORTS–TOURISM DEMAND CONTINUUM

Summary characteristics	INCIDENTAL	SPORADIC	OCCASIONAL	REGULAR	COMMITTED	DRIVEN
DECISION-MAKING FACTORS	Impromptu	Unimportant	Can be determining factor	Important	Very important	Essential
PARTICIPATION FACTORS	Fun or duty to others	If convenient	Welcome addition to tourism experience	Significant part of experience	Central to experience	Often sole reason for travel
NON-PARTICIPATION FACTORS	Prefer relaxation non-activity	Easily constrained or put off. Not essential to life profile	Many commitment preferences	Money or time constraints	Only unforeseen or significant constraints	Injury, illness or fear of illness
TYPICAL GROUP PROFILE	Family groups	Family and friendship groups	Often friendship or business groups	Group or individuals	Invariably groups of like-minded people	Elite groups or individuals with support
LIFESTYLE	Sport is insignificant	Sport is non-essential. Liked but not a priority	Sport is not essential but significant	Sport is important	Sport is a defining part of life	Sport is professionally significant
SPORTS EXPENDITURE	Minimal	Minimal except sporadic interest	High on occasions	Considerable	Extremely high and consistent	Extremely significant. Funding support from others

FIGURE 17.1 Sports-tourism demand continuum

Source: Derived from Jackson and Reeves (1996)

systematically isolated the sporting component of day-trip tourism, but it can reasonably be estimated as responsible for, or involved in, between 10 and 15 per cent of day trips in the UK (Collins and Jackson, 1999; Keynote, 2005). Accurate and consistent volume estimates are problematic and hinge largely around different definitions of what represents sport in such trips (e.g. whether the large number of the more rigorous walking/hiking trips are included) and at what point such recreational travel becomes a day trip. Also, there is a paucity of reliable data on the overall volume of spectator travel across the full range of sports.

As the deliberate development of sports facilities in tourism contexts has emerged, sport has also become increasingly significant in the generation of holiday tourism. Hotels and tourism packages increasingly specifically target the growing number of holiday-makers wanting 'activity' as part of their vacation. Again, whilst estimates vary, it appears that around 10 to 15 per cent of holidays involve sport as a significant component (BTA/ETB, 1992; Jackson and Reeves, 1998; Mintel, 2000, 2005; Smith and Jenner, 1990). Some estimates are significantly higher, but tend to include substantial levels of recreational (non-sport) holiday activity, particularly 'swimming' within the data. Beyond the former broad, but informed, estimates of the volume of the sector, assessing both the volume and the value of sports tourism remains a frustratingly imprecise science. As Collins and Jackson (1999: 171) note:

> there are very few reliable sources of data which are sufficiently precise to allow an accurate overall view of the volume and economic significance of sports tourism. This is a further indication of the inability of tourism statistics to accurately profile the behaviour of tourists, which has long been noted.

Major sports events can also be seen to generate significant tourism volumes, and the more identifiable tourism impacts of major events have generated interest amongst researchers and potential hosts. Getz (2003), for example, describes the significant growth in sports event tourism, as both demand and commercial suppliers have developed. Such growth provides opportunities for the many tourists for whom, both domestically and internationally, sports spectating has become a primary reason for holiday trips. Major 'hallmark' events (Olympic, Commonwealth and Pan-American Games, and world and European championships in individual sports etc.) provide opportunities for tourists to take a holiday based solely around high-class sports spectating, or to incorporate sports spectating into their holiday. Travel to a vast array of sports events is now possible, enabled by both traditional and new specialist tour and travel companies, and sports events have become major tourism generators. Examples abound, but the 1992 Barcelona Olympics attracted nearly half a million visitors to the region (Collins and Jackson, 1999; Truno, 1994), and in the 10 years following the Games, annual visitor numbers doubled (Weed, 2006). Furthermore, although the Games had significantly increased the city's number of tourist beds, average occupancy rates had still increased from 70 to 85 per cent during this period (Sanahuja, 2002). In the UK, the Euro 96 European Football Championships attracted 280,000 visiting spectators and media to the UK, spending £120m in the eight host cities and surrounding regions (Dobson et al.,

1997). More recently, the announcement that the Olympic Games of 2012 will be held in London has been described by Weed (2006: 53) as the 'B of the Bang' for the UK tourism industry, the start of a tourism phenomenon potentially lasting 15–20 years and leaving a lasting legacy for the organisation and co-ordination of UK tourism.

However, sports spectating is not limited to major events. Much spectator tourism involves travel to watch a family member or friend compete. The spectator following of events such as the London or New York Marathons and, indeed, many smaller mass participation events illustrate this point, as do the large numbers (mainly parents and family) who turn up to watch junior sports tournaments and events. In addition, the weekly leagues in a range of sports, although mostly football, in a range of countries around the world provide for regular domestic sports spectating day trips. However, the ever-increasing popularity of football and the growth of competitions such as the European Champions League lead to such trips becoming international in nature and, in the vast majority of cases, involving at least one overnight stay, with resulting economic benefits to the destination.

The term 'activity holiday' has entered our vocabulary and in the UK this is now a multi-billion-pound subsector of the tourism market (Mintel, 2005). The majority of activity holidays are sports related and this has boosted the sector, particularly the rural communities where much of this tourism activity takes place. A whole new 'genre' of tourism activity has emerged which is identifiably different from the exclusively relax-ation-oriented, sun-seeking tourism of the 1970s and early 1980s. The activity holiday consumer profile is diverse, including independent adults, parents and families, school parties, or groups of children at summer camps. Activity holiday markets in the UK are predominantly domestic, with 85 per cent of British consumers taking their activity hol-idays within the UK. Furthermore, many see activity holidays as an extra break, taken outside the traditional holiday period.

Found more outside the UK is the German concept of *Volkssports*, which translates as 'people's sports' or 'life sports'. Volkssports are family-oriented active recreations which originated in Germany, Austria and Switzerland in the early 1960s. The American Volkssports Association, which co-ordinates over 500 clubs in the United States, pro-motes the activities – walking, cycling, swimming and cross-country skiing – as sports in which anyone can participate with friends and family throughout his or her life. The con-cept is now found in over 20 countries around the world under the auspices of Der Internationale Volkssportverband (IVV) (The International Federation of Popular Sports). However, as Agne-Traub (1989) predicted, their increasing international popu-larity has led to their incorporation into business and pleasure travel and events are often scheduled to attract day-tripping tourists. A similar concept underpins the range of events established and calendared by local and municipal authorities to attract visitors and their spending, as well as providing a recreational, sometimes elite performance event, for the benefit of the local population, and sometimes to promote the city or area. British examples would be events such as the London (and others) Marathon, the Great North Run, the Scarborough Cricket Festival and the Worthing Bowls Festival.

There is great potential for such initiatives to stimulate sporting activity in a range of areas. Moreover, because many such activities lend themselves to universal participation, they can be linked to health promotion and active living programmes – something that has been largely neglected by sports development and health promotion professionals. The potential for sports tourism to play a role in the 'sports development process' was outlined in the early work by Jackson and Glyptis (1992), and more recently by Weed (2001a). Both studies noted that there are a vast number of people who only pick up a racquet or a ball while on holiday. If the playful and health-related benefits of sport are stressed by those organising sports activities on holidays, then this can have a great impact on developing active and healthy lifestyles when the tourist returns home. In this way, holidays can be used to entice individuals to take up a sport; activity holidays by schools and youth groups often generate interests for life. In addition, 'performance camps' away from home are increasingly common for some of the nation's best young sportspeople. Such examples show the potential for sport within the sport–tourism relationship.

SPORTS TOURISM SUPPLY

Turning to the *supply profile* of sports tourism, there has been a 'quiet revolution' in tourism supply development. This started with the provision of better hotel facilities (initially the inclusion of swimming pools in the product portfolio) and continued through the addition of health club facilities and access to tennis and golf provision, until the highest tariff/quality accommodation (outside city centres) now sees hotels set alongside their own golf and multi-sport complexes. Sport has became an integral part of the established tourism product, with conference and business tourists in particular now having high-class, prestigious facilities made available to them as competition increases for their custom. Manchester, for example, used its Olympic bids and its hosting of the 2002 Commonwealth Games to spearhead its push for the conference market. Sports facilities are now seen as almost essential in attracting the highly lucrative conference market. However, in addition to providing for the conference market, many 'country-house'-type hotels cater for the 'upmarket' sports tourist. It is often the range and quality of the facilities as well as the luxurious nature of the accommodation that define this product as 'upmarket' (Weed, 2001b; Weed and Bull, 2004). In fact, in a number of cases this market has been provided for by the addition of five-star accommodation to long-established and renowned sports facilities. For enthusiasts who cannot afford such hotels, many smaller hotel operators have agreements with local sports providers to attract visitors for mutual benefit. Furthermore a substantial number of farms have diversified into tourism and provide sport and recreation activities for those on a tighter budget.

Both major travel operators (e.g. Thomson) and smaller 'independents' have diversified their product offers into sports tourism holidays, particularly over recent years.

Within the latter group, the number of specialists and products available in activities of all types has grown significantly. Larger operators typically now offer multi-activity holidays, as well as sun/sea packages, and most of the latter include sports activity options. The UK now boasts over a hundred accredited independent tour operators (often specialising exclusively in activity tourism niches) offering sport and activity tourism ranging from golf holidays to high mountain range trekking. Several other independent operators directly market their multi-activity facilities and packages, such as walking, biking, pony trekking, canoeing adventure holidays; or aquatic-oriented pursuits such as sailing, surfing, windsurfing, diving, etc. These commercial operators are supplemented by education-sector centres and other commercial professional training/team-building centres. The diversity of sport/adventure tourism opportunities, as illustrated by these few examples, is substantial and still growing.

Sports holidays, particularly those in rural areas, have provided a whole range of tourism development opportunities ranging from those operated from enterprising small hotels, to the farm diversification projects mentioned earlier. As such, there is a range of examples of the effective use of countryside resources for sport and recreation from all around the world. Jackson (1999) notes the environmentally friendly nature of cycling as an activity in national parks in the United States, whilst in Crete and Thrace 'soft' forms of sports tourism, such as hiking, orienteering and cycling, have been promoted in rural areas (Vrondou, 1999; Vrondou and Kriemadis, 2006). In this Greek case, these 'soft' forms of sports tourism have been seen as having the potential to diversify tourism beyond the traditional 'mass' product for which Greece is known, and to have substantial potential for the future of the Greek tourism industry. Vrondou (1999) provides an example of a characteristic of sports tourism that is found elsewhere. Here, sports tourism is seen as a sustainable form of tourism that might 'minimise negative effects and maximise social, environmental and economic benefits' (Regional Programme for Crete, 1994–99) whilst also having the potential to promote local cultures, as the activities result in greater access to alternative routes and localities, with distinct natural and cultural characteristics. This is something which the World Tourism Organization (1988) has recognised and promoted for almost 20 years, commenting that the sport and recreation dimension can enrich the tourism experience by allowing greater interaction with destinations and a fuller appreciation of the social and cultural life of local communities.

Beneficially, there is also much evidence (see Jackson and Glyptis, 1992; Weed and Bull, 2004) that tourism can play a role, particularly in coastal or rural areas where the population may be dispersed, in supporting standards of sports facilities that would otherwise be unavailable to local residents. There is a range of examples of tourist support for the upkeep of recreational parkland and sports facilities in rural communities in France, North America, Australia and even Thailand. In many cases, as well as catering for the local market, facility developers find it essential to account for the recreational needs of tourists. In fact, in order to realise financial targets, leisure pool developments must often attract a high proportion of visitors from outside the immediate area. It is also important to ensure that these visitors spend money both inside and outside the facility, because without this visitor support many significant leisure developments would simply not be viable. Thus, tourism is sometimes essential in supporting local-level sports provision, as well as the local economy.

SPORTS TOURISM IMPACTS

As the above discussion intimates, there are clear *impacts* from sports tourism development. The economic impact is perhaps the most obvious and has already been evidenced in terms of adding value to individual facilities and sometimes to whole destinations. Broadly, sports tourism is a dynamic and expanding sector of the tourism economy, and by definition this is attractive economically. Sports-related facilities and events are clearly capable of generating visitors from outside the local area, and of attracting more and/or higher-spending visitors to existing tourist locations. There is economic benefit locally from sales of accommodation, food, beverages, gifts, admission fees, other spending at facilities, hire fees, use of transport, etc. Thus, there are clear benefits from attracting visitors, using sport or sports facilities as a key part of the tourism product offer. Sport and its events may also generate sponsorship income, inward investment, media exposure, ongoing tourist appeal and secondary multiplier effects. There are potentially significant economic benefits to be accrued from the additional revenue, employment, infrastructure, etc., to local and national economies which sports-oriented tourism provides.

Ten years ago Jackson and Reeves (1996) suggested that an estimate that 10–15 per cent of domestic holidays in Northern Europe have a sports orientation is not unreasonable and, while evidence is sparse, consumer preferences in the last 10 years seem to reinforce this view (Sport Business, 2005). However, the authors called for a more specific and consistent focus on this information gap in the collection of future tourism statistics. Three years later, Collins and Jackson attempted to synthesise a range of previous economic impact studies in disparate disciplines to present an overview of the economic impacts of the sport–tourism link, focusing on the UK. In doing so they commented that their work could only be considered 'indicative of the overall economic impact because of the inconsistent and invariably incompatible nature of the available data' (Collins and Jackson, 1999). Their 'conservative' estimates for the value of sports tourism in the UK are illustrated in Table 17.1, which suggests an overall value of over £2.5bn annually. A more 'bullish' estimate is provided by market analysts Mintel (2005), who value UK sports tourism at £3.4bn annually, but have a more 'inclusive' view of the sport component. That the Collins and Jackson estimate from 1999 remains the most recent 'academic' estimate of economic impact is an indication of the difficulty and complexity of disaggregating information on economic aspects of sports tourism.

TABLE 17.1   The economic impact of sports tourism in the UK

Types of sports tourism	Value (£m)
Sports as a prime activity on domestic holidays	1,640
Sports as a prime activity by overseas visitors	142
Sport as a prime activity on day trips	831
Total	2,613

Source: After Collins and Jackson (1999)

It has tended to be in the area of sports events that most economic impact research has been conducted, and it is therefore useful to review some of this research here. The obvious direct benefits of major sporting events (new facilities and visitor spending) are supplemented in most cases by a post-event tourism boost. Resulting publicity and the positive influence on local tourism are clear advantages of staging such events.

Although earlier Olympics made losses for the host cities (Munich and Montreal), since the commercial success of the Los Angeles Games in 1984 (which realised a surplus of £215m), there has been considerable competition for the privilege of being the host city for the Olympic Games. There is now far greater understanding of the broad and indirect benefits to cities, regions and governments of hosting major events, even where there is an initial cost to a city (see Preuss, 2004). The additional economic activity as a result of the event is invariably massive.

The act of winning the Olympic Games is a catalyst for bringing forward general infrastructure investments that may have been on the drawing board for a number of years. As a result of the 1992 Games, Barcelona gained a ring road, a new airport and the redevelopment of an area of derelict waterfront for the Olympic Village, as well as the associated spending in the wider region of 422,000 visitors and other event-related income. The worldwide publicity and infrastructure investment that the Games bring should enable a host city to attract further general investment, future events and more tourists. Even a failed Olympic bid can attract a large amount of public and private sector investment to provide some facilities and infrastructure. Manchester gained a world-class velodrome and several local infrastructure projects from its Olympic bid which helped it to bid for and host the Commonwealth Games of 2002. The level of public investment is usually justified along these lines, with many cities attaching importance to establishing an identity as a 'world-class city' in the circuits of international business, culture and tourism. At the city level, a major motivator for attracting sports tourism events may be the significant level of central government funding that is often attached to such projects. In fact, the group responsible for initiating Victoria's successful bid for the 1994 Commonwealth Games cite the infusion of federal funds into the city as one of the most important reasons for putting in a bid for the Games (D'Abaco, 1991). Rarely are major events viable without significant public sector investment. Invariably there is a cost to the host authority, but significant benefits to the wider economy (see Preuss, 2004).

Having staged a major games, it is important that cities seek to attract a string of future events. Subsequent events can be staged at a fraction of the cost of the original event as the infrastructure is already in place. However, the promotional, image and economic effects still persist. In this vein, Bramwell (1997) discusses the use of the 1991 World Student Games in Sheffield as part of a sustainable development strategy that promoted, and continues to promote, economic efficiency, social equity and environmental integrity in the city of Sheffield. Although initially unpopular and generating much local and external criticism, the continued legacy of these games is reflected in Sheffield's ongoing major sports events strategy that has attracted events such as Euro 96 and the World Masters Swimming Championships to the city with significant economic benefit (Gratton et al., 2005; Weed and Bull, 2004). However, it is not only large-scale events that can generate economic benefits for local communities, and this is a point that Dobson and Gratton (1997) make in relation to Sheffield's portfolio of events.

In order for major sports facilities built for mega-events to be sustainable in the long term, they need to be adaptable for local community use. One of the legacies of the World Student Games in Sheffield is the Ponds Forge International Sports Centre, which comprises a 50 m swimming pool, a pool with full diving facilities, a leisure pool and an indoor sports centre. This facility is perhaps the most flexible in the world, the pools having movable floors and bulkheads which make them adaptable for a large range of community uses. In fact, Bramwell (1997) describes the provision of new sport and recreation facilities for the long-term use of Sheffield residents as a key objective for the hosting of the World Student Games. However, it is important to note that many facilities built for major games may not be best suited to ongoing community use, either for participation or spectating.

It is also important to include factors other than economic impacts in the cost–benefit assessment of tourist-attracting sports events (Mules and Dwyer, 2005). For example, many such events, particularly those where regeneration is a major objective, often require the demolition of at least some existing provision or housing to make way for facilities, infrastructure or development. At worst, this can result in the traumatic break-up of entire communities. A displacement of indigenous communities occurred in the development of Barcelona's waterfront for the 1992 Olympic Games and in Beijing's preparation for the 2008 Games. Whilst many would see such redevelopment as a positive benefit that enhances the environment and image of the city, for those communities that are displaced the experience can be traumatic, and such socio-economic 'engineering' now receives very negative exposure, which denudes the positive impact which such developments and events are designed to secure.

Overall, however, sports tourism is viewed as having primarily positive impacts in comparison with many commercial development forms. Sports tourism has played a significant part in a number of countries in the generation of community identity and pride and in the economic and social regeneration of decaying urban areas. In addition, its economic potential has been harnessed in many rural areas to support the local economy and services. In the immediate aftermath of apartheid in South Africa, Nelson Mandela spoke of the role of the 1995 Rugby World Cup, hosted and won by South Africa, in 'nation building' after the years of internal turmoil and international isolation the country had suffered.

Both in the UK and the United States, sports-related tourism initiatives have been at the forefront of urban regeneration programmes (see Collins and Jackson, 1996; Roche, 1994; Stevens, 2005). In many urban areas, the use of sport within the tourism strategies of local government for regenerative purposes is also well documented (Law, 1992; SCLG, 1994; Silk and Amis, 2005). North American research by Rosentraub (2000) and Wilcox and Andrews (2003) discusses the substantial surge, since the early 1990s, in the number of new sports and entertainment facilities – largely aimed at staging sports events, concerts, conventions, conferences, exhibitions and any other events requiring a facility with a capacity of around 20,000 people. The prime objective identified in almost all of these cases has been economic development and revitalisation. An early example of this is provided by Chapin (1996), who specifically reviews the varying strategies of three facilities: Key Arena in Seattle, The Rose Garden in Portland, and GM Palace in Vancouver. The construction of the Key Arena in Seattle was part of a plan to revitalise an ageing, but culturally highly significant, civic centre. Here the former Seattle Coliseum arena was reconstructed and renamed as the Key Arena, as an integral part of the Seattle Center Entertainment District, resulting in a revamped city centre that retained much of its original heritage. In contrast, Portland chose to locate a new facility alongside an older, much smaller arena, and relatively new convention centre in an out-of-town development that is now specifically marketed as a Sports Entertainment District. Finally, Vancouver, like Seattle, located the GM Palace within its city centre, but focused on a newly built sports arena with the aim of enhancing the city centre as a 'metropolitan core'. These cases illustrate three widely popular strategies for urban regeneration utilising sports and entertainment facilities likely to attract visitors, namely reinvestment in existing facilities, development of new sports entertainment districts, and investment in inner-city revitalisation and redevelopment. However, a key factor in each of these cases, and one relevant to any town seeking to use sport in urban regeneration, is that it be developed alongside other leisure, entertainment and tourism facilities.

In rural areas too, sports tourism has made a number of significant impacts, particularly over recent years. Despite the evident sensitivity of rural environments and the fact that there will be some negative impacts of sports tourism development (see Hinch and Higham, 2004), sports tourism has for the most part maintained a reputation as 'soft' tourism (discussed earlier in the Greek example), capable of contributing to the rural economy in a range of contexts across the world. Countryside pursuits, such as hiking, climbing, orienteering, fell-running and cycling, all increasingly contribute to the rural economy, but perhaps the last has received the most recent attention in the literature. In the UK, the development of the National Cycle Network has seen rural districts and small local businesses invest in cycle tourism as a key element in rural economic development strategies (see Jackson and Morpeth, 1999). The authors note that the National Cycle Network is seen as having the potential to generate £150m in tourism receipts annually across the UK and over 3,000 jobs nationally, particularly focused in rural areas. The 'C2C Cycle Route' across the rural north of England, for example, is estimated to generate already £1.5m annually for the communities along its route. However, in more recent research, Lumsden et al. (2004) warn that the majority of this economic impact is generated by day visitors (70 per cent), and thus the impact is focused on 'hub' sites rather than evenly distributed along the route.

A cautionary note, however, should be sounded about an overreliance on the leisure economy. There is, of course, the long-documented concern about the part-time, seasonal and casual nature of many of the jobs that are created (see Shaw and Williams, 2002). Such dependency on recreation and tourism can also result in a neglect of ecological and environmental concerns. For example, Weiss et al. (1998) studied reactions to ski tourism among ski tourists and ski resort residents in Austria and Belgium. They found that ski tourists and locals who were not financially dependent on tourism had a much higher ecological awareness than tourism-dependent locals. This was clearly a result of the latter group's vested economic interest in the industry and was further highlighted by the fact that differences between these groups on general environmental issues were minimal. Environmental concerns in relation to ski tourism were found to vary according to the extent of the personal sacrifice involved in addressing such issues.

CONCLUSIONS AND FUTURE DIRECTIONS

This chapter has provided a broad overview of the significance and impacts of sports-related tourism from both a demand (participation) and supply (opportunity and facility provision) standpoint. It has also provided summary indications of the types of impact, both positive and negative, that sports tourism is now known to have. While conclusions per se are perhaps inappropriate in such a review chapter, there are some key points in this analysis that are worthy of emphasis. Most significant of these is that, despite a continued relative lack of recognition within leisure research and economic analysis, which often treat the sectors of sport and tourism separately, sports-related tourism is highly significant and continues its growth trend.

Notwithstanding the growth of security fears, further development of tourism seems assured worldwide, particularly as the Asia–Pacific region opens itself to visitation and trip generation. The Beijing Olympics are indicative of this process, and indicative too of sport's globalisation, as international competition and sport-associated travel filters from the traditional national representative matches and well-spaced world championships to embrace far more regular international competition and global 'tour' events almost weekly (fuelled by the emergence of a global television audience and attendant commercial opportunity). Even club and individual sports participation has developed an international element.

Clear corollaries are that international sports travel and spectator sports tourism will also grow and will have an increasing and significant economic impact. Whilst estimates of value in this area are notoriously difficult to extrapolate, if a conservative figure of 'around' 10 per cent of tourists have sport as a main or significant activity within their travel (Collins and Jackson, 1999; Sports Business, 2005; Standeven and De Knop, 1999), then sports tourism is a multi-billion-pound sector worldwide, and significant too within individual national economies. In addition, in terms of pure participation, it is clear that within holiday activity (i.e. a subset of overall tourism activity), the significance of sporting activity within the decision of whether and where to travel/stay is even more significant. In terms of participation, sports tourism is a significant element of the leisure and tourism market, and continues to grow.

We have shown through the concept of a 'sports tourism continuum' that within these macro-level figures there is a complete range of sports tourist types. These range from individuals who are 'driven' sports tourists (typically the professional or elite sports performer) through a continuum of interest types from those whose travel behaviour is regularly and significantly influenced by sport spectating or participation considerations in one or a number of sports, to those whose vacation time provides an occasional or irregular opportunity to experience sporting activity that everyday life largely precludes. In between lies a whole range of sports tourist types whose behaviour patterns vary in the level and type of activity. As noted earlier, this range of profiles has since been explored in further detail by Weed and Bull (2004).

Needless to say, our analysis shows that facility and other opportunity provision for sports tourism also continues to broaden and develop. An increasing proportion of accommodation, tour operating and other commercial companies, destination authorities and some national governments have identified and embraced the notion that sports tourism generates an important subset of the tourism market. This is particularly attractive as the tourism it generates is often supplementary to, rather than replacing, current demand. Consequently, sports events, large-scale sports facility developments and sports tourism have been seen, and continue to be viewed, as beneficial activity and/or facilities capable of maintaining the attractiveness, visitworthiness and the economic viability of destination settings as diverse as major industrial cities, ailing (or developing) coastal resorts and declining (or evolving) rural economies, looking for means to attract visitors and spending into peripheral regions, and limited and often tenuous local economic systems. The natural resources and space on which sports tourism often thrives are sometimes the only asset of such locations, other than an underemployed workforce.

Notwithstanding the fact that evidence can be found of events and facility developments where the proposed economic gains have not materialised, or have been over-stated, or where there has been unwise investment, inadequate and over-ambitious planning and poorly managed activity, the overall conclusion has to be that the great majority of sports tourism developments have resulted in positive economic impacts. In fact, economic considerations continue to serve as the primary motivation for most sports tourism developments. Consequently, better measured and more considered impact statements are now emerging for major events and facility developments of all scales, where previously these were under-analysed and sometimes fanciful.

We have also noted that in analysing the interrelationship between sport and tourism, it would be folly to focus solely on the economic impacts. Clearly there are socio-cultural and environmental externalities that must also be considered. In these two broad areas of analysis it is commonplace and understandable that negative impacts are highlighted and often emphasised. However, it is equally clear that while negative externalities exist – as with most forms of development and growth markets – a host of positive non-economic benefits may well result from sports-related tourism growth. This is particularly the case when the scale and pace of development are con-trolled, and if integrated and sustainable development and management approaches are implemented.

Although sports tourism's relatively 'clean', 'inexpensive' operation makes it acceptable to most locations, and certainly more suitable than many tourism forms, a cost–benefit approach juxtaposing economic gains and environmental impacts is fraught with danger, and unlikely to lead to an agreed 'bottom line' between those with very different per-spectives of 'value', who are invariably drawn into such debates. However positive we might want to be about sports tourism and its benefits, we have to pay attention to the fact that sports or active visitors (walkers, trekkers, runners, bikers, climbers and others) do intrude into sensitive, sometimes unspoilt locations. Furthermore, sports tourists do occasionally compete for scarce resources with local communities, who may not always share the profit from such economic developments – golf is often highlighted in this con-text. There are undeniable impacts on the physical and social environment from many sports tourism activities and to ignore these is myopic.

Again, the answer has to lie in considered and sensitive approaches, and sustainable development and management of sports tourism – as has been identified for other, often more intrusive types of tourism. Despite its reputation for having 'soft' impacts, sports tourism must embrace these considerations. In fact, as Standeven and De Knop (1999) and Hinch and Higham (2004) also identify, this may be one of the linchpins around which sports tourism can continue to develop, whilst also maintaining its reputation for primarily positive impacts. The future of sports tourism operations, particularly in some of the more sensitive coastal and rural locations, has to include those management policies and elements of self-regulation that have become the essence of sustainable tourism management, something that has been recognised for at least a decade (see Bramwell et al., 1996). Bramwell has also shown (e.g. in his 1997 analysis of sports tourism developments in Sheffield) that this is the case not solely in sensitive environments.

A secure future for sports tourism developments includes, for example, a sensitive level and pace of development, limiting environmental damage, inclusion of local residents in the decision-making processes, use of local products and services, etc. While self-regulation and responsible management within the tourism industry have been identified as ultimately far more valuable and beneficial, such responsible action will almost certainly have to be backed up by an appropriate level of state and local-level regulation and/or legislation, to ensure that sports tourism development and activity continue to grow, but in a sustainable way that does not damage the very resources on which they depend and flourish.

From this analysis then, it should be clear that sport and tourism interrelate in a multiplicity of ways, and this interrelationship is likely to continue to grow as participation and opportunity continue to increase. This has clear implications for both analysts and providers of sport and tourism activity, for policy makers, investors, developers and managers involved in these fields. Whilst long unrecognised or underemphasised, the extent of the overlap and interrelationship between sport and tourism, as two traditionally separately treated elements of the leisure market and industry, is now increasingly recognised as highly significant.

The sports tourism interrelationship is manifest in a number of substantial characteristics of contemporary leisure activity and supply. These, in turn, have significance for the future leisure industry. These characteristics can be summarised as:

1 the now substantial volume and continuing growth of sports-related tourism demand activity (both spectating and participatory);
2 the extent, nature and continued growth of joint provision and infrastructure (sports facilities and events designed to attract both tourists and the resident market; and the increasing level of tourism programmes focusing on, or marketed to, sports-oriented individuals or groups);
3 particularly the economic impacts, but also the social and environmental considerations, that result from this now significant and increasing integration of sport and tourism activity; and
4 the implications for future integrated management and policy making for sport and for tourism, particularly where the boundaries between them are blurred.

CHAPTER SUMMARY

» Sports tourism has developed significantly over the last two decades and the interrelationship continues to evolve in both the demand and the supply structure of contemporary leisure.
» Sports tourism demand can be conceptualised in terms of a continuum from, at one end, incidental participation in sport as part of a vacation, through to the other end where travel away from home is dictated by sports activity.
» Sports tourism supply has expanded rapidly and sport is now an important and integral part of the tourism product.
» The impact of sports tourism can be evaluated in terms of costs and benefits to the economy, to urban regeneration efforts and to the local environment.

FURTHER READING

Weed and Bull (2004) and Standeven and De Knop (1999) provide overviews of the field of sport tourism. Bianchini and Schwengel (1991) examine the impact of sports tourism on urban regeneration. Weiss et al. (1998) discuss environmental issues associated with winter sports tourism, and Collins and Jackson (1999) explore the economic impact of sports tourism. Bramwell (1997) and Roche (1994) both examine the wide-ranging impact of mega-events. Finally, Weed (2003) examines the policy context of sports tourism.

REFERENCES

Agne-Traub, L. (1989) 'Volkssporting and tourism: something for the working class', *Leisure Information Quarterly*, 15 (4): 6–8.

Bianchini, F. and Schwengel, H. (1991) 'Re-imaging the city' in J. Corner and S. Harvey (eds) *Enterprise and Heritage: Cross-currents of National Culture*. London: Routledge. pp. 212–63.

Bramwell, B. (1997) 'A sport mega-event as a sustainable tourism development strategy', *Tourism Recreation Research*, 22 (2): 13–19.

Bramwell, B., Henry, I.P. and Jackson, G.A.M. (1996) 'A framework for understanding sustainable tourism management', in B. Bramwell et al. (eds), *Sustainable Tourism Management: Principles and Practice*. Tilburg: Tilburg University Press.

British Tourist Authority/English Tourist Board (BTA/ETB) (1992) *Activities by the British on Holiday in Britain.* London: BTA/ETB/NOP Market Research Ltd.

Chapin, T.S. (1996) 'A new era of professional sports in the Northwest: facility location as an economic development strategy in Seattle, Portland and Vancouver', Paper presented to the 'Sport in the City' Conference, Sheffield, UK.

Collins, M.F. and Jackson, G.A.M. (1996) 'The economic impact of a growing symbiosis: sport and tourism', Paper presented at the 4th European Congress on Sports Management. Montpelier, France.

Collins, M.F. and Jackson, G.A.M. (1999) 'The economic impact of sport and tourism', in J. Standeven and P. De Knop, *Sport Tourism.* Champaign, IL: Human Kinetics.

Countryside Commission (1998) *UK Leisure Day Visits: Summary of the 1996 Survey Findings.*

D'Abaco, G. (1991) 'Marketing parks and recreational facilities as tourism attractions – experiences from the Victoria Tourism Commission's "Melbourne Now" campaign', in *Who Dares Wins – Parks, Recreation and Tourism*, Conference Proceedings, Vol. 2 Canberra: Royal Institute of Parks and Recreation.

De Knop, P. (1990) 'Sport for all and active tourism', *Journal of the World Leisure and Recreation Association*, Fall: 30–6.

Department of the Environment/Welsh Office (1991) *Planning Policy Guidance 17, Sport and Recreation.* London: HMSO.

Dobson, N. and Gratton, C. (1997) *The Economic Impact of Sports Events: Euro '96 and VI Fina World Masters Swimming Championships in Sheffield.* Sheffield: Leisure Industries Research Centre.

Dobson, N., Holliday, S. and Gratton, C. (1997) *Football Came Home: The Economic Impact of Euro '96.* Sheffield: Leisure Industries Research Centre.

Getz, D. (2003) 'Sport event tourism: planning, development and marketing', in S. Hudson (ed.), *Sport and Adventure Tourism.* New York: Haworth Hospitality Press.

Gibson, H. (1998) 'Sport tourism: a critical analysis of research', *Sport Management Review*, 1 (1): 45–76.

Glyptis, S.A. (1982) *Sport and Tourism in Western Europe.* London: British Travel Education Trust.

Glyptis, S.A. (1991) 'Sport and tourism', in C.P. Cooper (ed.), *Progress in Tourism, Recreation and Hospitality Management*, Vol. 3. London: Belhaven Press.

Gratton, C., Shibli, S. and Coleman, R. (2005) 'The economics of sport tourism at major sports events', in J. Higham (ed.), *Sport Tourism Destinations: Issues, Opportunities and Analysis.* Oxford: Elsevier.

Hall, C.M. (1992) 'Adventure, sport and health', in C.M. Hall and B. Weiler (eds), *Special Interest Tourism.* London: Belhaven Press.

Hinch, T. and Higham, J. (2004) *Sport Tourism Development.* Clevedon: Channel View.

Jackson, C. (1999) 'Pedalling in the parks', *National Parks*, March/April: 34–6.

Jackson, G.A.M. and Glyptis, S.A. (1992) *Sport and Tourism: a Review of the Literature.* Report to the Sports Council, Recreation Management Group, Loughborough University.

Jackson, G.A.M. and Morpeth, N. (1999) 'Local Agenda 21 and community participation in tourism policy and planning: future or fallacy?', *Current Issues in Tourism,* 2 (1): 1–38.

Jackson, G.A.M. and Reeves, M.R. (1996) 'Conceptualising the sport–tourism interrelationship: a case study approach', Paper presented at the LSA/VVA Conference, Wageningen, The Netherlands, September.

Jackson, G.A.M. and Reeves, M.R. (1998) 'Evidencing the sport tourism interrelationship: a case study of elite British athletes', in M.F. Collins and I.S. Cooper (eds), *Leisure Management: Issues and Applications.* Wallingford: CABI Publications.

Keynote (2005) *Travel and Tourism Market.* London: Keynote Market Intelligence.

Law, C. (1992) 'Urban tourism and its contribution to economic regeneration', *Urban Studies,* 29 (3–4): 599–618.

Lumsden, L., Downward, P. and Cope, A. (2004) 'Monitoring of cycle tourism on long distance trails: The North Sea Cycle Route', *Journal of Transport Geography,* 12 (1): 13–22.

Mintel (2000) 'Special interest holidays', *Leisure Intelligence,* London: Mintel.

Mintel (2005) 'Activity holidays', *Leisure Intelligence,* London: Mintel.

Mintel (2007) 'Cycling holidays', *Leisure Intelligence,* London: Mintel.

Mules, T. and Dwyer, L. (2005) 'Public sector support for sport tourism events: the role of cost-benefit analysis', *Sport in Society,* 8 (2): 338–55.

Preuss, H. (2004) *The Economics of Staging the Olympics – a Comparison of the Games 1972–2008.* Cheltenham: Edward Elgar.

Redmond, G. (1991) 'Changing styles of sports tourism: industry/consumer interactions in Canada, the USA and Europe', in M.J. Sinclair and M.J. Stabler (eds), *The Tourist Industry: an International Analysis.* Wallingford: CABI Publications.

Reeves, M.R. (2000) 'Evidencing the sport–tourism interrelationship', Unpublished PhD thesis, Loughborough University.

Roche, M. (1994) 'Mega events and urban policy', *Annals of Tourism Research,* 21: 1–19.

Rosentraub, M.S. (2000) 'Sports facilities, redevelopment and the centrality of downtown areas: observations and lessons from experiences in the Rustbelt and Sunbelt City', *Marquette Sports Law Journal,* 10 (2): 219–35.

Sanahuja, R. (2002) *Olympic City – the City Strategy Ten Years After the Olympic Games in 1992,* Sports Events and Economic Import Conference Copenhagen, April.

Shaw, G. and Williams, A.M. (2002) *Critical Issues in Tourism: a Geographical Perspective.* 2nd edn. Oxford: Blackwell.

Sheffield City Liaison Group (SCLG) (1994) *The Way Ahead – Plans for the Economic Regeneration of Sheffield.* Sheffield: SCLG.

Silk, M. and Amis, J. (2005) 'Sport tourism, cityscapes and cultural politics', *Sport in Society,* 8 (2): 280–301.`

Smith, C. and Jenner, P. (1990) 'Activity holidays in Europe', *Travel and Tourism Analyst*, 5: 58–78.

Sport Business (2005) *The Business of Sports Tourism*. London: Sport Business Group.

Standeven, J. and De Knop, P. (1999) *Sport Tourism*. Champaign, IL: Human Kinetics.

Standeven, J. and Tomlinson, A. (1994) *Sport and Tourism in South East England*. London: South East Council for Sport and Recreation.

Stevens, T. (2005) 'Sport and urban tourism destinations: the evolving sport, tourism and leisure functions of the modern stadium', in J. Higham, (ed.), *Sport Tourism Destinations: Issues, Opportunities and Analysis*. Oxford: Elsevier.

Truno, E. (1994) 'Sport for All and the Barcelona Olympic Games', Paper presented at the 2nd European Congress on Sport for All in Cities, Barcelona, Spain, October.

Vrondou, O. (1999) 'Sports related tourism and the product repositioning of traditional mass tourism destinations: a case study of Greece', Unpublished PhD thesis, Loughborough University.

Vrondou, O. and Kriemadis, A. (2006) 'Sport in the restructuring of tourism policy in Crete: public and private sector roles and perspectives', Paper presented at the 14th Congress of the European Association of Sport Management, Nicosia, Cyprus, September.

Weed, M.E. (2001a) 'Tourism and sports development: providing the foundation for healthy lifestyles', Paper presented at the International Conference, 'Sport and Quality of Life', Vila Real, Portugal, December.

Weed, M.E. (2001b) 'Developing a sports tourism product', Paper presented at the First International Conference of the Pan Hellenic Association of Sports Economists and Managers, 'The Economic Impact of Sport', Athens, Greece, February.

Weed, M.E. (2003) 'Why the two won't tango: explaining the lack of consensual policies for sport and tourism in the UK', *Journal of Sports Management*, 17 (3): 258–83.

Weed, M.E. (2005) 'A grounded theory of the policy process for sport and tourism', *Sport in Society*, 8(2): 356–77.

Weed, M.E. (2006) 'Olympic tourism? The tourism potential of London 2012', *e-Review of Tourism Research*, 4(2): 51–7.

Weed, M.E. and Bull, C.J. (1997a) 'Integrating sport and tourism: a review of regional policies in England', *Progress in Tourism and Hospitality Research*, 3 (2): 129–48.

Weed, M.E. and Bull, C.J. (1997b) 'Influences on sport–tourism relations in England: the effects of government policy', *Tourism Recreation Research*, 22 (2): 5–12.

Weed, M.E. and Bull, C.J. (2004) *Sports Tourism: Participants, Policy and Providers*. Oxford: Butterworth–Heinemann.

Weiss, O., Norden, G., Hilschers, P. and Vanreusel, B. (1998) 'Ski tourism and environmental problems', *International Review for the Sociology of Sport*, 33 (4): 367–79.

Wilcox, R. and Andrews, D. (2003) 'Sport in the city: cultural, economic and political portraits', in R. Wilcox, D. Andrews, R. Pitter, and R. Irwin (eds), *Sporting Dystopias: The Making and Meanings of Urban Sport Cultures*. New York: SUNY Press.

World Tourism Organization (1988) *Special Interest Tourism*. Madrid: WTO.

18

The Olympic Games

Winners and Losers

HOLGER PREUSS

OVERVIEW

» *An economic history of the Olympic Games*
» *Interests and the staging of the Olympic Games*
» *Macroeconomic aspects of the Olympic Games*
» *The winners and losers*
» *Conclusion*

'The best Games ever' was the remark former IOC President J.A. Samaranch (see Box 18.1) made at the conclusion of a 'successful' Games. Striving to host the best Games ever is an unwritten rule that has been passed on until now (TOROC, 2005). But how can we measure the success of the Olympic Games? Does Samaranch mean financial, social, organisational or sportive success? And from what point of view does he measure the success: from that of politicians, the construction industry, medal winners, prosperous citizens or the IOC – in other words, from the point of view of the 'winners'? Even if it were possible to answer these questions, a central problem would remain, namely that of comparing the recently completed Games with previous Games.

A comparative judgement of the Games is difficult because the aim of each Olympic host city is different. In Los Angeles, for example, the primary aim was to avoid a deficit and the organisers therefore used existing infrastructure whenever possible (Ueberroth et al., 1985), whereas in Barcelona the priority was urban regeneration (Millet, 1995) or in China it is to prove its economic strength in a new world order. The purpose of this chapter is not to identify the 'best Games ever', but to provide an analysis of the Games from Munich in 1972 and to identify the various interested parties and determine the 'winners' and 'losers' in an Olympic host city.

Box 18.1   Juan Antonio Samaranch

- Spaniard (1920–)
- Seventh IOC President (1980–2001)
- Economist and diplomat

The world of Samaranch:

1   Supporter of professionalism – liberalising the amateur regulations (1981)
2   Preservation of the Games after the financial crises of Montreal 1976 and opening the Games for commercialisation
3   Opponent of the political misuse of the Games (boycotts 1976, 1980, 1984) and of apartheid
4   Growth and unification of the Olympic Movement and financial independence through commercialisation

---

AN ECONOMIC HISTORY OF THE OLYMPIC GAMES

Economic considerations have been prominent throughout the entire history of the modern Olympics, although their precise significance has varied greatly. Dividing the history of the modern Olympic Games into four periods (Box 18.2) illustrates the developing relationship and the shifting pattern of winners and losers.

The first period, 1896–1968, is characterised by the financial problems experienced by many Organising Committees of the Olympic Games (OCOG). The first Games in Athens 1896 took place at a time when the Greek state had just been declared bankrupt, the Games only taking place due to the generosity of wealthy Greeks living abroad (Georgiadis, 2000: 208–17). After staging five Games, each of which had substantial financial problems, de Coubertin drew the conclusion that 'the question is not whether they will be held, but how they will be held, and at whose expense' (1913: 183). During this period it is notable how many governments developed new financing sources in an attempt to limit their financial obligations. Some financial sources were used only once, while others became established elements in the financing of the Games (see Landry and Yerlès, 1996: 183–7).

Box 18.2   The economic history of the
Olympic Games

Period 1 (1896–1968): recurring financial problems, identification of new sources of income

Period 2 (1969–80): publicly financed Olympic Games

Period 3 (1981–96): increasing importance of private finance

Period 4 (1997–2012): mixed financing, long-term relationships between sponsors, TV networks and IOC

In the second period, 1969–80, the urgency to develop new sources of finance increased in parallel with the scale of the Olympics. However, although the sale of broadcasting rights and sponsorship emerged as an additional source of finance, they were still of minor importance in comparison with public finance. Munich 1972 is a good example of publicly financed Games and especially the use of 'special financing means', which refers to those OCOG revenue sources that require government approval, such as the sale of Olympic coins or the organising of an Olympic lottery. Apart from the revenues generated by the OCOG itself, for example from ticket sales (approx. 19 per cent), the 1972 Games were financed by special financing means (approx. 50 per cent) and by federal government, state and city subsidies (approx. 31 per cent). The public deficit of US$743m[1] was covered by the federal government (50 per cent), by the states (25 per cent) and by the cities of Munich and Kiel (25 per cent) (OC Munich, 1974: 53–4).

The Montreal Olympics of 1976 also relied heavily on public subsidy, but differed from the 1972 Games in that the Canadian federal government did not give the City of Montreal a financial guarantee. Because of a 'written guarantee that the federal government would not be called upon to absorb the deficit nor to assume interim financing for organization' (OC Montreal, 1976: 55), the OCOG had to stage the Games relying solely on financial support from the city. At the conclusion of the Games the private revenues generated by the OCOG amounted to a mere 5 per cent of the funds required. The remaining 95 per cent was provided by special financing means and by the public sector (1976: 59). The deficit of US$2bn had to be covered exclusively by the City of Montreal, which had provided the official guarantee to the IOC. Montreal's taxpayers had to pay off the debt until 2006 from a special local tobacco tax. It should be noted that the deficit was not the result of low revenues; instead it was caused by large investment in infrastructure, mismanagement, strikes by construction workers and imbalance in the market (Commission of Inquiry, n.d.: 314). After the experience of Montreal, cities were reluctant to bid for the 1984 Games because the cost was no longer considered tenable (Figure 18.1). There is a lack of financial information concerning the Moscow Games, although it is safe to assume that they were financed overwhelmingly by state subsidy

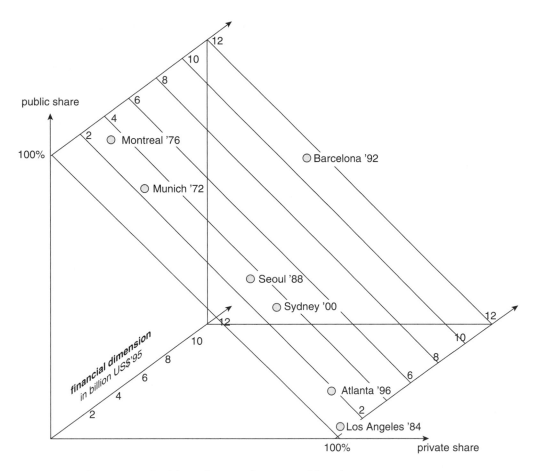

FIGURE 18.1   The pattern of public and private financing of the Olympic Games, 1972–2000

owing to the political aim to demonstrate the superiority of the communist system (see Ueberroth et al., 1985: 55–9). What Lord Killanin, IOC President during this period, said about the amateur issue in sport is also applicable to the financing of the Games: 'The word amateur unfortunately no longer refers to a lover of sports but, possibly, a lack of proficiency' (Killanin, 1982: 43).

The third period, 1981–96, paralleled much of the presidency of J.A. Samaranch. It was during this period that the removal of the word 'amateur' from the Olympic Charter during Lord Killanin's presidency was followed by the opening up of the Games to professional athletes in almost all sports. This contributed to the dramatic increase in sponsorship and television revenues for the Olympic Movement. The development of global markets and corporations which operate globally opened up the Games for worldwide sponsorship contracts (see also Box 18.3). Additionally, the pressure for Ueberroth to finance the Los Angeles Games without public money characterised the true beginning of commercialisation. In the previous period sponsorship constituted a few well-placed logos with the simple aim of brand recall, but during this period some sponsorships turned into close partnerships which opened up many new promotional opportunities for the Olympic Movement and host cities. The prospect of high revenues from both sponsorship and television attracted the interest of many cities to host the Olympics. This fundamental change secured the financial independence of the Olympic Movement and contributed to the ending of the political and financial crises of the 1970s and 1980s described in detail by Hoberman (1986).

Box 18.3   The history of financing sources

1896	Stamps, private donations, tickets, commemorative medals, advertisements in the official programme
1912	Olympic lottery
1924	Advertising inside the venue (once only)
1928	Copyright of Olympic emblems – first form of merchandising
1932	First Olympic pin (merchandising) and sponsoring
1948	Identification of television rights – which started in 1960
1951	First commemorative coin
1952	Concept of international marketing
1964	Surcharge on 'Olympic cigarettes' (merchandising)
1968	First mascot 'Schuss' (merchandising)
1972	Concept of licensees
1985	TOP-Program (worldwide sponsoring)
1996	International pin trade society
2005	Television rights include exclusive mobile phone and Internet rights

---

The first Games of this period were those in Los Angeles, 1984. At the election on 1 July 1978, there were no candidates except for Los Angeles, which had failed in its bid for the Games of 1980 and 1976. The deficit of Montreal's Games encouraged the citizens of Los Angeles to vote against public financial support of the Olympics (Agreement, 1978). The OCOG promised to meet the city's costs for security, transportation and other services which were not covered by the 0.5 per cent hotel tax and 6 per cent surcharge on the entrance tickets (Ueberroth et al., 1985: 121–2). The absence of other bidders and the lack of public financial support enabled, and indeed forced, the OCOG to impose conditions that the IOC would not otherwise have agreed to (Hill, 1992: 159; Reich, 1986: 24; Ueberroth et al., 1985: 53). After long negotiations, stipulations in the Olympic Charter were eventually declared void, thereby allowing the City of Los Angeles to decline a number of financial obligations associated with the Games (see Olympic Charter 1978 in comparison with that of 1979). These Games were the first in history without organisational links to the host city and the first to be financed from purely private sources; not surprisingly, little was invested in the transport infrastructure and in sports facilities. The overall cost of the Games amounted to a mere US$602m, which was covered by the OCOG revenues. There was even an official surplus of US$335m that was distributed between the United States Olympic Committee, the Amateur Athletic Foundation and the support of national institutions of Olympic sports (Taylor and Gratton, 1988: 34). The Los Angeles Games marked the transition from Games that relied overwhelmingly on public money to Games that were now increasingly dependent on private finance.

However, public finance was still important, especially when the state had clear objectives to achieve (see Box 18.4), as illustrated by the Seoul Games. The Korean state was keen to use the Games, *inter alia*, to demonstrate the country's economic growth, to improve its status in international sport, and to establish diplomatic relations with both communist and non-aligned nations (Park, 1991: 2–5). Additionally, the state wanted to promote the country for tourism and to market Korean products in order to stimulate foreign trade. Consequently, 53 per cent of the costs were covered by public finance (Kim et al., 1989: 42) and the alleged surplus of almost US$148m must be qualified in view of this large public contribution (Hill, 1992: 93).

The Barcelona public authorities also used the Games for the achievement of public policy objectives, in this case the redevelopment of the city and its promotion as a rival to Madrid, as an international site for industry and tourism. These reasons were used to justify the substantial public investment during the Olympiad and to create within the city and the province of Catalonia the desired impetus to make good the long-term underinvestment in leisure, culture, sport and transportation during previous decades (Millet, 1995: 191). Despite public investment amounting to US$6.2bn, the share of privately financed, Games-related expenditures at 38 per cent was still substantial. The official profit of the OCOG was only US$3m and must also be treated with some scepticism (Brunet, 1993: 113).

Box 18.4 Major objectives of host cities and countries

- *Promotion of a new image*: e.g. Munich 1972, Korea 1988, Sydney 2000
- *City redevelopment*: e.g. Munich 1972, Montreal 1976, Seoul 1988, Barcelona 1992, Athens 2004, Turin 2006, Beijing 2008, London 2012
- *Demonstration/promotion of upcoming economic power*: e.g. Tokyo 1964, Seoul 1988, Beijing 2008

- *Demonstration/promotion of a political system*: e.g. Moscow 1980, Los Angeles 1984
- *Increase in tourism*: e.g. Barcelona 1992, Sydney 2000, Athens 2004
- *Enhance city status*: e.g. Barcelona 1992, Atlanta 1996, Nagano 1998
- *Increasing inward investment*: e.g. Lillehammer 1994, Barcelona 1992, Atlanta 1996, Nagano 1998

Soon after the award of the Games to Atlanta, which appeared to be the most commercialised Games of the modern era, Samaranch commented:

> Marketing has become an increasing important issue … The revenues derived from television, sponsorship and general fundraising help to provide the Movement with its financial independence. However, in developing these programs, we must always remember that it is sport that must control its destiny, not commercial interests. (Samaranch, 1992: 2)

Similar to Los Angeles 1984, the city of Atlanta refused to accept any significant financial obligations. The OCOG had to use mainly private sources which promoted commercialisation. Compared with Seoul and Barcelona, the Games of 1996 had a very small budget with overall Games-related expenditure amounting to US$2bn (OC Atlanta, 1998: 222; see also French and Disher, 1997: 384). The city infrastructure hardly changed, although a few new sports facilities were erected. After the Games many facilities were reconstructed, seat capacity was reduced and temporarily erected facilities disappeared or moved to another location. With the exception of the publicly funded rowing facility, all sports sites were financed by the OCOG. As a result, the Games did not produce a surplus, much to the irritation of the IOC. The hoped-for surplus was supposed to support the Olympic Movement but instead was used to pay for the Olympic Stadium which was remodelled and subsequently served as a baseball stadium for the Atlanta Braves.

Box 18.5   Interest groups and the Olympic Games

- *IOC members*: cultural, geographical and power interests
- *State*: interests in improvement of international relations, positive psychological aspects for inhabitants and chance to demonstrate changes, such as modernisation
- *Politicians of the host city*: interest in

(Cont'd)

- increased tourism
- becoming a 'global city'
- getting better recognition in comparison with the capital city
- a huge one-time economic boost
- accelerated city development
- career enhancement and additional jobs

- *Local construction industry*: additional local demand for construction and international contracts
- *National sponsors*: interest in using the Games to improve relations with customers, contractors, partners and employees
- *TV networks*: interest in broadcasting the Games live during 'prime time', and selling expensive commercials

The final period, 1997–2012, started with the Olympiad of Sydney 2000. This time the OCOG was only responsible for staging the Games, while the Olympic Co-ordination Authority (OCA), established in 1995, was responsible for delivering the infrastructure for the Games. The investment in infrastructure was almost US$1bn (NSW Government, 2001: 6.5). Sydney staged the XXVII Olympic Games with a budget of US$3bn (Audit Office, 1999: 59, 161, 156, 157). Learning from the negative effects of the OCOG's independence from the city of Atlanta, this period is marked by mixed financing of the Games. Athens 2004 followed the form of an independent OCOG from a government-owned construction corporation. Owing to massive investments in infrastructure, security and oversized sport facilities the Games became the most expensive to date. The costs of the Games have been calculated to reach US$5.3bn. Disregarding the calculation of what infrastructure is Games-related and non-Games-related, the OCOG budget was approximately US$2.4bn (Athens OCOG 2003: 22) and in line with the average for previous OCOGs. The construction of the infrastructure and sports facilities to support and host the 2008 Olympic Games in Beijing is financially guaranteed by the Chinese central and Beijing municipal governments. The Bid Book forecasts an OCOG budget of only US$1.6bn (Bidding Committee Beijing 2008, 2001). This is very conservative, which is usual for bid cities in order not to overestimate revenues (interview, Payne, 2004). The city, region, state and private sectors are expected to invest US$33.7bn in total but only US$3.4bn in sport infrastructure (Lin, 2004).

For over 25 years commercialisation has had a decisive influence on the Olympic Movement. The extent of dependency on commerce has forced a reassessment of the relationships by the IOC in order to avoid over-commercialisation and to strengthen the

Olympic ideals. Consequently, the IOC puts increasing effort into raising the sponsors' understanding of how to use the Olympic ideals for their commercial purposes without corrupting them. Today the IOC tends to favour developing long-term contracts with sponsors and TV networks in order to develop a more mutually beneficial relationship. As a result, the IOC took direct control of the negotiations with both TOP sponsors and the television networks. On the one hand the power of the IOC increased; on the other hand the financial risk to bidding cities decreased owing to the fact that the IOC now provides approximately 40 per cent of the OCOG revenues before the selection of the next host is complete.

INTERESTS AND THE STAGING OF THE OLYMPIC GAMES

The range of interests involved in the staging of the Olympic Games is wide (Box 18.5) and differs from host to host. To identify the interested parties, and especially to identify 'winners', we have to look at the pattern of financial and ideological support at the bidding stage of the process of host selection. All interests that are mentioned here are drawn from specific Games and while some common patterns emerge, caution is required regarding generalisation because of the distinctive socio-cultural, political, historical and economic circumstances of each country.

The first interest is the *IOC members* collectively, who have a common concern to select the host city that will deliver the most successful Games as this is one way of ensuring that there will be strong competition to host future Games. The more cities that bid to host the Games, the greater will be the promises of investment from potential host cities and their governments. The second interest is the *regional groupings of IOC members* whose cultural identity is, according to Huntington (1996: 315–16), an important factor in determining how their vote is cast (see also Persson, 2000: 157–61; Preuss, 2000). The third interest is that of the *host governments*, which recognise the value of the Games in three particular areas, namely international relations, national morale and public relations. As regards international relations, the Seoul Games, for example, were an opportunity for the government to attempt to improve relations with North Korea and other socialist countries as well as to raise international awareness of Korean manufactured products (Kim et al., 1989: 48–66; Kramar, 1994: 141–84). The extra resources that are usually invested in developing the country's high-performance athletes prior to the Games provide a useful diplomatic resource, as the athletes give the country a higher profile at international sports events (Bernard and Busse, 2000). In addition, the host nation stages more international sports events before and after the Games; this provides further opportunities for strengthening links with foreign nations. Prior to the Sydney Games almost every member of the Olympic squad competed internationally between

September 1999 and March 2000, which included participation in seven world cups (OC Sydney, 2000: 75).

As regards improvements to national morale, the Seoul Olympics created 'a national perspective, a feeling of vitality, taking part, being recognised, modern and technologically up-to-date' (Denis et al., 1988: 229). This is also the aim of the Chinese government in staging the Games in 2008. However, in addition to feelings of enhanced national pride, hosting the Games can also lead to a deeper understanding of disability through hosting the Paralympic Games or a greater motivation to participate in sport as a result of watching the Games. Finally, the Games also provide important public relations opportunities. In earlier times one motivation to stage the Games was to demonstrate the superiority of a political system. The communist regimes of the 1970s and 1980s as well as the German Reich in 1936 saw the Games as a chance to prove the superiority of their systems. More recently, the motivation has been to announce or demonstrate to the world major changes in the host country. For example, Munich wanted to show that West Germany had rid itself of its Nazi past (Hattig, 2001). South Korea wanted to showcase its modern, high-technology national industries and replace its image as a developing country. Australia used the Games to enhance the tourist image of Australia as a whole and not just of Sydney (Morse, 2001) and was keen to raise its international profile as being more than merely 'a good source for raw material' (Parker, 2001: 9). Finally, Beijing is keen to demonstrate the growing importance of China to the world economy by delivering a 'High-Tech' Games (Lin, 2004).

In general, the Olympic Games are the biggest advertising opportunity that a city and a country can hope for. Years before the Games, companies will promote their association with the Games. In the months before the opening ceremony, reporters will write stories about the country. And in the weeks prior to the Games, the torch relay generates further media attention. The Opening Ceremony, which showcases the culture of the host, is watched by at least 3 billion people, while the Games themselves are watched by 92.5 per cent of all adults who have access to a television. The number of hours of Games coverage and the number of countries that broadcast the Games have increased at every Olympics (IOC, 2000: 5). The type and intensity of the promotion depend on the hosts and the media. In Sydney the Australian Tourist Commission (ATC) developed a strategy with well over 1,000 individual projects and provided not only good working conditions for the media, but also much additional information about Australia and Sydney (ATC, 2001: 3).

The fourth interest is the *politicians of the host city*, one of whose aims is to achieve a lasting increase in general tourist arrivals and in conference and convention business in particular (Dunn and McGuirk, 1999: 20; Hall, 1992: 17; Persson, 2001). This was a clear aim for Barcelona, Sydney and Athens, and is most often also the case for cities hosting the Olympic Winter Games. A second common objective of local politicians is to promote a city as a 'global city' with the ambition to generate international investment (Weirick, 1999: 70). At present there is evidence of the development of a network of 'global cities' based on combined global and transnational–regional links through which the international economic relations of industry are co-ordinated. Olympic hosts develop the location factors that are important to become a 'global city', such as new office space, improvements in telecommunications, gentrification of parts of the city, first-class tourist facilities and an international airport (Sassen, 1996: 123). In Seoul the increased awareness of the host city and its improved infrastructure stimulated the location of foreign industry and increased the sales of national products on foreign markets (Roulac, 1993: 18). A third, and related, objective of local politicians is to help host cities that are not the capital to become recognised nationally. Scott (1997) admitted that one objective of the Manchester bid was to project a sharper profile in comparison with other second-rank cities in the UK. Other examples include Barcelona establishing itself as a second centre of economic growth after Madrid, or Munich improving its status through the Games of 1972.

Local politicians are also concerned to stimulate the local economy by attracting funding that does not come from the city itself or which would otherwise have left the city. In this way they hope to create an economic impact, defined as a concentrated boost to the local economy (Preuss, 2004b). External or 'autonomous' money stems from the financial support of the state government and the OCOG. Most revenues of the OCOG are autonomous because they are from sponsors and television networks that are not located in the host city. Therefore, the argument of Olympic opponents that public funds used for the Games could be better spent on other projects has to be qualified (Preuss, 1998: 201). Politicians in Lillehammer aimed to improve the long-term employment situation by creating an autonomous economic impact through the Games in 1994 (Spilling, 2001). However, the assumption of a positive economic impact must be qualified. For a city the impact may be large because most money is external/autonomous, but for a nation the impact will be much smaller. In addition the economic situation at the time of investment has to be considered as Olympic-related investment can lead to 'crowding out' of other possible investment. Therefore, it should not be assumed that hosting the Games is the best way to stimulate the local or national economy (Baade and Matheson, 2002: 145; Szymanski 2002: 3).

The Games are often used as an instrument to help solve urban problems. When a city is elected host city, the time pressures that it experiences frequently lead to the breaking of deadlocks in urban planning. The Games offer the chance of achieving an acceleration of development and so may serve as a further motive for local politicians. Furthermore, association with the Games can positively affect the image of politicians. In the media the names of politicians involved in the Games are often mentioned, allowing them to 'bask in the reflected glory' (Snyder et al., 1986), as was clearly evident during Sydney 2000.

A fifth set of interests is the *local/regional construction industry*, which benefits most obviously from the building of infrastructure and sport facilities. During an economic boom, the price paid for building work increases, which means that the companies earn more money for the same work. During a recession, companies receive additional orders which they would not otherwise have obtained. Moreover, the companies also gain publicity. Multiplex, for example, which constructed Stadium Australia, has used its Olympic credentials to win large contracts overseas, such as the contract to build England's new National Stadium (Parker, 2001: 9). Other local businesses may be Olympic 'partners' and also see the Games as an important, though unique, opportunity to initiate business, develop contacts and promote their image internally and externally.

The final interest group is the *television networks*. Not only is broadcasting the Games a source of prestige, but the networks can generate profit from the sale of advertising, provided the Games can be broadcast during network 'prime time'. NBC bought the American rights to the Games between 2010 and 2012 for US$2bn. With the Games in Vancouver 2010 and London 2012 NBC has great potential to turn the investment into a profit.

One indicator of the significance of the interests identified above is the steady increase in the number of cities bidding to host the Games since the mid-1970s (see Figure 18.2). This figure shows that the number of bids for the Winter Games roughly equals that for the Olympic Games and that the number of bid cities for both the Winter and the Olympic Games increased after the financial success of the Games in 1984. A further rise in the number of bids was evident after 1992 owing to the success of Seoul and especially Barcelona in demonstrating the significant regenerative benefits that could be achieved through hosting the Games. The successful exploitation of the Games for country marketing by Australia added a further incentive to bid.

MACROECONOMIC ASPECTS OF THE OLYMPIC GAMES

The foregoing review of interests suggests a number of potential winners of the Olympic Games. The losers, however, best become visible through an examination of macroeconomic implications. The frequently claimed benefits to employment are dependent upon the size of the economic impact. Staging the Games increases demand at least temporarily, which usually creates employment and income. The additional income will be spent and induce further income and so on: in other words, a multiplier effect. However, imports, tax and savings reduce the event impact and within a certain period the one-time event-related economic impact has vanished completely. Only in the period directly associated with the Games and in some sectors (tourism, construction, services, etc.) is the economic impact significant in creating new employment or securing existing jobs. Through the induced post-Games impact, the employment effect might become greater. However, it is very difficult to measure this employment impact because the development of the markets without the Games is not known. In the case when the Games increase the attractiveness of the city and strengthen the location factors of a city it is most likely that permanent employment is created. This often happens in the tourism sector as well as for

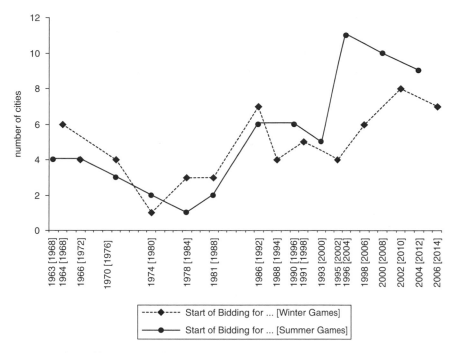

FIGURE 18.2   Number of bid cities (including applicant cities) and the year they started their bid

Sources: IOC (1997); Anon. 23 August (1993); Scherer (1995: 375); Schollmeier (2001: 27); www.gamesbids

conventions and other major sports events. However, what is critical is whether the investments have been directed at the most productive activity (Szymanski, 2002: 3). This very much depends on the fit between the Games and the structural needs of the city.

The initial economic response to increased demand due to Olympic-related investment is to increase production, while the second reaction is to regulate demand through price adjustments. New investment can only be expected if there is a strong expectation that demand will be sustained. While an increase in production or capital investment could satisfy the increased demand without the need to regulate through price, the limited capacity within business often results in price increases, thus leading to 'crowding out'. Crowding out can occur in sectors of high Olympic demand, such as construction, services and tourism. Many tourists, for example, avoid the Olympic region and some citizens of the host city will leave in order to escape the traffic congestion, noise and Olympic crowd. Consequently they spend their money outside the Olympic city. Some potential tourists may be lost for subsequent years if they thereby discover a new tourist destination (Preuss, 2005). Non-Olympic tourist attractions in the host city might be adversely affected by reallocation of consumption expenditure by local residents

(Development Action Group, 1996: 16). Local politicians might also reallocate public expenditure to Olympic priorities and away from established public services, thus creating the possibility of socially unjust distribution.

Price increases, which affect all who live in the host city, have three causes: first, the Games cause demand to exceed supply; second, speculation; and third, general inflation. Leaving aside speculation, which is a temporary phenomenon, it is important to consider whether, and to what extent, the Games have an independent effect on the cost of living within the city. From an examination of the Games over the last 30 years it is clear that, apart from Munich and Barcelona, there was no evidence of a link between the Games and price indexes for either the cost of living or rents (Preuss, 1998: 210). The sustained rise in both indexes in Munich and Barcelona is possibly explained by the increasing economic importance of both cities within their national economies to which hosting the Games might have contributed through an upgrade of location factors (see Preuss, 2004a).

However, hosting the Games increases overall demand, which leads to temporary price increases in specific sectors often due to the simple fact that shortages of some goods and services inevitably occur. Nevertheless, even temporary price rises may result in socially unjust reallocation as the poor may now be priced out of some markets (Development Action Group, 1996: 31).

The ecological effects of hosting the Games also need to be considered as most host cities commit themselves to the construction of new sports venues, parks and transport infrastructure. Because of the increasing emphasis within the IOC and at national level on environmental issues, one could assume that the overall ecological effect is beneficial for citizens. While there might be doubts about the beneficial effect on hosts of the Winter Games (because they are often staged in smaller cities where many sports facilities are constructed in open country), the analysis of summer host cities is more positive, as Table 18.1 shows. An examination of the locations of Olympic sports facilities since 1972 shows clearly that most often brown sites were chosen that were disused or had to be decontaminated. This pattern should not be surprising, since the construction of new sports facilities requires land relatively close to the city centre and only former industrial land is likely to be affordable.

London 2012 enters a new age of environmental planning with the OCOG trying to satisfy a twin principle of avoiding/reducing negative environmental impacts and, where this is not possible, offsetting them with appropriate environmental benefits (Levett, 2004: 69–89). The redevelopment of former brown areas is often expensive but the ecological benefit from the upgrading of the area may compensate for the costs in the form of social benefits in the long term. It is clear that the Games help to solve some urban problems and that the improved environment benefits all classes. However, time pressure may, as Hall (1992: 131) suggests, result in a relaxation of environmental guidelines or may 'crowd out' other ecologically superior projects.

There is often considerable time pressure on cities to complete the structural changes required of the host city. That became very clear for the Games in Athens 2004 and Turin 2006. From the moment a city is chosen as an Olympic host city, it suffers from great time

TABLE 18.1   Changed land utilisation caused by the Olympic Games

	Previous utilisation of selected areas (ecological view)	Post-Games utilisation of selected areas (benefit for the population)
Munich 1972	Disused estate, rubble, wasteland	Olympic park, traffic connection, recreational area, housing
Montreal 1976	Wasteland	Olympic park, recreational area
Seoul 1988	Contaminated site (Chamsil, Han River)	Olympic park, leisure-time venues (sports facilities), water purification, recreational area
Barcelona 1992	Decaying industrial site, old railway lines, run-down port, wasteland	Housing area, port atmosphere, parks, services complex, recreational area, sport
Atlanta 1996	Contaminated site (city centre)	Office buildings, recreational area
Sydney 2000	Contaminated site, wasteland, dump site	Olympic park, residential area, recreational area, 100,000 trees and shrubs planted
Athens 2004	Airport region, military base and industrial site at coastal area	Recreational area, wetland ecosystem, beach area
Beijing 2008	Underdeveloped residential area	Recreational area, 1 million trees planted in the city
London 2012	East London industrial area (Lower Lea Valley)	Upgrade and stimulation of economic activity, housing, community facilities and infrastructure

Sources: Garcia (1993: 251–70); Geipel et al. (1993: 287–9); Lee (1988: 60–1); Levett (2004: 82); Meyer-Künzel (2001); OCA (1998); Pyrgiotis (2001)

constraints as the Games cannot be postponed. If a city did not succeed in changing its infrastructure in time for the Games, it would be subject to worldwide criticism and the image of the city would be severely damaged. The time constraints and the fear of 'disgrace' provide such momentum for development activities that the period of 'normal' development is skipped (Cox et al., 1994: 35; Daume, 1976: 155; Garcia, 1993: 263; Geipel et al., 1993: 296). With the exceptions of the privately financed Olympics in Los Angeles and Atlanta, all other host cities used the period before the Games to carry out 'accelerated urban development' and realised long-term plans in a short timespan. Frequently, the external pressures help to resolve internal urban conflicts and break logjams between planners, politicians and citizens regarding important projects. Internal compromises are often a response to the pressure for unity in the face of potential external critics. For example, Seoul was driven by its rivalry with Japan. Barcelona's momentum came in part from its ambition for local autonomy in Spain, while Atlanta was concerned to demonstrate Southern capability to the Northern states and Beijing has a similar rivalry with Shanghai. Host cities were therefore concerned to demonstrate their efficiency and capacity not only to the world as a whole, but also to particular rivals.

While the 'acceleration effect' of the Games on planning decisions may be welcome, there is always the danger of irreversible planning errors due to time pressure, the 'crowding out' of other more worthwhile projects due to the shortage of public investment, or the infringements of social justice. The last point is especially important as there is considerable evidence that the deadline of the Games is used as an excuse for ignoring the interests of socially weaker groups. Evidence suggests that socially deprived groups are especially affected by airport expansion, road building or decisions on the location of the Olympic village. The Games have given urban planners a justification to evacuate whole suburbs and relocate the residents (Development Action Group, 1996: 9), as occurred in almost all cities including London, Beijing, Atlanta (Gladitz and Günther, 1995), Barcelona, Seoul (Denis et al., 1988: 230) and Munich.

Moreover, the impact of urban land use planning for the Games often alters the balance between public and private space and the capacity of certain groups to access remaining public space (Siebel, 1994: 18). Not only is public space privatised, but the remaining public space is redeveloped for use by the adult customer with purchasing power and not for children, the elderly or the poor. Thus, the city loses a major element of its urbanity, namely its openness to the public as a whole. Host cities appear to enhance the quality of public space by installing pedestrian precincts or public parks, but the precincts contain shops for the affluent and the parks often host fee-paying events. Poorer social groups gain little benefit if they are excluded by cost from the attractive post-Games leisure events or are priced out of the market for the housing that replaced their previous dwellings. The gentrification of residential areas produces socially exclusive housing near the city centre in an attractive and vibrant city atmosphere (Development Action Group, 1996: 9).

THE WINNERS AND LOSERS

The foregoing macroeconomic analysis helped to identify those social groups or interests that receive a net increase in benefits from the hosting of the Olympic Games (i.e. the winners) and that can be distinguished from those with a decrease in net benefits (i.e. the losers). However, due to the complexity of the interrelationships the effects can only be described on a relatively abstract level.

It is assumed in Figure 18.3 that the Games have had a positive effect on the city image and that there was a financial surplus. The first group of 'winners' is the local politicians, who have been able to use external resources flowing into the city, such as government subsidies, plus the reallocations within the city budget to change the structure of the city according to their political priorities. Frequently, their arguments for implementing certain projects are justified by claims that the Games 'demand' a certain structure or certain facilities within the city. The second group of 'winners' is the construction industry, which can confidently expect to receive contracts for extensive construction projects including parks, hotels, roads, sports facilities, housing, and sometimes convention and trade fair centres. Many of these projects contribute to the gentrification of areas of the

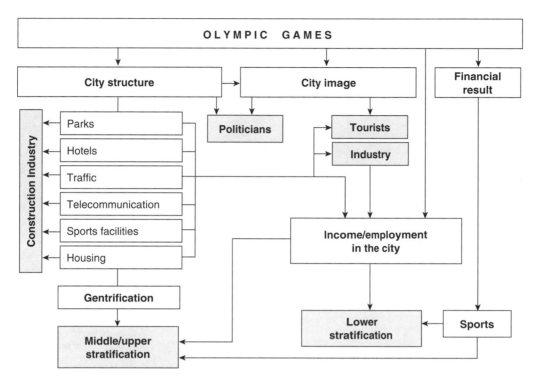

FIGURE 18.3   'Winners' of the overall economic effects of the Olympic Games

city, a process that benefits higher-income groups which constitute the third set of 'winners'. The fourth group is tourists who benefit from an improved tourism infrastructure and additional attractions in the host city.

A further group of 'winners' is the city's general population, many of whom benefit from the general upswing in economic activity produced by the improvements to the urban infrastructure, other location factors and consequently to the image of the city. Although the extent of Games-related economic activity differs greatly between host cities, the improved structure, the better image and the higher expenditures produced higher income and additional employment in all host cities. The frequently made criticism that additional income and employment only benefit members of the middle and upper classes must be rejected. Even if unskilled workers were underpaid, they did have work and their income was improved, irrespective of the duration of their employment. The capacity of the Games to create jobs and protect existing jobs is frequently overlooked. The generality of the city's population may also benefit if the Games produce a surplus. Normally, any surplus is distributed between the IOC, the NOC of the host country and various institutions that promote sport in the country. The last-mentioned recipients

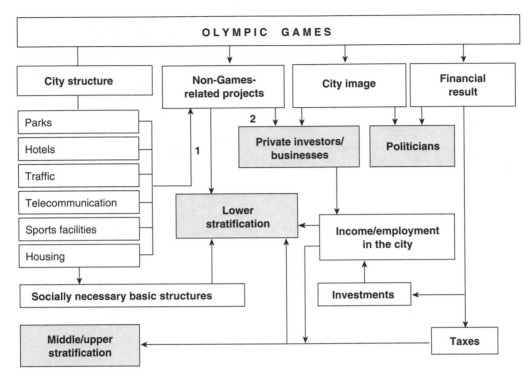

FIGURE 18.4   'Losers' of the overall economic effects of the Olympic Games

have the potential to use the income to the benefit of citizens irrespective of their social status. The city can maximise its financial benefit if it can persuade the OCOG to invest an anticipated surplus before the final balance is compiled, thus avoiding the risk of money being siphoned out of the city to the host country NOC or, via the IOC, to the NOCs of other countries and the international federations.

Turning attention to the 'losers', Figure 18.4 identifies the groups that were negatively affected by the Games. In this scenario it is assumed that the Games negatively affected the image of the city and that they were run at a financial deficit. The fact that even this scenario will produce winners is not ignored.

It is not surprising that many negative effects have the greatest impact on the poor, given the obvious priority within the low-income group for employment, affordable housing, adequate medical care and social integration. Hosting the Games means that other projects in the city are crowded out, as indicated by (1) in Figure 18.4. Additionally the opportunity costs have to be considered. The Games serve a particular complex of targets and the winners are those that benefit from the targets being reached. The money that was spent on the Games cannot be used for other projects and therefore the losers are those that have other targets which cannot be served but which would have been without the Games.

Prior to the Games, the sites of newly erected Olympic facilities were often housing areas of the poor (former workers' areas in the vicinity of industrial enterprises). It is exactly this sector of the population which suffers from expropriation and relocation caused by the construction activities, which leads to a loss of their social environment. Without doubt some municipal authorities tried to use the opportunity of the Games to expel from the area socially marginal groups, such as the homeless, street traders and prostitutes who, in their opinion, conflicted with the image of a modern city open to tourism which they were attempting to manufacture. (For Los Angeles and Seoul, see Anon., 1996; for Barcelona, see Garcia, 1993: 260–1; for Atlanta, see Gladitz and Günther, 1995; in general, see Lenskyj, 1996: 395). It must also be noted that the poor are forced out of their residential areas not just by major construction projects but also by the subsequent gentrification of areas (Cox et al., 1994: 75).

If the Games worsen the image of the host city or prevent investments in non-Games-related projects because of a strong reallocation of resources, the general economic activity in the host city (2) is negatively affected. Local enterprises in the city will not expand, nor will businesses be encouraged to relocate to the city. The reduced economic activity has a negative effect on income and employment with consequences for all citizens. Should the Games produce a deficit that has to be covered by the city, then there are consequences for future public investment and the level of municipal taxes which may well have to rise, again producing negative effects for all citizens. The Development Action Group (1996: 31) suggests that the lessons from previous Games are clear in so far as they stress that those who pay for the Games do not necessarily profit from the Games. After winning the bid, the city and the NOC have to organize the Games and therefore most of the benefits created are public goods. Private industry and others who benefit act as free riders and use the general infrastructure and better image which was built by public money.

The poor are less able to benefit than the upper-income groups and cannot direct the targets of the Games to their advantage. Furthermore the poor are more affected by capacity constraints and therefore are far more vulnerable to eviction and displacement than middle-income groups.

When bidding for the Games, the risk of possible negative effects and whether they can be borne from an economic point of view must be measured. This review has shown that hosting the Games runs the risk of deepening the social polarisation in the city.

CONCLUSION

Evidence from recent Olympic Games suggests that host cities benefit in three ways: improved infrastructure; increased income/employment; and a better city image.

Autonomous investments and consumption expenditures raise the general prosperity of the local population, but it is the upper-income groups that benefit disproportionately and, as has been suggested, there are some poorer income groups who suffer substantial dislocation of housing and community.

Even if one accepts the argument that the Olympic Games result in net benefits for the host city, the question remains whether an alternative project would have led to a higher net benefit for the city and/or a socially more just allocation. However, such a calculation is fraught with difficulty as it is so problematic to determine that the increase in benefits of one group is less valuable than that of another. Based on the Pareto optimum, it can be assumed that, economically, the Olympic Games produce greater benefits than costs to the citizens and that after taking all impacts and legacies into account, the Olympic Games are positive for a host city. The challenge for the future is to ensure that the general host city benefits are more evenly distributed. In future, the city could and should be integrated into the financing of the Olympic Games in order to enable the positive macroeconomic potential of the Olympic Games to be used for the greater benefit of socially deprived classes. However, the structure of city-based and national interest groups is such that prioritising social justice in the distribution of economic benefits over the profits of construction and redevelopment businesses is unlikely. It is possible that the IOC could link the awarding of Olympic Games to the publication of an acceptable plan for the distribution of economic benefits. However, given the close links between the IOC and international business and its general reluctance to interfere in the internal political decisions of the bid cities, such an expanded role for the IOC might be welcome but is unlikely.

CHAPTER SUMMARY

» Since the 1980s OCOGs can be confident that they will be able to host the Games and produce a surplus of revenues over operating costs.

» The Games now require a huge infrastructure for athletes, tourists and the media, which often involves substantial urban restructuring in most host cities affecting a wide range of interests and dividing them into winners and losers.

» Improvement of a city's image from media coverage can lead to increased tourism and conference business and also to business relocation and a consequent increase in jobs and tax income to the city.

» While some consequences of hosting the Olympic Games will benefit all social groups, in general upper-income groups derive greater advantages than the poor, who are less likely to benefit from gentrification, a new airport, less public space, expensive entertainment or a new fibre optic network.

FURTHER READING

A more detailed analysis of the economic consequences of hosting the Olympic Games is provided in Preuss (2004a). Studies of individual Games include Atlanta (French and Disher, 1997), Seoul (Kim et al., 1989; Park, 1991) and Barcelona (Millet, 1995). Lenskyj (2000, 2002) provides an extended critical review of the Sydney Games.

NOTE

1 All financial sums are expressed in 1995 dollars.

REFERENCES

Agreement (1978) between IOC and the City of Los Angeles (27 October), typescript.

Anon. (1993) 'Olympiasonderdienst des sid', News of the AGSPORT agency, 23 August.

Anon. (1996) 'Olympics 2004', *Argus* (South Africa), 14 February.

ATC (Australia Tourist Commission) (2001) 'Olympic Games tourism strategy. Overview', Sydney, typescript.

Athens OCOG (2003) *Liability, Underwriters, Information.* Athens: Typescript.

Audit Office (1999) 'Performance audit report. The Sydney 2000 Olympic and Paralympic Games. Review of estimates'. Sydney, typescript.

Baade, Robert and Matheson, Victor (2002) 'Bidding for the Olympics: fool's gold?', in C.P. Barros, M. Ibrahimo, and S. Szymanski (eds), *Transatlantic Sport: the Comparative Economics of North America and European sports.* London: Edward Elgar, pp. 127–51.

Bernard, Andrew B. and Busse, Meghan R. (2000) 'Who wins the Olympic Games? Economic development and medals totals', Working paper No. 7998. National Bureau of Economic Research, Cambridge, MA.

Bidding Committee Beijing 2008 (2001) *Bidbook.* Beijing.

Brunet, Ferrán (1993) *Economy of the 1992 Barcelona Olympic Games.* Lausanne: IOC Publications.

Commission of Inquiry (n.d.) 'Report of the Commission of Inquiry into the cost of the 21st Olympiad', Montreal, Vol. 1, typescript.

Coubertin, Pierre de (1913) 'La question d'argent', *Revue Olympique*, 13 (12): 183–5.

Cox, G., Darcy, M. and Bounds, M. (1994) 'The Olympics and housing. A study of six international events and analysis of potential impacts of the Sydney 2000 Olympics', Paper prepared for the Shelter NSW and Housing and Urban Studies Research Group, University of Western Sydney, Macarthur.

Daume, Willi (1976) 'Organising the Games', in Lord Killanin and J. Rodda (eds), *The Olympic Games. 80 Years of People, Events and Records*. London: Barrie & Jenkins, pp. 153–6.

Denis, M., Dischereit, E., Song, D.-Y. and Werning, R. (1988) *Südkorea. Kein Land für friedliche Spiele*. Reinbeck: rororo.

Development Action Group (1996) *The Olympics and Development. Lessons and Suggestions*. Observatory, South Africa.

Dunn, K.M. and McGuirk, P.M. (1999) 'Hallmark events', in R. Cashman and A. Hughes (eds), *Staging the Olympics. The Event and Its Impact*. Sydney: Griffin Press, pp. 18–34.

French, Steven P. and Disher, Mike E. (1997) 'Atlanta and the Olympics. A one-year retrospective', *Journal of the American Planning Association*, 63 (3): 379–92.

Garcia, S. (1993) 'Barcelona und die Olympischen Spiele', in H. Häusermann and W. Siebel (eds), *Festivalisierung der Stadtpolitik. Stadtentwicklung durch große Projekte*, in *Leviathan. Zeitschrift für Sozialwissenschaft*, Special vol. 13: 251–77, Opladen.

Geipel, R., Helbrecht, I. and Pohl, J. (1993) 'Die Münchener Olympischen Spiele von 1972 als Instrument der Stadtentwicklungspolitik', in H. Häusermann and W. Siebel (eds), *Festivalisierung der Stadtpolitik. Stadtentwicklung durch große Projekte*, in *Leviathan. Zeitschrift für Sozialwissenschaft*, Special vol. 13: 278–304, Opladen.

Georgiadis, Konstantinos (2000) 'Die ideengeschichtliche Grundlage der Erneuerung der Olympischen Spiele im 19. Jahrhundert in Griechenland und ihre Umsetzung 1896 in Athen', PhD dissertation, Johannes Gutenberg Universität, Mainz.

Gladitz, R. and Günther, W. (1995) 'Das Spiel mit den Spielen. Ein Themenabend: Atlanta und die Olympiade', Broadcast by the TV station *Arte* (18 January 1996, 23:05).

Hall, Colin M. (1992) *Hallmark Tourist Events. Impacts, Management & Planning*. London: Belhaven.

Hattig, Fritz (2001) Member of the Bid Committee for Munich 1972. Interview in Mainz.

Hill, Christopher R. (1992) *Olympic Politics*. Manchester: Manchester University Press.

Hoberman, John (1986) *The Olympic Crisis. Sport, Politics and the Moral Order*. New Rochelle, NY: Aristide D. Caratzas.

Huntington, Samuel P. (1996) *Kampf der Kulturen. Die Neugestaltung der Weltpolitik im 21. Jahrhundert*. Munich and Vienna: Europaverlag.

International Olympic Committee (IOC) (1997) *Report of the IOC Evaluation Commission for the Games of the XXVIII Olympiad 2004*. Lausanne: IOC Publications.

International Olympic Committee (2000) 'Marketing matters', No. 17.

Killanin, Lord (1982) 'The Olympic Movement since Varna', in IOC (ed.), *Report of the XIth Olympic Congress in Baden-Baden*, Vol. 1. Lausanne: IOC Publications.

Kim, J.-G., Rhee, S.-W., Yu, J.-Ch., Koo, K.-M. and Hong, J.-Ch. (1989) *Impact of the Seoul Olympic Games on National Development*. Korea Development Institute, Seoul: KDI Press.

Kramar, Mark A. (1994) 'Development of East European and Soviet direct trade relations with South Korea, 1970–1991', PhD dissertation, Florida State University, Tallahassee.

Landry, Fernand and Yerlès, Magdeleine (1996) *The International Olympic Committee: One Hundred Years. The Idea – the Presidents – the Achievements*, Vol. 3. Lausanne: IOC Publications.

Lee, Charles (1988) 'From wartime rubble to Olympic host', *Far Eastern Economic Review*, 140 (36): 60–5.

Lenskyj, Helen J. (1996) 'When winners are losers. Toronto and Sydney bids for the Summer Olympics', *Journal of Sport & Social Issues*, 20 (4): 392–410.

Lenskyj, Helen J. (2000) *Inside the Olympic Industry: Power, Politics and Activism*. New York: SUNY Press.

Lenskyj, Helen J. (2002) *The Best Olympics Ever? Social Impacts of Sydney 2000*. New York: SUNY Press.

Levett, Roger (2004) 'Is Green the New Gold? A sustainable Games for London', in Vigor Anthony, Mean Melissa and Tims Charly (eds), *After the Gold Rush. A sustainable Olympics for London*. London: ippr & Demos, pp. 69–90.

Lin, Xianpeng (2004) 'Economic impact of Beijing Olympic Games 2008', in Proceedings of the 2004 Pre-olympic Congress, 6–11 August, Thessaloniki, Greece, Vol. 1: 100.

Millet, Lluís (1995) 'The Games of the city', in Miguel de Moragas and Miguel Botella (eds), *The Keys to Success*. Barcelona: Centre d'Estudis Olímpics i de l'Esport.

Meyer-Künzel, Monika (2001) *Der planbare Nutzen. Stadtentwicklung durch Weltausstellung und Olympische Spiele*. Hamburg: Dölling & Galitz.

Morse, John (2001) 'The Olympic Games and Australian tourism', Paper presented at the World Conference on Sport & Tourism, Barcelona.

NSW Government (2001) *Budget Statement 2001–2002, Sydney 2000 Olympic and Paralympic Games*. Sydney: 6.1–10.

OC Atlanta (1998) *Official Report of the XXVI Olympic Games*, Vol. 1. Atlanta.

OC Montreal (1976) *Games of the XXI Olympiad, Montreal 1976, Official Report*, Vol. 1. Montreal.

OC Munich (1974) *Die Spiele – Die Organisation*, Vol. 1. Munich.

OC Sydney (2000) *The Games of the XXVII Olympiad. Sports Commission Report 1996–2000*. Sydney.

OCA (Olympic Co-ordination Authority) (1998) 'Environment fact sheet: clean up', Sydney.

Park, Seh-Jik (1991) *The Seoul Olympics. The Inside Story*. London: Bellew Publishing.

Parker, Lesley (2001) 'Business lands', *Clayton UTZ Magazine*, 7–9.

Payne, M.R. (2004) Interview with the TOC Marketing Director, Lausanne, January 2004.

Persson, Christer (2000) 'The Olympic host selection process', PhD dissertation, University of Technology, Lulea.

Persson, Christer (2001) President of the Bidding Committee Östersund 2002. Letter of 11 March.

Preuss, Holger (1998) 'Problematizing arguments of the opponents of Olympic Games', in R.K. Barney, K.G. Wamsley, S.G. Martyn and G.H. MacDonald (eds), *Global and Cultural Critique: Problematizing the Olympic Games. Fourth International Symposium for Olympic Research*. London, Ontario: University of Western Ontario, pp. 197–218.

Preuss, Holger (2000) 'Electing an Olympic host city: a multidimensional decision', in K.G. Wamsley, G.H. MacDonald, S.G. Martyn and R.K. Barney (eds), *Bridging Three Centuries: Intellectual Crossroads and the Modern Olympic Movement. Fifth International Symposium for Olympic Research.* London, Ontario: University of Western Ontario, pp. 89–104.

Preuss, Holger (2004a) *The Economics of Staging the Olympics. a Comparison of the Games 1972–2008.* Cheltenham: Edward Elgar.

Preuss, Holger (2004b) 'Calculating the regional economic impact of the Olympic Games', *European Sport Management Quarterly*, 4: 234–53.

Preuss, Holger (2005) 'The economic impact of visitors at major multi-sport-events', *European Sport Management Quarterly*, Special Issue: Sports Tourism Theory and Method, 3: 283–305.

Pyrgiotis, Yannis N. (2001) 'The Games in the XXIst century', in IOC (ed.), *Olympic Games and Architecture. The Future for Host Cities*, Lausanne: IOC Publications, pp. 25–9.

Reich, Kenneth. (1986) *Making It Happen: Peter Ueberroth and the 1984 Olympics.* Santa Barbara, CA: Capra Press.

Roulac, S.E. (1993) 'Place wars and the Olympic Games', *Futurist*, 6: 18–19.

Samaranch, Juan Antonio (1992) 'Message from the IOC President', in *Olympic Solidarity Itinerant School*, Marketing Manual. Lausanne: IOC Publications, p. 2.

Sassen, Saskia (1996) *Metropolen des Weltmarktes. Die neue Rolle der Global Cities.* Frankfurt and New York: Campus.

Scherer, K.A. (1995) 100 Jahre Olympische Spiele. Idee, Analyse and Bilanz, Dortmund.

Schollmeier, Peter (2001) *Bewerbungen um Olympische Spiele. Von Athen 1896 bis Athen 2004.* Germany: Books on Demand.

Scott, Robert (1997) President of the Manchester 2000 Bid Committee. Interview in Olympia.

Siebel, Walter (1994) 'Was macht eine Stadt urban?', in F.W. Busch and H. Haverost (eds), *Oldenburger Universitätsreden – Ausprachen, Auspräcke, Verträge*, 61, Oldenburg.

Snyder, C.R., Lassegard, M.A. and Ford, C.E. (1986) 'Distancing after group success and failure: basking in reflected glory and cutting off reflected failure', *Journal of Personality and Social Psychology*, 51 (2): 382–8.

Spilling, Olav (2001) Unpublished letter to author, 23 May.

Szymanski, Stefan (2002) 'The economic impact of the World Cup', *World Economics*, 3 (1): 1–9.

Taylor, Peter and Gratton, Chris (1988) 'The Olympic Games: an economic analysis', *Leisure Management*, 8 (3): 32–4.

TOROC (2005) 'Message from TOROC CEO', in *Torino 2006: the Environment and the Heart of the Games.* Torino, typescript.

Ueberroth, P., Levin, R. and Quinn, A. (1985) *Made in America. His Own Story.* New York: William Morrow.

Weirick, James (1999) 'Urban design', in R. Cashman and A. Hughes (eds), *Staging the Olympics. The Event and Its Impact.* Sydney: Griffin Press, pp. 70–82.

19

Sport and Recreation and the Environment

MICHAEL F. COLLINS

OVERVIEW

» *Growing professional/academic interest in sport and the environment*
» *Sport in the built environment*
» *Sport in the natural environment, especially noisy sports – can the countryside take it?*
» *Mega-events and facilities – case study of impacts from Albertville and Lillehammer to the London 2012 Olympics*
» *Conclusions*

GROWING PROFESSIONAL AND ACADEMIC INTEREST IN SPORT AND THE ENVIRONMENT

Awareness of the need to protect the natural environment has been growing since the 1960s, but was focused by the World Commission on Environment and Development's report *Our Common Future* in 1986 and subsequent international conferences (Da Costa, 2001). Six years later it was highlighted by the Rio (de Janeiro) Earth Summit Conference and the obvious adverse impacts of the Albertville Winter Olympic Games. Rio led to a popularisation of the concept of sustainability, which can be defined as: ways to meet 'the needs of the present without compromising the ability of future generations to meet their own needs'.

As Lenskyj (1998a: 341) pointed out, except for golf and downhill skiing, sport has received relatively little criticism for its environmental impact until recently. By the same token, there has been only limited research. Chernushenko (1994: 15–17) described how the great majority of sport is now undertaken in either modified natural settings like skiing pistes, grass pitches and courts, rowing courses, or in purpose-built facilities rather than natural environments. Vuolle (1991: 602) pointed out that this has a generational effect whereby younger people are socialised or acclimatised to taking part in these artificial settings, and 'distanced from nature'. Incidentally, it allows more of sport, both participant and spectator, to be packaged and 'commodified'.

Oittinen and Tiezzi (1998) argued for sustainable sport on three levels:

1 *The global*: **being responsible to the planet and future generations and protecting the quality of sites where sport is played.**
2 *The institutional*: **taking into account international obligations, the carrying capacity of sites, combining ecology with economy, and making environmental protection a criterion for marketing, financial and sponsorship decisions.**
3 *The individual*: **where every citizen has equal opportunity for sport as close to home as possible (to minimise transport costs), all year round, and wherever possible through multiple use (to reduce land and energy use).**

Oittinen and Tiezzi went on to provide perhaps the broadest view of sport's impacts, concentrating on those on the natural environment, referring in particular to golf, skiing, shooting, orienteering, motor sports, water sports and big events like the Olympics. The UK Sports Council (1998) in its *An Agenda for Sport and the Environment* drew up a more slender 'checklist' for commissioning new facilities involving prior assessment of biotic impact, energy-efficient construction, minimising transport and waste disposal, and requiring bidders and managers of events to adhere to environmentally green operating conditions.

In the UK greater attention has been paid to the impact of countryside sport rather than urban sport, particularly to walking on turf and disturbance of bird life (Sidaway, 1990, 1994). It could be argued that the impacts on townscapes are more neglected, and it is on those impacts that this chapter now focuses.

SPORT IN THE BUILT ENVIRONMENT

Much of the work has focused around high-profile events, mainly held in or near cities generally called hallmark (Whitson and Mcintosh, 1993) or mega-events (Roche, 1994; Rooney, 1976). The emphasis of such research has tended to be on economic impacts (see Collins and Jackson, 1999). Table 19.1 outlines the sorts of impacts mega-events can have. For all the furious competition to host mega-events like the Olympics or to attract

TABLE 19.1   Impacts of major facilities and events

Impact	Positive	Negative
Economic	• Increased expenditure and jobs (Euro 96, Sydney Olympics) • Base for winning subsequent events (Barcelona/Calgary Olympics, Sheffield World Student Games (WSG))	• Price 'hikes' during event (Atlanta OG) • Exaggerated benefits/legacy of debts (Montreal OG, Sheffield WSG) • Real estate speculation (Sydney OG, US stadiums) • Underused facilities after event (Montreal & Athens OGs, Calgary Ice Rink)
Tourism/ commerce	• Increased awareness of region for tourism/jobs (Lillehammer/Seoul/Olympics, Fremantle America's Cup)	• Poor reputation as a result of failures/ shortcomings (Atlanta Olympics, traffic/prices/ information) • Failure to attract/retain long-haul tourists (Fremantle Admiral's Cup) • Crowding out of regular/expected visitors (almost any mega-event)
Physical	• New/improved facilities/ regenerated environments (Barcelona/Sydney Olympics, Sheffield WSG) • Improved local facilities (Sheffield WSG)	• Environmental damage (Albertville Olympics) • Litter/noise/traffic accidents (Adelaide Grand Prix (GP)) • Overcrowding (almost any mega-event) • Reduction of local facilities (Sheffield WSG swimming)
Socio-cultural	• Permanent increase in interest/participation in sport after event • Strengthening regional traditions/values	• Commercialisation of personal/private activities (ice hockey in UK, Rugby Union World Cup) • Excessive drinking/thefts/muggings/ hooliganism (some England soccer matches overseas) • Modify event for tourism (Edinburgh Festival)
Psychological	• Increased national/regional pride (England 1966 World Cup, Seoul Olympics) • Greater awareness of outsiders' perceptions (Moscow Olympics)	• Defensive local attitudes • Misunderstandings/visitor hostility (Atlanta Olympics)
Political	• Enhanced reputation of host for investors (Barcelona OG, Adelaide GP) • Unify a nation (Montreal OG) • Distinguish region/nation (Seoul/Barcelona OGs) • Propagation of political values (Berlin/Moscow OGs)	• Exploitation of local people – displaced poor (Moscow/Mexico City/Los Angeles/Salt Lake/ Atlanta OGs) • Distortion of event to reflect political values (Berlin/Moscow OGs)

Sources: adapted from Burbank et al. (2001); Collins and Jackson (1999); Ritchie (1988); Whitson and Macintosh (1993)

franchises in the four main American stadium sports, some say that the economic effects are short-lived, and that they have either no long-term effect on a city's economy, or even a depressing one, through employing many unskilled, low-income workers. Indeed, it can also be argued that little account is generally taken of the opportunity cost of investing in the stadiums or arenas (Baade, 1995). UK Sport (UK Sports Council, 1998, 1999a, 1999b) measured the economic impacts of six world and European events, distinguished between spectator- and competitor-driven events, and constructed a typology (Box 19.1). The analysis later summarised data on 16 evaluated events (UK Sport, 2004), and produced a model that predicted financial outcomes to between 64 and 80 per cent accuracy.

Box 19.1 UK Sport's typology of events

		No. in UK, 1997
A:	Irregular, one-off events generating significant economic activity and media interest, e.g. World Cup, Olympics, Euro 96	None
B:	Also major events, part of an annual cycle, e.g. FA Cup Final, Wimbledon	43
C:	Irregular, one-off major events generating limited economic activity, e.g. European junior boxing, swimming, etc., championships, world badminton, IAAF grand prix	248 (for both C and D)
D:	Major events generating limited economic activity, part of an annual cycle, often not generating economic benefits commensurate to costs, e.g. national championships in most sports	

Wilson (2005) criticised this schema for neglecting the more common local events and suggested adding a group E of events involving 500 or fewer competitors, generating under £20,000 of local economic activity. Apart from these debates on the economic costs and benefits of major events, I suggest there are other significant impacts that have been neglected.

Visual Impact

Exciting as major stadiums and arenas can look when full of spectators, light and fireworks, their stands and halls are large and more often than not ugly concrete or brick constructions. Many stadiums, especially for soccer, date from the late nineteenth and early twentieth centuries, and are in inner cities, physically and psychologically over-shadowing the housing, often of the poorer groups (Bale, 1990; Churchman, 1995). Many modern stands are huge, unattractive and dominate their surroundings, even if it is possible occasionally to lessen the impact by burying them partly in holes or slopes.

Nevertheless not all stadium designs are poor or intrusive, and good design can lead to 'landmark' buildings that are a credit to their architects, clubs and communities. UK examples include the Reebok Stadium on the edge of Bolton and Pride Park on industrial wasteland near Derby rail station, and the Commonwealth Games/Manchester City stadium in east Manchester. To pay their large costs (£40–60m) they become multi-functional places for rallies and pop concerts, and have a multitude of meeting/conference/catering and indoor sport spaces under the stands, all increasing the range and weight of their environmental 'footprints', in terms of noise, litter, traffic and hours of operation.

Traffic and Noise

Stadiums provide theatres for spectacle for some of the largest frequent gatherings of humankind, especially young men. Consequently they generate large volumes of traffic and loud crowd noises. Moreover, whether drunk or sober, some spectators create prob-lems around the grounds, in rail and bus stations, on the streets parking their cars, often having to be shepherded by police to and from bus and rail stations. Humphries et al. (1983) termed and mapped these impacts as 'nuisance fields'. These issues, combined with the requirement for all-seater stadiums in the wake of tragic multiple deaths at Hillsborough in 1989, led to many clubs considering relocation, often on the outskirts of a city at a site adjacent to ring roads and inter-city motorways (Churchman, 1995). These may be at a distance from the homes of many fans; the news that both Liverpool and Everton were contemplating moving led a local MP to comment: 'It is essential that at least one club stays, otherwise the community is socially excluded' (Peter Kilfoyle, *Guardian Society*, 24 October 2001).

Many relocation attempts fail, however, as a result of planning authorities' demands, objections to impacts on protected landscapes, or local amenity groups' opposition. Thus many clubs opt instead for refurbishing or more expensive *in situ* redevelopment. For example, by late 2000, Southampton FC had obtained planning permission to move, after more than a dozen abortive attempts and having borne the costs of feasibility stud-ies on 19 alternative sites, environmental impact assessments and public inquiries. Likewise, with the restrictions inherent in a historic city and a fiercely protected Green Belt, Oxford United FC has been unable to devise a move from the Manor Ground despite 45 years of trying.

TABLE 19.2   Typical annual energy consumption, cost and CO_2 emissions in sports buildings (total area)

Type	Source	Use (kWh/m²) Good to poor		Cost 1996 (£/m²) Good to poor		CO_2 (kg/m²) Good to poor	
No pool	Fossil	215	325	2.6	4.0	41	62
	Electricity	75	85	4.7	5.3	47	54
With pool	Fossil	360	540	4.4	6.6	68	100
	Electricity	150	205	9.4	12.8	95	130
Pool only	Fossil	775	1,120	9.5	13.8	150	210
	Electricity	165	235	10.3	14.7	100	150

TABLE 19.3   Saving energy in sports facilities

Area	Aim	Measures
Fabric	Reduce air intake Better insulation	Door closers/draught lobbies/insulate walls/ roof/double glazing/reflective glass
Space heating	Reduce cost	Thermostats/time controls/recover exhaust heat/ modern boilers/combined heat and power plant
Water heating	Reduce costs	Insulate/small point-of-use devices
Swimming pool	Reduce heat loss	Fit pool cover/heat pump/clean filters
Ventilation	Reduce cost	Variable fans/clean filters/recover waste heat
Lighting	Reduce cost	Fluorescent instead of tungsten/time controls

Source: DETR (1994a, 1994b, 1996, 1997)

Sports Buildings and Energy Use

In the total energy budget, sport is not a major user, but in temperate climates buildings like sports halls, ice rinks and swimming pools can consume large amounts of electricity or fossil fuels. Table 19.2 gives some idea of the range of annual energy consumption and cost, and carbon dioxide emissions. Pools use 3,000–4,300 kWh per square metre of pool surface. Buildings pre-dating 1980 were rarely designed with much thought paid to energy conservation, and although the Building Research Establishment has estimated that 20 per cent of cost could be saved, worth close to £200m a year in the late 1990s, many operators have not been convinced to invest in the necessary technology, despite often short payback periods, as with flexible pool covers.

There are numerous ways to save energy, as shown in Table 19.3, ranging from better staff training to closing doors, turning off dripping taps and switching off lights in unused spaces, to installing computerised whole-building energy control systems. At the design stage, major savings can be made: for example, if an ice rink shares a site with a sports hall, or, better, a pool where the waste heat from the rink cooling plant can be used to warm the water in the pool and the air in either building.

While visual intrusion, noise, traffic congestion and energy consumption are important and generally under-researched issues for urban sport, it is the impact of sport on the countryside that causes the greatest friction between interest groups, and which poses the most awkward problems for policy makers.

SPORT IN THE COUNTRYSIDE: CAN THE COUNTRYSIDE TAKE IT?

Recreational Pressures on the Countryside

Most Britons and overseas visitors carry a 'chocolate-box' image of an idyllic countryside with small tree-lined fields, peaceful rippling streams and picturesque villages. It is not that such places do not exist in abundance, but that they coexist with:

- noisy arms testing, tree felling and quarrying;
- the huge fields of mechanised intensive agriculture;
- the spread of bracken on the hills;
- a shortage of jobs and affordable housing for agricultural workers;
- a high level of rural and urban deprivation; and
- 1.3 billion day trips in 2002–3, bringing motor cars into narrow valleys and bays, and into 'honeypot' villages and attractions in numbers never conceived or planned for (Countryside Agency, 2001; Commission for Rural Communication, 2006).

This has turned the countryside from a mainly productive area (crops, animals, wood, water, minerals) to a mixed economy where production coexists with consumption (nature study, sightseeing, sport and recreation). Vigorous debate about whether the countryside can 'take it' is no new thing, having ranged from the workers' mass trespasses in the Pennines in the 1930s to the recent debate over 'the right to roam' over 4 million acres (1.8 million ha) of mountain, moor, heath, down and common land legislated by the Countryside and Rights of Way Act 2000.

By far the most thoroughly studied impacts are those of walkers' wear and tear on vegetation, and the disturbance of birds, especially nesting or migrating waterfowl (Sidaway, 1995; see also Elson and Sidaway, 1995; Sidaway, 1991, 1994). These and other rural impacts of sport and recreation are spelled out in Table 19.4.

Despite the research of Sidaway and others, there is no consensus on the significance of the impacts. Arguments to suggest that fears of lasting and widespread environmental damage have been exaggerated include the following:

TABLE 19.4   Potential impacts of recreation

Biological effects	Environmental effects	Physical impacts
Damaging vegetation/soils	Wear and tear, vegetation loss, fires	Wear and tear on buildings, landscapes (cumulative in popular areas)
Incremental effects Disturbing fauna	Disturbing fauna, local communities	Damage/disturbance/intrusion, e.g. from motor sports, mountain biking
Removal of wildlife	Inappropriate development	Inappropriate infrastructure developments, e.g. golf courses, holiday villages
Habitat loss from development Habitat creation and improvement	Overcrowding	
Recreational traffic Pollution, noise Wave erosion/turbidity from power boats	Noise, emissions, nuisance to local communities	Traffic growth/parking

Sources: CPRE (1995); DoE et al. (1995); Sidaway (1994)

- The numbers of visits grew rapidly in the 1970s, but, whether because of a slowing down in acquiring cars, or greater commuting from home- or town-based leisure activities, the level plateaued, and even decreased in recent years, by 8 per cent from 1998 to 2003–4 (Countryside Agency, 2004). There is a growing interest in walking for health and using the countryside as a 'green gym' (Bull, 2005), but while health promotion interests would like to see this as a mass use, it is confined to relatively small groups at present.
- Peak visiting has been spreading into the spring and autumn.
- While the number of people seeking active and adventurous recreations has grown, the average size of countryside sporting clubs and groups is small, mostly under 50 people, except where larger numbers are needed to finance buying land or access rights, e.g. to fishing water, gliding and flying fields or water ski sites.
- Even when there are negative impacts, they are small compared with the impact of land use changes, for housing and industry, or the removal of thousands of kilometres of hedgerows, and the heavy use of herbicides and pesticides which have reduced biodiversity, food and cover for insects and birds throughout the UK and Europe (English Nature, 1995).

Focusing more closely on countryside sports, growth has slowed in recent years, with women's participation actually falling, possibly because more of them are in paid work and have less time for such activities. For children, outdoor activities have been down-graded in priority owing to changes in the National Curriculum for schools. Moreover, numerous local authority outdoor centres have been closed, and there are far fewer Sport Development Officers to help promote outdoor than urban sports (Glyptis et al., 1995).

A very different view was taken in the *Leisure Landscapes* study (CPRE/Lancaster University, 1994), whose authors felt that golf, holiday villages and other developments were so numerous that they were changing the ethos of the countryside in a radical way. They claimed that this was being misrepresented and misunderstood in its scale and seriousness by the main agencies (Sports Council, English Tourist Board and Countryside Commission).

A parliamentary Select Committee (HC, 1995: xiv) disagreed, expressing the view that:

> compared to other activities, leisure and tourism do not cause significant widespread ecological damage to the countryside. However … there are important issues to address, involving transport, rural culture, and leisure management, as well as local conflicts in specific areas.

One of the guardians of bird life, the Royal Society for the Protection of Birds, is of the same opinion: 'Is there a problem? Yes, there is, but only in some places, and for some habitats', instancing heathland in southern England near towns (Hounsden, 1999).

Thus experienced researchers (Curry, 1994; Elson and Sidaway, 1995; Sidaway, 1991) and the main agencies (Sports Council, Countryside Commission, English Tourist Board) believed that the pressures were seasonal or sporadic, localised and amenable to management solutions.

There is no space here to spell out in detail the planning and management techniques for dealing with impacts and conflicts (Elson and Sidaway, 1995; Sidaway, 1991), but they depend on two principles: that of separation in space and time and that of restriction on activity. The strengths and weaknesses of the principles, with examples of their use, are set out in Table 19.5. The techniques are difficult to apply, however, in the following situations:

- **where activities and impacts grow incrementally, and it is problematic to distinguish cumulative wear and tear from vandalism;**
- **where habitats are not resilient, e.g. mountain vegetation and sand dunes;**
- **where new activities are trying to obtain space to function amongst established activities, for instance mountain biking competing with ramblers and horse riders (Berridge, 2000) and jet skiing with anglers and sailors.**

Light Pollution

The volume of lights from roads, advertisements and buildings in urbanised zones is such as to make whole regions seem alight when viewed from space, especially in Western

TABLE 19.5   Managing recreation impacts

Strengths	Weaknesses	Examples
SEPARATION		
Zoning in space		
• Minimises impact	• Restricts freedom • May be difficult to change	• Density of use in Peak National Park • Different activities • Sefton coast, large reservoirs like Rutland Water
Seasonal or daily restrictions		
• Avoids disturbance at critical times • Easier to modify	• Restricts freedom	• Water skiing on River Crouch • Fishing seasons
RESTRICTION		
Voluntary		
• Works in clubs/peer groups • Works when clear target, justified and understood message • Works where pressure is not extreme	• Does not work where mainly unaffiliated/casual • Users, or high turnover • Does not work where messages vague, no clear responsibility on clubs, individuals	• Mountain bike routes on Snowdon • Climbing on sea cliffs where birds nest • Hierarchy of green lane routes in Lake District
Management control		
• Works where need is accepted • Signposted, evident	• Restricts freedom • May be temporary and difficult to police, e.g. chasing off motor cyclists • May be regarded as arbitrary	• Walking/cycling in the Goyt Valley • Separating cycling/riding on bridleways • Water ski 10 mph limit on Lake Windermere

Sources: Elson and Sidaway (1995); Glyptis et al. (1995); Sidaway (1991, 1995)

Europe and the North-eastern United States. The Council for the Protection of Rural England (CPRE, 2000) noted that many Britons cannot easily experience dark, and suggested that some rural areas should be designated to remain dark. With regard to sport, one of the most common local issues concerns light spilling into houses from the floodlights on playing fields; this often leads planning officers and inspectors to refuse planning permission, even when demand exists for more evening sports activity in the winter. Although lanterns and lamps have been redesigned and placed on lower poles to reduce lateral spillage, and although restrictions have been placed on hours of use, light remains a sensitive issue. Sport England (1999b: 46–7) agued that local authorities 'should avoid overly restrictive conditions when seeking to minimise impact on the amenity of neighbouring properties'.

Noisy Sports in 'Quiet' Landscapes

The 1995 Select Committee drew attention to different cultural perceptions of the countryside and nowhere is this more marked than in the matter of noisy sports. Under the 1949 National Parks and Access to the Countryside Act, National Parks were established for two original purposes, namely preserving and enhancing rural natural beauty, and promoting its enjoyment by the public. But while John Dower, a National Park architect, spoke of town dwellers 'enjoying the peace [of the countryside], and spiritual refreshment', another, Minister Lewis Silkin, spoke of the Act as a charter for hikers and ramblers.

From its inception in 1968, the Countryside Commission added riding, climbing, camping and cycling to walking as the main recreational beneficiaries. Quietness was first mentioned in policy documents concerned with common land in 1986, and in relation to designated areas in 1994 (Pearlman et al., 1999). In 1991 the Edwards Committee (NPRP, 1991), reviewing the purposes and management of the National Parks after 40 years, supported the emphasis on 'quiet enjoyment'. Commenting on this, Adrian Phillips, a former Director of the Countryside Commission, said: 'greater public awareness of environmental concerns means there is a growing impatience with forms of recreation which do violence to the qualities of national parks, noisy sports for example and those which disturb wildlife' (Phillips, 1994: 231). The Council for National Parks (CNP) (1994: 2) reinforced this view strongly: Quiet enjoyment should only include those activities which stem from the appreciation of natural beauty. They should be activities which require human muscle power for their pursuit, rather than rely on motorisation.

Attempts to insert the term 'quiet enjoyment' into a Private Member's Bill and into the 1995 Environment Act failed. The main reason given was that a legal definition of quiet behaviour existed for a very different purpose in landlord and tenant legislation which lawyers did not wish to compromise (Pearlman et al., 1999). In addition, the subjectivity of noise and disputes over how to measure it (UKCEED, 1993) would have made it very difficult to produce a legally robust definition. The outcome was that the 1995 Act referred to 'enjoyment of the special qualities of the National Parks', and soon thereafter DoE Circular 12/96 indicated that particular activities should not be excluded from the National Parks as a matter of principle, though they might not be appropriate everywhere, a stance ministers of state have maintained.

It is undoubtedly true that the noise of modern society – roads, railways, airports, industry – is spreading. The CPRE produced Tranquil Area maps for England in the 1960s and again in the 1990s, and its analysis showed a reduction of the tranquil areas by 21 per cent (from 70 per cent of the country to 56 per cent), and, perhaps more important in the long term, the fragmentation and hence reduction in the size of such areas by 73 per cent (CPRE, 1995). Respondents to Countryside Agency (2005a) research repeatedly asserted that tranquillity 'is about peace, and quietness, incorporating … absence of noise, and about being "at peace"'. I have asserted elsewhere (Collins, 1999) that noise in the countryside is a new target for environmental interest groups.

CASE STUDY 1: MOTORISED SPORTS IN THE LAKE DISTRICT

Water Skiing – Shut Out of the Local Policy Community

Water skiing at 40–70 mph (64–112 kph) requires large areas of water which are scarce inland in the UK. Boats are powerful and attractive to some onlookers, but a painful noise nuisance to others. They are also expensive, and so nearly 90 per cent of skiers take part through clubs, which can regulate usage effectively (Elson et al., 1989). Only 4 of the 15 larger lakes in the National Park have a public right of navigation, which, unlike the law for highway traffic, is indivisible and applies to all classes of boats. As activity grew and after a public inquiry, a 10 mph (16 kph) speed limit was imposed by by-law in 1973 on Coniston, Derwent and Ullswater. It was informally agreed with the Sports Council that Lake Windermere should remain for sports requiring powered boats which had used the lake since the 1920s.

But the number of boats registered trebled by the early 1990s, and 1,500 craft of all types could be found together on a busy summer's day. Two attempts to agree a management plan failed. Concerned about safety of other lake users, and the peaceful enjoyment of the valley by tourists and residents, the National Park Authority (NPA) applied for another 10 mph by-law, not challenging the legal right of navigation, but in effect regulating water skiing and power boating out of existence. The National Park's policy community was divided. Supporting the idea were the two District Councils, the Countryside Commission, the Council for National Parks (CNP), the Ramblers' Association, the Youth Hostels Association, the influential Friends of the Lake District (FoLD), and local amenity and sailing and canoeing groups. Opposing it were the British Water Ski Federation (BWSF), the Sports Council (with a further management plan proposal), the Cumbria Tourist Board and local lakeside businesses, concerned about job losses.

A long and costly 48-day public inquiry was held in 1994–5; the proponents on both sides had noise experts who argued about different measurements and their meanings. Many witnesses gave evidence about the growth of boat traffic, safety, conflicts and other amenity issues. The inspector, in a massive report in February 1996, rejected the Sports Council's proposals as not addressing the conflict issue, and recommended the by-law to John Gummer, then Secretary of State (Alesbury, 1996). After deliberation, however, Gummer rejected the proposal in a brief letter asking the parties to work on a new management plan. Incensed, the Park Authority considered a High Court appeal on the grounds of inadequate consideration. However, with the coming to power of the Blair Labour government with a manifesto pledge to protect the environment, the Minister, Chris Mullin, invited new submissions.

The Sports Council and BWSF were happy to discuss a management agreement, including registering boats and licensing drivers, but the Park Authority saw no change in circumstances and no need to re-enter debate (Collins and Ellison, 2001). In February 2000 the Minister confirmed the by-laws, to come into force in 2005, so as to give lake-side businesses time to adjust, saying: 'there was a fundamental problem of incompatibility in the confined area of the Lake … there is no reason why the Lake District should be expected to accommodate every recreational activity for which there is a demand'.

Now the howls of pain and cries of victory were reversed. The problem is that, having searched diligently at scores of sites, no adequate alternative for water skiing could be found within 100 km, and no one was planning a new or reclaimed suitable water site. As the ban came into effect in 2005, the affected employers still felt ignored and cheated by the government and sent a 100,000-signature petition (*Guardian*, 29 March 2005: 5) to no effect. Water skiers fear knock-on effects elsewhere: the Broads Authority accepts skiers from only one club on the 10 zones permitted, and expects each driver to log their visits (Millard, 2005).

Motor Sports: Getting into the Local Policy Community

Off-road motor cycling has been a real and widespread problem for three out of four English councils, dealt with more by the short-term response of using police or wardens to move trespassers on rather than attempting to produce a sustainable long-term solution by providing alternative sites. In the 1980s the search for satisfactory outcomes was hampered by the divided nature of motor sports and their poor image (Elson et al., 1986), even though major events like road rallies were well organised and caused only localised noise and negligible environmental impacts (e.g. the 1,000 Lakes Rally in Finland (Salo et al., n.d.)).

The Land Access and Rights Association (LARA) was formed to represent the interests of legitimate drivers, and started to negotiate with local planning and highway authorities, including National Parks. Often, the use of green lanes by motor cycles or four-wheel-drive cars is challenged by landowners and environmental groups, and LARA would sooner advise its members to avoid disputes rather than have use by motor vehicles selectively barred, which can be done by a Traffic Regulation Order (TRO) (LARA, 1996).

There are 250 such 'green lanes' in the National Park, and little had been achieved over 20 years of claim and counter-claim by motorists, landowners and walkers. The Park Authority sought in the late 1990s to fulfil an objective of eliminating unsustainable use (*Park Management Plan*, 1998), but recognised the legal claims of motorists and the need for a co-operative, user-led, non-statutory management approach. With LARA, therefore, it developed the idea of a Hierarchy of Trail Routes (LARA, 1997; Wilson and Robinson, 2005), identifying three categories of route:

1   those that can be used by the general public with little regulation (*green*, a total of 61);

2   those that should be publicised only to LARA members, in compliance with a strict code of conduct (*amber*, 23); and

3   those that should not be used at all, because of erosion, or disturbance to farming or wildlife (*red*, 23).

These routes totalled only 5 per cent of the Public Rights of Way in the National Park.

A Trail Management Advisory Group (TMAG) was set up (with a chairman from LARA, and a vice-chair from the NPA) involving representatives of riders, ramblers, cyclists, Forest Enterprise, the National Trust and landowners. A Trail Officer was appointed, and a three-year experiment launched costing nearly £0.5m, with signs erected on 250 miles (400 km) of routes. Initial problems arose with two Lancashire companies bringing in large groups of 4WD vehicles, but were resolved. LARA accepts that the NPA may have to impose TROs where damage is sustained, but that the existence of Category 3 will minimise this. Contraventions by non-LARA riders were few. After three years the regulation and signage was simplified by adopting a green/amber/red system. Obviously, LARA was able to persuade the other members of the local policy community to accept its legitimacy and consider its case. The FoLD and the CNP remain against the scheme, sceptical about compliance, and fearing an increase of traffic once riders discover rights of way they did not know they had. The CNP prefers the experimental use of TROs employed by the Yorkshire Dales National Park (O'Brien, 2005), emphasising that most of the environmental damage comes from the overwhelming majority of well-behaved motorists, not the tiny minority of 'cowboys'; it claimed that repairing damage to paths by off-road vehicles cost the Sussex Downs Conservation Board (English Heritage, 2005: 66).

Why were there such different outcomes to the two noisy sport issues? Collins and Ellison (2001) suggested that for water skiing the BWSF, Sports Council and Tourist Board were isolated against a local and national coalition of environmental amenity and recreation organisations behind which the Blair administration finally threw its weight; that the lack of flexibility in navigation law and of workable alternative waters made defence of water skiing on Windermere necessary if a lost cause. Also the situations for which the by-law could be precedential were fewer. In the case of green lane driving, a dispersed and difficult problem held many more potential precedents, and despite overt opposition from FoLD and CNP, the rest of the policy community wished a resolution, and LARA had worked skilfully and developed more and stronger alliances than BWSF.

Despite the success of the Hierarchy experiment, land-based motor sports could find their choices in and beyond National Parks curtailed as much as water skiing. The Minister of Rural Affairs, Alun Michael, in 2005 accepted that in the National Parks there was a place for motorised use that is 'responsible and appropriate' and set out a framework for clarifying the legal status of green lanes, a process some riders feared would lead to reductions in access, and set off a spate of claims. Sport England's current planning guidance (1999a) is seeking to get national governing bodies of sport to identify Significant Areas for Sport (SASPs) where it will oppose developments that threaten such sites, and will try to encourage planning authorities to acknowledge them. However, SASPs are most unlikely to gain statutory support because each serves only a small number of people compared with the community-wide benefits of national designations for landscape, nature or heritage conservation.

The Countryside Agency (CA, 2005b: 1) commented that the 'NPAs have not been as proactive as they might be in providing opportunities for outdoor recreation' and have been 'overly defensive in their approach to recreation'. But in the same year, copying earlier events in Wales and Scotland, the CA was merged with English Nature to form Natural England, an agency with a £400m budget, but where it remains to be seen how salient recreation is as a policy area. The real problem is that rural sports need to be planned at a regional level. Since the government abolished the advisory Regional Councils for Sport and Recreation in 1995, there has been no obvious mechanism for this. Meanwhile local authorities are heavily influenced by the NIMBY (Not In My Backyard) attitudes of local interest groups, or by co-ordinated pressure from well-organised regional or national environmental groups rather than sports governing bodies which have a poor record of mutual support. If recreation as a whole is a 'Cinderella' in the planning system in National Parks (Simkins, cited in Ravenscroft and Reeves, 1998), this is truer still of motor sports.

MEGA-EVENTS AND FACILITIES: THE OLYMPICS

Sport has found a potent partner in television: the global reach of major networks has not only brought major fees to the governing bodies and organisations that own the events, but also brought in third partners in the form of sponsors of goods and services which find exposure to new markets (Andreff, 2000; Maguire, 2000: 144–75). These income streams have become major financial lifelines for the sports organisations, and have totally transformed the finances of the Olympic Games. The Games have continued to grow in terms of participating nations and, in the Summer Games, in terms of number of events, athletes and media workers attending (Preuss, 2000; Toohey and Veal, 2000). TV revenues grew astonishingly from US$83.7m in 1976 to US$1.124bn in 2000, at 1995 prices (Preuss, 2000: 108). This rapid growth in scale has increased the impacts on the host cities and their countrysides.

Referring specifically to environmental impacts, Essex and Chalkley (1998) distinguished three types of Summer Games:

1   Low impact: involving mainly refurbished and few new facilities, e.g. Athens 1896, London 1948 and Mexico City 1968. After a period where state-of-the-art new buildings had prevailed, Los Angeles in 1984 showed how, using mainly existing 1932 and other sites, costs could be cut, leading to a surplus of US$215m, and rekindling the interest of cities in bidding, which had waned after major debts in Munich and Montreal.

2   New facility based: major stadiums, pools, and general and specialist arenas (for cycling, canoeing, rowing, riding, shooting, etc.) and new housing for the athletes, e.g. Stockholm 1912, Los Angeles 1932, Berlin 1936 and Atlanta 1996.

3   Stimulating: environmental transformation of a wide range and large scale, e.g. Rome 1960, Montreal 1976, Moscow 1980, Barcelona 1992, Sydney 2000 (see also Table 19.7 below). The soaring costs of Munich and Montreal with little after-use (e.g. the structural and locational unsuitability of the latter's Olympic village for housing) led to a crisis, for which Los Angeles gave a solution, but one where there was much more private entrepreneurial involvement.

The third type used the Summer Games as a trigger for a major transformation of the image and fabric of the host city, involving major public infrastructure and cultural investment, often compressing public investment into 8 or 10 years that might otherwise have taken 20 to generate, if indeed it would have come at all without such a 'flagship' event (see Table 19.6).

Developing Games facilities anywhere near the central city with its cultural, entertainment, hotel and shopping services involves using 'brown land' sites, usually of two main types. The first includes areas of low-cost housing occupied by lower-skilled, lower-paid workers who are needed in Games- and tourist-related services, but who are often displaced by the sports and related new facilities, as happened in Mexico City, Moscow and Barcelona. It is doubtful whether there are many environmental benefits to offset these social and economic costs. The second type includes industrial, often contaminated land where reclamation and redevelopment nominally present clear environmental gains but which requires generating high values to pay the costs, as in Homebush Bay, Sydney, and to some extent in London's Lee Valley. There are concerns that the tight timescale for preparing the Games and their high political and media profile result in overriding normal environmental checks and procedures (Lenskyj, 1996). The stirring of environmental awareness in the Olympic Movement led the Munich OCOG to invite all participating NOCs to plant a shrub in the Olympic Park and to support the slogan *Certatio sana in natura sana* (Healthy competition in an intact environment).

More recently a Rio Conference also committed the Olympic Movement to be a part of the worldwide environmental Agenda 21, and the IOC (1997) has developed a manual of requirements of bidders, as has UK Sport (n.d.). Nonetheless, Essex and Chalkley's

TABLE 19.6   Urban transformation through the Olympic Games

Host city/year	Urban developments
Rome 1960	New facilities, new Olympic Way, new water supply, airport
Tokyo 1964	New facilities, two new metro lines; new road link plus 22 other road schemes
Munich 1972	Reclaim 280 ha disused housing area for new sports facilities; pedestrianise historic quarter, improve expressways, shops, hotels, public transport and underground car parking
Montreal 1976	New Olympic park and village; 20 km of metro; new roads, hotels and airport
Moscow 1980	12 new sports facilities; hotels; airport terminal; TV and communications centres
Seoul 1988	New sports facilities and village; three metro lines, 47 bus routes, new arts centre, classical music institute, Chongju museum, refurbishing shrines; renewed rubbish collection and water supply systems, de-polluting the River Han and Chamsil site
Barcelona 1992	15 new sports venues; new airport link, ring road and rail station; new beaches and marina, offices, conference centre; Olympic village to become housing as part of revitalised historic quarter; energy saving
Sydney 2000	New sports facilities; improved roads, reclamation of polluted land and water sites; energy saving and waste reclamation
Athens 2004	New sports venues, new airport; new roads and improved metro

Source: Essex and Chalkley (1998) and author's update

(1998: 203) comment still holds, that 'what began as a festival of sport has grown into an unusually conspicuous element in urban global competition'.

CASE STUDY 2: FROM ALBERTVILLE 1992 TO LONDON 2012

Albertville 1992

Although the debt for the 1968 Grenoble Winter Games was still being paid off, Albertville bid and won the rights to host the 1992 Games. Concerns had built up about the impact of clearing forest and flora for skiing pistes, extending facilities and hotels to higher altitudes, and the trampling of much larger numbers of summer visitors. Despite reuse of derelict sites, improved river water quality and waste management, other worries were the pollution from increased car traffic, and the hydrological impact of snow-making equipment (Klausen, 1999; May, 1995), see also Table 19.7. To make 1 hectare of ski surface takes 200,000 litres of water – the equivalent of daily use of 1,000 people. Only 0.3 per cent of the construction budget was allocated to planting around buildings and pistes, though electricity and telephone cables were buried in 'sensitive' landscapes by the utility companies.

Seven Alpine countries and DGXI of the European Commission committed themselves to an Alpine Convention for sustainable activity, promoted by the Commission

Internationale de la Protection des Alpes (see Van't Zelfde et al., 1996). Already a French law of 1985 had required Environmental Impact Assessments in mountain areas, but May (1995) pointed out that such site-specific measures cannot cover the post-event and wider regional impacts, such as:

- the growth of 4WD and mountain bike use, scarring the landscape of Les Saisies;
- continuing debts of FF200m on the event and FF120m on the TV centre;
- increased demand for snow-making;
- the arrival of more summer visitors as a consequence of improved accessibility and new accommodation capacity, with extra pressures on other communal services; and
- reduced biological diversity and productivity in rivers.

Lillehammer 1994

Meantime Lillehammer, a small town of 20,000 people in Norway whose region had won the honour of coping with the 1994 Games, determined to do better. It sought to place Lillehammer on the same skiing map as the established and heavily invested resorts of the Alps and Rockies. The OCOG had budgeted for an estimated expenditure of $1.17bn, 46 per cent above income, on the grounds that 'the Games are expected to yield general spin-offs for the Olympic region and the country as a whole' (Lillehammer '94 Guide: 132–3).

The measures that Lillehammer took included: having regular meetings with citizens, employing energy-saving devices like heating the arenas with waste heat from the ice rink, educating its volunteers including army personnel, and requiring all suppliers to use recycled paper and non-carcinogenic or ozone-depleting agents (Chernushenko, 1994; Klausen, 1999).

Lenskyj (1998b) argued that Lillehammer had set a model for Sydney in waste management, use of biodegradable material in catering, energy saving, specifying for suppliers of goods and services and environmental legacy, but even after such efforts, and a very successful event, the following criticisms were made:

- the jumps and buildings made the White Mountain just like the developed slopes Lillehammer was trying to compete with, rather than preserving vernacular styles of structures and landscape;
- special places like the mating sites of capercaillies and lynx had been disturbed;
- a wetland area had been lost; and
- the area had been commodified to attract and satisfy tourists, for instance through creating Troll Park, with a consequential increased use of cars.

Ironically, one of Lillehammer's best legacies was not sporting: the expensive media centre was converted into a higher education centre for audio-visual arts and technology training for all of Scandinavia, making a year-round source of income from students it would have been most unlikely to achieve in the absence of the Games.

In 1995 at the first World Conference on Sport and the Environment, IOC President Samaranch said the IOC would consider environmental aspects as the third pillar of its future work, alongside sport and culture (Kidane, 1997). In 1997 it produced its *Manual on Sport and the Environment* (IOC, 1997), asking host cities to include an environmental action plan in their bids, to undertake EIAs, and to establish an awareness programme for partners, citizens and guests. The *Manual* covers not only impact on nature but issues of design, energy saving, water, air and waste treatment, and issues of transport, ticketing, catering and noise.

Sydney 2000

For the Summer Games in 2000 in Sydney, the OCOG wanted the event to be known both as the 'Athletes' Games' and the 'Green Games' (Stubbs, 2001), and worked with Greenpeace, Environment Australia and the lobby, Green Games Watch. The facilities and infrastructure cost A$3.03bn (two-thirds to government) and event operations A$3.46bn, all to government (Auditor General, 2002). The main site and the Bay had been very heavily polluted, and despite an acclaimed success in sporting and tourism terms (IOC President Samaranch called it 'the greatest ever'), it became clear that:

- the reclamation costs of A$667m had been underestimated (Toohey and Veal, 2000: 195–207), and needed much more money for completion;
- the legacy facilities will cost the NSW government A$11m a year to maintain (Auditor General, 2002), and there are concerns that they and the Australian Rules stadium are underused because of travel cost and distance from most of Greater Sydney;
- Sydney's western suburban residents – younger, more affluent, more likely to be married and more immigrant citizens – were more in favour of the event than those less affluent in other neighbourhoods (Waitt, 2003); and
- museums often expect little or no benefits from sporting mega-events because visitor profiles are seen as different and because of the deterrent effect of traffic, crowds and road closures, but two museums in Darling Harbour gained 25 per cent and 4 per cent extra visitors during the Games and in mounting related exhibitions subsequently (Scott, 2004).

Athens 2004

So, it is clear that later outcomes are complex and mixed; in this sense, the Athens Games were also a striking spectacle, but a step backwards environmentally. Costs escalated to Î7bn (£4.7bn), and were criticised substantially at the time and in retrospect for late completion of venues because of poor labour practices, damage to a Marathon wetland in constructing the rowing and canoeing centre (*The Times*, 20 February 2001: 12), failure to develop after-use plans, very high security costs, failure to use solar heating or sustainable waste water reclamation, and traffic management methods (*Guardian*, 25 August 2004: 11).

London 2012

The cumulative effect of very high-profile Games in Barcelona and Sydney was to raise interest in bidding, while seeking to contain the costs, protect the environment and play a role in urban renewal. These factors played a large role in the short-listed bids from Paris, Madrid, Moscow, New York and London. All received high marks for technicalities of sports provision. New York's bid was hindered by opposition to the US military intervention in Iraq, and was effectively torpedoed when the State Public Authorities Control Board refused to sanction the cost of the stadium in Manhattan (*Guardian*, 8 June 2005: 34). Paris, which had invested in updating its metro and had fewest new facilities to build (*Guardian* 11 March 2005: 29), was seen as the front runner by the media, but when an IOC evaluation group arrived they were faced with claims of business corruption by three members of the preparatory commission including a former sports minister, and by trade union demonstrations (*Guardian* 9 March 2005: 7; *London Evening Standard*, 9 March 2005: 6). London had been ranked lowly on government and public support, public transport to the village and key sites, on delivering mega-events (after the failure to build a new athletics venue for the 2005 World Athletics Championships, and problems over rebuilding Wembley Stadium) and environmental impact.

The London 2012 group was headed by Lord Sebastian Coe, a former Olympic champion, and went to work hard. Prime Minister Tony Blair put his signature to the bid, four out of five London and British citizens supported it, contracts for new road and rail works were signed and started, IOC members were visited and invited, and the candidate file was given a much higher-profile launch than that of Paris. The file (London 2012, 2005: 15, 19) stressed priority for:

- **the needs and experiences of athletes (a career-long mantra of Coe's and one that had the support of Samaranch), including a compact village and short journeys for most competitors (80 per cent less than 20 minutes);**

- harnessing London's passion for sport (and displaying some events in 'iconic' settings of historic and sporting splendour (Wembley, Wimbledon, Lord's cricket ground, Horse Guards Parade, Hyde Park and Eton) with as little new build as necessary – 'excellence without extravagance';
- creating a legacy to transform sport in the UK including a London Olympic Institute for sport, culture and the environment; and
- regenerating communities and environment in the most deprived areas of five North-East London Boroughs.

With an inspirational presentation focusing on sport for the youthful inheritors of the current actions, the Coe team confounded the pundits at the IOC meeting in Singapore on 6 July and outvoted Paris at each stage, finally wining with 54 votes to Paris's 50. It transpired that London had struck an understanding with Madrid to swing its votes behind London if it was eliminated (*Guardian*, 7 July 2005: 1–6). Tessa Jowell, Secretary of State for Media Culture and Sport, talked of 'embedding legacy in every aspect of our preparation' (Sport England press release, 26 October 2005). Within six months, the Olympic Delivery Authority and its chief officers were appointed, agreements made with English Partnerships over development sites, and facility designs progressed.

London 2012 (2005: 75–83) made large claims to run A One-Planet Olympics: 'we have only one planet … [and] … will respect the ecological limits of that planet, its cultural diversity, and create a legacy for sport, the environment and the local and global community'. Table 19.7 sets out how it will seek to meet the IOC framework.

The DCMS commissioned an independent assessment of the likely economic, social and environmental impacts of these Games (PWC, 2005). This showed they are likely to:

- generate £5.9bn of GDP and 39,000 jobs in London, mostly in construction, and another £1.9bn and 8,000 jobs elsewhere in the UK;
- promote £0.24bn valued added in tourism in London, and £0.5bn in the UK (lower than the estimates for Australia, but then London is already a larger tourist magnet than was Sydney); and
- create 3,600 houses and a major 200 ha park for parts of NE London where one-fifth of the wards are in the 5 per cent most deprived in England (and as many as 43 per cent in the Olympic Park area).

The main environmental disbenefits will be to the lower Lee Valley where sporting and general infrastructure building works will be concentrated. So to the basic facilities legacy there is now a worldwide understanding of the need for positive regeneration and environmental legacies of the Olympics (de Moragas et al., 2003) and the Commonwealth

TABLE 19.7   London 2012's environmental action plan

Sport	Environment	Community
• promoting healthier lifestyles • fostering excellence • engaging young people • increasing participation	• low carbon production • zero waste • conserving biodiversity • promoting environmental awareness and partnerships	• celebrating cultural diversity • boosting enterprise and economic development • improving quality of life

Theme	Proposed actions	Benefits
Low-carbon games Transport and air quality	• 00% public transport for spectators • maximise use of Channel Tunnel link to reduce air traffic • low emission zone for Olympic vehicles and Park • active spectator programme (encourage walking/cycling) • carbon offset for all Olympic travel	Significantly reduce CO_2 emission Improve air quality Powerful link to health agenda Innovative low-carbon strategy–benchmark for future Olympics
Resources	• combined heat/cool/power plants; renewable energy local and off-site	Exemplar integrated model for sustainable cities (including future bidders)
Sustainable construction	• build to highest standard consistent with One-Planet living	Buildings proofed against climate change and respecting local heritage
Zero-waste games Waste management Procurement	• closed loop system for recycling • sustainable purchasing of materials, services, food and merchandise	Divert waste from landfill Boost recycling market Healthy products and materials Resource-efficient, reducing waste at source
Conserving biodiversity Enhancing urban greenspace	• integrated restoration plan for lower Lee Valley • create large new urban park • Biodiversity plan for Olympic Park	Major gain in greenspace (200 ha) Biodiversity integral to built environment Bringing nature and people closer
Promoting environmental awareness and partnerships Community engagement International	• community-based sustainable sport programme • annual clean-up events • exchanges, scholarships, technology transfers and capacity building for developing countries	Raise public awareness and involvement in planning Legacy for future events Building global sustainability networks through sport

Games (e.g. Melbourne 2006), though clearly this has not yet spread to all other, sport-specific mega-events.

Interestingly, however, there is virtually no sound evidence of the sports development impact of mega-events (Brown and Massey, 2001) – that is, stronger national sports organisations and clubs, better school and youth programmes, improved coaching systems, and increased participation in sport and physical activity in increasingly sedentary, overweight/obese and substantially unhealthy societies. The exception is some comprehension of the potential of mega-events to encourage large-scale volunteering (Downward, 2005; MORI, 2003). Coalter (2004) reviewing the evidence, concluded:

1. for increasing participation in sport based on Australian evidence, it is difficult to attribute a modest increase to the Games, a view shared in Game Plan, the Department of Culture, Media and Sport's (2002) sport strategy: 'hosting events is not an effective, value for money, method of achieving … a sustained increase in mass participation'.
2. for impact on NSOs and clubs, based on New Zealand evidence, findings are also mixed – these bodies are interested in elite sport and are often not locked into any network or campaign.
3. for volunteering, sustained involvement is not automatic.

Thus the message is the same as for facility after-use and environmental benefits, these aspects have to be embedded in a longer term, wider sports development and community strategy and closely linked to the Olympic delivery plan; 'trickle-down benefits … are not automatic' (Hindsen et al., 1994: 22).

CONCLUSIONS

Ideally one would want to see approaches to countryside sport and recreation promoted that maximise its potential for positive environmental effects. While it is possible to compile a long list of environmental impacts associated with sport and recreation (including noise, traffic congestion, visual blight, high energy demands), one should not lose sight of the fact that these activities and events can also produce environmental benefits. Mention has been made of the reclamation of brownfield sites in preparing the facilities for major events like the Olympics. Sport does not always damage environments, it can create or restore them, by, for example:

*   reclaiming dry mineral workings/quarries for motor sports, climbing and shooting;
*   reclaiming wet pits for water sports, e.g. in Pugneys (Wakefield) and Rother Valley Country Parks (Glyptis et al., 1995);
*   replacing monocultural fields with greater biodiversity in the rough of new golf courses and with newly planted trees – 98 golf courses in England and Scotland contain Sites of Special Scientific Interest (see Wheat, 1995); and
*   providing access, recreation and culture, timber and other products through new National and Community Forests around cities (Countryside Agency, 1999).

In addition, one can point to modest help in supporting rural public transport. There are also a large number of specialised recreational public transport services in areas popular for landscape beauty and recreation, from Beeline Community Cars in Atherstone, Warwickshire, and the Hadrian's Wall bus to Tandridge's taxi vouchers (Countryside Agency, 2001). Many bus services, however, run only on summer weekends, and their patchy passenger loadings mean that most need substantial subsidies, although there are exceptions such as the normal scheduled services running from Huddersfield and Halifax to tourist and recreation attractions (Glyptis et al., 1995). There are also a few train services to day-trip and holiday areas, like the Hope Valley line in Derbyshire. Against all their shareholders' expectations, restored steam Railways are now making money as tourist attractions, e.g. the Severn Valley, the Great Central in Leicestershire and the Settle–Carlisle Railway, while also benefiting residents (Salveson, 1993).

As Chernushenko (1994) wrote, 'any harm done by the sports industry to the planet is thus a strike against the future of the sport itself'. Sport can bring great joy, boundless enjoyment and the creation of income and 'symbolic capital' for individuals, teams and clubs, and nations (Bourdieu, 1984). I have sought to show that sport can be a minor threat to the earth and/or a modest force for improving the environment. Therefore it needs to tread lightly on the earth, and sports planners and administrators still have much to learn in order to do that consistently and successfully. We are still a long way from Oittinen and Tiezzi's (1998) 'sustainable sport'.

CHAPTER SUMMARY

» The concept of sustainable sport can be operationalised at three levels: global; institutional; and individual citizens.

» Visual intrusion, traffic, noise and energy use are important elements of the environmental impact of sport in built environments.

» After growing in the 1970s, sporting use of the countryside has stabilised in recent years. However, environmental issues such as erosion of grass by informal recreation and light pollution and noise from active sports remain prominent sources of tension.

» Negotiating management agreements to cover the use of popular sites for outdoor sports has been widespread, but can prove difficult, as in the case of water sports on Lake Windermere. However, it is not impossible, as shown by the Hierarchy of Routes scheme covering motor sports in the same area.

» The IOC requires cities bidding to host the Olympic Games to undertake an environmental impact analysis. While some hosts, such as Lillehammer, Sydney and London, have sought to minimise the environmental impact, it is often achieved only at significant financial cost.

FURTHER READING

Curry (1994), Chernushenko (1994) and Da Costa (2001) provide overviews of the complex interrelationship between sport and the environment. Works that provide a more detailed focus on particular issues include Collins's (1999) study of noisy sports in the English countryside, and analyses of the Olympic Games by Essex and Chalkley (1998), Lenskyj (1998a) and Vigor and Mean (2004).

REFERENCES

Alesbury, A. (1996) *Report of the Inspector upon the Public Inquiry into Byelaws made by the Lake District Special Planning Board.* London: Dept of the Environment.

Andreff, W. (2000) 'Financing modern sport in the face of a sporting ethic', *European Journal of Sport Management,* 7 (1): 5–30.

Auditor General (2002) *Report to NSW Parliament on costs of Olympic and Paralympic Games.* Sydney: Auditor General.

Baade, R.A. (1995) 'Stadiums, professional sports and city economics: an analysis of the US experience', in J. Bale and O. Moen (eds), *The Stadium and the City.* Keele: Keele University Press, pp. 277–94.

Bale, J. (1990) 'In the shadow of the stadium: football grounds as urban nuisances', *Geography,* 75: 325–34.

Berridge, G. (2000) 'Mountain biking and access in the countryside', in M.F. Collins (ed.), *Leisure Planning in Transitory Societies.* Publication 58. Eastbourne: Leisure Studies Association, pp. 51–67.

Bourdieu, P. (1984) *Distinction: a Social Critique of the Judgement of Taste.* London: Routledge.

Brown, A. and Massey, J. (2001) *Literature Review: the Impact of Major Sports Events.* Manchester: Institute for Popular Culture, Manchester Metropolitan University.

Bull, M. (ed.) (2005) *Delivering a Countryside for Health and Well Being.* Seminar Proceedings, Birmingham, 10 May. Sheffield: Countryside Recreation Network.

Burbank, M.J., Heying, C.H. and Andranovich, G. (2001) 'Antigrowth politics or piecemeal resistance? Citizen opposition to Olympic-related economic growth', *Urban Affairs Review,* 35 (3): 334–57.

Chernushenko, D. (1994) *Greening Our Games: Running Sports Events and Facilities that Won't Cost the Earth.* Ottawa: Centurion Publishing and Marketing.

Churchman, C. (1995) 'Sports stadia and the landscape', *Built Environment,* 21 (1), 6–24.

Coalter, A.F. (2004) 'London 2012: a sustainable sporting legacy', in A. Vigor and M. Mean (eds), *After the Gold Rush: a Sustainable Olympics for London.* London: ippr & Demos.

Collins, M.F. (1999) 'Quiet, please! Sport in the British countryside', in M. Foley et al. (eds), *Leisure, Tourism and the Environment: Sustainability and Environmental Policies.* Publication 50.1. Eastbourne: Leisure Studies Association, pp. 77–101.

Collins, M.F. and Ellison, M. (2001) 'Insiders and outsiders to local policy networks: motorised recreations in National Parks', Unpublished paper.

Collins, M.F. and Jackson, G.A.M. (1999) 'The economic impact of sport tourism', in P. de Knop and J. Standeven (eds), *Sport Tourism.* Champaign, IL: Human Kinetics, pp. 169–202.

Commission for Rural Communities (2006) *Rural Disadvantage: Reviewing the Evidence.* Cheltenham: CRC.

Council for the Protection of Rural England (CPRE) (1995) *Tranquil Area Maps.* London: CPRE.

Council for the Protection of Rural England (2000) *Starry, Starry Night.* London: CPRE.

Council for the Protection of Rural England/Lancaster University (1994) *Leisure Landscapes: Leisure, Culture and the English Countryside.* Lancaster: Lancaster University.

Countryside Agency (1999) *Regeneration around Cities: the Role of England's Community Forests.* CAX33. Cheltenham: CA.

Countryside Agency (2001) *Great Ways to Go: Good Practice in Rural Transport.* CA62. Cheltenham: CA.

Countryside Agency (2004) *GB Day visits Survey 2002–03.* www.countryside.gov.uk (accessed 29 November 2004).

Countryside Agency (2005a) *Understanding Tranquillity.* Countryside Research Note 92. Cheltenham: CA.

Countryside Agency (2005b) *Demand for Outdoor Recreation in English National Parks.* Countryside Research Note 93. Cheltenham: CA.

Curry, N.C. (1994) *Countryside Recreation, Access and Land Use Planning.* London: E & FN Spon.

Da Costa, L. (2001) 'International trends in sport and the environment – a 2001 overview', Paper to ECSS Congress, Cologne, 24–28 July.

De Moragas, M., Kennett, C. and Puig, N. (eds) (2003) *The Legacy of the Olympic Games 1984–2000.* International Symposium, Lausanne, 14–16 November 2002. Barcelona: Olympic Studies Centre, Autonomus University.

Department of the Environment, Transport and the Regions (DETR) (1994a) *Good Housekeeping in Dry Sports Centres.* Good Practice Guide No. 129. London: DETR.

Department of the Environment, Transport and the Regions (1994b) *Good Housekeeping in Swimming Pools.* Good Practice Guide No. 130. London: DETR.

Department of the Environment, Transport and the Regions (1996) *Energy Efficiency in Sports and Recreation Buildings.* Good Practice Guide No. 51. London: DETR.

Department of the Environment, Transport and the Regions (1997) *Energy Efficiency in Swimming Pools.* Good Practice Guide No. 219. London: DETR.

Departments of the Environment/of Agriculture, Fisheries and Food/of Transport (1995) *Written Evidence to the House of Commons Committee into the Environmental Impact of Leisure Activities*. London: DoE/MAFF/DoT.

Downward, P. (2005) 'Some sports development implications of events volunteering: evidence from the Manchester Commonwealth Games', in M.F. Collins (ed.), *The Power of Sport*, EASM/ISRM European Sports Management Congress, Newcastle/Gateshead, 7–10 September, abstracts book, pp. 92–3.

Elson, M. and Sidaway, R. (1995) *Good Practice in the Planning and Management of Sport and Active Recreation in the Countryside*. Cheltenham: Countryside Commission/London: Sports Council.

Elson, M., Buller, H. and Stanley, D. (1986) *Providing for Motorsports: from Image to Reality*. Study No. 28. London: Sports Council.

Elson, M., Lloyd, J. and Thorpe, I. (1989) *Providing for Motorised Water Sports*. Study No. 36. London: Sports Council.

English Heritage (2005) *Heritage counts: the State of England's Historic Environment*. London: English Heritage.

English Nature (EN) (1995) *Written Evidence to the House of Commons Committee into the Environmental Impact of Leisure Activities*. London: English Nature.

Essex, S. and Chalkley, B. (1998) 'Olympic Games: catalyst of urban change', *Leisure Studies*, 17: 187–206.

Glyptis, S.A., Collins, M.F. and Randolph, L. (1995) *The Sporting Claim: a Countryside and Water Recreation Strategy for Yorkshire and Humberside*, Vol. 3: *Good Practice Case Studies*. Leeds: Y&H Council for Sport & Recreation.

Hindsen, A., Gidlow, B. and Peebles, C. (1994) 'The "trickle-down" effect of top-level sport: myth or reality? The case of the Olympic Games', *Australian Parks and Recreation*, 4.1: 16–24.

Hounsden, S. (1999) 'The overflowing honeypot: is there a problem, or is there not?', in J. Hughes (ed.), *Is the Honeypot Overflowing? How Much Recreation Can We Have?* CRN 1998 Conference Proceedings. Cardiff: Countryside Recreation Network, pp. 5–10.

House of Commons Select Committee on the Environment (HC) (1995) *The Environmental Impact of Leisure Activities*. London: HMSO.

Humphries, D.C., Mason, C.M. and Pinch, S.P. (1983) 'The externality fields of football: a case study of the Dell, Southampton', *Geoforum*, 14 (4): 401–11.

International Olympic Committee (IOC) (1997) *Manual on Sport and the Environment*. Lausanne: IOC.

Kidane, F. (1997) 'The Olympic movement and the environment', in L. Da Costa (ed.), *Environment and Sport: an International Overview*. Porto: University of Porto, pp. 246–54.

Klausen, A.M. (ed.) (1999) *Olympic Games as Performance and Public Event: the Case of the XVII Winter Olympic Games in Norway*. New York: Berghahn Books.

Land Access and Rights Association (LARA) (1996) *Access Guide: for Motorised Recreation and Motor Sport in the Countryside*. Rugby: LARA.

Land Access and Rights Association (1997) *Hierarchy of Trial Routes: First Report 1997*. Rugby: LARA.

Lenskyj, H.J. (1996) 'When losers are winners: Toronto and Sydney bids for the summer Olympics', *Journal of Sport and Social Issues*, 24: 392–410.

Lenskyj, H.J. (1998a) 'Sport and corporate environmentalism: the case of the Sydney 2000 Olympics', *International Review for the Sociology of Sport*, 33 (4): 341–54.

Lenskyj, H. (1998b) 'Green Games or empty promises: environmental issues and Sydney 2000', in R.K. Barnes et al. (eds), *Global and Cultural Critiques: Problematising the Olympic Games*. 4th International Symposium for Olympic Research. London, Ontario: University of Western Ontario, pp. 173–9.

London 2012 (2005) *Candidature file for the 2012 Games*. London: London 2012 Team.

Maguire, J. (2000) *Global Sport: Identities, Societies, Civilizations*. Cambridge: Polity Press.

May, V. (1995) 'Environmental implications of the 1992 winter Olympic Games', *Tourism Management*, 16 (4): 260–75.

Melbourne 2006 (n.d.) *2006 Melbourne Commonwealth Games – the Environmental Framework*. Melbourne: Office of Commonwealth Games Co-ordination.

Millard, J. (2005) 'Waterskiing on the Norfolk and Suffolk Broads', *Countryside Recreation*, 13 (2): 23–6.

MORI (2003) *The Sports Development Impact of the Commonwealth Games 2002: Pre-Games Research*. London: MORI.

National Parks Review Panel (NPRP) (the Edwards Committee) (1991) *Fit for the Future? Report of the NPR Panel*, CCP334. Cheltenham: Countryside Commission.

O'Brien, D. (2005) 'Recreational motor vehicle use – a National Park perspective', *Countryside Recreation*, 13 (3): 23–6.

Oittinen, A. and Tiezzi, E. (1998) '*Mens sane in corpore sano*': a scientific review of the information available on the links between the environment and sport. CDDS (98)45. Strasbourg: Council of Europe, Committee for the Development of Sport.

Pearlman, D.J., Dickinson, J., Miller, L. and Pearlman, J.J. (1999) 'The Environment Act 1995 and quiet enjoyment: implications for countryside recreation in the National Parks of England and Wales, UK', *Area*, 31 (1): 59–66.

Phillips, A. (1994) 'Access, recreation and tourism in the National Parks of England and Wales: "a third look at the second purpose"', in S.A. Glyptis (ed.), *Leisure and the Environment*. London: Belhaven Press, pp. 225–35.

Preuss, H. (2000) *Economics of the Olympic Games: Hosting the Games 1972–2000*. Petersham, NSW: Walla Walla Press.

PriceWaterhouseCoopers (PWC) (2005) *Olympic Games Impact Study – Final Report*. London: DCMS.

Ravenscroft, N. and Reeves, J. (1998) 'Planning for recreation in rural England', *Leisure Studies Association Newsletter*, 50: 24–30.

Richie, B. (1988) 'Assessing the impact of hallmark events: conceptual and research issues', *Journal of Travel Research*, 23: 2–11.

Roche, M. (1994) 'Mega-events and urban policy', *Annals of Tourism Research*, 21: 1–19.

Rooney, J.F. (1976) 'Mega-sports events as tourist attractions: a geographical analysis', Travel and Tourism Research Association Conference, *Proceedings*, Montreal, pp. 93–9.

Salo, H. et al. (n.d.) *The Neste 1000 Lakes Rally, Finland: Environmental, Economic and Social Impacts.* Jyvaskula: Institute for Environmental Research, University of Jyvaskula.

Salveson, P. (1993) *New Future for Rural Trains: the Full Report.* London: Transnet.

Scott, C. (2004) 'The Olympics in Australia: Museums meet mega and hallmark events', *International Journal of Arts Management*, 7.1: 34–41.

Sidaway, R. (1990) *Birds and Walkers: a Review of Research.* London: Ramblers' Association.

Sidaway, R. (1991) *Good Conservation Practice for Sport and Recreation.* London: Sports Council, Countryside Commission, Nature Conservancy Council and WWF.

Sidaway, R. (1994) *Recreation and the Natural Heritage: a Research Review.* Edinburgh: Scottish National Heritage.

Sidaway, R. (1995) 'Sport in the countryside: current trends, studies and practice', in C. Etchell (ed.), *Sport in the Countryside.* Cardiff: Countryside Recreation Network, pp. 3–8.

Sport England (1999a) *Motorsports.* Planning Bulletin 6. London: Sport England.

Sport England (1999b) *Planning policies for sport.* London: Sport England.

Stubbs, D. (2001) *Sydney Olympic Games 2000: The environmental Games.* Dorking: Committed to Green Foundation.

Toohey, K. and Veal, A.J. (2000) *The Olympic Games: a Social Science Perspective.* Wallingford: CABI Publishing.

UK Centre for Economic and Environmental Development (UKCEED) (1993) *Water Skiing and the Environment: a Literature Review.* London: Sports Council.

UK Sport (2004) *Measuring success – 2 The economic impact of major sports events.* London: UK Sport.

UK Sport (n.d.) *World class events: Practical environmental guidelines.* London: UK Sport.

UK Sports Council (1998) *An Agenda for Sport and the Environment.* London: UK Sports Council.

UK Sports Council (1999a) *Major Events – the Economics.* London: UK Sports Council.

UK Sports Council (1999b) *Major Events – the Economics: Measuring Success.* London: UK Sports Council.

Van't Zelfde, J., Richards, G. and van der Straaten, J. (1996) 'Developing sustainability in the Alps', in B. Bramwell et al. (eds), *Sustainable Tourism Management: Principles and Practice.* Tilburg: Tilburg University Press, pp. 73–86.

Vigor, A and Mean, M. (eds) (2004) *After the Gold Rush: a Sustainable Olympics for London.* London: ippr & Demos.

Vuolle, P. (1991) 'Nature and environments for physical activity', in P. Oja and R. Telama (eds), *Sport for All*. Amsterdam: Elsevier, pp. 597–606.

Waitt, G. (2003) 'Social impact of Olympic Games', *Annals of Tourism Research*, 30 (1): 194–215.

Wheat, S. (1995) 'Green golf', *Leisure Management*, 13 (11): 38–40.

Whitson, D. and Macintosh, D. (1993) 'Becoming a world class city: hallmark events and sports franchises in the growth strategies of western Canadian cities', *Sociology of Sport Journal*, 10: 221–40.

Wilson, G. and Robinson, D. (2005) 'Towards practical management of motorized recreational vehicle activity in a National Park. The Lake District Hierarchy of Trail Routes', *Countryside Recreation*, 13 (2): 12–18.

Wilson, R.J (2005) 'The economic impact of sport events: critiquing the UK Sport typology', in M.F. Collins (ed.), *The Power of Sport*, EASM/ISRM European Sports Management Congress, Newcastle/Gateshead, 7–10 September, abstracts book, pp. 293–4.

Part Four

International Comparison and Context

20

Sport in North America

The United States and Canada

TREVOR SLACK AND MILENA M. PARENT

OVERVIEW

» *Youth sport – community-level sport, high school sport*
» *Intercollegiate sport*
» *Professional team sport*

Sport is an integral and pervasive part of social life in North America and, for many people, North America, and in particular the United States, is the centre of the sporting world. North American athletes such as Shaquille O'Neal, Tiger Woods, Venus and Serena Williams, Wayne Gretzky, Barry Bonds and Mia Hamm are global icons who exemplify the pinnacle of excellence in their respective sports. North-American-based sporting goods companies such as Nike, Spalding and Brunswick are global brands that lead the sporting goods field. Teams such as the Chicago Bulls, the New York Yankees and the Montreal Canadiens are widely recognised in all corners of the world. North American athletes, particularly from the United States, dominate the Olympic Games and the events themselves are invariably scheduled so as to coincide with prime time television slots in the East Coast of the United States. The Super Bowl, the World Series and the National Basketball Association finals are some of the most watched sporting events, not just in North America, but throughout the world. Nowhere is sport more visible and more widely consumed.

In this chapter we look at the way sport is structured and organised in North America. We focus specifically on three levels. First we look at the way youth sport is delivered through community organisations and schools. We then look at intercollegiate sport and the way this is organised. Finally, we look at the highly commercialised professional sports leagues. We look critically at some of the problems and issues confronting these three levels of the sport system. As a result of its size and sporting prowess, the United States tends to dominate when one thinks of North American sport, but we also look at Canada which while geographically linked to the United States shows some marked differences in the way in which it organises and operates sport.

YOUTH SPORT

In both the United States and Canada sporting opportunities for the country's youth are delivered in one of two ways: either through community-based programmes or through schools. Ewing and Seefeldt (1996) suggest that in the United States community-based programmes serve twice as many participants as school programmes. They argue that diminishing resources in public schools (government-funded schools) have led to fewer school teams and fewer qualified staff to coach. In contrast, community programmes, which rely primarily on volunteers, have not been subjected to the same resource pressures. In Canada a 1992 World Health Organization study (King and Coles, 1992) found a similar but not as marked trend with 62 per cent of 11-year-old boys and 49 per cent of 11-year-old girls being involved in community sport programmes and 45 per cent of both boys and girls being involved in school programmes. Writing about Canada, Hall et al. (1991: 196) suggest that school sport, like other programmes within the public education system, has experienced 'pressures to cut back or at least do the same job with fewer resources'. They also note that as teachers' workloads have increased many have withdrawn their voluntary services, making it necessary to cut programmes and, as a result, fewer children are able to participate.

Weiss and Hayashi (1996) suggest that there are four types of community sport programmes and although they are writing about the United States these are for the most part also applicable to Canada. Agency-based programmes operate sport teams and leagues within the local community. They are primarily self-supporting with monies being raised through membership fees and fund-raising ventures. However, some may receive support or even be sponsored by service clubs such as Kinsmen or Rotary and they also obtain help from their local municipalities which provide, increasingly at a cost, the facilities where games are played. In the United States these agency-based programmes are often 'an affiliate of a larger national sponsor of a specific sport (e.g., Little League Baseball, American Youth Soccer Organization) that governs regulations for these sports' (Weiss and Hayashi, 1996: 44). In Canada the teams and leagues are frequently affiliated with a regional or provincial sport governing body which in turn is a part of a national organisation such as the Canadian Soccer Association or Hockey

Canada. In addition to being responsible for the staging of sports events in their community, many of these organisations also run coaching and officiating programmes which, while developed at the national level, are delivered locally through these community-based organisations.

As well as agency-based programmes which in both the United States and Canada have the largest number of participants, sporting opportunities are also delivered through national youth organisations (e.g. YM/WCA, Scouts and Guides, and Boys and Girls Clubs of America), privately operated sports clubs and municipal recreation programmes. National youth organisations such as the YM and YWCA have a long history of involvement in sport but it has been used primarily as an avenue for developing social skills and 'building character' rather than as an end in itself. Today such organisations while still involved in providing sporting opportunities offer relatively few programmes in comparison with agency-based programmes.

Private sport clubs are a growing phenomenon in both the United States and Canada but they are most prevalent in sports like gymnastics, figure skating and swimming. Here parents often pay significant fees and are involved in fund-raising to hire high-performance coaches and to help operate the club. While many of these clubs provide supportive and realistic programmes, Ryan (1995) has documented many examples of the abuse that some young athletes, specifically gymnasts and figures skaters, are subjected to in the pursuit of athletic excellence. In recent years the United States has also seen a rise in the number of club teams in basketball. Many of these are sponsored by the three major athletic footwear companies Nike, adidas and Reebok (which is owned by adidas) that financially endorse teams, leagues and camps:

> Kevin Gaines, a freshman at Michigan who attended the 1998 Nike camp prior to his senior year at Clark High School in Las Vegas [suggested that] it's for the guys who are going to college and hopefully the NBA. Then (once you are in the NBA) they'll get you down for a shoe contract. (Wetzel and Yaeger, 2000: 48)

Such is the pressure to secure the next Michael Jordan or Chamique Holdsclaw that athletic footwear companies can no longer wait until a player is in his or her junior year at college; they must now start identifying such talented youngsters at the junior high school level. Financially supporting non-school basketball clubs, leagues and camps is one way of doing this. As Weiss and Hayashi (1996: 44) also note, such clubs 'serve either as a farm system to high school or college sports or as a legal outlet for year-round participation'.

The final form of community-based sport delivery involves city and town recreation departments. In addition to the provision of facilities for agency-based programmes, these departments, in both the United States and Canada, also usually offer a range of introductory sports programmes as well as supporting such less competitive activities as camping, climbing, etc.

School sport in Canada and the United States incorporates both intramural and inter-scholastic competition, although intramural programmes are very much the poor cousins of the interschool programmes. High school sport in the United States is governed by the National Federation of State High School Associations (NFHS). The mission of the NFHS is 'to serve its members and its related professional groups by providing leadership and national coordination for the administration of interscholastic activities which will enhance the educational experiences of high school students and reduce risks of their participation' (www.nfhs.org). It is based in Indianapolis, has approximately 40 staff, and operates through 50 member state high school athletic associations plus the District of Columbia. The number of participants in high school sport in the United States is nearly 10 million. The most popular sports in 2006-07 in terms of participation were football[1] (1,104,548) and basketball (556,269) for boys and basketball (456,967) and outdoor track and field (444,181) for girls (http://www.nfhs.org/contentmanager/uploads/2006-07_Participation_Survey.pdf). Many schools and certainly most of the larger ones will employ athletic directors to co-ordinate interschool athletic teams and many of the bigger sports have paid coaches.

State high school athletic associations such as the California Interscholastic Federation, the New Hampshire Interscholastic Athletic Association and the Georgia High School Association are segmented into a number of regions and offer state championships in selected sport. The sports offered vary from state to state but most will include the major sports such as football, basketball, track and field, soccer, cross-country running, and swimming and diving. Schools compete against similar-size schools and there may be up to five different size classifications within some of the larger, more populous states. There are no formal national championships; most competition culminates at the state championship. However, in a number of sports there are All Star games such as the McDonald's All American High School Basketball Game and the Roundball Classic where the top players compete on representative teams. In many ways these events serve as showcases for college scouts looking to recruit players. There are also numerous 'All American' polls and ranking lists for the top high school teams produced by media organisations such as *USAToday* and *FOXSports.com* (see www.usatoday.com/sports/preps/softball/sbhssb.htm; http://msn.foxsports.com/story/1606815), Coaches Associations (see www.nscaa.com/scripts/runisa.dll?m2.131502:gp:586637:14028+awards/2001/HSAll) and sporting good manufacturers (see http://rivalshigh.rivals.com/default.asp? SID=950&FP=2301). Various bodies also produce lists of regional or state All Stars and Academic All Americans, athletes who have done well in their sport while maintaining a high level of academic work.

In Canada education is the role of the provincial not the federal government and high school sport is operated under the auspices of the various provincial organisations such as the Alberta Schools Athletic Association and the Ontario Federation of School Athletic Associations. Unlike the United States, schools are unlikely to employ athletic directors and coaches will be drawn primarily from the ranks of teachers or interested volunteers. There is a Canadian School Sport Federation (CSSF), but it plays a very minor role in the operation of high school sport. The various provinces hold championship tournaments in a number of sports such as volleyball, soccer, basketball, and track and field. Interestingly ice hockey, in many ways Canada's primary sport, is not played competitively in all provinces, within the school system. In large part this is because of the existence of a strong agency-based league system. As in the United States, provincial championships are held, but there is no national schools championship. Inter-provincial tournaments do take place but these are generally on a far less grandiose scale than their equivalent in the United States.

While organisations such as the NFHS, the CSSF and the various state and provincial governing bodies extol the virtues of high school competition, its emphasis on sporting ability and its links to educational goals, there have been and continue to be problems with high school sport. Although in many ways a number of these problems are more pronounced in the United States than in Canada, there are commonalties. First, there is a concern in both countries that coaches and athletic directors model their programmes on professional or high-level elite sport. As a result there is an overemphasis on winning and the higher-profile sports, which often cater to male participants. As Coakley (1998: 461) points out, 'in the process of trying to build high-profile sports programs they often overlook the educational needs of all students in their schools. Their goal is to be "ranked" rather than to respond to the needs of students.' Many US schools encourage students to focus on a single sport whereas in Canada seasons are generally shorter and students are encouraged to play in several sports (Hall et al., 1991). Because US coaches are hired primarily as coaches, their win–lose record is often more important than the educational values they impart to players. In Canada, where the majority of coaches are primarily hired as teachers, win–lose records are not a factor in continuing employment.

Linked to the increased emphasis on winning in youth sport there has also been a growing involvement from corporate sponsors. While most prevalent at the collegiate and professional levels of competition, both high school and community sport programmes in the United States and Canada have been appropriated by corporations anxious to capitalise on the qualities that are often associated with such activities. For example, many community-level teams carry the name of a local, regional or national business on their sweaters. High school sports organisations such as the Alberta Schools Athletic Association (McDonald's, adidas and Yonex) and the California Interscholastic Federation (Spalding, Marriott and Teamsports) are supported by corporate sponsors. Likewise many major tournaments and events are endorsed by corporations. While the financial support that is given certainly helps, youth sport sponsorship means that corporate interests may take priority over the educational interests of students. Wetzel and Yaeger in their aptly named book *Sole Influence: Basketball, Corporate Greed and the Corruption of America's Youth* provide numerous examples of the way major athletic footwear companies have prioritised their requirements over the educational or social needs of athletes.

High school sports have also been criticised for the fact that they focus mainly on participation opportunities for males. As noted above, in the United States, the figures for boys and girls show that males represent 59 per cent of the total participants in high school sport. In Ontario, Canada's most populous province, the situation is better with 55 per cent of participants being male. Prior to the early 1970s some US states actually had legislation which prohibited interscholastic sports for girls (Sage, 1998). However, since this time the number of girls involved in high school sports in the United States has increased dramatically as a result of the passage of Title IX of the Educational Amendment Act. This Act called for the abolition of sex discrimination in any educational programmes, including sports activities. However, while the participation of girls in high school sport has gone up, this has not been accompanied by a concomitant increase in the number of female coaches and administrators. As Coakley (1998: 226) notes, 'In North America … there has been a significant decline in the number and proportion of women coaches and administrators in many sport organizations, especially the athletic departments of high schools and colleges.' While there are a number of reasons for this decline, one of the main ones relates to the fact that, as women and girls' sports have become increasingly popular and more visible, they have offered sources of power and prestige and as such have been appropriated by men.

A final criticism of high school sport is that it may foster and perpetuate violence. There is some evidence to suggest that violence in sport is less common today than it was in the past (cf. Scheinin, 1994). Nevertheless, there is still a concern about the incidence of physical violence in youth sport and that participation in high school sport may be linked to violence off the field. Evidence suggests that male athletes in contact sports, such as ice hockey, basketball and football, accept a certain level of violence in sport and as the amount of contact in the sport increases so too does the acceptance of violence (Weinstein et al., 1995). Certainly there have been a number of incidents of violence in these sports at youth level (see http://news.mpr.org/features/199803/04_olsond_hockey/) some of which have resulted in criminal prosecution, but most are dismissed as part of the game. As Malina (http://ed-web3.educ.msu.edu/ysi/Spring%201999%20Bob.htm) notes, athletes involved in violence 'are often given a second, third, or fourth chance in sport essentially because of their skills. These athletes are also often preferentially treated by coaches and sport systems (and occasionally by the legal system) for the simple reason that they are central to winning and to the success of a coach or team.' Reports of violent behaviour by adults at youth sport events are also on the rise (Box 20.1). The most vivid recent examples involve a man in Boston accused of beating another father to death after their sons' hockey practice (www.washingtonpost.com/wp-dyn/articles/a54541-2002jan2.html) and another father accused of choking his son's coach because his son was on the bench (http://www.sportsnet.ca/othersports/shownews.jsp?content=s011787A).

Box 20.1 High school sport and violence

While no one can condone the violence that occurs during and after games, a far more disturbing link between high school sport and violence is evidenced in the events that took place at Columbine High School on 20 April 1999 and those graphically detailed in Lefkowitz's (1997) book *Our Guys: the Glen Ridge Rape and the Secret Life of the Perfect Suburb*. The Columbine situation involved two teenagers, allegedly youth sport dropouts, in a murderous rampage that left 13 dead and 21 wounded. Much of the aggression by the two teenagers was directed at high school athletes. When the killing began the two gunmen apparently began their rampage with the words 'All jocks stand up' and 'anybody with a white hat [a trademark of the school's athletes] or a shirt with a sports emblem is dead'. Columbine was apparently a school that favoured athletes. Adams and Russakoff (www.washingtonpost.com/wp-srv/national /daily/june99/ columbine12.htm) report that the state wrestling champion was regularly allowed to park his $100,000 Hummer [an all-terrain-type vehicle] all day in a 15-minute slot, a football player teased a girl about her breasts but was not reprimanded by the teacher who was also his coach, and the homecoming king, a football player, was on probation for burglary. Initiation rituals involved senior wrestlers twisting the nipples of freshmen wrestlers until they turned purple and tennis players volleying balls at younger players' backsides. They go on to suggest that 'some parents and students believe a schoolwide indulgence of certain jocks – their criminal convictions, physical abuse, sexual and racial bullying – intensified the killer's feelings of powerlessness and galvanized their fantasies of revenge' (Adams and Russakoff, www.washingtonpost.com/wp-srv/national/ daily/june99/ columbine 12.htm). While thankfully a rare occurrence, the Columbine situation is not the only one where suggestions have been made that killings have been linked to the favouritism shown to high school athletes. After a March 2001 shooting at Santana High School in Santee, California, (http://www.signonsandiego.com/news/ metro/santana/), an angry reader wrote to the *Los Angeles Times* stating:

For school personnel to be at a loss as to the motives of the shootings at Santana High School is hypocritical. Anyone who has attended high school knows there is the 'in crowd' made up of sports heroes, class officers and their entourage. To this group the teachers and administrators pander allowing them to do pretty much as they please. Those not in the 'in group' become the subjects of bullying, taunting and ridicule.

The situation described by Lefkowitz involved a group of high school athletes who lured a retarded girl to a basement with a promise that if she joined them she would get a date with one of their friends. They then raped her with a broomstick, a baseball bat and a stick. Lefkowitz documents how the 'gang-rape – which town residents euphemistically called the boys' 'alleged misconduct' – provoked no community introspection in Glen Ridge. Instead adults and fellow students rallied around the accused athletes … and dismissed the victim, who had the mental age of an 8-year old, as a slut' (www.salon.com/aug97/mothers/guys970813.html).

Such issues certainly raise debate about the status that is attached to outstanding high school athletes and teams in North America, particularly in the United States. While the United States is often held up as the epitome of athletic excellence, the excesses of such a system, as has been shown, often lead to broader social problems.

INTERCOLLEGIATE SPORT

Unlike many countries of the world, intercollegiate sport in North America, particularly the United States, is a highly structured and commercialised activity. Student input is minimal and programmes are operated by paid professional staff. The governing body of intercollegiate sport in the United States is the National Collegiate Athletic Association (NCAA); in Canada it is Canadian Interuniversity Sport (CIS) which prior to September 2001 was known as the Canadian Interuniversity Athletic Union (CIAU). The 2001–2 NCAA manual describes its members' competitive athletic programmes as 'a vital part of the educational system' and 'the athlete is an integral part of the student body'. This it is suggested helps 'retain a clear line of demarcation between intercollegiate athletics and professional sports'. As Zimbalist (1999: 4) cynically states, 'whom do they think they are kidding?' At its highest levels interuniversity sport in the United States is very much the same type of entertainment spectacle as is professional sport. In Canada the situation is less severe and it is generally accepted that university sport has stronger links to the educational ambitions of the university than it does in the United States.

The NCAA is a large complex organisation which in the 2004–5 year had budgeted revenues of $564m. Of this amount $508.25m (90 per cent) came from television revenues (http://www1.ncaa.org/finance/2006-07_budget.pdf) thus showing the entertainment orientation of US collegiate sport. Its national offices are in Indianapolis, Indiana, and there is a staff of more than 350 (http://www.ncaa.org/about/what_is_the_ ncaa.html). The NCAA is governed by over 1,100 NCAA school representatives sitting on 125 committees (http://www1.ncaa.org/eprise/main/Public/hr/about.html). The member institutions of the NCAA are divided into three divisions, I, II and III. There are 329 Division I institutions, 282 Division II institutions and 422 at Division III level (http://www1.ncaa.org/membership/membership_svcs/membership_breakdown.html). To be classified as a Division I school (the US term used to denote a college or university) an institution must meet a number of criteria. These include but are not limited to: sponsoring at least seven sports for men and seven for women (or six for men and eight for women) with at least two team sports for each gender; playing a minimum percentage of games against Division I opponents (this is slightly different for football and basketball); and meeting minimum financial aid award (scholarship) levels. Schools that have football are classified as Football Bowl Subdivision (formerly Division 1–A) or NCAA Football Championship Subdivisions (formerly Division 1–AA). Bowl subdivision schools are usually fairly elaborate programs. Football Bowl Subdivision teams have to meet minimum attendance requirements (average is 15,000 people in actual or paid attendance per home game), which must be met once in a rolling two-year period. NCAA Football Championship Subdivision teams do not need to meet minimum attendance requirements.

Division II institutions must sponsor at least five sports for men and five for women with at least two team sports for each. Like Division I there are scheduling requirements as regards who member institution's teams can play against (other than for football and basketball). There are no attendance requirements but there is a maximum for financial aid awards that Division II schools can offer. Division II schools are in many ways more regionally focused than Division I schools which compete nationally. Division III schools must sponsor at least five sports for each sex, again with a minimum of two team sports. There are minimum contest and participation requirements but Division III student athletes receive no financial aid. The NCAA description of the three divisions suggests that 'Division III athletics departments place special importance on the impact of athletics on the participants rather than on the spectators', perhaps further emphasising the entertainment focus of the higher divisions' sport programmes (www.ncaa.org/about/div_criteria. html). Universities such as Ohio State and the University of Southern California are examples of Division I schools; North Dakota and New Haven, Division II; and Colby-Sawyer and Frostberg State, Division III. The NCAA's total Division I expense and allocation for 2006–7 is $389,776,600 compared with a mere $24,646,800 for Division II and $17,935,200 for Division III (http://www1.ncaa.org/finance/2006-07_budget.pdf).

The vast majority of universities compete in one of the nearly 90-member collegiate athletic conferences. These function in the same way as leagues, with position in the conference determining eligibility for post-conference tournaments (or bowls in football). The NCAA sponsors 88 national championships, 10 of which all divisions are eligible for and the rest being evenly spread between Divisions I, II and III. The biggest events are the men's basketball championship, colloquially know as 'March Madness', the women's basketball championship and the various football bowl games, of which there are currently 24 certified by the NCAA. The best known of these is the Rose Bowl. National championships in most sports are decided through tournament play. In football the national championship is decided by polls. The NCAA itself does not conduct polls for most Division I sports but these are carried out by agencies such as USAToday/ESPN, Associated Press, etc. Because of the number of polls it is possible that some will produce different 'national champions'.

University sport in Canada is far less grandiose than that of the United States. It is also fair to say that its links to educational objectives are closer than those found in many US programmes. This notwithstanding, Canadian university sport is still more commercially oriented than student sport in countries like England and Australia and it is primarily operated by paid staff hired by their respective universities primarily for this purpose. The CIS, located in Ottawa, Ontario, operates with a staff of 11 and in 2000–1 had a revenue budget of C$2,822,179 (http://www.cisport.ca/e/plans/documents/strategicplans 07-11.pdf), figures which pale in comparison with those of the NCAA. The CIS serves over 10,000 students through four conferences: the Canada West Universities Athletic Association (14 universities); Ontario University Athletics (18 universities); the Quebec Student Sport Federation (8 universities); and the Atlantic University Sport Conference (11 universities). Member universities compete within their respective units for conference and ultimately national titles in 19 national championships (9 for men and 10 for women) in 11 different sports. The CIS is involved in the selection of 'All Canadians' and in conjunction with the Royal Bank selects 'Academic All Canadians', athletes who apart from performing at a high level also maintain a high grade point average. Some of the national championships and semi-final games in major sports (football, ice hockey and basketball) are shown on TSN (Canada's Sport Network); however, there is nowhere near the type of TV exposure to collegiate sport that is found in the United States. Likewise it is fair to say that with the possible exception of eastern Canada where university sport is very popular (probably due to the absence of any professional sport franchises) intercollegiate competitions do not engender the type of passion and community interest that characterises US campuses (see also Box 20.2).

Box 20.2 Sports scholarships

One issue that has long plagued Canadian interuniversity sport is the awarding of athletic scholarships. Unlike the United States where scholarships are an integral part of university sport, Canadian universities have for a long time resisted the awarding of scholarships a fact that perhaps underscores the different priorities attached to university sport in the two countries. While there were 'unofficial' scholarships given to athletes (mainly in Atlantic province universities) these were disguised as part-time jobs and were technically against CIAU rules. Over the years athletic awards have become more prevalent and in June 2000 CIS members agreed to report all athletic awards. The results of a study released in December showed that $2,396,500 were awarded to CIS student athletes, with the average amount of an award being $1,160 (again a figure which pales in comparison with US awards). The sports that received the largest amount of awards were football, ice hockey and basketball for men and basketball, volleyball and soccer for women.

In addition to their primary roles in interuniversity sport the NCAA and CIS also perform other functions. These involve co-operating with national sport organisations in the preparation of athletes for national teams, running drug awareness programs, working towards gender equity, and enhancing leadership skills. Individual universities will also often have community-based programmes and will run summer sport camps for local athletes.

As with high school sport, interuniversity sport in both the United States and Canada generates a number of issues and concerns. Again many of these are more pronounced in the US system than they are in Canada. Here we look briefly at three issues: gender equity, increasing commercialisation and lack of student involvement.

While both the CIS and the NCAA have a stated commitment to gender equity, the figures of each of these organisations show they have some way to go before equity is achieved. Statistics released by the NCAA in March 2002 show that approximately 42 per cent of participating athletes in NCAA competition are female (http://www.ncaa.org/about/fact_sheet.pdf). The numbers have, however, improved considerably since 1971, the year before the passage of Title IX, when only 7.4 per cent of total participants were female (Zimbalist, 1999). The 2001 scholarship and expenditure figures showed more pronounced inequalities with the average number of scholarship equivalents per Division I university being 91.8 for men and 61.3 (40 per cent of total) for women. Total average operating expenses for Division I men's programmes are $4,649,667 and for women $1,776.160 (27.6 per cent of the total). A major argument for these inequities has been that men play football, often seen as a revenue-generating sport at Division I-A level, and there is no equivalent for women. However, Messner et al. (1996) have argued that women's sport could be revenue generating if it were to be marketed properly and that the inequities which exist are because athletic administrators are not interested in promoting women's programmes. The majority of these administrators are men. In fact Zimbalist (1999) reports that since 1972, when over 90 per cent of women's athletic programmes were directed by women, the figures have declined and in 1996 only 18.5 per cent were in this category. A similar situation exists in coaching where the 1972 and 1996 figures were 90 per cent and 47.7 per cent, respectively.

Figures for CIS athletes are not as readily available but a February 2004 press release (http://www.universitysport.ca/e/story_detail.cfm?id=1910) notes that 65 per cent of athletic awards in Canadian university sport went to male athletes. In addition Danylchuk and MacLean (2001: 368) report that within Canadian university sport 'there are still slightly more male participants overall, primarily due to the large roster size of football and a larger roster size for men's wrestling than women's due to three additional weight classes'. In addition they add that of the 49 CIS member universities only 11 (22 per cent) have female athletic directors and only 30.2 per cent of coaches of women's teams are female. While the number of athletic directors has increased from 13 per cent five years ago, the situation of coaches has worsened with a drop of just over 10 per cent from 40.6

per cent. Marketing efforts, it is claimed, are similarly directed primarily at the major men's sports of football, basketball and ice hockey. Clearly, while progress has been made in both countries, total gender equity is some way off.

The high-profile nature of college sport means that it is of decided interest to commercial sponsors. In 1995 the average NCAA Division IA school earned $459,000 in sponsorship and signage income, $96,000 in programme advertising and sales, and $833,000 in miscellaneous income, which included licensing (Zimbalist, 1999). Sponsorship comes from companies such as those involved in the production of athletic footwear, soft drinks and beer. A single sponsorship for a high-profile Division I university can be in the millions of dollars. TV contracts also bring in considerable revenue for individual universities and conferences, which negotiate for transmission of regular season games. In addition, in November 1999 the NCAA announced that it had reached a deal with CBS Sports which gave it exclusive TV rights to the NCAA men's Division I basketball championship event and associated marketing. The deal, which began in the 2002–3 academic year, runs for 11 years and is worth a minimum of $6bn (www.ncaa.org/releases/make page.cgi/champother/1999111801co). The various football bowl games are sponsored by such corporate bodies as FedEx, Jeep, Nokia and Toyota. Commercial connections also exist through the sale of designated seats and boxes at games primarily football and basketball) to corporate bodies which use them for entertainment purposes.

As we have seen in other areas, although Canada in some ways mirrors the United States it is on a much smaller scale. For example, the 2000–1 CIS revenue budget shows C$281,900 coming from sponsorship. The majority of the budget for CIS comes from public funds with Sport Canada, the federal government agency responsible for sport, giving nearly C$350,000. Danylchuk and MacLean (2001: 374) predict that the funds available from Sport Canada are likely to decline in the future and this will 'force an increase in reliance on marketing initiatives'. But they note that this will be difficult as the CIS has no critical mass of corporate support and in fact in 1999 the Board of Directors (of the then CIAU) overturned a consultant's suggestion to open a second office in Toronto, the heart of corporate Canada.

The Canadian problems notwithstanding, in the United States increased commercialisation has meant that intercollegiate sport has become an 'entertainment conglomerate, with operating methods and objectives totally separate from and mainly opposed to, the educational aims of the schools that house its franchises' (Sperber, 1990: 56). The involvement of commercial bodies and media organisations in intercollegiate sport has meant that in many cases it has lost its educational objectives and become a business. In this situation the academic progress of players becomes less important than the win–lose record of the team and the TV ratings that are generated. The big sports of football and basketball, which are the main revenue generators, become all important and other sports such as field hockey and cross-country running are marginalised because they have little spectator appeal. Sack and Staurowsky (1998) suggest that the commercialisation of college sport has led to the professionalisation of college athletes. These athletes as a group tend to have a markedly different demographic profile from the rest of the student body. 'Teams tend to have a higher proportion of blacks than can be found on their campuses as a whole. Also the overall gap between athletes and nonathletes in academic prepared-ness tends to be rather large' (Sack & Staurowsky 1998: 5).

In Canada this situation is not as grave as it is in the United States, a fact which reflects the relative lack of importance of intercollegiate sport on Canadian campuses. However, this is not to say that Canadian university sport is immune from the pressures and prob-lems of commercialism (cf. Hall et al., 1991). Football and ice hockey, two sports pre-dominantly played by men, are the major recipients of commercial support and men's basketball teams are often given scheduling priority over women's because of their 'com-mercial' appeal. There are instances where staff who are primarily hired to coach have sacrificed students educational objectives for their involvement in sport. It is important to note, however, that the problems that do exist in Canada as a result of commercial pres-sures are minuscule compared with those that exist in the United States.

As noted earlier, student sport in the United States and Canada is different from many countries in that it is primarily run by paid staff. As a result there are often concerns about the lack of student input into an activity which is ostensibly for the benefit of students (see Sage 1998: 230–1 for a brief history of the decline of student control of sport in the United States). Eitzen (1999: 115) notes that 'students, who typically help the athletic department through their fees (which total more than $1 million annually at most big-time programs) have no influence over how their money is spent'. Yet, as he goes on to note, alumni and other donors who give large but significantly less sums often have considerable input into the oper-ation of programmes. In the United States where the demand for seats at the major sporting events is relatively high, students are given a relatively small allocation, most seats going to alumni and boosters. Eitzen (1999) gives the example of the University of Louisville which only allocates 10 per cent of its seats to students and the University of Arizona which holds a lottery to choose which students can attend basketball games. In Canada student input into university athletic programmes is, like the United States, relatively limited. However, students are usually able to obtain seats at university sporting events as the popularity of these events is limited in comparison with the United States. Sack and Staurowsky (1999) suggest that one of the solutions to many of the problems of intercollegiate sport in the United States would be to turn back control to the students. However, neither they nor any other observer of intercollegiate sport seriously expect this to happen.

PROFESSIONAL SPORT

The major professional team sports leagues in North America are the National Football League (NFL), the National Hockey League (NHL), the National Basketball Association (NBA), Major League Baseball (MLB) and the Women's National Basketball

Association (WNBA). Although the NBA (1), NHL (6) and MLB (1) have teams in Canada, the majority of franchises of these leagues are located in the United States. The NFL is entirely US based. The Canadian equivalent is the Canadian Football League (CFL)[2] which has teams in nine cities in Canada. In addition to these team sports North Americans are of course extensively involved in professional sports such as golf, tennis, boxing and auto racing. Here we focus on the professional team sports. The NFL has 32 teams which compete in two conferences, the American Football Conference (AFC) and the National Football Conference (NFC). Each conference is divided into four divisions. The winners of each division plus selected 'wild cards' enter the playoffs with the AFC and NFC champions competing in the Super Bowl. The NHL has 30 teams, which compete in an Eastern and a Western Conference, each of which is split into three divisions. As with football, division winners as well as the seven best teams (based on regular season points total) in each conference enter the playoffs. The winners of the two conferences meet for the Stanley Cup. All playoff games and the Stanley Cup Final are seven-game series.

Major League Baseball has 30 teams which compete in two leagues, the American League (AL) and the National League (NL). Each league has three divisions. The division winner and the team with the best record compete in the semi-finals of the league championship with the ultimate winner of the AL meeting the winner of the NL in a seven-game 'World Series'. The WNBA is the only major professional team sport league for women. The NBA Board of Governors announced the formation of the league in April 1996 and play began in June 1997. The WNBA has been extremely successful and has grown from an initial 8 teams to 13 teams which play in an Eastern and a Western Conference.

Professional sport franchises are extremely valuable. The 2006 report by *Forbes* magazine estimated the most valuable franchises in each of the men's leagues as follows: NFL, Washington Redskins $1,423,000,000; MLB, New York Yankees $1,2000,000,000; NBA, New York Knicks $ 592,000,000; NHL, Toronto Maple Leafs $332,000,000. In the 1997–8 season the average player salary in the NBA was over $4 million, in MLB over $2.5 million; the NFL just over $1 million; and NHL $1.75 million (Quirk and Fort, 1999; Ozanian, http://forbes.com/lists/2004/09/01/04nfland. html). Money comes to teams from TV revenues, merchandising and licensing, ticket sales (particularly corporate hospitality suites), parking revenues, and concessions. Unlike professional sport franchises in many other countries, franchises in North America are portable, that is to say they can be moved from one city to the next. One of the most recent moves involved the struggling Vancouver Grizzlies of the NBA moving to Memphis.

Like all professional sport the major North American leagues face a number of problems. These include but are not limited to escalating player salaries, increasing violence, drug abuse, labour relations between players and owners, and free agency issues. Here we

Weiss, M.R. and Hayashi, C.T. (1996) 'The United States', in P. De Knop, L.M. Engström, B. Skirstad and M.R. Weiss (eds), *Worldwide Trends in Youth Sport.* Champaign, IL: Human Kinetics, pp. 43–57.

Wetzel, D. and Yaeger, D. (2000) *Sole Influence: Basketball, Corporate Greed and the Corruption of America's Youth.* New York: Warner Books.

Whitson, D., Harvey, J. and Lavoie, M. (2000) 'The Mills Report, the Manley Subsidy proposals and the business of professional sport', *Canadian Public Administration,* 43.

Zimbalist, A. (1999) *Unpaid Professionals: Commercialism and Conflict in Big-time College Sports.* Princeton, NJ: Princeton University Press.

Web Sources

Adams, L. and Russakoff, D. 'Dissecting Columbine's cult of the athlete'
www.washingtonpost.com/wp-srv/national /daily/june99/columbine12.htm
Accessed 6 January 2002

Associated Press national ranking
www.latimes.com/sports/highschool/la-preps-bbb-aprank.story
Accessed 6 January 2002

Bast, J. 'Sport stadium madness: why it started. How to stop it'
www.heartland.org/studies/sports/madness-sum.htm
Accessed 12 January 2002

Canadian Interuniversity Sport announces results of data collection on athletic awards
http://www.universitysport.ca/e/story_detail.cfm?id=1910
Accessed 19 January 2005

Canadian Interuniversity Sport Strategic Plans and 2007-08 Operational Plans and Budget
http://cisport.ca/e/plans/documents/Strategicplans07-11.pdf
Accessed 14 September 2007

CBC News Indepth: Tragedy in Taber
http://www.cbc.ca/news/background/taber/
Accessed 19 January 2005

Did Glen Ridge raise its sons to be rapists?
www.salon.com/aug97/mothers/guys970813.html
Accessed 6 on January 2002

FOXSports.com 'Polls'
http://msn.foxsports.com/story/1606815
Accessed 19 January 2005

Malina, R.M. 'Sport, violence and Littleton – a perspective'
http://ed-web3.educ.msu.edu/ysi/Spring%201999%20Bob.htm
Accessed 6 January 2002

National Collegiate Athletic Association 'About us'
http://www1.ncaa.org/eprise/main/Public/hr/about.html
Accessed 14 September 2007

National Collegiate Athletic Association 'Composition of the NCAA'
http://www1.ncaa.org/membership/membership_svcs/membership_breakdown.html
Accessed 14 September 2007

National Collegiate Athletic Association 'Fact sheet'
http://www.ncaa.org/about/fact_sheet.pdf
Accessed 19 January 2005

National Collegiate Athletic Association revised budget for the fiscal year ending 31 August 2007
http://www1.ncaa.org/finance/2006-07_budget.pdf
Accessed 14 September 2007

National Collegiate Athletic Association 'What is the NCAA?'
http://www.ncaa.org/about/what_is_the_ncaa.html
Accessed 14 September 2007

National Collegiate Athletic Association 'What is the difference between Divisions I, II and III?'
http://www.ncaa.org/about/divcriteria.html
Accessed 14 September 2007

National Federation of State High School Associations
www.nfhs.org
Accessed 14 September 2007

National Federation of State High School Associations, 2003–4 High School Athletics Participation Survey
http://www.nfhs.org/core/contentmanager/uploads/2006-7_Participation_Survey.pdf
Accessed 14 September 2007

National Soccer Coaches Association of America, High School All-Americans
www.nscaa.com/scripts/runisa.dll?m2.131502:gp:586637:14028+awards/2001/HSAll
Accessed 6 January 2002

NCAA reaches rights agreement with CBS Sports
www.ncaa.org/releases/makepage.cgi/champother/1999111801co
Accessed 12 January 2002

Olson, D. 'Body checking in high school hockey'
http://news.mpr.org/features/199803/04_olsond_hockey/;
Accessed 6 January 2002

Ozanian, M.K. 'The business of football'
http://forbes.com/lists/2004/09/01/04nfland.html
Accessed 24 January 2004

Questions raised about why push to stop parental hockey violence not working
http://www.sportsnet.ca/othersports/shownews.jsp?content=s011787A
Accessed 19 January 2005

Rivals High: The inside source for High School sports
http://rivalshigh.rivals.com/default.asp?SID=950&FP=2301
Accessed 6 January 2002

Santana High School Shooting
http://www.signonsandiego.com/news/metro/santana/
Accessed 24 January 2005

Trial begins in beating death stemming from sports fight
www.washingtonpost.com/wp-dyn/articles/a54541-2002jan2.html
Accessed 6 January 2002

USAToday 'Super 25 softball rankings'
www.usatoday.com/sports/preps/softball/sbhssb.htm
Accessed 6 January 2002

What's the difference between Divisions I, II and III?
www.ncaa.org/about/div_criteria.html
Accessed 12 January 2002

21

Sport in Australia

MURRAY PHILLIPS AND TARA MAGDALINSKI

OVERVIEW

» *Australia's sporting heritage*
» *Government involvement in Australian sport*
» *Commodification of Australian sport*
» *Gender dimensions of Australian sport*
» *Ethnic identity and Australian sport*
» *Racial dimensions of Australian sport*
» *Conclusion*

The success of the Sydney 2000 Olympics and the recent Melbourne 2006 Commonwealth Games confirmed for many that Australia is a nation 'obsessed' with sport. Sport pervades the national media, and news bulletins dedicate around a third of their broadcasts to reporting Australia's latest sporting achievements. Icons and sporting heroes are commemorated and revered by politicians, the media and the general public. Throughout these two world-class sporting events, the national obsession with sport was displayed on a global stage, and the world reaffirmed what Australians believed they had known all along: that Australia celebrates sport like nowhere else on earth.

The validity of these claims is, however, part of an ongoing debate about the nature of sport and physical activity in Australia. Whilst large-scale sporting events suggest an expertise in event management, what do they really reveal about sport in Australia? Are Australians more likely to participate in sport and enjoy greater levels of physical fitness than other nations? Do all Australians enjoy similar levels of access to sporting experiences?

Do citizens purchase larger amounts of merchandise than citizens of other developed nations? What is it that makes Australia stand out as a 'sporty nation'?

The claims about Australia's 'obsession' with sport derive from several sources. First, those who promulgate this mythology turn to attendance figures at sporting events to prove that Australians are 'sports mad'. Others claim that international sporting success, given the nation's relatively small population, reveals a national dedication to physical activity. Finally, the ability and willingness to host global sporting events such as the Olympics suggest that the nation is geared to produce memorable sporting experiences. Such arguments invariably conclude that there is something 'special' about Australia's infatuation with sport.

Throughout the 1990s, several academic texts sought to expose the Australian sporting psyche, and a brief look at the titles is useful. From Brian Stoddart's *Saturday Afternoon Fever* (1986) and Richard Cashman's *Paradise of Sport* (1995) through to Jim McKay's *No Pain, No Gain?* (1991) and Douglas Booth and Colin Tatz's *One-Eyed* (2000), the academic debate has gradually adopted a more critical edge, initially supporting, then qualifying, questioning and gradually rejecting this notion of a national 'obsession'. Challenging these myths has certainly been difficult, yet through the careful analysis of sport participation, attendance, coverage and rituals, a series of authors have carefully deconstructed these widely held beliefs.

Whilst this debate is interesting, it is time to move on and focus on what actually constitutes the national sporting cultures. We discuss sport in terms of 'cultures' to highlight that sport may be interpreted in contrasting ways by different sections of Australian society. In this chapter, we pose the following questions: What has contributed to the creation of sporting cultures in Australia, and what makes them distinct from or similar to other countries' sporting practices? And what, if any, are the defining features of Australia's sporting cultures? Of course, these are simple questions requiring complex answers for which we simply do not have the space. Instead, we focus here on the intersection between Australian sport and government, business, gender, ethnicity and race.

SPORTING HERITAGE

Whilst Australia was settled prior to the codification of modern sport in Europe, its primary sporting cultures remain highly derivative, a result of Australia's establishment as an outpost of the British Empire. Throughout the nineteenth century, colonisers brought British cultural practices with them to Australia, just as British social structures were disseminated to other parts of the Empire (Cashman, 1995). This 'cultural baggage' of the Anglo-Celts included sports such as boxing, cricket, horse racing, hunting, rowing, Rugby Union, soccer, and track and field; gambling too was firmly entrenched in early colonial sport.

Despite the dominance of British physical culture in Australia, local games and sports emerged, though without the might of an Empire to facilitate their diffusion to the rest of the world, they remained parochial practices. The nation's most popular, unique and locally created sport is Australian Rules football. 'Aussie Rules' was identifiable by 1859 and codified some seven years later, around the same time that other games, such as soccer and rugby, were undergoing similar processes in the UK (Hess and Stewart, 1998). The development of such a sport was a rebellion against the 'overriding dominance of the British Empire', which assisted in stressing 'national independence and cultural difference' (Cronin, 1998: 170).

On the whole, it can be said that Australians have contributed little to sporting forms in other nations, whilst domestic conditions have created a distinctly local tenor to British and American sporting forms. City life has been crucial to organised sport, as leagues were established in Adelaide, Brisbane, Darwin, Hobart, Melbourne, Perth and Sydney. Suburban-based teams in a range of sports engaged in city-wide competitions, yet it took some time before national leagues developed. Communication and transport restrictions in a large continent as well as the parochial nature of colonial life ensured that sport remained largely local for most of the late nineteenth and early twentieth centuries (Cashman, 1995). The historical exceptions to localised, city-based competitions were cricket, some individual sports, and to a lesser degree the rugby codes.

As in other parts of the British Empire, social class and status have played a central role in defining the contours of Australian sport. For instance, Rugby League was closely linked to working-class culture whereas Rugby Union was fostered in the fee-paying, exclusive schools and by university graduates in New South Wales and Queensland. In other sports, including Australian Rules football, class affiliations have been structured differently. Australian Rules football has traditionally been played and watched by a cross-section of people; however, individual clubs established initially in Melbourne, Adelaide, Perth and Hobart suburbs have been aligned to the socio-economic status of their communities (Stoddart, 1986). The class affiliations in the football codes support the large-scale empirical studies of participation patterns which indicate that sport and physical activities are inextricably linked to income, education and occupation (McKay, 1990, 1991). The evidence clearly indicates that 'economic class and social status determine what sports Australians play and how, when and where they play' (Booth and Tatz, 2000: 8). In addition to the class affiliations, gender, ethnic and racial issues have influenced Australian sport.

GOVERNMENT INVOLVEMENT IN SPORT

Many of the structural changes to Australian sport throughout the twentieth century were closely aligned to government involvement. For over 70 years, federal governments, whether Liberal/National or Labor, had only an ad hoc involvement with the organisation, administration and/or provision of sport, and developed no formal national policies or strategies. Athletes and sporting organisations were, for the most part, expected to fund their activities largely independently of the public purse. This is not to say that there was no governmental support at all. Indeed, the considerable growth of sport through the second half of the nineteenth century and beyond was only possible by the 'in-kind' support by local and state governments (Cashman, 1995). Facilities were built and subsidised by ratepayers, and local politicians allocated resources to the development of sporting communities and talents. Gradually, the federal government became more involved, first placing restrictions on sport during the First World War, passing the National Fitness Act during the Second World War, and making irregular financial contributions to the Olympic Games, Commonwealth Games and other teams competing in the Asian region, as well as providing federal assistance to the Life Saving Movement (Armstrong, 1988). When Gough Whitlam came to power in 1972, these attitudes changed and the Labor Party's period of office until 1975 is recognised as a 'watershed in government involvement in sport, recreation and other forms of culture' (Armstrong, 1994: 189). The Whitlam government established the first federal Ministry for Tourism and Recreation, aimed at 'catering for the masses', whilst state governments followed suit and founded their own respective departments of sport (Cashman, 1995: 124).

Growing recognition of the political and electoral mileage of international sporting success and two critical reports about the state of Australian sport paved the way for the creation of the Australian Institute of Sport in 1981 (Daly, 1991). The following Hawke/Keating Labor governments (1983–96) further increased financial and political support for sport and initiated the formation in 1985 of the largest sporting bureaucracy, the Australian Sports Commission. Four years later, the Australian Sports Commission became a statutory authority and subsumed the Australian Institute of Sport (AIS) (Shilbury and Deane, 1998). There is little doubt that sporting administrators argued for and welcomed the financial assistance from governments, yet at the same time this jeopardised their autonomy.

As international sport has grown in importance, and government involvement has increased in many countries, a host of domestic and foreign policy issues have emerged. In Australia, two issues, namely apartheid in sport and Olympic boycotts, were highly contested political terrain. While the 1971 Springbok rugby tour and the 1980 Moscow Olympic Games caused heated public debate and divided the Australian sporting public, more recently domestic concerns have dominated. Some critics have questioned government funding of Olympic and Commonwealth Games bids, the staging of the major sporting festivals, and the financing of elite sport on the basis that expenditure is redirected from more needy areas of education, health and welfare (Booth and Tatz, 1994; Lenskyj, 2000). The support of elite sport and events is justified on the grounds that sporting success promotes Australia internationally, inculcates national identity, provides economic benefits and stimulates activity levels of the population (Houlihan, 1997, 2000).

The promotion of elite sport, however, has come at a cost, as there have been continual reductions in funding of participation-based activities. Even though the Whitlam government championed participation over sporting success, this trend was reversed from the late 1970s (McKay, 1991), typified by the establishment of the AIS, and this has continued through successive governments. In the years 1999–2000, for example, elite sport consumed 78 per cent of the total sports budget (Hogan and Norton, 2000: 210), justified on the assumption that sporting success encourages the public to be physically active. Yet, politicians do not recognise that 'gender, age, ethnicity, race and income and wealth are far more significant than elite role models' (Booth and Tatz, 2000: 175). Questions have also been raised about the inequities of funding models which privilege Olympic over non-Olympic sports, Olympic over Paralympic sports, and Olympic medal-winning sports over less successful sports (Cashman and Hughes, 1998).

COMMODIFICATION OF AUSTRALIAN SPORT

Interwoven with government involvement has been the process of commodification. In reality, sport in Australia has always been a commodity. Until the 1960s, spectator-orientated sports in Australia were similar to those in the UK and in North America, where gate receipts raised financial capital to be spent according to the dictates of the administrators or owners (Holt, 1989; Horne et al., 1999). Gradually, many spectator-orientated sports created markets for commercial companies which invested in order to sell goods and services (Sage, 1990). The key dimensions in the commercial trajectory of sport in Australia were the businesses that have sponsored sporting events, the television companies that have broadcast mainly male sports, and the sport organisations themselves. Following Rowe's (1999) work, we refer to this tripartite alliance as the media sports cultural complex.

The media sports cultural complex was a post-1960s phenomenon. Commercial sponsors have been involved in sport from the late nineteenth century, but only in an irregular, transient and peripheral way. Similarly, the symbiotic relationship between sport and television in Australia was not widely recognised before the middle of the 1970s. Following the introduction of television in 1956, sport administrators were happy to have their events televised as long as they could regulate the coverage (partial and often delayed) to ensure that gate receipts were not affected. Television networks covered football, cricket and some international sport, but were reluctant to invest heavily because they were unsure of the ability of televised sports to attract regular, long-term audiences (Stoddart, 1986). Television stations, commercial companies and sport had yet to realise their mutual strengths and benefits.

The nascent relationship between the constituents of the sports media cultural complex changed with the introduction of colour television in 1975. This medium presented sport to viewers in a far more appealing visual package, as colour images were enhanced by innovations in camera positions and presentation techniques principally derived from American televised sport. Ratings boomed. The increased audience prompted greater interest from commercial sponsors, particularly those selling cigarettes and alcohol, which became close partners with televised spectator sports. Today there is a visual saturation of corporate logos and insignia to the point where some athletes represent little more than mobile corporate billboards (Phillips, 1998). In this respect, Australian sport differs from American professional sports where television has traditionally required 'clean screens' free from commercial clutter (Barnett, 1990). The visual display of corporate capitalism in Australian sport reminds us that the media sports cultural complex, while a useful analytical tool, needs to be both culturally and historically contextualised (Rowe et al., 1994).

Box 21.1 Pyjama cricket

Kerry Packer's cricket revolution is an example of the importance of spectator-orientated sports for television and also the power of media organisations in the emerging media sports cultural complex. Packer, the owner of Channel Nine in Australia, sought to purchase cricket for his station, but was thwarted by the Australian Cricket Board when the traditional broadcasters, the Australian Broadcasting Commission (the equivalent of the British Broadcasting Corporation), retained the rights. In retaliation, Packer established a rebel competition with disgruntled local and international players and eventually forced the Australian Cricket Board to compromise. Channel Nine was delivered the broadcast rights to cricket that it has since retained.

World Series Cricket, as it was known, provided a fillip to one-day cricket on the international scene, and introduced the game under lights, coloured clothing for players and new technological advances. While televised sport in Australia before colour television mimicked an 'imported BBC house style' with a small number of fixed cameras widely sweeping as much of the action as possible in a simulation of a single spectator getting the 'best seat in the house' (Rowe, 2000: 135), after World Series Cricket, sport on television increasingly resembled American versions of broadcasting which emphasise action, drama and entertainment.

The introduction of colour television was followed by three key events: the Kerry-Packer-inspired one-day cricket revolution (1977), victory by Australia in the America's Cup yachting (1983) and, as we have already discussed, government involvement in sport, each of which have been regarded as catalysts accelerating the commodification of Australian sport and leisure. While World Series Cricket (Box 21.1) indicated a paradigm shift in the presentation style of televised sport, Packer's involvement highlighted the increasing importance placed on sport in television profiling, marketing and scheduling. Sport had become a valuable television commodity. The most prized asset is 'live' sport, but in recent years a host of hybrid shows have adopted current affairs format or merged sport into comedy, quiz shows or discussion formats (Rowe, 2000). 'Live' coverage of a select group of sports, such as Australian football, cricket, Rugby League, Rugby Union and soccer, as well as the Commonwealth and Olympic Games, commands large fees for exclusive broadcast rights. These rights vary according to the competition between stations and the state of the television industry, and have raised issues about the role of media companies in shaping Australian sport.

The most recent example of media dominance over sport in Australia is Rupert Murdoch's News Corp's foray into Rugby League. Murdoch's Australian corporate arm, News Limited, acquired a large stake in one of the licences available during the introduction of pay television in 1995. Rugby League, as a consequence, became a bloody battleground for pay television (Rowe, 1997). Thwarted by the rival pay television station holding the exclusive Rugby League rights, News Limited bought half of the competition in Australia as well as leagues in New Zealand, England and elsewhere. After two court cases, divided competitions and a massive decline in public support, a compromise was reached. A united, smaller competition was formed which resulted in the loss or merger of several foundation clubs and large-scale resistance from supporters of vanquished clubs. Through this turmoil and at an unprecedented cost, News Limited secured broadcast rights to Rugby League. The Rugby League case points to a number of crucial issues in Australian sport: the changing power relationship in the media sports cultural complex; the increasing global forces, including powerful transnational media companies; and the growing difficulty separating the ideologies, structures and practices of the media and sporting organisations.

GENDER

As with most countries, sport in Australia has been a gendered activity and a site for the reproduction of perceived differences between appropriate female and male physicality. In the nineteenth century, sport was deemed a natural activity for men, while women were actively discouraged from playing sports. For men, sport became a central part of an emerging masculine nationalist ethos, particularly in international competition within the British Empire. Courage, aggression, strength, endurance and physical prowess were the qualities built through sport and instilled in the young male participants. Early women's physical activity was conducted within the grounds and behind the walls of private schools and the competitive model of male sport was initially rejected. At the same time, men had a wide range of sporting opportunities, whilst the only sports initially available to women were those that complemented traditional notions of femininity, fitted within the ideology of biological determinism, did not threaten the procreative functions of women and were recognised as having health benefits (King, 1979). As a consequence, women played only a limited range of 'feminine' sports, such as croquet, golf and tennis, and their incursions into 'masculine' sports were resented, resisted and prevented by conservative women and men alike.

Despite these social, structural and ideological barriers, women developed separate competitions in some Olympic sports as well as in cricket, netball, softball, hockey and water polo. In these sports, Australian women have a very impressive record, winning world championships and/or Olympic medals (Phillips, 1992). A new dimension for sporting women since the 1980s has been their increasing participation in former male-only contact sports – Australian football, boxing, Rugby Union, Rugby League, soccer – and physical activities centring on muscularity, strength and power such as powerlifting and bodybuilding. The involvement of women in these activities has extended the debate about the appropriateness of specific sports for female athletes, a debate rarely entertained in regard to male sporting participation. Women in violent or strength-based activities continually have to reconfirm their femininity by reproducing acceptable gendered practices. The consequences of not reproducing traditional femininity have meant that women are 'marginalized and criticized for being too masculine, [have] their sexuality called into question and [are] labelled as not being "real" women' (Burroughs and Nauright, 2000: 189).

The discrimination faced by women with respect to participation also extends to the labour and power dimensions of sport (McKay et al., 2000). Women perform a disproportionate amount of ancillary work in the sport setting (cooking, cleaning and fundraising) and provide the labour for sporting children and partners (Thompson, 1999). In terms of power, women have struggled to gain access and develop careers in coaching and administration (McKay, 1997). In coaching, female aspirants have many barriers not faced by their male counterparts, including limited career opportunities and few female role models, as well as the growing trend of male coaches being employed in women's sport (Phillips, 2000).

Another common feature shared by sporting women in the Western world is minimal media coverage. A succession of reports (Gordon, 1989; Menzies, 1989; Phillips, 1997; Stoddart, 1994) have detailed the quantitative differences in media coverage in Australia accorded to male and female athletes in Australia. As Table 21.1 indicates, women's sports receive minimal attention compared with their male counterparts in newspapers, and on television and radio (Phillips, 1997). In many cases, international sport, including American basketball and European soccer, and animal sports such as horse and greyhound racing, receive more coverage than female athletes. The effect of this marginalisation is debilitating. As two prominent feminist researchers contend:

This underrepresentation by the mass media does more than simply create an impression that women are absent from the sporting arena. Rather, it creates a false impression of women's athleticism by denying the reality of the modern feminine athlete. (Kane and Greendorfer, 1994: 36)

TABLE 21.1   Media coverage of women's, mixed and men's sports, 1996

	Newspaper (%)	Television (%)	Radio (%)
Women	10.7	2.0	1.4
Mixed	10.2	41.8	3.5
Men	79.1	56.2	95.1

Source: Phillips (1997)

Compounding this under-representation are the messages contained in the portrayals of female athletes. What has appeared in the printed and electronic press has tended to sexualise or trivialise female athletes, consigning them to the roles of wives and mothers, sex objects, and in the case of contact sports, freaks. Achieving appropriate recognition for their athletic performances has been difficult, and McKay (1994) argues that women are forced to market their sports according to voyeuristic potential, confirming their appeal and availability to men, in short, their 'heterosexiness'. Where female athletes transgress such boundaries, the media have treated them harshly, such as in the coverage of lesbian athletes (McKay et al., 1999), of women who have used steroids (Magdalinski, 2001) or of women who play violent sports such as Rugby Union (Carle and Nauright, 1999).

Male athletes, on the other hand, have not been subject to the same levels of sexploitation. Whilst there have been a proliferation of 'beefcake' calendars in Australian men's sport, organised primarily to attract a larger female demographic, none of these has included full-frontal nudity. Indeed, when the genitals of Rugby League player Andrew Ettingshausen were exposed in a women's magazine, he successfully sued for defamation (Burroughs and Nauright, 2000). Thus, whilst there have been moves to use sexiness to sell both men's and women's sports, the coverage of men's sports still focuses primarily on the active physical moving body as subject, while women sporting stars are still framed most often as objects for the male voyeuristic gaze (Box 21.2).

```
          Box 21.2  'Sex sells'
```

In the majority of cases, the sexualisation of elite female athletes has been the dominant form of coverage and is used by sports organisations to try to attract sponsorship and greater media coverage. Magazines such as *Inside Sport* promote an 'emphasized femininity' by exclusively depicting semi-naked 'sports models' on their covers and in centrefold sections (Lenskyj, 1998).

But it has not only been male editors and publishers who have relied on the 'Sex Sells' concept. Women too have been willing contributors to the reproduction of a masculine hegemony within sport. For example, former Australian heptathlete Jane Fleming organised the production of the 1995 Golden Girls Calendar, which portrayed a range of Australian female track and field athletes, naked and bodypainted, in highly suggestive poses (Lenskyj, 1995; Mikosza and Phillips, 1999). More recently, the Australian women's soccer team, the Matildas, posed nude for a calendar shoot, designed to 'raise the profile' of women's soccer. The publisher's rationale for producing such a display was that: 'It is not appetising to watch women in baggy shorts and tops and socks up to their knees. There are feminine, athletic bodies underneath' (*Sunday Herald Sun*, 1999).

Women's exterior appearance rather than their playing skill is thus suggested as sufficient for interest in the sport. Female athletes themselves have been complicit in their sexual exploitation, choosing to strip for promotional purposes or adopting explicit sportswear that displays advertisers' logos in suggestive places. Throughout the 1990s, a plethora of women's sports leagues and teams, such as basketball and hockey, have adopted skintight bodysuits as uniforms, and some netball teams even took to wearing sponsors' logos on their athletic briefs worn under their skirts (Burroughs and Nauright, 2000).

ETHNICITY

The discrimination faced by female athletes has also been experienced in different ways by sporting immigrants in Australia. As the British settled in Australia, it is not surprising that their traditional sports were transported as part of the cultural baggage. Traditional British sports served to introduce those born in the colonies to the ways of the 'home country' and became an important mechanism for the sustenance of English cultural values and norms, in short, of 'civilisation'. Besides the English, notable immigrant minorities in the colonies who added to the sporting tapestry were the Irish, the Scottish and, from the late 1830s, the Germans. Irish sports such as hurling and the Scottish Caledonian Games were enjoyed by those from their homelands, while the Germans who settled in South Australia established shooting and rifle clubs, and were responsible for the introduction of *kegel* and gymnastics through the Turner Movement (Mosely et al., 1997).

Ethnic diversity in Australia increased with the migration waves that resulted from the discovery of gold in the 1850s. Men from Western Europe, China and the Americas joined British and Irish settlers. Amongst these immigrants, the Irish played an early version of Gaelic football, the Scots were crucial in the establishment and growth of golf, bowls and soccer, Germans spread the Turner Movement beyond South Australia, Norwegians introduced the locals of the Snowy Mountains to skiing, the Chinese played the gambling games of *fan-tan* and *pak-a-pu*, and the Americans built bowling alleys. All of these activities created distinct sporting cultures inextricably linked to ethnic groups and served an important role in maintaining migrant cultural traditions (Mosely et al., 1997). In the social milieu of colonial Australia, these sporting activities raised questions, which persisted throughout the twentieth century, about whether immigrants should assimilate by abandoning their own customs and traditions, or whether cultural pluralism should be adopted by embracing non-British ethnic cultures as part of the nation's identity.

The tension over assimilation and cultural pluralism grew in intensity as a consequence of the mass migration following the Second World War. Under the federal government policy of 'populate or perish', 1.5 million Europeans, mostly from Italy, Greece, Yugoslavia, Holland, Germany and Poland, came to Australia between 1945 and 1965 (Mosely et al., 1997). Many of these immigrants found affordable accommodation in the inner suburbs of Australian cities and, as a result, distinctive 'ethnic enclaves' were created (Booth and Tatz, 2000). These 'new Australians', like the colonisers before them, brought their regional and national sporting practices, and associations were quickly established to service these groups. As Mosely et al. (1997: xv) argue: 'It was in leisure activities or church organisations, rather than at work, that most immigrants of the 1950s and 1960s found the social, educational and support networks so necessary for newcomers in a strange land.' Sport served the important function of connecting pre-existing ethnic groups. Immigrants expressed their cultural heritage through new activities like *bocce* (Italian bowls), through existing sports like soccer, and through specific styles of participation and spectatorship. These endeavours, however, proved problematic in the context of the federal government social policy of assimilation which mandated the submission of imported customs and traditions to the dominant Anglo-Australian way of life (Booth and Tatz, 2000).

The pressure to assimilate ethnic cultures into Australian society was no more evident than in the sport of soccer. Although Australia was one of the first places in the world to form a soccer association (1882), prior to the Second World War soccer was largely underdeveloped and did not enjoy the popularity it did throughout the rest of the world. It was regarded as a working-class game, flourishing in the New South Wales mining districts, and as a 'pommie' game, organised by English and Scottish migrants, at a time when Australian sports, run by locals, were gaining popularity during a period of emerging nationalism. This was compounded by the fact that Australian sports teams were organised around regions and districts, whilst the British-inspired soccer teams more often represent ethnic groupings, such as the Caledonians or the Rangers (Mosely and Murray, 1994).

With the influx of Southern European migrants, soccer soon became associated almost exclusively with 'new Australians'. By 1949, teams that represented Italian, Maltese, Dutch, Yugoslav, Greek and Macedonian communities were founded, quickly followed by Jewish, Hungarian, Czechoslovakian, Polish, Serbian, Croatian and Ukrainian teams, amongst others. The British influence on soccer slowly dissipated as clubs came to represent much more than simply an avenue for physical expression. As Mosely and Murray (1994: 223) contend, there was simply less of a need for British migrants to 'seek shelter in a club of their own language and culture'.

But the greatest challenge to migrant clubs was the Australian post-war policy of assimilation, and 'those groups which more easily fitted into the "Australian way of life" were more easily accepted' (Mosely and Murray, 1994: 224). Assimilation was based on assurances that the Australian 'way of life' would not change despite the influx of immigrants unfamiliar with the culture (Murphy, 2000). As a result, challenges to that 'way of life' were viewed with suspicion, and soccer clubs were considered to be exclusive ethnic enclaves which deliberately resisted assimilation (Hughson, 1997). Such attitudes are ironic, given that these clubs became a 'haven' for migrants suffering from racism, discrimination and a lack of familiarity with local customs.

Since this era, soccer has undergone a process of mainstreaming, whereby traditional 'ethnic' clubs have been forbidden from identifying with an ethnic community. In 1997, David Hill, then President of Soccer Australia, argued that:

> If you take some of the old Sydney and Melbourne clubs, we are saying, look we really don't want you to play any more, decked out with the colours and insignia of a European country. We don't want you presenting yourselves as exclusively a team for Australian Croatians or exclusively for Australian Greeks. You should be appealing to all people in Australia. (Cited in Brabazon, 1998: 54)

The stance by soccer officials contradicts the contemporary appreciation of the multicultural dimensions of Australian society. Multiculturalism encourages and endorses members of ethnic groups 'to flaunt their ethnicity, [but] soccer clubs are expected to hide it' (Mosely and Murray, 1994: 229–30). The problem is not 'ethnicity' per se, but the kinds of ethnicities that are deemed undesirable. For example, Perth Glory, a soccer team that actively and loudly celebrates its Englishness, is not asked to ban the Union Jack flag from its games, nor is it asked to forbid the singing of English anthems. The rationale is that Englishness is a 'safe or invisible ethnicity, whereas Greekness or Croatianness is [regarded as] dangerous to the sport' (Brabazon, 1998: 55). Soccer, as perhaps the only truly national game, is expected to appeal to 'all Australians', rather than minority segments. Overall, soccer indicates the historical and contemporary tensions in Australia, during periods of the contrasting social policies of assimilation and multiculturalism, that have shaped ethnic involvement in a predominantly Anglo-Australian sporting culture.

Box 21.3 Racial vilification and Australian
Rules football

Athletes still face racial slurs on and off the field, and the problem of racial vilification is best highlighted in a 1993 incident where fans of Collingwood Football Club taunted St Kilda player, Nicky Winmar, who responded by lifting his shirt and pointing to his skin. Collingwood President Allan McCalister's retort revealed the levels of racism inherent in Australian sport. McCalister suggested: 'as long as they [indigenous players] conduct themselves like white people ... everyone would admire and respect them' (cited in Nadel, 1998: 243). Following a public and media outcry, the Australian Football League Commission was forced to react, eventually implementing a code of conduct in 1995 to rid the game of racism and ethnic taunts (Nadel, 1998).

RACE

Like ethnicity, the concept of race, as well as racism, has permeated Australia's sporting cultures since the arrival of white colonisers in the late eighteenth century. To celebrate the centenary of the federation of Australia and as part of the ongoing process of reconciliation, in early 2001 Prime Minister John Howard announced that a cricket match would take place between black and white Australians. Howard revealed that the forthcoming match was 'a very important event symbolically because it recognises the importance of sport and particularly cricket to all Australians, indigenous and other Australians' and thus was 'an aid to reconciliation' (Howard, 2001). That an adversarial event would be used as a vehicle for reconciliation reveals much about racial tensions in Australian sport.

Whilst cricket may be depicted as a national pastime, one that is important to 'all Australians', the reality is that for most of Australia's history, sport has been enmeshed in racial politics. Academics have taken two contrasting approaches to Aboriginal history. One side of the debate, that of the 'oppositionists', stresses 'racial discrimination and the structures of colonial dominance' while their antagonists, the 'revisionists', emphasise 'Aboriginal agency in resisting or accommodating colonial power' (Broome, 2000: 130). Our stance in this debate supports the oppositionists' view of history. Sport remained the preserve of the white Anglo-Celtic man, and a means of maintaining racial exclusivity. Whilst some Aborigines have excelled in elite, competitive sport, the history of indigenous involvement in sport is a tale of prejudice, racism, discrimination, intolerance, active exclusion and denial of access to funding, selection and facilities (Tatz, 1995). This is not to say that Aborigines have not enjoyed a robust sporting culture (Tatz and Tatz, 2000), however, their inclusion in formal organised sporting structures has been sporadic at best, and only since the 1970s has there been any real effort to address the inequalities faced by Aboriginal athletes (Tatz, 1995).

Regarded by scientists as a 'doomed race', Aborigines were placed at the bottom of the human evolutionary chain. Many scientists in the nineteenth century thought that 'primitive' races had either to adapt to modern civilisation or face extinction. Whilst some early settlers treated Aborigines no better than wild animals, others believed that Aborigines should be taught the virtues of British and Christian civilisation. In this process, sport, particularly cricket, played a key role (Whimpress, 1999). Many believed that in order to 'become civilised', British cultural values had to be inculcated into indigenous Australians. As a result, cricket and other British cultural activities were established on Aboriginal mission stations and were used to teach indigenous peoples the values of 'sportsmanship' and 'fair play' (Tatz, 1995).

During the 1850s and 1860s, Aborigines were able to pursue a range of sporting activities and succeeded in cricket, pedestrianism (running) and boxing. Cricket remained popular and 'Aborigines played talented and enthusiastic cricket in an era which, while free legally, saw geographic isolation, rigid missionary control, settler animosity, poor diet, rampant illness and, of course, killing' (Tatz, 1994: 3). This limited access to sports ended by the late nineteenth century with greater legal and physical separation from white Australian society, an institutionalised racism that heralded the era of forced relocations and removals of mixed-race children. As Booth and Tatz (2000: 88) note, the exclusion of Aborigines from mainstream sport was 'virtually complete' by 1911. Settlements and reserves often had few or no facilities, many without even a patch of grass upon which to play, and many of these conditions remain today. Most Aborigines, particularly those living in remote communities, continue to have little if any access to adequate health and educational facilities, let alone formal organised sport.

Aboriginal athletes have endured active isolation and exclusion as well as overt racism within sport that has served to inhibit, if not destroy, the careers of some. Whilst many are still subjected to racist attacks within sport (see Box 21.3), increasingly, sports federations and leagues are being required to implement policies that will ensure protection from verbal assault, as well as greater access to facilities, funding and programmes. Critical commentators acknowledge these positive initiatives, but realise that racial ideologies are deeply embedded and change requires continuing reform from players, spectators, the media, sports organisations and governments.

CONCLUSION

The Sydney 2000 Olympic Games and the Melbourne 2006 Commonwealth Games illustrate the increasing involvement of government in Australian sport. For the Olympic and Commonwealth Games bids to be successful, state and federal governments had to underwrite these events and commit large amounts of capital to finance the infrastructure. Few people criticised this expenditure at the same time that budgets for education, welfare and other social programmes were stripped (Booth and Tatz, 1994, 2000; Lenskyj, 2000). Equally importantly, state and federal governments poured more money than ever before into producing international sporting stars. For example, after the Olympic Games were awarded to Sydney, the Australian Sports Commission began a six-year elite development programme aimed at winning 60 medals. One of the programmes implemented, the Olympic Athlete Programme (OAP), received over A\$400m through a combination of state and federal government funding, including A\$72m from the Australian Olympic Committee (Magdalinski, 2000). When Australia won a record number of medals, the links between governments, government-funded sporting agencies and elite sport were further enhanced.

The Olympic and Commonwealth Games also illustrate the continuing commodification of Australian sport. The rights to broadcast the Sydney Olympic Games were hotly contested between the two leading networks, Channel Seven and Channel Nine. Seven won the rights to televise the Games at a cost of A\$100m and for this received exclusive broadcasting throughout Australia. The Games rated very well, rarely slipping below 65 per cent of the total viewing audience and producing some of the highest-rating shows in television history. Channel Seven sold advertising according to expected ratings, and used its broadcasts to satisfy other commercial needs, including station profiling, personality exposure and programming identification.

The Olympic strategy was extremely effective. As a result of the Games, Channel Seven beat Channel Nine in the annual ratings for the first time in 44 years (*The Australian*, 2001) and earned a surplus revenue estimated at A\$170–180m (*The Australian*, 2000). To counter Channel Seven's corporate success associated with the Sydney Games, Channel Nine purchased the exclusive broadcast rights for the Melbourne 2006 Commonwealth Games. Channel Nine provided saturation coverage, interrupted only by news bulletins, which focused almost exclusively on the personal lives, successes and tragedies of Australian athletes to steal the ratings race from their rivals. International sporting festivals featuring Australian athletes, as the Olympic and Commonwealth Games demonstrate, are absolutely crucial to the national television industry.

Similarly, commercial companies tendered for the rights to be 'official' Olympic and Commonwealth Games sponsors. The Olympic rights were sold to international sponsors, National Olympic Committee sponsors and Sydney 2000 sponsors who could advertise their association, in exclusive product categories, with the Games. These companies sought to take commercial advantage of this alliance while other competing businesses devised methods to circumvent their lack of Olympic association. The most obvious corporate battle was fought between the airline companies, Ansett, the 'official' Olympic airline, and Qantas. Qantas implemented a number of corporate ploys including running advertisements on Channel Seven during major Olympic events to create the impression they were associated with the Games. Their corporate battle was mimicked by telecommunications companies Optus and Telstra, sport equipment multinationals Nike and adidas, car manufacturers Holden and Mitsubishi, and computer giants IBM and Microsoft. As the television networks and the commercial companies illustrate, the Olympic and Commonwealth Games, like much of Australian sport, have become enmeshed in local, national and transnational corporate strategies.

Whilst the Olympic and Commonwealth Games were a playground for corporate battles, they worked at a different level to interact with the racial, ethnic and gendered nature of Australian sport. Racial issues were always going to be central to the Olympic Games, with Aboriginal sprinter Cathy Freeman lighting the flame during the opening ceremony and winning Australia's only gold medal on the track. Her athletic successes were achieved against a backdrop of the federal government's refusal to apologise to Australia's indigenous people about past injustices, and massive street marches urging reconciliation. In this context, Freeman is regarded as a 'success' story. Her life is the kind of rags-to-riches drama that elides greater structural inequalities facing most Aboriginal athletes. She represents the struggle of a 'poor black kid from the bush' who, through hard work and determination, has 'made it' in sport and is held up as an exemplar for other Aboriginal Australians. Like cricket in the nineteenth century, Freeman is, in a sense, a modern-day 'civilising tool' that espouses individual effort over structural constraints. Her role is well summed up in her earlier athletic career by a newspaper comic, where an overweight white Australian male, with a beer in one hand, speaks to a group of Aboriginal women, who sit in front of ramshackle accommodation, cooking their meals over an open fire. He asks 'Why can't you all be like Cathy Freeman?' (*The Australian*, 1996). If Cathy Freeman's profile does little to address white Australia's treatment of its indigenous people and promote reconciliation issues, her success will remain just one more gold medal to add to the list.

As much as Cathy Freeman's medal victory, her role in lighting the Olympic flame and the centrality of Aboriginal culture in the opening and closing Olympic ceremonies belie the historical and contemporary plight of Aborigines in Australia, the same argument can be put forward for Australian sporting women. In some ways, the Olympic and Commonwealth Games showcase women's sport. These international sporting festivals represent rare opportunities for female athletes to gain the recognition that is commonplace for their male counterparts. Previous research during the Olympic Games indicates that unlike any other time, women's sport is accorded larger amounts of media coverage (Mikosza, 1997). For two weeks successful female athletes like Freeman, Susie O'Neill and others are afforded the attention their athleticism deserves. From a quantitative perspective, women's sport is recognised, but much of this attention focuses on traditional aspects of femininity (Phillips, 1997), thereby reinforcing rather than confronting stereotypes. Of course, some female athletes use this media attention and profile to attract large endorsements and to establish careers built around their prowess, similar to male athletes.

The coverage during Olympic and Commonwealth Games, however, is illusory. The reality for many is that there are still fewer activities available for female athletes, as well as fewer coaching and administration positions.

The recent Melbourne Commonwealth Games also highlight tensions in the ways immigrants are accepted or rejected in Australia. On the one hand, the federal government treats illegal refugees fleeing neighbouring countries by detaining them in specialised, security-dominated and isolated centres. These centres have been widely condemned by domestically and internationally based humanitarian organisations. On the other hand, recent immigrants, such as Russian-born pole vaulter Tatiana Grigorieva, are hailed as successful members of the Australian team, and coaches and athletes from former European communist countries are accepted as part of the Australian sporting landscape. The ethnic origins of Australian athletes and coaches are ignored and the team members are incorporated into a generic 'Aussieness' that masks the tensions, struggles and controversies generated by national immigration policies.

The Sydney Olympic and Melbourne Commonwealth Games are outstanding examples of nationalism overriding the gendered, racial and ethnic dimensions of Australian sport. For a fleeting nationalistic moment, successful women, Aborigines and non-Anglo-Saxons, and in the case of the Paralympics, people with disabilities, are embraced by the wider Australian community. Unfortunately, when the flames were extinguished, so too was the equal sporting citizenship temporarily accorded to these athletes. In stark contrast, the Olympic and Commonwealth Games reinforced the increasing role for governments as well as the inextricable link with local, national and transnational companies and corporations, as political and economic incentives increased with the exposure provided by these popular sporting events.

CHAPTER SUMMARY

» The development of Australian sport is a mixture of local, British and American sport.
» Government involvement in Australian sport has existed at local, state and national levels.
» Australian sport has always been a commodity but the level of commodification has increased with the development of the media sports cultural complex.
» Opportunities for men and women have been important in creating gendered identities through sport.
» The social policies of assimilation and multiculturalism have shaped ethnic involvement in a predominantly Anglo-Australian sporting culture.
» Racial ideologies have limited indigenous participation to a small number of sports and have been a dominant feature of the sporting landscape.

FURTHER READING

There have been four relatively recent books which have looked at Australian sport from contemporary and historical perspectives. McKay (1991) is an excellent analysis of contemporary Australian sport, while Adair and Vamplew (1997), Booth and Tatz (2000) and Cashman (1995) analyse contemporary sport in Australia from a historical basis.

REFERENCES

Adair, D. and Vamplew, W. (1997) *Sport in Australian History*. Melbourne: Oxford University Press.

Armstrong, T. (1988) 'Goldlust: federal sports policy since 1975', Unpublished PhD thesis, Macquarie University, Sydney.

Armstrong, T. (1994) 'Government policy', in W. Vamplew, K. Moore, J. O'Hara, R. Cashman and I. Jobling (eds), *The Oxford Companion to Australian Sport*. 2nd edn. Melbourne: Oxford University Press, pp. 188–200.

The Australian (1996) 3–4 August: 20.

The Australian (2000) 7–8 October: 12.

The Australian (2001) 12 February: 3.

Barnett, S. (1990) *Games and Sets: the Changing Face of Sport on Television*. London: BFI Publishing.

Booth, D. and Tatz, C. (1994) '"Swimming with the big boys"? The politics of Sydney's 2000 Olympic bid', *Sporting Traditions*, 11 (1): 3–23.

Booth, D. and Tatz, C. (2000) *One-Eyed: a View of Australian Sport*. St Leonards, NSW: Allen & Unwin.

Brabazon, T. (1998) 'What's the story Morning Glory? Perth Glory and the imagining of Englishness', *Sporting Traditions*, 14 (2): 53–66.

Broome, R. (2000) 'Review of: Bernard Whimpress, *Passport to Nowhere: Aborigines in Australian Cricket 1850–1939. Sporting Traditions*', 16 (2): 129–31.

Burroughs, A. and Nauright, J. (2000) 'Women's sport and embodiment in Australia and New Zealand', *International Journal of the History of Sport*, 17 (2/3): 188–205.

Carle, A. and Nauright, J. (1999) 'Women playing a "man's game": a case study of women playing Rugby Union in Australia', *Football Studies*, 2 (1): 55–74.

Cashman, R. (1995) *Paradise of Sport: the Rise of Organised Sport in Australia*. South Melbourne, Victoria: Oxford University Press.

Cashman, R. and Hughes, A. (1998) 'Sydney 2000: cargo cult of Australian sport?', in D. Rowe and G. Lawrence (eds), *Tourism, Leisure, Sport: Critical Perspectives*. Sydney: Hodder Headline, pp. 216–25.

Cronin, M. (1998) '"When the World Soccer Cup is played on roller skates": the attempt to make Gaelic Games international: the Meath-Australia matches of 1967–68', in M. Cronin and D. Mayall (eds), *Sporting Nationalisms: Identity, Ethnicity, Immigration, and Assimilation.* London: Cass, pp. 170–88.

Daly, J.A. (1991) *Quest for Excellence: the Australian Institute of Sport.* Canberra: Australian Government Publishing Service.

Gordon, S. (1989) *Drop-out Phenomenon in Organised Sport.* Perth: Department of Human Movement and Recreation Studies, University of Western Australia.

Hess, R. and Stewart, B. (1998) *More Than A Game: an Unauthorised History of Australian Rules Football.* Melbourne: Melbourne University Press.

Hogan, K. and Norton, K. (2000) 'The "price" of Olympic gold', *Journal of Science and Medicine in Sport,* 3 (2): 203–18.

Holt, R. (1989) *Sport and the British: a Modern History.* Oxford: Clarendon Press.

Horne, J., Tomlinson, A. and Whannel, G. (1999) *Understanding Sport: an Introduction to the Sociological and Cultural Analysis of Sport.* London: E & FN Spon.

Houlihan, B. (1997) *Sport, Policy, and Politics: a Comparative Analysis.* London and New York: Routledge.

Houlihan, B. (2000) 'Politics and sport', in J. Coakley and E. Dunning (eds), *Handbook of Sport Studies.* London: Sage, pp. 213–27.

Howard, J. (2001) 'Transcript of the Prime Minister the Hon. John Howard MP. Joint Press Conference with Mr Geoff Clark, Chairman of ATSIC–SCG, Sydney, 3 January 2001. http://www.pm.gov.au/news/interviews/2001/interview636.htm (accessed 17 January 2001).

Hughson, J. (1997) 'The Croatian community', in P.A. Mosely, R. Cashman, J. O'Hara and H. Weatherburn (eds), *Sporting Immigrants: Sport and Ethnicity in Australia.* Sydney: Walla Walla Press, pp. 50–62.

Kane, M. and Greendorfer, S. (1994) 'The media's role in accommodating and resisting stereotyped images of women in sport', in P. Creedon (ed.), *Women, Media and Sport: Challenging Gender Values.* Thousand Oaks, CA: Sage, pp. 28–44.

King, H. (1979) 'The sexual politics of sport: an Australian perspective', in M. McKernan and R. Cashman (eds), *Sport in History: the Making of Modern Sporting History.* St Lucia, Brisbane: University of Queensland Press.

Lenskyj, H. (1995) 'Sport and the threat to gender boundaries', *Sporting Traditions,* 12 (1): 47–60.

Lenskyj, H. (1998) '"Inside sport" or "On the margins"?', *International Review for Sociology of Sport,* 33 (1): 19–32.

Lenskyj, H. (2000) *Inside the Olympic Industry: Power, Politics and Activism.* Albany, NY: SUNY Press.

Magdalinski, T. (2000) 'The reinvention of Australia for the Sydney 2000 Olympic Games', *International Journal of the History of Sport,* 17 (2/3): 305–22.

Magdalinski, T. (2001) 'Drugs *Inside Sport*: the rehabilitation of Samantha Riley', *Sporting Traditions*, 17 (2): 17–32.

McKay, J. (1990) 'Sport, leisure and social inequality in Australia', in D. Rowe and G. Lawrence (eds), *Sport and Leisure: Trends in Australian Popular Culture*. Sydney: Harcourt Brace Jovanovich, pp. 125–60.

McKay, J. (1991) *No Pain, No Gain? Sport and Australian Culture*. New York: Prentice Hall.

McKay, J. (1994) 'Embodying the "new" sporting woman', *Hectate*, 20 (1): 68–83.

McKay, J. (1997) *Managing Gender: Affirmative Action and Organizational Power in Australian, Canadian and New Zealand Sport*. Albany, NY: SUNY Press.

McKay, J., Martin, R. and Miller, T. (1999) 'Mauresmo, the media and homophobia', Paper presented at the Teams and Fans Conference, Mudjimba Beach, Queensland, 15–18 July.

McKay, J., Hughson, J., Lawrence, G. and Rowe, D. (2000) 'Sport and Australian society', in J.M. Najman and J.S. Western (eds), *A Sociology of Australian Society*. 3rd edn. Melbourne: Macmillan, pp. 275–300.

Menzies, H. (1989) 'Women's sport: treatment by the media', in K. Dwyer (ed.), *Sportswomen towards 2000: a Celebration*. Adelaide: University of Adelaide, pp. 220–31.

Mikosza, J. (1997) *Inching Forward: Newspaper Coverage and Portrayal of Women's Sport in Australia: a Quantitative and Qualitative Analysis*. Canberra: Womensport Australia.

Mikosza, J. and Phillips, M. (1999) 'Gender, sport and the body politic: framing femininity in the *Golden Girls of Sport Calendar* and *The Atlanta Dream*', *International Review for Sociology of Sport*, 34 (1): 5–16.

Mosely, P. and Murray, B. (1994) 'Soccer', in W. Vamplew and B. Stoddart (eds), *Sport in Australia: a Social History*. Melbourne: Cambridge University Press, pp. 213–30.

Mosely, P.A., Cashman, R., O'Hara, J. and Weatherburn, H. (eds) (1997) *Sporting Immigrants: Sport and Ethnicity in Australia*. Sydney: Walla Walla Press.

Murphy, J. (2000) *Imagining the Fifties: Private Sentiment and Political Culture in Menzies' Australia*. Sydney: University of New South Wales Press.

Nadel, D. (1998) 'The League goes national, 1986–1997', in R. Hess and B. Stewart (eds), *More Than A Game: an Unauthorised History of Australian Rules Football*. Melbourne: Melbourne University Press, pp. 243–55.

Phillips, D. (1992) *Australian Women at the Olympic Games 1912–92*. Kenthurst, NSW: Kangaroo Press.

Phillips, M.G. (1997) *An Illusory Image: a Report on the Media Coverage and Portrayal of Women's Sport in Australia 1996*. Canberra: Australian Sports Commission.

Phillips, M.G. (1998) 'From suburban football to international spectacle: the commodification of Rugby League in Australia, 1907–1995', *Australian Historical Studies*, 29 (110): 27–48.

Phillips, M.G. (2000) *From Sidelines to Centre Field: a History of Sports Coaching in Australia*. Sydney: University of New South Wales Press.

Rowe, D. (1997) 'Rugby League in Australia: the Super League saga', *Journal of Sport and Social Issues*, 21 (2): 221–6.

Rowe, D. (1999) *Sport, Culture and the Media: the Unruly Trinity*. Buckingham: Open University Press.

Rowe, D. (2000) 'Sport: the genre that runs and runs', in G. Turner and S. Cunningham (eds), *The Australian TV Book*. Sydney: Allen & Unwin, pp. 130–41.

Rowe, D., Lawrence, G., Miller, T. and McKay, J. (1994) 'Global sport? Core concern and peripheral vision', *Media, Culture & Society*, 16 (4): 661–75.

Sage, G.H. (1990) *Power and Ideology in American Sport: a Critical Perspective*. Champaign, IL: Human Kinetics.

Shilbury, D. and Deane, J. (1998) *Sport Management in Australia: An Organisational Overview*. Burwood, Victoria: Bowater School of Management and Marketing, Deakin University.

Stoddart, B. (1986) *Saturday Afternoon Fever: Sport in Australian Culture*. North Ryde, Sydney: Angus & Robertson.

Stoddart, B. (1994) *Invisible Games: a Report on the Media Coverage of Women's Sport*. Canberra: Australian Sports Commission.

Sunday Herald Sun (1999) 28 November.

Tatz, C. (1994) 'Aborigines in sport', in W. Vamplew, K. Moore, J. O'Hara, R. Cashman and I. Jobling (eds), *The Oxford Companion to Australian Sport*. Melbourne: Oxford University Press, pp. 3–7.

Tatz, C. (1995) *Obstacle Race: Aborigines in Sport*. Sydney: University of New South Wales Press.

Tatz, C. and Tatz, P. (2000) *Black Gold: the Aboriginal and Islander Sports Hall of Fame*. Canberra: Aboriginal Studies Press.

Thompson, S. (1999) *Mother's Taxi: Sport and Women's Labour*. Albany, NY: SUNY Press.

Whimpress, B. (1999) *Passport to Nowhere: Aborigines in Australian Cricket 1850–1939*. Sydney: Walla Walla Press.

22

Sport, the Role of the European Union and the Decline of the Nation State?

IAN P. HENRY

OVERVIEW

» *The evolution of the European project*
» *The nature of national sovereignty and its erosion in the later twentieth century*
» *Evolving competences for the EU in respect of leisure policy*
» *Five rationales for EU intervention in sport*
» *The debate around sport and the Draft Constitution for Europe*
» *The future of the EU and the nation state in sport policy – some conclusions*

The rapid intensification and expanding scope of interactions between societies and polities in the contemporary world has led some authors to project a significant weakening of nation states and occasionally even to question whether we are likely to see the demise of the nation state as an institution (Mann, 1997; Morris, 1997; Schachter, 1997; van Deth, 1995). The decline of the nation state is, for many commentators, most strongly evidenced in the construction of the European Union. Core functions of the nation state, such as the production of a national currency, and the macroeconomic policy associated with this, have already been ceded to a European institution. However, such predictions of the nation state's demise are keenly contested (Hirst and Thompson, 1995; Shaw, 1997). The emergence of political, economic or cultural transnational bodies, it is pointed out, are controlled, regulated and legitimated at local level by local institutions, often by the nation state itself. Within this context, this chapter seeks to evaluate the impact of the European project on the relationship between the European Union and the nation state, focusing in particular on its implications for sports policy.

The aim of this chapter is to evaluate not simply the nature, but also the significance of, and rationales for, policy shifts in sport in relation to the European Union. The chapter is divided into six sections: the first considers the stages in the development of the unfolding European project; the second deals with the changing nature of national sovereignty in contemporary Europe; the third highlights the shifting of competences[1] in sport from the national to the European level; the fourth provides a typology of the rationales behind policy intervention in the leisure field at the European level; the fifth examines the debate around sport and the draft of the new European constitution; and the final section considers the implications of this for the relationship between the European Union and member states, arguing that claims for the demise of the state are exaggerated, and that a new set of tensions and balances is being negotiated between the European Union, the nation state and civil institutions.

The first two of these sections relate to the generic context of the European project, while the remainder focus more specifically on sports policy issues.

THE EVOLUTION OF THE EUROPEANISATION PROJECT: INTERGOVERNMENTAL VERSUS SUPRAGOVERNMENTAL APPROACHES

The development of sports policy in the European Union is inevitably a reflection of the nature of the union itself, and in particular the tension between those who would wish to see it operate as an *intergovernmental* body rather than a *supranational* entity. The distinction here is between a body which has power by virtue of agreements between governments – thus intergovernmental – and one that can require governments to act in particular ways whether or not they so wish to act – supranational. The changing nature of the union and its conception are evident in the evolving nomenclature which is used to refer to it, which reflects three principal stages in the development: from 'Common Market', which indicated a primary concern with elimination of tariff barriers; through 'European Community', which implied a wider communal set of interests; to 'European Union', with a clearer emphasis on political integration, and, some might argue, federalism. The significance of these name changes is that each implies a different stage in the development of the project, and a different relationship between the EU and the nation state with further implications for policy.

The Development of the 'Common Market'

The European Economic Community, or the Common Market as it was initially popularly titled, was established in 1957 with the Treaty of Rome. It set itself the principal goal of eliminating tariff barriers within approximately 15 years. While it is clear that for many of those involved in the inception of the EU, the Treaty of Rome was intended as a road that would lead to political union, this was not reflected in the wording of the Treaty itself.

However, although the Treaty dealt almost exclusively with the requirements to establish a common market area of free trade, there was a declared intention to move forward on matters relating to European union. Discussions at the time of the drawing up the Treaty had clearly signalled the intention to introduce majority voting for certain policy issues, which would have removed the possibility of any given state vetoing action in those areas and thus reduced the power of the governments of the member states.

This was a matter of real contention. General de Gaulle, promoting the notion of *l'Europe des Patries*, tipped the balance in favour of those who opposed stronger integration by simply refusing to have France represented at European Community meetings – the 'empty chair' policy – thereby frustrating any advance on this and other issues such as the UK's membership. The 'Luxembourg compromise', which was agreed as a way out of this impasse, *de facto* set back the introduction of majority voting, offering member states a virtual veto by allowing them to appeal against the use of majority votes on matters that they deemed to be of 'national interest'.

With de Gaulle's political demise, there was progress towards a more centralised and interventionist stance for the EC, with the resourcing of the Common Agricultural Policy from European sources rather than from national funds, and the introduction of a targeted regional funding system. However, the global economic and oil crises of the early 1970s turned governments back to more national goals. Progress at the beginning of the 1970s had seemed possible. The term 'European Union' was, for example, actually introduced at the Paris Summit of 1971 but it was vague and undefined and met with little opposition because it signified very little. European Monetary Union originally envisaged to be achieved by 1980 was also deferred in the aftermath of crises of global economies.

The European Community

Despite these delays and frustrations, the establishment of a European Community, as opposed to a common market of European nations, was to be effected in the 1980s following the enhancement of the power of the Commission, the increased legitimacy of the European Parliament, which was directly elected from 1979, and the institutionalisation of the Council of Ministers from 1974. Enlargement, with the accession of the Southern European states in the 1980s, also implied an extension to the majority voting procedure if political paralysis were to be avoided and this itself also implied some weakening of the sovereignty of states.

The move to European union was to be promoted at the Fontainebleau Summit of 1983 which established two groups, the Dooge Committee, which was to assess the options for political change, and a *Committee for a People's Europe*, which was charged with evaluating how the EC might promote the growth of a European identity across the populations of the member states. In terms of the significance of sport in the process of Europeanisation, the Adonino Report of the Committee for a People's Europe (European Commission, 1988) is of key importance.

However, it was the Single European Act (SEA), ratified in the late 1980s to take effect in 1992, which represented the springboard to the next stage of development. On the face of it, this establishment of a frontierless internal market via the SEA was the core of the minimalist view of the Common Market. However, allowing the free flow of capital, people, goods and services across frontiers is more than a simple matter of economics. Put crudely, the move to a single market would mean increasing pressure to move to one business culture (Southern European business hours and practices differ from those of Northern Europe) and perhaps one language of business – which was likely to be English.

The European Union

The SEA thus opened the back door to the deepening of co-operation between member states in more than just economic matters, and, though being concerned with market reform, it made explicit reference to areas such as regional disparity, improvement in living and working conditions, and the quality of life. The next major move was also in effect in the economic domain, with the establishing of a Single European Currency. However, the Treaty on European Union negotiated at Maastricht, and its successor Treaty of Amsterdam in 1997, not only incorporated the mechanism and timetable for organising monetary union, but also included for the first time an article on culture and, in the Amsterdam Treaty, a declaration on sport, reflecting the twin deepening of the cultural and the economic dimensions of the union. This set of concerns in relation to sport was also to be developed further in the fuller statement on sport in Appendix IV of the Nice Treaty in 2001. Indeed the further deepening of the union in terms of the development of the Draft Constitution for Europe represented a further extension of this logic. However, the progress of the Constitution was halted in 2005 with three major defeats in national referenda in member states to ratify the proposed Constitution even though it had been approved by heads of state in the forum of the Council of Ministers.

What is provided above is a thumbnail sketch of the history of the development of the EU. Nevertheless it serves to illustrate how the construction of simply a common market requires a degree of political integration to enforce common rules. This in turn implies a requirement for greater cultural integration to ensure public acceptance and legitimacy for this political project. Each of these elements is bound up with questions of national sovereignty and thus before going on to discuss EU intervention in sport, some clarification of the nature of sovereignty is required.

THE NATURE OF NATIONAL SOVEREIGNTY AND ITS EROSION IN THE LATER TWENTIETH CENTURY

It is perhaps ironic that while we are discussing the purported erosion of the significance of the nation state by the European project, the notion of the nation state itself is generally attributed to its roots in Europe. The flexibility of the European state system has been apparent in its ability to adapt to changing circumstances with, for example, the absolute monarchies of the eighteenth century transforming into the industrial and national states of the nineteenth century, and into the welfare states of the twentieth century (Laffan et al., 2000). The question that faces the state at the beginning of the twenty-first century is whether, in the context of a globalised political economy, it has exhausted its capacity for transformation and adaptation, or whether new forms of governance are likely to supplant it. It is in this context that we are evaluating the emerging division of labour and responsibility in sports policy between the EU and the nation state.

If we wish to evaluate the nature of the erosion of sovereignty for European states, it will be important to distinguish different types of sovereignty – legal, political and popular – since, as Laffan et al. (2000) point out, there are different trajectories in respect of each of these three forms. The loss of sovereignty of member states to the EU is most clearly evident in respect of *legal* sovereignty, since the EU has, through the European Court of Justice, established a legal order such that 'each member state now has two interlocking constitutions' (Temple-Lang, 1996: 126). The ways in which the EU imposes legal obligation on its member states generally takes one of two forms: a directive, which requires that national legislation be adapted to achieve specified ends; or a regulation, which in effect specifies a legal requirement directly. Since EU legislation can be made without reference to domestic parliaments, it is argued by some commentators that this fosters a democratic deficit.

In terms of *legal* sovereignty then, there are clearly grounds to make the claim that aspects of sovereignty have been eroded and this, as we shall see, can have specific implications, for example in a nation's laws in respect of sport or leisure. *Political* sovereignty, the right to make political decisions in respect of one's own territory and people, might also be said to have been undermined by the introduction of majority voting. As we have already noted, there is a considerable amount of disagreement as to whether one should regard the EU as an intergovernmental body, or a supragovernmental body. The matter is complicated by the fact that EU arrangements are framed by intergovernmental agreements, the founding treaties, for example, and when certain aspects such as the removal of passport controls under the Schengen Agreement, the social chapter in the Maastricht Treaty, or the establishment of European Monetary Union have not been to a government's liking, it has been possible for that state to opt out. Nevertheless the process of centralisation of power in the institutions of the Community has proceeded apace. With the likelihood of further extension of majority voting, decisions affecting the internal affairs of member states will, in principle at least, be subject to decisions made externally, but only where intergovernmental agreement exists. It seems, therefore, that the most one can claim about political sovereignty is that it has been compromised or 'pooled', through processes of voluntary collaboration in intergovernmental agreements, rather than diluted (Laffan et al., 2000).

Popular sovereignty stands in contrast to the other two forms of sovereignty in that democracy in the form of voting arrangements and political representation is organised solely along national lines. Nationally defined popular sovereignty remains in place, even for elections to the European Parliament, though there has been recent debate about direct election of a European President, counting votes across national boundaries which would breach the principle of national, popular sovereignty.

One of the reasons why nationalism is so deeply entrenched is that it is a key element of the cultural identity of individuals. It is partly imbued through what Smith (1983) calls myths of shared 'primordial' national origins, and is promoted through the construction of 'imagined communities', to coin Anderson's term (Anderson, 1983). Thus, if the nation state were to be weakened as an organising unit, then alternative sources of identity would be required. Leisure, culture and sport are of course important elements in the development of national identities and thus leisure, cultural and sports policy are likely to be key to discussions about the diminution of the nation state.

EVOLVING COMPETENCES FOR THE EU IN RESPECT OF LEISURE POLICY AND THE GOVERNANCE OF RELATED POLICY DOMAINS

Intrinsically bound up with the development of the European project and with the erosion, pooling or loss of sovereignty are issues of subsidiarity. Subsidiarity is a concept related to governance which is central to the philosophy of the European Community. Vertical subsidiarity is the principle by which decisions are taken at the lowest level of government possible. Decisions about, for example, whether to teach in minority languages, such as Basque, are a matter for local decision makers, while policy relating, for example, to the monitoring and control of pollution can only really be effective if agreed at the transnational level, since pollution produced in one country may potentially affect many others. Horizontal subsidiarity is the principle by which matters of policy are only decided by government if they cannot be effectively displaced onto the voluntary or commercial sector.

Which policy domains then lend themselves to 'governmental' intervention at the European or supranational level? There are some obvious candidates, such as environmental policy or trade policy, and some contested areas such as defence and foreign policy. But what of cultural and leisure policy – at what levels are decisions best taken for this policy domain? There are some aspects, such as broadcasting policy, which clearly require supranational regulation because broadcasts cannot be restricted by national boundaries. Nevertheless other areas of cultural policy, such as sport, at first glance seem likely to lend themselves to the application of the principles of vertical and horizontal subsidiarity. Such a suggestion is, however, at odds with the fact that the Maastricht Treaty defined a new competence for the EU in respect of culture, and its revision at Amsterdam in 1997 incorporated a declaration on sport, effectively laying down a marker for future definition of the EU's legitimate interest in sport, which was partially articulated in an appendix on sport to the Nice Treaty in 2001. Nevertheless, there is a problem for those who advocate European intervention in sport or culture of defending the basis or the rationale for such intervention.

FIVE RATIONALES FOR EU INTERVENTION IN SPORT

1   Sport as Trade

While the EU may have no clear and unambiguous competence in matters of sport, it certainly does in respect of trade. Policy in respect of trade provides one of the *raisons d'être* of the European Community, and sport is an increasingly significant area of trading activity representing an estimated 3 per cent of gross domestic product for all Council of Europe member states. Intervention in the sports field in the early years of the European Community was restricted solely to that justified by policy relating to trade, as the 1973 decision of the European Court of Justice (ECJ) in the Walrave and Koch case illustrates, when the Court declared that: 'the practice of sport is subject to Community law so far as it constitutes an economic activity in the meaning of Article 2 of the Treaty'.

The economic rationale for intervention in sport also underpins the Heylens decision of the ECJ in 1986. Heylens was a Belgian football coach employed in France who was taken to the French courts for practising his trade without obtaining a French football coaching qualification. He did, however, hold a Belgian qualification which the ECJ accepted was of equivalent standing. In this case the ECJ overruled the French court's decision that a specific French qualification could be required. This decision, although made on the grounds of restraint of trade, had clear implications for vertical subsidiarity in sport. National legislation could be subordinate to European rulings in the field of sport.

While the Heylens case illustrates the erosion of vertical subsidiarity, the Bosman case of 1995 illustrates the clear erosion of horizontal subsidiarity in respect of sport. Professional sport could no longer, after Bosman, be regarded simply as a matter for voluntary or commercial sector interests. The Bosman case related to two significant elements. The first was freedom of movement of professionals at the end of their period of contract with clubs. But it is the second which concerns us here, in that Bosman successfully appealed against a UEFA and French Football Association ruling which limited the number of foreign nationals playing in professional teams in domestic or European competition. This element of the Bosman appeal was based on the argument that such quotas for foreign players restricted freedom of movement of professionals within the EU.

The Bosman ruling has important implications for the production of 'local' talent. Among the anticipated economic effects of the removal of European tariff barriers was an expectation that production would develop in a borderless Europe on the basis of regional specialisation. Cars, for example, would be produced in those regions where production could be accomplished most cheaply, or where the greatest level of required skills was available. This logic implies that some nations/regions will not have a car production capacity, but that this will be compensated for by those industries where the region does possess key market advantages. If this economic rationale were applied to professional sport (as implied by the Bosman ruling), then a likely consequence would be a major decline in the local production of sporting talent for some member states. A national or regional economy can, of course, survive without the capacity to produce cars, but can a national culture survive without a capacity to produce sporting stars, when sport is a strong feature of national identity? The impact of the Bosman ruling is visible throughout Europe. In the UK, expensive imports of high-quality players dominate the Premier Leagues of English and Scottish football, while cheaper (often Eastern and Central European) imports are increasingly taking up places in the lower divisions of the domestic leagues, restricting the opportunities of the development of home-grown talent. UEFA requested in 2000 that the EU reconsider the position of sport as a special case, arguing that culture and broadcasting had been treated as exceptions to aspects of competition law, but this request was rejected.

If the rationale that underpins the Bosman case is that sport is an industry like any other, and should therefore be treated in exactly the same manner, a different type of argument has been mobilised in the revision of the *Television without Frontiers* Directive (1997). According to the directive, access via television to selected sporting events for the general population can be protected by national governments which may reserve for free-to-air television the broadcasting of a limited number of sporting events of particular national importance. In other words the rationale here is that sport is more than simply a product, and that its broadcasting rights cannot therefore be simply sold to the highest bidder. Sport is, in effect, part of a nation's cultural heritage and may be subject to protectionism. This provision of special treatment for sport stands in stark contrast to the thinking behind the Bosman ruling.

One aspect of the special status of sport is, however, reflected in the revisions to the transfer system agreed in 2001 between the Commission, FIFA and UEFA. This agreement limited the length of contracts to five years, but incorporated a form of compensation for the costs of education and training for a player, so that the smaller clubs, which produced players who then moved on, would be compensated for their efforts.

2 Sport as a Tool of Economic Regeneration

While the initial development of the European Community took place in the period of post-war growth which continued up until the 1970s, it was clear by the time of the first enlargement of the Community, with the addition of the UK, Ireland and Denmark in 1973, that regional disparities were growing, not simply in the non-industrialised regions, but also in those traditional industrial regions which had gone into decline. The development of the Structural Funds (including the establishment of the European Regional Development Fund (ERDF), targeted principally at lagging and deindustrialising regions, and the expansion of the European Social Fund, aimed at combating unemployment) has been used in the funding of sport and leisure on a quite significant basis (Bates & Wacker, 1993). Although regional funding should form part of an integrated strategy and have clear economic goals, it is clear that some applicants, while rehearsing economic arguments in order to attract funding, are themselves more concerned to achieve social objectives (Matthews and Henry, 2001). The European Social Fund (ESF), which is designed to generate new employment opportunities, also has social goals in the sense of targeting disadvantaged groups. Sport and leisure, as elements in the growing service sector, represent areas in which employment opportunities may be generated (Le Roux et al., 1999). Thus in the 1980s a variety of sport-related schemes were developed at local level with social as well as economic implications, such as the Comsport scheme funded under the ESF in the East Midlands of England, which generated job training for women in community sports development (Seary, 1992).

The competitive position of lagging regions is deemed to be a product of a mix of factors including physical, service, educational and cultural infrastructures, and regional policy. Thus, improvement of cultural infrastructure to make regions more effective in attracting capital is legitimately funded for economic development purposes. Nevertheless there are significant potential social gains claimed by applicants for much of this funding in respect of reducing inequalities. However, as commentators such as Harvey (1989) and Lash and Urry (1994) point out, much of the sporting or cultural infrastructure developed for economic regeneration purposes targets groups such as service-class professionals, who will need to be retained in lagging or deindustrialising regions; consequently the investment in such cultural provision may reinforce rather than challenge social inequities in leisure. The examples of Sheffield in the UK and Bilbao in Spain illustrate this point.

Sheffield attracted ERDF funding for some of the facilities required for the World Student Games which it staged in 1991. The intention of the local authority was to use the Games as a vehicle for reimaging the city and providing new 'state-of-the-art' facilities. However, the Games provided a huge financial burden for the local authority, and though the facilities inherited have allowed the staging of a programme of international sporting events in Sheffield, prices for ordinary members of the community using these new sports facilities have risen considerably (Henry and Paramio-Salcines, 1999). In the case of swimming, despite the provision of new pools to replace old dilapidated facilities, the number of people swimming in the city declined in the post-Games period against a national background of growth in participation (Taylor, 1998).

Similarly, the Guggenheim project in Bilbao represented an attempt to put Bilbao on the global cultural map. Although redevelopment of the riverfront benefited from European funding, the scheme attracted criticism that local culture was being sacrificed to pander to the tourist market and that cultural budgets on behalf of local governments were totally absorbed by the prestige project (Henry and Paramio-Salcines, 1998). Thus the use of sport and leisure for economic regeneration purposes is not unproblematic.

3   Sport and Social Integration

Although the initial phase of development of the EC was dominated by economic concerns to set up an area of free trade, the implications of this process for the social as well as economic exclusion of some of its citizens were well recognised, and were reflected in the inception of the ESF in 1962. However, although social policy has been a continuing and growing concern of the EU, with, for example, the introduction of the social chapter in the Treaty of Maastricht, the focus of concern has been predominantly with economic exclusion, or economically related aspects of social exclusion, such as sex discrimination in pay and conditions, or the use of employment initiatives to integrate ethnic minorities into the workforce.

There has, however, been some use of other European funds directly on sport, and this has in large part been aimed at aspects of social exclusion. A budgetary line in relation to sport was first inserted in the EC budget in the early 1990s in response to the expressed interests of members of the European Parliament.[2] The budget represented a small amount, but was not without controversy. In the budget negotiations of the first half of the decade, the EC (in which sport's interests were relatively weakly represented in a smaller directorate) eliminated the budget only to have it reinstated at the insistence of the European Parliament.[3] The original sports budget incorporated the European Awareness Budget (to which we return below) and funds directed at young people and socially excluded groups, particularly disability sport. The budget was consolidated into the Eurathlon Programme in 1996, with broadly the same objectives. However, despite enthusiasm in some quarters, particularly among a small group of MEPs who had formed the Sports Intergroup in the Parliament, there were worries that there was no legal justification for EU expenditure on sport per se, since sport had not been incorporated as a competence in the founding treaties, and there was some concern on the part of officials that the justification of expenditure was rather tenuous. Apparently as a result of this, the Eurathlon Programme was abruptly discontinued in 1998, when a number of European Commissioners came under investigation for activities in other policy fields, and subsequently resigned over issues relating to use of European funds for activities without appropriate legal justification.

In the period 1995–7, some of the key actors in the European sports scene had been involved in lobbying member states and European Commissioners to establish a competence in the field of sport in the revisions of the Treaty on European Union at Amsterdam (Arnedt, 1998). The support for such a move was by no means universal. UEFA, for example, and some of the other European bodies representing professional sports were very wary, having been profoundly and (as they saw it) adversely affected by the EU through the Bosman decision. This and issues such as the ban on tobacco sponsorship made a number of people in the sports world nervous about increasing the powers of the EU to intervene in sport; nevertheless the amateur sports group were broadly supportive. In the end the lobby was not entirely successful, a competence was not incorporated in the Amsterdam Treaty, but a Declaration on Sport[4] was adopted which dealt specifically only with amateur sport, but which was seized upon by interested MEPs, who subsequently called for a full review of the EU's role in sport (Pack, 1997). This has been used as the stimulus for discussions (such as the First European Conference on Sport in Olympia in 1999) that have incorporated concerns in particular with broadcasting and interpenetration of sports and media ownership, and has also resulted in a fuller statement on sport being added in an appendix to the Nice Treaty in 2001.

4 Sport as an Ideological Tool

The role of sport in helping to construct a European identity was recognised by the EU explicitly in the 1980s (Shore, 1993). By the 1980s it had become widely acknowledged that progress with the European project was likely to be impossible without a strong element of financial and political integration. Political integration itself could not be achieved without winning over the consent and the commitment of European citizens: that is, it could not be achieved without citizens of the member states relating to a European identity.

This concern exercised the minds of the European Council of Ministers when it received the Adonino Report, *A People's Europe*, in 1985. The report highlighted ways in which a cultural identity for European citizens might be developed, such as the adoption of a European anthem, an EU flag, and the promotion of EU policy in the cultural sphere.

Among some of the ideas rehearsed in the Adonino Report were the establishing of a pan-European Games, the entering of a European Olympic team, and the provision of support for sporting events that promoted European identity. Some of the more radical ideas have not been acted upon but others found their way into EU policy. For example, the EU has funded the establishment of sporting events such as a European Clubs Swimming Championship, and supported the European Ryder Cup team (even though that represents more than simply the EU states). It also supported during the 1990s developments such as the European Yacht Race – a race which was routed to join various European ports – and the extension of the Tour de France into other countries (The Netherlands, Belgium, Germany, the UK, etc.).

This symbolic use of sport to 'unite' the territory has precursors in the premodern and the modern eras, at the levels of the local and the nation state respectively. In the premodern era, marching or riding the bounds (e.g. in Scottish border towns) was a means of reasserting annually the extent of the boundaries of the township and expressing civic community. Similarly the Breton *pardon*, the tradition in Catholic parishes in Brittany of procession round the boundaries of the parish, on the feast day of the saint after whom the parish church had been named, reaffirmed the sense of religious and political community of the parish. Dine has illustrated how in the modern era in the early twentieth century, the Tour de France was inaugurated partly as a means of asserting the unity of the French nation, formed as it had been out of diverse regions, sometimes with aspirations for separate identity (1997). In the late modern or high modern period of the late twentieth century, it may be argued that the EU support for the European Yacht Race seeks to perform in symbolic terms much the same function, of publicly asserting a symbolic unity of a political entity. Indeed the funding of this event in the early 1990s came from an EC budget line entitled the European Awareness Budget.

Whether one accepts this assertion or not, it is difficult to deny that sport has an ideological function. Culture and sport and identity politics are intrinsically interrelated and there is a tension in the period of late modernity between their use in promoting national, supranational or local identities (Roche, 1998).

5 Sport as a Tool of International Relations

The use of sport by nation states as a tool for cementing international relations is well established from the Berlin Olympics of 1936 to the ping-pong diplomacy of Richard Nixon re-establishing relations with China. A number of nation states employ sports development aid as part of a wider programme of international relations. For example, in 1989 the UK signed a Memorandum of Understanding with Saudi Arabia incorporating the provision of sporting advice, as part of a wider deal between British Aerospace and the Saudi Arabian government to supply military aircraft. UK Sport (formerly the Sports Council) also has a programme of aid for Southern Africa and Eastern Europe.

Although sport has been used by nation states in such a manner, it is interesting to note that in the mid-1990s when Nelson Mandela visited Europe, members of the Sports Intergroup sought to ensure that the provision of sport aid was included in a package to be discussed by representatives of the EU and President Mandela. Sport as a tool of diplomacy was clearly an issue for development for certain parties in the EU arena.

THE DEBATE AROUND SPORT AND THE DRAFT OF THE NEW EUROPEAN CONSTITUTION

In June 2004 a European Constitution was adopted by the Council of Ministers which was to be subject to ratification in most member states by referendum or parliamentary approval. Part of the function of the proposed Constitution was a tidying up of the situation with regard to the competences of the EU. The legislation proposed three types of competence: those which would be *exclusive* to the EU; those which would be *shared* and thus where action by the EU and/or by the member states would be possible; and *supporting, co-ordinating or complementary competences* where the EU would have the right to carry out actions to support, co-ordinate or supplement the actions of the member states, without thereby superseding their competence in these areas. Sport, it was proposed, would be added as part of this third type of competence.

Sport was to be incorporated in Article III-182 of the Constitution in the following terms:

> 1 ... The Union shall contribute to the promotion of European sporting issues, while taking account of its specific nature, its structures based on voluntary activity and its social and educational function ... developing the European dimension in sport, by promoting fairness and openness in sporting competitions and cooperation between bodies responsible for sports, and by protecting the physical and moral integrity of sportsmen and sportswomen, especially young sportsmen and sportswomen ... The Union and the Member States shall foster cooperation with third countries and the competent international organisations in the field of education and sport, in particular the Council of Europe.

However, the ratification process, which was due to have been completed in all member states by 2006, faltered in 2005 when the citizens of France and The Netherlands rejected the new Constitution in national referenda. As a consequence some consideration has been given as to how EU action in sport might be promoted in other ways. In 2005, under the UK Presidency, the European Council of Ministers, in co-operation with UEFA, commissioned a report, The Independent Sport Review, which was published in May 2006 (Arnaut, 2006: 934). This document might more accurately be entitled 'the Independent European Football Review' since it deals almost exclusively with football, but many of the issues are of generic relevance in sport. The report identifies actions which could broaden the competence of the EU on the basis of existing legislation via a range of instruments such as the establishing of a European Sports Agency, modification of existing Treaty articles, and the use of 'soft law' instruments such as voluntary agreements, White and Green Papers and Memoranda of Understanding, regulation, agreement of legislation (Arnaut, 2006). The reaction to this report will reflect the strength of political will of the Council of Ministers to clarify the situation of sport and to formalise the roles which the EU might play.

The support for the use of sport in other facets of EU policy was evident in the adoption of the European Year of Education through Sport in 2004, in which a wide range of projects were supported by the Community but legitimated through its competence in relation to education. In the same year the Sport Unit of the EC commissioned four major studies on the education of young elite sportspersons, on sport and employment, sport as a tool for generating multicultural dialogue, and the role of sport in promoting exercise and health (Amara et al., 2004a, 2004b; Brettschneider, 2004; EOSE, 2004). The ∈2m invested in these research projects reflects the significance to the EC of sport in achieving other social goals related to health, education and the protection of minors, employment and social cohesion.

THE FUTURE OF THE EU AND THE NATION STATE IN SPORT POLICY: SOME CONCLUSIONS

Notwithstanding the growing role of the EU in sport policy, this does not imply a diminishing of interest on the part of the nation state in sport policy. Indeed, as the nation state finds its role challenged to some degree by the rise of transnational entities, so it may use sport to reassert the existence and importance of national identity.

This characteristic is well illustrated in the British case by the circumstances surrounding the publication of the governmental statement *Sport: Raising the Game* (Department of National Heritage, 1995) in the run-up to the UK's general election of 1997. *Sport: Raising the Game* was the first major policy statement on sport in the UK for 22 years. The importance of sport for key actors in the government was underlined by the fact that the Prime Minister himself chose to write a preface to the document outlining the significance of sport. The document, and in particular the preface, were fairly unequivocally nationalistic, if not jingoistic. John Major for example wrote:

Sport is a central part of Britain's National Heritage. We invented the majority of the world's great sports and most of those we did not invent, we codified and helped to popularise throughout the world. It could be argued that nineteenth-century Britain was the cradle of the leisure revolution every bit as significant as the industrial and agricultural revolutions we launched in the centuries before … Sport is … one of the defining characteristics of nationhood and of local pride. (Department of National Heritage, 1995: 2)

The document focused policy interest in sport on two areas: youth and national performance. It also indicated the then government's intention of investing £100m in the establishment of a National Academy of Sport.

This policy statement came at a time when the Conservative Party had reached a low ebb of public support and when the Party itself was manifesting deep and electorally damaging divisions on the issue of Europe and the erosion of national sovereignty by the growing power of the EU. Sport was one policy area in which the government could demonstrate, at least in symbolic terms, its affiliation to the protection of national identity, in a way that was likely to have a wide appeal. Attempts to rectify the decline of the UK's national performance would almost invariably attract cross-party support from among the electorate. Thus ironically sport is being used both to undermine and to reinforce national identity.

There are other good reasons why the nation state seems likely to remain as a significant actor in the sports policy process, including for example its continuing interest in education, or in the economics of the sports industries. Nevertheless there are also important reasons why the role of transnational bodies such as the EU will grow, for example, in professional sport. The interpenetration of media and sports club ownership (particularly in soccer) and the globalisation of sports talent production (e.g. football clubs having feeder clubs in other European countries' lower divisions) mean that transnational regulation will be required if these transnational phenomena are to be controlled. The EC's attempts to promote discussion about a *European Model of Sport* in opposition to a North American model reflect concerns about phenomena such as the potential breakaway European Football League. With the G14 group of clubs such as Manchester United or Barcelona in a dominant market position, their ability to act as a cartel, effectively excluding other clubs because of the lack of a promotion and relegation system, can perhaps only be effectively regulated by a transnational body. On the other hand, issues such as the production of local talent may require national sporting systems to act in a protectionist manner. Indeed, UEFA has since the Bosman ruling sought to reopen negotiations with the EU on the matter of re-establishing national quotas of players in professional football, and though its most recent attempt met with rejection in 2000, it seems likely to be a running issue.

Although the EU has traditionally sought to distinguish between professional sport as economic activity (where economic regulation generally applies) and amateur sport (which is more directly subject to the principle of subsidiarity) there are important ways in which legitimate policy concerns have emerged even in relation to amateur sport at the EU level. Although the Declarations on sport incorporated in the Treaties of Amsterdam and Nice fall short of according a competence, they indicate a clear concern on the part of the EU with a whole range of issues associated with the governance of sports organisations, in terms of transparency, democracy and solidarity: the need to protect and foster the economic and social role of volunteers; the need to preserve training policies; to protect young sportsmen and women, particularly in terms of health and from the use of drugs in sport; the need to mutualise revenues from broadcast sales; the need to regulate the transfer market for professional sportsmen and women; the need to protect clubs from concentration of ownership (particularly in the hands of transnational media). The Nice Declaration also explicitly recognises the potential role of sport in combating aspects of social exclusion. The Declaration makes it clear that the basis for recognising the competence of the sports federations is their role in assuring such outcomes:

> These social functions entail special responsibilities for federations and provide the basis for the recognition of their competence in organising competitions ... While taking account of developments in the world of sport, federations must continue ... providing a guarantee of sporting cohesion and participatory democracy. (Annex IV, Treaty of Nice)

It also acknowledges the EU's concerns to ensure that the principles of good organisational governance for sports organisations are identified and, by implication, monitored. The implication of all this may be that if sports organisations fail to deliver on these social gains, the EU may be forced to rethink its position in relation to sport.

To conclude I would argue that, in effect, the European project and the various national projects are incomplete and ongoing. Both are organised around the trinity of politics, economics and culture. Sport, culture and leisure are integral to the processes involved in both types of project, and sport, leisure and cultural policies are of significance in each of the three elements identified here. In economic terms sport, for example, is a major contributor to national economies, but as a transnational phenomenon it has to be subject to transnational regulation. In cultural terms sport, culture and leisure contribute to the notions of cultural identity, which are central to issues of the political legitimacy of both nation state and the EU. In political terms the ceding of policy control by nation states to the EU or vice versa, or to the commercial and voluntary sectors, is politically non-viable and in policy terms impractical, since both the EU and member states are mutually reliant.

The relationship between Europe and the member states is thus both complementary and competitive. I would argue therefore that reference to the impending demise of the nation state is mistaken. It is rather more appropriate to refer to a relatively fluid process of mutual adjustment between these tiers of government as they negotiate and respond to what has been an increasingly complex global context.

CHAPTER SUMMARY

» The transition from Common Market, through European Community, to European Union, has marked a steady widening in the scope of the organisation to include, among other policy areas, an interest in culture and sport.
» As the European Union has expanded into new policy fields, it has challenged traditional views of state sovereignty and consequently stimulated renewed interest in debates on identity and the role of sport in establishing and maintaining identity.
» Growth of European Union interest in sport is based on sport's significance for trade, economic regeneration, social integration, ideology and international relations.
» While the European Union is of increasing significance to sport, the nation state remains important: the relationship between the European Union and its members is both complementary and competitive.

FURTHER READING

Seary (1992) and Bates & Wacker (1993) provide general overviews of the role of European institutions in cultural and sports policy. Matthews and Henry (2001) provide an analysis of the capacity of the EU to influence sport through the use of its funding resources. Mann (1997) examines the arguments regarding the future of the nation state. Shore (1993) provides a challenging analysis of European cultural policy. Henry (2001: ch. 8) provides an overview of the relationship between the role of the EU, the nation state and the city with reference to debates about globalisation.

NOTES

1 The term 'competence' refers to an area of policy making in which the EU has a legal authority or competence to act, as defined by Treaty.
2 Interview with John Tomlinson MEP, Chair of the EP Sports Intergroup, February 1996.
3 This was described to the author and a co-researcher (Nicola Matthews) in an interview with a Commission official as part of a 'game' where the Commission would eliminate from budget proposals items which it was confident would be reinstated by the Parliament.
4 A 'Declaration' is of lesser significance than an article. The latter defines the EU as having legal competence, in a policy field; the former simply declares the EU's intention to act in particular ways.

REFERENCES

Amara, M., Aquilina, D., Calvey, C., Delaney, H., Henry, I. and Taylor, M. (2004a) *Education of Elite Young Sportspersons*. Brussels: European Commission, DG Education and Culture.

Amara, M., Aquilina, D., Henry, I. and Taylor, M. (2004b) *Sport and Multiculturalism*. Brussels: European Commission, DG Education and Culture.

Anderson, B. (1983) *Imagined Communities*. London: Verso.

Arnedt, R. (1998) 'European Union law and football nationality restrictions: the economics and politics of the Bosman decision', *Emory International Law Review*, 12 (2).

Arnaut, J. L. (2006) *Independent European Sport Review* 2006. Brussels: *www.independentsportreview.com*.

Bates & Wacker (1993) *Community Support for Culture*. (A study carried out for the Commission of the EC (DGX) by Bates & Wacker S.C.) Brussels: European Commission.

Brettschneider, W. D. (2004) *Young People's Lives and Sedentariness*. Paderborn: University of Paderborn.

Department of National Heritage (1995) Sport: *Raising the Game*. London: Department of National Heritage.

Dine, P. (1997) 'Peasants into sportsmen: modern games and the construction of French national identity', in P. Dine and I. Henry (eds), *The Symbolism of Sport in France*. Stirling: University of Stirling.

EOSE (2004) *Vocational Education and Training related to Sports in Europe: Situation, Trends and Perspectives*. Lyons: European Observatoire of Sport and Employment.

European Commission (1988) *A People's Europe*. (COM (88) 337 final of 24 June 1988).

Harvey, D. (1989) *The Condition of Postmodernity*. Oxford: Basil Blackwell.

Henry, I. (2001) *The Politics of Leisure Policy*. 2nd edn. London: Palgrave.

Henry, I. and Paramio-Salcines, J.L. (1998) 'Leisure, culture and urban regimes in Bilbao', in I. Cooper and M. Collins (eds), *Leisure Management: International Perspectives*. Wallingford: CABI, pp. 97–112.

Henry, I. and Paramio-Salcines, J. (1999) 'Sport and the analysis of symbolic regimes: an illustrative case study of the City of Sheffield', *Urban Affairs Review*, 34 (5): 641–66.

Hirst, P. and Thompson, G. (1995) 'Globalization and the future of the nation state', *Economy and Society*, 24 (3): 408–42.

Laffan, B., O'Donnell, R. and Smith, M. (2000) *Europe's Experimental Union: Rethinking Integration*. London: Routledge.

Lash, S. and Urry, J. (1994) *Economies of Signs and Space*. London: Sage.

Le Roux, N., Chantelat, P. and Camy, J. (1999) *Sport and Employment in Europe: Final Report*. Brussels: European Commission, DGX.

Mann, M. (1997) 'Has globalization ended the rise and rise of the nation state?', *Review of International Political Economy*, 4 (3): 472–96.

Matthews, N. and Henry, I. (2001) 'The funding of sport and leisure through the European Structural Funds in Britain', in C. Gratton and I. Henry (eds), *Sport in the City*. London: Routledge.

Morris, L. (1997) 'Globalization, migration and the nation state: the path to a post-national Europe?', *British Journal of Sociology*, 48 (2): 192–209.

Pack, D. (1997) *Rapport sur le rôle de l'Union européenne dans le domaine du sport*. Commission de la culture, de la jeunesse, de l'éducation et des médias. Brussels: European Commission.

Roche, M. (1998) *Sport, Popular Culture and Identity*. Aachen: Meyer & Meyer.

Schachter, O. (1997) 'The decline of the nation state and its implications for international law', *Columbia Journal of Transnational Law*, 36 (1–2): 7–23.

Seary, W. (1992) *Brussels in Focus: EC Access for Sport*. London: Sports Council.

Shaw, M. (1997) 'The state of globalization: towards a theory of state transformation', *Review of International Political Economy*, 4 (3): 497–513.

Shore, C. (1993) 'Inventing the Peoples' Europe – critical approaches to European Community cultural policy', *Man*, 28 (4): 779–800.

Smith, A. (1983) *Theories of Nationalism*. 2nd edn. London: Duckworth.

Taylor, P. (1998) 'Sports facility development and the role of forecasting: a retrospective on swimming in Sheffield'. Paper presented at the Sport in the City Conference, Sheffield.

Temple-Lang, J. (1996) 'Community constitutional law', in B. Laffan (ed.), *Constitution-building in the European Union*. Dublin: Institute of European Affairs.

van Deth, J.W. (1995) 'Comparative politics and the decline of the nation-state in Western Europe', *European Journal of Political Research*, 27 (4): 443–62.

23

An Introduction to the Study of Sport in the Muslim World

MAHFOUD AMARA

OVERVIEW

» *Introduction: Basic information about Islam*
» *Sport in Islam*
» *Sport in Muslim countries*
» *Conclusion*

Sport in its modern form emerged largely in the nineteenth century in codified forms such as Association Football, and was promoted and developed in the early twentieth century under Western cultural hegemony through organisations such as the IOC, FIFA and the IAAF. The key question concerning sport in/and Islam is how such an essentially 'Western', 'modernist' and 'secular' form of cultural practice can articulate with what is portrayed as 'non-Western', 'non-secular' and 'traditionalist' world views. This question is amenable to analysis from a variety of disciplinary perspectives, including history, sociology, philosophy, and religious studies.

The chapter distinguishes between two types of endeavour relating to sport and Muslim thought. These are: (a) sport in Islam, including the question of sport in Islam in the West; and (b) sport in Muslim societies. The chapter argues that each of these domains has its own ontological and/or epistemological positions; in other words, diverse ways of questioning the existence of, and knowing about, sport.

INTRODUCTION

Before we begin our debate on sport in Islam and Muslim societies the aim of the following is to provide a non-Muslim reader with some brief information about Islam.

What is Islam? Islam literally means, in Arabic, *Salaam*, peace, humbleness and submission. It is the name of a monotheistic religion belonging – similar to Christianity and Judaism – to the *Abrahimic* tradition, revealed to the Prophet Muhammad (peace be upon him) in the seventh century. The attachment of Muslims to the *Abrahimic* teachings is celebrated in *Id al-Adha*, meaning 'the feast of the sacrifice', which marks the end of pilgrimage (El-Hajj in Arabic). The second most important religious festival is *Id-El Fitr* which celebrates the end of Ramadan.

The holy book of Islam is the QURA'AN (or *Qur'an*), which contains the revelations, the Words of God, received by Muhammad in *Mecca* and *Medina*. It is made up of 114 *souras*, or chapters, of varying length, each composed of a number of *ayas* (*signs*), or verses. Divided into *Mecciya* (revealed in Mecca) which organises the life of Muslims in relation to the transcendental, and *Medaniya* (revealed in Medina) which organises the life of Muslims in relation to the temporal, the *Qur'an* remains unchanged since its compilation was completed in 645 (Box 23.1).

Box 23.1   The Pillars of Islam

Chapter The Cow, verse 177, summarises the basic foundations of Islam, known as the five pillars of Islam, and the ethical code of Islam:

> It is not righteousness that ye turn your faces to the East and the West; but righteous is he who believeth in Allah and the Last Day and the angels and the Scripture and the prophets; and giveth wealth, for love of Him, to kinsfolk and to orphans and the needy and the wayfarer and to those who ask, and to set slaves free; and observeth proper worship and payeth the poor-due. And those who keep their treaty when they make one, and the patient in tribulation and adversity and time of stress. Such are they who are sincere. Such are the Allah-fearing. (The Cow: 2.177)

The five pillars of Islam are as follows:

1. the testimony that there is no deity other than God (Allah) and that Muhammad is God's last messenger;
2. the five daily prayers;
3. the daytime fast during the holy month of Ramadan;
4. the annual payment of a proportion of one's wealth for charitable and communal use;
5. the pilgrimage to the holy city of Mecca, made at least once in a lifetime, if possible.

Although the first Muslims were Arabs, the community quickly expanded to include members of other ethnic groups. It has today a global following of approximately 1.4 billion adherents. The majority of Muslims belong to the Sunni school of jurisprudence, composed of *Hanafi*, *Shafi*, *Hanbali*, *Maliki*. The other main minority groups are *Shi'aa* and *Ibadi*. *Sunnis* represent those Muslims who did not question the legitimacy of the 'caliphs' (or 'successors' to the Prophet) who headed the *Umma* (community of Muslim believers) from the time of the Prophet's death, whereas *Shi'a* maintain that the succession to the Prophet should be restricted to his first cousin and son-in-law Ali, and his descendants after him.

Distinction should be made between Islam as a belief system and Islam as a cultural form, interpreted, conceived and manipulated by nation states, political movements and different interest groups to legitimate their political agenda, social conduct and traditional (sometimes pre-Islamic) practices. The same distinction should be made between Islam and 'Islamism' (the so-called political Islam) which in Arkoun's (1995) terms is a type of discourse or collective affirmation linked to a category of actors who share a strong will/determination to re-establish 'religious' (Islamic) values, and exactly a 'religious' model of societal organisation.

Accepting the divinity of Islamic religion, or at least acknowledging its place within a monolithic tradition, should not restrict the study of Islam to the domain of theology. On the other hand, opening Islam to human questioning (which is obligatory to every Muslim) should not confine the study of Islam to (purely secularised) sociological, anthropological and historical sciences or interpretations. We have to take into consideration the lived religion or the religiosity of Muslim populations, their degree of Islamisation, and social interpretations. Lamchichi (1996) in his approach to the sociology of Islam, outlines the complexity, diversity and richness of Islam/Muslim societies and communities with the following statement:

> We have to take into consideration the history of societies, of men, and institutions … the history of Muslim societies is not determined solely by the credo of religion … this history is the result of a permanent invention of political, social and cultural actors in their different struggles … Each of those societies incorporate a multitude of [micro] societies, and plurality of 'Islamic' expressions … Therefore we need to avoid any globalist approach that consists of reducing this richness and complexity, by locking Muslims into abstract, extemporal and homogeneous religiosity, without any consideration of concrete societies, nor reflection about the huge geographic, anthropological, human, cultural, social, institutional and intellectual diversities of countries where Islam exists. (24–6).

Although much has been written about sport within the discourse about Islam, most of it lacks serious philosophical debate when it comes to linking the values of Islam to modern sport. The majority of this literature refers to the *Islamist* (political Islam) point of view as representing one homogeneous group or discourse (particularly regarding women's participation in sport), which is normally discussed in opposition to the 'modern (Western) liberal' view.

In the subsequent section we shall highlight the difference between two types of endeavour relating to sport and Muslim thought. These are: (a) sport in Islam, including the question of sport in Islam in the West; and (b) sport in Muslim societies.

SPORT IN ISLAM

To undertake an Islamic study of any phenomenon, including the study of modern sport, one should consider the fundamentals of Islamic belief, or at least the internal logic and the core of Islam as a monotheistic religion. A primary condition is to understand the muslimness of a Muslim believer (*Homo islamicus*). This involves the following:

- The Islamic ontology of *Tawhid*: the Islamic belief in the absolute Oneness of the Creator, the impossibility of there being a representation of Him, and the truth of His word revealed in the *Qur'an*.
- The Islamic sources of jurisprudences: (a) the teachings of the *Qur'an*; (b) the authenticated sayings of the Prophet Muhammad and the precedents he set, collectively called the *Sunna*, or 'Tradition'; (c) the consensus of learned opinion, explicit or implicit (called *ijma'*); and (d) reasoning by analogy (called *qiyas*), to help Muslims decide how to deal with new situations that arise in new places or with the passage of time.
- Principles of Islamic *Shari'a* or Islamic path: the domain of belief, morality and law. Its formulation and codification take two forms: law (*al Hukm*) and *Fetwa*. The law is a fixed norm, while *Fetwa* is a mobile norm. The sum of laws and *Fetwas* (moral, juridical, cultural) are classified into five levels: obligations, recommendation, permission, undesirability, prohibition.
- Islamic parameters which guide the process of *Ijtihad* or the endeavour of attaining a level of knowledge from the primordial texts, *Qur'an* and *Sunna*, and applying it to real-world situations: some of these parameters include the forbidden, blameable, permitted, recommended and obligatory in Islam (*Halal* and *Haram*); public good (*Istislah*); overall promotion of social, economic and cultural justice (*Adl*).

It can be stated that Islamic legal judgments in relation to modern sport practices may depend on many variables such as the purpose, the individual and societal benefits of the sporting activity. Furthermore, the type of sporting activity or the place and the cultural settings where it is taking place may also be relevant. There are universal principles or values in Islam which are unchangeable (*Thabit*) and not affected by time and space, and others that are subject to change (*Mutaghayir*), changing from one cultural setting or society to another. Put in other terms, in Islam everything is permitted except that which is explicitly forbidden by an undisputed text. There are matters where the margin of interpretation is virtually nil, for instance questions related to *Akida* (Islamic belief or creed in the Oneness of *Allah*, prophethood, angels, Hereafter, destiny), and other issues where the scope for the exercise of reason and creativity is huge (Oubrou, 2002; Ramadan, 2004).

As a general rule, most Islamic scholars agree that Islam permits the Muslim (both genders) to practise sports and games as long as such sports are balanced and beneficial for the person's physical fitness. The argument usually put forward is that Islam encourages a Muslim to be strong and to seek the means of strength. Examples of *Fetwa* which seeks to give an Islamic (theological) reading of contemporary sport practices (e.g. sport rules and etiquette, the question of boxing, Islam's stance on women practising sport) are available in Islam online (http://www.islamonline.net) (Box 23.2). Islam online has a strong link with The European Council for Fatwa and Research, one of the leading Islamic organisations in Europe, which includes on its board some prominent Islamic scholars, preachers and thinkers.

Box 23.2 Sheikh 'Atiyyah Saqr's Fatwa on the question of sport (definition, etiquette and ruling)

In research terms, this is an interesting text to investigate – from a discursive analytical perspective – in order to explore how meaning systems around sport practice are constructed/developed in Islamic thought – *usul al dine and usul al fiqh* – or what Arkoun (2002, 2003) defines as 'the root/divine origins/foundations of religion and Law'. Sheikh Atiyyoh Saqr is the former head of the Al Azhar Fatwa Committee.

'From the time immemorial, people have sought means of physical training and invented all kinds of sports to make their bodies strong, but each to its purposes and conditions. A nation where fighting and battles were the norm, sports like weightlifting, archery and duelling would be very common, while swimming became the favourite sports to people living on sea-shores. In the Arabian peninsula, people got used to hunting and horse-riding due to their conditions of frequent travelling and moving from one place to another.

How does Islam view sports?

Islam does not oppose having a strong body via practicing sports. Muslims are commanded to be of sound bodies and sound minds in addition to having sound morals. In the Hadith, we read: 'A strong believer is better and more beloved to Allah than a weak one.' (Reported by Muslim) A sound strong body is capable of fulfilling both the religious and the worldly duties. Islam never accepts anything that leads to neglecting these duties, save in some cases where some exemptions are made so as to make matters easy for believers.

The effects of sports on the body:

In his well known book 'Zad-Al-Ma'aad', Imam Ibnul-Qayyem states that movement is the core of sports. It helps the body get rid of waste food in a very normal way. It makes it active, enhances its immunity and protects it from diseases. Each organ has its own sport that suits it. As for horse-riding, archery, wrestling and racing, they are sports that benefit the whole body.

Sports appearing in Islamic rituals:

In Islam, we see that many Islamic rituals contain sports that help the body attain physical fitness once they are practiced properly. The rituals of pilgrimage, paying visits to Muslim brothers, visiting the sick, going to and from the mosque and participating in many social activities are no more than sports.

Etiquette of sports in Islam:

The fact that Islam encourages the practicing of sports makes one realize how great, flexible and comprehensive is this course of Allah given to mankind. In this context, Islam stresses the importance of spiritual and moral training that should accompany physical training so that the latter yield its desired effects.

In supporting a team, hooliganism should be avoided. Also, there is no place for gloating. Having an upper hand in games does not warrant jeering at a defeated opponent. Islam views sports as a means of enhancing mutual love and cooperation among people, not a means of hurting feelings. That's why the winning party should never be carried away with joy to the extent of insulting the opponents, nor must the defeated party be eaten up with envy at his counterpart's advantage. He must keep in mind that his today's loss will pave way for his success tomorrow, if he keeps patience and tries to improve himself.

This reminds us of the occasion when a nomad's camel outpaced the Prophet's she-camel which was known to be ever-first in racing, Muslims felt sad. Commenting on the issue, the Prophet, peace and blessings be upon him, said: '*Almighty Allah has decreed that nothing shall have a permanent glory (meaning that every situation has its ups and downs and no condition is permanent).*' The Prophet, peace and blessings be upon him,

(Cont'd)

made this statement to cool down the feelings of those who found his camel being outpaced a difficult thing to swallow.

In contests, a true Muslim never forgets the etiquette of giving the counterparts good treatment. Casting aside morals in contests and competitions is a form of hypocrisy to which the Prophet referred when saying: *'There are four characteristics if found in a person, he is a pure hypocrite. If one of them is found in a person, it gives him a characteristic of hypocrisy until he drops that: if trusted with something, he breaches trust, if talks, he tells lies, if makes a promise, he does not keep his word and if is in a quarrel with someone, he proves deviant (resorts to vile speech and corrupt conduct.)'*

Tips for a Muslim practicing sports:

1   A Muslim should not occupy himself with sports to the extent that leads to neglecting religious and other duties.
2   A Muslim is not permitted to give himself loose rein in practicing sports in a way that involves inflicting harm on others. Practicing sports in crowded streets, for example, thus causing traffic jam is not an Islamic way for example.
3   Blind fanaticism in favour or against a team has nothing to do with Islam, for this really contradicts the Islamic teachings calling for unity and love.
4   While practicing sports there should be no room for foul words, bad behaviour and slandering.
5   Islam does not allow matches or games that involve both sexes, in a way that opens channels for seduction, temptation and corruption.
6   Islam rejects also all games and sports that stir sexual urge or encourage moral perversion such as women practicing dancing and being watched by the public.

Males are to practice sports that suits their nature and vice versa. In Islam, it is not allowed for females to practice sports that are unique for men.

In conclusion, it is to be made clear that upon declaring something permissible, Islam places some stipulations that aim at maintaining morality and that cope with the general wisdom of legislation. Sports are to be practiced following these stipulations so as to avoid any undesired harms. The general rule of Shari'ah is that any act that involves transgressing limits whether in eating, drinking, clothing or anything else, is prohibited. The Qur'an declares: *'O ye who believe! Forbid not the good things which Allah hath made lawful for you, and transgress not. Lo! Allah loveth not transgressors.' (Al-Ma'idah: 87)*
Almighty Allah knows best.'

Source: http://www.islamonline.net

Prior to concluding this first component of our discussion the aim of the following is to explore the question of sport in Islam in a non-Muslim (and secular) context, the West.

Sport in Islam in the West

Islam is no longer confined to traditional Muslim countries (*Dar Al-Islam* or the House of Islam). Muslim settlements in Europe and North America have given rise to intense debate over the legal conditions connected to Muslim minority status in non-Muslim societies, principally the reconciliation between the exigencies of Islam with secular life, without losing Islam's soul (Césari, 2004: 160). This raises concerns regarding the application of the (*Shari'a*) Islamic path in a non-Muslim context. It includes questions such as:

- personal law (marriage, inheritance, citizenship, protection of faith, investment);
- the practice of Islamic rituals (fasting, prayer, *Halal* meat);
- the subject of dress code, particularly for Muslim women, in a public space;
- participation of Muslims in the political life and democratic debates of their societies;
- the institutionalisation of Islam in the West through the establishment of Islamic councils representing different Islamic tendencies in the public domain (e.g. Muslims Executive of Belgium, Islamic Commission of Spain, French Council on Islam, etc.);
- the question of loyalty to religion versus loyalty to the nation state. Regarding this last point we can cite the example in sport (the product of the nation state system) of the NBA suspension of Mahmoud Abdul-Rauf, a professional basketball player for the Denver Nuggets and a Muslim since 1991. He was suspended for repeatedly not standing while the national anthem was played. The reason he put forward was that nationalism implied in the song ran counter to his belief of 'Islam is the only way'. According to Mahmoud Abdul-Rauf, 'Islam has given him more maturity and a new perspective on life' (Siddiqui and Moharram, 1995).

New questions are being raised in relation to the practice of sport in the West. Demands are being made by Muslim communities – in the name of democracy, citizenship and rights to cultural and religious differences – to accommodate specific times for Muslim women and young girls at local leisure centres, to allow men to wear long swimming trunks in public swimming pools (Silverstein, 2002; Tabeling, 2005; Walseth, 2006) and, moreover, to allocate specific training/nutrition programmes for professional athletes to meet their religious duty of fasting during the month of Ramadan.

It should be said that the question of sport practice among Muslim communities is not always that of conforming the practice of modern sports to religious exigencies (although not all Muslims by cultural heritage who are living in the West want to be categorised in relation to their faith – perceived by some as a private matter – in their everyday social relations). There are other cultural, socio-economic and even historical variables (e.g. history of colonialism and decolonisation) that need to be taken into account, as follows:

- **The complex forms of self-affirmation of the 'Muslim' population (local/transnational, religious/secular).**
- **The status of religion in Western societies, organised according to Césari (2004) into three main types: (a) the co-operation between church and state (Austria, Belgium, Italy, Spain and Germany); (b) the existence of state-sponsored religion (the UK, Denmark and Greece); (c) or the total separation of religion and politics (France).**
- **Differences in the needs and aspirations of generations (first, second and third/even fourth). For third and fourth generations the question of integration is not a concern, because they already are members of the national community (born and raised in the West).**
- **Place of origin (nationality, region, urban/rural) (Baillet, 2003; Fleming, 1994).**
- **Forms of migration (economic or forced). In particular, the differences in the socio-economic status and cultures (including the desire to practise sport and leisure activities) between well-established ethnic minorities and the so-called newly established minorities or newcomers (refugees and asylum seekers) (Henry et al., 2004b).**
- **Contemporary policy discourses in Europe about citizenship and integration of ethnic minorities. The idea of pluri-ethnic and pluri-religious Europe is challenged today by two antagonistic and conflicting definitions of national identity and citizenship. The first is based on a demand by some members of, and groups from, immigrant and ethnic minorities for a more inclusive and comprehensive conception of citizenship and thus one which is more sensitive to their particular circumstances and cultures. The second is claimed by some 'nationalist' movements, defenders of the well-established national sovereignties and 'national preference', for more exclusionary forms of citizenship (Barry, 2001; Benhabib, 2002).**
- **The question of girls'/women's participation in sport. We have to be aware of the difficult position of Muslim women who have to deal today with both family and community environments in a crisis of identity and in search of new cultural references and representations of their collective 'self'; that is, a redefinition of what it is to be a member of a community. The return to community is seen as the best way to resist the challenges of mass production of culture and material civilisation (Beck et al., 2003). That said, we agree on the other hand with Mandaville's argument that:**

Islam often offers the easy way out, both for analysts seeking a quick explanation and for the policy-makers of the societies in question who want to sidestep the structural causes of gender inequality and mistreatment of women by referring to 'cultural' causes which are 'conveniently out of their hands'. (2003: 58)

To face these multiple dilemmas Muslim scholars living in the West, principally those who identify themselves as both Muslims and citizens of the West, are calling today for the application of new forms of *Ijtihad* which takes into account the specificity of addressing Islamic issues in Western liberal democracies (i.e. in relation to the secular tradition of Western legislation, science and values of human rights). Groups of Muslim scholars are demanding the application of exceptional jurisprudence (*Fiqh* or episte-mology of minority rights) based on the Islamic ethical principle of *maslaha* or common benefit, which can be divided in terms of priority and individual/societal needs into the indispensable, the necessary and the aesthetic (Oubrou, 2002). For instance, if we were to apply the notion of *maslaha* to the sport context then the practice of sport to prevent health problems would be seen as indispensable, while for instance bodybuilding would be perceived as aesthetic, although if it were concerned with vanity it would be conse-quently discouraged.

Others reject the necessity of minority law which they regard as a sign of *ghettoisation* (ethnisation) of Islam, and instead believe that the West now constitutes part of the Muslim world (i.e. space of safety, space of testimony) and therefore it is indeed possible to live there according to Islamic principles (Ramadan, 2004: 77). They thus encourage Muslim citizens to be more visible in the public domain and fully active in all domains of (their) Western society (in politics, economy, sport, media, art, etc.).

Some research questions which are worth exploring in future studies of the same topic are as follows:

- How are the meanings ascribed to Islam reinterpreted by Muslim minorities in Western contexts? How are the values of modern sport perceived and defined by Muslim minorities in Western contexts?
- What different social roles does sport play in the different types of Muslim 'reli-giosity' across different Muslim communities in Western socio-cultural and politi-cal settings?
- How is sport employed in the service of civil participation and common benefit (*maslaha*) of Muslim communities in the West?

SPORT IN MUSLIM COUNTRIES

To examine the question of sport in Muslim countries means studying sport in socially and historically changing contexts, in nation states where Islam represents the religion (faith, form of identity, and cultural reference) of the majority of the population. The purpose of what follows is to highlight some of the parameters we believe are significant for such a study.

First, the pluralistic cultural, social organisations and modern histories of Muslim societies. The Islamic world should be investigated as a heterogeneous group of cultures, histories and traditions belonging to the same civilisation and fundamental principles of Islam.

Despite the shared sense of belonging to the Islamic faith, Muslim countries can be divided in relation to the practice of Islam as a source for their legislation into:

- Revolutionary–modernist: such as Tunisia, Algeria, Turkey, Syria, Libya, Malaysia, Indonesia, as well as Muslim countries of the former Soviet Union. Ranging from semi-secularist to secularist (e.g. Kemalism, in reference to Kamel Ataturk forced secularisation of the Turkish society), they adopt a hybrid judicial system inspired by *Shari'a* law (particularly in relation to questions of civil law: such as inheritance, property and family) and are heavily influenced by the Western juridical system.
- Conservative or 'traditionalist': such as Iran, Sudan and Afghanistan. These states claim to adopt an 'Islamic system of governance' and the rule of the Islamic court inspired from *Shari'a* law (including criminal law).
- Monarchy states: such as Oman, Kuwait, Qatar, UAE, Saudi Arabia, Bahrain, Morocco, Jordan, which rely in their political systems on the traditional legitimacy of the ruling family, a legitimacy according to Kamrava (1998: 76) deeply rooted in the history and Arabo-Islamic cultural heritage of the country. This heritage takes a different (religious) dimension in Morocco, Jordan and Saudi Arabia, where dynastic rulers justify their positions on the grounds of being descendants of the Prophet (*Sharifs*), and for the Saudi family, the guardian of Islam and its two holiest cities (Mecca and Medina).

Muslim countries can be divided also in terms of their state's Islamic school of thought. These are: *Sunni*, which includes the majority of Muslim countries; *Shi'a* in Iran; and *Ibadi* in Oman. Each of these have their own *Shi'a, Sunni, Ibadi*, 'non-orthodox' Muslim and non-Muslim minorities. There are also multi-religious countries where Muslims are in the majority, such as Lebanon, Malaysia, Egypt, Syria, Iraq, Sudan, or representing the second biggest majority, as in the case of Nigeria where Muslims are in the majority in several states. There are also Muslim countries where the population, in addition to sharing the same Islamic identity or belonging to the same Islamic doctrine (or for the case of Iraq to both *Sunna* and *Shi'a*), forms different ethno-linguistic groups, such as in Afghanistan, Iraq, Syria, Iran, Turkey, Algeria, Morocco and Indonesia.

The other important element that needs to be addressed while studying sport in Muslim societies is the history of modernisation and different responses towards Western modernity. These include the colonial and post-colonial histories and post-colonial endeavours for nation state formation which have had important effects on the social organisations and governance of (ex-colonised) Muslim societies. The latter has also influenced the debate on authenticity and modernity, and thus 'Islamisation' (versus Westernisation) of the society. For instance, the diffusion of modern sport in the Arab world happened primarily as a result of the various forms of colonial and foreign presence. This is not to say that there was not a culture of physical activities in the Arab world prior to colonialism or the foreign presence in the region (we should emphasise here that not all Arabs are Muslims and not all Muslims are Arabs). Arab traditions of racing horses and camels, sailing boats, chess, polo, fishing, water diving and hunting are just some to serve as testimony to the richness of the physical culture of the Arab people. Nonetheless, modern sport in its Western rationalised and competitive format has been assimilated (without negotiation) and used for different purposes during the colonial and post-colonial eras. After being employed during the colonial period in reinforcing social stratification, and in the struggle against colonialism (the case of Algeria in the past and Palestine today), sport became in the post-colonial period a tool *par excellence* for party–state regimes in their projects of popular mobilisation around nation state building and integration into the international bipolar world system. As for today, in the alleged era of globalisation and 'the end of history' (so-called triumph of Western liberalism) (Fukuyama, 1992), sport is an ingredient of the general strategy of transformation from socialism or controlled liberalism to the market economy and thus openness towards the 'liberal' world (see Amara and Henry, 2004; Fates, 1994, 2004; Henry et al., 2003; Morgan, 1998; Sfeir, 1985).

As a case in point, large investments are being poured into Gulf countries in staging and sponsoring the world's leading sporting events and building sports infrastructure. Investment in sport goes beyond the national space to include sponsorship of major regional and continental events like the Pan Arab Games (Henry et al., 2003) and other 'globalised' sports events, namely Dubai Duty Free sponsorship of the WTA Tour and Fly, Emirates official partner of the 2006 FIFA World Cup Germany. The aim is to open up the Arabian peninsula to the world of business and finance and to establish a global reputation as a leading destination for international sporting events (Amara, 2005).

The Arab media space is witnessing a significant rise in the number of sports channels (e.g. Art Sport, Al-Jazeera Sport, Abu Dahabi Sport, Dubai Sport, Saudi Sport, Iraq Sport) battling for the broadcasting rights of regional, international and foreign sporting events – particularly Spanish, Italian, French and North African football leagues – as well as the sponsorship of regional football competitions.

The other domain worth investigating is the history of Muslim countries' participation, including by women athletes, in international events. In the aftermath of independence, the appropriation of the dominant model of sport by major Muslim countries was seen as inevitable, taking into account the multiple uses of sport as an element for political, social

TABLE 23.1   Sport and national identity: the developing role of sport in Algerian society

1926–57	Colonialism and Algerian nationalist movements	Sport organised in terms of ultra-nationalist and European groups (representing cultural richness)
		Initial forms of sporting exclusion of indigenous population
		Subsequently used as a colonial too for integration
		Finally sport becomes a privileged site used by nationalist movements for individual liberation (from colonialism) and an instrument of subversion or political expression and rejection of colonial oppression
1954–62	Algerian Revolution	Integrated as a part of dynamic break with colonial society
		Sport (football, the heritage of the colonial power) used for the internationalisation of the Algerian cause
1962–88	FLN state	Sport as a tool for nation state building
		Externally, tool for national representation
		Internally, an important element for political legitimation and integration into socialist and popular values of the nation (social positivism)
		Strengthening friendship and co-operation with other socialist countries
		Era of official amateurism
1988–92	Economic crisis and pluralism	Increased interest in sporting spectacles
		An arena for political agitation and social protest or rejection of social inequalities
From 1992	Market economy	End of amateurism
		Commercial sport in a local (Algerian–specific) form

Source: Amara and Henry (2004: 20)

and cultural recognition. One can nevertheless suggest that the adhesion of formerly colonised nations to the international sporting community did not happen in a straightforward manner. The newly independent countries, including Muslim ones, have also used international sporting events, and particularly the media coverage that such events attract, as a space to express their regional political and ideological concerns (e.g. anti-imperialism and pan-Africanism), which had led sometimes to a real situation of crisis, for example the struggle over the Games of the New Emerging Forces (GANEFO) in 1965 (Adams, 2002); Black September at the Munich Olympics in 1972 (Macdonald, 1999); and the boycott of the Olympic Games to denounce apartheid in South Africa in 1976 (Guttmann, 2002).

Table 23.1 illustrates how the meaning and functionality of modern sport have been negotiated in colonial and post-colonial (socialist and post-socialist) Algeria.

Turkey was the first Muslim country to send women athletes to the Olympic Games, followed by Iran in 1964 (it was the first and last time until the Atlanta Games). Algeria, Libya and Syria did so in 1980 and Egypt in 1984 (Aldeeb, 1996). The first gold medal for a Muslim woman, Nawel Moutawakel, in the 1984 Los Angles Olympic Games, announced the beginning of a new era in women's participation in international sporting events. The other factor in the change of attitude towards women's participation in sport could be the Islamic Women Games (Box 23.3), newly created in 1993, which may increase Muslim women's participation in other sports, though in the context of closed (to males and the media) sports events (see also Boxes 23.4 and 23.5).

Box 23.3   Islamic Women Games, Tehran

Organised by the Islamic Federation of Women Sport (IFWS) (http://www.ifws.org).

Mission statement of the Games:

> Sport and physical education is regarded as a necessity for women since they take on their shoulders some specific responsibilities in families and societies which are very important. The holy religion of Islam deeply concerns sport and advises the training in sport activity by parents of their children as a religious duty.

Objectives of the IFWS are as follows:

- To provide suitable conditions for the participation of women in sports activities in compliance with the Islamic codes.
- To consolidate the basis for peace, friendship, understanding and solidarity.
- To develop the culture of physical education and sport in the societies.
- To safeguard the well-being, and to provide for the delight and livelihood among the women.
- To endeavour towards the development of sports for all and competition sports.
- To promote the managerial, executive and technical ability of women in the member countries.
- To promote women's scientific knowledge in sports.
- To strengthen the co-operation and co-ordination among members on matters of common interest.

In an attempt to rebuild the sense of Islamic unity, shaken by severe political crises among Muslim countries, and to reinforce the universal values of Islam and its global status as the second largest religion in the world, the first ever Islamic Solidarity Games (open also to Christians living in Muslim countries), said to be the largest sporting event after the Olympic Games, were hosted by the Saudi cities of Makkah, Taif, Madinah and Jeddah (8–20 April 2005). These are highly symbolic places in the history of Islam. The Games were organised under the patronage of the Organization of the Islamic Conference (OIC) and the Islamic Solidarity Sports Federation.

Box 23.4   President lifts ban on women watching football in Iran

The Iranian president, Mahmoud Ahmadinejad, has announced that women will be allowed to attend football matches in big stadiums for the first time since the 1979 Islamic revolution.

> Under a decree reported on state television yesterday [24 April 2006], the president has ordered the head of the country's sports organisation to provide separate areas for women. 'The best stands should be allocated to women and families in the stadiums in which national and important matches are being held', Mr Ahmadinejad was quoted as saying. The reason given by the president seems to have been intended to placate hardliners. 'The presence of women and families in public places promotes chastity', he said. (Whitaker, 2006)

On the same topic see the film Offside, directed by Jafar Panahi and starring Sima Mobarak Shahi, Safar Samandar, Shayesteh Irani, M. Kheyrabadi and Ida Sadeghi (Iran 2005, 88 min). '"Offside" report of a screening at the 2006 Berlin International Film Festival', http://www.signandsight.com/features/619.html.

Box 23.5   Hassiba Boulmerka's victory at the Tokyo World Athletics Championships in August 1991

Both representatives of state (official) Islam and certain personalities within the so-called 'Islamist' (political) movements criticised the non-Islamic dress of the gold medallist Hassiba Boulmerka at the Tokyo World Athletics Championships in August 1991, which was described by one of the imams of Algiers as 'scandalous' (Fates, 1994: 10). This view was not shared by all Algerians, however. For the so-called 'secularist' women's associations in Algeria Hassiba Boulmerka's victory was considered as a victory against men's domination, and as a symbol of resistance against the Family Law (adopted from Islamic Shari'a law), approved by the Algerian National Assembly in 1984, which for some has accorded Algerian women a legally inferior status. For them Hassiba did not need prior permission from her tutor (a father or husband) to participate and succeed, as is the case for the rest of Algerian women who represent more than half of the population and who, like Hassiba, if opportunities were offered to them, would be able to represent their country with dignity.

As for Hassiba: 'when I won in Tokyo, I wasn't comfortable with being the centre of attention … I like to keep things simple, not to be a star. But I've become a representative of all Algeria, and of young women in particular. I've gotten so many letters wishing me courage', she said. She added that 'in athletics, on the track, I learned to suffer, to love my country, to concentrate, to take responsibility. I believe you can express yourself in sport maybe better than in other field. All that, and it brings everyone together, too' (Moore, 1992: 58 and 61).

CONCLUSION

The dominant line in Western literature argues that the emergence of modern sport in nineteenth-century Europe was associated with the advent of capitalism, industrialisation and urbanisation. Such forms of social organisation were linked to the institutionalisation and rationalisation of sports practices. Sport, however, may also be characterised as part of the discourse on modernity which takes the West or Western philosophy of enlightenment as 'the master signifier' to define the meaning of modern sport. Sporting meanings and value systems were often constructed in opposition to traditional and 'indigenous' sports practices. Indeed the acceptance of modern sport practice by native (colonised) populations was explained by some Western historians and anthropologists as a sign of 'assimilation' of (Western) modernist values, and thus of the growth of Occidental universalism.

Having said that the aim of a Muslim (and non-Muslim) reconsideration of the evolutionist version of the history of sport and modern sports values should not be directed towards the so-called return to 'purity' characterised by the complete rejection of modern sport and the return to pre-colonial identity and forms of (Islamised) sports practices. Islam is open to creative innovation in the service of human progress and respects of human dignity and thus should not deny a role for modern sport, or completely reject modern sport without providing an accepted (inclusive) alternative (i.e. the replacement of a Western-centric (secular) definition of sport with an Islamo-centric meaning of sport).

Questioning the why (purpose) and the how (form of practice) of sport in Islam should acknowledge the kernel of Islamic belief, the universal values (i.e. respect for equality, justice and human dignity) and the notion of constructive dialogue. The aim should be directed towards reaching what the *Qur'an* itself defines as the 'Middle Nation' or just balance. The potential is of negotiating ideological extremes and providing a common ground by seeking a median course between:

Ascetic spiritualism and obsessive materialism, between selfishness and altruism, between complete freedom and restriction in mate selection, between monogamy and polygamy; and, in more modern context between capitalism and socialism, and between democracy and authoritarianism. (Ba-Yunus, 2002: 101)

Abu Hamid Al Ghazali (1058–1111) one of the most eminent Muslim theologious and philosophers, inspired by the life and teachings of the Prophet, understood as early as in the eleventh century the health and pedagogical benefits of physical activities. He promoted 'innocent games which children should practice after school, to avoid killing the spirit' (reported in Fates, 1994: 26; original text in French). Nowadays, however, it should be said that sport is not seriously considered by Muslim academics (sociologists, economists, psychologists, historians, philosophers) and, we have to say, is neglected by Islamic scholars. Despite the increasing interest, in relation to media coverage, governments and private investment, sport is still regarded as a non-academic, non serious activity restricted to the domain of play, and, for some, a deviation from religious teachings. Islam has been reduced to its strict religious domain and disaggregated from its civilisational constituent of scientific innovation and artistic creativity.

The following statement from Ramadan sums up the deficit of Islamic thinking about sport and leisure today:

If there was a domain where we are finding difficulty to promote an alternative project, it is definitely that of leisure and recreation. If we were to study the offered activities here and there we would notice three major deficits: either everything, or almost, is 'forbidden'; or we perpetuate activities coming from 'elsewhere' which are inadequate to our reality; or lastly, we propose activities most of the time child-like, and sometimes childish, without considering the age of those (male and female) to whom those activities are offered. By looking at adolescents (he/or she) as if they were perpetual children of eight or ten, we will end up pushing them to search, elsewhere, for what they think are fitting leisure activities for their age and expectations. It is necessary to distinguish between ages and levels; to take into account the respective realities of the child, adolescent and young adult. We need to embark upon the universe of leisure by intelligent selection and ethical complement. To be able to develop a spirit of a critical and responsible way of thinking. To think about cultural and artistic alternatives, which is stimulating and good for one's status. A knowledge of the environment is more than appreciated in this case, in addition to good management of available competences. (2002: 60–3, translated by the author from the French)

To add to Ramadan's viewpoint, and based on the Islamic values of *Istislah* (public good), *Adl* (overall promotion of social, economic and cultural justice) and *Istihsane* (seeking excellence), Ministries of Youth and Sports, national federations, National Olympic Committees, as well as representatives of civil society (including sports associations) in Muslim countries or within Muslim communities, should play an active (world) role in:

- Tackling doping in sport or all other forms of cheating, based on the Prophet (peace be upon him). *Hadith* 'He who cheats us does not belong to us.'
- Implanting sports policies, including and fostering a cross-cultural dialogue:

O mankind! We created you from a single (pair) of a male and a female, and made you into nations and tribes, that ye may know each other (not that ye may despise each other). Verily the most honoured of you in the sight of Allah is (he who is) the most righteous of you. And Allah has full knowledge and is well acquainted (with all things). (*Qur'an*, 049.013)

- The celebration of humanity, exemplified by the Prophet saying:

No Arab has any superiority over a non-Arab, nor does a non-Arab have any superiority over an Arab. Nor does a white man have any superiority over a black man, or the black man any superiority over the white man. You are all the children of Adam, and Adam was created from clay.

CHAPTER SUMMARY

» There is a need today to apply different research paradigms to the study of sport in Islam, and sport in Muslim societies and communities.
» Distinction needs to be made between

- Islam as a religious belief, and Muslims' religiosity (identity-politics usage of religious rhetoric to legitimise social practices);
- modernity as a project for society, which may take different (local and global) forms, and the exclusive Western historicity and scientific positivism of modernity.

» *Sport in Islam*: to examine sport based on the fundamentals of Islamic belief, the foundations of Shari'a (Islamic path, Islamic law), and Islamic roots of Ijtihad (intellectual effort and critique of legal formulations in the light of the texts, Qur'an and Sunna). There are universal principles or values in Islam which are unchangeable (Thabit) and not affected by time and space, and others that are subject to change (Mutaghayir), thus changing from one cultural setting to another, from one society to another. In Islam everything is permitted except that which is explicitly forbidden by an undisputed text.
» *Sport in Muslim countries*: to study sport as a social phenomena in nation states where Islam represents the religion (faith, form of identity, and cultural reference) of a majority of the population. The Muslim world should be investigated as heterogeneous groups of cultures, ethnicities, histories (of colonialism, decolonisation and nation state building) and traditions that belong to the same Islamic civilisation and the fundamental principles of Islam.

FURTHER READING

There are a number of studies that explore sport in Arabo-Muslim contexts such as the Pan-Arab Games (Henry et al., 2003), sport in the Gulf region (Amara, 2005), Islam's view on physical activity and sport in Egypt (Walseth and Fasting, 2003), sport and Islamism (Fates, 2004), Muslim women, leadership and the Olympic Movement (Henry et al., 2004a), religion and football in Iran (Fazooni, 2004). There are also studies that focus on the question of sport and Muslim identities and cultures in the West such as sport, Islam and North African culture in France (Silverstein, 2002), perceptions of young Muslim women in the UK about sport and physical activity (Zaman, 1997), sport and different forms of belonging of Muslim women in Norway (Walseth, 2006), leisure behaviour of American Muslims post September 11 (Livengood and Stodoloska, 2004).

REFERENCES

Adams, I. Pancasila (2002) 'Sport and the building of Indonesia – ambitions and obstacles', *International Journal of the History of Sport*, 19 (2–3): 295–318.

Aldeeb Abu-Sahlieh (2004) 'Limites du sport en droit Musulmans et Arabe', *Confluences Méditerranée*, No. 50, Summer.

Amara, M. (2005) 'A "modernization" project from above? Asian Games – Qatar 2006', *Sport in Society*, 8 (3): 495–516.

Amara, M. and Henry, I.P. (2004) 'Between globalization and local modernity: the diffusion and modernization of football in Algeria', *Soccer and Society*, 51: 1–26.

Arkoun, M. (1995) *Clarifier le passé pour construire le future*. No. 16 http://confluences.ifrance.com (accessed 2001).

Arkoun, M. (2002) *The Unthought in the Contemporary Islamic Thought*. London: Saqi book in association with Institute of Islamaili Studies.

Arkoun, M. (2003) 'Rethinking Islam today', *ANNALS, AAPSS*, 588 (July): 18–39.

Baillet, D. (2003) 'Pratiques sportives et jeunes issus de l'immigration maghrébine', *Migrance*, 22 (2): 60–9.

Barry, B. (2001) *Culture and Equality, an Egalitarian Critique of Multiculturalism*. London: Polity Presss.

Ba-Yunus, I. (2002) 'Ideological dimensions of Islam: a critical dimension', in D. Hasting (ed.), *Interpreting Islam*. London: Sage, pp. 99–110.

Beck, U., Bonss, W. and Lau, C. (2003) 'The theory of reflexive modernisation: problematic, hypotheses and research programme', *Theory, Culture and Society*, 20(2): 1–33.

Benhabib, S. (2002) *The Claims of Culture, Equalities and Diversity in the Global Era.* Princeton, NJ: Princeton University Press.

Césari, J. (2004) *When Islam and Democracy Meet: Muslims in Europe and in the United States.* New York: Palgrave.

Fates, Y. (1994) *Sport et Tiers Monde, Pratiques corporelle.* Paris: Presses Universitaires de France.

Fates, Y. (2004) 'L'islamisme algérien et le sport: entre rhétorique et action', *Confluences Méditerranée*, No. 50, Summer. Available online http://confluences.ifrance.com/numeros/50.htm (accessed 3 October 2007).

Fazooni, B. (2004) 'Religion, politics and class: conflict and contestation in the development of football in Iran', *Soccer and Society*, 5, (3): 356–70.

Fleming, S. (1994) 'Sport and South Asian youth: the perils of "false universalism" and stereotyping', *Leisure Studies*, 13 (3): 159–77.

Fukuyama, F. (1992) *The End of History and the Last Man.* New York: Free Press.

Guttmann, A. (2002) *The Olympics: A History of the Modern Games*, Urbana, IL: University of Illinois Press.

Henry, I.P., Al-Tauqi, M. and Amara, M. (2003) 'Sport, Arab nationalism and the Pan Arab Games', *International Review of the Sociology of Sport*, 38 (3): 295–310.

Henry, I., Radzi, W., Rich, E., Shelton, C., Theodoraki, E. and White, A. (2004a) *Women, Leadership and the Olympic Movement.* Loughborough: Institute of Sport and Leisure Policy, Loughborough University and the IOC.

Henry, I., Amara, M., Aquilina, D., Coalter, I. and Taylor, F. (2004b) *The Roles of Sport and Education in the Social Inclusion of Asylum Seekers and Refugees: An Evaluation of Policy and Practice in the UK.* Loughborough: Institute of Sport and Leisure Policy, Loughborough University & Stirling University.

Kamrava, M. (1998) *Democracy in the balance: Culture and Society in the Middle East.* London: Chatham House.

Lamchichi, A. (1996) 'Crise Social, Islamism et perspectives politique', in G. Manceron (ed.) *Algerie: Comprendre la Crise.* Paris: Interventions, pp. 115–38.

Livengood, J.S. and Stodoloska, M. (2004) 'The effects of discriminations and constraints negotiation on leisure behaviour of American Muslims in Post-September 11 America', *Journal of Leisure Research*, 36 (2): 183–208.

Macdonald, K. (1999) *One Day in September*, Documentary (94 min), Arthur Cohn Production (Academy Award Winner 1999 Best Documentary Feature).

Moore, K.E. (1992) 'A scream and prayer: politics and religion are inseparable from sport in the lives of Algeria's world champion runners Nourdine Morceli and Hassiba Boulmerka', *Sport Illustrated*, 77 (5): 46–61.

Morgan, J.W. (1998) 'Hassiba Boulmerka and Islamic Green: international sports, cultural differences, and their postmodern interpretation', in G. Rail (ed.), *Sport and Postmodern Times.* Albany, NY: SUNY Press.

Oubrou, T. (2002) 'Shari'a de minorité: réflexions pour une intégration légale de l'Islam', in F. Frégosi (ed.), *Lectures Contemporaines du Droit Islamique: Europe et Monde Arabe*. Strasbourg: Presse Universitaire de Strasbourg.

Ramadan, T. (2002) *Musulmans d'occident: Construire et Contribuer*. Paris: Tawhid.

Ramadan, T. (2004) *Western Muslims and the Future of Islam*. London: Oxford University Press.

Sfeir, L. (1985) 'The status of Muslim women in sport: conflict between cultural tradition and modernisation', *International Review for Sociology of Sport*, 20 (4): 283–303.

Siddiqui. Y. and Moharram, J. (1995) 'Muslims in sports', www.colostate.edu/Orgs/MSA/muslims_in_sport.htm (accessed June 2005).

Silverstein, P.A. (2002) 'Stadium politics: sport, Islam and Amazigh consciousness in France and North Africa', in T. Magdalinski (ed.), *With God on their Side: sport in the service of religion*. London: Routledge, pp. 37–54.

Tabeling, P. (2005) 'Muslims and swimming lessons: separating the boys from the girls', trans. from the German by John Bergeron, *Qantara Newsletter*, 26 August. http://www.qantara.de/webcom/show_article.php/_c-478/_nr-322/i.html (accessed 3 October 2007).

www.islamonline.net/English/In_Depth/Religious/Sportsinislam/Ethics/articles/01.shtml (accessed November 2007).

Walseth, K. (2006) 'Young Muslim women and sport: the impact of identity work', *Leisure Studies*, 25 (1): 75–94.

Walseth, K. and Fasting, K. (2003) 'Islam's view on physical activity and sport: Egyptian women interpreting Islam', *International Review for the Sociology of Sport*, 38/1: 45–60.

Whitaker, B. (2006) 'President lifts ban on women watching football in Iran', *Guardian*: 25 April.

Zaman, H. (1997) 'Islam, well-being and physical activity: Perceptions of Muslim young women', in G. Clarke and B. Humberstone (eds) *Researching Women and Sport*. London: Macmillan Press, pp. 50–67.

24

Sport and Globalisation

BARRIE HOULIHAN

OVERVIEW

» *Globalisation as a process*
» *Globalisation as an outcome*
» *Reach and response*
» *Conclusion*

In a humorous guide to revision for chemistry examinations, school students were told 'When in doubt say it's "osmosis". If osmosis is the default explanation of chemical processes, then it has a lot in common with much of the use of the concept of globalisation. Whether the focus of discussion is the spread of Olympic sports, or changes in eating habits, intergenerational relationships, welfare policy or manufacturing work practices, the default explanation is a reference to the often poorly specified concept of globalisation. Globalisation has established itself across the social sciences to the extent that Featherstone and Lash were moved to suggest that globalisation had become the 'central thematic for social theory' (1995: 1). However, paralleling the growing dominance of globalisation as an explanation within the social sciences was a sceptical reaction against the paradigmatic status that the concept seemed to be assuming. Unease focused on the utility of the concept, its descriptive accuracy and its explanatory potential. For Bauman it was 'a fad word fast turning into a shibboleth' (1999: 1), Fitch dismissed much of the theorising of globalisation as 'globaloney' (1996), and Rosenberg (2005: 3) argued that 'the "age of globalization" is over'.

The overextension and casual use of the concept will add little to our understanding of global change and its implications for sport. There are three aspects of the concept of globalisation in the study of sport that require consideration before the concept can be used with confidence. The first is the need to distinguish between different dimensions of globalisation such as the political, economic and cultural, and consider their interrelation and relative significance as well as distinguishing between globalisation as a process and globalisation as an outcome. Second, there is a need to specify how that outcome of globalisation would be recognised and specify the criteria that would have to be fulfilled before we could confidently state that we now live in a globalised world. The third aspect concerns exploring the reach of globalising forces and the response of the 'receiving' nation/community.

GLOBALISATION AS A PROCESS: DIMENSIONS AND FLOWS

Political scientists make the important distinction between *democratisation*, which is the process of making progress towards democracy, and *democracy* itself, which is the outcome of the process. There is a need to be aware of a similar distinction between process and outcome when considering globalisation and sport. If we use the term 'globalisation' primarily to refer to the *process* of movement away from a world of discrete nation states and their social systems, cultural patterns, political systems and economies, then there is still the problem of defining the outcome of the process. More will be said about the outcome of globalisation in the next section while the focus in this section remains on an examination of globalisation as a process.

Scholte (2000) identifies five common uses of the term 'globalisation', namely as internationalisation, liberalisation, universalisation, Westernisation/Americanisation and deterritorialisation (see Box 24.1). Each usage of the term is based on a different balance between economic, political and cultural processes. Some definitions give priority to one process: liberalisation gives clear priority to economic forces whereas universalisation focuses more on the role of culture in globalisation. Other conceptualisations of globalisation, such as Westernisation/Americanisation, reflect a combined emphasis on economic, political and cultural factors.

Box 24.1   Varieties of globalisation

Globalisation as a process of

Internationalisation, reflecting greater cross-border exchanges, especially trade, but also people and ideas, between countries

Examples from sport

Trade in athletes; an increase in the number of international competition circuits

Liberalisation, whereby government restrictions on cross-border business are removed and to a large extent reflect the efforts of the World Trade Organization and at a regional level the European Union and the North American Free Trade Area	The impact of the European Union ruling regarding the transfer of players and the number of non-national players that a team may field (Bosman ruling), and also the liberalisation of cross-border TV media ownership and broadcasting
Universalisation of culture, a synthesis of existing cultures producing a homogeneous cultural experience	The global coverage of the Olympic Games in terms of both the number of countries participating (more countries than are members of the United Nations) and the number of countries receiving TV broadcasts, contributing to an increasingly homogeneous sports diet
Westernisation/Americanisation whereby the social structures of modernity, capitalism, rational bureaucracy, industrialism and representative democracy are spread throughout the world	Rational bureaucratic sports structures (written rules, leagues and records of achievement), a scientific approach to talent identification and development, specialisation both on and off the field of play (physiotherapists, psychologists, dieticians, etc.), and commercialisation
Deterritorialisation whereby the spatial organisation of social relations is altered as a result of a dramatic change in our perception of space, location and distance	The development of large fan groups for English and Scottish football teams not just outside the locality but outside the national state boundaries; the live transmission of international sports events

Source: Adapted from Scholte (2000)

Because so much of the discussion of sports globalisation focuses on sport as an element of culture, it is important to consider, if only briefly, the relative importance of the various dimensions of globalisation. For most Marxists the answer is fairly clear: economic factors dominate with cultural practices being broadly a reflection of the underlying mode of production. In relation to sport, Marxists would emphasise the commodification of sport and athletes, the domination of sport by powerful media interests which increasingly determine what sport is practised, especially at the elite level, and what sport will reach a global television market. Thus media interests, especially television, and the major international federations (football, cricket, Rugby Union/League and athletics) share a common concern to produce a marketable global product. Sport is no different from any other product in the capitalist economy where markets are carefully managed and where labour is exploited as the primary source of profit. The spectacular wages of footballers such as Ronaldinho, Beckham and Shevchenko detract attention from the more modest wages and short careers of most footballers and the ruthless exploitation of footballing talent of many poorer nations, particularly in Africa (Darby, 2001). Support for this argument comes from the work of Klein (1991), who demonstrated how the United States Major League Baseball teams undertook a crude form of asset-stripping of talent in the Dominican Republic. Although a number of players from the Republic became major stars in the United States, most of the talented young players who were exported there were abandoned when they did not 'make the grade'. However, such was the exodus of talent that the domestic Dominican Republic league was systematically undermined.

For Marxists and others who prioritise economic processes, culture is either a tool for incorporating economies through the manipulation of values and attitudes – cultural imperialism – or mere froth and not worthy of serious consideration. Examples of the former include Hamelink, who refers to a process of worldwide 'cultural synchronisation' (1983: 3), and Levitt who refers to the world's preference structure becoming relentlessly homogenised (1983). Scholte summarises the arguments as follows: 'Globalisation introduces a single world culture centred on consumerism, mass media, Americana, and the English language' (2000: 23) and one might add a diet of Olympic sport and Western-defined world championships in sports such as soccer, Formula One, athletics and swimming. Rather more bluntly, Brohm argues that global sport

> ideologically reproduces bourgeois social relations ... spreads an organisational ideology specific to the institutions of sport and ... transmits on a huge scale the general themes of the ruling bourgeois ideology like the myth of the superman, individualism, social advancement, success, efficiency etc. (1978: 77)

According to Brohm, the value of sport to capitalism is not just as a source of profit but also as a subtle vehicle for infiltrating capitalist values into a society because awareness of the manipulative capacity of sport is so low. Adopting a slightly different view, Harvey (1989), also arguing from a Marxist standpoint, retains confidence in a traditional base–superstructure relationship between economic processes and cultural forms and rejects the suggestion that the cultural dimension of globalisation – prominent though it undoubtedly is – requires a new conceptual language for its analysis: modern culture including sport is essentially epiphenomenal. Wallerstein (1991) is equally dismissive, viewing the cultural dimension as a slight ideological impediment to socialism by comparison with the underlying economic relations.

Priority to the economic dimension draws attention to the commodification of sport, the creation and management of global markets for sports products, and the increasing vertical integration between television media companies and the sports they broadcast. Christian Aid (Brookes and Madden, 1995) provided a powerful indictment of the practices of sports goods companies. They found that the manufacture of sports shoes was located in countries with the lowest labour cost where employment conditions, especially for children, were very poor and, perhaps most damning of all, that less than 5 per cent of the final retail price was received by the factory workers in South East Asia (see also Katz, 1994; Maguire, 1999: ch. 6; Sage, 1996). As regards the role of sports media in furthering the vertical integration within the industry, companies such as BSkyB, Canal and NTL have all sought to purchase football clubs or at least a shareholding (Brown, 2000), thus enabling them to exercise greater control over their key product.

Events such as the Olympic Games are also examples of the careful development of sports products and more importantly the extent to which even an event as profitable as the Olympics is so heavily dependent on US corporations. Around 60 per cent of all income to the Olympic Movement comes from US businesses either in the form of sponsorship (8 of the 10 largest sponsors are US based) or in the income generated from the sale of broadcasting rights. It is no wonder that the Games have been awarded to US cities four times since 1980 and that a recurring preoccupation for the local organising committee for the Games is how best to schedule events to meet the requirements of US East Coast television viewers.

Such is the interconnection between economic power and sport that it should come as no surprise that, with a small number of notable exceptions, the same countries that dominate the world economy also dominate international sport. The G8 countries (USA, UK, France, Germany, Canada, Italy, Russia and Japan) share 65 per cent of world trade with the remaining 200 or so other national economies accounting for the remaining 35 per cent. As in world trade so in Olympic medals where the same G8 countries dominate, accounting for 42 per cent of all gold medals at the Athens Olympics. If China had been included then the nine leading economies would have accounted for over half of all gold medals. The figures would undoubtedly have been closer to the G8 level had it not been for the residual effect of the prominence of sport in the former socialist countries of Central Europe and the continuing high political status of sport in the remaining socialist countries such as Cuba. In a study of a range of structural factors that might account for success in Olympic competition, Stamm and Lamprecht (2001) concluded that the structural factors of population size and level of economic development were the primary indicators of Olympic success and were becoming more pronounced.

In the study of the globalisation of sport, economic processes are clearly of central importance. However, this does not mean that culture should be written off as a mere cipher for more significant economic processes. There are a number of students of globalisation who are willing to grant the cultural sphere a substantial degree of autonomy. Hall (1983), for example, arguing from a broadly Marxist position, suggests that despite the clear power of business interests, there is still scope for a reconstruction of everyday practices and a rearticulation of cultural practices, such as in the area of sport. For Hall, capitalist power determines culture in the first, rather than the last, instance. Hannerz (1990) provides a useful attempt to disaggregate dimensions of globalisation and to investigate their interrelationship. He identifies three cultural 'flows', namely: (a) that of cultural commodities which circulate within the marketplace to include sports fashionwear and individual sports or competitions; (b) that which concerns the actions of the state, to include decisions about funding for sport; and (c) that which concerns the 'form of life', which refers to deeply embedded patterns of behaviour, attitudes and values. What is especially significant about this conceptualisation is, first, that it does not suggest that cultural phenomena are only to be found at the superficial or superstructural level and, second, that in order to ask significant questions about global sport, we need to be able to disaggregate culture and distinguish between levels or depths of embeddedness.

For example, within the realm of social relations, we could ask whether sport globalisation is evident 'merely' at the commodity level or has penetrated to the level of deep structural values and practices. A number of the major European football clubs have extensive worldwide networks of supporters' clubs with their own local fan magazines and club products. While such a phenomenon is evidence of some form of globalisation, we might be tempted to dismiss it as functioning only at the surface of society as a fashion. Like all fashions, it will exhaust itself and be supplanted by a new passion for a different team, sport or other cultural product and remembered in later years with a degree of fond embarrassment. However, if the support for European clubs were to be extended through the emulation of some of the less attractive patterns of fan behaviour such as hooliganism and racism, it might prompt the government to regulate fan behaviour. The intervention of the state would indicate that the degree of cultural change was of a more significant kind. If the growing popularity of football led to the establishment not only of national men's leagues, but also of leagues for women and, more significantly, to a decline in local or regional sports, then we might have evidence of cultural change of a far more profound kind.

Similarly, if we were to focus on the political dimension of culture, we would be rightly sceptical of bestowing too much significance on the attendance of politicians, even from countries with a strong football tradition, at major football matches, as this is likely to be an aspect of the froth of electioneering and cheap populist politics rather than an indication of deeply rooted state commitment. However, if the popularity of football were to prompt the government to reorder its funding priorities for sport with the intention of establishing a national professional league or strengthening the chances of the national team qualifying for the World Cup, we would be right to see this as a change of deeper significance. Furthermore, if the state began to undermine the traditional autonomy of sports clubs in order to pursue its policies, then the degree of cultural change would be far more significant. As should now be clear, there is a danger of reading too much significance into the fact that such a high proportion of the world's population watch some part of the Olympic Games or the football World Cup. What is more significant is when the state intervenes to manipulate, support or impose emergent cultural trends. More significant still is when there is evidence of changes to long-established sporting traditions or to deeply embedded societal attitudes and values in relation to patterns of social deference, gender roles or intergenerational relations, such as a move closer to the rational bureaucratic model of sports organisation or an acceptance of women's participation in the same elite competitive sports as men.

There are two conclusions that emerge from the discussion of globalisation as a process. The first is an acknowledgement that the significance of cultural change must be conceptualised in terms of depth of social embeddedness and that we must be wary of granting too much importance to shifts in the popularity of particular teams, sports or events. The second conclusion is that while the political and cultural dimensions have a degree of autonomy from economic processes, it is economic interests that have become much more prominent in sport in the last 25 years as major sports and sports events have become increasingly a focus for private profit rather than state subsidy.

GLOBALISATION AS AN OUTCOME

In the opening section of this chapter an analogy was drawn between democratisation and democracy on the one hand and globalisation as process and globalisation as outcome on the other. What was not made clear at the time is that while there is a reasonable degree of agreement about what might constitute evidence of democratisation, there is far less agreement about the grounds for declaring that a country qualifies as a democracy. There is disagreement about the criteria for democracy and the relative weight each criterion should be given. It should come as no surprise that there is an equal degree of uncertainty regarding the threshold for a globalised world and the form that that world would take.

The contemporary complex mix of globalising pressures and their ebb and flow over time make it extremely difficult to predict the precise trajectory of the process of globalisation. From the point of view of sport globalisation, there are at least three fairly clearly observable trajectories of globalisation visible in contemporary sport (see Table 24.1). The first is a globalised sporting world where nation and nationality mean little in terms of defining identity, the provision of funding or the regulatory framework within which sport takes place. Sports teams, leagues and events are deterritorialised and no longer defined primarily by national affiliation, but structured according to some other principle such as commercial opportunity, religion, sexuality or ideology. Professional road cycling, where multinational teams compete in a global competition circuit, is probably the best example of organisation around a commercial principle, although it is interesting to note the extent to which regional and national communities adopt teams as their own, even though the link with the territory is often tenuous.

The second trajectory of globalisation leads to an outcome which is characterised by a pattern of intense international sporting competition. In other words, the internationalised sporting world is defined by the volume of competition between athletes, squads and teams drawn from clearly defined nation states and where these international competitions are considered, by regional and national communities, to be more important than domestic competitions. Whether Liverpool FC beat Everton FC and whether Liverpool FC win the Premier League would be clearly of less interest to their fans than whether Liverpool FC won the European Champions League. A third possible outcome is best described as multinationalised sport, where the nation is still an important reference point for identity and the state a key source of resources for sports development, but the pattern of sports participation and fan identification reflects the increasingly common multiple or nested identities that a growing proportion of the world's population experience, especially in the industrialised countries. In the UK, for example, there has long been a capacity among Rugby Union supporters to support the England team in the Six Nations Championships and also the British and Irish Lions (a team drawn from the four home countries plus Ireland, a foreign country) who compete against southern hemisphere countries such as Australia and New Zealand. England supporters seem quite able to cheer on the Irishman Brian O'Driscoll when he is playing for the Lions even though he regularly plays against England in the Six Nations competition. Furthermore English football supporters of Irish descent seen quite capable of supporting both England and Ireland in international matches and coping with the split loyalty when the two teams have to play each other.

Split, hybrid, multiple or nested loyalty in sport is not the only dimension of an increasingly fragmented identity. Previous generations in the early and mid-twentieth century inhabited societies, in Western Europe in particular, in which identity was subject to powerful homogenising forces of class, religion and nationality. Since then identity has become more multi-faceted with an increasing range of dimensions which now include gender, sexuality, ethnic origin and education, and a fragmentation and decline in significance of traditional homogenising forces. The rapid decline of the industrial working class, the rise of new Christian churches and the import of eastern religions through immigration, and the effect of European Union membership on national identity have all contributed to a much more complex and heterogeneous social fabric which is reflected in sport. When the Conservative Party MP Norman Tebbit questioned the 'Britishness' of Asian immigrants who supported touring Indian or Pakistani cricket

TABLE 24.1 Sport and the outcomes of globalisation

Characteristic	Globalised sport	Internationalised sport	Multinationalised sport
Nation as the defining unit of international sport and nationality as the defining characteristic of sportsmen and sportswomen	Multinational/nationally ambiguous teams the norm, as in Formula One motor racing and professional road cycling	Teams defined by their country of origin, e.g. as in the Olympic Games, and international soccer club competitions	The nation is an important, and perhaps primary, reference point for team/athlete definition. However, athletes/teams will represent their nations, but also other politically defined units whether sub-national (Quebec's participation in the Francophone Games or the participation of Scotland in the World Cup) or supranational (a European team in the World Athletics Championships or the Irish rugby or hockey teams which comprise players from Northern Ireland and the Irish Republic)
Extent of global diversity in sport	Diminishing diversity and/or the overlaying of regionally/nationally distinctive sporting traditions with an increasingly uniform pattern of Olympic and major international team/individual sports	Maintenance of a vigorous national/regional sporting culture which exists alongside or takes precedence over Olympic and major international team/individual sports	Increasing diversity in terms of opportunities for competitions, although there may be a decline in diversity among sports themselves with those without an international stage being especially vulnerable to marginalisation through the adoption by governments of selective funding policies
Extent of state patronage of elite sport	Minimal, sports either are financially self-sufficient or attract commercial patronage	Substantial, most Olympic and major international sports depend on state subsidy	Substantial, although some wariness regarding the allocation of national funds to support supranational teams
Extent to which sports businesses and organisations operate within a national framework of regulation	Self-regulation by the industry or no regulation	National framework of regulation, e.g. licensing of clubs, coaches, sports venues and television broadcasting or supranational framework of regulation, e.g. by the European Union	National regulatory frameworks important but both businesses and sports organisations operate within multiple regulatory frameworks, especially within the European Union

TABLE 24.1 *(Continued)*

Characteristic	Globalised sport	Internationalised sport	Multinationalised sport
Extent to which international sports federations and the IOC are subject to domestic control	Immune from domestic regulatory and legal systems or in countries where the legal system is 'protective' of corporate/organisational interests	Subject to legal challenge and regulatory oversight at state level, but also at supranational level	Subject to legal challenge and regulation at both national and supranational levels

Source: Adapted from Hirst and Thompson (1999)

teams, he not only failed to appreciate the extent to which the concept of 'Britishness' had changed, but also failed to appreciate the long-established capacity of Britons to manage multiple/nested identities. Norman Tebbit did not apply his 'test' to Scots or Welsh who cheered for their countries when playing football and who, it appears, can cope quite adequately with being both British and Scottish or Welsh without running the risk of becoming the 'lost souls' described by Scholte (2000: 161).

Taking each criterion identified in Table 24.1 in turn, the first is the role and significance of the nation as the defining factor or reference point in international sport. The extent to which a nation was ever a clear and unambiguous concept is often exaggerated, but it is undoubtedly the case that the reality underpinning the 'imagined community' of the nation is often both frail and pragmatic. On the one hand governments have frequently been enthusiastic in allowing applications for naturalisation from elite athletes and have, on occasion, actively 'bought' elite athletes from other countries. For example, the South African, Zola Budd, was awarded British citizenship remarkably rapidly so that she could compete for her new country. Fiona May, the British-born long jumper, was granted Italian nationality and subsequently went on to win a world title in 1995. When May lost her title four years later, she lost it to an athlete, Niurka Montalvo, whose nationality was equally complex. Montalvo originally competed for Cuba but when she took May's title she was a Spaniard. There are also examples of Ethiopian-born athletes competing as naturalised Turks and Sudanese-born athletes competing as naturalised Qataris. Finally, Mohammed Mourhit, previously of Morocco, won bronze in the world 5000 m cross-country event in 2000 in Seville for Belgium and then posed wrapped in a Moroccan flag with his former team-mate Salah Hissou.

On the other hand, there are many examples of athletes who have sought to maximise their opportunity to compete at the highest level by changing sporting nationality. Athletes can thus retain legal nationality with one country while adopting the sporting nationality of another by virtue of ancestry or even residence. For example, the Canadian tennis player Greg Rusedski adopted British sporting nationality; many British-born footballers have opted to represent the Republic of Ireland; and there are always a substantial number of non-English-born members of the England cricket team as players from Wales, Ireland and South Africa have joined the squad.

Merged, blurred and ambiguous national identities would be expected in truly globalised sport. By contrast, under conditions of internationalised sport, the nation would be protected as the defining unit of international sport. The status of the nation as an organising concept for sport is intimately linked to the significance of the state with which it has, in the vast majority of cases, a mutually dependent if not symbiotic relationship (see Houlihan, 1997). Under conditions of multinational sport, the state would retain a central role as a reference point for the organisation of international sport and for the identity of athletes, but it would lose a degree of exclusivity. Increasingly, other geopolitical reference points would emerge based either on supranational organisations (such as the European Union) or on geography, with the increasing construction of 'continental' teams (e.g. the European team that competes against the United States in golf's Ryder Cup; the presence of a European team, alongside other national and continental teams, in the IAAF Athletics World Championships).

The second characteristic is the extent of sports diversity throughout the world. Maguire (1999) refers to 'diminishing contrasts and increasing varieties' with regard to sport, while Hannerz (1990: 237) identifies a major impact of globalisation as producing the 'organisation of diversity'. An illustration of Maguire's conclusion would be the increase in the variety of running events (new distances, new contexts, or new combination of running with other sports, e.g. triathlon) but the decline or exclusion of events and sports that are more sharply differentiated from the dominant Olympic programme, such as dog-fighting, bear-baiting and bare-knuckle fighting.

Though Maguire's conclusion is a compelling one, the measurement of diversity is problematic; indeed, determining when a variation becomes a contrast is far from easy. Nevertheless, the conclusions of both Maguire and Hannerz suggest that under conditions of globalised sport, one might expect to find that local/regional sporting forms were retreating in the face of a largely European diet of Olympic sports and major commercial sports and the rational bureaucratic form of organisation with which they are underpinned. At the very least, one would expect to find evidence of a 'third culture' (Featherstone, 1991) which overlays more localised sports cultures. In essence it would be the anational holders of power, such as the international federations and transnational sports businesses, that would provide the direction and momentum for change at the domestic level. By contrast, under conditions of internationalised sport, the dynamics of change in sporting culture would be substantially national. Moreover, while engagement with, and adoption of, non-traditional sports might be common, it would be the result of choice rather than imposition or coercion. Multinationalist sport would result in an increasing diversity of competition opportunities with, for example, the European Union providing a context for new competitions, but not necessarily any increase in the diversity of sports available at the elite level.

Third, under conditions of globalised sport, one would expect the role of the state as a patron of, and organisational focus for, elite sport to be slight, by comparison with commercial patrons for example. The influence of the state in determining the pattern of engagement with global sport would be minimal. Internationalised sport would be characterised by a key role for the state, which would play a central role in funding and organising elite sport, reflecting a situation where engagement with global sport is determined significantly by nationally set priorities. Under conditions of multinational sport, state patronage would remain important, although supranational state organisations would provide both an additional source of patronage and a further set of constraints on the decision-making freedom of sports governing bodies.

The fourth characteristic refers to the degree to which commercial sports organisations, including professional football clubs, broadcasting companies and event organising bodies, operate within national frameworks of regulation. Globalised sport would be typified by minimal regulation or a pattern of self-regulation while under conditions of internationalised sport national or regional (e.g. European Union) systems of licensing, certification and training would create a mosaic of distinctive regulatory systems and consequently of sports practices. The conditions of multinationalised sport would be similar to those of internationalised sport, except that there would be clear evidence of dual regulation from the domestic and the supranational levels.

The final characteristic is the degree to which international sports organisations, such as the Commonwealth Games Federation, the IOC and the international federations, are subject to control by the domestic political/administrative/legal system. Under conditions of globalised sport, one would expect these engines of globalisation to be substantially immune from domestic systems of regulation or to be located in countries traditionally protective of corporate interests, such as Switzerland and Monaco. Within an internationalised system, international federations and the IOC would be open to legal challenge and interest group lobbying and enjoy no privileges arising solely from their status as global sports organisations. Multinationalised sport would be characterised, in Europe at least, by dual-level oversight and regulation.

A cursory reflection on the pattern of engagement between sport in the UK and international sport would quickly indicate that it corresponds neatly to none of the three ideal types, but rather exhibits a hybrid profile. The nation clearly remains the primary reference point for sports identity, but paradoxes and ambiguities abound. Chelsea FC still attracts passionate support from over 40,000 fans for each home game as well as from the many thousands who are not able to attend matches. Yet Chelsea regularly fields eight or nine non-English players and on one occasion fielded a team that had no English players. Moreover its current and three previous managers have been foreigners. The lack of any depth of association between the team members and England, let alone West London, has done nothing to undermine the intensity of support. In marked contrast to this apparent embrace of cosmopolitanism and globalisation, the proposals to merge Oxford FC with a neighbouring club or to move Wimbledon FC out of London to Milton Keynes was met with passionate parochial opposition. In tennis and boxing there is the strong impression that the British public are more at ease supporting Andy Murray, Tim Henman and Amir Khan than Greg Rusedski and Lennox Lewis. Similarly, in Formula One motor racing the fact that many of the top teams are based in the UK is given little weight if the driver is not British. Thus it appears that for some sports (e.g. football), place is important in affecting the public's sense of identity, while for others (Formula One) it is not; for some sports the nationality of the players does not prevent strong identification, while for other sports (e.g. tennis and boxing), nationality, or at least accent, remains important.

In considering the extent of sports diversity in the UK, the role of the state becomes sharply apparent. The Conservative government of John Major reshaped the National Curriculum for physical education to ensure that traditional British sports were embedded in the education system and it initiated the reorientation of elite funding policy to prioritise the major traditional team sports and Olympic sports. Given the relative poverty of most sports governing bodies, the power of state patronage is of considerable if not defining importance. The importance of the state and supranational state organisations in shaping the UK's engagement with globalisation is further emphasised by an examination of the regulatory framework within which sport operates. While at the national level state regulation is still modest, it is undoubtedly growing in areas such as the vetting of coaches who work with children, the licensing of major sports grounds, and the integration of coach training into the national system of vocational qualifications. At the European Union level, where a regulatory culture is more deeply entrenched, the impact on sport has been substantial particularly in relation to the movement of players and the control of sports broadcasting.

If the evidence so far seems to be indicating that the current trajectory of globalisation is towards internationalised or multi-nationalised sport, the relative immunity of international federations and the IOC from domestic state or supranational state regulation and oversight provides contrary evidence. However, the capacity of the United States to call the IOC to account over the Salt Lake City bribery allegations and the role of countries such as Canada, Australia and the UK along with the European Union in forcing the IOC to agree to an independent anti-doping agency (the World Anti-Doping Agency) both demonstrate the capacity of states to challenge the transnational status of international federations and the Olympic Movement.

From the foregoing discussion of the three-fold ideal typology, it should be clear that, as in the discussion of the process of globalisation, the state commands a central position in any discussion of the outcome of globalising processes. Whichever examples of globalisation are selected, anti-doping efforts, the development of sports broadcasting, the movement of sportsmen and women between clubs and countries, or the response to football hooliganism, the state is of central significance in determining the pattern of engagement between national and global sport and is far from the residual institution that is sometimes suggested (see Houlihan, 2003). This is not to argue that the state is a natural adversary of globalisation. Indeed some states, especially those with an ideological commitment to liberal economics, may well be the primary source of momentum for the intensification of flows between the national and the international. Moreover, it is argued that the capacity of the state to adapt to a changing global environment should not be underestimated. Any cursory review of the nature of globalisation in sport will provide ample examples of the close relationship between globalisation and regulation by the state or by international governmental bodies. As Vogel (1996: 2) argues, 'the rhetoric of globalisation … serves only to obscure what is really going on … [L]iberalism requires reregulation.'

In summary, it can be argued that sport globalisation as a process has no predetermined outcome. Indeed there are a variety of possible outcomes which would conform to the conventional definitions of globalisation, which stress the more extensive and intensive connections between people and places due to the increasing transnational flow of people, ideas, information, commodities and capital. However, a significant determinant of the trajectory of globalisation in general and of sport globalisation in particular is the behaviour of states.

REACH AND RESPONSE

In the wake of the US-led invasion of Afghanistan and the defeat of the Taliban following the September 11 attack on the World Trade Center and the Pentagon, the Western press was keen to produce stories and pictures of the return to 'normal' life within the country. Two stories that received wide coverage were, first, the contact between the Afghan sports authorities and the IOC concerning the future involvement of the country in the Olympic Games and, second, the revival of a local sport (involving a headless goat and teams of horsemen) previously banned by the Taliban. The celebration of local sporting culture and the conscious embrace of global sport is by no means unusual. Many, perhaps most, countries can provide examples of dual sporting cultures sitting comfortably alongside one another. The Irish have various Gaelic sports yet participate enthusiastically in the soccer World Cup and the Olympic Games; Australia has its parochial sport of Australian Rules football, but is also active across a wide range of Western team and individual sports; and the United States seems unconcerned that few other countries play American football or baseball.

Just at the time when we are coming to terms with the impact of globalisation, there appears to be a contradictory phenomenon emerging, namely that of localisation. If globalisation reflects the power of universalistic socio-cultural flows, then localisation emphasises spatial definition and socio-cultural specificity. This phenomenon is evident in politics, especially in Europe, where the enlargement of the European Union has been paralleled by the creation of 16 new states since 1989. For Rosenau (1994) the relationship between the two processes is described as 'fragmegration' aiming to capture, if not very elegantly, the dual processes of fragmentation and integration. Robertson (1995) identified a similar phenomenon which he referred to as 'glocalisation'. For Robertson global culture is contested terrain where 'what is taken to be a worthy direction of societal aspiration – is something which is constructed in the global arena in relation to the constraints upon (most) societies to maintain their own identities and senses of community' (1987: 38). Globalisation involves the reconciliation of a paradox which is the 'particularization of universalism (the rendering of the world as a single place) and the universalization of particularism (the globalized expectation that societies … should have distinct identities)' (Robertson, 1989: 9).

The capacity of globalisation to reach into every community is not denied, but what is less clear is the impact of that 'reach'. As mentioned above, for a number of writers, the impact of globalisation on culture is to lead to synchronisation, Americanisation or homogenisation and, as Scholte observes, 'Depending on one's perspective, this homogenisation entails either progressive cosmopolitanism or oppressive imperialism' (2000: 23). However, there is little evidence of a consensus on the impact of globalisation on culture generally or on sports culture in particular. In contrast to those who see only cultural homogeneity and the 'end of the national project' (Brown, 1995), there is an equally strong view that globalisation not only is compatible with continuing cultural heterogeneity but may even stimulate greater heterogeneity.

Underlying much of the discussion of the impact of globalisation is an appreciation that the basis on which national identity is defined has subtly shifted. It has long been accepted that defining national/regional identity is a mutually constitutive process in so far as identity is defined in relation to contrasts with 'foreigners'. More recently, it can be argued that there is a set of globally recognised reference points which are now also important in establishing identity and against which each nation or community has to position itself. These reference points range from the relatively mundane, such as distinctive postage stamps, military uniforms, national flags and anthems, to the more significant such as membership of the World Trade Organization and the United Nations, participation in UN peacekeeping/making activities, and attitudes towards global 'principles' of human rights, state sovereignty and internal democracy (see Meyer et al., 1997). One of these reference points is clearly participation in international sport and the Olympic Games in particular. Sport is thus an example of the common paradox of utilising a uniform vehicle for the demonstration of difference.

On one level therefore the reach of globalisation should not be equated with homogeneity, as its 'arrival' may be a welcome opportunity to demonstrate community/ national distinctiveness. At another level, the capacity of communities to modify and adapt global culture should not be underestimated. Jensen, in a study of the local response to television news programmes in a range of countries, noted how 'respondents consistently redefined and reinterpreted the agenda offered by journalists and political actors appearing on the news' and emphasised the extent to which 'the varied local cultures manifest themselves in the interpretation of foreign as well as domestic news. Culture shines through' (1998: 194, 195). Hannerz reinforces Jensen's conclusion and observes that peripheral cultures have a clear capacity to absorb 'the influx of meanings and symbolic forms from the centre [and] transform them to make them in some considerable degree their own' (1990: 127). For Hannerz engagement with global culture is an active process according to which communities/groups appropriate selectively global cultural commodities and use them to refine and reform their own distinctive cultural identity.

Hannerz's marketplace model of globalisation overemphasises the element of choice and discretion in peripheral communities but it does have a resonance in developed countries, where engagement with global culture is on more equal terms. Warde (2000) demonstrates the capacity of communities to adapt global culture in his study of eating habits in the UK. He illustrates a number of responses to non-traditional food, including the domestication of the exotic whereby previously exotic ingredients are incorporated into traditional British dishes and where foreign recipes are modified to suit British taste. These closely related processes can be seen in many British sports in recent years, where sports such as tennis, football, cricket, swimming and hockey have imported foreign elite coaches who have each brought with them 'foreign' training methods and playing strategies. Similarly, the influx of foreign players into the Premier League has required an adaptation on their part to aspects of the traditional English game, such as the pace and aggression.

There are a number of parallel examples to the British experience. In his study of baseball and the relationship between the Dominican Republic and the United States, Klein (1991) argues strongly that the game of baseball has been metamorphosed and that far from simply reflecting American cultural hegemony, it has become a vehicle for demonstrating Dominican excellence. Baseball has been reshaped to infuse it with distinctive Dominican characteristics and qualities, suggesting a clear capacity for a community to import, redefine and re-export a sports cultural product. Similar conclusions were reached by a number of writers in relation to the impact of cricket in the West Indies. James (1963) argued that cricket was significant in establishing a West Indian identity, while St Pierre suggests that cricket 'has been reshaped in sympathy with the cultural ethos of the West Indies [and] has been used as a tool to foster and further nationalist sentiment and racial pride' (1990: 23). For Burton the form of cricket might remain English but it has been 'injected with a new, specifically West Indian content and meaning' (1991: 8). The use of four fast bowlers and the panache and flamboyance of play are considered to be in marked contrast to the English playing norms of seriousness, respectability and moderation.

Just as it was difficult to pin down the particularities of the process of globalisation, so it is equally difficult to be precise regarding the process by which outcomes are determined. Table 24.2 suggests a model for investigating the mediation of global culture at the community level (see Houlihan, 1997).

Passivity generally implies an inability to challenge the external culture and would come close to descriptions of cultural imperialism with the relationship between the United States and the Dominican Republic being a good example. By contrast, the

TABLE 24.2   Global reach and local response in sport

Reach of globle culture	Response of the local community		
	Passive	Participative	Conflictual
Commodities	Unmediated reception of satellite television sports broadcasts	Gradual widening of participation in major international sports events such as the soccer World Cup and the Olympic Games through the formation/action of non-governmental sports bodies	The manufacturing of high-retail-value football kit and equipment in low-wage countries
Actions of the state	Ignoring the issue of doping by national athletes	Shifts in public funding to protect/promote particular sports	Olympic boycotts
Deep structure of societal processes	The gradual marginalisation of local sports or their repackaging for global consumption	The arranging of specific sports events for women, e.g. in Iran	Banning of female athletes in Olympic squads in many Islamic countries

development of sport in much of Western Europe and in English settler states such as Canada and Australia suggests not only a deep penetration by external culture, but more significantly, a strongly participative relationship in shaping and mediating external culture through control over media businesses or through influence within international sports bodies such as the IOC. Further examples of participative relationships between the domestic and the external culture include Japan and many of the countries of South East Asia, where the depth of penetration might be lower and where cultural adaptation and reinterpretation are greater. A conflictual response to external sports culture was seen briefly in both Russia and China in the immediate post-revolutionary period and more recently in the 1960s, when a group of mainly Asian states organised GANEFO (Games of the New Emerging Forces) as a challenge to the perceived dominance by Western capitalist and pro-Israeli states of the Olympic Movement and the major federations.

CONCLUSION

There can be no doubting the importance of current debates concerning globalisation in aiding our understanding of a number of key issues in sport, including: the significance of sport in the cultural fabric of a community; the interpenetration of sport with business in general and the international media in particular; and the significance of sport to governments and supranational governmental organisations. Yet, as this chapter has demonstrated, the analysis of globalisation and the consequent refinement of the concept is still in its infancy. As a result there is a need for caution both in the use of the concept and in the conclusions drawn about the nature and consequences of globalising trends.

This chapter has touched on three key debates over the nature of globalisation: globalisation as process; globalisation as outcome; and the reach of globalisation and the response of local communities. In all three of these areas there is a notable lack of consensus which reflects not only the shortage of empirical study, but also the complexity and multi-faceted character of the processes under consideration. As regards the process of globalisation, the significance of economic power in sport must be acknowledged, but simply to treat global sport as a cipher for, or a tool of, economic interests is an overextension of the limited evidence available. Moreover, claims that sport is capable of penetrating and altering deeply rooted local cultural practices must also await more substantial evidence. This scepticism is not to deny the possibility that sport may be a leading factor in, for example, bringing about greater equality for women, but rather to suggest that while sport may indeed be in the vanguard of cultural change, it may also be simply a highly visible reflection of change which has originated elsewhere – in the workplace for example.

The discussion of globalisation as an outcome highlighted the importance of treating globalisation as an open-ended set of processes which do not necessarily lead to a fixed destination. Globalisation is a complex and contingent set of processes within which the state plays a key role in shaping their pace, character and trajectory. The state is still the primary reference point for international sport and a central actor in determining the pattern of engagement between domestic sport and international sport. The final discussion concerned the need to appreciate the resilience, dynamism and interpretive capacity of local cultures. The language of sport may be universal but the meaning it carries is as much determined locally as it is in the boardrooms of multinational sports corporations.

CHAPTER SUMMARY

» The concept of globalisation refers to both a process and an outcome.
» Globalisation in sport has been described in relation to some or all of the following: internationalisation, liberalisation of government control, universalisation of culture, Westernisation/Americanisation and deterritorialisation.
» There is a tension between those theorists of globalisation who emphasise the economic basis of globalisation and those who emphasise the cultural basis.

> » As an outcome, there is a need to specify the criteria by which a globalised sports world would be recognised.
> » It is valuable to distinguish between the outcomes of globalisation, internationalisation and multinationalisation in sport.
> » Just as it is important to determine the 'reach' of globalising culture, it is also important to examine the response of recipient cultures which may be passive, participative or conflictual.

FURTHER READING

Scholte (2000) provides a good overview of the debates on the nature of globalisation while Maguire (1999) provides a wide-ranging analysis of globalisation in sport. More detailed studies of aspects of globalisation include Brookes and Madden's (1995) review of the economics of sports shoe production, Darby's (2001) examination of Africa's relationship with global football, and Klein's (1991) exploration of the relationship between the Dominican Republic and the United States in baseball. Rosenberg (2005) provides a vigorous critique of much recent globalisation theory.

REFERENCES

Bauman, Z. (1999) *Globalization: the Human Consequences.* Cambridge: Polity Press.

Brohm, J.-M. (1978) *Sport! A Prison of Measured Time.* London: Pluto Press.

Brookes, B. and Madden, P. (1995) *The Globe-trotting Sports Shoe.* London: Christian Aid.

Brown, A. (2000) 'Sneaking in through the back door? Media company interests and dual ownership of clubs', in S. Hamil et al. (eds), *Football in the Digital Age: Whose Game Is It Anyway?* London: Mainstream Publishing.

Brown, R. (1995) 'Globalisation and the end of the national project', in J. MacMillan and A. Linklater (eds), *Boundaries in Question: New Directions in International Relations.* London: Pinter, pp. 54–68.

Burton, R.D.E. (1991) 'Cricket, Carnival and street culture in the Caribbean', in G. Jarvie (ed.), *Sport, Racism and Ethnicity.* London: Falmer Press.

Darby, P. (2001) *Africa and Football's Global Order.* London: Frank Cass.

Featherstone, M. (1991) 'Global culture: an introduction', in M. Featherstone (ed.), *Global Culture: Nationalism, Globalisation and Modernity.* London: Sage.

Featherstone, M. and Lash, S. (1995) 'Globalisation, modernity and the spatialisation of social theory: an introduction', in M. Featherstone, S. Lash and R. Robertson (eds), *Global Modernities. 10th Anniversary Conference*. London: Sage.

Fitch, R. (1996) *The Assassination of New York*. London: Verso.

Hall, S. (1983) 'The problem of ideology – Marxism without guarantees', in B. Matthews (ed.), *Marx: a Hundred Years On*. London: Lawrence & Wishart.

Hamelink, C.J. (1983) *Cultural Autonomy in Global Communications: Planning National Information Policy*. London: Longman.

Hannerz, U. (1990) 'Cosmopolitans and locals in world culture', *Theory, Culture & Society*, 7: 237–51.

Harvey, D. (1989) *The Condition of Postmodernity*. Oxford: Blackwell.

Hirst, P. and Thompson, G. (1999) *Globalisation in Question*. 2nd edn. Cambridge: Polity Press.

Houlihan, B. (1997) 'Sport, national identity and public policy', *Nations and Nationalism*, 3 (1): 113–37.

Houlihan, B. (2003) 'Sport globalisation, the state and the problems of governance', in T. Slack (ed.), *The Commercialisation of Sport*. London: Frank Cass.

James, C.L.R. (1963) *Beyond a Boundary*. London: Stanley Paul.

James, C.L.R. (1977) *The Future in the Past*. New York: Lawrence Hill.

Jensen, C.B. (1998) 'Conclusion', in C.B. Jensen (ed.), *News of the World*. London: Routledge.

Katz, D. (1994) *Just Do It: the Nike Spirit in the Corporate World*. New York: Random House.

Klein, A. (1991) *Sugarball: the American Game, the Dominican Dream*. New Haven, CT: Yale University Press.

Levitt, T. (1983) 'The globalisation of markets' *Harvard Business Review*, May/June 61. 3, pp. 92–100.

Maguire, J. (1999) *Global Sport: Identities, Societies, Civilizations*. Cambridge: Polity Press.

Meyer, J.W., Boli, J., Thomas, G.M. and Ramirez, F.O. (1997) 'World society and the nation-state', *American Journal of Sociology*, 103 (1): 144–81.

Robertson, R. (1987) 'Globalization and societal modernization: a note on Japan and Japanese religion', *Sociological Analysis*, 47 (Summer): 35–43.

Robertson, R. (1989) 'Globalization, politics and religion', in J.A. Beckford and T. Luckman (eds), *The Changing Face of Religion*. London: Sage, pp. 10–23.

Robertson, R. (1995) 'Glocalization: time–space and homogeneity–heterogeneity', in M. Featherstone, S. Lash and R. Robertson (eds), *Global Modernities. 10th Anniversary Conference*. London: Sage.

Rosenau, J.N. (1994) 'New dimensions of security: the interaction of globalizing and localizing dynamics', *Security Dialogue*, 25 (3): 255–81.

Rosenberg, J. (2005) 'Globalization theory: a post mortem', *International Politics*, 42: 2–74.

Sage, G. (1996) 'Patriotic images and capitalist profit: contradictions of professional team sports licensed merchandise', *Sociology of Sport Journal*, 13: 1–11.

St Pierre, M. (1990) 'West Indian cricket: a cultural contradiction?', *Arena Review*, 14 (1): 13–24.

Scholte, J.A. (2000) *Globalisation: a Critical Introduction*. Basingstoke: Palgrave.

Stamm, H.-P. and Lemprecht, M. (2001) 'Sydney 2000 – the best Games ever? World sport and relationships of structural dependency', Paper presented at the First World Congress of Sociology of Sport, Seoul, July.

Vogel, S.K. (1996) *Freer Markets, More Rules: Regulatory Reform in Advanced Industrial Countries*. Ithaca, NY: Cornell University Press.

Wallerstein, I. (1991) 'Culture as the ideological battleground', in M. Featherstone (ed.), *Global Culture: Nationalism, Globalisation and Modernity*. London: Sage.

Warde, A. (2000) 'Eating globally: cultural flows and the spread of ethnic restaurants', in D. Kalb et al. (eds), *The Ends of Globalisation: Bringing Society Back In*. Lanham, MD: Rowman & Littlefield.

Index